A Pocket

CANTONESE

廣州話袖珍字典

Roy T. Cowles

香港大學出版社

HONG KONG UNIVERSITY PRESS

Hong Kong University Press
14/F, Hing Wai Centre
7 Tin Wan Praya Road
Aberdeen
Hong Kong

© Hong Kong University Press 1986
First Edition, 1914
Second Edition, 1949
Third Edition, 1986
Fourth Impression, 1999

ISBN 962 209 122 9

http://www.hkupress.org

Printed in Hong Kong by Ko's Art Printing Company Limited

FOREWORD

In presenting the first edition of this work, published in 1914, the author remarked:

"A convenient pocket dictionary of Cantonese is so evident a need that no apology is necessary for the presentation of this volume."

The reception given that volume fully justifies the above quoted remark. In the years that have passed since then, hundreds of missionaries and others have found that the book met their needs, and though it has long been out of print, well used copies are treasured by their owners. We have had continuous request for a reprint or new edition, and it is now with a real sense of satisfaction that we are able to bring out the new volume.

Back in 1922 work was begun on a revised and enlarged edition, the printing of which was undertaken by the old Fukuin Printing Company of Yokohama. The work was very close to being finished when the great earthquake of 1923 hit Yokohama, and everything was destroyed utterly, printed stock and plates.

There was, however, a bit of silver lining to the cloud of loss. Practically all of the original manuscript had been returned to me with proof sheets from Japan, and had thus been saved from the disaster. These sheets were carefully preserved up to the present.

Since that time, though there has been the desire to undertake the work again, no practical opening for doing so presented itself. Being in the homeland, difficulties in the way of my undertaking the work of republication were multiplied.

But with the return of my son, Rev. Milton S. Cowles, to Hong Kong in the early part of 1947, and the establishing by him of a mission press there, with offset lithograph equipment, the way opened for taking up the work again.

The present volume is a further revision of the manuscript that was prepared for the Japan printing, and incorporates several additional ideas in make up to increase its usefulness, the result of suggestions that have been gathered through the years.

We believe that most of the shortcomings and faults of the earlier edition have been eliminated, and that due to the printing process used, wherein the carefully prepared and checked and rechecked sheets sent from here to Hong Kong, have there been reproduced photographically for the printing, typographical errors are practically eliminated.

There is no doubt room for further improvement, and any suggestions from users of the book that would lead to making a future edition of the work more conveniently useful to the great body of missionaries and other students of Cantonese, will be welcomed.

I wish to express my gratitude to God, that though circumstances have kept me from returning to the mission field in South China, He has, in giving me the opportunity to work again on this dictionary, allowed me the privilege of helping other missionaries in the language field, and thus having a share still in the missionary work in the land that is very near to my heart.

R.T. COWLES

Waterford, California, U.S.A.
September 30, 1948

INTRODUCTION

This work is designed as a handbook of the spoken language, and aims at usefulness only in that field. Consequently some things that might be looked for in a dictionary of Cantonese will not be found. The contents are confined practically to only such characters and information as pertain in some measure to the spoken colloquial.

The first section of the book is a Cantonese-English Dictionary. Some 5300 characters, including duplicates pronounced variously, are listed, with about 4000 phrases. These phrases have been carefully chosen, in most cases to show some use or meaning of the characters which is not evident from the separate definitions. In order to keep down the size of the book, combinations of characters which are readily definable from a combination of the definitions under the different characters, are for the most part excluded.

It has been the endeavor to include every character in colloquial use. These have been gathered from the colloquial Bible, colloquial literature and everyday conversational language. These characters have been classified according to their use and frequency of use.

The definitions are necessarily brief. It should be borne in mind that often where a verb definition is given, a noun may be made of it, and vice versa. The aim in the definitions has been to give as concisely as possible the colloquial meaning commonly met with.

The spelling used is the system of Romanization adopted by the Missionary body of South China in 1888. This Romanization is the only system in practical use today. Other systems are found only in dictionaries or instruction books dealing with the language. This system may not be the best possible, as some aver, but the fact that it is the *only* Romanized Cantonese in which a literature exists, compels it recognition as the *Standard Romanization*. All publications in Romanized issued by the British and Foreign Bible Society, the China Baptist Publication Society, and the Pakhoi Mission Press have conformed to this standard.

Included in this section are over 200 of the commonest geographical names.

Following this section is the Radical Index, printed on green paper, to make it very easy to turn to. It has been the endeavor to give a page arrangement here that will make it unusually convenient for use.

The third section of the book is the English Index. This makes an English-Cantonese dictionary within the same covers in a minimum of pages.

Publisher's Notes:
The 1986 edition is reproduced photographically from the original 1949 edition published by the author, and the opportunity has been taken to correct some textual errors and delete a list of biblical names.

CANTONESE – ENGLISH

CHINESE-ENGLISH SECTION

Explanatory Notes

The arrangement is alphabetical according to the Standard Romanization, each tone of each syllable being given a separate heading. Under each of these headings the first entry is the commonest in use of the characters of that sound and tone. The others follow as nearly as possible in the order of relative frequency of use.

Note: In the alphabetical arrangement the double opening consonants are treated as separate initial letters, as are the aspirated letters also. It is a phonetic departure from the strict alphabetical arrangement. Tabulated, the initials under which the characters are listed is:

a
ch
ch'
e
f
h
i
k
k'
kw
kw'
l
m
n
ng
o
p
p'
s
sh
t
t'
ts
ts'
u
w
y.

Each <u>main</u> entry is numbered, the numbers being consecutive from first to last. The sub-entries, or phrases, are numbered (a), (b), (c), etc. These numbers are for reference from the Radical and English Indices.

Beneath many of these numbers will be found marks indicating classifications which will be useful especially to beginners. These class designations are as follows:

** The double star is used to mark several hundred of the very commonest characters.

(Unmarked) The large number of common colloquial characters in every day use, but not of such frequency of use as to´put them in the ** class, are left without any mark.

* Indicates characters that are used colloquially, but of infrequent occurrence.

' Indicates a class of characters which have hardly any claim to being called "colloquial", but which are met with occasionally in conversation, especially in names.

" Indicates a class of "unauthorized" forms, and some phonetic characters very commonly seen. Some of these are recognized in Eitel's Dictionary, and some are not. The fact that these exist and are in more or less common use, to the confusion of the student, is sufficient excuse for including such. Where the sign " occurs and <u>no definition</u> follows the character, the indication is that it is a character of purely <u>phonetic</u> use.

"' Some characters, having no claim whatever to being called "colloquial" are included because they are found in proper names or transliterations very frequently. For many of these no definition is given.

To the right of each character is the designation of its composition, Radical and number of strokes. Example, see No. 454. After the character ch'ăm appears the number 149 above the bar. This indicates that it belongs under the 149th Radical. Below the bar the figures 17 indicate that there is a count of 17 strokes, in addition to the Radical, to complete the character.

The definition first given usually indicates the most frequently met with meaning of the character, as used colloquially.

Sometimes, following the definition, will be found another Romanized spelling, enclosed in parenthesis. This indicates that the character may be read differently and, if with a different meaning, will be found listed under the alternative pronunciation.

The following abbreviations are used:

C, for classifier.
F, for final particle.
S, for surname.
aw, for also written.
uf, for used for.
cp, for correctly pronounced.
ph, for photographic term.
pr, for printing term.
pl, for plumbing term.
mus, for musical term.
naut, for nautical term.
surv, for surveying term.

A verticle line drawn past two or more characters indicates that they are interchangeable, or are different forms of the same character.

The phrases are given in Romanized only and definitions are necessarily the briefest possible. Note No. 1031a, for example. The phrase is heí-shaú. The syllable hei is, of course, the character 起 under which this phrase appears.

The student desiring to know which character the shaú stands for, will note the figures following, 3860. Turning over to that serial number, it is seen that the character is 首, meaning head, or beginning. Where the phrase is made up of three or more characters, the numbers referring to each appear, as see 1031d.

Standard Romanization

In the Standard Romanization no diacretical marks whatever are used to indicate sounds, these being represented entirely by combinations of letters. The spelling is very close to that used in Chalmer's English-Cantonese Dictionary. The main differences are:

Standard	Chalmers
a	u
u	uu
ei	i
o	oh(sometimes)
ui	ue(")

The Standard differs more widely from the spellings in Eitel's Cantonese-English Dictionary, and the differences are:

Standard	Eitel
aa	á
e	é
eu	éu
i	í
iu	íu
oh	o
ue	ü
ei	í
oo	ú
o	ò

In this Standard Romanization, diacretical marks are used to indicate tones only. The tone marking scheme is:

Upper even,	unmarked.
Upper rising,	´
Upper going,	`
Lower even,	¯
Lower rising,	˘
Lower going,	^
Upper entering,	unmarked.
Middle entering,	°
Lower entering.	¯

In this dictionary the arrangement of succession of the tones is in the order of the above list.

NOTE: Syllables with opening vowel sound are often heard with "ng" initial put on. And where "ng" initial rightly belongs it is occasionally dropped. "L" initial is often heard substituted for "n" initial and vice versa. Also "s" initial may be heard for "sh" initial and vice versa. In use of a dictionary arranged by Romanization these quite commonly heard variations should be borne in mind.

A

1. 吖 $\frac{30}{3}$ Ah! F-emphatic, interrogative or euphonic.

2. 丫 $\frac{6}{2}$ Forked.
 * (nga, ngà)

(a) a-t'aū 4339.
   Slave girl.
(b) a-kok,-kaí 1744-1517.
   Hair dressed in two tufts.
(c) a-a-hoi 1124.
   Irrelevant.

3. 呀 $\frac{30}{4}$ F-surprise.
 **

(a) kóm-a 1753.
   Alas!

4. 鴉 $\frac{196}{4}$ Raven. Crow.
 *

(a) lŏ-a 2420.
   Crow. Raven.
(b) a-tseuk. 4519.
   Raven.
(c) a-p'ĭn 3491.
   Opium.
(d) a-p'ĭn-naī 2845.
   Raw opium.
(e) a-p'ĭn-kwaí 2061.
   Opium sot.
(f) a-p'ĭn-tŭk 4260.
   Opium curse.
(g) a-p'ĭn-tsaú 4500.
   Laudanum.
(h) a-p'ĭn-tsing 4560.
   Morphine.
(i) a-p'ĭn-shĭ 3902.
   Opium dross.

5. 椏 $\frac{75}{8}$ Fork in branches. Forked.

Á

6. 啞 $\frac{30}{8}$ Dumb.
 *
7. 瘂 $\frac{104}{8}$ Mute.
 *

(a) á-kwaí 2061.
   A mute.
(b) á-haú 1006.
   Dumb. Mute.
(c) á-tsai 4482,
   or
(d) á-ló 2404.
   A dumb person.

À

8. 呀 $\frac{30}{4}$ F-emphatic or calling attention.
 **

9. 亞 $\frac{7}{6}$ A prefix to names of persons.
 **
(a) à-pa 3159.
   Papa.
(b) à-má 2555. Amah.
   Nurse. Mother.
(c) à-paak. 3172.
   An uncle.
(d) à-shuk 4010.
   Uncle.
(e) à-ī 1270.
   Maternal aunt.
(f) à-kung 1878.
   Grandfather.
(g) à-p'ōh 3528.
   Grandmother. Old woman.
(h) à-tsé 4508.
   Elder sister.
(i) à-mooī 2776.
   Younger sister.
(j) à-chaat. 102.
   Small footed woman.

(k) à-feī 759.
   Fat man.
(l) à-ch'oh-koh 572-1728.
   A novice.
(m) à-māng 2630.
   Amen.
(n) à-sāi-à 3589 or
   à-sai-à 3584.
   Asia.
(o) à-meī-leī-ka 2661-
   2293-1409.
   America.
(p) à-meī-neī-à 2873.
   Armenia.
(q) à-mā-suen 2561-3704.
   Amazon.
(r) à-chin-taī-ying 253-
   4071-5221.
   Argentine.
(s) à-ting 4168.
   Aden.

10. 噁 $\frac{30}{8}$ Phonetic.

   (a) à-moōn 2783.
      Amen.

11. 阿 $\frac{170}{5}$ Used for No. 9.
   (oh)

Â

12. 呀 $\frac{30}{4}$ Contraction for
   shāp 3845.

AAI

13. 挨 $\frac{64}{7}$ To lean on. Towards. Against.

   (a) aai-maǎn 2575.
      Evening.
   (b) aai-tó 4197.
      To lean against.

AAÌ

14. 嗌 $\frac{30}{10}$ ⎫
15. 嗌 $\frac{30}{18}$ ⎬ To quarrel.
   *   ⎭

   (a) aaì-kaau 1494.
      To squabble,
      wrangle.

16. 隘 $\frac{170}{10}$ Narrow.
   '   Crowded.

AAK

17. 軛 $\frac{159}{4}$ A yoke or col-
   *   lar. To re-
           strain.

AAK。

18. 鈪 $\frac{167}{4}$ A bracelet.
   *   Bangle.

AÀM

19. 陷 $\frac{170}{8}$ To wallow.
   *   (haâm)

AÀN

20. 晏 $\frac{72}{6}$ Late in the day
           or year.

   (a) shīk-aàn 3925.
      To eat lunch.
   (b) aàn-chaù 165.
      Afternoon.

-2-

AANG

21. 甖 98/14
22. 罌 121/14 Earthenware vessel. Jar.

AAP。

23. 押 64/5 To arrest. detain. (aat。)

24. 鴨 196/5 Duck.

(a) shuí-aap。 4004.
 Wild duck. Teal.
(b) faan-aap。 655.
 Muscovy duck.
(c) aap。-miú 2764.
 Duckling.

AAT。

25. 壓 32/14 To repress, subdue.

26. 押 64/5 To pawn. Pawnshop. uf No.23 (aap。)

(a) aat。-p'iù 3508
 Pawnticket.

27. 遏 162/9 To repress, bar.

AAU

28. 坳 32/5 Distress. Poor. Destitute.

(a) aau-oô-sheng 3131½- 3880. Caterwaul.

AAÚ

29. 拗 64/5 To break off. Bent. (aaù)

AAÙ

30. 凹 17/3 A hollow. Valley. Pass.(nap)

31. 拗 64/5 Bent. Warped. (aaú)

AI

32. 唉 30/7 Exclamation: surprise, pain.
33. 嗌 30/10

(a) ai-ya: 5082.
 Alas! Oh dear! Oh!

AÍ

34. 矮 111/8 Short in stature. Stunted. Dwarf. Low.
35. 躷 158/8

AÌ

36. 翳 124/11 Shaded. Screened.
(a) paì-aì 3207.
 Sorrowful. Sad.

37. 屭 44/21 Strong,
(a) paì-aì 3209.
 Sorrowful. Sad.

38. 縊 120/10 To strangle, hang.

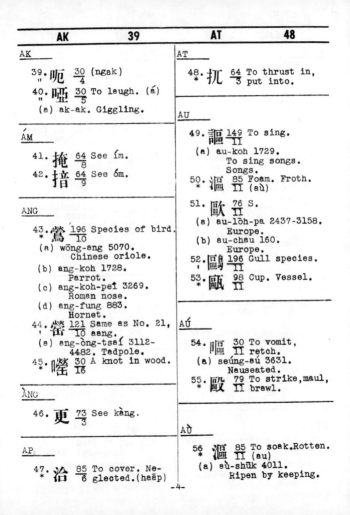

AK

39. " 呃 $\frac{30}{4}$ (ngak)

40. " 啞 $\frac{30}{5}$ To laugh. (á)

(a) ak-ak. Giggling.

ÁM

41. 掩 $\frac{64}{8}$ See ím.

42. 揜 $\frac{64}{9}$ See óm.

ANG

43. * 鶯 $\frac{196}{10}$ Species of bird.

(a) wōng-ang 5070.
    Chinese oriole.
(b) ang-koh 1728.
    Parrot.
(c) ang-koh-pei 3269.
    Roman nose.
(d) ang-fung 883.
    Hornet.

44. ' 鶊 $\frac{121}{10}$ Same as No. 21,
    aang.
(e) ang-òng-tsai 3112-
    4482. Tadpole.

45. * 嚌 $\frac{30}{16}$ A knot in wood.

ÀNG

46. 更 $\frac{73}{3}$ See kàng.

AP.

47. * 洽 $\frac{85}{6}$ To cover. Ne-
    glected. (haāp)

AT

48. * 扰 $\frac{64}{3}$ To thrust in,
    put into.

AU

49. 謳 $\frac{149}{11}$ To sing.

(a) au-koh 1729.
    To sing songs.
    Songs.

50. * 漚 $\frac{85}{11}$ Foam. Froth.
    (aù)

51. 歐 $\frac{76}{11}$ S.

(a) au-lōh-pa 2437-3158.
    Europe.
(b) au-chau 160.
    Europe.

52. ' 鷗 $\frac{196}{11}$ Gull species.

53. * 甌 $\frac{98}{11}$ Cup. Vessel.

AÚ

54. 嘔 $\frac{30}{11}$ To vomit,
    retch.

(a) seúng-aú 3631.
    Nauseated.

55. * 毆 $\frac{79}{11}$ To strike, maul,
    brawl.

AÙ

56. * 漚 $\frac{85}{11}$ To soak. Rotten.
    (au)

(a) aù-shūk 4011.
    Ripen by keeping.

CHA

57. 揸 64/9 To grasp, sieze, To manage, work. A handful.
(a) cha-pán 3225.
Manager.

58. 喳 30/12 F-cautioning or restraining.

59. 渣 85/9 Sediment. Leavings. Dregs.
(a) cha-tsź 4671.
Sediment. Refuse.
(b) tsź-káng-cha 4670-1555. Shellac.

CHÁ

60. 鲊 195/5 See lǎ, là, 2148.

CHÀ

61. 詐 149/5 Deceitful. To feign.
(a) chà-ká 1419.
To falsify.
(b) chà-ngaí 3017.
A sham. False.

62. 榨 75/10 To press or extract juices.

63. 醡 164/10 A press for such use.

64. 搾 64/10 To crush. A press.

65. 咋 30/5 F-emphatic, restraining or cautioning.

66. 痄 104/5
(a) chà-soi 3694.
Mumps.

67. 炸 86/5 To burst, explode.
(a) chà-taán 4058.
A bomb.

68. 蚱 142/5 Locust species.
(a) chà-maǎng 2587.
Grasshopper.

CHAAI

69. 齋 210/3 Abstain from. To fast. Vegetables.
(a) shīk-chaai 3925.
To be vegeterian.

70. 嚌 30/16 F-emphatic.

CHAAÌ

71. 債 9/11 To owe. A debt.
(a) chaaì-chué 328.
Creditor.
(b) chaaì-yān 5117, or
(c) chaaì-tsaí 4482.
A debtor.
(d) chaaì-tán 4093.
A bankrupt.
(e) fòng-chaaì 795.
To lend money.

CHAAÎ

72. 寨 40/11 A hold. Fortress. Castle. No. 73 also used.

73. 岩 112/5 Den. Brothel.
(a) yíng-chaaî 5235.
Barracks. Station.
(b) mīng-chaaî 2690.
Licensed brothel.
(c) sz-chaaî 3758.
Sly brothel.

74. 豸 R 153 Fabled unicorn.

CHAAK。

75. 責 154 4 To reprove, punish.
 (a) chaak。yâm 5105.
   Official charge or duty.
 (b) chaak。faât 734.
   To punish.
 (c) chaak。mân 2629.
   To question, torture.
 (d) chaak。shîng 3948.
   To reprimand, rebuke.
76. 窄 116 5 Narrow. Contracted.
77. 磧 112 11 To crush, press.
78. 喋 30 10 To crush, press.
 (a) chaak。-sź 3767.
   To crush to death.

CHAAK

79. 摘 64 11 To pick, pull, pluck.
80. 擇 64 13 To choose, select.
81. 澤 85 13 Benefits. Moist. Fertile.
82. 擲 64 15 To throw down, shake.
 (a) chaak-shik 3917.
   Dice playing.
 (b) chaak-kau-tsai 1571-4482. To gamble.
83. 宅 40 3 Family dwelling.
84. 謫 149 11 To punish.

 (a) chaak-fât 734.
   To punish by fine.

CHAAM

85. 斬 69 7 To cut down or off, behead.

CHAAM

86. 站 117 5 Stage of a journey. To stand.
 (a) yat-chaam-lô 5133-2426. Ten leǐ.
 (b) chaam-t'aū 4339.
   (Railway) station.

CHAAN

87. 盞 108 8 Classifier for lamps, etc.
 (a) tang-chaan 4094.
   Old style lamp saucer.

CHAAN

88. 賺 154 11 To make profit, gain. (waăn)
89. 綻 120 8 Seam open. To rip.
90. 棧 75 8 Warehouse. Boarding house.
91. 饌 184 12 Food. Delicacies.

CHAANG

92. 爭 87 4 To wrangle, debate, contest, fall short.
 (a) chaang-taù 4110.
   To scuffle.
 (b) chaang-aaù 31.
   To dispute.

(c) chaang-tsûng 4655.
Litigation.
(d) chaang-ti(k) 4140.
A little short or
different.

93. 琤 30/8 Used for No. 92.

94. 踭 130/8 The heel. Elbow. Tendon of

95. 蹖 157/8 heel or elbow.

96.* 撜 64/8 To wedge in. (chaàng)

(a) tá-chaàng 4027.
To caulk.

CHAAP。

97. 劄 118/8 To write out. A document.

98.* 眨 109/5 To wink.

CHAAP

99. 閘 169/5 A gate. A pass. To shut up.

(a) shuí-chaāp 4004.
A waste weir. Sluice gate.

100.* 极 75/4 Camp stool. Inclined.

101. 鈒 167/4 To cut. Grass shears.

CHAAT。

102. 扎 64/1 To pierce. To bind. Bundle. C.

(a) chaat。-keuk 1638.
Bound feet.

103. 札 75/1 Used for No. 102.

104.* 紮 120/5 To tie up, bind. uf No. 102.

CHAAU

105. 啁 30/8 Chirping of birds.

106. 嘲 30/12 To rail, jest, abuse.

CHAAÚ

107.* 爪 R/87 Claws. Talons.

(a) chaaú-wa 4953.
Java.

108. 找 64/4 To seek. To change (as money).

(a) chaaú-t'aū-lō 4339-2426. To look for employment.

(b) chaaú-ts'ín 4761.
To exchange money.

(c) chaaú-ts'ām 4710.
To seek after.

109.* 抓 64/4 To scratch.

CHAAÙ

110. 燋 86/12 To fry in oil or fat.

111.* 罩 122/8 Cover. Shade.

(a) tang-chaù 4094.
Lamp shade, globe.

112. 笊 118/4

(a) chaaù-leī 2283.
Bamboo ladle.

113. 櫂 75/14 To row, propel.

114. 棹 75/8 To row, propel.

115. 掉 64/8 To hit.

(a) chaaū-tseúng 4525.
To row (as a boat).

CHAI
116. 擠 $\frac{64}{14}$ To put, place. (tsai)

CHAÌ
117. 制 $\frac{18}{6}$ To govern, stop, cut off. Valve. (Electric) switch.
(a) chaì-fūk 874 or 876. To overcome.
(b) chaì-kwan 2075, or
(c) chaì-t'oî 4422. Governor General.
(d) chaì-m̄-chuê 2551-339. Ungovernable.
(e) chaì-tsô 4594. To invent, make.
118. 掣 $\frac{64}{8}$ To obstruct, draw lots.
119. 製 $\frac{145}{8}$ To compound, make.
(a) chaì-tsô 4594. To manufacture.

CHAÎ
120. 滯 $\frac{85}{11}$ Sluggish. Obstinate.

CHAK
121. 側 $\frac{9}{9}$ By the side. Inclined.
(a) tá-chak 4027. To lurch.
(b) chak-shat 3850. Concubine.
122. 仄 $\frac{9}{2}$ Oblique. Uneven.

CHAM
123. 針 $\frac{167}{2}$
124. 箴 $\frac{118}{9}$
125. 鍼 $\frac{167}{9}$
A needle. Pin. Probe. Index pointer. Indicating instrument. To warn, sew. Pierce. To prick.

(a) t'aū-cham 4339. A pin.
(b) cham-tēng 4129. Thimble.
(c) ch'uen-taal-cham 611-4031. Bodkin.
(d) fòng-shuí-cham 795-4004. Trocar.
(e) chî-naām-cham 215-2823. Magnetic needle. Compass.
(f) hōn-shuè-cham 1164-3986. Thermometer.
(g) fung-uê-cham 879-4889. Barometer.
(h) cham-în 1350. (book of)Proverbs.

126. 砧 $\frac{112}{5}$ Block. Anvil.
(a) cham-paán 3187. Chopping board.
127. 斟 $\frac{68}{9}$ To deliberate, pour.
(a) cham-cheuk₀ 178. To consult, plan.

CHÁM
128. 枕 $\frac{75}{4}$ A pillow.
(a) chám-t'aū 4339. A pillow.
(b) chám-t'aū-toî 4224. Pillow case.
(c) chám-kwat 2083. The occiput.
(d) chám-poón 3390. Bedfellow.
(e) chám-pin. 3886. In private. A wife.

129. 胈 $\frac{74}{8}$ Callous.

130. 怎 $\frac{61}{5}$ A Mandarin particle of interrogation.

CHĂM
131. 枕 $\frac{75}{4}$ To pillow, lean on.

132. 浸 $\frac{85}{7}$ See tsăm.

CHÂM
133. 朕 $\frac{74}{6}$ A puff (of smoke, etc.)

134. 吮 $\frac{30}{7}$ | To drown.

135. 沉 $\frac{85}{4}$ |

CHAN
136. 眞 $\frac{109}{5}$ True. Genuine.
** Sure. S.

137. 珍 $\frac{96}{5}$ Precious. Rare. Delicate.
(a) chan-chue 314.
Pearls.

CHĂN
138. 震 $\frac{173}{7}$ To shake, tremble. Terror.
(a) chăn-tŭng 4277.
To shake.
(b) teí-chăn 4125.
Earthquake.

139. 振 $\frac{64}{7}$ To restore,
* shake.

140. 鎭 $\frac{167}{10}$ A mart. To keep,
* protect.

CHĂN
141. 陣 $\frac{170}{7}$ | C. for gusts,
blasts, showers,
142. 陳 $\frac{170}{8}$ | etc. A period of
time. Battle array. Ranks.
(ch'ăn)

CHANG
143. 箏 $\frac{118}{8}$ Harpischord.
(a) laai-chang 2151.
Thrum the guitar.

(b) fung-chang 879.
Singing kite.

144. 淨 $\frac{15}{8}$ Used for tsíng, 4564.

145. 撐 $\frac{64}{12}$ See ch'aang.

CHĂNG
146. 掙 $\frac{64}{8}$ To cut.
(chaăng)

CHAP
147. 執 $\frac{32}{8}$ To hold, grasp, gather.
(a) chap-ch'aŭ 480.
To draw lots.
(b) chap-tsź-nap 4672-2859. To set type.
(c) chap-sź 3776.
A manager. To manage business.
(d) chap-ma 2553.
A midwife.
(e) chap-chíng 277.
Powers of government.

148. 汁 $\frac{85}{2}$ Juice. Sap. Gravy.

149. 㪫 $\frac{30}{11}$ A handful. A tuft.

CHAT
150. 質 $\frac{154}{8}$ Substance. Matter. To confront.

151. 栀 $\frac{75}{5}$ A plug. Cork.
(chí)

CHĀT
152. 姪 $\frac{38}{6}$ Nephew. Niece.
(a) chāt-tsź 4667.
Brother's son.
(b) chāt-nuí 2949.
Brother's daughter.
(c) ngoí-chāt 3070.
Wife's nephew or niece.

(d) noî-chāt 2937.
Wife's brother's
child.

153. 桎 75/6 Fetters.
' 6 Spike.

154. 窒 116/6 To obstruct.

155. 蟄 142/11 To hibernate.
' 11 Hidden.

---

156. 周 30/5 Complete. Everywhere. All. S.
(a) chau-wai 5001.
All around.
(b) chau-tsai 4484.

157. 賙 154/8 To bestow, as
alms, help.
s.a. 156.

158. 週 162/8 To revolve. A
year. s.a. 156.

159. 州 47/3 A political division. Dis-
trict. Conti-
nent.

160. 洲 85/6 Island. Conti-
nent. u.f. 159.
(a) ngō-uĕ-chau 3052-4872
Whampoa Island.
(b) ch'eūng-chau 512.
Dumbell Is., H.K.

161. 舟 R/137 A boat. Ship.
Ark.
(a) fong-chau 779.
The Ark.
(b) chau-shaan 3793.
Chusan.

162. 肘 130/3 Forearm. Elbow.
' 3 Cubit.

163. 箒 118/8 A kind of
broom.

---

164. 呪 30/5 To curse.

164½. 咒 30/5 An imprecation.

(a) chaù-chòh 298.
To curse, swear.

165. 晝 72/7 Daylight.

(a) sheūng-chaù 3896.
Forenoon.
(b) hâ-chaù 908.
Afternoon.

166. 冑 13/7 A helmet.

167. 遮 162/11 To cover, screen.
An umbrella.
(a) che-pai 3208.
To overspread, hide.
(b) che-k'oî 1994.
To cover, hide.
(c) che-îm 1301.
To conceal, hush up.
(d) uĕ-che 4888.
Oil paper umbrella.

168. 呎 30/5 F-limiting.

168½. 遮 30/18 (chek。)

168¾. 睹 30/9

169. 者 125/4 Impersonal pronoun. Used to
form nouns. One.
That. Those. A
personality.
Something.
(a) sik。-ché 3635.
Formerly.
(b) tsoî-ché 4607.
Furthermore.

170. 赭 $\frac{155}{9}$ Ochre color.
' Reddish.
   (a) ché-shĕk 3879.
       Haematite iron ore.

CHÈ
171. 蔗 $\frac{140}{11}$ Sugar cane.
   (a) t'it.-chè 4366.
       Dark brown cane.
   (b) kom-chè 1750.
       Sweet cane.
   (c) chuk-chè 364.
       Small cane.
   (d) chè-liŭ 2392.
       Sugar mill or shed.
172. 鷓 $\frac{196}{11}$ Partridge.
   (a) chè-koo 1792.
       Partridge.
173. 啫 $\frac{30}{9}$ F-implying lim-
' itation or de-
       lay.
174. 這 $\frac{162}{7}$ A Mandarin
'" word, this.

CHEK. -- See also chik.
175. 隻 $\frac{172}{2}$ C of birds,
       ships, limbs,
       etc.
176. 只 $\frac{30}{2}$ Only.
176². 咮 $\frac{30}{5}$ Merely.
       (che)

CHEUK.
177. 著 $\frac{140}{9}$ To clothe. No.
       184 also used.
178. 酌 $\frac{164}{3}$ To consult, de-
' liberate, plot.
179. 芍 $\frac{140}{3}$ Peony.
   (a) cheuk.-yeūk 5183.
       Peony.
180. 斫 $\frac{69}{5}$ To cut, hew.

181. 勺 $\frac{20}{1}$ A ladle.
182. 棹 $\frac{75}{8}$ A table.
183. 灼 $\frac{86}{3}$ To burn,
' blister.

CHEŪK
184. 着 $\frac{123}{6}$ Completed ac-
       tion. Right.
   (a) uĕ-cheŭk 4896.
       To meet with.
   (b) cheŭk-fóh 767.
       To ignite.

CHEUNG
185. 張 $\frac{57}{8}$ To open out. A
       sheet. C for
       paper, etc. S.
   (a) cheung-hoi 1124.
       To expand.
186. 章 $\frac{117}{6}$ Chapter. Rules.
       System. S.
   (a) cheung-ch'ing 561.
       Rules. Bylaws.
   (b) cheung-uĕ 4872.
       Cuttlefish.
187. 樟 $\frac{75}{11}$ Camphor tree.
*'
   (a) cheung-nŏ 2926.
       Gum camphor.
188. 嫜 $\frac{38}{11}$ Husband's
' father.
189. 彰 $\frac{59}{11}$ To display.

CHEŪNG
190. 長 $\frac{R}{168}$ Old. Exalted.
       To grow.
       (ch'eŭng)
   (a) tô-cheŭng 4207.
       Taoist abbot.
   (b) cheŭng-lŏ-ooĩ 2420-
       3143. Presbyterian
       Church.
   (c) cheŭng-k'ei 1948.
       Nagasaki.

(d) oo͡i-cheúng 3143.
   Head of a society
   or guild.
(e) kūk-cheúng 1875.
   Head of an estab-
   lishment.
(f) cha͡ám-cheúng 86.
   Station master.

191. 掌 $\frac{64}{8}$ Palm of hand.
   To control.

(a) cheúng-kwa͡i 2072.
   An accountant.
(b) cheúng-k'uén 2007.
   To wield authority.

CHEÙNG
192. 賬 $\frac{154}{8}$ An account. A
   debt. A time.
   Times.

(a) cheùng-mūk 2798.
   An account.
(b) yat-cheùng 5133.
   Once.

193. 仗 $\frac{9}{3}$ Warfare.
   Weapons.
   (cheùng)

(a) tá-cheùng 4027.
   To make war, battle.

194. 帳 $\frac{50}{8}$ A curtain. Awning. Screen.

(a) mán-cheùng 2613.
   Mosquito net.
(b) pò-cheùng 3336.
   Awning.
(c) cheùng-fóng 798.
   A tent.

195. 唱 $\frac{30}{14}$ Time. Times.
   uf No. 192.

196. 脹 $\frac{130}{8}$ Dropsical.

(a) shuí-cheùng 4004.
   Dropsy.

197. 漲 $\frac{85}{11}$ To flood, overflow.

198. 瘴 $\frac{104}{11}$ Malaria.
   Miasma.

199. 障 $\frac{170}{11}$ Screen. Partition. Barricade.

200. 悵 $\frac{61}{8}$ Disappointed.
   Vexed.

CHEÛNG
201. 丈 $\frac{1}{1}$ Ten feet. One
   worthy of re-
   spect. Senior.

(a) cheûng-foo 801.
   A husband.
(b) fong-cheûng 779.
   Buddhist abbot.

202. 杖 $\frac{75}{3}$ Staff. Club.

203. 仗 $\frac{9}{3}$ Warfare. Weapon.
   (cheûng)

CHI
204. 之 $\frac{4}{3}$ Sign of gene-
** tive. Posses-
   sive.

(a) chi-koo͡-laát 1796-
   2195. Chocolate.
(b) chi-ha͡ú 1013.
   Afterwards.

205. 知 $\frac{111}{3}$ To know.
** Wisdom.

(a) chi-foo 814.
   A prefect.
(b) chi-uén 4933.
   Magistrate of a
   district.
(c) chi-tò 4203.
   To know.
(d) chi-sź 3776.
   A secretary.

206. 枝 $\frac{75}{4}$ Branch. C for
   branches,
   sticks, etc.

(a) chi-kon 1768.
   Trunk and branches.
(b) pok₀-chi 3355.
   To engraft
(c) suen-chi 3702.
   Ebony.

(d) chi-ch'a 401.
   A fork.

207. 支 $\frac{R}{65}$ Branch.
   To pay.

(a) chi-p'aal 3418.
   Descendants.Tribe.

(b) chi-kaang 1479.
   A watchman.

208. 肢 $\frac{130}{4}$ The limbs.

(a) chi-t'ai 4315.
   The body.

209. 吱 $\frac{30}{4}$ F-emphatic.

210. 蜘 $\frac{142}{8}$

(a) chi-chue 317.
   A spider.

211. 脂 $\frac{130}{6}$ Fat. Grease.
   Cosmetics.

212. 芝 $\frac{140}{4}$

(a) chi-má 2557.
   Sesaman.

213. 栀 $\frac{75}{7}$ Gardenia.

214. 卮 $\frac{49}{4}$ A goblet.
   News.

CHI

215. 指 $\frac{64}{6}$ Finger. Toe.
   To point, indi-
   cate.

(a) shaú-chí-kung 3859-
   1878. Thumb.

(b) i-chí 1287.
   Forefinger.

(c) chìng-chí 275.
   Middle finger.

(d) chí-kaap. 1488.
   Finger(toe) nail.

(e) chí-kaap₀-fa 650.
   Balsam.

(f) chí-shî 3910.
   To indicate.

(g) chí-tím 4152.
   To direct.

(h) chí-mŏng 2764.
   To expect, hope.

216. 紙 $\frac{120}{4}$ Paper.

(a) faan-chí 671.
   Sized paper.

(b) king-uén-chí 1669-
   4910. Soft cotton
   paper.

(c) sha-chí 3780.
   Tough native paper.

(d) sha-chí 3779.
   Sand paper.

(e) kai-p'eî-chí 1515-
   3468. Brown paper.

(f) ts'ó-chí 4777.
   Coarse paper.

(g) yàn-shuî-chí 5116-
   4004. Blotter.

(h) chí-paāk 3179.
   Paper effigies.

(i) chí-iū 1393.
   A kite.

(j) chí-t'ung-fa 4452-650.
   Artificial flowers.

217. 止 $\frac{R}{77}$ To halt, stop,
   end. The end.
   Only.

218. 址 $\frac{32}{4}$ Foundation.

219. 旨 $\frac{72}{2}$ Purpose. Will.
   Decree. Excel-
   lent.

220. 只 $\frac{30}{2}$ This. So. Only
   (chek₀ chik)

(a) chí-koón 1819.
   Only (emphatic).

221. 祇 $\frac{113}{4}$ Only. Reverent.
   uf 220 and 224.

222. 枳 $\frac{75}{5}$ Hawthorn.
   (chat)

223. 祇 $\frac{145}{5}$ uf No. 220.
   (chik)

224. 祇 $\frac{113}{5}$ Reverent.
   Only.

225. 祉 $\frac{113}{4}$ Happiness.
   Felicity.

226. 趾 157/4 Toes. uf No. 218.

CHI
227. 至 R 133/** To reach. Superlative degree.
(a) chì-tò 4203.
Until.
(b) yàt-chì 5137.
The solstice.

228. 致 133/3 To come to, cause, reach.

229. 智 72/8 Wisdom. Knowledge.
(a) chì-waî 5016.
Wise. Wisdom.
(b) chì-leî 2293.
Chili.

230. 志 61/3 Will. Purpose. Annals.
(a) chì-heî 1033.
Purpose. Ambition.

231. 置 122/8 To get rid of, * put in position of, judge.

231½. 緻 120/10 Fine. Delicate.

232. 質 154 See chat.

233. 痣 104/7 Black spot. Mole.
(a) mìn-chì 2687.
Freckles.

234. 誌 149/7 Annals. To record. s.a. 230.
(a) mô-chì 2727.
Epitaph.

CHÎ
235. 治 85/5 To govern, rule. (ch'Î)
(a) chî-luen 2474.
Suppress rebellion.

236. 痔 104/6 Piles.
(a) chî-ch'ong 578.
Piles.

237. 雉 172/5 Pheasant species.

CHIK -- See also chek.
238. 織 120/12 To weave, plait, knit.
(a) chik-fông 787.
To spin.
(b) chik-kei 1601.
A loom.

239. 職 128/12 Office. Duty. To manage.
(a) chik-tô 4207.
Taotoi.
(b) chik-fân 723.
Duty. Title.

CHIK。-- See also chek。.
240. 炙 86/4 To roast. * (chek。)

241 只 30/2 (chek。, che) uf No. 175.

CHÎK
242. 直 109/3 Straight.
(a) chîk-laî(taî) 2214.
Chihli province.

243. 值 9/8 Price. Worth. To happen.
(a) chîk-leî 2285.
A director.

244. 植 75/8 To plant. *
(a) chîk-laâp 2190.
To stand upright, be established.

245. 殖 78/8 To grow, prosper.

CHIM
246. 沾 85/5 To moisten, re- * ceive benefits, imbue with.

247. 占 25/3 To divine. A lot. (chìm)

(a) ohim-sing-hok 3652-
1140. Astrology.

248. 粘 $\frac{115}{5}$ White rice.
* (nǐm)

249. 粘 $\frac{119}{5}$ Glutinous.
, Sticky.

250. 黏 $\frac{202}{5}$ (nǐm)
"

CHIM
251. 占 $\frac{25}{3}$ To usurp, sieze.
, (chim)

252. 佔 $\frac{9}{5}$ (tim)
, uf No. 251.

CHIN
253. 氈 $\frac{82}{13}$ Felt. Blanket.
* Rough goods as

254. 毡 $\frac{82}{13}$ rugs, etc.
,

(a) tei-chin 4125.
Carpet.

(b) paāk-chin 3178.
Blanket.

255. 顫 $\frac{181}{13}$ To shake,
, tremble.

256. 羶 $\frac{123}{13}$ Rank.
, Frowzy.

257. 鸇 $\frac{196}{13}$ A hawk.
,

258. 鱣 $\frac{195}{13}$ A sea monster.
,

CHÍN
259. 碾 $\frac{112}{10}$ To roll,
* crush.

260. 展 $\frac{44}{7}$ To open out,
* unroll.

261. 甂 $\frac{107}{13}$ To peel, rip
, off.

262. 闡 $\frac{169}{12}$ To enlarge upon,
, expound.

CHIN
263. 戰 $\frac{62}{12}$ To fight, war.
Terrified.

(a) chǐn-shue 3982.
Declaration of war.

(b) chǐn-shuēn 3999.
Warship.

(c) chǐn-ch'eūng 510.
Battlefield.

(d) chǐn-sǐn 3646.
Battle front line.

CHIN
264. 纏 $\frac{120}{15}$ To bandage, bind
* up. (ch'ǐn)

CHING
265. 貞 $\frac{154}{2}$ Pure.
, Chaste.

266. 正 $\frac{77}{1}$ (chǐng)
,

(a) ching-uēt 4937.
The first month.

267. 蒸 $\frac{140}{10}$ To heat, dry
, up. (ching)

268. 烝 $\frac{86}{6}$ To steam, dis-
* till.

(a) ching-shuí-wōk 4004-
5066. Steam boiler.

269. 征 $\frac{60}{5}$ To subjugate,
, make war.

(a) ching-shau 3857.
Collect by force.

270. 徵 $\frac{60}{12}$ To testify,
, summon.

271. 楨 $\frac{75}{9}$ Waxtree.
,

(a) nuí-ching 2949.
Waxtree.

272. 偵 $\frac{9}{9}$ To spy, re-
, connoiter.

273. 癥 $\frac{104}{15}$ Obstruction of
, bowels.

CHING
274. 整 $\frac{66}{12}$ To make,
* To do.

(a) ching-hó 1099.
To repair.

(b) ching-waaï 4965.
To spoil.

CHÌNG
275. 正 77/1 Straight. Right. Exact. Just as. When.

(a) chìng-faat。 682.
Capital punishment.

(b) chìng-sam 3593.
To reform.

(c) chìng-kaaù 1507.
Orthodox.

(d) chìng-ngaam 2993.
Just right.

276. 證 149/12 To witness. Evidence.

277. 政 66/5 To govern, rule. Rules. Laws.

(a) kwok。-chìng 2103.
The government.

278. 症 104/5 Disease.

279.* 証 149/5 uf No. 276.

280.* 蒸 140/10 To heat, dry up. (ching)

CHÍNG
281.'" 鄭 163/12 S.

CHIP。
282. 摺 64/11 To fold. A document.

(a) chip。-to 4195.
A claspknife.

CHIT。
283. 折 64/4 To break, bend, To decide, (as a case at law.

284.* 浙 85/7 To spout, spatter.

(a) shuí-chit。4004.
Syringe.

(b) chit。-kong 1771.
Chekiang.

285.* 哲 30/7 Wise. Sagacious.

(a) chit。-hók 1140.
Philosophy.

286. 蜇 142/7 Sting of insect. Kind of crab.

CHIU
287. 朝 74/8 Morning. Early. S. (ch'iū)

(a) chiu-sìn 3641.
Chosen; Korea.

288. 招 64/5 To receive, entertain, call.

(a) chiu-p'aal 3420.
Shop sign.

(b) chiu-t'ip。4364.
Poster.

(c) kaai-chiu 1430.
Street placard.

(d) chui-tsip。4569.
To entertain (as guests).

289.' 照 72/5 Illustrious. Bright.

CHIÚ
290.' 沼 85/5 Fishpond. Pool.

CHIÙ
291.** 照 86/9 To shine upon, enlighten. Like.

(a) oò-chiù 3128.
Passport.

(b) chiù-i 1247.
In accordance with.

292.* 詔 149/5 Imperial proclamation.(chiû)

(a) chiù-shue 3982.
Imperial mandate.

CHIÛ
293. 召 30/2 To call, summon.

294. 兆 10/4 Omen. Sign.

(a) chiû-t'aū 4339.
A sign. Portent.
295. 趙 156/7 To hasten to. S.
,"

CHÓH
296. 阻 170/5 To hinder, oppose, obstruct.
(a) chóh-chuē 339.
To hinder.
(b) chóh-ngoî 3071.
To retard.
297. 咀 30/7 Sign of past tense. F.

CHÒH
298. 詛 149/5 To curse; revile.

CHÓH
299. 助 19/5 To help, assist.

CHŌK
300. 濯 85/14 To wash, rinse.
*

CHONG
301. 裝 145/7 To pack, load, dress. Fashion.
(a) chong-paān 3190.
Costume.
(b) chong-hong 1178.
Vain.
(c) chong-tseuk₀ 4518.
To decoy birds.
302. 妝 38/4 } To adorn, dress,
303. 粧 119/6 } disguise, feign.
(a) chong-līm 2343.
Ladies toilet.
304. 椿 75/11 A stake, post.
* Piling. C.
(a) faū-chong 743.
A buoy.

305. 眈 109/6 To stare at,
,, watch, peep,
306. 覘 147/11 spy.
*
(a) chong-ngaau 3007.
Bopeep.
307. 莊 140/7 Sedate.
* Correct. S.
308. 庄 53/3 Farm house.
, Building.

CHŌNG
309. 壯 33/4 Strong.
Robust.
(a) chǒng-kīn 1666.
Hale. Healthy.
(b) chǒng-yŭng 5281.
Volunteers.
(c) chǒng-shāt 3854.
Plethora.

CHÒNG
310. 撞 64/12 To strike against.
(a) seung-chǒng 3625.
To meet, affront.
(b) chǒng-paán 3187.
To disappoint.
(c) chǒng-paau-sin-shaang.
3198-3639-3802.
A quack.
(d) chǒng-ngaam 2993.
Well met!
311. 狀 94/4 Form. Appearance. Complaint. Lawsuit.
(a) hāng-chǒng 986.
Biography.
(b) kung-chǒng 1882.
A plea.
(c) chǒng-sz 3757.
Attorney.

CHUE
312. 豬 94/9 } Pig.
313. 豬 152/9 } Swine.

(a) shaan-chue 3793.
Porcupine.

(b) tsìn-chue 4556.
Hedgehog.Porcupine.

(c) t'ó-chue 4380.
Badger.

(d) chue-uē 4872.
Porpoise.

(e) chue-lŭng-ts'ó 2533-
4777. Pitcher plant.

314. 珠 $\frac{96}{6}$ Pearl.
Bead.

(a) nap-chue 2859.
A knob.

315. 諸 $\frac{149}{9}$ All.
The whole.

(a) chue-kwan 2074.
Gentlemen— as a
company addressed.

316. 朱 $\frac{75}{2}$ Red.Vermillion.
Scarlet. S.

317. 蛛 $\frac{142}{6}$ Spider.

(a) chue-sz 3761.
Spider web.

318. 株 $\frac{75}{6}$ Trunk of
a tree.

(a) chue-lìn 2350.
To implicate.

319. 脾 $\frac{130}{6}$ The cheeks.

320. 硃 $\frac{112}{6}$ Vermillion.
Imperial.

(a) chue-sha 3779.
Cinnabar.

(b) chue-sha-kat 1561.
Mandarin orange.

(c) ngān-chue 3028.
Vermillion powder.

321. 侏 $\frac{9}{6}$ Pigmy.

322. 菜 $\frac{140}{6}$ A kind of tree.

323. 誅 $\frac{149}{6}$ To punish,
exterminate.

324. 詶 $\frac{113}{6}$ To curse.

325. 洙 $\frac{85}{6}$ S.

326. 潴 $\frac{85}{16}$ A pool.

327. 銖 $\frac{167}{6}$ S.

328. 主 $\frac{3}{4}$ Lord. Master.
To rule.

(a) chué-chî 235.
To govern.

(b) chué-ì 1258.
Resolve. Decision.

(c) ts'ói-chué-lò 4803-
2404. Capitalist.
Rich man.

(d) uk-chué 4944.
Landlord.

329. 煑 $\frac{86}{9}$ To cook,
prepare food.

330. 麈 $\frac{198}{5}$ The yak.

331. 渚 $\frac{85}{9}$ Name of an
island.

332. 鑄 $\frac{167}{14}$ To cast metals.

333. 註 $\frac{149}{5}$ To define,
annotate.

(a) chuè-ch'aak 423.
To register.

334. 蛀 $\frac{142}{5}$ Worm eaten.

335. 駐 $\frac{187}{5}$ To sojourn.
To colonize.

(a) chuè-chaat 104.
To be stationed at.

336. 著 $\frac{140}{9}$ To manifest.
(cheuk.)

337. 炷 $\frac{86}{5}$ Wick. C. for
incense sticks,
etc.

338. 注 85/5 To fix the mind on.

CHUĒ
339.** 住 9/5 To stop, abide, dwell.
(a) chuē-ka 1410.
   A residence.
(b) cha-chuē 57.
   To hold fast.
340. 筯 118/7 } Chopsticks.
341. 箸 119/9 }

CHUEN
342. 磚 112/11 } Brick.
343. 甎 98/11 } Tile.
(a) ts'ing-chuen 4764.
   Burnt brick.
(b) kaai-chuen 1435.
   Red floor tiles.
344.* 專 41/8 Only. Solely. Exclusive attention.
345. 鱄 195/11 A kind of fish.

CHUÉN
346. 轉 159/11 To turn, change, revolve.(chuén)
(a) chuén-aau 28.
   Turn a corner.
(b) chuén-waan 4971.
   Turn a bend, veer.

CHUÈN
347. 轉 159/11 To turn about, roll, change. (chuèn, ch'uèn)
(a) chuèn-k'eī 1953.
   Turncoat.

CHUÊN
348. 傳 9/11 (ch'uēn)

CHUET
349.* 啜 30/8 To suck, sip, sob, kiss.
350.* 拙 64/5 Stupid. Clumsy.
351. 劚 18/8 To carve, engrave.
352. 惙 61/8 Mournful.
353. 掇 64/8 To pluck.
354. 歠 76/15 To drink.
355. 輟 159/8 To stop, suspend.

CHUI
356. 追 162/6 To pursue, reach, reflect.
357.* 錐 167/8 An awl. Gimlet. To pierce.
358. 隹 R/172 Short tailed birds.
(a) sha-chui 3778.
   A snipe.

CHUÎ
359.* 贅 154/11 To repeat. Over and over.
(a) chuî-luî 2496.
   Repetition. Verbose.
(b) chuî-ìn 1350.
   Verbiage.
(c) chuî-wâ 4960.
   Tittle-tattle.
360.* 墜 32/12 To fall, sink.
(a) chuî-lōk 2454.
   Prolapse.
(b) chuî-sing 3652.
   Meteor.
361. 縋 120/10 A cord. To let down.

-19-

CHUK

362. 祝 $\frac{113}{5}$ To invoke. S.

  (a) chuk-fuk 867.
    To bless.

  (b) miŭ-chuk 2709.
    Temple keeper.

363. 捉 $\frac{64}{7}$ To arrest, catch, seize. (chuk)

  (a) chuk-tsź-shat 4672-3849. To cavil.

364. 竹 $\frac{R}{118}$ Bamboo.

  (a) chuk-shāt 3854.
    Bamboo seeds.

  (b) chuk-wōng 5070.
    Bamboo silica.

  (c) chuk-sún 3740.
    Bamboo sprouts.

  (d) chuk-paāk 3179.
    Padacarpus nageia.

  (e) taâm-chuk-ĭp 4042-1367. Commolina.

  (f) naām-t'in-chuk 2823-4355. Nandina Domestica.

  (g) shēk-chuk 3879.
    Dianthus.

365. 粥 $\frac{119}{6}$ Congee. Gruel. S.

366. 燭 $\frac{86}{13}$ A candle. To light.

  (a) laāp-chuk 2192.
    Wax candle.

  (b) chuk-t'oĭ 4422.
    Candlestick.

367. 囑 $\frac{30}{21}$ To order, bid, enjoin upon.

368. 築 $\frac{118}{9}$ To raise entrenchments. Fortifications.

CHUK₀

369. 捉 $\frac{64}{7}$ Arrest, seize, catch. (chuk)

CHŪK

370. 逐 $\frac{162}{7}$ To expel, drive out.

  (a) kón-chūk 1765.
    To expel.

  (b) chūk-kwaí 2061.
    To exorcise.

  (c) chūk-kôh 1734.
    To particularize.

  (d) chūk-tsź 4672.
    Verbatim.

  (e) chūk-yat 5133.
    One by one. In order.

371. 軸 $\frac{159}{5}$ Axle. Pivot. Axis.

  (a) lūn-chūk 2518.
    An axle.

  (b) chìng-chūk 275.
    Principal axis.

  (c) têng-chūk 4132.
    Fixed axis.

  (d) ts'z-chūk 4851½.
    Magnetic axis.

  (e) shî-chūk 3911.
    Visual axis.

372. 濁 $\frac{85}{13}$ Muddy. Turbid.

  (a) paāk-chūk 3178.
    Gonorrhea.

CHUN

373. 嚀 $\frac{30}{8}$ "   To babble.
374. 吨 $\frac{30}{4}$ "   Gibberish.
375. 諄 $\frac{149}{8}$ "   To impress upon. Earnestly.

CHÚN

376. 准 $\frac{15}{8}$ To allow, permit, authorize.
377. 準 $\frac{85}{10}$ To adjust. A water level. Exactly.

378. 隼 $\frac{172}{2}$
379. 雛 $\frac{196}{8}$ Falcon species.
380. 鷷 $\frac{196}{11}$

381. 嗒 $\frac{30}{15}$
382. 噸 $\frac{30}{12}$ Confused.

383. 中 $\frac{2}{3}$ Middle. Center. Within.(chùng)
(a) chung-kaan 1463. Within. Between.
(b) chung-ì. 1258. To like.
(c) chung-hŏk 1140. Middle school.
(d) chung-kwok. 2104. China.

384. 忠 $\frac{61}{4}$ Devoted. Loyal. Faithful.

385. 鐘 $\frac{167}{12}$ Bell. Clock.
(a) shì-shān-chung 3905-3838. A clock.

386. 舂 $\frac{134}{5}$ To pound out, hull grain.
(a) chung-hŏm 1145. A mortar.
(b) chung-fooi-sha. 845-3778. Beat chunam.
(c) chung-ts'eūng 4738. Build concrete wall.

387. 盅 $\frac{108}{4}$ A bowl. Cup.

388. 終 $\frac{120}{5}$ Final. The end. S.

389. 鍾 $\frac{167}{9}$ A cup.

390. 螽 $\frac{142}{11}$ A locust.

391. 種 $\frac{115}{9}$ Seed. Germ. Yeast.(chùng)
(a) yàn-chúng-hŏk 5117-1140. Ethnology.
(b) tá-chúng 4027. To copulate (of animals).
(c) tsaáp-chúng 4475. Mongrel.

392. 腫 $\frac{130}{9}$ A swelling.
393. 瘇 $\frac{104}{9}$ To swell.
(a) shuí-chúng 4004. Dropsy.

394. 踵 $\frac{157}{9}$ Heel. To follow.

395. 眾 $\frac{143}{6}$ Many. A crowd.
396. 中 $\frac{2}{3}$ To hit the center. Exactly. (chung)
397. 種 $\frac{115}{9}$ To plant, sow. (chúng)
(a) chùng-taú 4118. To vaccinate.

398. 重 $\frac{166}{2}$ Still. Yet. More. (ch'ùng, chùng)
399. 仲 $\frac{9}{4}$ Second brother. S.

399½. 絀 $\frac{120}{5}$ Deficiency. (fat)
399½. 黜 $\frac{203}{5}$ To dismiss, degrade. (fat)

400. 差 $\frac{48}{7}$ Different. Wrong.(ch'aai)

-21-

(a) ch'a-ts'òh 4791.
   A mistake.
(b) ch'a-pat-toh 3236-
   4215. Almost. Near-
   ly.
(c) ch'a-tak-uên 4081-
   4929. Very different.

401. 叉 $\frac{29}{1}$ A fork. To be
   caught in fork.

402. 杈 $\frac{75}{3}$ A (wooden)
   fork.
(a) ch'a-kai-ts'aāk 1516-
   4682. A pickpocket.

403. 扠 $\frac{64}{3}$ To fork up,
   pitch out.

CH'À
404. 詫 $\frac{149}{6}$ To boast.
(a) ch'à-î 1293.
   Incredible.

CH'Ā
405. 查 $\frac{75}{5}$ To examine, investigate.
(a) ch'ā-ch'aat 444.
   To scrutinize.

406. 搽 $\frac{64}{10}$ To rub on, anoint, smear.

407. 喳 $\frac{30}{9}$ Whisper.

407½. 嗏 $\frac{30}{10}$ Twitter.

408. 鵪 $\frac{196}{5}$
(a) chue-shí-ch'ā 312-
   3902. Black thrush.

409. 茶 $\frac{140}{6}$ Tea.
(a) ch'ā-îp 1367.
   Tea leaves.
(b) ch'ā-shuê 3996.
   Tea plant.
(c) ch'ā-moŏt 2792.
   Refuse leaves and
   stems.

(d) ch'ā-kui 1846.
   Tea house.
(e) ch'ā-lām 2226.
   Tea shop.
(f) ch'ā-po 3326.
   Tea kettle.
(g) ch'ā-oō 3122.
   Teapot.
(h) ch'ā-kang 1551.
   Teaspoon.
(i) ch'ā-kei 1609.
   Teapoy.
(j) ch'ā-sheung 3887.
   Tea merchant.
(k) ch'ā-sz 3756.
   Tea taster.
(l) chuen-ch'ā 342.
   Brick tea.
(m) ts'ing-ch'ā 4763.
   Black tea.
(n) hūng-ch'ā 1235.
   Dark red teas.
(o) lūk-ch'ā 2507.
   Green teas.
(p) oo-lūng-ch'ā 3115-
   2532. Oolung tea.
(q) pó-chúng-ch'ā 3331-
   391, or
   paau-chúng-ch'ā 3198.
   Paochung tea.
(r) kung-foo-ch'ā 1877-
   801. Congou.
(s) siú-chúng-ch'ā 3674-
   391. Souchong.
(t) paāk-hŏ-ch'ā 3178-
   1104. Pekeo.
(u) hei-ch'un-ch'ā 1026-
   629. Hyson.
(v) hei-p'eī-ch'ā 3468.
   Old Hyson.
(w) ngōh-meī-ch'ā 3063-
   2657. Young Hyson.
(x) p'eī-ch'ā 3468.
   Hyson skin.
(y) chue-laān-ch'ā 314-
   2182. Scented ca-
   pers.

(z) siú-chue-ch'ā 3674-
314. Gunpowder tea.

(aa) uēn-chue-ch'ā 4918-
314. Imperial gun-
powder tea.

(bb) shuí-sin-ch'ā 4004-
3640. Water fairy.

(cc) lūng-tséng-ch'ā 2532-
4515. Dragon well.

CH'Ǎ
410. 搻 $\frac{64}{10}$ Writing.
ˌ (ch'ā)

CH'AAI
411. 差 $\frac{48}{7}$ An office. Messenger. (ch'a)

(a) ch'aai-yĭk 5211.
A policeman.

412. 搓 $\frac{64}{10}$ To rub or roll
ˌ between the
hands.(ch'aaí)

413. 猜 $\frac{94}{8}$ To suspect,
* doubt, guess.

414. 釵 $\frac{167}{3}$ Hairpin.

CH'AAÍ
415. 踹 $\frac{157}{9}$ To treed under
foot, crush,
bruise.

(a) cn'aaí-taáp 4063.
To trample.

416. 搓 $\frac{64}{10}$ To knead,
* as bread.

CH'AAÌ
417. 嘬 $\frac{30}{12}$ To suck, sip.
ˌ (shaal)

418. 瘵 $\frac{104}{11}$ Wasting
disease.

CH'AAĪ
419. 柴 $\frac{75}{5}$ Firewood.
Kindling.

(a) ch'aaī-t'aū 4339.
Knotty log.

(b) fóh-ch'aaī 767.
Matches.

420. 豹 $\frac{153}{3}$
(a) ch'aaī-lōng 2459.
A wolf.

421. 儕 $\frac{9}{14}$ Sign of
ˌ'" plural.

CH'AAK。
422. 拆 $\frac{64}{5}$ To open, pull
to pieces, de-
stroy.

423. 册 $\frac{13}{3}$ A register.List.
Issue (of per-
iodical).

(a) oô-haú-ch'aak。3129-
1006. A census.

(b) sheùng-ch'aak。3895.
To register.

424. 策 $\frac{118}{6}$ To plan, whip,
ˌ scheme.

425. 坼 $\frac{32}{5}$ To burst,
ˌ crack.

CH'AAM
426. 篸 $\frac{118}{11}$ Basket. Hod.
ˌ Scuttle.
(tsaam,ts'aám,
ts'aàm)

CH'AÀM
427. 杉 $\frac{75}{3}$ A log. Timber.
Pine.

CH'AĀM
428. 撑 $\frac{64}{17}$ To support,
ˌ hold up.

CH'AǍM
429. 桭 $\frac{75}{8}$ Doorsill.
ˌ (ch'aan)

CH'AÁN
430. 産 $\frac{100}{6}$ To produce,
bear. Produc-
tion. Estate.

(a) ch'aán-îp 1368.
Property.

(b) t'ó-ch'aán 4380.
Local products. Products of the soil.

(c) shaang-ch'aán. 3802.
To breed, rear.

(d) ch'aán-moōn 2779.
The vagina.

431. 鏟 $\frac{167}{11}$ To shovel.
* A shovel.

432. 剗 $\frac{18}{8}$ To level.
*

433. 剗 $\frac{18}{11}$ To cut off,
* extinguish.

434. 串 $\frac{2}{6}$ A skewer.

CH'AÁN

435. 根 $\frac{75}{8}$ Doorsill. To
. cleanse.
(ch'aàm)

CH'AANG

436. 撐 $\frac{64}{12}$ To pole a boat,
. push off, prop
437. 撐 $\frac{64}{12}$ up. (ch'aàng)

CH'AÁNG -- See 440.

CH'AÁNG

438. 瞠 $\frac{109}{12}$ To dazzle.
*

439. 撐 $\frac{64}{12}$ To stretch open,
* prop. See 436.

CH'AÁNG

440. 橙 $\frac{75}{12}$ Common orange.
. (ch'aàng)

441. 根 $\frac{75}{8}$ See 429 and
. 435.

CH'AAP

442. 插 $\frac{64}{9}$ To insert, drive
* into, put up.
(a) ch'aap.-sheang 3802.
To grow from slip.

(b) ch'aap.-shiu 3965.
Lean of roast pork.

(c) ch'aap.-shiu-tsai
4482. Children of
concubine.

(d) ch'aap-shaú-ló 3859-
2404. Pickpocket.

443. 扱 $\frac{64}{4}$ uf 442.
(ngāp, yap)

CH'AAT

444. 察 $\frac{40}{11}$ To examine, know,
judge, investi-
gate.

445. 獺 $\frac{94}{16}$ The otter.
*
(a) shuí-ch'aat. 4004.
Common otter.

(b) hoí-ch'aat. 1125.
The seal.

446. 刹 $\frac{18}{6}$ Monastery.
.

CH'AAU

447. 抄 $\frac{64}{4}$ To transcribe,
* copy. To con-
fiscate.

CH'AAÚ

448. 炒 $\frac{86}{4}$ To fry, roast,
. grill.
(a) ch'aaú-t'it. 4366.
To puddle iron.

(b) siú-ch'aaú-yŭk 3674-
5249. Fried hash
and vegetables.

(c) ch'aaú-uk 4944.
To speculate in
houses.

(d) ch'aaú-ch'â 409.
To fire tea.

449. 吵 $\frac{30}{4}$ Clamor. Din.
Uproar.

CH'AAÙ

450. 鈔 $\frac{167}{4}$ Dues. Taxes.
. Paper money.

(a) shuı-ch'aaù 4005.
Imposts. Transit
dues.

(b) shuĕn-ch'aaù 3999.
Tonnage dues.

CH'AAŪ
451. 巢 $\frac{47}{8}$ A nest.

452. 繰 $\frac{120}{10}$ Wrinkled.(tsaù)
Shriveled.

CH'AK
453. 測 $\frac{85}{9}$ To fathom, es-
* timate, measure.
(ch'aak)

CH'AM
454. 讖 $\frac{149}{17}$ Prognostic.
, Omen.

455. 譖 $\frac{149}{14}$ ⎫
" , ⎬ Slander.
456. 僭 $\frac{9}{14}$ ⎭
" ,

CH'AM
457. 沈 $\frac{85}{4}$ Lost. Ruined.
To sink, drown.

458. 沉 $\frac{85}{4}$ S.

(a) ch'ăm-lūn 2519.
To be lost, ruined.

459. 霃 $\frac{173}{7}$ Cloudy.

(a) yam-yam-ch'ăm-ch'ăm
5090. Rainy looking.

460. 魡 $\frac{195}{4}$ Roe of fish.
" ' (shám)

CH'AN
461. 診 $\frac{149}{5}$ ⎫
⎬ To examine,
462. 睒 $\frac{154}{5}$ ⎭ diagnose,
* verify.

---

463. 疹 $\frac{104}{5}$ Eruption.
* Diagnosis.

464. 繽 $\frac{120}{10}$ To tie.
, Close knit.

465. 軫 $\frac{159}{5}$ A carriage.
" '

CH'ÀN
466. 趁 $\frac{156}{5}$ To embrace an
opportunity.
At the time of.
When.

467. 襯 $\frac{145}{16}$ Inner garments.
" To assist.

468. 櫬 $\frac{75}{16}$ An (inner)
, coffin.

CH'ĀN
469. 塵 $\frac{32}{11}$ Dust. Dirt.
The world.

(a) ch'ān-oi 3096.
Dust. Dirt.

(b) fung-ch'ān 879.
Dusty from travel.

470. 陳 $\frac{170}{8}$ To arrange, display. Old. Dry.

CH'AU
471. 抽 $\frac{64}{5}$ To lift, draw
out, levy,whip.

(a) ch'au-kan 1539.
Spasm. Cramps.

(b) ch'au-heı 1033.
To gasp.

CH'AÚ
472. 丑 $\frac{1}{3}$ 1 to 3 a.m.
* Buffoon. Clown.

473. 醜 $\frac{104}{10}$ Ugly. Deformed.
* Vile.

CH'AÙ
474. 臭 $\frac{132}{4}$ Stench.
Smell.

(a) ch'aù-ch'ūng 646.
   Bedbugs.
(b) ch'aù-shuí 4004.
   Carbolic. Disinfec-
   tant.
(c) ch'aù-ts'ó 4777.
   Rue.
(d) ch'aù-hang-hang 982.
   Nasty smell.

CH'AŪ

475. 仇 $\frac{9}{2}$ To hate,
   oppose.

476. 讎 $\frac{149}{16}$ An enemy.
   Rival.

477. 讐 $\frac{149}{16}$

(a) pò-ch'aū 3337.
   To take revenge.

478. 綢 $\frac{120}{8}$ Silk. Pongee.
   Fine texture.

(a) shaang-ch'aū 3802.
   Stiff or raw pongee.
(b) shŭk-ch'aū 4011.
   Soft silk or pongee.
(c) uě-ch'aū 4893.
   Bombazettes.

479. 囚 $\frac{31}{2}$ To imprison. A
   prisoner.(ts'aū)

480. 籌 $\frac{118}{14}$ To compute.A lot
   or tally. Game.

(a) kaang-ch'aū 1479.
   To strike the hour.

481. 稠 $\frac{115}{8}$ Thick. Close.
   Crowded.

482. 酬 $\frac{164}{6}$ To pledge.

483. 酧 $\frac{164}{6}$ An offering.
   Thanksgiving.

484. 儔 $\frac{9}{14}$ Class.
   Clique.

485. 紬 $\frac{120}{5}$ uf 478.

486. 裯 $\frac{145}{8}$ Cover.
   Curtain.

487. 躊 $\frac{157}{14}$

CH'AŬ

488. 趨 $\frac{156}{10}$ To walk,
   or
489. 蹂 $\frac{157}{10}$ sprain ankle.

CH'E

490. 車 $\frac{R}{159}$ Cart. Vehicle.
   Engine. Motor.
   To turn in a
   lathe. S. (kui)

(a) ch'e-lūn 2518.
   Wheels.
(b) ch'e-tsaí 4482.
   Ricksha.
(c) shuí-ch'e 4004.
   Fire engine.
(d) fóh-ch'e 767.
   Locomotive.
(e) tīn-ch'e 4163.
   Tram. Motor car.
   Electric motor.
(f) kung-foo-ch'e 1877-
   801. Sewing machine.
(g) ch'e-ch'ōng 587.
   A lathe.
(h) taan-ch'e 4046, or
   keuk-ch'e 1638.
   Bicycle.
(i) shaú-ch'e 3859.
   Wheelbarrow.
(j) ch'e-tseūng 4529.
   A turner.
(k) taaī-ch'e 4033.
   Chief engineer.
(l) ch'e-ts'ĭn-ts'ó
   4760-4777.Plantago.
(m) tsź-yaū-ch'e 4673-
   5148. Automobile.

491. 奢 $\frac{37}{9}$ Wasteful.
   Extravagant.

(a) ch'e-ch'í 522.
   Wanton.

CH'É
492. 且 $\frac{1}{4}$ Also. Moreover.

493. 扯 $\frac{64}{4}$ To go away, send off. To haul, drag, pull apart.

494. 撦 $\frac{64}{12}$

  (a) ch'é-heī 1033. Death rattle.

  (b) laai-ch'é-suen 2151-3708. To strike an average.

  (c) ch'é-peī-hōn 3269-1165. To snore.

495. 扭 $\frac{64}{5}$ Wrongly used for 490 and 493.

CH'EK₂ -- See also ch'ik₀.
496. 尺 $\frac{44}{1}$ Chinese foot measure. A standard.

  (a) p'aaī-ts'īn-ch'ek₀ 3419-4761. Tailor's foot, 14.8 in. Eng.

  (b) chau-t'ung-ch'ek₀ 158-4452, or kaú-ng-ch'ek₀ 1571-2962. Mason's foot, 14.1 inches, Eng.

  (c) leūng-t'īn-ch'ek₀ 2313-4355. Quadrant. Sextant.

  (d) k'uk-ch'ek₀ 2029. Carpenter's square. Pipe elbow.

CH'EUK₀
497. 戳 $\frac{62}{14}$ To stamp, stab. A seal.

498. 卓 $\frac{24}{6}$ Surpassing. Lofty.

CH'EUNG
499. 窓 $\frac{116}{7}$

500. 窻 $\frac{116}{9}$ A window.

501. 窗 $\frac{116}{7}$

  (a) ch'eung-moōn 2779. A window.

  (b) t'in-ch'eung 4355. Skylight.

  (c) paak₀-īp-ch'eung 3170-1369. Venetians.

  (d) t'ong-ch'eung 4434. To open sliding windows.

  (e) ch'eung-hâ 908. At school.

  (f) t'ūng-ch'eung 4459. Fellow students.

  (g) ch'eung-yaŭ 5160. Fellow students.

502. 娼 $\frac{38}{8}$ Singing girls.

  (a) ch'eung-keī 1632. Prostitutes.

  (b) ch'eung-liū 2392. A brothel.

  (c) tong-ch'eung 4230. To lead a life of prostitution.

503. 倡 $\frac{9}{8}$ A leader. uf 502.

504. 菖 $\frac{140}{8}$ The sweet flag.

  (a) ch'eung-p'ō 3519. Calamus.

505. 昌 $\frac{72}{4}$ Prosperous. Shining.

506. 猖 $\frac{94}{8}$ Frenzied. Wild.

CH'ÈUNG
507. 唱 $\frac{30}{8}$ To sing, recite.

508. 暢 $\frac{72}{9}$ Joyous.

509. 鬯 $\frac{R}{192}$ Thorough.

CH'EŪNG

510. 場 $\frac{32}{9}$ A field. Threshing floor.

511. 塲 $\frac{32}{11}$ Place. C.

　(a) faat-ch'eūng 682.
　　Execution ground.

512. 長 $\frac{R}{168}$ Long. (cheūng)

　(a) ch'eūng-hei 1033.
　　Tiresome. Tedious.

513. 腸 $\frac{130}{9}$ Bowels. Intestines.

　(a) sam-ch'eūng 3593.
　　Inward thoughts.Tem-
　　perament. Feelings.

　(b) chĭk-ch'eūng 242.
　　Rectum.

　(c) siú-ch'eūng 3674.
　　Urinary intestines.

　(d) siú-ch'eūng-hei 1033.
　　Hernia.

　(e) chue-ch'eūng 312.
　　Sausage.

　(f) ngaū-ch'eūng 3039.
　　Tripe.

CH'I

514. 黐 $\frac{202}{11}$ Glutinous. Sticky.

515. 嗒 $\frac{30}{11}$ To stick, adhere.

　(a) ch'i-kaau 1495.
　　Birdlime.

516. 癡 $\frac{104}{14}$ Stupid. Idiotic.

517. 痴 $\frac{104}{8}$ Lustful.

518. 笞 $\frac{118}{5}$ To flog, bastinade.

519. 嗤 $\frac{30}{10}$ To laugh heart-ily. To hiss.

520. 褫 $\frac{145}{10}$ To strip, doff.

521. 鴟 $\frac{196}{5}$ An owl.

CH'Í

522. 侈 $\frac{9}{6}$ Extravagant. Wasteful.

523. 始 $\frac{38}{5}$ To begin. First.

　(a) ch'í-ch'oh 572.
　　(At) the beginning.

524. 齒 $\frac{R}{211}$ Front teeth. Age. Serrated.

　(a) haú-ch'í 1006.
　　Promise. Word.

525. 恥 $\frac{61}{6}$ Disgrace. Shame.

526. 耻 $\frac{128}{4}$ To be shamed. Ashamed.

　(a) haú-ch'í 1006.
　　Mealy mouthed.

　(b) sau-ch'í 3604.
　　Shame.

527. 弛 $\frac{57}{3}$ To relax. To annul.

528. 矢 $\frac{R}{111}$ An arrow. To shoot. To take an oath. Straight.

529. 豕 $\frac{R}{152}$ Swine.

530. 豸 $\frac{R}{153}$ Reptiles.

CH'Ì

531. 翄 $\frac{124}{4}$ Wings.

532. 翅 $\frac{124}{4}$ Fins.

533. 幟 $\frac{50}{13}$

CH'Ī
534. 持 64/6 To grasp, hold, support.

535. 池 85/3 Pond. Pool. Cistern. S.

536. 遲 162/11 Tardy. Slow. To wait.

(a) ch'ī-chaī 120. Stagnant.

537. 匙 21/9 Spoon. Key. (shī)

538. 馳 187/3 Fleet. Rapid. Known far and wide.

539. 鯔 195/5 Mackerel.

540. 剮 18/11 To dismember.

541. 治 85/5 To govern, rule. (chī)

CH'Ǐ
542. 恃 61/6 To trust in, depend on.

CH'IK -- See also ch'ek.
543. 斥 69/1 To blame, expel.

(a) ch'ik-faat₀ 682. Jugglery.

544. 蠚 142/11 Venomous.

(a) ch'ik-ch'ūng 646. Scorpion.

545. 敕 66/7 Order. Warrant. Charter.

546. 勅 19/7 (Imperial) orders.

CH'IK -- See also ch'ek₀.
547. 赤 R Reddish. 155 Flesh color.

(a) ch'ik₀-tô 4207. The equator.

(b) ch'ik₀-shan 3830. Naked.

(c) ch'ik₀-sam 3593. Sincere.

(d) ch'ik₀-pò 3336. Nankeen cloth.

(e) ch'ik₀-maī 2603. Red rice.

(f) ch'ik₀-uê 4872. Catfish.

CH'ÍM
548. 諂 149/8 To flatter, fawn.

549. 謅 149/16

CH'ĪN
550. 纏 120/15 To wind about, involve in, bind.(chīn)

(a) ch'īn-chuê 339. To take hold on.

(b) ch'īn-t'āng-fa 4332-650. Convolvulus.

551. 躔 157/15 Revolution. Orbit.

(a) ch'īn-tô 4208. Zodiac.

552. 廛 53/12 Market.

CH'ĪNG
553. 稱 115/9 To style, designate.

554. 秤 115/5 To weigh.

CH'ÍNG
555. 拯 64/6 To rescue save.

(a) ch'íng-kaù 1582. To save.

556. 逞 162/7 Bold. Forward.

557. 檉 75/13 Tamarisk.
"t

CH'ING
558. 稱 115/9 A steelyard. To weigh. Competent. Worthy.
559. 秤 115/5 (ch'ing)

CH'ING
560. 埕 32/7 Earthenware jar.
561. 程 115/7 A road. Journey. To travel. A rule. Measure. One tenth. Percentage.
562. 懲 61/15 To correct, reprove.

CH'IT.
563. 設 149/4 To set up, set forth, devise.
**
(a) ch'it.faat. 682. To devise means.
(b) ch'it.sz 3768. Supposing that.
(c) ch'it.laap 2190. To establish.
564. 撤 64/12 To remove, reject, issue.
*
(a) tsau-ch'it.tsz 4500-4667. Syphon.
565. 轍 159/12 A rut. Track of a wheel.
*
566. 澈 85/12 Clear.
"t
567. 徹 60/12 To penetrate, investigate.
"t

CH'IU
568. 超 156/5 To surpass, release, save.
*

(a) ch'iu-uĕt-hōk 4938-1140. Transcendentalism.
568½. 釗 167/2 To incite, To pare.
"t

CH'IŪ
569. 朝 74/8 Court. To go to court. (chiu)
(a) kwok.-ch'iū 2103. Dynasty.
570. 潮 85/12 Tide. Moist. Damp.
(a) cheúng-ch'iū 190. Rising tide.
(b) lōk-ch'iū 2454. Ebb tide.
(c) ch'iū-shap 3843. Damp.
571. 晁 72/6
"t

CH'OH
572. 初 18/5 To begin. At first.
(a) ch'oh-hōk 1140. Beginning studies. Elementary school.
573. 芻 140/4 Hay. Straw.
"t

CH'ÓH
574. 楚 75/9 Painful. Distressing. Clear.

CH'ŌH
575. 鉏 167/5 Hoe. Mattock.
576. 鋤 167/7 To hoe, till.
(a) ch'ōh-t'aŭ 4339. A hoe.
577. 雛 172/10
"t

-30-

CH'ONG

578. 瘡 104/10 Sore. Boil. Abscess.

(a) ch'ong-laû 2267.
An ulcer.

(b) hŏn-ch'ong 1164.
Chilblains.

(c) ch'ong-na 2810.
A scar.

CH'ÓNG

579. 廠 53/12 Shed. Store-house. Warehouse.

(a) p'ūng-ch'óng 3564.
A shed.

(b) p'aāng-ch'óng 3431.
A mat shed.

580. 敞 66/8 Spacious. Open.

581. 怆 61/10 Sad. Sorrowing.

582. 憅 61/10 Alarmed.

583. 閶 169/10 Nervous. To burst forth.

CH'ÒNG

584. 創 18/10 To begin, invent.

585. 刱 18/6 To found.

(a) ch'òng-tsô 4594.
To create.

CH'ŌNG

586. 牀 90/4 Bed.

587. 床 53/4 Couch.

(a) ch'ōng-p'o 3511.
Bedding.

(b) p'o-ch'ōng 3511.
To make a bed.

588. 幢 50/12 (t'ōng)

CH'UÊ

589. 處 141/5 To manage, set-tle. (ch'uê, shuè)

(a) ch'uê-chì 231.
To judge in the matter. To punish.

CH'UÊ

590. 處 141/5 A location. Place. (shuè)

CH'UÊ

591. 厨 27/12 A kitchen.

592. 廚 53/12

(a) ch'uê-fŏng. 798.
A kitchen.

(b) tsô-ch'uê 4593.
A cook.

593. 除 170/7 To deduct, re-move. Besides. (ch'uî)

594. 儲 9/16 To collect, store. S.

595. 樞 75/11 Pivot. Axis. (shue)

595½. 躇 157/13 Undecided. Irresolute.

CH'UĚ

596. 柱 75/5 Pillar. Post.

(a) ch'uě-tán 4092.
Pedestal.

597. 杵 75/4 Pestle. Beater.

598. 楮 75/9 The paper mulberry.

599. 苧 140/5 A kind of hemp.

600. 貯 154/5 To store up.

601. 署 122/9 Public office.
Acting appointment. (shuě)
  (a) ch'uě-yâm 5105.
    Acting in office.

602. 杼 75/4 A shuttle.
Long.

CH'UEN

603. 穿 116/4 To dig, drill, or perforate through.
  (a) ch'uen-cheuk₀ 177.
    To wear (clothes).
  (b) ch'uen-shaan-kaap₀ 3793-1488. The scaly anteater.

604. 川 R/47 A stream.
  (a) sz̄-ch'uen 3770.
    Szechuen province.

CH'UÉN

605. 揣 64/9 To feel with the hand. (ch'uí)

606. 喘 30/9 To gasp, pant.
  (a) ch'uén-faî 695.
    Wheezing cough.
  (b) heî-ch'uén 1033.
    Asthma.

607. 擩 64/18 To seduce.

608. 竄 116/13 To skulk off, hide.

609. 舛 R/136 Contradictory.

610. 遄 162/9 Quickly.

CH'UÈN

611. 串 2/6 To string. A string of. C.

612. 釧 167/3 A bracelet. S.

CH'UĒN

613. 傳 9/11 To narrate, announce. Annals. Traditions. (chuén)
  (a) ch'uēn-tô 4207.
    To preach, propagate doctrine.
  (b) ch'uēn-shaû 3866.
    To impart, as knowledge.
  (c) ch'uēn-shût 4025.
    To publish, make known.

CH'UI

614. 吹 30/4 To blow, play a wind instrument.
  (a) ch'ui-yam 5089.
    To whistle.
  (b) tang-ch'ui 4094.
    Blowpipe.
  (c) ch'ui-tâ-lô 4027-2404.
    Musicians.
  (d) ch'ui-hong 1175.
    To winnow.
  (e) ch'ui-heî 1033.
    To breathe upon.
  (f) ch'ui-heî 1031.
    To blow.

615. 推 64/8 (t'ui)
  (a) ch'ui-ch'ak 453.
    To calculate.

616. 炊 86/4 To blow. To cook. uf 614.

CH'UÍ

617. 揣 64/9 To estimate. (ch'uén)

CH'UĪ

618. 除 170/7 To deduct. Laying aside. (ch'uē)

619. 錘 167/8 A hammer.

620. 鎚 167/10 A weight. To pound.

621. * 椎 75/8 Hammer.

622. * 槌 75/10 Wrench.

  (a) mŭk-ch'uī 2795.
    A mallet.

  (b) tá-chong-ch'uī 4027-304. A pile driver.

  (c) koó-ch'uī 1802.
    Drumstick.

623. * 搥 64/10 To beat.

CH'UK

624. 束 75/3 To bind, tie.
    A bundle. S.

625. 畜 102/5 Cattle.
    Beasts.

  (a) ch'uk-shaang 3802.
    Animals.

  (b) lŭk-ch'uk 2504.
    Domestic animals.

  (c) ch'uk-má 2561.
    To breed horses.

626. * 蓄 140/10 To gather up.
    To rear.

  (a) ch'uk-lĭk 2330.
    To husband strength.

  (b) ch'uk-pei 3248.
    A reservoir.

  (c) ch'uk-a-t'aū 2-4339.
    To keep slave girls.

627. , 觸 148/13 To strike against, butt, move.

  (a) ch'uk-chōng 310.
    To butt.

  (b) ch'uk-sheung 3885.
    To gore.

628. , 搐 64/10 To writhe.

---

629. * 春 72/5 The spring season.

  (a) ch'un-kwaī 2066.
    Springtime.

  (b) ch'un-fan 696.
    Vernal equinox.

  (c) san-ch'un 3596.
    New Year.

  (d) ch'un-ts'īng 4766.
    Venereal.

630. , 椿 75/9 A long lived tree.

  (a) heung-ch'un 1046.
    Cedrela odorata.

  (b) ch'aù-ch'un 474.
    Allanthus glandulosa.

631. , 橁 130/11 Eggs of birds or reptiles. Testicles.

  (a) ngōh-ch'un-yeûng 3057-5201. Oval.

  (b) uē-ch'un 4872.
    Fish roe. Spawn.

  (c) shēk-ch'un 3879.
    Pebbles.

  (d) shat-ná-ch'un 3851-2811. Nits.

---

632. 蠢 142/15 Stupid. Foolish.

  (a) uē-ch'ún 4874.
    Foolish, Silly.

  (b) ch'ún-chĭk 242.
    Simple minded.

633. , 蹍 157/9 Mixed. Obstinate.

---

634. 充 10/3 To fill, satisfy.

  (a) ch'ung-tīn 4163.
    Electric charge.

(b) foô-ch'ung 839.
  Negative charge.
(c) chîng-ch'ung 275.
  Positive charge.

635. 冲 $\frac{15}{4}$ To dash against, pour.

636. 沖 $\frac{85}{4}$ infuse, dash.

  (a) ch'ung-ch'â 409.
    To make tea.

637. * 衝 $\frac{144}{9}$ To rush towards, collide with.

638. * 涌 $\frac{85}{7}$ Creek. Canal.

639. * 裏 $\frac{145}{4}$ Good. Central. The inner man.

CH'UNG

640. * 寵 $\frac{40}{16}$ Grace. Favor.

641. * 塚 $\frac{32}{10}$ A tomb. A mound.

642. ' 冢 $\frac{14}{8}$ A mound. Eminent.

CH'UNG

643. * 扰 $\frac{64}{6}$ To leap, hop, skip.

644. * 銃 $\frac{167}{6}$ Firearms. A mortar.

  (a) ch'ung-tsz 4667.
    Shot. Ammunition.

CH'ŪNG

645. 重 $\frac{166}{2}$ Heavy. Serious. Weighty. S.
    (ch'ŭng, chŭng)

646. 蟲 $\frac{142}{12}$ Worms.

647. 虫 $\frac{R}{142}$ Insects. Reptiles.

  (a) teí-taí-ch'ŭng 4125-4071. Grub.

  (b) ngaâng-hok。-ch'ŭng 3001-1137. Wood louse.

CH'ŬNG -- See 645.

CH'UT

648. ** 出 $\frac{17}{3}$ Out. To go out, put out.

  (a) ch'ut-sheng 3880.
    To utter, cry out.
  (b) ch'ut-kaai 1430.
    To go out (on the street).
  (c) ch'ut-haú 1006.
    To leave port, export.
  (d) ch'ut-haú-taan 4046.
    Clearance.
  (e) ch'ut-kung 1881.
    To go to stool.
  (f) ch'ut-yam 5106.
    To let out (as property).
  (g) ch'ut-lîk 2330.
    To exert strength.
  (h) ch'ut-shaí 3818.
    To be born.
  (i) ch'ut-ts'ai 4697.
    To divorce a wife.

E

649. " 唉 $\frac{30}{10}$ F-interrogative. Exclamation. (ai)

FA

650. ** 花 $\frac{140}{4}$ Flowers. Ornament. Vice. S.

  (a) fa-hôk 1140.
    Botany.
  (b) fa-wông 5072.
    Gardener.
  (c) fa-yuí 5243.
    Pistil and stamens.
  (d) fa-shaang 3802.
    Peanuts.
  (e) fa-mêng 2669.
    Nickname.

(f) fa-wâ 4960.
   Exaggeration.
(g) fa-hŭng 1235.
   Reward. Bonus.
(h) fa-kong-shĕk 1772-
   3879. Granite.
(i) fa-fa-kung-tsź 1878-
   4667. A rake.
(j) fa-saàn 3576.
   To dissipate.
(k) fa-k'eī-kwok₀ 1953-
   2103. U.S, America.
(l) fa-t'ĕng 4347.
   Pleasure barge. A
   floating brothel.

FÀ
651. 化 $\frac{21}{2}$ To change,trans-
       mute, melt.
(a) fà-hōk 1140.
   Chemistry.
(b) kóm-fà 1755.
   To influence.

FAAÌ
651** 快 $\frac{61}{4}$ Quick. Lively.
       Cheerful.
(a) faaì-ts'uì 4826.
   Speedy.
(b) faaì-tsź 4667.
   Chopsticks.
(c) faaì-leî 2293.
   Sharp. Smart.
652. 塊 $\frac{32}{10}$ Clod. Lump.
       Piece. C.

FAAK
653.* 拂 $\frac{64}{5}$ | To whisk,
                    | beat,
654." 沸 $\frac{85}{5}$ | brush.
                    | (fat)

FAAN
655. 番 $\frac{102}{7}$ | To return,
656. 番 $\frac{102}{6}$ | repeat.
                     | Foreign.
(a) faan-shuē 3991.
   Sweet potatoes.
(b) faan-shĕk-laū 3879-
   2253. Guava.
(c) faan-kaán 1469.
   Soap.
(d) faan-t'aan 4294.
   Gambling game.
(f) lō-faan 2420.
   The(Mr.) foreigner.
657. 翻 $\frac{124}{12}$ To return,
       change. Again.
658. 繙 $\frac{120}{12}$ To translate,
       interpret.
659. 幡 $\frac{50}{12}$ A banner.
       (faān)
660. 旛 $\frac{70}{14}$ Tassels.
       Flag.

FAÁN
661. 反 $\frac{29}{2}$ To turn back,
       turn over,rebel.
(a) seung-faán 3625.
   Contrary.
(b) tsok₀-faán 4610.
   To rebel.
662.* 返 $\frac{162}{4}$ To return,
       turn back.

FAÀN
663. 泛 $\frac{85}{5}$ To float, over-
       flow. Reckless₀
(a) faàn-īn 1350.
   Vague words.
(b) faàn-sheúng 3890.
   Ordinary.
664.* 販 $\frac{154}{4}$ To traffic,
       trade, deal in.

665. 氾 $\frac{85}{2}$ Overwhelming.

666. 汎 $\frac{85}{3}$ uf 663.

FAAN

667. 凡 $\frac{16}{1}$ All. Common.

668. 凣 $\frac{16}{1}$ Everyone. S.

669. 煩 $\frac{86}{9}$ To annoy, worry, trouble.

(a) faan-iŭ 1403.
To vex, annoy.

(b) toh-faan-neĭ 4215-2875. May I trouble you to—.

670. 燔 $\frac{86}{12}$ To burn, roast for sacrifice.

671. 礬 $\frac{112}{15}$ Alum.

(a) paăk-faan 3178.
Alum.

(b) fei-faan 750.
Burnt alum.

(c) ts'ing-faan 4764.
Sulphate of iron.

(d) taám-faan 4038.
Sulphate of copper.

(e) lŭk-faan 2509.
Acetate of copper.

(f) faan-shĕk 3879.
Alum shale.

672. 帆 $\frac{50}{3}$ A sail.

(a) faan-pò 3336.
Canvas.

672½. 藩 $\frac{140}{15}$ Fence. Boundary.

673. 繁 $\frac{120}{11}$ Troublesome. Manifold.

673½. 番 $\frac{140}{12}$ Flourishing. S.

674. 樊 $\frac{37}{11}$ A fence. A cage.

674½. 蟠 $\frac{142}{15}$ A species of small grasshopper.

675. 蹯 $\frac{157}{12}$ A paw.

FAĀN

676. 酓 $\frac{164}{5}$ Evil spirits or influences.

FAÂN

677. 飯 $\frac{184}{4}$ Cooked rice. Food. A meal.

(a) faân-shĭk 3925.
Victuals.

(b) faân-shĭ-t'aŭ 3906-4339. The viper.

(c) faân-yuĭ-oh'ong 5243-578. A wart.

678. 犯 $\frac{94}{2}$ To offend, commit wrong.

679. 範 $\frac{118}{9}$ Pattern. Mold. Rule. S.

680. 梵 $\frac{75}{7}$ Brahmin. Buddhist.

680½. 范 $\frac{140}{5}$

FAAT

681. 發 $\frac{105}{7}$ To send forth. To start, become. S.

(a) faat.-ĭt 1372.
To have fever.

682. 法 $\frac{85}{5}$ Law. Rules. Doctrines. Means. S.

(a) faat.-tsź 4667. Plan. Device. Remedy.

(b) faat.-laăn-sai 2182-3584, or
faat.-kwok.yăn 2103.
France.

(c) faat.-laan-yăn 2179-5118. Flannel.

(e) mŏ (or mō)-faat。2719 (or 2711). No recourse. No help for it.

683. 髮 $\frac{190}{5}$ Hair of the head. S.

(a) seuk。-faat。3624. To shave the entire head.

(b) shĕk-faat。3879. Moss.

(c) faat。-ts'oì 4800. Edible algae.

684. 哱 $\frac{30}{9}$ "

(a) faat。-leî-ts'oì 2300-4802. Pharisee.

FAI
685. 輝 $\frac{159}{8}$ Bright. Glorious. *

686. 虧 $\frac{141}{11}$ Wanting. Defective.(kw'ai)

(a) fai-k'uet。2010. A loss.

687. 煇 $\frac{86}{9}$ Same as 685. '

688. 徽 $\frac{60}{14}$ Excellent. '

(a) on-fai 3107. Anhui province.

689. 麾 $\frac{200}{4}$ Signal (flag). '

FAÎ
690. 廢 $\frac{53}{12}$ To throw away, ruin, destroy.

691. 費 $\frac{154}{5}$ To spend, lavish, waste.

(a) lô-fai 2426. Traveling expenses.

(b) faì-sz̄ 3776. Troublesome.

692. 肺 $\frac{130}{4}$ The lungs. *

(a) faì-lô-chìng 2414-278. Consumption.

693. 痱 $\frac{104}{5}$ Pimples. Skin eruption. *

(a) ìt-faì 1372. Prickly heat.

694. 沸 $\frac{85}{5}$ To bubble up, boil.(fat,faak)

FAÎ
695. 吠 $\frac{30}{4}$ To bark, yelp. *

FAN
696. 分 $\frac{18}{2}$ To divide. A part. Candareen. (fân) **

(a) shăp-fan-hô 3845-1099. Excellent. Perfect.

(b) fan-meî-hŏk 2656-1140 Differential calculus.

(c) fan-kŭk 1875. Branch office.

697. 吩 $\frac{30}{4}$ To give orders.

(a) fan-foô 822. To command.

698. 婚 $\frac{38}{8}$ To marry a wife. Marriage. *

699. 昏 $\frac{72}{4}$ To confuse, bewilder. *

(a) wōng-fan 5070. Dusk.

700. 葷 $\frac{140}{9}$ Meats. Strong flavored vegetables. *

701. 紛 $\frac{120}{4}$ Confused. Disorderly. *

702. 熏 $\frac{86}{10}$ To smoke (as *

703. 燻 $\frac{86}{14}$ meats, hams, etc.). *

704. 曛 $\frac{72}{14}$ Twilight. '

705. 勳 $\frac{19}{14}$ Patriotic '

706. 勛 $\frac{19}{10}$ merit. '

-37-

707. 惽 $\frac{61}{8}$ Dull. Stupified.

708. 枌 $\frac{75}{4}$ White elm tree.

709. 棻 $\frac{75}{7}$ Wood burnt for perfume.

710. 氛 $\frac{84}{4}$ Miasma. Pirates. Sedition.

711. 芬 $\frac{140}{4}$ Fragrant.

712. 闇 $\frac{169}{8}$ A gate.

FÁN
713. 粉 $\frac{119}{4}$ Flour. Powder. To whitewash.
(a) fa-fán 650. Pollen.
(b) fán-tsai 4482. Vermicelli.
(c) fán-sz 3761. Vermicelli.
(d) t'ung-sam-fán 4452-3593. Macaroni.
(e) chi-fán 211. Cosmetics.
(f) fóh-shēk-fán 767-3879. Chalk.

714. 扮 $\frac{64}{4}$ (paàn)

FÀN
715. 瞓 $\frac{109}{10}$ To lie down, sleep.
(a) ngaǎn-fàn 2999. Sleepy.
(b) fàn-kaau 1509. Asleep.

716. 訓 $\frac{149}{3}$ To instruct, teach. Teachings.

717. 糞 $\frac{119}{11}$ Excrement. To dung, till.

FĀN
718. 墳 $\frac{32}{12}$ A grave. A mound.

(a) fān-mó 2727. A tomb.

719. 焚 $\frac{86}{8}$ To burn. Cremation.

FẢN
720. 忿 $\frac{61}{4}$ Anger. Resentment. (fān)
(a) fǎn-hàn 981. To hate bitterly.

721. 憤 $\frac{61}{12}$ Zeal. Ardor. Boiling rage.

722. 奮 $\frac{37}{13}$ To earnestly endeavor. Energetic.

FÀN
723. 分 $\frac{18}{2}$ Position. Reputation. A share.
(a) sz-fàn-yat 3770-5133. One fourth.
(b) saam-fàn-lūk 3572-2504. A five cent coin.

724. 份 $\frac{9}{4}$ A share. uf 723.

FÂNG
725. 撝 $\frac{64}{8}$ To swing. (fìng)

FAT
726. 忽 $\frac{61}{5}$ Suddenly. To disregard. S.
(a) fat-īn 1349. Suddenly.
(b) hing-fat 1071. To make light of.

727. 拂 $\frac{64}{5}$ To bring, take away. (faak)

728. 揗 $\frac{64}{8}$ To remove dirt.

729. 窟 $\frac{116}{8}$ An opening.

730. 掘 $\frac{64}{8}$ A hut.

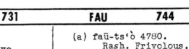

731. 弗 $\frac{57}{2}$ Not. Negative.

732. 沸 $\frac{85}{5}$ To sprinkle, bubble up.

733. 笏 $\frac{118}{4}$ Ivory tablet.

__FĀT__

734. 罰 $\frac{122}{9}$ To fine, forfeit, punish. (faāt)

(a) yīng-fāt 5231. Punishment.

735. 佛 $\frac{9}{5}$ Buddha.

(a) fāt-kaaù 1507. Buddhism.

(b) fāt-shaú 3859. Citron. Citrus.

(c) fāt-song 3699. Hibiscus syriaca.

(d) fāt-ts'ing 4764 Ultramarine.

736. 乏 $\frac{4}{4}$ Needy. Poor.

737. 伐 $\frac{9}{4}$ To fell wood. To cut down.

__FAU__

738. 缶 $\frac{R}{121}$ Earthenware.

739. 罘 $\frac{122}{4}$ Screen. Snare.

740. 坯 $\frac{32}{4}$ Unburnt bricks. (p'ooi)

741. 抔 $\frac{64}{4}$ To take up in both hands.

__FAÚ__

742. 否 $\frac{30}{4}$ Negative. No.

__FAŪ__

743. 浮 $\frac{85}{7}$ To float. Volatile.

(a) faū-ts'ò 4780. Rash. Frivolous.

(b) faū-shuí-huen 4004-1201. A life belt.

744. 蜉 $\frac{142}{7}$ Kind of ant.

__FAÙ__

745. 埠 $\frac{32}{8}$ A port. Mart on river or sea. (faù)

746. 阜 $\frac{R}{170}$ Mound. Abundant.

747. 復 $\frac{60}{9}$ Further. Once again. (fūk)

748. 覆 $\frac{146}{12}$ To cover. (fūk)

__FEI__

749. 非 $\frac{R}{175}$ Opposed to. Not false.

(a) fei-sheūng 3890. Notable.

750. 飛 $\frac{R}{183}$ To fly.

(a) fei-shué 3985. The bat.

751. 妃 $\frac{38}{3}$ Imperial concubine.

752. 啡 $\frac{30}{8}$

__FEÍ__

753. 匪 $\frac{22}{8}$ Vagabond. Seditious.

(a) feí-t'ò 4390. Rowdies.

754. 榧 $\frac{75}{10}$ Yew tree.

755. 菲 $\frac{140}{8}$ Coarse. Poor.

756. 斐 $\frac{67}{8}$

(a) feí-līp-paaī 2380-3168. Philippines.

757. 棐 75/8 To assist. Yew tree.

758. 誹 149/8 To slander, grumble.

FEI
759. 肥 130/4 Fat. Fertile. Flourishing.
(a) feī-chòng 309. Robust.
(b) feī-taaī 4033. Portly.
(c) feī-meī 2661. Plump.
(d) feī-yùn 5258. Fertile.

760. 腓 130/8 (feī)

FEI
761. 翡 124/8
(a) feī-ts'uì-yūk 4827-5250. Chrysoprase.

FIK
762. 味 30/5 Fitful. (ît)

FING
763. 拼 64/8 To swing, fling. To slap, jerk. (fâng)

FIT
764. 慸 183/5 To whip, whisk, brush.

FOH
765. 科 115/4 Series. Rank. Department.
(a) noī-foh 2937. Medical practice.

(b) ngoī-foh 3070. Surgery.

766. 蝌 142/9 Tadpole.

FOH
767. 火 R/86 Fire. Fever. To burn.
(a) fóh-chuk 366. Conflagration.
(b) fóh-îm 1327. Flame.
(c) fóh-shí 3902. Sparks.
(d) fóh-fei 750. To sparkle.
(e) fóh-lo 2401. Soot.
(f) fóh-lŏ 2406. Fireplace. Stove.
(g) fóh-shaan 3793. Volcano.
(h) fóh-tséng 4515. Oil well.
(i) fóh-sìng 3652. Planet Mars. Stars.
(j) fóh-shuí 4004. Kerosene.
(k) fóh-ts'eung. 4736. Firearms.
(l) fóh-yeùk 5183. Gunpowder.
(m) fóh-ts'at 4721. Sealing wax.
(n) fóh-t'uí 4448. Ham.
(o) fóh-kai 1515. The turkey.
(p) fóh-shĕk 3879. Flint.
(q) fóh-shĕk-laū 2253. Flowering pomgranate.

768. 伙 9/4 Tools. Gear. Goods.

(a) fóh-shĭk 3925.
Provisions.
(b) fóh-t'aū 4339.
A cook.
(c) fóh-keĭ 1630.
Assistant.Employee.
(d) fóh-cheŭng 190.
First mate.

(e) ĭ-fóh 1287.
Second mate.
769. 夥 36 Comrade.
　　 11 Partner.
(a) fóh-keĭ 1630.
Partner. Mate.
770. 顆 181 C. for things
　　 8 small and round.

FÒH
771. 貨 154 Goods. Wares.
　　 4 Cargo.
(a) heĭ-fòh 1031.
To discharge cargo.
(b) fòh-ts'ong 4807.
Storehouse.
772. 課 149 A lesson.
※ 　 8 A task.

FOK。
773. 藿 140 A fragrant
　　 16 plant.
(a) fok₂heung 1046.
Betony.Bishopwort.
774. 霍 173
　　 8
(a) fok₂luĕn-chĭng 2474-
278. Cholera.
775. 縛 120 To bind, tie
※ 　 10 up.
776. 廓 53 To cut off.
　　 11
777. 擴 64 To extend.
　　 15 (kwok。)
778. 攉 64 To beckon.
　　 15

FONG
779. 方 R Square.
　　 70 Region. Area.
(a) fong-t'ĭn 4356.
Plane mensuration.
(b) fong-faat。682.
Means. Method.
(c) fong-leŭk 2309.
A stratagem.
(d) fong-pĭn 3295.
Convenient.
780. 慌 61 Nervous. Fear-
　　 10 ful. Alarmed.
781. 荒 140 Wilderness.
　　 6 Waste. Uninhab-
　　 ited.
(a) fong-ts'ó 4777.
Speargrass.
782. 坊 32 Street.
※ 　 4 Shop.
(a) kaai-fong 1430.
Neighbor.
783. 枋 75 A kind of wood.
　　 4
784. 妨 38 To oppose,
　　 4 impede.
(a) mō-fong 2711.
No objection.
Harmless.

785. 肪 130 Fat.
　　 4 Grease.
786. 芳 140 Fragrant.
※ 　 4 Agreeable.
(a) fong-ts'ó 4777.
Fresh grass.

FÓNG
787. 紡 120 To spin, reel,
※ 　 4 twist.
788. 訪 149 To inquire into,
※ 　 4 search out.
789. 誮 149 A lie.
※ 　 9 Falsehood.
790. 舫 137 A boat.
　　 4

-41-

791. 説 149/6 Same as 789.

792. 倣 9/8 To resemble.

793. 恍 61/6 Wild. Mad.

794. 幌 50/10 Curtain.

FŎNG

795. 放 66/4 To release, let loose, give license to.

(a) fòng-ka 1423.
    To give a holiday.

(b) fòng-kung 1877.
    To quit work.
    Quitting time.

(c) fòng-fóh 767.
    Arson.

(d) fòng-tòng 4238.
    Dissolute.

(e) fòng-sż 3775.
    Intemperate.

796. 況 85/5 Moreover. Still more.

797. 況 15/5 Comparatively.

(a) fòng-ch'é 492.
    Moreover.

FŌNG

798. 房 63/4 Room. Dwelling. S.

(a) fōng-chung-taan 383-4048. Aphrodisiacs.

(b) hāng-fōng 986, or t'ūng-fōng 4459.
    Copulation. Sexual intercourse.

799. 防 170/4 To guard against. Beware.

800. 魴 195/4 The bream.

FOO

801. 夫 37/1 Husband. Man. Nobility. S.

(a) foo-tsź 4667.
    Complimentary address.

(b) kiú-foo 1703.
    Chair coolie.

802. 呼 30/5 To call out, shout.

803. 枯 75/5 Dried. Withered.

(a) foo-kó 1724.
    Dry rot.

(b) foo-fai 690.
    Mortification.

804. 骷 188/5 Skeleton.

(a) foo-lŏ-t'aū 2410-4339.
    A skull.

805. 箍 118/8 To bind, hoop. (k'oo)

806. 敷 66/11 To proclaim, propagate.

(a) foo-yeŭk 5183.
    To apply medicine.

807. 麩 199/5 Bran of wheat.

808. 孚 39/4

809. 俘 9/7 To capture. Booty.

810. 枹 75/8 A drumstick.

811. 膚 130/11 The skin.

812. 麱 199/7 Same as 807.

FOÓ

813. 苦 140/5 Bitter. Affliction.

(a) foó-ch'óh 574.
    Distressing.

(b) foó-lìn 2359.
    Pride of India.

814. 府 $\frac{53}{5}$ District. Prefecture. Office.
(a) t'ó-foó 4380.
     A tower.

815. 虎 $\frac{141}{2}$ Tiger species. Tigerlike.
(a) ló-foó 2420.
     The tiger.
(b) foó-paan-má 3182-2561.
     The zebra.
(c) foó-moōn 2779.
     Bocca Tigris.

816. 斧 $\frac{69}{4}$ Axe. Hatchet.
(a) foó-t'aū 4339.
     Hatchet.
(b) kai-tsuí-foó 1515-4627. Pickaxe.

817. 撫 $\frac{64}{12}$ Comfort.
* To soothe.

818. 俯 $\frac{9}{8}$ To stoop, condescend.
*

819. 琥 $\frac{96}{8}$ Signet.
'
(a) foó-p'aak。 3425.
     Amber.

820. 釜 $\frac{167}{2}$
" '
(a) foó-shaan 3793.
     Fusan.

821. 甫 $\frac{101}{2}$ S.
'   (pó)

822. 咐 $\frac{30}{5}$ To order, command. Used with 697 and 367.

823. 富 $\frac{40}{9}$ Rich. Wealthy. Abundance.
(a) foó-haù 1014.
     Wealthy.

824. 褲 $\frac{145}{10}$ Trousers.

825. 袴 $\frac{145}{6}$ Drawers.

(a) t'ò-foo 4386.
     Leggins. Overalls.

826. 副 $\frac{18}{9}$ To aid, second. C.
(a) foó-līng-s2 2376-3776.
     Vice-consul.

827. 庫 $\frac{53}{7}$ Storehouse. Treasury.
(a) foó-ngàn 3028.
     Revenue.

828. 賦 $\frac{154}{8}$ To bestow, levy.
* An idyl.

829. 戽 $\frac{63}{4}$ To bale out, lift water.
*

830. 扶 $\frac{64}{4}$ To uphold, help.
(a) foō-ch'Í 534.
     To sustain.

831. 乎 $\frac{4}{4}$ (oo)

832. 符 $\frac{118}{5}$ To verify.
* A charm. S.
(a) foō-hōp 1193.
     To tally.
(b) foō-lūk 2513½.
     A charm.

833. 芙 $\frac{140}{4}$
*
(a) foō-yūng-fa 5278-650.
     Hibiscus mutabilis.

834. 鳬 $\frac{196}{2}$ Mallard. Duck.

835. 婦 $\frac{38}{8}$ Married woman. Female.

836. 父 $\frac{R}{88}$ Father. Fatherly.
(a) foō-ts'an 4712.
     Father.

(b) shān-foô 3835.
Roman Catholic
priest.

(c) foô-hing 1070.
Fathers and breth-
ren.

837. 傅 $\frac{9}{10}$ To superintend,
teach.

(a) sz-foô 3757.
Master workman.

838. 附 $\frac{170}{5}$ Neighboring.
Adjacent.

839. 負 $\frac{154}{2}$ Ungrateful.
To owe.

840. 付 $\frac{9}{3}$ To transfer,
give to.

(a) foô-t'ok 4427.
To entrust with.

841. 赴 $\frac{156}{2}$ To go, come,
reach, attend.

842. 腐 $\frac{130}{8}$ Rotten.
Decayed.

(a) foô-laân 2186.
Putrid.

843. 輔 $\frac{159}{7}$ To help, aid.

844. 耐 $\frac{113}{5}$ To inter.

844½. 鮒 $\frac{195}{5}$ A kind of fresh
water fish.

FOOI

845. 灰 $\frac{86}{2}$ Ashes. Lime.
Plaster.

(a) fooi-shui 4004.
(White)wash.

(b) shaang-fooi 3802.
Quicklime.

(c) ngā-fooi 2977.
Tooth powder.

(d) pat-fooi-mūk 3236-
2795. Asbestos.

846. 詼 $\frac{149}{6}$ To play with,
jest, banter.

(a) fooi-haaī 915.
To banter.

---

847. 魁 $\frac{194}{4}$ First.
Chief.

FOOI

848. 續 $\frac{120}{12}$ To embroider,
sketch,

849. 繪 $\frac{120}{13}$ paint.
(kw'oof)

850. 賄 $\frac{154}{6}$ To bribe.

(a) fooi-lō 2428.
A bribe.

851. 憒 $\frac{61}{12}$ Troubled.
Confused.

852. 鮨 $\frac{195}{6}$ Sturgeon.

FOOI

853. 悔 $\frac{61}{7}$ To repent.
Contrition.

(a) fooi-hān 981.
To repent, regret.

854. 誨 $\frac{149}{7}$ To teach,
exhort,

855. 晦 $\frac{72}{7}$ Obscure.

FOON

856. 歡 $\frac{76}{18}$ To rejoice.
Delighted.

(a) foon-hei 1030.
Happy. To like.

857. 寬 $\frac{40}{12}$ Broad. Indulgent. Forbear-
ing. To show
mercy.

(a) foon-yūng 5269.
To pardon.

858. 貛 $\frac{153}{18}$

(a) kaú-foon 1574.
The badger.

FOÓN

859. 欵 76/7 * To treat courteously. An article. Item. C for treaties, petitions, business, etc.

860. 款 76/8 *

(a) shī-foon 3905.
  The fashion.
(b) foon-tung-fa 4273-650.
  Coltsfoot.

861. 盥 108/11 ' To wash.

862. 窽 116/10 ' Empty.

863. 窾 116/12 ' Vacant.

FOÒN

864. 喚 30/9 To call out, name.
  (a) shai-foòn 3814.
    To employ.
  (b) shai-foòn-yàn 5117.
    A servant.

FOOT.

865. 闊 169/9 Broad.

866. 濶 85/14 Wide.

FUK

867. 福 113/9 Divine blessing. Happiness. Felicity.
  (a) ñg-fuk 2962.
    The Five Blessings.
  (b) fuk-seung 3625.
    Jolly.
  (c) fuk-yam 5089.
    The Gospel.
  (d) fuk-chau 159.
    Foochau.
  (e) fuk-kìn 1664.
    Fukien.

---

868. 覆 146/12 To and fro. To turn over, throw down. (faù)

  (a) fuk-chuèn 346.
    To capsize.

869. 幅 50/9 C of walls, pictures, maps, cloth, etc.

  (a) fuk-yàm 5101½.
    A valance.

870. 腹 130/9 * Stomach. Abdomen.

871. 輻 159/9 * Spoke of a wheel.

872. 薔 140/9 ' Pokeweed.

873. 蝠 142/9 ' The bat.

FŪK

874. 服 74/4 Garments. To serve. Mourning apparel.

  (a) fūk-sz̀ 3776.
    To serve.
  (b) fūk-shuí-t'ó 4004-4380. To be acclimated.
  (c) ñg-fūk 2962.
    Five degrees of mourning.
  (d) cheuk.-fūk 177.
    To go into mourning.
  (e) t'uet̄-fūk 4446.
    To lay off mourning.
  (f) fūk-yeùk 5183.
    To take medicine.
  (g) yat-fūk 5133.
    One dose.

875. 復 60/9 To come back. Again. (faù)

  (a) fūk-shaang 3802.
    Resurrection.

876. 伏 9/4 To fall prostrate, hide, overcome. S.

(a) maaī-fūk 2568.
To hide.

877. 袚 140/6 China root.
*

(a) fūk-lìng 2366.
China root.

(b) t'ó-fūk-lìng 4380.
Smilax pseudo china.

(c) paāk-fūk 3178.
Szechuan root.

878. 袱 145/6 A wrapper.
* Wrapping cloth.

FUNG
879. 風 R/182 Wind. Rumor.
Fashion. Custom.

(a) taaî-fung 4033.
A gale.

(b) fung-kaù 1598.
Typhoon.

(c) fung-shān 3835.
Aeolus.

(d) fung-shuî 4004.
System of geomancy.

(e) fung-ŭĕ-hōk 4888-1140.
Meteorology.

(f) fung-sheng 3880.
Rumor.

(g) fung-k'ăm 1911.
Organ (musical).

(h) fung-seung 3626.
Bellows.

(i) fung-kwaî 2071.
Winnowing machine.

(j) fung-lō 2406.
Portable stove.
Furnace.

(k) tak-lūt-fung 4082-
2546. Telephone(HK).

(l) fung-shap 3843.
Rheumatism.

(m) fung-lūt 2548.
Chestnut.

(n) fung-ch'e-fa 490-650.
Passion flower.

880. 封 41/6 Feudal or vassal
territory. To
seal, close.

(a) fung-sùn 3743.
A letter.

(b) sùn-fung 3743.
An envelope.

881. 豐 151/11 Abundant.
Prolific. S.

(a) fung-tsuk 4636.
Plentiful.

882. 瘋 104/9 Leprosy. Paraly-
* sis. Insanity.

(a) mā-fung 2558.
Leprosy.

883. 蜂 142/7 | Bee species.
*

884. 蠭 142/17 |

(a) māt-fung 2637.
Bees.

(b) wōng-fung 5070.
Wasps.

(c) ang-fung 43.
Hornets.

(d) fung-hit。 1087.
Scorpions.

(e) pìn-t'aù-fung 3291-
4339. The cobra.

885. 鋒 167/7 Edge of knife
* or sword.

886. 楓 75/9 Kind of tree.
' The maple.

887. 葑 140/9 Kind of mustard.
'

888. 丰 2/3 Graceful.
' Refined.

889. 峯 46/7 A peak.
'

890. 烽 86/7 A beacon.
'

FÚNG
891. 俸 9/8 Salary.
Emolument.

-46-

892. 捧 $\frac{64}{8}$ To hold in both hands. (p'úng)

<u>FÙNG</u>
893. 諷 $\frac{149}{9}$ To intone. Sarcasm.

<u>FÜNG</u>
894. 縫 $\frac{120}{11}$ To sew.

895. 逢 $\frac{162}{7}$ To meet with. To happen.
(a) mooí-fūng 2774. Each time.

896. 馮 $\frac{187}{2}$ S.

<u>FÛNG</u>
897. 奉 $\frac{37}{5}$ To offer respect, homage. To serve.

898. 鳳 $\frac{196}{3}$ Male phoenix. S.
(a) fûng-sin-fa 3640-650. China balsam.

<u>HA</u>
899. 蝦 $\frac{142}{9}$ Shrimp species.
900. 鰕 $\frac{195}{9}$
(a) ngān-ha 3028. Small sea shrimps.
(b) ha-maí 2603. Dried shrimps or prawns.
(c) míng-ha 2690. Prawns.
(d) lūng-ha 2532. Lobster. Crawfish.

901. 瘕 $\frac{104}{9}$ A disease of the throat.
(a) ha-sheng 3880. Wheezing.

902. 暇 $\frac{30}{9}$

(a) ha-aat. 25. To intimidate.
(b) ha-ha. Aha!

<u>HĀ</u>
903. 瑕 $\frac{96}{9}$ A flaw. S.
(a) hā-ts'z 4851. A fault. Blemish.

904. 霞 $\frac{173}{9}$ Lurid. Red tinged. S.

905. 遐 $\frac{162}{9}$ Long. Far.

<u>HǍ</u>
906. 下 $\frac{1}{2}$ (hâ)

907. 吓 $\frac{30}{3}$ A while. Once. A moment. C.
(a) sz-hǎ 3758. On the sly.

<u>HÂ</u>
908. 下 $\frac{1}{2}$ To go down. Below. Next. S. (hǎ)
(a) hâ-ng 2965. Afternoon.
(b) hâ-ts'z 4854. Next time.
(c) hâ-hǒm 1154, or hâ-p'a 3412. The chin.
(d) hâ-tsok. 4610. Groveling.
(e) hâ-mǎ-wai 2561-4985. A humbug.

909. 夏 $\frac{35}{9}$ Summer. S.
(a) hâ-po 3336. Grass cloth.

910. 廈 $\frac{53}{10}$
(a) hâ-moŏn 2779. Amoy.

HAAI
911. 揩 $\frac{64}{9}$ To wipe, rub, scrape.
*

HAAĪ
912. 鞋 $\frac{177}{6}$ | Shoes.
913. 鞵 $\frac{177}{8}$ | Sandals.

(a) uō-yung-haaī 4881-5261. Slippers.
(b) ts'ó-haaī 4777. Grass sandals.
(c) haaī-ch'au 471. Shoe horn.
(d) haaī-huèn 1209. Shoe last.
(e) haaī-taī 4071. Shoe sole.
(f) haaī-taaī 4031. Shoe lace.
(g) haaī-māk 2606. Shoe blacking.
914. 唯 $\frac{30}{16}$ An interjection.
* Rough.
915. 諧 $\frac{149}{9}$ To be in harmony. To laugh, ridicule.

HAAĬ
916. 蟹 $\frac{142}{13}$ Crab species.

HAAÎ
917. 械 $\frac{75}{7}$ Weapons. Manacles.
*
918. 解 $\frac{148}{6}$ S. (kaaī)
(a) haaī-ì 1258. To talk by signs.
919. 懈 $\frac{61}{13}$ Lazy.
920. 薤 $\frac{140}{13}$ Scallions. Garlic.

HAAK。
921. 客 $\frac{40}{6}$ Stranger. Visitor. Guest. Customer. S.
(a) taap。-haak。 4059. Passengers.
(b) haak。-tìm 4154. Hotel. Inn.
(c) haak。-ka 1410. The Hakkas.
922. 刻 $\frac{18}{6}$ To carve, cut (hak)
(a) haak。-pók 3361. Malignant. To browbeat.
923. 嚇 $\frac{30}{14}$ To frighten, terrify.
924. 赫 $\frac{155}{7}$ Bright.
"' Fiery.
(a) haak。-sui-laī 3718-2200. Huxley.

HAĀM
925. 喊 $\frac{30}{9}$ To weep, call out. (hǎm)
(a) tá-haàm-lô 4027-2427. To yawn.
(b) haàm-yê-laàng 5176-2187. Auction sale.

HAÀM
926. 鹹 $\frac{197}{9}$ Salty. Brackish.
(a) haàm-shui-wâ 4004-4960. Pidgin English.
(b) haàm-hoí 1125. Aral Sea.
927. 涵 $\frac{85}{8}$ To soak, submerge.
*
928. 咸 $\frac{30}{6}$ All.
"' S.
929. 函 $\frac{17}{6}$ To enfold.
"' S.
930. 銜 $\frac{167}{6}$ A bit.
' To control.

HAÂM
931. 陷 170/8 To fall, become involved in, cause to fall.

932. 餡 184/8 Meat in pastry. *

(a) haân-chaì 117. To restrict.
(b) haân-têng 4132. To fix, assign.
(c) yaû-haân 5159. "Limited".

HAAN
933. 慳 61/11 Saving. Avaricious. *

(a) haan-lìm 2342. Economical.
(b) haan-kìm 1659. Thrifty.
(c) haan-ts'ìn-yän 4761-5117. A miser.

HAÂN
934. 閒 169/4 Vacant. Idle.

(a) tak-haân 4081. Leisure.
(b) haân-yĕ 5173. Something. Small thing.
(c) hó-haân 1099. Trifling. Unimportant.
(d) haân-wâ 4960. Gossip.
(e) haân-sz̄ 3776. Trifling matters.

935. 嫻 39/12 Accomplished. Refined. '

936. 癇 104/12 Convulsions. Fits. '

937. 閑 169/4 Barrier. Bar. '

938. 鷴 196/12 Silver pheasant. '

HAÂN
939. 限 170/6 A limit. Boundary. To restrict.

HAÀNG
940. 坑 32/4 A pit. Ditch. Ravine. Gully. S.

(a) mooì-haang 2766. Coal mine.
(b) haang-k'uì 2021. Sewer. Drain.

HAĀNG
941. 桁 75/6 Rafters. Cross beams. *

HAAP。
942. 呷 30/5 To suck, sup. *

943. 嗑 30/10 To suck, drink. *

HAÁP
944. 狹 94/7 Straitened. Narrow. (kìp) *

945. 峽 46/7 A mountain defile. A strait. *

(a) p'oh-kei-haáp 3527-1606. The cobra.

946. 洽 85/6 Suitable. (ap。) '

947. 狎 94/5 To caress, toy with. '

948. 匣 22/5 A chest. Small box. '

949. 柙 75/5 Kind of tree. Cage. '

950. 俠 9/7 Generous. Bold. "'

951. 掐 64/8 To dig the nails, lacerate. '

952. 陝 $\frac{170}{7}$ Pass. A defile.

HAAU

953. 敲 $\frac{66}{10}$ To knock, rap.

954. 哮 $\frac{30}{7}$ To roar, howl, gasp, pant.
(a) haau-ch'ún 605. Croup.

955. 拷 $\frac{64}{6}$ To flog, torture.

956. 尻 $\frac{44}{2}$ Extremity of spine.

HAAÚ

957. 考 $\frac{125}{3}$ To examine, question.
(a) haaú-kaù 1585. To examine thoroughly.
(b) haaú-shì 3903. Literary examinations.
(c) haaú-shò 3972. To audit accounts.

958. 巧 $\frac{48}{2}$ Cunning. Skilful. Art.
(a) haaú-shaú 3859. Dexterous.
(b) haaú-pìn 3297. Sophistry.

959. 栲 $\frac{75}{6}$ Tree yielding varnish sap.

HAAÙ

960. 孝 $\frac{39}{4}$ Filial piety. S.

HAAŪ

961. 姣 $\frac{38}{6}$ Petty. Intriguing. Artful. Unchaste.
(a) faat。-haaū 681. Female puberty.
(b) haaū-p'òh 3528. A whore.

HAAÛ

962. 效 $\frac{66}{6}$ To imitate, copy, follow.

963. 効 $\frac{19}{6}$ To toil.
(a) haaû-faat。 682. To imitate.
(b) haaû-ìm 1329. Proven efficacy. Result.

964. 校 $\frac{75}{6}$ School. School house.

HAÍ

965. 喺 $\frac{30}{9}$ To be in, at, on, under.
(a) haí-shuè 3987. Here.

HAĪ

966. 兮 $\frac{12}{2}$ An interjection.

967. 蹊 $\frac{157}{10}$ A path.

HAÎ

968. 係 $\frac{9}{7}$ To be. Is. Are. Affirmative.

969. 繫 $\frac{120}{13}$ To tie, fasten.

970. 系 $\frac{120}{1}$ Link. Succession. Nerves. S.
(a) shaì-haî 3818. Geneaology.

HAK

971. 黑 $\frac{R}{203}$ Dark. Black.
(a) hak-òm 3106. Darkness.
(b) hak-ma-ma 2552. Pitch dark.

972. 刻 $\frac{18}{6}$ To engrave, cut into. (haak。)

973. 克 10/5 To repress, deny one's self. (haak。)
  (a) hak-chai 117. To overcome.

974. 剋 18/7 To subdue, repress.

___

HÂM
975. 喊 30/9 (haâm, haàm)
  (a) hâm-pa(ng)-lâng 3235-2234. All.

___

HÁN
976. 懇 61/13 Earnest. Urgently.
  (a) hán-ts'it。4769. Urgently.

977. 很 60/6 Quarrelsome. Intractable. Harsh.

978. 狠 94/6 Snarling of dogs.
  (a) hán-heúng 1047. Shrill.

979. 墾 32/13 To break new land.

___

HĀN
980. 痕 104/6 A scar. Mark. Stain.
  (a) hó-hān 1099. Itching.
  (b) hān-tsìk 4534. Marks. Prints.

___

HÂN
981. 恨 61/6 To hate, resent, crave. Alas!
  (a) hân-ts'ìn 4761. Avaricious.

___

HANG
982. 哼 30/7 To moan.

___

983. 鏗 167/11 Ringing sound of metals. To thump.

984. 亨 8/5 Successful.

___

HÁNG
985. 肯 130/4 Willing. Will.

___

HĀNG
986. 行 R/144 To walk, go, act. (haāng, hâng, hồng)
  (a) hāng-waī 5013. Conduct.
  (b) hó-hāng 1099. Farewell!
  (c) hāng-hím 1055. Adventure.
  (d) hāng-leī 2288. Baggage.
  (e) hāng-sing 3652. A planet.

987. 恒 61/6 Permanent. Constant.

988. 恆 61/6 S.

989. 珩 96/6 Girdle ornaments.

990. 莖 140/7 Stalk. Stem. Penis.

991. 衡 144/10 Balance. To weigh. (waāng)

___

HĀNG
992. 行 R/144 Conduct. Practice. S. (hãng, haāng)
  (a) hó-hâng 1099. Very tight.

993. 幸 51/5 Fortunate. Lucky. S.

994. 杏 75/3 Apricot. S.

___

-51-

(a) hāng-yān 5118.
Almonds. Apricot pits.

995. 倖 $\frac{9}{8}$ Lucky. Fortunate.

HAP

996. 恰 $\frac{61}{6}$ Timely. Exact. Fitting.
(a) hap-ngaǎn-fān 2999-715. To doze.

997. 哈 $\frac{30}{6}$ S.
(a) hap-ĭ-paàn 1284-3190. Harbin.

HAT

998. 乞 $\frac{5}{2}$ To beg alms, implore. S.
(a) hat-ĭ 1266. A beggar.
(b) tá-hat-ch'ì 4027-516. To sneeze.

999. 吃 $\frac{30}{3}$ To laugh, stammer.

HĀT

1000. 轄 $\frac{159}{10}$ To govern, control.
1001. 核 $\frac{75}{6}$ Stone or kernel of fruit.(hŏp)
(a) hāt-tsź 4667. Nuts.
1002. 劾 $\frac{19}{6}$ To investigate, inquire.
1003. 檄 $\frac{75}{13}$ Urgent. A despatch.
1004. 瞎 $\frac{109}{10}$ Blind.

HAU

1005. 吼 $\frac{30}{4}$ Roaring.

HAÚ

1006. 口 $\frac{R}{30}$ Mouth. Hole. Port. C. S.
(a) shaang-haú 3802. Living things.
(b) yān-haú 5117. People in general.
(c) hoí-haú 1125. Estuary. Firth.
(d) kóng-haú 1780. A port.
(e) haú-heī 1033. Breath.
(f) haú-ts'oĬ 4804. Eloquence.
(g) haú-ts'oĬ-hŏk 1140. Art of oratory.
(h) haú-fa 650. Loquacious.
(i) haú-leūng 2311. Provisions.
(j) yat-haú 5133. A mouthful.

1007. 詬 $\frac{149}{6}$ Shame.

HAŪ

1008. 喉 $\frac{30}{9}$ The throat.
(a) haū-lūng 2535. The gullet.
(b) ngaǎng-haū 3001. Windpipe.
(c) haū-laám 2162. Adam's apple.
(d) haū-kap 1558. Hasty.
(e) ngaū-haū 3039. Fire hose.
(f) shuí-haū 4004. Water pipe.

1009. 侯 $\frac{9}{7}$ Rank of nobility. S.
1010. 瘊 $\frac{104}{9}$ Wart. Mole. Pimple.
1011. 猴 $\frac{94}{9}$ Kind of monkey. Clever.

1012. 餱 184/9 Provisions.

HAÛ

1013. 後 60/6 After. Behind, of time or place. S.
  (a) haû-yât 5137.
      Day after tomorrow.
  (b) haû-loî 2445.
      Afterwards.
  (c) haû-mǒ 2720.
      Stepmother.
  (d) haû-yuî 5245, or haû-yân 5117.
      Descendants.
  (e) haû-yân 5115½.
      Afterbirth.
  (f) haû-shaang 3802.
      A youth.

1014. 厚 27/7 Rich. Thick.
  (a) haû-taaî 4033.
      Massive.

1015. 候 9/8 To wait. A period of time.

1016. 后 30/3 Empress. Queen. S. uf 1013.

1017. 鱟 195/13 The king crab.

HE

1018. 唏 30/7 An interjection. (heî)

HEI

1019. 欺 76/8 To deceive, oppress, cheat.
  (a) hei-p'în 3490.
      To cheat.

1020. 希 50/4 To hope. Rare. S.
  (a) bei-hón 1159.
      Rare.
  (b) hei-k'eî 1950.
      Curious. Rare.

  (c) hei-laāp 2191.
      Greece.

1021. 咥 30/6 To laugh loudly.

1022. 嘻 30/12

1023. 稀 115/7 Far apart. Rare. Watery. S.
  (a) hei-hei-teî 4124.
      Insipid.

1024. 禧 113/12 Divine blessing. Joy.

1025. 嬉 39/12 Pretty. To play.
  (a) hei-siù 3675.
      To titter.
  (b) siù-hei-hei 3675.
      Giggling.

1026. 熙 86/9 Splendid.

1027. 犧 93/16 Perfect sacrificial victims.

1028. 絺 120/7 Fine linen. (ch'i)

1029. 羲 123/11 Breath. Vapor.

HEÍ

1030. 喜 30/9 To rejoice, be happy. Joy. S.
  (a) heí-tseuk₀ 4519.
      Magpie.

1031. 起 156/3 To rise, raise, begin. From. Beginning with. S.
  (a) heí-shaú 3860.
      To begin.
  (b) heí-shan 3830.
      To arise.
  (c) heí-fóh 767.
      A rocket.
  (d) heí-meî-chuè 2663-338.
      To abscond.

-53-

1032. 豈 $\frac{151}{3}$ Interrogative particle, implying a negative answer.

1041. * 汽 $\frac{85}{5}$ Steam.

1041½ " 汔 $\frac{85}{4}$

HEÌ

1033. 氣 $\frac{84}{6}$ Air. Breath. Temper.
  (a) heì-chat 150.
      Gases.
  (b) heì-hŏk 1140.
      Pneumatics.
  (c) heì-tseûng-hŏk 4531.
      Meteorology.
  (d) shaang-heì 3802.
      To get angry.
  (e) heì-koón-ìm 1819-1323.
      Bronchitis.

1034. 棄 $\frac{75}{8}$ To reject, discard.
1035. 器 $\frac{30}{13}$ Dish. Implement. Ability. S.
  (a) heì-mìng 2696.
      Vessels.
  (b) heì-kuî 1856.
      Tools.

1036. 戲 $\frac{62}{13}$ To jest, make sport of. The-
1037. 戲 $\frac{62}{11}$ atrical performance. S.
  (a) heì-siù 3675.
      Ridicule.
  (b) heì-lùng 2544.
      To make sport of.
  (c) heì-uén 4916.
      Theater.
  (d) heì-tsź 4667.
      An actor.

1038. * 餼 $\frac{184}{10}$ Fodder. To feed.
1039. " 气 $\frac{R}{84}$ Vapor.
1040. ' 憇 $\frac{61}{11}$ To rest.

HENG--See also hing.

1042. 輕 $\frac{159}{7}$ Light weight. To esteem lightly.(hing)
  (a) heng-p'aau-p'aau 3436.
      Light weight.
  (b) heng-heng-teî 4124.
      Lightly. Gently.
  (c) heng-pŏk 3361.
      Levity.
  (d) heng-î 1291.
      To disregard.
  (e) heng-heì-k'aū 1033-1937. A balloon.
  (f) heng-sè-yeŭk 3617-5183. Aperient.
  (g) heng-fán 713.
      Calomel.

HEU

1043. * 嘘 $\frac{30}{10}$ Sound of expelling breath.
  (a) heu-teu 4133.
      A trumpet.
1044. 靴 $\frac{177}{4}$ Boots.

HEUNG

1045. 鄉 $\frac{163}{10}$ Village. Countryside. S.
  (a) heung-ts'uen 4813.
      Village.
  (b) heung-hâ(hă) 908.
      Rural. Country. Native place.
  (c) heung-leî 2286.
      Neighbors.

1046. 香 $\frac{R}{186}$ Fragrance. Aroma. Incense. S.
  (a) keuk-heung 1638.
      Incense sticks.

(b) hāng-heung 986.
To worship.

(c) heung-haak。921.
Worshippers.

(d) heung-īp 1367.
Geranium.

(e) heung-fa-ts'oì 650-
4800. Mint.

(f) heung-ch'ām 457.
Aloes.

(g) heung-leī 2280.
Civet cat.

(h) heung-kóng 1780.
Hong Kong.

HEÚNG
1047. 響 180/13 A sound.
1048. 响 30/6 Noise. Noisy.

(a) ooī-heúng 3135.
Echo.

(b) ooī-heúng 3140.
Sonorous.

(c) heúng-kung 1883.
Aeolian harp.

(d) heúng-shuè 3987.
uf 965a.

1049.* 餉 184/6 Taxes. Duties. Rations.

1050.* 享 8/6 To enjoy, receive.

1051.ʹ 嚮 30/16 uf 1053.

1052. 饗 184/13 To feast, To offer up.

HEÙNG

1053. 向 30/3 From. Facing towards. S.

HIM
1054. 謙 149/10 Respectful. Humble. Modest.

(a) him-pei 3244.
Humility.

HÍM
1055. 險 170/13 Dangerous. Risky.

(a) hím-shuè 3987.
Danger!

HÌM
1056. 欠 R 76 To owe. Deficient.

(a) hìm-k'uet。2010.
Deficiency.

(b) hìm-hòng 1191.
Debts. Liabilities.

HIN
1057. 牽 93/7 To pull, connect, implicate.

1058. 愆 61/9 Sin. Guilt.

1059.ʹ 軒 159/3 Porch. Chariot. Pleased.

1060.ʹ 騫 187/10 Defective. To fail.

HÍN
1061. 顯 181/14 To make manifest,

1062. 顕 181/10 display. S.

(a) hín-īn 1349.
Evident.

(b) hín-ín 1361.
To appear unto.

(c) hín-mìng 2690.
To make plain.

(d) hín-tsik 4534.
An apparition.

(e) hín-meī-kèng 2656-
1637. Microscope.

(f) hín-yìng 5228.
To develope (ph).

(g) hín-yìng-yeŭk 5183,
or
hín-tseùng-shuí 4531-
4004. Developer(ph).

1063. 遺 162 / 10 To depute, send.
* (a) ch'aai-hin 411.
To send as envoy.

1064. 蜆 142 / 7 Small bivalves.
* (a) hín-hok. 1137.
Bivalve(shells).
(b) sha-hín 3778.
Clams.

1065. 譴 149 / 14 To reprove, reprimand.
*

1066. 繐 120 / 14 A parasite.
'

1067. 獻 94 / 16 To present, offer. S.
*

1068. 憲 61 / 12 Laws. Regula- tions. S.
(a) hin-faat. 682.
A constitution.

1069. 讞 149 / 20 To pronounce judgement.
'

1070. 兄 10 / 3 Elder brother. Senior.
(a) hing-taí 4077.
Brethren. Male relatives.

1071. 輕 159 / 7 See heng.

1072. 興 134 / 9 To rise, raise, set in motion. S. (hìng)
(a) hing-wông 5081.
Prosperous.

1073. 馨 186 / 11 Fragrance. (heng)
*

1074. 卿 26 / 9 A rank of nobil- ity. S.

1075. 興 134 / 9 To rejoice, ex- cite. Joyful. (hing)
(a) ko-hìng 1713.
A jolly time.

1076. 慶 61 / 11 To congratulate. Joyful. Happy. S. uf 1075.

1077. 熹 86 / 11 Feverish. To dry by fire.
'

1078. 磬 112 / 11 Stone chimes.
'

1079. 罄 121 / 11 Exhausted. Empty.
'

1079½. 謦 149 / 11 To hawk, cough.
'

1080. 怯 61 / 5 Timorous. Timid.
*

1081. 挾 64 / 7 To grasp, clasp under arm.(hip.)
* (a) hīp-chaì 117.
To oppress.

1082. 脅 130 / 6 The sides, be- low the arms.
* (a) hīp-kwat 2083.
The ribs.

1083. 協 24 / 6 Mutual. To aid.
(a) hīp-lìk 2330.
To cooperate.

1084. 叶 30 / 2 To harmonize, rhyme.

1085. 愜 61 / 9 Pleased. Satisfied.

1086. 歇 76 / 9 To stop, desist, rest, halt.
(a) pat-hit. 3236.
Incessantly.

(b) hit。-tìm 4154.
An inn.

1087. 蠍 142/13 Scorpion

1088. 蝎 142/9 species. (k'it。)

HIU

1089. 曉 30/12 Action complet-
** ed. Sign of the
past tense.

1090. 嚣 30/18 Clamor.

1091. 枵 75/5 Empty.
, To waste.

1092. 梟 75/7 Owl.

1093. 嶢 157/12 Cross legs.
, Tiptoe.

1094. 驍 187/12 Brave.

HIÚ

1095. 曉 72/12 To understand,
, know.

HIÙ

1096. 簝 116/13 Curving upwards.
, (k'iù)

HO

1097. 薅 140/13 To pull up,
* weed.

1098. 蒿 140/10 Name of plant. S.
(a) t'ong-ho 4438.
Kind of celery.

HÓ

1099. 好 38/3 Good. Right.
** Very. (hò)
(a) hó-ti 4138. Better.
(b) hó-ts'ż 4868.
Like unto.

HÒ

1100. 好 38/3 To like, love,
be fond of. S.

1101. 耗 127/4 To squander.
, Waste.

1102. 靠 175/7 (k'aaù)

1103. 犒 93/10 To reward.

HŌ

1104. 毫 82/7 The least part.
, A mite.
(a) yat-hō 5133.
Ten cents.
(b) (yat)-hō-tsż 4667.
Ten cent coin.
(c) taan-hō 4046.
Ten cent coin.
(d) sheung-hō 3886.
20 cent coin.

1105. 蠔 142/14 The oyster.
(a) shaang-hō 3802.
Oysters.
(b) hō-t'ong 4438.
An oyster bed.

1106. 濠 85/14 City moat.

1107. 豪 152/7 Martial.
, Brave. S.

1108. 壕 32/14 Ditch.
, Moat.

HÔ

1109. 號 141/7 A name. Designation. Mark.

1110. 号 30/3 Number. Signal.
Day of month.
(a) lūk-hô 2504.
Number 6.
(b) mēng-hô 2669.
Cognomen.
(c) hô-t'ūng 4461.
Trumpet.
(d) òm-hô 3106. Password.

1111. 浩 85/7 Vast.
' Great.

1112. 皓 106/7 Luminous.
'

1113. 顥 181/12 White.
'

HOH

1114. 呵 30/5 To gape, scold.
*
 (a) hoh-hìm 1056. To yawn.

1115. 訶 149/5 To upbraid, ridicule, blame.
'

1116. 苛 140/5 Petty.
' Annoying. S.

HÓH

1117. 可 30/2 Can. May. Possible. To permit.
**
 (a) hóh-Ì 1278. May. Can.
 (b) hóh-lìn 2351. To pity.
 (c) hóh-lūn-poh 2515-3348. Colombo.

1118. 坷 32/5 Rough.
"' Uneven.

HŌH

1119. 河 85/5 A river. A canal. S.
 (a) hōh-naām 2823. Honan Province. Honam, Canton.

1120. 何 9/5 How? What? Why? S.
 (a) hōh-fòng 796. How much less (or more)?
 (b) keì-hōh-hòk 1624-1140. Mathematics.

1121. 荷 140/7 Water lily. To sustain. (hòh)
 (a) hōh-paau 3198. Purse. Pouch.
 (b) hōh-ìp-lìn 1367-2353. Nasturtium.
 (c) hōh-laān 2182. Holland.

 (d) hōh-laān-taù 4016. Peas.
 (e) hōh-laān-shuē 3991. Common potatoes.
 (f) hōh-laān-shuí 4004. Aerated water.

HÔH

1122. 賀 154/5 To congratulate. S.
1123. 荷 140/7 To carry, wear. (hōh)
*

HOI

1124. 開 169/4 To open, begin, enumerate.
 (a) hoi-shan 3830. To set sail, start.
 (b) hoi-sam 3593. To amuse.
 (c) hoi-fa 650. To bloom.
 (d) hoi-p'ìk 3483. The creation.
 (e) hoi-p'ìk-lùn 2528. Cosmogony.

HOÍ

1125. 海 85/7 The sea. Rivers. Waters. S.
 (a) kwòh-hoí 2100. To cross river or harbor.
 (b) hoí-t'ó 4384. An island.
 (c) hoí-shì 3908. A mirage.
 (d) hoí-ts'oí 4800. Sea weed.
 (e) hoí-kau 1574. The seal.
 (f) hoí-mǎ 2561. Hippocampus. Walrus.
 (g) hoí-sham 3824. Sea slugs.

(h) hoí-wŏng-sing 5072-
    3652. The planet
    Neptune.
(i) hoí-kwan 2075.
    Navy.
(j) hoí-kwaan 2051.
    Maritime customs.
(k) hoí-chue-ts2 314-4677.
    Dutch Folly, Canton.
(l) hoí-haú 1006.
    Hoihow.
(m) hoí-naām 2823.
    Hainan;
(n) hoí-fong 799.
    Haiphong.
(o) hoí-sham-suí 3824-
    3723. Vladivostok.
(p) hoí-haāp-chĭk-mǎn-teî
    945-245-2618-4125.
    Straits Settlements.
(q) hoí-ngā 2977.
    The Hague.

1126. 愷 61 / 10 Kind.
    ' Triumphant.
1127. 凱 16 / 10 Triumphant.
    ' (oí)
1128. 鎧 167 / 10 Mail.
    ' Armor.
1129. 剴 18 / 10 To sharpen,
    ' influence.

HOĪ
1130. 骸 188 / 6 Bones of
    * the body.
1131. 咳 30 / 6 Infant's laugh.
    * (k'at)
1132. 駭 187 / 6 Startled.
    ' Alarmed.
1133. 孩 39 / 6 A child.
    ' A youth.
    (a) hoī-ī-kuk 1266-1867.
        Valerian.
1134. 頦 181 / 6 The chin.
    '

HOĪ
1135. 害 40 / 7 To wound, in-
    ' jure, illtreat.
1136. 亥 8 / 4 9 to 11 P.M.
    '

HOK。
1137. 壳 33 / 4 Husks. A cover-
    ' ing.
1138. 殼 79 / 8 Shells, animal
    ' or vegetable.
1139. 㲉 79 / 6 Dipper. Ladle.
    '
    (a) t'aū-hok。 4339.
        Skull.
    (b) to-hok。 4195.
        Scabbard.
    (c) siù-mĭn-hok。 3675-
        2687. A mask.

HŌK
1140. 學 39 / 13 To learn, study,
    ' imitate, prac-
1141. 孝 39 / 4 tice, follow
    ' after. Science.
    (a) hŏk-haaû 964.
        School. Academy.
    (b) hŏk-shaang 3802.
        Student.
    (c) mung-hŏk 2803.
        Primary school.
    (d) hŏk-ló 2404.
        Fukien men.
1142. 鶴 196 / 10 The crane.
    * S.

HOM
1143. 堪 32 / 9 Fit for. Able
    ' to. Worthy of.S.
1144. 龕 212 / 6 Shrine for
    * an idol.

HÓM
1145. 砍 112 / 4 A mortar.
    ' To chop, cut.

(a) hóm-hoi 1124.
To split.

1146. 坎 $\frac{32}{4}$ A pit.
' Uneven. S.

1147. 扻 $\frac{64}{7}$ To knock,
1148. 揪 $\frac{64}{7}$ strike.
"

HÒM

1149. 勘 $\frac{19}{9}$ To revise, col-
' late, investi-
gate.

1150. 墈 $\frac{32}{11}$ Cliff.
' Brink.

1151. 戡 $\frac{62}{9}$ To subdue,
' stab.

HǑM

1152. 含 $\frac{30}{4}$ To hold,cherish,
To hold in

1153. 哈 $\frac{30}{7}$ the mouth.
' (ngām)

(a) hǒm-mūk-laám 2795-
2162. To keep
silence.

HǑM

1154. 頷 $\frac{181}{7}$ The chin.
*

HǑM

1155. 冚 $\frac{14}{3}$ To cover, fit.
* A cover.

(a) hǒm-chung 387.
Jar. Gallipot.

(b) hǒm-t'aŭ 4339.
Covered dish.

1156. 憾 $\frac{61}{13}$ Resentful.
' Vexed at.

(a) hǒm-hân 981. To
cherish resentment.

1157. 嵌 $\frac{46}{9}$ To inlay,
' inchase.

HON

1158. 看 $\frac{109}{4}$ To watch,guard,
' care for. S.
(hòn)

(a) hon-toì 4223.
To behave towards.

(b) hon-kaang-lò 1479-
2404.Night watchman.

HÓN

1159. 罕 $\frac{122}{3}$ Rare. Seldom.
* A net. S.

1160. 刊 $\frac{18}{3}$ To carve, en-
* grave. (haan)

1161. 侃 $\frac{9}{6}$ Straight for-
' ward. Bold.
uf 1160.

HÒN

1162. 看 $\frac{109}{4}$ To look at,view,
' examine. (hon)

1163. 漢 $\frac{85}{11}$ Chinese.

(a) hòn-haú 1006.
Hankow.

(b) hòn-yeŭng 5196.
Hanyang.

HÒN

1164. 寒 $\frac{40}{9}$ Cold. Freezing.
' Humble. Poor.S.

1165. 鼾 $\frac{209}{3}$ To snore.

1166. 韓 $\frac{178}{8}$ S.
" '

HǑN

1167. 旱 $\frac{72}{3}$ Dry.
' Drought.

(a) hǒn-luì 2479. Thun-
der without rain.

HÒN

1168. 汗 $\frac{85}{3}$ Perspiration.

1168½. 釬 $\frac{167}{3}$ To solder.

-60-

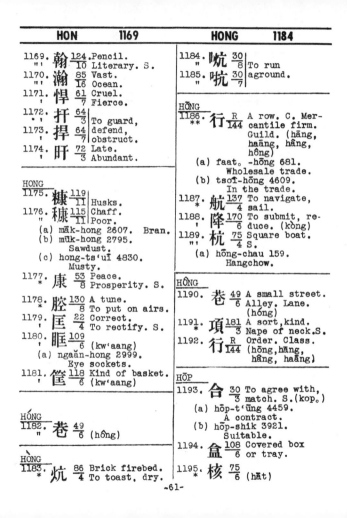

1169. 翰 124/10 Pencil. Literary. S.
1170. 瀚 85/16 Vast. Ocean.
1171. 悍 61/7 Cruel. Fierce.
1172. 扞 64/3 To guard,
1173. 捍 64/7 defend, obstruct.
1174. 旰 72/3 Late. Abundant.

HONG
1175. 糠 119/11 Husks.
1176. 穅 115/11 Chaff. Poor.
(a) māk-hong 2607. Bran.
(b) mūk-hong 2795. Sawdust.
(c) hong-ts'uī 4830. Musty.
1177. 康 53/8 Peace. Prosperity. S.
1178. 腔 130/8 A tune. To put on airs.
1179. 匡 22/4 Correct. To rectify. S.
1180. 眶 109/6 (kw'aang)
(a) ngaăn-hong 2999. Eye sockets.
1181. 筐 118/6 Kind of basket. (kw'aang)

HŎNG
1182. 巷 49/6 (hŏng)

HŌNG
1183. 炕 86/4 Brick firebed. To toast, dry.

1184. 沆 30/8 To run
1185. 吭 30/7 aground.

HŌNG
1186. 行 R144 A row. C. Mercantile firm. Guild. (hāng, haāng, hâng, hōng)
(a) faat₀ -hōng 681. Wholesale trade.
(b) tsoī-hōng 4609. In the trade.
1187. 航 137/4 To navigate, sail.
1188. 降 170/6 To submit, reduce. (kòng)
1189. 杭 75/4 Square boat. S.
(a) hōng-chau 159. Hangchow.

HŎNG
1190. 巷 49/6 A small street. Alley. Lane. (hŏng)
1191. 項 181/3 A sort, kind. Nape of neck.S.
1192. 行 R144 Order. Class. (hōng,hāng, hâng, haāng)

HŌP
1193. 合 30/3 To agree with, match. S.(kop₀)
(a) hŏp-t'ūng 4459. A contract.
(b) hŏp-shik 3921. Suitable.
1194. 盒 108/6 Covered box or tray.
1195. 核 75/6 (hāt)

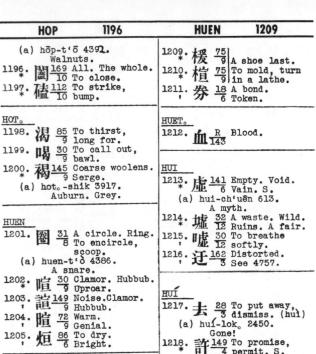

(a) hōp-t'ŏ 4392.
   Walnuts.

1196. 闔 169/10 All. The whole.
*   To close.

1197. 磕 112/10 To strike,
*   bump.

HOT。

1198. 渴 85/9 To thirst,
   long for.

1199. 喝 30/9 To call out,
   bawl.

1200. 褐 145/9 Coarse woolens.
*   Serge.
(a) hot。-shik 3917.
   Auburn. Grey.

HUEN

1201. 圈 31/8 A circle. Ring.
   To encircle,
   scoop.
(a) huen-t'ŏ 4386.
   A snare.

1202. 喧 30/9 Clamor. Hubbub.
*   Uproar.

1203. 諠 149/9 Noise.Clamor.
'   Hubbub.

1204. 暄 72/9 Warm.
'   Genial.

1205. 烜 86/6 To dry.
'   Bright.

HUÉN

1206. 犬 R/94 A dog.
*

HUĔN

1207. 勸 19/17 To advise,
1208. 劝 19/2 exhort.
(a) huen-kaàn 1476.
   To admonish.

1209. 楥 75/9 A shoe last.
*

1210. 楦 75/9 To mold, turn
*   in a lathe.

1211. 券 18/6 A bond.
'   Token.

HUET。

1212. 血 R/143 Blood.
*

HUI

1213. 虛 141/6 Empty. Void.
*   Vain. S.
(a) hui-ch'uen 613.
   A myth.

1214. 墟 32/12 A waste. Wild.
*   Ruins. A fair.

1215. 噓 30/12 To breathe
'   softly.

1216. 迂 162/3 Distorted.
'   See 4757.

HUÍ

1217. 去 28/3 To put away,
   dismiss. (huì)
(a) huí-lok。 2450.
   Gone!

1218. 許 149/4 To promise,
*   permit. S.
(a) huí-p'ing 3495.
   To betroth (of
   women)

1219. 栩 75/6 Kind of tree.
'

1220. 詡 149/6 To boast,
'   brag.

HUÌ

1221. 去 28/3 To go away,
**   depart. (huí)

-62-

HUK

1223. 哭 30/7 To cry, weep, wail, lament.

  (a) huk-song 3698. To wail for the dead.

1224. * 曲 73/2 (k'uk)

HŪK

1225. * 酷 164/7 Cruel. Inhuman.

HUNG

1226. 空 116/3 Empty. Void. Vain. S. (hŭng)

1227. 兇 10/4 Violent. Malvonent. Savage.

  (a) hung-shaú 3859. A murderer.

1228. 胸 130/6 The breast.

1229. 匈 20/4 Thorax. Affections.

  (a) hung-ngā-leî 2977-2293. Hungary.

1230. ' 凶 17/2 Unfortunate. Malignant. Baleful.

HÚNG

1231. 恐 61/6 To fear. Alarm. Doubt.

  (a) húng-p'à 3410. To fear. Lest.

1232. * 孔 39/1 An aperture. S.

  (a) húng-foo-tsź 801-4667. Confucius.

  (b) húng-kaaú 1507. Confucianism.

  (c) húng-tseuk₀ 4518. The peacock.

HÙNG

1233. * 控 64/8 To accuse, appeal higher.

1234. ' 空 116/3 To leave a space. (hung)

HŪNG

1235. 紅 120/3 Red. Ruddy. Lucky. S.

  (a) taaî-hūng 4033. Scarlet.

  (b) ngān-hūng 3028. Light vermillion.

  (c) hūng-fa 650. Safflower.

  (d) hūng-laām-fa 2167. Saffron.

  (e) hūng-ts'oî-t'aū 4800-4339. Beetroot.

  (f) hūng-mō-yān 2712-5117. Foreigners.

  (g) hūng-mō-naî 2844. Portland cement.

  (h) hūng-hoî 1125. The Red Sea.

1236. 洪 85/6 Vast. Overflowing.

  (a) hūng-shuî 4004. The Deluge.

1237. * 虹 142/3 The rainbow.

1238. * 鴻 196/6 Swan. Vast. Profound. S.

  (a) hūng-kuk 1870. A swan.

  (b) hūng-yan 5108. Profound kindness.

1239. * 熊 86/10 The bear. S.

  (a) hūng-yān 5117. A bear.

1240. ' 雄 172/4 Male bird. Martial. S.

  (a) hūng-wŏng 5070. Red sulphuret of arsenic.

1241. 葒 140/9 A water plant.

1242. 烘 $\frac{86}{6}$ To roast, dry.

HŬNG

1243. 哄 $\frac{30}{6}$ To impose on, deceive. Din. Hum of a crowd.

1244. 汞 $\frac{85}{3}$ Quicksilver.

1245. 鬨 $\frac{169}{6}$ To quarrel. Hubbub.

HWOI

1246. 誊 $\frac{30}{17}$ Exclamation. Calling to a person.

I

1247. 依 $\frac{9}{6}$ In accord with. To rely on. S.
   (a) i-laai 2156, or i-k'aau 1896.
       To rely on.
   (b) i-chue 339.
       According to.

1248. 衣 $\frac{R}{145}$ Clothes. S. (1)
   (a) i-fūk 874. Clothing.

1249. 醫 $\frac{164}{11}$ To heal, cure.
   (a) i-hŏk 1140.
       Science of medicine.
   (b) i-uen 4910. Hospital.
   (c) i-shaang 3802.
       Physician.

1250. 噫 $\frac{30}{13}$ Sound of regret. Alas!
   (a) i-lo-lo 2403.
       A low idle fellow.

1251. 翳 $\frac{124}{11}$ Dimness. (ai)

1252. 鷖 $\frac{196}{11}$ Widgeon.

1253. 伊 $\frac{9}{4}$ S.

1254. 移 $\frac{115}{6}$ To remove. (I)
   (a) i-i-yuk 5247.
       Rickety.

Í

1255. 倚 $\frac{9}{8}$ To rely on, depend on, trust in.
   (a) í-laai 2156.
       To depend upon.

1256. 椅 $\frac{75}{8}$ A chair. A seat.
   (a) huen-shaú-í 1201-3859.
       An arm chair.

1257. 綺 $\frac{120}{8}$ Variegated silk.

Ì

1258. 意 $\frac{61}{9}$ Thought. Will. Motive. Purpose.
   (a) ì-sz 3773.
       Idea. Thought.
   (b) tse-ì 4509. Metaphor.
   (c) ì-ngoî 3070.
       Accidental.
   (d) ì-taat-leî 4033-2293.
       Italy.

1259. 薏 $\frac{140}{13}$ Name of a plant. Plantago.
   (a) ì-maî 2603.
       Pearl barley.

1260. 懿 $\frac{61}{16}$ Admirable.

1261. 衣 $\frac{R}{145}$ To clothe.

Ī

1262. 而 $\frac{R}{126}$ And. And yet. Still.
   (a) Ī-ch'é 492.
       Also. Besides.
   (b) Ī-ka 1410. Now.

1263. 疑 $\frac{103}{9}$ To doubt, sus-pect, Doubtful.
(a) Ĭ-waǎk 4968.
To mistrust.

1264. 移 $\frac{115}{6}$ To remove, transplant.(i)

1265. 宜 $\frac{40}{5}$ Natural. Reason-able. Suitable.

1266. 兒 $\frac{10}{6}$ A male child. Infant. S.
(a) Ĭ-heĭ 1036. Child's-play. Trifling.
(b) Ĭ-ch'ā 409. Catechu.

1267. 儀 $\frac{9}{13}$ Etiquette.Rites. Presents. S.

1268. 夷 $\frac{37}{3}$ Foreign. Barbarian.

1269. 怡 $\frac{61}{5}$ Concord. Harmony.

1270. 姨 $\frac{38}{6}$ Maternal aunt. Sister in law.

1271. 嶷 $\frac{46}{14}$ Mountain peaks.

1272. 薐 $\frac{140}{6}$ Plant name.

1273. 彝 $\frac{58}{15}$
(a) mǒ-Ĭ-ch'ā 2723-409. Bohea tea.

1274. 杙 $\frac{75}{6}$ A kind of tree.

1275. 栭 $\frac{75}{6}$ A kind of chestnut.

1276. 迻 $\frac{162}{6}$ uf 1264.

1277. 貽 $\frac{154}{5}$ To bequeath. transmit.

Ǐ

1278. 以 $\frac{9}{3}$ To cause. To use.
(a) Ĭ-waĭ 5013.
To regard as.
(b) shŏh-Ĭ 3977.Therefore.

1279. 已 $\frac{R}{49}$ Finished. Complete.

(a) Ĭ-king 1668.
Already. Past time.

1280. 耳 $\frac{R}{128}$ The ear.
(a) Ĭ-tsaĭ 4482. The ear.
(b) Ĭ-tŏh(teú) 4218.
Lobe of the ear.
(c) Ĭ-shĭ 3902. Ear wax.
(d) Ĭ-mĭng 2692.
Buzzing ears.
(e) Ĭ-lŭng 2534. Deaf.
(f) Ĭ-pin-fung 3286-879.
Rumor.

1281. 擬 $\frac{64}{14}$ To deliberate, decide.

1282. 議 $\frac{149}{13}$ To discuss, cri-ticize, judge.
(a) Ĭ-lŭn 2528. To sit in judgement on.
(b) Ĭ-uĕn 4910.
Parliament.

1283. 矣 $\frac{111}{2}$ Implying com-pleteness or finality.

1284. 爾 $\frac{89}{10}$ You. Just so.

1285. 苡 $\frac{140}{5}$ A plant. Plan-tago species.
(a) Ĭ-maĭ 2603.
Pearl barley.

1286. 呓 $\frac{30}{5}$

Î

1287. 二 $\frac{R}{7}$ Numeral two.

1288. 貳 $\frac{154}{5}$ Second. Additional.

1289. 弍 $\frac{56}{2}$ Substitute. No. 1290 is

1290. 川 $\frac{2}{1}$ running hand form.
(a) taĭ-Î 4076.
Second. The next.
(b) Î-ts'z̆ 4854. Twice.
(c) à-Î 9. Second son.

(d) î-só 3683.
Second son's wife.

1291.** 易 72/4 Easy. S. (yik)

1292. 義 123/7 Good. Righteous.
Right. Public.

1293. 異 102/6 Foreign.
Strange.

___

IM

1294. 醃 164/8 To pickle, salt down, tan.

1295. 腌 130/8 The side of

1296." 腌 130/9 the body. (îm)

(a) siú-im 3674.
The side. Loins.

1297.* 閹 169/8 To castrate, geld.

1298.* 劊 18/8 A eunuch.
A doorkeeper.

1299.' 淹 85/8 To soak,detain.
Deep in.

1300.' 俺 61/8 To love.

(a) im-ts'im 4749.
Petulant.

(b) im-tsim 4550.
Fastidious.

___

ÎM

1301. 掩 64/8 To shut, hide.

1302. 揜 64/9 (ám)

(a) îm-peî 3269.
To stop the nose.

(b) îm-maaî 2568.
To shut (door).

(c) îm-hoî 1124.
To open (door).

1303.' 揜 32/8 To cover with earth, bury.

1304.' 弇 55/6 To cover, hide.

___

1305.' 檿 75/14 Wild mulberry.

1306." 广 R/53 A roof.

1307." 腌 130/8 The side of

1308.' 臉 130/9 the body. (im)

1309.' 魘 194/14 Nightmare.

1310.' 厭 27/12 To conceal, hate. (îm)

___

ÎM

1311. 厭 27/12 To dislike,

1312. 懨 61/14 loathe. (îm)

(a) îm-heî 1034.
To disdain.

1313.' 饜 184/14 Satiated.

___

ÎM

1314. 鹽 197/13 Salt.

1315. 塩 108/8 Salts.

(a) ts'ing-îm 4764. Soda.

(b) îm-t'în 4356.
Salt marsh.

1316.' 嚴 30/17 Strict. Firm. S.
Stern.Majestic.

1317.* 嫌 38/10 To object to,be weary of, dis-like.

1318.* 檐 75/13 Eaves of a roof.

1319.* 簷 118/13 Eaves of a roof.

1320.* 蚺 142/4 A species

1321.' 蚺 142/5 of snake. S.

-66-

(a) Īm-shē 3874. A lizard.

1322. 閻 169 Village.Hamlet.
        8 Lane. S.

(a) Im-lōh-wōng 2437-5072.
        The Chinese Pluto.

1323. 炎 86 To flame.
        4

1324. 焰 86 Ardent.
        8 Hot.

ĬM

1325. 染 75 To infect, dye.
        5 Infection.

ÎM

1326. 燄 86 Blazing.
        12

1327. 焰 86 Brilliant.
        8 Fierce.

1328. 爓 86 A flame.
        16

1329. 驗 187 To fulfill,
        13 verify, assay,

1330. 驗 187 investigate.
        8 Fulfilment.

(a) Îm-shi 3900.
        An inquest.

(b) Îm-taan 4046. Certifi-
        of inspection or
        analysis.

1331. 艷 151 Beautiful.
        20

1332. 艷 151 Fascinating.
        17

1333. 艷 151 Brilliant.
        22

IN

1334. 煙 86 Smoke.
        9

1335. 烟 86 Tobacco.
        6 Opium.

(a) in-fóh 767.Fireworks.

(b) in-t'ūng(t'ung) 4461.
        Chimney.

(c) yān-in 5117.
        Population.

(d) oo-in 3115.Lampblack.

(e) in-yūk 5249. Bacon.

(f) in-tun 4265. Beacon.

(g) in-Ip 1367. Tobacco.

(h) in-tsaí 4482.
        Cigarettes.

(i) in-lām 2226.
        Tobacco shop.

(j) shuí-in 4004.
        Scented tobacco for
        water pipes.

(k) shīk-in 3925.
        To smoke.

(l) kung-in 1878.
        Licensed opium.

(m) in-ts'eung 4735.
        Opium pipe.

(n) in-t'oī 4423. Chefoo.

1336. 胭 130 Throat.
        6 Rouge.

1337. 焉 86
        7 (In)

1338. 於 140 To fade out,
        8 rot. uf 1365.

1339. 蔫 140 To rot, decay.
        11 Diseased.

ÍN

1340. 燕 86 The swallow.
        12 Feast. Easy.(ìn)

(a) in-tsź 4667.
        The swallow.

(b) paāk-ín 3178. Canary.

(c) ín(ìn)-woh 5056.
        Edible bird's nests.

(d) t'ek₅ín(ìn) 4343.
        Shuttlecock.

(e) ín(ìn)-shoh 3976.
        Insurance.

1341. 演 85 To practice,per-
     * 11 meate, lead on.

(a) Ín-t'aān 4303.Pulpit.

IN	1342	IN	1355

(b) ín-ch'ut 648.
   To evolve.

1342. 蜒 142/9 Kind of lizard.
   (a) ín-t'íng 4363.
      Chameleon.

1343. 偃 9/9 To rest, cease, bend over.

1344. 堰 32/9 To raise a dam.

1345. 衍 144/3 Ample. To overflow.

İN

1346. 宴 40/7 Comfortable. At ease.

1347. 燕 86/12 To feast. Comfortable. (ín)

1348. 讌 149/16 To converse, feast.

ÍN

1349. 然 86/8 Thus. So. Right. Existant. To be. S.
   (a) ín-tsak 4487.
      Well then.
   (b) ín-haû 1013.
      Afterwards.

1350. 言 R Word. Words. 149 Sayings.
   (a) ín-uě 4890.
      Conversation.
   (b) ín-hăng 986.
      Biography.
   (c) yăn-ín 5117. Arsenic.

1351. 筵 118/7 A mat spread out. Banquet.

1352. 延 54/5 Slow. Protracted. To invite.

1353. 絃 120/5 String of a lute.
   (a) î-ín 1287. A fiddle.

1354. 弦 57/5 String of a lute. Moon at quarter.

(a) sheûng-ín 3896.
   First quarter (moon).
(b) hâ-ín 908.
   Last quarter (moon).

1355. 研 112/6 To grind, rub fine. To play a fiddle.

1356. 賢 154/8 Worthy. Virtuous.

1357. 涎 85/7 Spittle. Saliva.

1358. 蜒 142/7 See 5157.

1359. 焉 86/7 A demonstrative particle. (in)

1360. 燃 86/12 To burn, light.

ÍN

1361. 現 96/7 To manifest, appear.
   (a) ín-shī 3905. Now.
   (b) ín-shīng 3948.
      Ready made.
   (c) ín-ngăn 3028.
      Ready money. Cash.
   (d) ín-tsoî 4609. Now. At the present moment.

1362. 莧 140/7 Greens. Spinach.
   (a) ín-ts'oî 4800.
      Spinach.
   (b) ma-ch'î-ín 2561-524.
      Purslane. Long leaved spinach.
   (c) ts'z̄-ín 4855.
      Prickly spinach.

1363. 硯 112/7 A smooth stone. To rub.
   (a) măk-ín 2606.
      Ink stone.

1364. 彥 59/6 Handsome. Talented.

1365. 諺 149/9 Proverb. Saying.

-68-

IP	1366	IT	1375

IP₀

1366. 腌 130/8 * To preserve, pickle, salt down. (im)

IP

1367. 葉 140/9 Leaf of tree or book.
  (a) ngaū-paak₅-Ip 3039-3170. Tripe.
1368. 業 75 Property. Profession. Trade.
  (a) sz̄-Ip 3776. Affairs.
  (b) ka-Ip 1410. Patrimony.
  (c) waī-Ip 5003. Assets.
1369. 頁 R Leaf. 181 Page.
  (a) paak₅-Ip 3170. Venetian blinds.

IT₀

1370. 噎 30/12 * To hiccough, choke.
  (a) tá-sz-it₀ 4027-3761. Hiccough.
1371. 謁 149/9 An interview. A visit.

IT

1372. 熱 86/11 Hot.
1373. 熱 86/11 Heat. Burning.
1374. 热 86/5 Fervent.
  (a) It-t'aū 4339. The sun.
  (b) chung-It 383. Sunstroke.
  (c) t'in-It 4355. Hot weather.
  (d) It-pêng 3278. Fever.
  (e) It-sam 3593. Zealous. Affectionate.

1375. 臬 132/4 Law. Justice. Boundary.
1376. 孼 39/16 Retribution.
1377. 孼 39/16 Ills. Evil.

IU

1378. 喓 30/9 To call out, cry out. A shrill call.
1379. 腰 130/9 Loins. Waist. Middle. Isthmus.
  (a) iu-taal 4031. A girdle.
  (b) iu-kwat 2083. The backbone.
  (c) iu-tsz 4667. The kidneys.
  (d) iu-yaū 5149. Suet.
1380. 妖 38/4 * A phantom. A sprite. Magical. Supernatural.
  (a) iu-kwaal 2048. An elf.
  (b) ók₀-iu 3100. Diabolical.
1381. 呦 30/3 * To cry out.
  (a) iu-iu-lok₀ 2450. Hush! Hush!
1382. 幺 R Small. Minute. 52 Tender.
1383. 邀 162/13 To invite, engage.
1384. 蔞 140/9 A plant. Luxuriant.
1385. 要 146/3 To seek for. To make agreement. (iū)
1386. 夭 37/1 Tender. Young.
1387. 妖 78/4 Premature death.

IÙ

1388. 要 146/3 ** To want, need. Important. Necessary. Must. (iu)

IÙ

1389. 搖 64/10 To shake, move, agitate.
(a) iū-hǎ 907. To dandle.

1390. 窯 116/10 A brick kiln.

1391. 窰 116/10 A furnace.

1392. 橈 75/12 A paddle. To paddle.

1393. 鷂 196/10 * A harrier. Paper kite. (iú)

1394. 瑤 96/10 ' A green jasper.

1395. 愮 61/10 ' Perturbed.

1396. 傜 60/10 ' Forced labor.

1397. 堯 32/9 "ı' Eminent. S.

1398. 薚 140/12 ' Stubble. Fuel.

1399. 謠 149/10 ' Rumor.

1400. 遙 162/10 ' Far. Distant.

1401. 饒 184/12 ' Abundant.

1402. 鰩 195/10 ' A kind of fish.

IÛ

1403. 擾 64/15 To give trouble, disturb, confuse.

1404. 舀 134/4 * To dip out, bale out.

1405. 繞 120/12 ' To wind around.

IÛ

1406. 燿 124/14 Dazzling.

1407. 曜 72/14 Bright. Glory. Glorious.

1408. 燿 86/14 Brightness as the sun.

KA

1409. 加 19/3 To add to, increase, promote.
(a) ka-lūn 2515. Gallon.
(b) ka-nǎ-taaî 2813-4033. Canada.
(c) ka-lô-wai-sî-tûn 2426-4985-3777-4268. Galveston.
(d) ka-poh-leî-suen 3347-2275-3702. Carbolic acid.

1410. 家 40/7 Household. Family. Profession. Professional man. S.
(a) ka-yān 5117. Household. Family.
(b) leūng-ka 2321. Both (of us, of them)
(c) taaî-ka 4033. All (of us, of them)
(d) shaî-ka 3818. Aristocracy.

1411. 傢 9/10
(a) ka-fóh 768. Furniture. Thing(s).

1412. 枷 75/5 * Stocks. Cangue. A flail.

1413. 嘉 30/11 * Commendable. Excellent. S.
(a) ka-uē 4872. The barbel.

1414. 茄 140/5 " S. (k'ē) See 4803a.

1415. 咖 30/5 "

(a) ka-fei 752. Coffee.

1416. 葭 140/9 Bulrush. Reed.

1417. 迦 162/5

1418. 伽 9/5

KÁ

1419. 假 9/9 False. To pretend. (kà)

(a) ká-ì 1258. Falsely.

(b) ká-mô 2731. To impersonate.

1420. 檟 75/13 A kind of tree. (Gardenia).

KÀ

1421. 價 9/13 Price. Value.

(a) kà-ts'ìn 4761. Price.

(b) kà-shaì 3819. Showy.

1422. 假 9/9 Leisure time. Leave of absense. (ká)

1423. 嫁 38/10 To marry a husband.

1424. 架 75/5 A frame. Staging. C.

(a) shàp-tsẑ-kà 3845-4672. A cross.

(b) tá-kà 4027. To fight.

1425. 駕 187/5 To mount on. C. for vehicles.

1426. 嗎 30/15 F-declarative and interrogative.

1427. 㗎 30/9

1428. 枷 75/5 Same as 1424.

1429. 稼 115/10 To sow. Husbandry.

KAAI

1430. 街 144/6 Street. Thoroughfare.

1431. 皆 106/4 All. Every. The whole.

1432. 階 170/9 Steps. Ascent.

(a) kaai-k'ap 1924. A step. A grade.

1433. 佳 9/6 Elegant. Good. Nice.

1434. 偕 9/9 Together with.

1435. 堦 32/9 Pavement. Same as 1430.

KAAÍ

1436. 解 148/6 To loosen, explain. To put up. To saw (as wood). (haaí, kaaí)

(a) kaaí-hot₀ 1198. To quench thirst.

(b) kaaí-tūk 4260. An antidote.

(c) kaaí-shuet₀ 4001. To apologize.

KAAÌ

1437. 戒 62/3 To warn, caution. Warnings. uf. 1441.

(a) kaaì-chí 215. A finger ring. A washer (mech.).

1438. 界 102/4 A region. The world. Boundary.

(a) shaì-kaaì 3818. The world. The age. The times. Employment.

(b) nuí-shaì 2949. The female world.

1439. 芥 140/4 Mustard plant.

(a) kaai-moŏt 2792.
Mustard.

1440. 鋸 167/9 To saw. *

1441. 誡 149/7 To forbid, warn, instruct. Commandments. *

1442. 解 148/6 To take, forward. (kaaí) *

1443. 介 9/2 Excellent. Great. S. '

(a) kaai-luī 2494.
Conchology. Things in the sea.

1444. 蚧 142/4 Kind of lizard. '

1445. 价 9/4 A servant. '

1446. 届 44/5 To reach. A limit. '

1447. 疥 104/5 Itch. '

KAAK。

1448. 隔 170/10 To separate. A partition.

(a) kaak。-chí 216.
To interleave.

(b) kaak。-cha 59.
To strain out.

(c) kaak。-leī 2274.
Neighboring.

1449. 革 R 177 To remove, change. S. *

1450. 格 75/6 Model. Pattern. S. *

(a) laám-wāt-kaak。 2162-5044. Lattice.

(b) kaak。-paán 3187.
A shelf.

(c) kaak。-māt 2636, or kaak。-chī-hŏk 228-1140. Natural philosophy.

(d) kaak。-līng-laān 2364-2182. Greenland.

(e) kaak。-lām-wai-ch'Ī 2226-4985-535.
Greenwich.

1451. 胳 130/6 The neckbone. Armpit. '

(a) kaak。-laāk-taí 2161-4071. The armpits.

1452. 絆 120 To form the woof. '

1453. 搯 64/6 To strike. '

1454. 膈 130/10 The diaphragm. '

KAAM

1455. 監 108/9 Prison. To superintend. S. (kaàm)

(a) kaam-tuk 4255.
Superintendent.

(b) kaam-tán 4093.
A jailbird.

(c) kaam-tsŏ 4593.
Compelled to do.

1456. 緘 120/9 To tie up, close, seal. '

KAÁM

1457. 減 85/9 To diminish, lessen. S.

1458. 减 15/9 To diminish, lessen. S.

(a) kaám-shiú 3966.
To diminish.

(b) kaám-pat 3237.
Abbreviated form of writing.

KAÀM

1459. 鑒 167/14 To look upon, examine.

1460. 鑑 167/14 Mirror. Reflection.

(a) kaàm-kaai 1437.
An example.

1461. 監 108/9 To examine. An office. (kaam)
(a) kaàm-tsź 4677, or t'aai kaàm 4283. A eunuch.

1462. 鑒 30/22 Whilst.
" kaàm-shaang 3802. To bury, or plunge in, alive.

KAAN

1463. 間 169/4 Separate. Between. Within.
1464. 閒 169/4 C. for rooms, houses, etc. (kaàn) (1464 haān)
1465. 艱 138/11 Difficult. Hardship. Calamity.
(a) kaan-naān 2834. Difficult. Difficulty. Distressing. Dangerous.
1466. 姦 38/6 Illicit intercourse. Adultery.
(a) kaan-yâm 5097. Adultery.
(b) k'eúng-kaan 1964. To rape.
(c) kai-kaan 1515. Sodomy.
1467. 奸 38/3 Inordinate. Deceitful. False. uf 1466
(a) kaan-chà 61. Fraudulent.
(b) kaan-kaaú 1504. Villianous. Crafty.
(c) kaan-tsái 4482. A rascal.

KAÁN

1468. 揀 64/9 To choose, select.

(a) kaán-chaāk 80. To select.
(b) kaán-pooí-ch'ā 3382-409. Campoi tea.

1469. 鹼 197/7 Soap.
(a) óon-kaán 3146. Coarse soap.
(b) laāp-kaán 2192. Fine soap.
(c) kaán-shuí 4004. Lye.
(d) kaán-sha 3778. Sediment of lye.
1470. 繭 120/13 Cocoon.
(a) kaán-ch'ūng 647. A chrysalis.
(b) kaán-ch'aŭ 478. Undyed pongee.
1471. 鰜 197/10 Potash.
1472. 鹼 197/13 Soda. Natural salts.
1473. 簡 118/12 To abridge. Document. Rude. Simple.
(a) kaán-leŭk 2308. To abridge.
1474. 柬 75/5 A visiting card. To select.
1475. 癇 104/12 A sickness with foaming at the mouth.

KAÀN

1476. 諫 149/9 To remonstrate, warn, exhort. S.
1477. 間 169/9 To partition, separate. (kaàn)
(a) kaàn-waāk 4966. Supposing. If.
(b) kaàn-sìn 3646. To rule (paper).
1478. 澗 85/12 Rivulet. Creek. Brook.

KAANG

1479. 更 73/3 See kang.

1480. 耕 127/4 To plow, cultivate. (kang)

1481. 樬 64/13 To form the warp. To reel (silk). To spin (as a spider).

1482. 經 120/7 (king)
  (a) lōh-kaang 2437.
    A compass.

KAÀNG

1483. 梗 64/7 To stir up, find by touch, wade.

1484. 逕 162/7 To passby, approach. A dangerous spot.
  (a) tá-kaàng 4027.
    A footpad. Robber.

KAAP₀

1485. 夾 37/4 To press together, squeeze, smuggle, secrete.
  (a) kaap₀-maaí 2568.
    To put or press together.
  (b) shue-kaap₀ 3982.
    Portfolio.
  (c) i-kaap₀ 1248.
    Portmanteau.
  (d) kaap₀-maân 2576.
    A chest. A safe.

1486. 唊 30/7 " To hold fast.

1487. 硤 112/7 " To press.

1488. 甲 102/1 Scales. Finger nails. Armor.
  (a) kaap₀-chaû 166.
    Armor.

  (b) kaap₀-ch'ūng 647.
    Beetle.

1489. 頰 181/7 The cheek. Jaws.

1490. 筴 118/7 Pincers.
  (a) kaap₀-tsaí 4482.
    Tweezers.

1491. 鋏 167/7 Tongs. Pincers.
  (a) lô-shue-kaap₀ 2420-3985. A vice.

1492. 莢 140/7 Pods. Seeds. S.

KAĀT

1493. 甴 73/1
  (a) kaāt-tsaāt 4479.
    Cockroach.

KAAU

1494. 交 8/4 To deliver to. Friendship. Acquaintance.
  (a) kaau-kit₀ 1694.
    To make friends.
  (b) kaau-tsip₀ 4569.
    To entertain.
  (c) kaau-yīk 5220.
    Commercial intercourse.
  (d) sam-kaau 3593.
    Intimacy.
  (e) kaau-hōp 1193.
    Sexual intercourse.
  (f) kaau-t'ok₀ 4427.
    To entrust to.
  (g) tá-kaau 4027.
    To fight.
  (h) kaau-kwaan 2051.
    Serious. Terrible.
  (i) kaau-keuk₀ 1638
    To cross the legs.
  (j) kaau-ch'í 524.
    To dovetail.

(k) kaau-í 1256.
   An armchair.

(l) kaau-chí-chi-nōh 226-
   207-2934. Cochin
   China.

1495. 膠 130/11 To adhere to.
   Glue. S.

(a) uō-kaau 4872. Fish
   glue. Isinglass.

(b) kaau-hōp 1193.
   Union. To stick to-
   gether.

1496. *郊 163/6 Waste or un-
   occupied land.

(a) kaau-yè 5173. Country.
   Wilderness.

1497. 茭 140/6 Dried grass.
   Fodder.

(a) kaau-sún 3740.
   Cane shoots.

1498. 鮫 195/6 A large shark.

1499. 餃 184/6 Meat dumplings.
   (kaaù)

1500. 咬 30/6 (ngaaù)

1501. 教 66/7 To cause, in-
   duce. (kaaù)

KAAÚ

1502. 攪 64/20 To mix, disturb,
   excite.

(a) kaaú-iū 1403.
   To embroil.

(b) kaaú-shuí 4004.
   To dilute.

(c) kaaú-wàn 5037.
   To mix.

(d) kaaú-ch'eūng-sha 513-
   3781. Cholera mor-
   bus.

1503. 絞 120/6 To burst, strangle. To turn, as
   a screw. S.

(a) kaaú-t'aū-pò 4339-
   3336. Turban.

(b) kaaú-p'oōn 3553.
   Capstan.

(c) kaaú-pèng 3277.
   A crank.

1504. *狡 94/6 Wily.
   Crafty.

1505. *姣 38/6 Handsome. Artful. Salacious.

1506. 皎 106/6 White.
   Spotless.

KAAÙ

1507. 教 66/7 To teach. Doctrine. Relig-
   ious system.
   (kaau)

(a) kaaù-fàn 716.
   To instruct.

(b) kaaù-tsaāp 4476.
   Teacher. Professor.

(c) saam-kaaù 3572.
   The Three Religions
   (of China).

(d) Yē-So-kaaù 5172-3681,
   Kei-Tuk-kaaù 1606-
   4255, or
   fuk-yam-kaaù 867-5089.
   The Protestant
   Churches.

(e) yāp-kaaù 5132.
   To join the church.

(f) kaaù-oot 3143.
   A church.

(g) T'in-Chué-kaaù 4355-
   328. The Roman
   Catholic Church.

(h) kaaù-wōng 5072.
   The pope.

(i) chué-kaaù 328.
   R.C. bishop.

(j) hūng-i-chué-kaaù 1235-
   1248. R.C. cardinal.

1508. 較 159/6 To compare.

(a) peí-kaaù 3251.
   Compared with.

(b) m̄-shaí-kaaù 2551-3814.
   Trustworthy.
(c) kaaù-ch'eüng 510.
   Parade ground.
(d) kaaù-sín 3646.
   To tune.
1509. 覺 147/13 To sleep. (kok.)
1510. 鉸 167/6 A hinge.Shears. To shear.
   (a) kaaù-tsín 4554.
   Scissors.
1511. 酵 164/7 Leaven. Yeast.
   (a) kaaù-chúng 391.
   Yeast.
1512. 窖 116/7 Cellar. Vault. Pit. To store.
1513. 珓 96/6 Divining blocks.
1514. 校 75/6 To compare. S. (haaû)

KAI

1515. 鷄 196/10 The fowl. Chickens.
   (a) shaan-kai 3793.
   Pheasant.
   (b) kam-kai 1527.
   Golden pheasant.
   (c) kam-ts'ín-kai 4761.
   Peacock.
   (d) paák-shìng-kai 3178-3947. Jacana.
   (e) kai-hóng 1182.
   A pullet.
   (f) sìn-kai 3648.
   Capon.
   (g) kai-t'aí 4322.
   Cockcrow.
   (h) kai-taân-ko 4057-1716.
   Sponge cakes.
   (i) t'ín-kai 4356.
   Frogs.
   (j) ngān-kai 3028.
   Police whistle.

(k) kát-kai 1566.
   Cook of a gun.
(l) kai-ngaán 2999.
   Corns.
(m) shui-kai 4004. Bamboo
   water pipe (for smoking).
1516. 雞 172 The cock. uf 1515.
   (a) kai-koon-fa 1816-650.
   Cockscomb.
1517. 笄 118/6 A hair pin. To do up the hair.
1518. 枅 75/6 Tie beam. Davit.

KAI

1519. 髻 190/6 See kaì.
1520. 偕 9/9 See kaí.

KAÌ

1521. 計 149/2 To calculate, plan. S. (kei)
   (a) kaì-shò 3972.
   To reckon up accounts.
   (b) kwat-kaì 2083.
   Ginglymus joint.
1522. 繼 120/14 To follow in line. Lineage. Hereditary.
   (a) kaì-foô 836.
   Stepfather.
1523. 髻 190/6 Coiffure. Tuft of hair. Crest of a bird.(kaí)
1524. 彑 R/58 Hog's head.

KAÎ

1525. 偈 9/9 Enigma. Secret code. Buddhist stanzas. (kaí)

-76-

KAM

1526. 今 $\frac{9}{2}$ The present time. Now.

1527. 金 $\frac{167}{}$ Gold. Money. Precious. S.

(a) kam-pŏk 3361.
Gold leaf.

(b) kam-fa-ts'oĭ-hūng 650-4796-1235. Tinsel.

(c) kam-fūng 898.
Acacia.

(d) kam-sún 3740.
Carrots.

(e) kam-kai-naăp 1515-2836. Quinine.

(f) kam-sing 3652.
Planet Venus.

(g) kam-sing-shĕk 3879.
Friable mica.

(h) kam-kong-shĕk 1772.
Diamond.

(i) kam-shaan 3793.
California.

(j) san-kam-shaan 3596.
Australia.

(k) kam-shaan-taaĭ-faû 4033-745.
San Francisco.

(l) kam-pin 3286.
Cambodia.

KÁM

1528. 錦 $\frac{167}{8}$ Embroidered. S.

1529. 嘞 $\frac{30}{16}$ To take a part.

KÂM

1530. 禁 $\frac{113}{8}$ To restrain, forbid. Against. S. (k'am)

1531. 嘑 $\frac{30}{13}$ Difficult to speak. (t'âm, k'am)

KÂM

1532. 搝 $\frac{64}{10}$ To press down. (k'am)

1533. 撍 $\frac{64}{13}$ To press down. uf 1532, 1909.

KAN

1534. 斤 $\frac{R}{69}$ A catty. S. Equal to

1535. 劤 $\frac{148}{2}$ 1⅓ pound adv.

(a) tá-kan-taú 4027-4109.
Somersault.

1536. 跟 $\frac{157}{6}$ To follow, imitate.

(a) kan-paan 3183.
Attendants.

1537. 巾 $\frac{R}{50}$ A cloth. Towel. Napkin.

(a) shaú-kan 3859.
Handkerchief.Towel.

(b) mĭn-kan 2687.
A towel.

(c) t'oĭ-kan 4418.
Table napkin.

1538. 根 $\frac{75}{6}$ Root. Origin. S.

(a) kan-k'eǔng 1967.
Roots.

1539. 筋 $\frac{118}{6}$ Sinews. Muscles. S.

1539½. 肋 $\frac{130}{2}$ Used for 1539 (lăk).

(a) huet₀-kan 1212.
Blood vessels.

1540. 齦 $\frac{211}{6}$ The gums. To gnaw. (kān)

KÁN

1541. 緊 $\frac{120}{8}$ Important. Urgent. Makes the present participle.

(a) kán-iû 1388.
Necessary.Important.

(b) shuí-kán 4004.
Strong current.

1542. 謹 149 Cautious. Wary.
11 Watchful. S.

(a) kán-shân 3839.
To be careful.

1543. 僅 9 Scarcely. Bare-
11 ly. Hardly.

1544. 菫 140
8

(a) kán-ts'oì 4800.
The pansy.

1545. 槿 75 Hibiscus.
11

1546. 瑾 96 Brilliant
11 gem.

KÀN

1547. 艮 R Perverse.
138 Obstinate.

1548. 覲 147 To have
11 audience.

KÂN

1549. 近 162 Adjoining. Near
4 (in time or
place) (k'ǎn)

KANG

1550. 更 73 Night watches.
3 (kaang, kàng)

(a) kang-foo 801.
A watchman.

(b) kang-laū 2248.
Watch tower.

(c) t'ai-kang 4314.
To keep watch.

(d) lò(lò)-kang 2420(2404)
A watchman.

1551. 羹 123 Soup.
13 Chowder.

1552. 羹 123 A spoon.
9 (kaang)

(a) ch'ī-kang 537.
Large spoon.

1553. 耕 127 See kaang.
4

1554. 庚 53 Age.
5 To change. S.

KÁNG

1555. 梗 75 Straight. Stiff.
7 Obstinate.
Fixed. uf 1541.

1556. 耿 128 Bright. Upright
4 Honorable. S.

KÀNG

1557. 更 73 Again. More.
3 Further. Still.
(kang, kaang)

KAP

1558. 急 61 Quick. Haste.
5 Urgent. Anxious.

(a) kap-uě 4888.
A shower.

(b) kap-shuí 4004.
A torrent.

KAT

1559. 刮 18 To pierce,
6 prick.

1560. 吉 30 Fortunate.
3 Lucky. S.

(a) kat-lâm 2226.
Kirin.

1561. 桔 75 Kind of orange.
6

(a) kat-tsaí 4482.
Small smooth orange.

(b) sż-kwai-kat 3770-2066.
Nutmeg oranges.

(c) kam-ts'ín-kat 1527-
4761. Tomato.

1562. 拮 64 To grasp
6 firmly.

1563. 吃 30 To stammer.
3 To eat. (hat)

-78-

1564. 訖 $\frac{149}{3}$ To finish.
' Until. To date.

KĀT

1565. 跛 $\frac{157}{3}$ To limp.
*
1566. 跰 $\frac{157}{4}$ Lame.
'

  (a) kāt-ko 1713.
      To curl up.
  (b) kāt-ko-t'aū 4339.
      To stand on tiptoe
      to look.
  (c) kāt-heí-t'aū 1031.
      To sit up (in bed).
  (d) kāt-keuk, 1638.
      To tiptoe.
  (e) kāt-t'ok, 4429.
      Cackle of a hen.
  (f) kāt-la! 2146.
      Begone!

KAU

1567. 鳩 $\frac{196}{2}$ Turtle dove.
' Pigeon.
  (a) kau-huí 1221.
      To rush off.
  (b) kau-kau-sheng 3880.
      Noisy swagger.
1568. 勾 $\frac{20}{2}$ To hook, entice,
* inveigle. S.
1569. 鉤 $\frac{167}{5}$ A hook. To hook.
* S. (k'aù,ngau)
  (a) kau-keuk, 1638.
      To trip up.
1570. 溝 $\frac{85}{10}$ A ditch. Drain.
'

KAÚ

1571. 九 $\frac{5}{1}$ The numeral
nine.
1572. 玖 $\frac{96}{3}$ S.

1573. 爻 $\frac{R}{34}$ op chi. Used as
running hand
form of numeral
nine.

  (a) kaú-ng 2962. Almost.
      Most likely. Prob-
      ably.
  (b) kaú-kong 1771.
      Kiukiang.
  (c) kaú-lūng 2532.
      Kowloon.
1574. 狗 $\frac{94}{5}$ Dog. Brat. Term
of contempt.
  (a) yě-kaú 5173. Jackal.
  (b) kaú-shat 3851. A flea.
  (c) kaú-mō-ch'ūng 2712-
      647. Caterpillar.
1575. 久 $\frac{4}{2}$ A long time.
  (a) kaú-pat-kaú 3236.
      Frequently.
1576. 苟 $\frac{140}{5}$ Illicit.
* Irregular. S.
  (a) kaú-hōp 1193.
      Fornication.
1577. 笱 $\frac{118}{5}$ A shrimp trap.
'
1578. 韭 $\frac{R}{179}$ Leeks.
" '
1579. 韮 $\frac{140}{9}$
'
1580. 垢 $\frac{32}{6}$ Dirt. Foul.
' Disgrace.
1581. 糾 $\frac{120}{2}$ To collect.
' A league.

KAÙ

1582. 救 $\frac{66}{7}$ To save, help.
S.
  (a) kaù-měng 2671.
      Save! Help!
  (b) kaù-fôh 767.
      To fight fire.
  (c) kaù-chuē 328.
      The SAVIOR.

(d) kaù-shaì-kwan 3818-2075. Salvation Army.

1583. 夠 36/8 Enough. Plenty. Complete.

1584. 疚 104/3 Poor. Sick. Tired out.
(a) kaù-kwooì 2110. Weary.

1585. 究 116/2 To investigate.
(a) kaù-kíng 1677. To inquire into. After inquiry. Finally. After all. Even then. Indeed.

1586. 灸 86/3 To cauterize, blister. S.

1587. 咎 30/5 Crime. Fault.

1588. 姤 38/6 To pair, copulate.

1589. 媾 38/10 Marriage. Favor. Copulation.

1590. 搆 64/10 To drag. To incur.

1591. 構 75/10 To roof, finish. To mix.

1592. 覯 147/10 To meet with, see.

1593. 購 154/10 To buy, procure.

1594. 舊 134/12 Old. Former.

1595. 旧 72/1 Ancient. S.

1596. 㧅 9/8 A lump. C. for stone and heavy articles.

1597. 礭 30/17

1598. 颶 182/8 A great wind. (kuî)

1599. 柩 75/5 Corpse in coffin.

1600. 嘅 30/11 Sign of possessive. With nouns makes adjective. F.

1601. 機 75/12 } Opportunity.

1602. 机 75/2 Spring. Moving power.
(a) kei-heì 1035. Machine. Machinery.
(b) fei-kei 750. Flying machine.
(c) kei-ooì 3143. An opportunity.
(d) mō-kei-ma̍t 2711-2636. Amorphozoa.

1603. 饑 184/12 Dearth. Hunger.

1604. 飢 184/2 Famine. S.
(a) kei-fong 781. Famine.

1605. 譏 149/12 To ridicule. Satire.
(a) kei-siù 3675. To taunt, scoff at.

1606. 基 32/8 Foundation. Base.
(a) Kei-Tuk 4255. CHRIST.
(b) kei-lōh 2437. Kilogramme.
(c) kei-maì 2603. Kilometer.

1607. 箕 118/8 Basket. Sieve. S.

1608. 肌 130/2 Muscles. Flesh.
(a) kei-sz 3761. Muscle fibers.
(b) chì-kei 230. Voluntary muscles.

1609. 几 R/16 A stand. Small table.

-80-

1610. 幾 $\frac{52}{9}$ Nearly. Almost.
*

1611. 几 $\frac{R}{16}$ (kei)

1612. 奇 $\frac{37}{5}$ Odd. Odd numbers. Surplus. (k'eī)
*

1613. 磯 $\frac{112}{12}$ Obstacle, checking the current.
" '

1614. 期 $\frac{74}{8}$ A full period. (Year.) (k'eī)
" '

1615. 嘻 $\frac{30}{11}$
" '

(a) kei-lô-ping 2431-3302. Cherubim.

1616. 占 $\frac{5}{5}$ To divine. Planchette.
'

1617. 姬 $\frac{38}{6}$ A beauty. S.
'

1618. 綦 $\frac{120}{8}$ Very. Dark grey.
'

1619. 羈 $\frac{146}{19}$ A halter.
'

1620. 羈 $\frac{122}{19}$ To restrain, detain.
'

1621. 羈 $\frac{122}{17}$ To sojourn.
'

1622. 凱 $\frac{188}{2}$ Same as 1608.
" '

1623. 己 $\frac{R}{49}$ One's self. S.

1624. 幾 $\frac{52}{9}$ How many? How? A few. Several.

(a) keí-shî 3905. When?

(b) keí-kòh 1734. Several.

(c) keí-toh 4215. How many?

(d) taî-keí 4076. Which one (of them)?

(e) keí-hôh 1120. Quantity (math.).

1625. 紀 $\frac{120}{3}$ A record. To narrate. Age.S.

(a) kei-nîm 2891. To remember.

(b) nîn-kei 2895. Age.

(c) shaî-kei 3818. Century.

(d) tsz̄-kei 4673. Autobiography.

1626. 杞 $\frac{75}{3}$ Kind of tree. S.
" '

1627. 記 $\frac{149}{3}$ To remember, recollect, note down.

(a) keî-tak 4081. To remember.

(b) keî-nîm 2891. To remember, memorialize.

(c) yât-keî 5137. Diary.

(d) sź-keî 3769. History.

(e) keî-hô 1109. Trade mark. Mark. Sign.

1628. 既 $\frac{71}{7}$ Already. Since.

(a) keî-în 1349. Seeing that. Since.

(b) keî-haî-kóm 968-1754. It being so.

1629. 寄 $\frac{40}{8}$ To lodge, send, dispatch.

(a) keî-kui 1846. To lodge at.

1630. 計 $\frac{149}{2}$ (kaî) See 768c, 769a.
*

1631. 忌 $\frac{61}{3}$ To be jealous. To envy, hate, avoid. S.
*

(a) keî-la-sz̄-koh 2145-3777-1728. Glasgow.

1632. 妓 $\frac{38}{4}$ A prostitute.

1633. 技 $\frac{64}{4}$ Dexterous. Skillful.

1634. 伎 $\frac{9}{4}$ Talent. Cleverness.

1635. 媳 $\frac{38}{7}$ Anger. Envy.

KÉNG--See also kíng.

1636. 頸 $\frac{181}{7}$ The neck. (kíng)

(a) kéng-taal 4031. Necktie.

(b) kéng-léng 2305. Collar.

(c) noî-sheung-kéng 2937- 3885. Nervous.

(d) hó-kéng 1099. Good tempered.

(e) fóh-kéng 767. Irascible.

(f) kéng-hot 1198. Thirsty.

KÈNG--See also kìng.

1637. 鏡 $\frac{167}{11}$ Mirror. Glass. Lens. (kìng)

(a) mîn-kèng 2687. Looking glass.

(b) kèng-chong 303. Dressing case.

(c) oô-sam-kèng 3128-3593. Breastplate.

(d) t'aû-kwong-kèng 4338- 2105. A lens.

(e) nap-kèng 2860. Concave lens.

(f) tāt-kèng 4106. Convex lens.

(g) ngaǎn-kèng 2999. Spectacles.

(h) fòng-taaî-kèng 795- 4033. Magnifier.

(i) ts'in-leî-kèng 4754- 2286. Field glasses. Telescope.

KEUK.

1638. 腳 $\frac{130}{9}$ The feet.

1639. 脚 $\frac{130}{9}$ Legs.

(a) keuk nŏng 2942. Calf of the leg.

(b) keuk ngaǎn 2999. The ankle.

(c) keuk pooî-waan 3377- 4970. Instep.

(d) keuk paǎn 3187. Sole of the foot.

(e) keuk naú 2867, or t'oî-shaang-keuk 4417-3802. Clubfoot.

(f) keuk tsìk 4554. Footprints.

(g) keuk chaǎp 99. Stocks.

(h) t'in-keuk 4355. The horizon.

(i) shuî-keuk 4004. Fare. Passage money.

(j) keuk -heî 1033. Beriberi.

KEUNG

1640. 薑 $\frac{140}{13}$ Ginger.

(a) tsź-keung 4667. Stem ginger.

(b) t'ŏng-keung 4437. Preserved ginger.

(c) wōng-keung-fán 5070- 713. Curry powder.

1641. 疆 $\frac{102}{14}$ A boundary. Frontier.

1642. 韁 $\frac{177}{13}$ A bridle. Halter.

1643. 蜣 $\frac{142}{8}$ Dung beetle.

1643½. 僵 9/13 Stiff. Rigid.

1644. 姜 38/6 S.

1644½. 殭 78/13 Stiff. Rigid.

1645. 羌 123/2 S.

1646. 蠶 142/13 Silkworms dying immature.

__KEUNG__

1647. 強 57/8 | Stiff.

1648. 彊 57/13 | Inflexible.

__KIK__

1649. 激 85/13 To provoke, excite, rouse. S.
   (a) kik-nau 2865.
       To exasperate.
   (b) kik-siu 3675.
       To banter.
   (c) kik-yeŭk 5183.
       Stimulants.

1650. 棘 75/8 Thorny bushes. To prick. S.

1651. 擊 64/13 | To strike,

1651½. 撽 64/13 | attack.

1652. 亟 7/6 Haste. Urgency.

1653. 戟 62/8 Lance. Halberd.

__KĪK__

1654. 極 75/8 The extreme. Utmost. Superlative degree.
   (a) pak-kīk 3215.
       North pole.

__KIM__

1655. 兼 12/8 Also. Finally. Both. S.
   (a) kim-yaŭ 5159.
       Moreover.

__KÍM__

1656. 撿 64/13 To revise, gather up, search.

1657. 檢 75/13 To label, examine. Attentive. S.

__KÌM__

1658. 劍 18/13 Two edged sword.
   (a) kìm-hok 1138.
       Scabbard.
   (b) kìm-shŭt 4024.
       Art of fencing.
   (c) mŏ-kìm 2721.
       To fence.

__KĪM__

1659. 儉 9/13 Economical. Frugal. S.

__KIN__

1660. 堅 32/8 Strong. Stable. Firm. S.
   (a) kin-koŏ 1810.
       Lasting. Strong.

1661. 肩 130/4 Shoulder. To sustain. S.

__KÍN__

1662. 蹇 157/10 Halt. Lame.

__KÌN__

1663. 見 R 147 To see, observe, perceive. S.
   (a) yăn-kìn 5121.
       To introduce.

(b) kìn-chìng 276.
A witness. Testimony.

(c) ì-kìn 1258.
Opinion.

(d) m̄-kìn 2551.
Not seen. Lost.

1664. 建 54/6 To establish,
* build. S.

KÌN

1665. 件 9/4 An item. C. for
** clothing, busi-
ness, affairs,
things in gen-
eral.

1666. 健 9/9 Strong. Robust.
Vigorous. S.

1667. 鍵 167/9 Bolt of a lock.

KING

1668. 經 120/7 Past. A classic.
** S. (kaang)

(a) king-shaú 3859, or
king-keí 1625.
A broker.

(b) king-hōk 1140. Gov-
ernmental science.

(c) shìng-king 3945. The
Bible. Confucian
sacred books.

(d) king-lìk 2331. Time
passed by. A sec-
retary.

(e) uët-king 4937.
The menses.

1669. 京 8/6 A high peak.
Capital city. S.

(a) king-t'aan 4300.
Charcoal.

(b) pak-king 3215.
Peking.

(c) naàm-king 2823.
Nanking.

1670. 驚 187/13 To terrify,
frighten,
alarm. (keng)

(a) king-fong 780.
Frightened.

(b) king-maì 2601.
Stunned.

(c) haàm-king 925.
To exorcise by in-
cantations.

1671. 矜 110/4 To boast, pity.

(a) king-kw'a 2111.
To brag, boast.

1672. 荊 140/6 Thorn. Thorny.
* Brambles. S.

(a) king-kik 1650.
Thorns. Brambles.

1673. 兢 10/12 Fear. Dread.
*

KÍNG

1674. 儆 9/13 To warn,
caution.

1675. 警 149/13 To awake.

1676. 境 32/11 A boundary. District. Region.
Place.

(a) kíng-kaaì 1438.
Boundary. Frontier.

1677. 竟 117/6 Finally.
* After all.

1678. 景 72/8 Scenery. View.
* Prospect.
Light. S.

(a) kíng-chì 231½.
Prospect. View.

1679. 頸 181/7 See kéng.

KÌNG

1680. 敬 66/9 To honor,
revere.

1681. 鏡 167/11 Mirror. Glass.
Lens. S.(kèng)

1682. 徑 60/7 Direct.

1683. 徑 9/7 Short path.
Diameter.

(a) kìng-ló 2426.
By path. Short cut.

(b) kìng-sin 3646.
Diameter.

(c) kìng-ts'Ing 4766.
Straightforward.

(d) ts'ē-kìng 4731.
Tricky. Smart.

1684. 脛 130/7 Leg. Shin.
Shank. (kèng)

(a) k'uk-kìng 2029.
Bandy legged.

1685. 逕 162/7 Direct. An ap-
proach.Bypath.
(kaàng)

KÌNG

1686. 競 117/15 To quarrel,
compete

1687. 勁 19/7 Strong.

KIP。

1688. 刮 18/5

1689. 刦 18/5 To rob by force.

1690. 劫 19/5

1691. 呷 30/7 Percussion cap.
Cartridge.

KĪP

1692. 狹 94/7 To pinch,
(haàp)

KIT。

1693. 潔 85/12 To purify.
Pure. Clean.

1694. 結 120/6 To connect, ally.
To produce, as
fruit. Bonds.
To tie.

(a) kit-t'aù 4339.
A knot.

(b) oòt-kit 3157.
A halter. A noose.

(c) kit-maaī 2568.
To coagulate.

(d) kit-kùk-hòk 1875-1140.
Teleology.

1695. 絜 120/6 To regulate,
adjust.

KĪT

1696. 傑 9/10 Hero.
Eminent.

1697. 偈 9/9 Martial.
Ardent. (kaī)

1698. 桀 75/6 S.
S.

KIU

1699. 驕 187/12 Proud. Arrogant.
Haughty.

1700. 澆 85/12 To sprinkle,
splash water.

(a) kiu-pòk 3361.
Unfaithful.

1701. 嬌 38/12 Delicate. To
pet. Fascinating.

1701½. 僥 9/ Lucky.

1702. 驍 187/12 Brave.
(hiu)

KIÚ

1703. 轎 159/12 Sedan chair.
Palanquin.(kiû)

1704. 撟 64/12 To wipe.
(kiû)

1705. 矯 111 / 12 To feign. Martial. Forced.
1706. 繳 120 / 13 To hand in, pay.
1707. 蹺 157 / 12 Cross legs. Unsettled.

KIÙ

1708. 叫 30 / 4 To call,
1709. 叫 30 / 3 call out. To style.
　(a) kiù-tsô 4593. To name, style. It is called. S.

KIÛ

1710. 撬 64 / 12 To pry up, pry open, trip up.
1711. 橋 64 / 12 To raise, grasp, trip up, pin together. (kiú)
1712. 轎 159 / 12 (kiú)

KO

1713. 高 R 189 Exalted. Tall. Lofty. Eminent. S.
　(a) ko-kìn 1663. Your honorable opinion.
　(b) ko-sìng 3657. Your honorable surname.
　(c) ko-laū 2248. A tower.
　(d) ko-laū-koón 1820. An eating house.
　(e) ko-hìng 1075. Showy. Show. Festive time.
　(f) ko-laī 2212. Corea.
1714. 膏 130 / 10 Ointment. Rich. To anoint.
　(a) ko-yeúk 5183. Salve. Medicinal plaster.
1715. 羔 123 / 4 A young lamb.

1716. 糕 119 / 10 Cakes. Pastry. Dumplings.
1717. 篙 118 / 10 A bamboo pole. To pole a boat.
1718. 餻 184 / 10 Same as 1716.
1719. 皋 132 / 5 Marsh.
1720. 皐 106 / 5 Pool.
1721. 睪 132 / 5 High. Eminent.

KÓ

1722. 稿 115 / 10 Stalks of grain. Rough draft.
1723. 藁 115 / 10 Printer's copy. Proof sheet.
　(a) uén-kó 4919. Original copy (pr).
1724. 槁 75 / 10 Stalks of grain.
1725. 槀 75 / 10 Dry. Withered.

KÒ

1726. 告 30 / 4 To announce, complain, accuse. S.
　(a) kò-paʰk 3178. An advertisement.
　(b) kò-shī 3910. Proclamation.
　(c) kò-cheūng 192. To sue for debt.
　(d) kò-tsùng 4655. To prosecute.
　(e) uén-kò 4919. Plaintiff.
　(f) peī-kò 3262. Defendant.
　(g) leúng-kò 2321. Parties to a case.
　(h) kò-kà 1422. Leave of absence.
　(i) kò-t'uì 4449. To resign.

(j) kò-kaaí 1436. To
confess. (Rom.Cath.)

1727. 誥 149/7 To enjoin upon.
' A decoration.

___

KOH

1728. 哥 30/7 An elder brother.
A particle. S.

(a) à-koh 9 Elder brother.
(b) liù-koh 2399.
The grackle.

1729. 歌 76/10 Local ditties.
To recite.

1730. 謌 149/10 To sing,
' chant.

___

KÓH

1731. 個 9/8 Emphatic

1732. 嗰 30/10 demonstrative
pronoun.

1733. 个 9/1 That.
(kòh)

(a) kóh-kóh 1734.
That one.

___

KÒH

1734. 個 9/8 Classifier of
wide applica-

1735. 箇 118/8 tion. Persons.
Things. Imper-

1736. 个 9/1 sonal pronoun.
(kóh)

(a) kòh-kòh
All. Everyone.

___

KOI

1737. 該 149/6 Ought. Right.
Altogether. To
owe. Due. S.

(a) m̄-koi 2551. Beg par-
don! Thank you!

1738. 嗐 30/13 See 3583.
"

___

KOÍ

1739. 改 66/3 To change, alter, amend. S.

___

KÒI

1740. 蓋 140/10 A cover.
*

1741. 盖 108/6 To cover,
* screen, hide.

1742. 蓋 108/7 (k'oi)
*

___

KOK。

1743. 各 30/2 All. Every.
**

1744. 角 R/148 A corner. Horn
of animal. S.

(a) kok。-t'aü 4339.
Angle. Corner.
(b) yuí-kok。 5246.
Acute angle.
(c) ching-kok。 275.
Right angle.
(d) tûn-kok。 4269.
Obtuse angle.
(e) saam-kok。 3572.
Triangular.
(f) saam-kok。-yïng 5230.
A triangle.
(g) saam-kok。-faat。 682.
Trigonometry.
(h) saam-kok。-maí 2603.
Buckwheat.
(i) yat-kok。 5133. One
quarter. A ten cent
piece. One corner.
(j) a-kok。 2. Antler.
(k) kok。-t'üng 4461.
Syphon.
(l) hoi-kok。 1124.
To borrow money.
(m) haú-kok。 1006.
Eloquent.
(n) tiu-ngaǎn-kok。 4182-
2999. To ogle.

(o) ʻkok₀-tsaí 4482.
　　Patties.

1745. 覺 147/13 To perceive, understand, feel.
　　S. (kaaừ).

1746. 桷 75/7 Rafters.
　*　Lath.

1747. 閣 169/6 Vestibule. Hall. Council chamber. S.
　*

(a) noī-kok₀ 2937.
　　Council.

1748. 咯 30/6 To cackle.
　*　(lok₀).

(a) kok₀-tʻok₀ 4429.
　　Cackling.

1749. 擱 64/14 To hinder, delay, run aground.
　'

KOM

1750. 甘 R/99 Sweet. Pleasant. Seasonable. S.

(a) kom-tsʻó 4777.
　　Liquorice.

(b) kom-yam-yam 5094.
　　Delicious.

(c) kom-suk 3738.
　　Kansu province.

1751. 柑 75/5 A kind of loose skinned orange.

1752. 疳 104/5 Ulcers. Sores.

(a) ngā-kom 2977.
　　Gum boil.

(b) kom-chʻong 578.
　　Venereal ulcers.

KÓM

1753. 噉 30/12 Thus. So. Adverb of quality.
　**

1754. 敢 66/8 To presume upon. To dare.

1755. 感 61/9 To influence, affect, move.

(a) kóm-tsě 4510.
　　To give thanks.

1756. 橄 75/12
　　(a) kóm-laám 2162.
　　The Chinese olive.

1757. 鹹 195/9 A kind of fish.
　'

KÒM

1758. 咁 30/5 Thus. So. So much. Adverb of quantity.

KON

1759. 乾 5/10 To clean.

1760. 乹 5/8 Dried up.

(a) kon-tsěng 4516.
　　Pure. Bright. Clean.

(b) kon-kwóh 2096.
　　Dried fruit.

(c) kon-tsʻó 4777. Hay.

(d) péng-kon 3276.
　　Biscuits. Crackers.

(e) kon-má 2555.
　　Dry nurse.

(f) shuí-kon 4004.
　　Ebb tide.

1761. 干 R/51 Concern. Matter. S.

1762. 杆 75/3 Club or stick. Felled timber.
　*

1763. 肝 130/3 The liver. Feelings.

(a) kon-taám 4038.
　　Courage.

1764. 竿 118/3 Pole. Staff. Cane.

(a) tiừ-kon 4191.
　　Fishing rod.

KÓN

1765. 赶 156/3 To drive out, eject, expel.

1766. 趕 156/7 To pursue.

   (a) kón-faaî 651½. In a hurry.

1767. 稭 115/7 Stubble. Straw.

KÒN

1768. 幹 51/10 Ability. Skill. Business. S.

   (a) nâng-kòn 2858. Ability. Talent.

1769. 榦 75/10 Stem. Trunk. Physique.

KONG

1770. 缸 121/3 Pottery. A jar.

1771. 江 85/3 River. S.

   (a) kong-haú 1006. Mouth of river.

   (b) kong-sai 3584. Kiangsi province.

   (c) kong-so 3677. Kiangsu province.

   (d) kong-moōn 2779. Kongmoon.

1772. 剛 18/8 Hard. Firm. Just. Exactly. S.

   (a) kong-ngaî 3019. Confident. Bold.

   (b) kong-k'eūng 1966. Violent. Strong.

1773. 鋼 167/8 Steel. Hard.

   (a) shūn-kong 4016. Pure steel.

1774. 綱 120/8 Bound up in. Summed up in.

1775. 岡 46/5 Hill. Ridge. Heap.

1776. 肛 130/3 Large intestine.

   (a) kong-moōn 2779. The anus.

1777. 䋧 121/8 uf 1770.

1778. 堈 32/8 uf 1770.

KÓNG

1779. 講 149/10 To talk, discourse, explain.

   (a) kóng-sam 3593. To speak one's mind.

1780. 港 85/9 Port. Harbor. Anchorage.

KÒNG

1781. 降 170/6 To descend, come down from heaven. To condescend. (hōng)

   (a) kòng-lām 2224. Condescend to visit.

   (b) kòng-k'ap 1924. To degrade.

   (c) kòng-shaang 3802. To become incarnate.

1782. 絳 120/6 Dark red. Purple.

1783. 杠 75/3 Ship's yard. Cross bar. Boom. Thill.

1784. 蜂 142/6 uf 1237.

KÔNG

1785. 抗 64/4 Wilful. Obstinate. (k'ong)

KOO

1786. 姑 38/5 Husband's mother or sisters. S.

   (a) à-koo 9. A girl.

(b) koo-neŭng 2880.
  Young lady. Miss.
(c) chaai-koo 69. A nun.
(d) neî-koo 2873.
  Buddhist nun.
(e) tô-koo 4207.
  Taoist nun.

1787. 孤 $\frac{39}{5}$ Fatherless. Orphan. Neglected. Solitary. Alone.

1788. 辜 $\frac{160}{5}$ Fault. Crime. uf 1787.
(a) koo-foô 839.
  To be ungrateful.

1789. 菰 $\frac{140}{8}$ Kind of

1789½. 苽 $\frac{140}{5}$ water plant.
(a) ts'z̄-koo 4867.
  Caladium.

1790. 罛 $\frac{122}{5}$ A large net. To haul.

1791. 沽 $\frac{85}{5}$ To buy or sell.
(a) taaî-koo 4033.
  Taku.

1792. 鴣 $\frac{196}{5}$ See 172a.

1793. 菇 $\frac{140}{8}$

1794. 咕 $\frac{30}{5}$
(a) koo-lei 2273. Coolie.

1795. 酤 $\frac{164}{5}$ To sell spirits.

KOÓ

1796. 古 $\frac{30}{2}$ Ancient. Old. Formerly. S.
(a) kóng-koó 1779.
  To tell stories.
(b) tá-koó-tsaí 4027-4482.
  To ask riddles.
(c) koó-mât-hŏk 2636-1140.
  Archaeology.
(d) koó-tŭk 4260. Sullen.

(e) koó-pa 3158. Cuba.

1797. 估 $\frac{9}{5}$ To guess, think, estimate, value.
(a) koó-shuî 4005.
  To assess.

1798. 股 $\frac{130}{4}$ Thighs. Rump. Leg.

1799. 肷 $\frac{130}{4}$ Division. Share of stock.
(a) tāt-koó 4106.
  Panelled.

1800. 蠱 $\frac{142}{17}$ Worms in abdomen. Dropsy. Poisonous.
(a) koó-waāk 4968.
  To delude.
(b) koó-cheúng 196.
  Dropsy.

1801. 牯 $\frac{93}{5}$ Male.
(a) mǎ-koó 2561.
  Stallion.

1802. 鼓 $\frac{R}{207}$ A drum. To drum up, excite.
(a) koó-mŏ 2721.
  To rouse, excite.
(b) koó-heî 1031.
  To inflate.
(c) koó-heî 1033.
  Sullen. Sulky.

1803. 臌 $\frac{130}{13}$ Petruding. Bulging.

1804. 賈 $\frac{154}{6}$ Trader. Market.
(a) taaî-koó 4033.
  Wholesale dealer.

1805. 咕 $\frac{30}{5}$ To mutter, coo, chatter.

1806. 瞽 $\frac{109}{13}$ Blind.

1807. 罟 $\frac{122}{5}$ A net.

1808. 詁 $\frac{149}{5}$ Sayings. Stories.

KOO

1809. 故 $\frac{66}{5}$ To cause, make. Old. To die.
  (a) koò-ts'ź 4852.
      Therefore.
  (b) uən-koò 4914.
      A reason.
1810. 固 $\frac{31}{5}$ Strong. Stable. Firm. S.
  (a) koò-ì 1258.
      Wilful. Purposely.
1811. 顧 $\frac{181}{12}$ To look after, upon, take care of, regard. S.
1812. 僱 $\frac{9}{12}$ To hire, rent.
1813. 雇 $\frac{172}{4}$ To borrow.
1814. 錮 $\frac{167}{8}$ To caulk, stop, restrain.

KOOI--See kwooi.

KOON

1815. 官 $\frac{40}{5}$ Officer. Official. S.
  (a) koon-lò 2426.
      Public road.
  (b) koon-wà 4960.
      Mandarin language.
  (c) tá-koon-sz 4027-3756.
      To go to law.
  (d) kwai-koon 2057.
      To confiscate.
  (e) taaì-à-koon 4033-9.
      A beau.
1816. 冠 $\frac{14}{7}$ Cap. Crown. Crest. S.(koòn)
  (a) koon-mìn 2683.
      A crown.
  (b) hà-koon 908.
      Wattles.
1817. 棺 $\frac{75}{8}$ Coffin.

  (a) koon-ts'oï 4805.
      A coffin.
1818. 觀 $\frac{147}{18}$ To look up to. New. S.
  (a) koon-môŋ 2764.
      To look forward to, gaze, watch.
  (b) koon-yam-laù 5089-2261. Tamarisk.

KOÓN

1819. 管 $\frac{118}{8}$ To oversee, control, look after. A tube. S.
  (a) koón-leï 2285.
      To govern.
  (b) koón-ka 1410.
      A butler.
  (c) koón-sź 3776.
      A steward.
  (d) koón-tìm 4154. Shop or house coolie.
  (e) koón-ch'uk 624.
      To curb, restrain.
  (f) koón-hàt 1000.
      To control.
  (g) heì-koón 1033.
      The windpipe.
  (h) huet-màk-koón 1212-2609. The arteries.
  (i) ooì-huet-koón 3135.
      The veins.

1820. 館 $\frac{135}{10}$ Inn. Eating house.

1821. 館 $\frac{184}{8}$ Resort. Hall. School.
  (a) hoi-koón 1124.
      To open school.
  (b) koón-shôh 3977.
      A public hall.

1822. 莞 $\frac{140}{7}$

KOÒN

1823. 罐 $\frac{121}{18}$ Vessel.
*   Jar.
1824. 礶 $\frac{112}{18}$ Pitcher.
*   Can.
  (a) t'aàm-koòn 4289.
      Spittoon.

1825. 貫 $\frac{154}{5}$ Strung together.
       Full.Complete.S.
  (a) koòn-ch'uèn 611. To
      string, as beads.

1826. 灌 $\frac{85}{18}$ To water, irri-
'   gate. To force
       water.

1827. 冠 $\frac{14}{7}$ To cap (ceremo-
'   ny). To excell.
       S. (koon)

1828. 觀 $\frac{147}{18}$ To look at, ex-
'   amine. (koon)

KOP。

1829. 鴿 $\frac{196}{6}$ Dove.
       Pigeon.
  (a) paāk-kop。-piu 3178-
      3319.Lottery ticket.

1830. 蛤 $\frac{142}{6}$ Frog.
*   Lizard.
  (a) kop。-ná 1830. Frog.
  (b) kop。-kaai 1436.
      Gecko. Lizard.

1831. 合 $\frac{30}{3}$ To join, agree.
*   (hòp).

KOT。

1832. 割 $\frac{18}{10}$ To cut, injure,
       inflict.
  (a) kot。-laì 2205.
      Circumcision.

1833. 葛 $\frac{140}{9}$ Creeping plant.
'   Dolichos. S.

KUEN

1834. 捐 $\frac{64}{7}$ To contribute,
       subscribe, pur-

       chase. To re-
       ject. To buy
       office.
  (a) luen-kuen 2470.
      To wriggle.
  (b) kuen-lung 2529. To
      squeeze through a
      hole.

1835. 鵑 $\frac{196}{}$
  (a) tô-kuen 4212.Cuckoo.
  (b) tô-kuen-fa 650.
      Azalea.

1836. 娟 $\frac{38}{7}$ Graceful.

1837. 鐲 $\frac{142}{17}$ Pure. Clear.

KUÉN

1838. 卷 $\frac{26}{6}$ C. for pictures,
*   maps, books,etc.
       A roll. A book.
       (kuèn)
  (a) kuén-paak。3173.
      Lycopodium.

1839. 捲 $\frac{64}{8}$ To roll up.
*
  (a) kuén-faat。 683.
      Curly hair.
  (b) kuén-taan 4048.
      Tiger lily.

KUÈN

1840. 眷 $\frac{109}{6}$ To love, care
*   for, draw near
       to. Family. S.

1841. 絹 $\frac{120}{7}$ Taffeta. Lus-
*   tring.Sarcenet.

1842. 卷 $\frac{26}{6}$ Rolled up. A
*   book. Volume.
       (kuén)

KUÈN

1843. 倦 $\frac{9}{8}$ Weary.
       Tired.

KUET.

1844. 橛 75/12 A piece.

1845. 橛 75/12 Half.

KUI

1846. 居 44/5 To dwell, inhab-
it. A dwelling.
S.
  (a) kui-chuě 339.
    To reside.
  (b) kui-yăn 5117.
    Occupants.
  (c) kui-măn 2618.
    Inhabitants.
  (d) kui-seung 3629.
    Widowed.
  (e) oōn-kui 3153.
    Sandpiper.

1847. 俱 9/8 All. Altogether.
Both. (k'ui)

1848. 車 R/159 Large cart. Vehicle. Chariot.
(ch'e)
  (a) taaī-kui 4033. Wagon.

KUÍ

1849. 舉 134/11 To raise up,
elevate.

1850. 舉 67/3 The whole.
All. S.
  (a) kuí-tsín 4557.
    To recommend.
  (b) lō-kuí 2420. A whore.

1851. 矩 111/5 Rule. Pattern.
Custom. Manner.

1852. 櫸 75/17 Kind of
willow.
  (a) kuí-laǔ 2261.
    Willow boxwood.

KUÏ

1853. 句 30/2 Sentence.
Phrase. C.

1854. 鋸 167/8 A saw.
To saw.

KUÎ

1855. 據 64/13 Evidence. Testimony. According
to. (kuī)

1856. 具 12/6 Implements.Uten-
sils. To pre-
pare, arrange.S.

1857. 懼 61/18 To fear,

1858. 懼 61/8 stand in awe of.

1859. 颶 182/10 A great wind.
Typhoon.(kaǔ)

1860. 炬 86/5 A torch.

1861. 踞 157/8 To squat,
crouch.

1862. 倨 9/8 Haughty.
Strong.

1863. 巨 48/2 Great.

KUK

1864. 穀 119/10 Grain.

1865. 穀 115/10 Cereals. S.
  (a) nğ-kuk 2962.
    Grain in general.
  (b) sha-kuk-maī 3778-
    2603. Sage.

1866. 谷 R/150 Valley. Ravine.
To nourish. S.
  (a) shaan-kuk 3793.
    A ravine.

1867. 菊 140/8 Chrysanthemum
species.
  (a) kong-naăm-kuk-fa 1771-
    2823-650. Chrysan-
    themum.
  (b) maăn-shaǔ-kuk 2576-
    3867. Marigold.

(c) kom-kuk-fa 1750-650.
    Chamomile.

1868. 搹 $\frac{64}{8}$ To rouse, raise.
" To force,

1869. 𥚃 $\frac{20}{6}$ irritate, make a spurt.

(a) kuk-hei 1033.
    Irritated.

1870. 鵠 $\frac{196}{7}$ Swan.
" White goose.

(a) wŏn-kuk 5060.
    Java sparrow.

1871. 㖡 $\frac{30}{7}$ Cluck of a fowl.
" To cackle.

1872. 鞠 $\frac{177}{8}$ To nourish. Exhausted. A football. uf 1873.

1873. 鞫 $\frac{177}{9}$ To examine, hear a case, judge. uf 1872.

1874. 麯 $\frac{199}{8}$ Yeast. Barm.

KŪK

1875. 局 $\frac{44}{4}$ Shop. Establishment. Game. C. (k'ūk) uf 1876.

(a) ts'în-kūk 4761.
    A mint.

(b) t'ung-sheung-kūk 4452-3887. Board of Trade.

(c) tsok͙-kūk 4610. Trick.
    Sharp practice.

(d) kūk-sź 3767. To smother to death.

1876. 焗 $\frac{86}{7}$ To bake,
" smother.

(a) kūk-lô 2406.
    A stove.

(b) kūk-p'oŏn 3552. Oven.

KUNG

1877. 工 $\frac{R}{48}$ Work.
** Labor.

(a) kung-foo 801. Work.
    Employment.

(b) yat-kung 5133.
    One day's work.

(c) yāt-kung 5137.
    Day work.

(d) yê-kung 5176.
    Night work.

(e) saàn-kung 3576.
    Job or piece work or workers.

(f) ch'eūng-kung 512.
    Permanent employment.

(g) hoi-kung 1124.
    To begin work.

(h) shau-kung 3857.
    Stop work.

(i) kung-pô 3342. Board of Public Works.

(j) kung-mô-koon 2729-1815. Surveyor general.

1878. 公 $\frac{12}{2}$ Just. Right.
** Public. Male. S.

(a) kung-tô 4207.
    Equitable.

(b) kung-î 1292.
    Righteousness.

(c) lô-kung 2420.
    Husband.

(d) kung-tsai 4482. Statuettes. Pictures. Toys.

(e) naî-à-kung 2844-9.
    Clay idol.

(f) kung-sz 3756. A trading or mercantile company.

1879. 功 $\frac{19}{3}$ Merit.
" Meritorious.

(a) kung-lô 2408.
    Merit

(b) kung-foo 801. Ability.

(c) kung-haaû 962.
    Effect. Effectual.

1880. 攻 66/3 To strike, attack, assault, censure.

(a) kung-k'it, 1987.
To accuse.

1881. 恭 61/6 To revere, respect. Polite.S.

1882. *供 9/6 To contribute, give evidence, accuse.S.(kung)

1883. ' 弓 R/57 A bow(weapon).

1884. " ' 宮 40/7 Mansion. Palace. S.

1885. 躬 158/3 Person. Personality.

KÚNG

1886. *拱 64/6 To fold hands in salute, bow. To lift up. An arch. S.

(a) kúng-p'ūng 3564.
Canopy. Archway.

1887. 鞏 177/6 Strong.To warp, turn up. S.

1888. " ' 廾 R/55

KÙNG

1889. " ' 貢 154/3 Tribute. **Presents. S.**

(a) sai-kùng 3584. Saigon.

1890. *供 9/6 To offer, as in worship. (kung)

1891. " ' 塡 32/10

KŬNG

1892. 共 12/4 Together with. All. S.

K'Á

1893. ' 卡 25/3 A guard house. Station.

K'AAI

1894. ' 楷 75/9 Model. Pattern.

K'AAĬ

1895. 搣 64/7 To take in the hand, grasp,use.

K'AAÙ

1896. 靠 175/7 To lean on, trust in. (hò)

1897. *銠 167/6 To fetter. Fetters.

K'AI

1898. *溪 85/10 Mountain brook. Rivulet.

(a) k'ai-kaàn 1478.
A brook.

1899. ' 稽 115/10 To investigate.

K'AÍ

1900. 啟 30/8 | To open, reveal,

1901. 啓 30/8 | divide, separate. S.

(a) k'aí-shī 3910.
To reveal.

K'AÌ

1902. 契 37/6 Covenant.Union. Bond. Property. Deed. S.

(a) k'aì-yē 5171.
Adopted father.

(b) k'aì-ná 2811.
Adopted mother.

(c) k'aì-ka-lò 1410-2404.
A lover.

(d) k'aì-ka-p'ōh 3528.
A sweetheart.

(e) lŏ-k'aì 2420.
A kept mistress.

(f) k'ai-tai 4077. Sodomite.	1914. 蟾 142/13
	1915. 蟆 142/12
K'AK	(a) k'ām-k'uī 2024. Toad.
1903. 喀 30/9 To retch. Rough.	(b) k'ām-lō 2419. A long legged spider.
K'AM	**K'ĂM**
1904. 啿 30/9 To endure, last. Lasting.	1916. 姶 38/4 Wife's sisters.
1905. 襟 145/13 Lapel. Opening of coat.	**K'ĂN**
(a) k'ām-t'aū-cham 4339-123. A brooch.	1917. 勤 19/11 Laborious. Diligent.
1906. 禁 113/8 To forbid, restrain. (kàm)	(a) k'ăn-lĭk 2330. Industrious.
1907. 噤 30/13 Difficult to speak. (kàm)	1918. 懃 61/13 Earnest. S.
	(a) yan-k'ăn 5110. Diligent. Attentive.
K'ĀM	1919. 芹 140/4 Malvaceous plants.
1908. 嗛 30/10	To cover,	(a) k'ăn-ts'oī 4800. Celery.
1909. 搇 64/10	close up. (kăm)	(b) shuī-k'ăn-ts'oī 4004. Watercress.
	(c) k'ăn-ts'ó 4777. Parsley.
K'ĀM	**K'ĂN**
1910. 禽 114/8 Birds. S.	1920. 近 162/4 Near. (kân)
(a) k'ām-shaù 3863. Birds and beasts.	**K'ÁNG**
1911. 琴 96/8 Lute. Organ. S.	1921. 鯁 188/7 To choke. (káng)
(a) yeūng-k'ām 5194. Piano. Organ.	(a) kai-k'áng 1515. Pip of a fowl.
(b) t'aān-k'ām 4304. To play an instrument.	**K'ÀNG**
1912. 擒 64/13 To seize, climb.	1922. 掯 64/8 To oppress, extort.
(a) k'ām-p'ā 3412. To scramble.	
1913. 尋 41/9 (ts'ām)	
(a) k'ām-yāt 5137. Yesterday.	

(a) hó-k'àng 1099. Strong (smell).Oppressive.
(b) k'àng-chü̂ 339.
To entangle.

K'AP

1923. 給 $\frac{120}{6}$ To put on (as a seal), affix, grant to.
*

1924. 級 $\frac{120}{4}$ Steps. Grades of rank.
*

1925. 汲 $\frac{85}{4}$ To draw water. S.
*

1926. 吸 $\frac{30}{4}$ To attract, inhale.
*

(a) k'ap-lĩk 2330. Attractive force. Gravity.
(b) k'ap-t'üng 4461. Suction pipe.

K'ĀP

1927. 及 $\frac{29}{2}$ A conjunction. And. To reach to, attain.Concerning. About.
**

K'AT

1928. 咳 $\frac{30}{6}$ To cough. (hoī)
*

(a) k'at-ch'i 519. Sneeze.

K'AU

1929. 摳 $\frac{64}{11}$ To mix up, adulterate, scrape.
(a) k'au-wān 5029. To mix.
(b) k'au-p'ūng 3564. To tack (naut).

K'AÙ

1930. 扣 $\frac{64}{3}$ To knock, deduct. Discount.
*

1931. 叩 $\frac{30}{2}$ To strike, put the hands to the head, implore.
*

(a) k'aù-t'aū 4339. To kowtow.

1932. 鉤 $\frac{167}{5}$ To backstitch. (kau)
*

1933. 蔻 $\frac{140}{11}$ Cardamom seeds.
'

(a) taū-k'aù 4116. Nutmeg.
(b) paāk-taū-k'aù 3178. Cardamom.

1934. 釦 $\frac{167}{3}$ A button. Ornament. Clasp.
'

1935. 寇 $\frac{40}{8}$ To rob. Violent.
'

K'AŪ

1936. 求 $\frac{85}{2}$ To ask, beg, entreat. Seek. S.
*

1937. 毬 $\frac{82}{7}$ A ball. Knob. Globe.
*

1938. 球 $\frac{96}{7}$ Round gem. Ball. Sphere. Balloon. uf 1937.
*

1939. 逑 $\frac{162}{7}$ To gather, collect, match, pair.
*

1940. 裘 $\frac{145}{7}$ Fur garments.
'

1941. 絿 $\frac{120}{7}$ Urgent.
'

K'AŬ

1942. 舅 $\frac{134}{7}$ Maternal uncle. S.
*

1943. 柏 $\frac{75}{6}$ The tallow tree.
*

1944. 臼 $\frac{R}{134}$ A mortar. S.
'

K'Ē

1945. 騎 $\frac{187}{8}$ To ride on a horse. (k'eī)
*

1946. 茄 $\frac{140}{5}$ Solanum.

(a) faan-k'ē 655.
Tomato.

(b) k'ē-tsź 4667. Egg-
plant. Brinjal.

(c) tin-k'ē 4159.
Belladona.

1947. 伽 $\frac{9}{5}$ (ka)

K'EI
1948. 崎 $\frac{46}{8}$ Steep. Abrupt.

K'EÍ
1949. 踦 $\frac{157}{6}$ See 4944.

K'EĪ
1950. 奇 $\frac{37}{5}$ Odd. Strange.
Extraordinary.
Mysterious.(kei)

(a) k'eī-î 1293. Wonder-
ful. A miracle.

(b) ch'ut-k'eī 648.
Wonderful. Strange.

1951. 祈 $\frac{113}{4}$ To pray,
beseech.

(a) k'eī-t'ó 4381.
To pray.

1952. 期 $\frac{74}{8}$ An appointed
time. A period.
(kei)

(a) yāt-k'eī 5137.
A fixed date.

1953. 旗 $\frac{70}{10}$ A flag.
Banner.

(a) k'eī-hô 1109.
Signal flag.

(b) k'eī-hâ-lô 908-2404.
A bannerman.

1954. 騎 $\frac{187}{8}$ To ride on a
horse or beast.
(k'ē)

1955. 其 $\frac{12}{6}$ A demonstrative
particle. S.

(a) k'eī-uê 4871.
As to the rest.

(b) k'eī-chung 383.
Among them.Therein.

(c) k'eī-shāt 3854. In
point of fact. In
truth.

1956. 棊 $\frac{75}{8}$ Chess.

1957. 棋 $\frac{75}{8}$ Draughts.

(a) tseûng-k'eī 4531.
Chinese chess.

(b) k'eī-p'oôn 3552.
Chess board.

(c) k'eī-p'oôn-pô 3336.
Tartan.

1958. 蜞 $\frac{142}{8}$ Kind of crab.
Grub.

1959. 蟣 $\frac{142}{8}$ Worm.
Leech.

(a) k'eī-ná 2811. Leeches.

1960. 示 $\frac{R}{113}$ Spirits of the
earth. S.

1961. 祁 $\frac{113}{3}$ S.

K'EĪ
1962. 企 $\frac{9}{4}$ To stand on tip-
toe.Erect.(k'eī)

(a) k'eī-tó 4197.
To stand.

K'EK--See k'ik.

K'EUK。
1963. 郤 $\frac{163}{7}$ To decline,
reject.

K'EŪNG
1964. 強 $\frac{57}{8}$ Strong. Violent.
S.(k'eûng)
See 1647.

(a) k'eūng-shuí 4004.
  Acids.

(b) siu-k'eūng-shuí 3669.
  Nitric acid.

1965. 彊 57/13 Strong. Violent. Overbearing. (keūng)

K'EŪNG

1966. 強 57/8 To force, compel. S.(k'eūng)

1967. 藭 140/12 Small roots.

K'IK (k'ek)

1968. 摑 64/10 To tie a knot, join or tie fast.

(a) lŏ-shué-k'ik 2420-3985. A noose.

K'ĪK (k'ēk)

1969. 屐 44/7 Pattens. Clogs. Wooden shoes.

1970. 劇 18/13 Troublesome. Stage play.

(a) tsak-k'ĭk 4487. To amuse.

K'ĪM

1971. 鉗 167/5 Pincer. Tongs. Tweezers. Fetters. S.

(a) mă-k'ĭm 2561. The bit of a bridle.

(b) haú-k'ĭm 1006. Pronunciation.

(c) haū-k'ĭm 1008. Stillson wrench.

1972. 箝 118/8 To stop the mouth. To gag.

1973. 拑 64/5 To pinch, nip, seize. S.

K'IN

1974. 搇 64/11 To lift up, pull up, turn over.

K'ĪN

1975. 虔 141/4 Sincere. Pious. Devout. S.

1976. 乾 5/10 S. (kon)

K'ING

1977. 傾 9/11 To overthrow, test by talking. To talk. (k'eng)

K'ÍNG

1978. 頃 181/2 A moment. Presently. Just now. 100 mau (2643).

K'ING

1979. 凝 15/14 To settle, as dregs.

(a) k'ing-tùng 4275. To congeal.

(b) k'ing-kon 1759. To dessicate.

1980. 鯨 195/8 King of fishes. The whale.

1981. 墥 32/11 The brim. Margin. (k'eng)

1982. 擎 64/13 To raise up, lift.

1983. 瓊 96/15 A red stone. Precious.

K'IT。

1984. 揭 64/9 To open, lift off, raise. S.

1985. 詰 149/6 To question, examine.

1986. 竭 117/9 To exhaust, exert great effort.

1987. 許 149/3 To accuse, divulge.

K'IÙ

1988. 竅 116/13 Aperture. Pore. (hiù)

K'IŪ

1989. 橋 75/12 A bridge. Crossbeam. S.

1990. 蕎 140/12 Buckwheat.

1991. 喬 30/9 Lofty. S.

1992. 翹 124/12 Tail feathers. To elevate.

K'IŬ

1993. 繑 120/12 To wind (as a spring).

K'OÌ

1994. 蓋 140/10 | A cover.
1995. 盖 108/6 | To cover, screen, hide.
1996. 葢 108/7 | (koì)

(a) sheūng-k'oì 3896. Canopy.
(b) ngaăn-k'oì 2999. Eyelids.
(c) k'oì-ngă 2981. To lay tiles.
(d) teì-k'oì 4125. Edible toadstools.

1997. 槪 75/11 | The whole.
1998. 槩 75/11 | Altogether. In general.

(a) taaì-k'oì 4033. Probably. About.

1999. 漑 85/11 To flow, wash.

K'OK。

2000. 確 112/10 Really. Surely. Verily.
2001. 涸 85/8 Dried up.

K'ONG

2002. 扛 64/3 To carry on the shoulder.

K'ÒNG

2003. 抗 64/4 To withstand, oppose. (kŏng)
2004. 炕 86/4 To run aground. See 1184.

K'OO

2005. 軲 159/5 A wheel. To revolve, tangle, trouble, roll.
2005½. 箍 118/8 To hoop, bind. (foo)
(a) k'oo-chuê 339. To bind, undergird.

K'OOT。

2006. 括 64/6 To fasten together, include.
(a) paau-k'oot。 3198. To contain.

K'UĒN

2007. 權 75/18 Authority. Power.
(a) k'uēn-pèng 3277. Power. Authority.
2008. 拳 64/6 The fist. S.
(a) k'uēn-t'aū 4339. The clenched fist.

(b) k'uĕn-t'aū-kwat 2083.
   The knuckles.
(c) k'uĕn-tá 4027.
   To box.
(d) k'uĕn-feí 753. The
   "Boxers" of 1900.
2009. 顴 181 Cheek bones.
   ' ‾18

K'UET。

2010. 缺 121 Broken. Maimed.
   ‾4 Defective. Of-
        ficial post.
(a) ts'aān-k'uet。 4695.
   To maim, ruin.
(b) hoi-k'uet。 1124. To
   make a vacancy.
(c) pó-k'uet。 3330.
   To fill a vacancy.
(d) kaán-k'uet。 1473.
   An easy post.
(e) faān-k'uet。673.
   A wearisome post.
(f) haū-k'uet。 1015. Can-
   didate for a post.
(g) uĕt-k'uet。4937.
   Wane of the moon.
2011. 決 15 | To decide.
   * ‾4 |
2012. 決 85 | Certainty.
   * ‾4 |
(a) k'uet。ĭ 1258.
   Determination.
2013. 亅 R A barb or hook.
   " ' ‾6
2014. 訣 149 Farewell words.
   " ‾4 Secret arts.

K'UI

2015. 俱 9 All. Altogether.
   ' ‾8 (kui)
2016. 拘 64 To seize,grasp,
   ' ‾5 hold. (kui)
(a) k'ui-ch'uk 624.
   To restrain.

(b) m̄-k'ui 2551. No mat-
   ter. No importance.
2017. 驅 187 To drive ahead,
   ' ‾11 drive off. S.
(a) ts'ín-k'ui 4760.
   A forerunner.
2018. 區 23 Place. Region.
   ' ‾9 Small. Petty.
        Trifling.(au)
2019. 軀 158 Body.
   ' ‾11 Physique.
2020. 嶇 46 Precipitous.
   ' ‾11.

K'UÏ

2021. 渠 85 A drain.
   * ‾9 Sewer. S.
2022. 劬 19 Toil. Labor.
   ' ‾5 Anxiety.
2023. 蕖 140 Water lily.
   * ‾12
2024. 蠂 142 See 1915a.
   * ‾12
2025. 瞿 109 Timid.
   ' ‾13 S.

K'UǏ

2026. 佢 9 Third person
   ** ‾5 pronoun. He.
        She. It.
2027. 拒 64 To resist, op-
   ' ‾5 pose, refuse,
        reject.
(a) k'uǐ-chuè 339.
   To stop one.
2028. 距 157 A spur. Hook.To
   ' ‾5 jump. Distance.
(a) kai-k'uǐ 1515.
   Cock's spurs.

K'UK

2029. 曲 73 Crooked. Bent.
   ' ‾2 Perverse. S.
        (huk)

(a) wat-k'uk 5040.
　　To bend.
(b) waan-k'uk 4970.
　　A bend.
(c) k'uk-chit。283.
　　Labyrinth. Tricky.
(d) sz-k'uk 3758.
　　A trick.
(e) chi-k'uk 207.
　　A song.
(f) ts'ż-k'uk 4862.
　　Lyrics.

K'ŪK

2030. 局 $\frac{44}{4}$ Shop. Establish-
　　　　　ment. (kŭk)

K'ŪNG

2031. 窮 $\frac{116}{10}$ ⎫ Poor
2032. 窮 $\frac{116}{14}$ ⎬ Impoverished.
　　　　　　　　　 ⎭ Destitute.
(a) mō-k'ūng 2711. Inex-
　　haustible.Abundance.
2033. 夐 $\frac{35}{11}$ ⎫ A bunch.
　＊　　　 ⎬ Branch.
2034. 喀 $\frac{30}{8}$ ⎭ C.
　"　　　　　(k'ung)
2035. 穹 $\frac{116}{3}$ Vast. Lofty.
　'
2036. 蛩 $\frac{142}{6}$ Cricket.
　'　　　　 Locust.

KWA

2037. 瓜 $\frac{R}{97}$ Melon. Gourd.

(a) wōng-kwa 5070.
　　Cucumber.
(b) aí-kwa 34.
　　Eggplant.
(c) sai-kwa 3584.
　　Watermelon.
(d) tung-kwa 4273.
　　Coarse pumpkin.

(e) faan-kwa 655.
　　Small squash.
(f) heung-kwa 1046. Musk-
　　melon. Canteloupe.
(g) kwa-tsź 4667.
　　(Water)melon seeds.
(h) yam-kwa 5090.
　　Orange gourd.
(i) mūk-kwa 2795.
　　Papaya. Quince.
(j) t'in-kwa 4355.
　　Bryony.
(k) tsit。-kwa 4570.
　　Hairy brinjal.
　　Vegetable marrow.
(l) kwa-moōn 2779.
　　Panelled door.
(m) keuk。-kwa 1638.
　　Calf of leg.

KWÁ

2038. 寡 $\frac{40}{11}$ Widowed.
　　　　　Solitary. Few.

KWÀ

2039. 挂 $\frac{64}{6}$ ⎫ To hang up,
　　　　　　　　 ⎬ suspend,
2040. 掛 $\frac{64}{8}$ ⎬ be in suspense.
　　　　　　　　 ⎭ Anxiety.
(a) kwà-luî 2496.
　　Anxiety.
(b) kwà-hô 1109.
　　To register,record.
2041. 啩 $\frac{30}{8}$ F—implying
　＊　　　 probability.
　　　　　　(kwa)
2042. 褂 $\frac{145}{8}$ Outer jacket.
　'　　　　 Robe.
(a) hô-kwà 1109.
　　Soldier's uniform.
2043. 卦 $\frac{25}{6}$ To divine. The
　'　　　　 eight diagrams.

-102-

KWAAI

2044. 乖 $\frac{4}{7}$ Good (as a child) Obedient. Artful. Crafty.

KWAAÍ

2045. 枴 $\frac{75}{5}$ A staff.

(a) kwaaí-cheúng 202. A walking stick.

2046. 拐 $\frac{64}{5}$ To decoy, seduce, kidnap.

(a) kwaaí-tsz-ló 4667-2404. A crimp.

2047. 蒯 $\frac{140}{10}$ Rushes. Straw.

KWAAÌ

2048. 怪 $\frac{61}{5}$ Strange. Weird. Supernatural. To wonder. To blame.

KWAAK。

2049. 摑 $\frac{64}{11}$ To slap. (kwok。)

2050. 嘓 $\frac{30}{15}$ A loop. To encircle, noose. (kw'aak)

KWAAN

2051. 關 $\frac{169}{11}$ A bar. Barrier.

2052. 關 $\frac{169}{10}$ Serious. To bolt, bar.

(a) hoí-kwaan 1125. Maritime customs.

(b) shuí-kwaan 4005. Customs service.

(c) kwaan-haú 1006. Customs house.

(d) pò-kwaan 3337. To pass customs.

(e) kwaan-p'ìng-ngân.3497-3028. Haikwan taels.

(f) kwaan-ship. 3959. Concerned with.

(g) kwaan-haí 968. Serious (matter).

(h) m̄-kwaan-ngôh 2551-3065.Not my concern.

(i) ngâ-kwaan-kwat 2977-2083. A jawbone.

(j) sai-kwaan 3584. Western suburbs.

2053. 鰥 $\frac{195}{10}$ A bachelor. Widower.

KWAÀN

2054. 慣 $\frac{61}{12}$ Accustomed to. Habitual.

(a) m̄-kwaàn 2551. Unskilled.

(b) faàn-kwaàn 661. Playful.

(c) kwaàn-teí 4125. To tumble down.

KWAANG

2055. 逛 $\frac{162}{7}$ To ramble, stroll, (kw'aang)

KWAAT。

2056. 刮 $\frac{18}{6}$ To rub, scrape, brush away.

(a) kwaat。-tsź 4672. To erase.

(b) kwaat。-ts'aat。4696. To grate.

(c) kwaat。-sha 3781. To cauterize.

(d) yat-kòh-kwaat。 5133-1734. One quarter.

KWAI

2057. 歸 77 To return.
14 To go home.

(a) kwai-yat 5133.
   To harmonize, adjust.
(b) kwai-ching 275.
   To reform.
(c) mō-shóh-kwai 2711-3977. Vagabond.
   Homeless.
(d) kwai-mō 2711.
   Annihilation.
(e) kwai-wing 5049.
   To glorify.

2058. 龜 R 213 The tortoise.
*

2059. 亀 5/9

(a) uén-kwai 4918.
   The great tortoise.
(b) ts'ün-kwai 4842.
   The land tortoise.
(c) pan-kwai 3223.
   Three footed tortoise.
(d) kwai-keuk。 1638.
   Sea anemone.
(e) mín-kwai 2688.
   Pastry.
(f) kwai-tsai 4482.
   Bastard (abusive).
(g) kwai-kung 1878.
   A cuckold. Pimp.

2060. 閨 169 Zenana.
   6 Virgin.

KWAI

2061. 鬼 R 194 Disembodied spirit. Devil.
   Ghost.
(a) moh-kwai 2735.
   The devil.
(b) kwai-fóh 767.
   Ignis fatuus.
(c) kwai-t'aū-fung 4339-879. A whirlwind.

(d) kwai-tsai-hei 4482
   1036. Puppet show.
(e) kwai-shān-hōk 3835-1140. Mythology.
(f) moōn-kwai 2779.
   A door latch.

2062. 詭 149 Cunning. Deceitful. Crafty.
   6

(a) kwai-kwat 2084.
   Deceitful. Treacherous.
(b) kwai-kai 1521.
   Wily scheme.

2063. 軌 159 A rut. Groove.
   2

(a) kwai-tô 4207.
   An orbit.

2064. 晷 72 Shadow.
   8

(a) yāt-kwai 5137.
   Sun dial.

KWAI

2065. 貴 154 Valuable.
   5 Expensive.
(a) kwai-sing 3657.
   Your surname.
(b) kwai-chau 159.
   Kweichow.

2066. 季 39 Season.
   5 Quarter. S.

2067. 桂 75 Cassia species.
   6
(a) yuk-kwai 5249.
   Cinnamon.
(b) taan-kwai 4048.
   Laurel.
(c) kwai-fa 650.
   Olea fragrans.
(d) kwai-p'ei 3468.
   Cassia lignea.
(e) kwai-lām 2226.
   Kweilin.

2068. 瑰 96 Jasper.
   10 Reddish jewel.

2069. 癸 105/4 The tenth stem character: Water. Menstruation.

KWAÎ

2070. 跪 157/6 To kneel, make obeisance.

2071. * 匱 22/12 Wooden chest,

2072. * 櫃 75/14 Cabinet. Place of

2073. * 槶 75/12 records. (kwaî)

　(a) shue-kwaî 3982. Bookcase.

　(b) kwaî-t'úng 4454. A drawer.

　(c) lōh-kwaî 2437. Winnowing machine.

　(d) kwaî-waî 5001. Counter.

KWAN

2074. 君 30/4 Honored. Royal. Sovereign. S.

　(a) kwan-sẑ-t'aán-ting 3777-4296-4168. Constantinople.

2075. 軍 159/2 Army. Legion. Multitude. S.

　(a) kwan-faat。 682. Martial law.

　(b) kwan-heí-kūk 1035-1875. Arsenal.

2076. * 昆 72/4 Afterwards.

2076½. " 蜫 142/8 Descendants. S.

　(a) kwan-chúng 399. Brothers.

　(b) kwan-ch'úng 646. Crawling things. Insects.

2077. 均 32/4 Equal. Uniform.

KWÁN

2078. * 滾 85/11 To boil, seethe. (kw'án)

KWÀN

2079. 棍 75/8 A stick. Club. A rod.

　(a) kwàn-keuk。 1638. Rascal. Scamp.

KWÂN

2080. 郡 163/7 Prefecture. District.

KWANG

2081. * 轟 159/14 Rumble. Roar. Sound of crash.

　(a) kwang-kwang. Roaring.

　(b) kwang-lang 2232. Jingling.

2082. * 甍 140/13 Humming sound.

KWAT

2083. 骨 R/188 The bones.

　(a) kwat-kaak。 1450. Whole skeleton.

　(b) faân-shî-kwat 677-3906. Shoulder blade.

　(c) kaau-kwat 1494. Os pubis.

　(d) ts'uî-kwat 4828. Cartilage.

　(e) kwat-suî 3720. Marrow.

　(f) kwat-p'aaî 3420. Dominoes.

2084. 譎 149/12 To deceive. (k'uet。)

2085. * 橘 75/12 Citrus fruit.

(a) kwat-p'eī 3468.
　　Dried orange peel.

KWĀT

2086. 掘 64/8 To dig, excavate.

2087. 榾 75/8 A felled tree.
*

(a) kwat-t'aū 4339.
　　A stump.

2088. 倔 9/8 Perverse. Dull.
'　　　　Blunt. Rude.

(a) kwāt-t'aū-lô 4339-
　　2426. Cul-de-sac.

KWIK

2089. 隙 170/10 A fissure.
'　　　　Grudge. Strife.

KWING

2090. 叮 R/13
"'

(a) kwing-lang 2232.
　　To jingle. Jingling.

KWÍNG

2091. 炯 86/5 Clear.

2092. 焗 86/7 Bright. Hot.

KWIT。

2093. 唰 30/8 Smart (as of
"　　　　children).

2094. 嘥 30/13 Squeaking.
"　　　　Shrill. (wǎ)

KWOH

2095. 戈 R/62 Lance.
"'　　　　S.

(a) kwoh-pik 3284. Gobi.

KWÓH

2096. 果 75/4 Fruits in general. Results. Actual.

(a) kwóh-ïn 1349.
　　Indeed. Really.
(b) uē-kwóh 4873.
　　If really so.
(c) kwóh-shāt 3854.
　　Absolutely certain.
(d) kit。-kwóh 1694.
　　To produce fruit or results.

2097. 菓 140/8 Fruits, berries, nuts and like.

(a) shaang-kwóh 3802.
　　Unripened or uncooked fruit.
(b) t'ông-kwóh 4437.
　　Preserves.
(c) suen-kwóh 3702.
　　Pickles.

2098. 裹 145/8 To bind up,
'　　　　wrap.

2099. 餜 184/8 Pastry.
'　　　　Confectionery.

KWÒH

2100. 過 162/9 To pass by,
2101. 过 162/3 pass over. Finished.

(a) kwòh-yê 5176.
　　To pass the night.
(b) kwòh-shan 3830.
　　To die.
(c) kwòh-k'eī 1952.
　　Late.
(d) kìn-kwòh 1663.
　　Seen.
(e) hó-kwòh 1099.
　　Better than.
(f) (toh)-kwòh-t'aū(4215)-
　　4339. Too (much).

2102. 嘓 30/13 F—implying doubt. (kwoh)
"

KWOK。

2103. 國 31/8 Nation.

2104. 国 31/4 Kingdom. Country.

　(a) kwok。-ka 1410.
　　　The government.

　(b) maân-kwok。 2576.
　　　International.

　(c) ngoî-kwok。 3070.
　　　Foreign nations.

　(d) kwok。-mân 2618.
　　　The people.

　(e) kwok。-ch'îng 277.
　　　Administration of
　　　government.

　(f) kwok。-ch'îng-hŏk 1140.
　　　Political science.

2104½. 郭 163/8 Outer wall. Suburb. S.

KWONG

2105. 光 10/4 Light. Bright. Glory. Naked. Uncovered.

　(a) t'in-kwong 4355.
　　　Daybreak. Dawn.

　(b) yāt-kwong 5137.
　　　Daylight.

　(c) shat-kwong 3849.
　　　To tarnish.

　(d) kwong-kwong.
　　　Dazzling.

　(e) kwong-hŏk 1140.
　　　Optics.

　(f) kwong-t'ō 4393.
　　　Spectrum.

　(g) kwong-t'aū 4339.
　　　A baldhead.

2106. 桄 75/6 Species of palm.

KWÓNG

2107. 廣 53/12 Broad. Enlarged. S.

　(a) kwóng-foot。 865.
　　　Extensive.

　(b) kwóng-hŏk-ooî 1140-3143. The C.L.S.(of China.)

　(c) kwóng-tung 4272.
　　　Canton province.

　(d) kwóng-sai 3584.
　　　Kwangsi province.

　(e) kwóng-chau 159.
　　　Canton city.

KWÒNG

2108. 礦 112/15 Raw metals.
　* ── Ore.

2109. 鑛 167/15 A mine.
　* ── (kw'òng)

KWOOÎ

2110. 癗 104/13 Weary. Ill. (kooî, fooî)

KW'A

2111. 誇 149/6 ┐
　　　　　　　 │ To brag,
2112. 夸 37/3 ┘ boast.

KW'À

2113. 跨 157/6 To bestride.

KW'AANG

2114. 框 75/6 Door frame. A frame.
　* ──
　(a) t'it。-kw'aang 4366.
　　　Printer's chase.

2115. 筐 118/6 Kind of basket. uf 2114.(hong)

KW'AÁNG

2116. 莖 140/7 A stem. Stalk.
　* ── (hāng)

(a) chi-kw'aáng 206.
Twigs.

KW'AÀNG

2117. 躓 157／12 To tumble over,
* stumble.

2118. 繽 120／15 To fasten with
* loops, tie up.
run against.
(kw'òng)

(a) kw'aàng-chuê 339.
To entangle.

2119. 逛 162／7 (kwaâng)
*

(a) haān-kw'aàng 934.
Gadabout.

(b) kw'aàng-sheng 3880.
Twang.

KW'AI

2120. 規 147／4 Rule. Law. Custom. Usage. Com-
passed.

(a) kw'ai-kuí 1851.
Custom. Manners.

2121. 虧 141／11 To be deficient
* in. (fai)

(a) kw'ai-hìm 1056.
In debt. Arrears.

(b) kw'ai-foô 839.
Deficient in. To
wrong, injure.

2122. 窺 116／11 To peep stealth-
* ily. To spy.

(a) kw'ai-t'aàm 4287.
To spy out.

(b) yāt-kw'ai 5137.
Sundial.

2123. 盔 108／6 Helmet.
*

(a) kw'ai-kaap。 1488.
Armor.

KW'AÌ

2124. 愧 61／10 Ashamed.

2125. 媿 38／10 Abashed.
Mortified.

KW'AĪ

2126. 攜 64／10 To take by
* the hand,

2127. 攜 64／18 To lead. S.
*

2128. 葵 140／9 Mallows. Palm.
* S.

(a) kw'aī-ts'oì 4800.
Edible mallows.

(b) kw'aī-fa 650.
Althoea rosa.

(c) wōng-chūk kw'aī 5070-
372. Manihot.

(d) chiù-yāt-kw'aī 291-
5137. Sunflower.

(e) p'ō-kw'aī 3519.
Fan palm.

(f) kw'aī-p'ūng 3564.
Palm leaf thatching.

KW'AN

2129. 坤 32／5 Earth. Female.
,

KW'ÁN

2130. 綑 120／7 To bind, tie,
bale. A bale.
Ream.

2131. 滾 85／11 To roll, Water
· rolling. (kwán)

(a) shēk-kw'án 3879.
Stone roller.

2132. 菌 140／8 Mushroom.
, Fungus. Mold.

(a) saì-kw'án 3589.
Bacteria. Germs.

2133. 丨 R／2 Perpendicular.
"'

<u>KW'ÀN</u>

2134. 困 31/4 Weary. Exhausted. To confine.
 (a) kw'àn-chuè 339.
    To restrain.
2135. 窘 116/7 Distressed. Persecuted. straitened.
 (a) kw'àn-pik 3281.
    To harass.
2136. 𡇒 30/7 To confine.

<u>KW'ĀN</u>

2137. 羣 123/7 Flock. Herd. Crowd.
2138. 群 123/7 Multitude. To group. S.
 (a) kw'ān-chùng 395.
    The multitudes.
 (b) maaī-kw'ān 2568.
    To consummate marriage.
2139. 裙 145/7 Skirt. Petticoat.
 (a) waī-kw'ān 5001.
    Apron.

<u>KW'ÓNG</u>

2140. 壙 32/15 Tomb. To excavate. (fòng)

<u>KW'ÒNG</u>

2141. 曠 72/15 Waste. Wild. Desert. (fòng)
 (a) kw'òng-yè 5173.
    Wilderness.
2142. 纊 120/15 Floss. Silk. (kw'aàng)

<u>KW'ŌNG</u>

2143. 狂 94/4 Furious. Mad. Wild. Rash.

 (a) ch'eung-kw'ōng 506.
    Madly rushing about.

<u>LA</u>

2144. " 喇 30/9 F— emphatic or euphonic.
 (a) la-ma 2554.
    Lama (Tibetan).
2145. "↑ 拉 64/5 (la) See laai.
 (a) la-luèn 2474.
    Uproar.
 (b) la-saat。 3582.
    Lhassa.
2146. "↑ 啦 30/8

<u>LÁ</u>

2147. , 擸 64/16 To pull, clutch.

<u>LÀ</u>

2148. * 罅 121/11 A crevice. Rift. Crack. Fissure. (là)
 (a) là-kwik 2089.
    A crevice. Fissure.
 (b) laû-là 2262.
    A loophole. A leak.
 (c) kà-là-sé 1424-3616.
    To write between the lines.
 (d) là-chá 60. Dirty.
2149. " 嘞 30/19 F—implying urgency or completion; certainty.
2150. " 嘞 30/17

<u>LAAI</u>

2151. 拉 64/5 To draw, pull, drag, move, arrest. (la)
 (a) laai-kuì 1854.
    To saw.

(b) laai-laām 2173.
　　To tow a boat.

(c) laai-māng 2631.
　　To pull along, bor-
　　row money.

(d) laai-tak-fōh 4081-771.
　　To get goods on
　　credit.

(e) laai-taai 4029.
　　Untidy.

(f) laai-shí 3902.
　　To go to stool.

2152. 孻 39/14 Late in season
* or in series.
　　uf 2151.

LAAÍ

2153. 𦧡 135/16 To lick, lap.
*

LAAÌ

2154. 癩 104/16 Skin disease.
* Itch.
(a) laaì-sín 3642.
　　Ringworm.

LAAĪ

2155. 嘞 30/16 To omit.
* (laaì)

LAAÎ

2156. 賴 154/9 | To depend on,
2157. 顂 181/7 | trust in, rely
on. To be left
out, behind.

2158. 勵 19/15 | To exert one's
* strength, rouse,
excite. (laî)

2159. 瀬 85/16 To moisten.
*
(a) laaî-niû 2921.
　　To urinate uncon-
　　sciously.

2160. 醉 164/7 To pour out li-
' bation, sprinkle.

LAĀK

2161. 肋 130/2 Rib.
* (lāk, laak。)

LAAM

2162. 欖 75/21 The Chinese
* olive.
(a) paāk-laām 3178. Large
　　olive (canarium al-
　　bum).
(b) oo-laām 3115. Sweet
　　olive (canarium
　　pimela).
(c) laām-wāt 5044. Olive
　　seed. Trellised.

LAÀM

2163. 蹃 157/12 To step over.
*
(a) laàm-yāt 5137.
　　Every other day.
(b) laàm-lā 2148.
　　Alternately.

LAĀM

2164. 籃 118/14 | A large
2165. 篸 118/8 | basket.
"

2166. 婪 38/8 To covet. Avar-
* icious. Greedy.
　　(laam)

2167. 藍 140/14 Blue. Indigo.
*
(a) laām-tīn 4166.
　　Native indigo.

2168. 嵐 46/9 Mountain mist.
' Vapor.

-110-

LAÃM

2169. 攬 64/14 * To grasp, seize, gather, pick up,

2170. 攣 64/14 * To hug.

2171. 攬 64/21 (laǎm)

　(a) laǎm-t'aū 4339.
　　A foreman.
　(b) laǎm-tsoì-chí 4608-216. Bill of lading.

2172. 覽 147/14 ' To look at, inspect. S.

LAÃM

2173. 纜 120/21 Cable.

2174. 纜 120/16 Rope.
　(a) hoí-laǎm 1125.
　　Submarine cable.
　(b) kaap₀-laǎm 1488.
　　Armored cable.
　(c) laǎm-lô 2426.
　　Towing path.
　(d) kaaí-laǎm 1436.
　　To weigh anchor.

2175. 檻 75/14 * A cage. Bars. Railing.

2176. 濫 85/14 * To go to excess. At random.

LAAN

2177. 欄 75/17 * A market place. (laan)
　(a) ka-laan 1410.
　　Home made.
　(b) maaí-laan 2568.
　　To turn hawker.

2178. 躝 157/17 * To pass over, crawl, creep.
　(a) laan-sheǔng 3895.
　　To climb.

　(b) laan-t'āng 4332.
　　Creepers.
　(c) laan-sz 3761.
　　Tendrils.
　(d) laan-ch'ūng 647.
　　Reptiles.

2179. 嘛 30/17 "

LAÃN

2180. 攔 64/17 * To obstruct, hinder, fence off.

2181. 欄 75/17 * A fence. Railing. Pen. (laan)
　(a) laǎn-laǎm 2175.
　　Bulwarks.

2182. 蘭 140/17 * Orchid species.
　(a) mǎ-laǎn 2561.
　　Iris pumila.
　(b) yūk-laǎn 5250.
　　Magnolia yulan.
　(c) tiù-laǎn 4189.
　　Epidendrum.
　(d) laǎn-p'oōn-yeǔng 3552-5201. Cyathiform.

2183. 瀾 85/17 ' Swelling waters. Billows.

2184. 闌 169/9 ' Late. Screen.

LAÃN

2185. 懶 61/16 * Lazy. Reluctant.
　(a) laǎn-tôh 4220.
　　Lazy. Slothful.

LAÃN

2186. 爛 86/17 * Broken. Torn. Decayed. Worthless. Bad.
　(a) haú-laǎn 1006.
　　Thrush.

(b) laân-haú 1006.
   Obscene language.
   A blackguard.

LAĀNG

2187. 冷 15 Cold. Cool.
       5 Chilly. S.
   (a) laǎng-taâm 4042. In-
       different. Dull.
   (b) laǎng-ngaǎn 2999.
       Indifferent.
   (c) laǎng-siù. 3675.
       To simper, sneer.
   (d) laǎng-chân 138.
       To shiver.
   (e) laǎng-ngaâng 3001.
       To freeze.

LAÂNG

2188. 吟 $\frac{30}{7}$

LAAP。

2189. 插 $\frac{64}{5}$ Altogether.

LAĀP

2190. 立 R To set up,
   ** 117 establish.
   (a) laǎp-sam 3593.
       Determined.
   (b) laǎp-luên 2474.
       Confused.
   (c) laǎp-uê 4872.
       The snapper.
2191. 臘 $\frac{130}{15}$ Dried and salt
   * meats.
   (a) laǎp-aap。 24.
       Dried duck.
   (b) laǎp-ch'eûng. 513.
       Dried sausage.
2192. 蠟 $\frac{142}{15}$ Wax. Beeswax.
   * Candle.

(a) wŏng-laǎp 5070.
   Beeswax.
(b) paāk-laǎp 3178.
   Insect wax.
(c) paāk-laǎp-shuê 3996.
   Freximus Chinesis.
(d) yaū-laǎp-shuê 5149.
   Photmia serrulata.
(e) laāp-mooī-fa 2767-650.
   Chimonanthes frag-
   rans.
(f) laāp-shēk 3879.
   Greasy quartz.
(g) laāp-péng 3276.
   Coiled wax taper.
(h) laāp-uên 4923.
   Wax coated pills.
(i) laāp-tsuí 4627.
   The hawfinch.

2193. 擸 64 To crush, mix
   * 15 up. (laap。, lip)
   (a) laāp-tsaāp 4475.
       Mixed.
   (b) laāp-saáp。3578.
       Rubbish.

LAĀT

2194. 辢 $\frac{160}{7}$ Pungent.
   * Hot.
2195. 辣 $\frac{160}{7}$ Biting.
   * Acrid.
   (a) kaàl-laāt 1439.
       Mustard.
   (b) laāt-tsiu 4575.
       Pepper. Cayenne.
   (c) lŏ-laāt 2420.
       Precocious.
2196. 剌 $\frac{18}{7}$ To cut, slash.
   *
2197. 角 $\frac{101}{1}$ (lat)
   *

LAAŪ

2198. 撈 64 To fish for,
   * 12 grapple, dredge.
       (lo)

LAĬ

2199. 师禮 30 To turn, as the
    * 18 neck, To sprain,
         impeach.

(a) fàn-laĭ-kéng 715-1636.
    Stiff neck.

LAĪ

2200. 嚟 30 To come, become.
    ** 15 In order to.
         F—indicating
         present perfect
         tense.

2201. 犂 93 A plow.
    * 8

2202. 犁 93 To plow.
    * 15

(a) laī-t'aū-tsuí 4339-
    4627, or
    laī-to 4195.
    Plowshare.

(b) laī-p'ā 3414.
    A harrow.

(c) foō-laī 830.
    To plow.

(d) laī-lō 2426.
    A furrow.

2203. 黎 140 A kind of wood.
    ' 15

(a) laī-lō 2409.
    Hellebore.

(b) tsāt-laī 4496.
    Thistle.

2204. 鱺 202.S.
    " 3

(a) saam-laī-uē 3572-4872.
    The shad.

LAĬ

2205. 禮 113 Ceremony. Rite.
    * 13 Worship.

2206. 礼 113 Etiquette.
    " 1 Conduct.

(a) laĭ-Ī 1267.
    Ceremony. Rite.

(b) siú-laĬ 3674.
    Etiquette.

(c) hui-laĬ 1213.
    Mere formality.

(d) hāng-laĬ 986. To
    exchange courtesies.

(e) mō-laĬ 2711.
    Impolite.

(f) laĬ-pô 3342.
    Board of rites.

(g) laĬ-paal 3168.
    Obeisance. Worship.

(h) yat-kòh-laĬ-paal 5133-
    1734. A week.

(i) laĬ-paal-(yāt) 5137.
    Worship day. Sunday.

(j) laĬ-paal-yat 5133.
    Monday.

(k) laĬ-paal-lūk 2504.
    Saturday.

(l) laĬ-paal-t'ōng 4435.
    Christian place of
    worship.

(m) laĬ-paal-tsź 4677.
    A mosque.

LAȊ

2207. 例 9 Laws. Regula-
    * 6 tions. Custom.
         Rule.

(a) hoi-laȊ 1124.
    To initiate.

(b) shȊng-laȊ 3948.
    A precedent.

(c) chiù-laȊ 291.
    Legal.

(d) laȊ-foón 859.
    Ordinance.

2208. 曬 109 To stare at.
    * 19

2209. 矖 109
    " 13

2210. 勵 19 To exert one's
    * 15 strength. (laaȊ)

2211. 荔 $\frac{140}{6}$
*
  (a) laî-chi 206.
     The lichee.
  (b) faan-laî-chi 655.
     Custard apple.

2212. 麗 $\frac{198}{8}$ Beautiful.
'   Elegant.

2213. 礪 $\frac{112}{15}$ Grindstone.
'   Whetstone.

2214. 隸 $\frac{171}{}$
'' |

2215. 隸 $\frac{171}{}$ (taî)
'' |

2216. 厲 $\frac{27}{13}$ Severe.
'   To oppress.

2217. 勒 $\frac{19}{9}$ A bridle. To
         strangle, re-
         strain.
  (a) lāk-sok。3697.
     To extort.
  (b) lāk-sź 3767.
     To strangle to
     death.

2218. 竻 $\frac{118}{2}$
* |

2219. 竻 $\frac{118}{11}$ Thorns.
         | Brambles.

2220. 竻 $\frac{140}{11}$
* |
  (a) fóh-yeung-lāk 767-
     5189.Euphorbium.
  (b) lāk-tāk 4083.
     Queer.

2221. 肋 $\frac{130}{2}$ Rib. (lak,laak,
          laak。, laāk)
  (a) hip-lāk 1082, or
     lāk-shaak。-kwat 3790-
     2083. The ribs.
  (b) lāk-k'ak。1903.
     Rugged.
  (c) kóng-tak-lāk-k'ak
     1779-4081. To stam-
     mer.

2222. 啉 $\frac{30}{8}$ To vociferate.
*   A bud.
  (a) lam-lut 2545. To re-
     iterate, grumble,
     scold.
  (b) à-lam-tsaî 9-4482.
     A street girl.
  (c) lam-lam-tseuk。4518.
     Hooting owl.

2223. 林 $\frac{14}{8}$ To bend.
  (a) ling-lam-koó 2360-
     1802. A rattle.

2224. 臨 $\frac{131}{11}$ To come down, as
         from heaven.
         To look on.
  (a) lām-p'oōn 3553.
     A childbirth.

2225. 淋 $\frac{85}{8}$ To fall in tor-
         rents, soak.
         To water plants.
  (a) lām-laaî 2159. To
     irrigate, moisten.
  (b) niû-lām 2921.
     Diabetes.

2226. 林 $\frac{75}{4}$ A grove. Col-
*   lection of
         (shrubs, etc).
  (a) shuê-lām 3996.
     Forest.

2227. 痳 $\frac{104}{8}$ Diseases of
'   the bladder.
  (a) shēk-lām 3879.
     Calculus.
  (b) sha-lām 3779.
     Gravel.
  (c) paāk-lām 3178.
     Stringy urine.

2228. 廩 $\frac{53}{13}$ A granary.
*

2229. 琳 64/8 To soften or smooth. (lâm)

LÂM

2230. 琳 64/8 To pile up, build (a wall). (lâm)

2231. 霖 122/8 To lump together, heaping.

LAN -- See lun.

LANG

2232. 唥 30/7 A bundle. To jingle. (làng, lâng, laâng)

2233. 舲 137/5 Kind of boat.
    (a) ma-lang-t'èng 2552-4347. Slipper boat.

LÂNG

2234. 唥 30/7 See 2232.

LAP

2235. 笠 118/5 A basket. Crate. Hamper.
    (a) shaú-lap 3859. Gloves.
    (b) lap-chuê-shaú 339. To glove.
    (c) lap-chuê-haú 1006. To muzzle.

LÂP

2236. 啦 30/5 Confused.
2237. 蝶 117/12 Disorderly.

LAT

2238. 甩 101/1 To loose, take off, get rid of. (laat)

LAU

2239. 摟 64/11 To hold, enfold, embrace, urge. (laū)

2240. 褻 140/11 A coat.
2241. 褸 145/11 Cloak.
    (a) pok。-lau 3358. A shawl.
    (b) taat-lau 4033. Cloak. Overcoat.
    (c) haú-shuí-lau 1006-4004. A bib.

2242. 蒌 140/6 Betel pepper.
2243. 䮫 187/10 (laū)
    (a) mǎ-lau 2561. The monkey.
    (b) mǎ-lau-tsing. 4560. Hobgoblin. Smart as a monkey.

2244. 嘍 30/11 Loquacious. Chattering.

LAŪ

2245. 流 85/7 To flow along. A current. Scattered. Spread about.
    (a) laū-leî 2293. Fluent.
    (b) laū-k'aū 1941. Unmannerly.
    (c) laū-sing 3652. Meteor.
    (d) tîn-laū 4163. Electric current.
    (e) uên-laū 4919. Primary current.
    (f) sheūng-laū 3890. Continuous current.
    (g) hāng-laū 987. Constant current.
    (h) kaan-laū 1463. Intermittent current.

2246. 雷 102/7 To keep,
stay, stop,
2247. 留 102/5 restrain,
leave behind.
- (a) laū-lōk 2454.
  To leave behind.
- (b) laū-sam 3593. Be careful. Give attention to.
- (c) pat-laū 3236.
  Continually.
- (d) laū-sheng-kei-heī 3880-1601-1035.
  Phonograph.

2248. 樓 75/11 A loft. Story.
Tower.
- (a) chung-laū 385.
  A belfry.
- (b) k'eī-laū 1954.
  Verandah.
- (c) laū-sheūng 3896.
  Upstairs.
- (d) sheūng-laū 3895.
  To go upstairs.
- (e) laū-paán 3187.
  Flooring.
- (f) laū-t'ai 4313.
  A staircase.

2249. * 硫 112/7 Sulphur.
- (a) laū-wōng 5073.
  Sulphur.
- (b) shēk-laū-wōng 3879.
  Brimstone.
- (c) laū-wōng-moōt 2792.
  Flowers of sulphur.
- (d) laū-wōng-heung 1046.
  Bituminous sulphur.
- (e) t'ó-laū-wōng 4380.
  Sulphur gangue.

2250. * 旒 70/9 Pennants.
2251. * 斿 70/7 Tassels.

2252. * 榴 75/11
2253. * 榴 75/11 The pomgranate.
2253½. ṇ 雷 102/7
- (a) shēk-laū 3879.
  The pomgranate.
- (b) laū-uēt 4937.
  Fifth moon, month.

2254. ' 僂 9/11 Deformed
Hunchback.

2255. ' 琉 96/11
2256. ' 瑠 96/12 Glazed
Vitreous.
2256½. ' 瑠 96/11
- (a) laū-leī 2282.
  Beryl.
- (b) laū-leī-ngă 2981.
  Glazed tiles.

2257. ' 瘤 104/11 Swelling
Tumor. (laū)
- (a) yūk-laū 5249.
  Fleshy tumor.
- (b) huet-laū 1212.
  Vascular tumor.

2258. ' 摟 64/11 To hold, enfold. (lau)
2259. ṇ' 劉 18/13 S.
2260. ṇ' 婁 38/8 S.

LAŪ

2261. * 柳 75/5 Willows.
Willowlike. S.
- (a) shuī-sz-laŭ 4007-3761.
  Tamarisk.
- (b) shuī-yeūng-laŭ 5195.
  Weeping willow.
- (c) laŭ-suī 3728.
  Willow catkins.
- (d) fa-laŭ-ch'eūng 650-510. A brothel.

(e) laŭ-t'iŭ 4375.
   Striped.
(f) heí-laŭ 1031.
   To groove.

LAÛ

2262. 漏 85/11 To leak, drip, escape, drop, overlook.
(a) tik-laŭ 4141.
   To drip. Clepsydra.
(b) tsaú-laŭ 4500.
   A strainer.

2263. 遛 162/10 To ramble.
*
(a) taŭ-laŭ 4119.
   To loiter, linger.
(b) laŭ-fa 650.
   To trot.
(c) laŭ-haú 1006.
   To stutter.

2264. 撞 64/12 To shake
*
2265. 搖 64/11 (laù)
(a) laŭ-hǎ 907.
   To dandle.

2266. 溜 85/11 Slippery.
'
(a) waāt-laŭ 4984.
   Slippery. Tricky.

2267. 瘦 104/11 An ulcer.
'
2268. 瘺 104/12
"

2269. 陋 170/6 Vile. Evil.
'   Sordid.

LE

2270. 哩 30/7 F—affirmative.
   (le, lei, leī)

LÈ

2271. 唎 30/7 F—emphatic, affirmative, imperative. (lei)

LEI

2272. 唎 30/7 Slovenly.
"

2273. 喱 30/9 See 1794a.
"

LEĪ

2274. 離 172/11 To leave, separate.
2275. 氂 166/11 A thousandth. Small.
2276. 厘 166/2 Minute.
(a) leī-kam 1527.
   Likin tax.
(b) fōng-leī 798.
   House tax.
(c) leī-tâng 4100. Small balance for silver.

2277. 籬 118/19 Hedge. Fence.
*
(a) taŭ-leī 4116.
   Trellis for peas.
(b) tseŭng-ngaǎn-leī 4531-2999. Lattice.

2278. 梨 75/8 Chinese pear.
*
2279. 棃 75/7
*
(a) suet-leī 3714.
   Russet pear.
(b) sha-leī 3773.
   Coarse native pear.
(c) fa-leī-mūk 650-2795.
   Chinese rosewood.

2280. 狸 94/7 Catlike or foxlike animals.
*
2281. 貍 153/7
*

(a) oŏ-leĭ 3119.
   The fox.

(b) oŏ-leĭ-tsing 4560.
   Brownie. Witch.

(c) yĕ-leĭ 5173.
   Siberian wildcat.

2282. 璃 96 Vitreous sub-
   $\frac{96}{11}$ stance.

2283. 篱 118 Kind of basket.
   $\frac{118}{11}$ Ladle. (lei)

2284. 犛 93
   $\frac{93}{11}$

(a) leĭ-ngaū 3039.
   The yak.

LEĬ

2285. 理 96 To govern,
   $\frac{96}{7}$ manage.

(a) tá-leĭ 4027.
   To manage.

(b) hŏp-leĭ 1193.
   Reasonable.

(c) māan-leĭ 2616.
   The written style.

(d) tŏ-leĭ 4207. Doctrine.
   Teaching. Reasonable.

(e) teĭ-leĭ 4125.
   Geography.

2286. 里 R Chinese mile;
   $\frac{R}{166}$ 1894.12 English
   feet. S.

(a) lūn-leĭ 2516, or
   heung-leĭ 1045.
   Neighbor.

2287. 裡 50 A (mat) sail.
   $\frac{50}{7}$

(a) leĭ-laâm 2173.
   Halliards.

(b) ch'é-leĭ 493.
   To hoist sail.

2288. 李 75 Plum. Prune.
   $\frac{75}{3}$ S.

(a) yuk-leĭ 5248.
   Prunus Japonica.

(b) leĭ-tsaí 4482.
   Cherry.

2289. 鯉 195 The carp.
   $\frac{195}{7}$

2290. 唎 30 (lei, le)
   $\frac{30}{7}$

2291. 履 44 Shoe.
   $\frac{44}{7}$ To tread.

2292. 裏 145 Inside.
   $\frac{145}{7}$ (luĭ)

LEÎ

2293. 利 18 Gain. Interest.
   $\frac{18}{5}$ Sharp. S.

(a) leî-sik 3633.
   Interest.

(b) leî-sheûng-sik 3896.
   Compound interest.

(c) leî-yik 5204.
   Advantages.

(d) k'aū-leî 1936.
   Mercenary.

(e) leî-heî 1035.
   Edged tools.

(f) mŏh-leî 2740.
   To sharpen.

2294. 脷 130 The tongue.
   $\frac{130}{7}$

(a) leî-yam 5089.
   A final particle.

(b) leî-haaĭ 914.
   Furred tongue.

2295. 吏 30 Subordinate
   $\frac{30}{3}$ officers. S.

2296. 俐 9 Clever. Sharp.
   $\frac{9}{7}$

2297. 莉 140 White jasmine.
   $\frac{140}{7}$

2298. 詈 149 To scold,
   $\frac{149}{5}$ blame.

(a) leî-mâ 2567.
   To abuse, curse.

2299. 痢 104 Bowel disease.
   $\frac{104}{7}$

(a) hūng-paâk-leî 1235-
   3178. Dysentery.

(b) huet.-leî 1212.
   Bloody flux.

(c) kàm-haú-leî 1530-1006.
Cholera morbus.

2300. 唎 $\frac{30}{7}$ (lei, le)

___

LĒK

2301. 瀝 85 A ridge. Row.
* $\frac{16}{16}$ To cut. (lĭk)
(a) sha-lēk 3778.
Shallows.

2302. 癧 104 Scrofula.
' $\frac{16}{16}$ (lĭk)
(a) lēk-lóh 2434.
Scrofulous swelling.

___

LÈNG--See also ling.

2303. 靚 174 Pretty.
* $\frac{7}{7}$ (lèng, lìng)
(a) shíp.-lèng 3961.
Glossy.
(b) lèng-fóh 767.
Lightning.

___

LĒNG

2304. 零 173 Remainder. Sur-
$\frac{5}{5}$ plus. In numer-
al= 0. (lìng)
(a) shāp-lēng 3845.
Over ten.

___

LĔNG

2305. 領 181 A collar.
* $\frac{5}{5}$ (lìng)

___

LEU

2306. 𡃤 135 To dribble.
* $\frac{11}{11}$

___

LÈÙ

2307. 搮 64 To confuse.
* $\frac{13}{13}$

___

LEŪK

2308. 略 102 A few.
$\frac{6}{6}$ Little.

2309. 畧 102 In general.
$\frac{6}{6}$ S.

2310. 掠 64 To plunder, rob.
* $\frac{8}{8}$

___

LEŪNG

2311. 糧 119 Provisions.
$\frac{12}{12}$ Rations.

2312. 粮 119 Taxes paid
$\frac{7}{7}$ in kind.
(a) ch'ut-leūng 648.
To pay wages.
(b) kip.-leūng 1688.
To forage.

2313. 量 166 To weigh, esti-
$\frac{5}{5}$ mate, measure.
(leūng)
(a) leūng-tōk 4228.
To measure.

2314. 良 138 Virtuous. Ex-
$\frac{1}{1}$ cellent.Good. S.
(a) leūng-keung 1640.
Galangal (ginger).
(b) wŏng-leūng 5070.
Rhubarb.

2315. 涼 15 Cool. Fresh.
$\frac{8}{8}$

2316. 凉 85 Cold. Coldly.
$\frac{8}{8}$
(a) leūng-t'ìng 4361.
Summer house.
(b) leūng-shóng 3981.
Airy.

2317. 樑 75 Beam. Mast.
* $\frac{11}{11}$

2318. 梁 75 Ridgepole. S.
' $\frac{7}{7}$

2319. 粱 119 A grain.
$\frac{7}{7}$
(a) ko-leūng 1713.
Sorghum vulgare.

(b) ko-leūng 1714.
A dainty dish.

2320. 黃 $\frac{140}{7}$

(a) shuě-leūng 3991.
Gambier.

LEŬNG

2321. 兩 $\frac{11}{6}$ Two. A pair.
**

2322. 两 $\frac{1}{6}$ Double.

2323. 两 $\frac{1}{6}$ A tael, weight or money.

2324. 倆 $\frac{9}{8}$ Skill. Cleverness.
,

LEŪNG

2325. 亮 $\frac{8}{7}$ Clear. Bright. Transparent. S.

2326. 量 $\frac{166}{5}$ Capacity. To judge, estimate. (leūng)
*

(a) leūng-faat -hŏk 682-1140. Mensuration.

2327. 諒 $\frac{149}{8}$ Faithful. To suppose. S.

2328. 喨 $\frac{30}{9}$ Wailing.
,

LIK

2329. 瀝 $\frac{85}{16}$ A drop. To drip, filter. (lĕk)

(a) lik-ts'ing 4764.
Bitumen.

LĪK

2330. 力 $\frac{R}{19}$ Strength. Force. S.
**

(a) tīn-lĭk 4163.
Electric energy.

(b) lĭk-leŭng 2326.
Capacity. Ability.

(c) lĭk-kan 1538.
Horseradish.

2331. 曆 $\frac{72}{12}$ Almanac.

2332. 歷 $\frac{77}{12}$ Calendar. To pass over,

2333. 歷 $\frac{77}{10}$ experience.

(a) lĭk-loi 2445.
Hitherto.

(b) lĭk-sź 3768.
History. Biography.

2334. 叻 $\frac{30}{2}$ (lik)
,,

(a) lĭk-la 2144. Cracking and creaking.

2335. 鬲 $\frac{R}{193}$ A tripod.
,, ,

2336. 瀝 $\frac{85}{16}$ A ridge. (lĕk)
*

LĪM

2337. 舔 $\frac{135}{8}$ To lick, taste, try with the tongue.
,

LĪM

2338. 簾 $\frac{118}{13}$ Curtain.
*

2339. 帘 $\frac{50}{13}$ Screen.
*

2340. 鎌 $\frac{167}{10}$ Instrument
*

2341. 鐮 $\frac{167}{13}$ for reaping.
*

(a) wŏh-līm 5060, or līm-to 4195.
A sickle.

(b) ch'eūng-līm 512.
A scythe.

2342. 廉 $\frac{53}{10}$ Frugal. Sparing. Pure. S.
*

2343. 奩 $\frac{37}{11}$ Dressing case. Dowry.
,

-120-

2344. 腒 130/13 Calf of leg.
Shin. Spleen
of animals.
(a) lǐm-t'ip。 4364.
Spleen.

LǏM

2345. 斂 66/13 To gather up,
collect, draw
within. S.
2346. 殮 78/13 To enshroud a
corpse, bury.
2347. 臉 130/13 Face. Reputation. (lǐm)
(a) mō-lǐm 2711.
Brazenfaced.

LÎM

2348. 臉 130/13 Face. Reputation. (lǐm)
2349. 輦 159/8 Imperial char-
iot.Court.(lǐm)

LĪN

2350. 連 162/7 Including.
Successive.
(a) līn-maaī 2568.
Together with.
(b) līn-waān-ts'eung 4974-
4736. A revolver.
2351. 憐 61/12 To pity,
sympathize.
(a) līn-mǎn 2621. To pity,
sympathize with.
2352. 鏈 167/11 A chain. Lead
or tin ore.(lîn)
(a) sóh-līn 3691.
Shackles.
2353. 蓮 140/11 Name of flower.
(a) līn-fa 650. The lotus.
Water lily.
(b) līn-hing-fa 1073.
Primrose.

(c) wōng-lîn 5070.
Yellow gentian.
2354. 鏈 195/11

LǏN

2355. 揵 64/11 To remove,carry,
transport(goods)

LÎN

2356. 煉 86/9 To refine,smelt,
discipline.
2357. 鍊 167/9 To smelt,refine.
A mineral.
(a) sau-lîn 3603.
Ascetic.
(b) lîn-yūk 5254.
Purgatory.
2358. 練 120/9 To practice.
Skilled.
(a) lîn-taāt 4068.
Experienced.
(b) lō-lîn 2420.
Clever.
2359. 楝 75/9 Pride of India
(tree).

LING

2360. 哈 30/13 Tinkling.
A fender. (leng)

LĪNG

2361. 靈 173/16 Spirit. Force.
Cleverness.
(lēng)
(a) līng-wān 5028.
The soul.
(b) līng-t'ung 4452.
Quickness of under-
standing.
2362. 凌 15/8 To insult,
disgrace. S.
(a) līng-yūk 5255. Dis-
grace. To violate,
mock.

(b) lǐng-siu-fa 3673-650.
Begonia.

2363. 伶 9/5 Clever. Active. Smart.

(a) lǐng-leî 2296.
Smart. Sharp.

2364. 陵 170/8 Mound over a grave. Elevated.

2365. 鴒 196/5 Lark species.

(a) tsik-lǐng 4541.
The wagtail.

(b) paāk-lǐng 3178.
The lark.

(c) kok-lǐng 1744.
The skylark.

2366. 苓 140/5 China root. Tuber.

2367. 鈴 167/5 Small tinkling bell. (ling)

(a) lǐng-ī-tsʻó 1266-4777.
Blue harebells.

(b) kam-lǐng 1527. Yellow chrysanthemums.

2368. 羚 123/5 Chamois.

(a) lǐng-yeūng 5193. Ante-(lope.

2369. 蛉 142/5

2370. 呤 30/13 Tinkling. (ling)

2371. 綾 120/8 Damask.

2372. 翎 124/5 Plumage. Feathers.

2373. 菱 140/8 Calthrops.

2374. 零 173/5 Seo lēng.

2375. 鯪 195/8 Kind of fish. (lēng)

<u>LǏNG</u>

2376. 領 181/5 To receive. A collar. (lěng)

(a) lǐng-sz-koon 3776-1815. A consul.

(b) mūk-fung-lǐng 2795-879. The cangue.

2377. 嶺 46/14 Mountain range. Ridge.

<u>LÎNG</u>

2378. 令 9/3 To cause, make. Your (polite address.

2379. 另 30/2 Separate. Alone. Distinct.

(a) lîng-ngoî 3070.
Extra. Additional.

<u>LĪP</u>

2380. 獵 94/15 To pursue animals.

(a) tá-līp 4027. To hunt.

2381. 擸 64/15 To take hold of. (laāp)

2382. 鱲 195/15 A kind of fish. Wrasse.

<u>LIT.</u>

2383. 纈 120/15 A knot. A knob.

(a) shaú-chí-lit. 3859-215.
The knuckles.

(b) shaang-lit. 3802.
A loose knot.

(c) sz-lit. 3767.
A fast knot.

<u>LĪT</u>

2384. 列 18/4 To arrange. In order.

(a) lǐt-waî 5014. All (polite address).

2385. 裂 145/6 To crack, split, rip. A flaw.

2386. 烈 86/6 Blazing. Fierce. Chaste.

2387. 唎 $\frac{30}{6}$ " Disk of moon.

LIÛ

LIU

2388. 蹓 $\frac{157}{11}$ * To run away. (mau)

LIÚ

2389. 撩 $\frac{64}{12}$ ' To excite, incite, stir up. (liū)

LIŪ

2390. 鐐 $\frac{167}{12}$ * Fetters.

2391. 聊 $\frac{128}{5}$ ' To depend on. Inclined to

2392. 寮 $\frac{40}{12}$ ' A hovel. (Living) quarters. (liú)

(a) shuí-liū 4004.
    Peddler's boat.

2393. 嫽 $\frac{38}{12}$ ' To trifle, dally with.

2394. 撩 $\frac{64}{12}$ ' To rouse, excite. (líú)

2395. 療 $\frac{104}{12}$ ' To heal, control disease.

(a) liū-hōk 1140.
    Therapeutics.

2396. 繚 $\frac{120}{12}$ ' To wind. Leech lines of sails.

2397. 鷯 $\frac{196}{12}$ ' Small birds, as wren, tomtit, etc.

(a) paāk-liū 3178.
    The butcher bird.

2398. 遼 $\frac{162}{12}$ ' Distant.

LIŬ

2399. 了 $\frac{6}{1}$ ' Finished. Past. Extreme. Quick.

(a) liū-pat-tak 3236-4081.
    Exceedingly.

LIÛ

2400. 料 $\frac{68}{6}$ ' Stuff. Material. To calculate, manage. The expected.

(a) liû-pit 3315. To expect, suppose.

LO

2401. 摍 $\frac{64}{11}$ * To shake violently, strip. Aggressive.

(a) lo-lo. To stir as in cooking.

(b) wōk-lo 5066. Soot.

(c) lo-waāt 4984. Sly.

(d) lo-keuk. 1638. A loafer.

(e) lo-ka-tsaí 1410-4482. Blackleg. Sharper.

2402. 撈 $\frac{64}{12}$ * Bother. (laaū)

2403. 嘮 $\frac{30}{12}$ "

LÓ

2404. 佬 $\frac{9}{6}$ ' A fellow. Brother.

(a) taaî-ló 4033. Elder brother.

(b) saî-ló 3589. Younger brother.

(c) saî-ló-koh 1728. My lad!

2405. 獠 $\frac{94}{12}$ ' uf 2404.

LŌ

2406. 爐 $\frac{86}{16}$ ' Stove. Furnace.

2407. 炉 $\frac{86}{4}$ Fireplace. Stove.

2408. 勞 19/10 Toil. Service.
Distress. To
trouble. S.

2409. 蘆 140/16 Kind of reed.
Rushes.
(a) lō-suk 3737.
Sweet sorghum.
(b) lō-wai(ooī) 4998.
Aloes. Hellebore.

2410. 顱 181/16 The skull.
* Forehead.

2411. 牢 93/3 Dungeon.
* Jail.
(a) teī-lō 4125.
Basement.

2412. 櫨 75/16 A kind of
' fruit.
(a) lō-kwat 2085.
The loquat.

2413. 鱸 195/16 The perch.
'
(a) t'aū-lō 4339.
Red headed labrax.
(b) paan-lō 3182. The
spotted wrasse.

2414. 癆 104/12 Wasting disease.
(a) lō-pĕng 3278.
Tuberculosis.

2415. 轤 159/16 Windlass.
' Pulley.

2416. 嘮 30/11
(a) lō-ts'ō 4783.
To babble.

2417. 盧 108/11 Rice vessel.
"' Black.

2418. 臚 130/16 Spread out.
'

2419. 螑 142/12 Kind of cicada.
Spider.

2419½. 鑪 167/16 Stove.
' Brazier.

2420. 老 R Aged.
** 125 Venerable.
(a) lǒ-kung 1878.
My husband.
(b) lǒ-p'ōh 3528.
My wife.
(c) lǒ-shaú 3859.
Experienced.
(d) lǒ-foo-ī 815-1280.
Saxifrage.
(e) lǒ-wŏng 5070.
Tawny.

2421. 櫓 75/15 A scull. Oar.
Sweep.
(a) iū-lǒ 1392.
To scull.
(b) t'ui-lǒ 4447. To
starboard the helm.
(c) maan-lǒ 2573. To
port the helm.

2422. 擄 64/13 To capture,
*

2423. 虜 141/7 seize, plunder.

2424. 魯 195/4 Stupid. Dull.
Rude.

2425. 鹵 R Salt. Rude.
' 鹵 197 Violent.

2426. 路 157/6 A road. Path-
** way. S.
(a) yat-lô 5133.
All along.
(b) lô-faī 691.
Traveling expenses.
(c) shuī-lô 4004. By wa-
ter. The water road.
(d) lô-shò 3972.
Prosperity. Luck.
(e) to-lô 4195.
An incision.

2427. 露 173/13 Dew. To reveal.

(a) lô-ch'ut 648.
  To disclose.
(b) lô-shuí 4004.
  Dew.
(c) fa-lô-shuí 650.
  Eau de Cologne.

2428. 賂 154/6 To present. A bribe.

2429. 鷺 196/13 Heron species.

(a) paāk-lô 3178.
  The egret.
(b) chue-lô 316.
  The bittern.

2430. 澇 85/13 To pour.

2431. 咯 30/13

___

LOH

2432. 囉 30/19 F—emphatic or affirmative. (lôh)

(a) loh-soh 3689.
  Teasing.

___

LÓH

2433. 攞 64/19 To get, obtain.

2434. 瘰 104/11 Scrofulous disease.

2435. 裸 145/8 Bare. Naked.

___

LÒH

2436. 爐 86/19 Smelling of burning matter. Smoky.

___

LŌH

2437. 羅 122/14 A (fowler's) net.

(a) lōh-mǒng 2759.
  A net.

(b) lōh-taú 4109.
  A strainer.
(c) lūt-lōh 2549.
  A pulley.
(d) lōh-faū 743. Name of a mountain in South China.
(e) lōh-mǎ 2561.
  Rome.
(f) lōh-mǎ-neī 2873.
  Roumania.

2438. 籮 118/19 Bamboo basket.

2439. 鑼 167/19 A brass gong.

2440. 蘿 140/19 Turnip. Parasite plant.

(a) lōh-paāk 3180.
  Turnips.
(b) wōng-lōh-paāk 5070.
  Carrots.
(c) hūng-lōh-paāk 1235.
  Carrots.
(d) hūng-lōh-paāk-tsaí 4482. Radishes.
(e) oō-lōh-paāk 3125.
  Parsnips.
(f) shaang-lōh-paāk 3802.
  Chilblains.
(g) tsín-pin-lōh 4555-3286. The pink (Dianthus).

2441. 騾 187/11 A mule.

2442. 贏 187/13

(a) lōh-mǎ 2561.
  A mule.
(b) hoī-lōh 1125.
  The beaver.

2443. 螺 142/11 Spiral univalve shells.

2444. 蠃 142/13 Snails. Conch. (lōh·)

(a) faū-shuí-lōh 743-4004.
  Nautilus.

(b) t'ĭn-lōh 4356.
   Fresh water snails.
(c) pĭn-lōh 3291.
   Limpet.
(d) heúng-lōh 1047. Conch
   shell trumpet.
(e) lōh-sĭn 3646.
   A spiral.
(f) lōh-sz 3761.
   A screw.

LOĪ

2445. 來 $\frac{9}{6}$

2446. 来 $\frac{119}{2}$ | To come, reach, obtain.

2447. 未 $\frac{R}{127}$ | Future.

(a) poón-loī 3388.
   Originally.
(b) loī-wòng 5079. To go
   and return. Commer-
   cial or social in-
   tercourse.
(c) loī-lô 2426.
   Imported.
(d) loī-shaì 3818.
   The next world.
(e) loī-shaì-lūn 2528.
   Eschatology.

2448. 萊 $\frac{140}{8}$ Kind of plant. Weeds.

LOÎ

2449. 耒 $\frac{R}{127}$ A plow.

LOK。

2450. 咯 $\frac{30}{6}$ F—emphatic of affirmative.

2451. 駱 $\frac{187}{6}$

(a) lok。-t'ōh 4408.
   The camel.

2452. 烙 $\frac{86}{6}$ To sear, brand, burn, roast.

2453. 絡 $\frac{120}{6}$ To tie up.

(a) lūng-lok。2533.
   To ensnare.
(b) luēn-lok。2471.
   To join together.

LŌK

2454. 落 $\frac{140}{9}$ Down. To go down, fall, put down.

(a) lōk-pat 3237.
   To begin to write.
(b) lōk-lǐk 2330.
   Energetic.
(c) lōk-shuēn 3999.
   To board ship.
(d) lōk-faat。683.
   Tonsure.

2455. 樂 $\frac{75}{11}$ To rejoice, de-light in. Joy.

(a) lōk-uēn 4916.
   Garden of delight.
   Paradise.
(b) lōk-t'in-ché 4355-169.
   Optimist.

LÓNG

2456. 喨 $\frac{30}{10}$ To rinse, spread thin.

(a) lóng-yaù 5149.
   Enamel.

LÒNG

2457. 晾 $\frac{72}{8}$ | To shore up, put on trestles.

2458. 撽 $\frac{64}{10}$ | (lòng)

LŌNG

2459. 狼 $\frac{94}{7}$ Wolf. Cruel. S.

-126-

LONG

2460. 郎 163/7 (lóng)
*
  (a) san-lōng 3596.
     A bridegroom.
  (b) tiù-uē-lōng 4189-4872.
     The kingfisher.

2461. 廊 53/10 Courtyard.
*   Verandah.

2462. 椰 75/10 Name of a tree.
  (a) pan-lōng 3219. The
     betel nut (areca).

2463. 根 75/7 Palm tree.
  (a) kwong-lōng 2106.
     The caryota palm.

2464. 浪 85/7 Fluctuating. Dis-
'   solute. (lòng)

2465. 琅 96/7 Kind of gem.

2466. 蜋 142/7 Dung beetle.
'   Mantis.

LŎNG

2467. 朗 74/7 Clear. Bright.
'   Brilliant.

LÔNG

2468. 浪 85/7 Waves. Billows.
    (lōng)

2469. 晾 72/8 To dry in the
*   air. To sun,
    air. (lòng)
  (a) lông-shóng 3981.
     To air.

LUEN

2470. 攣 64/19 Crooked.
'   Warped.
  (a) luen-maaī 2568.
     To curl.
  (b) luen-shaang 3802.
     Twins.

LUĒN

2471. 聯 128/11 United. A seam.
*   To sew.
  (a) luēn-māng 2633.
     An alliance.
  (b) luēn-kwan 2075.
     Allied troops.
  (c) luēn-i 1248.
     To sew clothing.
  (d) luēn-kwat 2083.
     A seam.

2472. 鸞 196/19
  (a) luēn-kai 1515.
     Argus pheasant.

LUĔN

2473. 孌 38/19 Beautiful.
*   To be fond of.
  (a) luĕn-t'ŭng 4463.
     Sodomy. Sodomite.

LUĒN

2474. 亂 5/12 Rebellion.
     Confusion.

2475. 乱 5/6 Anarchy.

2476. 戀 61/19 To be fond of.
    (luēn)
  (a) luēn-mô 2728.
     To long for.

LUET₂

2477. 捋 64/7 To grasp, scrape,
*   gather.
  (a) luet₂-so 3678.
     To stroke the beard.
  (b) luet₂-maaī 2568.
     To scrape together.
  (c) luet₂-sheng-t'an 3880-
     4329. To gobble up.

2478. 劣 19/4 Inferior.
*   Feeble. Poor. *

LUĪ

2479. 雷 173/5 Thunder. S.

  (a) shuí-luī 4004.
    Torpedo.

  (b) luī-kung-uē 1878-4872.
    Tadpole.

  (c) luī-kung-shē 3874.
    The gecko.

2480. *驢 187/16 A donkey. Ass.

  (a) siú-luī 3674.
    A squirrel.

  (b) luī-mīng 2692.
    Bray of a donkey.

2481. ' 縲 120/11 To bind.

  (a) luī-sit。 3663.
    Bonds.

2482. 閭 169/7 Village. Village gate.

2483. ' 纍 120/15 uf 2481.

LUǏ

2484. 裏 145/7 | Inside.

2485. 裡 145/7 | Within.

  (a) luǐ-t'aū 4339.
    The inside.

2486. *屢 44/11 | Often.

2487. 屡 63/11 | Repeatedly.

  (a) luǐ-ts'z 4854.
    Frequently.

2488. *旅 70/6 Travellers. Guests.

  (a) luǐ-shūn 4022.
    Port Arthur.

  (b) luǐ-koón 1820.
    An inn.

2489. '"' 呂 30/4 S.

  (a) luǐ-sùng 3751.
    Luzon. Manila.

2490. ' 侶 9/7 Comrade. Associate.

2491. 褸 145/11 Ragged. (lau)

2492. ' 壘 32/15 Rampart. Fortified camp. Intrenchments. S.

2493. ' 累 120/5 (luǐ)

LUÎ

2494. *類 181/10 Class. Race. Category. Sort. Species.

  (a) luî-shue 3982.
    An encyclopedia.

  (b) yān-luî 5117.
    Human kind.

2495. 慮 61/11 To care for, be anxious.

2496. 累 120/5 To accumulate, involve in, embarrass.(luǐ)

  (a) luî-k'āp 1927.
    To implicate.

  (b) luî-shai 3818.
    Tiresome.

2497. 淚 85/8 | Tears.

2498. 泪 85/5 |

2499. 蕾 140/13 Flower buds.

2500. *戾 63/4 To offend. Perverse.

  (a) pó-luî 3345.
    Cruel. Savage.

LUK

2501. *轆 159/11 A pulley. Wheel. Windlass. uf 2502.

(a) sīn-luk 3646.
   A spool of thread.
(b) ch'e-luk 490.
   A wheel.
(c) luk-lo(lóh) 2415
   A windlass.
(d) luk-tsaí 4482.
   A trundle.

2502. 摝 64 II To move, roll,
   rattle, shake.
   uf 2501.

(a) luk-naī 2844. To roll
   ground smooth.
(b) luk-ngaū 3036. Game
   of rolling coppers.

2503. 碌 112/8 A green stone.
   Toilsome.

(a) poh-luk 3347.
   Pumelo.
(b) luk-yaū 5158
   Shaddock.

LŪK

2504. 六 12/2 The numeral 6;
2505. 陸 170/8 common, complicated and run-
2506. R/8 ning hand forms.

(a) lūk-haú-līn 1006-2350.
   A revolver.
(b) lūk-kaap。 1488.
   Pregnancy.

2507. 綠 120/8 Green.

(a) ts'ing-lūk 4763.
   Grass green.
(b) lūk-faān 671.
   Green vitrol.
(c) lūk-i 1248. Police,
   (H.K. and Shameen).

2508. 陸 170/8 Dry land.

(a) lūk-kwan 2075.
   Land army.

2509. 錄 167/8 To record, copy

(a) mūk-lūk 2798. An index.

2510. 鹿 R/198 Deer. Stag.

(a) pak-taaī-lūk 3215-
   4033. Reindeer.
(b) lūk-niú 2920.
   The cassowary.

2511. 爈 86 II To scald.

2512. 戮 62 II To kill,
   slaughter.

2513. 祿 113 Emolument.

2513½. 籙 118/16 A chart.
     A list.

LUN

2514. 唄 30/8 To gnaw,
   hesitate.

(a) lun-chun 373.
   Stammering.

LŪN

2515. 倫 9/8 Constant.
   Regular. S.

(a) lūn-tun 4262. London.

2516. 鄰 163/12 Near to.
2517. 隣 170/12 Neighboring.

(a) lūn-shè 3872.
   Neighbor.

2518. 輪 159/8 A wheel. To revolve. In turn.

(a) lūn-laū 2245. In ro-
   tation. In turn.
(b) lūn-shuēn 3999.
   Steamship.
(c) lūn-ooī 3133.
   Transmigration.

2519. 淪 85/8 Eddy. Whirl.
   Perdition.

2520. 鱗 195/12 Fish scales.
* Scaly creatures.

2521. 掄 64/8 To select.
† By turns.

2522. 嗑 30/10 To hurry.
"

2523. 崙 46/8 } Rugged
"†

2524. 崙 46/8 } mountains.
"†

2525. 綸 120/8 Silk threads.
†

2526. 麟 198/12 Female unicorn.
*†

LŬN

2527. 卵 26/5 Eggs. Roe of
* fish. (lún)
(a) lŭn-shaang 3802.
Oviparous.
(b) lŭn-tsź 4667.
Testicles.

LÛN

2528. 論 149/8 To discuss, reason, discourse.
Concerning.
Ism. Ology.
(a) lûn-k'áp 1927.
With reference to.
(b) t'aäm-lûn 4288.
To converse.
(c) pín-lûn 3297.
To argue.
(d) m̄-lûn 2551. Irrespec-
tive. No matter.
(e) lûn-chūn 381. Disor-
derly. Confused.
(f) poón-t'ai-lûn 3388-
4315. Ontology.
(g) moōt-shai-lûn 2792-
3818. Eschatology.

LUNG

2529. 寵 116/16

2530. 宂 116/4 A hole.
" Hollow.

2531. 窄 116/4 Cavity.
"

LŪNG

2532. 龍 R 212 Dragon.
2532½. 竜 117/5 S.

(a) lūng-sheŭng-shuí 3895-
4004. Waterspout.
(b) nğ-chaaú-lūng 2962-
107. Lilac convol-
vulus.
(c) lūng-ngaăn 2999.
The lungan.
(d) lūng-shuēn-fa 3999-
650. Clerodendrum.
(e) lūng-so-ts'oǐ 3678-
4800. Asparagus.
(f) lūng-ĭn-heung 1357-
1046. Dragon's
blood. Ambergris.
(g) lūng-nŏ-heung 2926.
Baroos camphor.

2533. 籠 118/16 A cage.
To snare.
(a) chue-lūng 312.
A pig basket.
(b) tseuk₀-lūng 4518.
Bird cage.
(c) mă-lūng-t'aū 2561-
4339. A halter.
(d) tang-lūng 4094.
A lantern.

2534. 聾 128/16 Hard of hearing.
Deaf.

2535. 嚨 30/16 The throat.
*

2536. 櫳 75/16 Bars. A pen.

2537. 襱 75/16 Cage. Lattice.
Screen.

2538. 攏 64/16 To collect,drag,
grasp.(lŭng,
lúng)

   (a) lūng-tsúng 4652.
All. The whole.

2539. 朧 74/16 The rising moon.
Obscure.

2540. 隆 170/9 Eminent.
Abundant.

LŬNG

2541. 壟 32/16 A grave. Mound.
(lung)

2542. 櫳 75/16 A trunk.

2543. 籠 118/16 A box.

LŪNG

2544. 弄 55/4 To toy with,
mock.

   (a) mŏ-lúng 2722.
To make sport of.

LUT

2545. 哷 30/6 A noise.
To speak.

LŪT

2546. 律 60/6 Statutes. Laws.

   (a) lūt-faat。682.
Laws. Ordinances.

   (b) lūt-ching-sz 277-3756.
Attorney general.
(H.K.)

2547. 慄 61/10 To shudder.
Terrified.

2548. 栗 75/6 Chestnut
species.

   (a) shuí-lūt 4004.
Water chestnut.

   (b) fung-lūt 879.
Common chestnut.

   (c) shĕk-lūt 3879.
Aleurites.

2549. 縲 120/11 To let down
slowly.

2550. 聿 R/129 A pencil.

M̄

2551. 唔 30/7 A negative.
No. Not.

MA

2552. 孖 39/3 Twins.
Two of a kind.

   (a) ma-maaí 2568.
To join.

   (b) ma-koo-ín 1788-1334.
Cigarettes.

   (c) ma-se-ló 3615-2426.
Marseilles.

2553. 媽 38/10 Nurse. Mother.
(má, mǎ)

   (a) naaí-ma 2819.
A wet nurse.

   (b) kon-ma 1759.
Dry nurse.Procuress.

2554. 嘛 30/11 See 2144.

MÁ

2555. 媽 38/10 Nurse. Mother.
(ma, mǎ)

MǍ

2556. 麻 R/200 Hemp.

2557. 蔴 140/11 Linen.
S.

(a) mā-sìn 3646.
Linen thread.

(b) mā-pò 3336. Grass
cloth. Linen.

(c) mā-wōng 5070.
Ephidra.

(d) mā-kan 1538.
Oakum.

(e) mā-maī-yaū 2603-5149.
Linseed oil.

(f) mā-tseuk₀ 4518.
Sparrow.

(g) shaan-mā-tseuk₀ 3793.
The lark.

(h) mā-ying 5223.
The hawk.

(i) mā-leî 2296. Shrewd.

2558. 麻 104/8 Numbness.
* Paralysis.

(a) mā-fung 882.
Leprosy.

(b) mā-mā-peî 3259.
Creeping sensation.

(c) mā-yeŭk 5183.
Anesthetic.

2559. 蔴 140/11 | Sesamum
'
2560. 蔴 140/13 |
"

(a) mā-tseŭng 4527.
Ground sesamum.

MǍ

2561. 馬 R The horse.
** 187

(a) mǎ-wōng 5072.
A groom.

(b) mǎ-pīn 3288.
Riding whip.

(c) mǎ-taāp-tàng 4063-
4099. A stirrup

(d) mǎ-on 3108.
A saddle.

(e) mǎ-fōng 798.
A stable.

(f) mǎ-laān 2181.
A paddock.

(g) mǎ-lô 2426.
Main road. Highroad.

(h) mǎ-sheŭng 3896.
Suddenly.

(i) mǎ-lĭk 2330.
Horsepower.

(j) mǎ-t'aū 4339.
A jetty.

(k) hôh-mǎ 1119.
Hippopotamus.

(l) mǎ-ts'ĭn 4760. Nux
vomica. Strychnine.

(m) mǎ-haū 1006.
Mouth of urethra.

(n) mǎ-neī-la 2873-2144.
Manila.

(o) mǎ-loī 2445.
Malay.

(p) mǎ-loī-sai-à 3584-9.
Malaysia.

(q) mǎ-lāk-kaak₀ 2217-
1450. Malacca.

(r) mǎ-taāt-ka-sz-ka 4068-
1409-3763.
Madagascar.

2562. 嗎 30 F—interroga-
. 10 tive.(ma, má)

2563. 瑪 96 Agate.
* 10 Veined stones.

(a) mǎ-nô 2927. Agate.
Carnelian. Sardius.

(b) ch'ik₋mǎ-nô 547.
Hyacinth.

2564. 碼 112 Weights used in
* 10 commerce.
uf 2563.

(a) mǎ-(ch'ek) 496.
A yard (measure).

(b) mǎ-t'aū 4339.
A landing. Jetty.

(c) mǎ-chuê 339.
To rivet.

2565. 螞 142 Leech.
10 Locust.

(a) mǎ-fung 883.
The wasp.

2566. 媽 38 Mother, Nurse.
十 10 (ma, má)

MÂ

2567. 罵 122 To rail, scold,
十 10 vilify.

MAAĪ

2568. 埋 32 With. Beside. To
十 7 conceal, bury.
(a) maaī-kaai 1430.
To go ashore.
(b) maaī-t'aū 4339.
To make a landing.

MAAǏ

2569. 買 154 To buy, pur-
十 5 chase.
(a) maaǐ-maaî 2570. To
engage in trade.
(b) maaǐ-shuí 4004. To
buy water (at a
parent's death).
(c) maaǐ-paân 3191.
Compradore.

MAAÎ

2570. 賣 154 To sell, betray.
十 8
(a) maaî-fòh-shaú 771-
3889. A salesman.
(b) maaî-yän-haú 5117-
1006. To sell peo-
ple.
(c) maaî-chue-tsaí 312-
4482. To sell
coolies.
(d) maaî-shan 3830.
To be a prostitute.
(e) maaî-fung 882. To
infect with leprosy.

2571. 邁 162 Old. Aged.
十 13 To surpass.

MAAK。

2572. 擘 64 To open, break
十 13 apart with the
hands. (mēk)

MAAN

2573. 攬 64 To pull, draw,
* 十 24 port the helm.

MAĀN

2574. 蠻 142 Savage. Truou-
* 蛮 19 lent. Boorish.
(a) maān-shēk 3879.
Rubble.
(b) hó-maān 1099.
Unreasonable.

MAǍN

2575. 晚 72 Late.
十 7 Evening.
(a) maǎn-hak 971.
Night.
(b) maǎn-ts'aan 4692.
Supper. The Lord's
Supper.

MAÂN

2576. 萬 140|
九 9 | Ten thousand.
2577. 万 1-|Many. Myriad.
二 2|
(a) maân-yän 5117.
All men.
(b) maân-fa-t'ūng 650-
4461.Kaleidoscope.

2578. 慢 61 Slow. Rude.
II Dilatory.

2579. 幔 50 A curtain.
* II A screen.

2580. 鳗 195/11 The eel.

2581. 曼 73/7 S.

   (a) maân-kuk 1866.
       Bangkok.

2582. 卍 24/4

2583. 嫚 38/11 To treat with contempt.

2583½. 漫 85/11 Boundless.

MAANG

2584. 繃 120/11 To draw, pull tight.

MAĀNG

2585. 盲 109/3 Blind.

MAǍNG

2586. 猛 94/8 Savage. Cruel. Violent. Fierce.

2587. 蜢 142/8 Grasshoppers.

   (a) chà-maǎng 68.
      A grasshopper.

2588. 艋 137/8 A kind of boat. A junk.

MAÂNG

2589. 孟 39/5 "

   (a) maâng-oh 3092.
      Mencius.
   (b) maâng-maaǏ 2569.
      Bombay.

MAAT。

2590. 抹 64/5 To wipe, rub out. (moot。)

MAĀT

2591. 襪 145/15 Stockings. Hose.

MAAU

2592. 猫 94/9 The cat. (maaū)

MAAŪ

2593. 貓 153/9 ⎱ Cat species.
2594. 猫 94/9 ⎰ (maau)

   (a) ch'aù-maaū 474.
      Polecat.
   (b) maaū-leǏ 2280.
      Striped fox.
   (c) maaū-Ǐ-t'aū-ying 1266-
      4339-5223. The owl.

2595. 茅 140/5 Thatched hut. Booth. Poor. S.

2596. 矛 R 110 A lance. Contradictory.

MAAŬ

2597. 牡 93/3 Male of quadrupeds. (maŭ)

2598. 卯 26/3 Smooth. 5 to 7 A.M.

MAAÛ

2599. 貌 153/7 Form. Likeness.

MAI

2600. 咡 30/6 To pucker. (maǐ)

MAĪ

2601. 迷 162/6 To deceive, bewitch, be possessed by.

(a) maī-waāk 4968.
    To delude.
(b) maī-sùn 3743.
    Infatuated.
(c) yāp-maī-lō 5132-2426.
    Bewildered.
(d) maī-yeŭk 5183.
    Narcotics.

2602. 咪 30/6 (mai) To pucker.

MAĬ

2603. 米 R 119 S. Rice.
(a) sai-maĭ 3584.
    Sago. Tapioca.
(b) sha-kuk-maĭ 3779-1864.
    Sago.
(c) siú-maĭ 3674. Millet.
    Canary seed.
(d) maĭ-tsai 4482.
    Broken rice.
(e) lìn-maĭ 2353.
    Lotus nuts.
(f) hak-maĭ 971.
    Opium.
(g) maĭ-ngaŭ 3039.
    Weevils.
(h) tek-maĭ 4126.
    To buy rice.
(i) t'iù-maĭ 4373.
    To sell rice.

2604. 咪 30/6 Don't. Do not.

MAÎ

2605. 謎 149/10 A riddle. Conundrum.

MĀK

2606. 墨 32 12 S. Ink. Black.
(a) māk-shuí 4004.
    Liquid (foreign) ink.

(b) māk-shuí-hōp 1194.
    Inkstand.
(c) māk-shuí-ch'ī 535.
    Inkwell.
(d) māk-uē 4872.
    Cuttle fish.
(e) māk-sai-koh 3584-1728.
    Mexico.
(f) māk-sz-foh 3763-765.
    Moscow.

2607. 麥 R 199 Wheat. Bearded grain.
(a) oo-māk 3115, or
    saam-kok₂-māk 3572-
    1744. Buckwheat.
(b) ts'o-māk 4775.
    Oats.
(c) māk-fán 713.
    Oatmeal. Cereal.
(d) taaf-māk 4033.
    Barley.
(e) māk-t'aū 4339, or
    māk-suĭ 3721.
    Grits.
(f) māk-hong 1175, or
    māk-foo-tsź 807-4667.
    Bran.
(g) māk-uē-tsź 4871.
    Wheat chaff.
(h) māk-ts'au 4724.
    Wheat harvest.
(i) māk-sai-koh 3584-1728.
    Mexico.

2608. 脈 130/6 Blood. Kindred.
2609. 脉 130/5 The circulation. The pulse.
2610. 峫 143/5 (maāk)

2611. 默 203/4 Dark. Retired. Secret.
(a) māk-shī 3910. Inspiration. Revelation.

MAN

2612. 文 R 67 A coin.
(mān)
  (a) yat-man 5133.
      One dollar.One cash.

2613. 蚊 142 Mosquito.
      4 Gnat.

2614. 伇 9 Small.
      4
  (a) saı̄-man-tsaı́ 3589-
      4482. A child.

MĀN

2615. 眠 30 Brink. Verge.
      5 Edge.

MĂN

2616. 文 R 67 Literature.
      Literary. Civil.
      Elegant. S.
      (mân, man)
  (a) hōk-mān 1140. Learn-
      ing. Educated.
  (b) mān-hōk 1140.
      Literature.
  (c) laı̄-mān 2205.
      Courtesy.
  (d) t'in-mān 4355.
      Astronomy.
  (e) mān-faat 682.
      Grammar.
  (f) huèn-shaı̄-mān 1207-
      3818. Tracts.

2617. 聞 128 To hear, smell,
      8 learn. Fame. S.
  (a) fung-mān 879.
      Rumor.
  (b) san-mān 3596.
      News.

2618. 民 83 The people.
      1 Public.
  (a) tsź-mān 4667, or
      kwok-mān 2103.
      The people.

  (b) mān-kwok.
      A republic.
  (c) kwok-mān-tóng 4232.
      Republican Party.

2619. 紋 120 Texture. Pat-
      tern. Figures.
  (a) tsàu-mān 4502.
      A wrinkle.
  (b) poh-mān 3347.
      Ripples.
  (c) mān-shan 3830.
      Tattooed.
  (d) mān-ngàn 3028.
      Sycee.

2620. 珉 96 Fine stone.
      5 Alabaster.

MĂN

2621. 憫 61 To sympathize
      12 with, grieve.

2622. 吻 30 Corners of the
      4 mouth. Lips.
  (a) tsip-mān 4569.
      To kiss.

2623. 抆 64 To rub, smooth
      4 off.
  (a) mān-fooı̄ 845.
      To plaster.
  (b) mǎn-chuen-haú 342-
      1006. To point
      bricks.

2624. 黽 R A toad.
      205

2625. 刎 18 To cut the
      4 throat.

2626. 敏 66 Quick. Clever.
      7 Energetic.

2627. 泯 85 Exhausted.
      5 Destroyed.

2628. 鰵 195 Kind of fish.
      11 Perch. Codfish.

MÂN

2629. 問 30 To ask, inquire,
      8 examine into. S.

MANG

2630. 呎 血 30/8 Coarse. (māng)
  (a) mang-kai 1515. Scars about the eyes.

MÀNG

2631. 挷 血 64/13
2631½. 搎 血 64/8 | To pull, stretch, pluck.
2632. 呎 血 30/11

MĀNG

2633. 盟 血 108/8 To covenant. An alliance.
2634. 萌 140/8 To bud, sprout.

MAT

2635. 乜 5/1 What? Something. Any. (mi)
  (a) mat-yě 5173. What?
  (b) mat-shui 4006. Who?
  (c) tsô-mat 4593. Why?

MĀT

2636. 物 93/4 Things in general. Articles.
  (a) māt-kin 1665. Things. Articles.
  (b) shaang-māt 3802. Living things.
  (c) shīk-māt 3925. Eatables. Viands.
  (d) fôh-māt 771. Merohandise.
  (e) māt-ip 1368. Property.

(f) māt-ip-taan 4046. Inventory.
(g) kam-māt 1526. Today.
(h) k'ām-māt 1913. Yesterday.
(i) māt-leǐ-hōk 2285-1140. Physics.

2637. 蜜 142/8 Honey. Sweets.
  (a) māt-t'ōng 4437. Honey.
  (b) shēk-māt 3879. Rock honey.
  (c) māt-laāp 2192. Beeswax.
  (d) māt-wōng 5072. The queen bee.
  (e) māt-lūng 2533. A beehive.
  (f) māt-t'ōh-sang 4414-3599. Litharge.

2638. 密 40/8 Inner. Hidden. Thick. Close.S.
2639. 勿 20/2 Do not. No. None.

MAU

2640. 躇 157/11 To squat, roost, rap. (liu)

MAŪ

2641. 謀 149/9 To plot, plan.
  (a) maū-faán 661. Treason.

MAŬ

2642. 某 75/5 A certain one. Such a time.
2643. 畝 102/5 Chinese acre: 6.1 maǔ equals 1 English acre.

2644. 厶 R Evil minded.
28 uf 2642.

MAÛ

2645. 茂 140/5 Flourishing. Luxuriant.

2646. 謬 149/11 Error. Misleading. S.

2647. 貿 154/5 To barter, trade, S.

ME

2648. 咩 30/6 F--interrogative. Bleating of sheep.

2649. 舿 154/3
2650. 孭 39/7 To carry on the back.

(a) me-taaî 4031. A pack sling or wrapper.

2651. 哶 30/7 Bleating of sheep.

MÉ

2652. 歪 77/5 Awry. Slanting. Not straight.

MEI

2653. 尾 44/4 To terminate. (meǐ)

2654. 咪 30/6 To sip.

2655. 蝞 142/9 See 4440a.

MEĪ

2656. 微 60/10 Small. Minute.

(a) meī-leî-yeŭk 2293-5183. A laxative.

(b) meī-shaang-māt 3802-2636. Germs. Bacteria.

(c) meī-moōt 2792. Atoms.

2657. 眉 109/4 The eyebrows. S. (meǐ)

(a) paāk-wā-meī 3178-4961. Garrulax (thrush).

(b) wâ-meī-tseuk。 4518. White eyed thrush.

2658. 糜 119/11 Boiled to pieces. Scum.

2659. 楣 75/9 Lintel.

2660. 麋 198/6 Tailed deer. Doe.

MEǏ

2661. 美 123/3 Beautiful.

2662. 美 123/4 Excellent. S.

(a) meǐ-kwok。 2103. America.

(b) meǐ-sok。-pat-taāt-maī-a 3697-3236-4068-2601-9. Mesopotamia.

2663. 尾 44/4 The tail. End. S.

(a) meǐ-lūng-p'ā 2532-3413. Sirloin steak.

2664. 靡 175/11 To waste. Extravagance. Not.

MEÎ

2665. 未 75/1 Not. Not yet. 1 to 3 P.M.

(a) meî-ts'āng 4713. Not yet.

(b) meî-ts'uî 4825. A bachelor.

2666. 味 30/5 Taste. Flavor. Smell. (mi)

(a) ng̃-mei 2962.
　　　The five spices.
(b) ng̃-mei-kā 1424.
　　　A cruet.
(c) yĕ-mei 5173.
　　　Game.
(d) mei-tò 4207.
　　　A relish. Taste.

2667. 媚 38/9 To flatter,
* 　　　　smirk.

2668. 寐 40/9 To close the
" 　　　　eyes.

(a) mei-shui 4004.
　　　To dive.

___

MĒNG—See also ming

2669. 名 30/3 Name. Fame. Rep-
** 　　　utation. (ming,
　　　　méng)

(a) mēng-hŏk 1140.
　　　Logic.

2670. 咯 30/6 uf 2665a.
"

___

MĚNG

2671. 命 30/5 Life or lot.
　　　Luck. Fate. Com-
　　　mand. Decree.
　　　　(mìng)

(a) shaang-měng 3802.
　　　Life, Being.
(b) wŏng-měng 5072.
　　　A death warrant.

___

MI

2672. 乜 5/1 What?
　　　　(mat)

2673. 味 30/5 (mei)
"

(a) mi-ni 2881.
　　　A minute.

___

MĪK

2674. 冖 R/14 To cover.
" "

___

2675. 覓 147/4 To seek,
' 　　　　demand.

___

MĪN

2676. 棉 75 Cotton plant.
*

(a) mīn-fa 650. Cotton.

2677. 綿 120/9 Soft.
*

2678. 綿 120/8 Downy.
* 　　　　S.

2679. 冖 R/40 To cover.

2680. 眠 109/6 Sleep.
'

___

MĬN

2681. 免 10/5 To avoid, for-
　　　　give. S.

2682. 勉 19/7 To force, urge,
　　　stimulate.

(a) mĭn-k'eŭng 1966.
　　　To compel.

2683. 冕 13/9 A crown.
　　　Diadem.

2684. 挽 39/7 To give birth.
'

2685. 娩 38/7
' '

2686. 緬 120/8
" '

(a) mĭn-tìn 4167.
　　　Burmah.

___

MĪN

2687. 面 R/176 The face.
* 　　　A surface.

(a) mīn-ts'ìn 4760.
　　　Before. In front of.
(b) tui-mīn 4250. Oppo-
　　　site. Facing.
(c) shue-mīn 3982.
　　　Title page.

2688. 麪 199/9 Flour.

2689. 麫 199/4 Vermicelli.

  (a) mîn-fán 713.
    Flour.

  (b) mîn-paau 3202.
    Bread.

  (c) mîn-shĭk 3925.
    Pastry.

MĪNG—See also meng.

2690. 明 72/4 Clear. Bright.
**   Plain. (mēng)

  (a) mīng-paāk 3178. Plain.
    To understand.

  (b) ts'ung-mīng 4843.
    Wise. Perspicacious.

  (c) mīng-yăt 5137.
    Tomorrow.

  (d) tá-mīng-fóh 4027-767.
    Burglary.

  (e) mīng-ngă-là 2931-2148.
    Calcutta.

2691. 銘 167/6 To record, carve,
*   engrave.

2692. 鳴 196/3 Cry of bird or
'   animal. Sound
    of bell or drum.

2693. 螟 142/10
'

  (a) mīng-lĭng 2369.
    Caterpillar.

2694. 冥 14/8 Dark.
'   Obscure.

2695. 名 30/3 (mēng)
'

MĬNG

2696. 皿 R 108 Vessel.
    Utensil.

2697. 茗 140/6 Teaplant.

MÎNG

2698. 命 30/5 See mêng.

MIT

2699. 搣 64/10 To peel, pull,
*   pinch.

MĪT

2700. 篾 118/11 Splints. Bamboo
*   hoop. Bamboo
    thongs.

2701. 滅 85/10 To destroy,

2702. 威 86/6 extinguish,
    exterminate.

MIÚ

2703. 呦 30/7 To purse the
"   lips, wriggle.

MIŪ

2704. 苗 140/5 Sprout. Descend-
'   ants. Miao
    tribes. S.

2705. 描 64/9 To trace, draw,
'   sketch, copy,
    picture.

MIŬ

2706. 藐 140/14 To despise,
*   slight, disdain.

2707. 渺 85/9 Vast. Boundless.
'   Vague.

MIÛ

2708. 妙 38/4 Mysterious. Ex-
*   cellent. Subtle.

  (a) miû-shaú 3859.
    An artist. Skilled.

2709. 廟 $\frac{53}{12}$ Temple.

2710. 庙 $\frac{53}{5}$ Shrine.

MŌ

2711. 無 $\frac{86}{8}$ Negative. No. Not. Without. None. S.

(a) mō-l 1263.
   Undoubted. Plain.
(b) mō-fei 749.
   Simply.
(c) mō-nol-hōh 2940-1120.
   No help for it.
(d) mō-shóh-pat-nāng 3977-3236-2858. Almighty.
(e) mō-shóh-pat-chi 205.
   Omniscient.
(f) mō-shóh-pat-tsol 4609.
   Omnipresent.
(g) mō-fa-kwóh 650-2097.
   The fig.

2712. 毛 $\frac{R}{82}$ Hair. Fur. Feathers. S.

(a) mō-hung 1232.
   Pores of the skin.
(b) faat, -mō 681.
   To become moldy.
(c) mō-ch'ūng 645.
   Weight.
(d) ch'uē-mō 593.
   Deduct tare.
(e) mō-tel-wōng 4125-5070.
   Foxglove.
(f) mō-chin 253.
   Felt.

2713. 模 $\frac{75}{11}$ A pattern. Model. Example.

2714. 巫 $\frac{48}{4}$ Divination. A witch. S.

(a) mō-shūt 4024. Sorcery.
   Magic arts.

2715. 誣 $\frac{149}{7}$ To slander, malign, accuse falsely.

2716. 毋 $\frac{R}{80}$ Negative. No. S.

2717. 模 $\frac{119}{11}$

(a) mō-oō 3120.
   To blur.

2718. 无 $\frac{R}{71}$ No.

MŌ

2719. 冇 $\frac{13}{2}$ Negative. No. Not.

2720. 母 $\frac{80}{1}$ Mother. Female.

(a) lŏ-mō 2420.
   Mother.

2721. 舞 $\frac{136}{8}$ To make postures. to music. To dance, play. S.

(a) t'iù-mō 4371.
   To dance.

2722. 侮 $\frac{9}{7}$ To insult, ridicule, disrespect.

2723. 武 $\frac{77}{4}$ Military. Martial. S.

2724. 鵡 $\frac{196}{7}$ Parrot. Cockatoo.

2725. 姆 $\frac{38}{5}$ Female relatives. Old woman. Matron.

MÔ

2726. 帽 $\frac{50}{9}$ A cap. Hat.

(a) t'ùng-mô-tsź 4462-4667. Percussion cap.

2727. 墓 $\frac{32}{11}$ Grave. Tomb. Burial spot.

2728. 慕 $\frac{61}{11}$ To love, long for. S.

2729. 務 $\frac{19}{8}$ To attend earnestly to. Business. Function. S.

(a) hōk-mô 1140.
Education.
(b) kwok.-mô 2103.
National affairs.

2730. 霧 173 Fog. Vapor.
* 11 Mist.

2731. 冒 13 To falsely as-
* 7 sume, pretend
to be.

2732. 募 19 To call, enlist,
' 11 levy.

MOH

2733. 摩 64
11 | To touch, feel
2734. 攎 64 | with the hand.
15 | (móh)

(a) moh-wai-wai-à 4985-
5006-9. Bolivia.
(b) moh-lūk-ka-kw'ān-t'ó
2510-1409-2137-4384.
Moluccas.
(c) moh-leī-mān 2276-2612.
Bremen.
(d) moh-loh-yān 2432-5117.
Mussulman. Hindoo.

2735. 魔 194 Demon.
* 11 Devil.

(a) shuī-moh 4008.
Nightmare.
(b) tsaú-moh 4500.
Delirium tremens.
(c) ts'ē-moh-pēng 4732-
3278. Delirium.

2736. 麼 200 F--interroga-
* 3 tive.(móh,mōh)

2737. 嘛 30 Slow.
" 15 Late.

MÓH

2738. 攎 64
15 | To feel with
2739. 摸 64 | the hands,catch.
11 | (mok。)

MŌH

2740. 磨 112 To grind, rub,
* 11 sharpen, polish.
(môh)

(a) mōh-foó 813.
To afflict.

MŎH

2741. 莫 140 To stop, wait.
* 7 (mōk)

MÔH

2742. 磨 112 A mill. Mill-
* 11 stone. (mōh)

MOK。

2743. 剝 18 To flay, peel,
8 lay bare.

2744. 摸 64 To feel with
11 the hand.(móh)

2745. 嘆 30 About. To
" 11 guess at.

MŌK

2746. 幀 50
11 | Curtain.
2747. 幕 50 Screen.Awning.
11 | Tent.
2748. 寞 40 Still. Silent.
11 Solitude.

2749. 莫 140 Not. None.
* 7 Don't. S. (mŏk)

(a) mōk-taaī 4033.
None greater.

2750. 膜 130 A film.
11 Thin skin.

(a) i-mōk 1248.
Membrane.
(b) ko-mōk 1714.
Mesentery.
(c) taaī-ch'eung-mŏng-mōk
4033-513-2759. A
caul.

MONG

2751. 橺 $\frac{75}{8}$

   (a) mong-kwóh 2097.
     Mango.

2752. 芒 $\frac{140}{3}$ (mŏng) uf 2751.

MŌNG

2753. 亡 $\frac{8}{1}$ Destroyed. Gone. Ruined. Dead.

2754. 忘 $\frac{61}{3}$ To forget. Unconscious.(mông)

   (a) mōng-kei 1627.
     To forget.
   (b) mōng-yan 5108.
     Ungrateful.
   (c) mōng-yīng 5230.
     Abstracted.
   (d) mōng-wān 5028.
     Comatose.
   (e) mōng-yan-tsʻó 5141-4777. The iris.

2755. 忙 $\frac{61}{3}$ Hurried. Flurried.Perplexed. S.

2756. 蝱 $\frac{142}{9}$ A stinging fly.

   (a) ngaū-mōng 3039.
     The gadfly.

2757. 芒 $\frac{140}{3}$ Beard of grain. S. (mong)

2758. 鋩 $\frac{167}{7}$ Edge or point of sword. Sharp.

MŎNG

2759. 網 $\frac{120}{8}$ Net. Web. To entrap

2760. 妄 $\frac{38}{3}$ False. Erroneous. Wrong. (mông)

2761. 蟒 $\frac{142}{11}$ A huge serpent. Python. Boa constrictor.

2762. 网 $\frac{R}{122}$ A net.

2763. 罔 $\frac{122}{3}$ To trap.

MÔNG

2764. 望 $\frac{74}{7}$ To hope, anxiously look for, expect.

MOOI

2765. 妹 $\frac{38}{5}$ Girl. Slave girl.(mooí,mooî)

MOOĪ

2766. 煤 $\frac{86}{9}$ Coal.

   (a) mooī-tʻaàn 4300.
     Coal.
   (b) mooī-heī 1033.
     Coal gas.
   (c) mooī-yaū 5149.
     Gasoline.

2767. 梅 $\frac{75}{7}$ Plum species.

   (a) mooī-tsź 4667.
     Prunes.
   (b) hak-mooī 971.
     Dried prunes.
   (c) siú-mooī 3674.
     Damson.
   (d) yeūng-mooī 5196.
     Arbutus.
   (e) oo-mooī-mūk 3115-2795.
     Ebony.
   (f) suen-mooī 3702.
     A laughing stock.
   (g) mooī-fa-teng 650-4128.
     Syphilitic sores.
   (h) yeūng-mooī-teng 5195.
     A bubo.

2768. 霉 $\frac{173}{7}$ Mildew. Mouldy.

   (a) shap-mooī 3843.
     Slatternly.

2769. 莓 140/7 Edible berries.
  (a) mooI-t'oI 4424.
    Moss.
  (b) shē-mooI 3874.
    Wild strawberry.

2770. 玫 96/4 Fine red stone.
  (a) mooI-kwaI-fa 2068-650.
    The rose.

2771. 胸 130 Brisket.

2772. 媒 38/9 A go-between.

2773. 枚 75/4 Stalk. Stem. C for coins, fruits, etc.

MOOǏ

2774. 每 80/3 Each. Every.

2775. 浼 85/7 To defile.

MOOÎ

2776. 妹 38/5 Younger sister. Female relatives. (mooi)

2777. 昧 72/5 Dark. Obscure.

2778. 瑁 96/9 Tortoise shell.

MOŌN

2779. 門 R 169 Door. Entrance.
2780. 门 Sect. C.
  (a) waāng-moōn 4981.
    A side door.
  (b) moōn-p'aaI 3420.
    Census ticket.
    House number.
  (c) naú-moōn 2868.
    A buttonhole.

  (d) fàn-moōn 717.
    The anus.
  (e) moōn-shaang 3802.
    A disciple.
  (f) ch'ut-moōn 648.
    To marry a husband.

2781. 捫 64/8 To hold, cover. (moon)
  (a) moōn-shat 3851.
    To crack lice.
  (b) moōn-hung 1228.
    A bodice.

2782. 瞞 109/11 To deceive, conceal. S.

2783. 閂 30/8

2784. 們 9/8 Sign of plural in Mandarin.

MOǑN

2785. 滿 85/11 Full. Entire. Complete.
  (a) moǒn-chau 160.
    Manchuria.

MOÔN

2786. 悶 61/8 Sad. Distressed.
2787. 憫 61/8 Melancholy.
2788. 懣 61/14 Chagrined. Melancholy.

MOOT

2789. 咪 30/5 To compress the lips.

MOOT。

2790. 抹 64/5 To rub, blot out, wipe out, strike out. (maat。)

(a) moot。-kéng 1636 .
　　To cut the throat.

2791. 沬 85 5 Froth. Foam.
　Bubbles.

MOŌT

2792. 末 75 1 The end. Last.
Final. Dust.
Atoms.

(a) moōt-yāt 5137 .
　　End of the world.

(b) tsiu-moōt 4575 .
　　Powdered pepper.

2792½. 沒 85 4 To perish.
Loss.

(a) moōt-yeŭk 5183 .
　　Myrrh.

(b) moōt-shĕk-tsź 3879-
4667. Gall nuts.

2793. 茉 140 5

(u) moōt-leî 2297.
　　The moly or jasmine.

MUK

2794. 呋 30 4 To bud, guess,
reckon mentally.

MŪK

2795. 木 R 75 Wood. Tree. Lum-
ber. Wooden.

(a) paāk-mŭk 3178 .
　　Quassia.

(b) paāk。-heung-mŭk 3173-
1046. Cedar.

(c) mŭk-t'ung 4452 .
　　Clematis.

(d) mŭk-heung 1046 .
　　Putchuck.

(e) mŭk-ǐ 1280 .
　　Edible fungus (on
trees).

(f) mŭk-shat 3851 .
　　Bug. Louse.

(g) mūk-sing 3652 .
　　Jupiter.

2796. 牧 93 4 To tend cattle
or sheep. A
shepherd.

(a) mūk-sz 3757 .
　　A pastor.

2797. 睦 109 8 Harmony.
　Peace.

2798. 目 R 109 Eye. Index.
Items.To view.

(a) shò-mūk 3972 .
　　Numbers.

(b) t'aī-mūk 4323 .
　　Topic. Index.

2799. 沐 85 4 S.
　To wash, bathe.

2800. 穆 115 11 S.
　uf 2797.

MUNG

2801. 懵 61 16 Dull.
Senile. Stupid.

2802. 懞 61 14 uf 2804.

2802½. 檬 75 14 See 2807.

MŪNG

2803. 蒙 140 10 To teach, favor.
Thankful. S.

(a) mūng-hŏk 1140 .
　　Primary school.

(b) mūng-moōt 2777 .
　　Dullness.Ignorance.

(c) mūng-koō 1796 .
　　Mongolia.

2804. 曚 72 14 About dark.
Before dawn.

2805. 朦 74 14 Darkened. Dim.
Obscured.

2806. 矇 109 14 Dim. Blind.
Dull.

2807. 檬 75 14 (mung)

-145-

MŬNG

2808. 夢 36/11 To dream.

2809. 梦 36/8 A dream.

NA

2810. 痲 104/9 A scab. Scar. To-gether with. To stick. S.

NÁ

2811. 嬤 80/4 A mother. Female.
(a) ná-yīng 5230. Effeminate.
(b) shat-ná 3851. A louse.

NĀ

2812. 拏 64/5 To grasp,

2813. 拿 64/6 carry, bring.

2814. 嗱 30/9 Exclamation. Now!

NÂ

2815. 那 163/4 F--emphatic.(nā; ná) That; there; the (mand.)

NAAI

2816. 奶 38/2 Title of respect for women. Madam. (naaĭ)
(a) sz-naai 3757. A lady. Mrs.

NAAÍ

2817. 跐 157/2 To step.

NAAÌ

2818. 奶 30/2 To tie, fasten, tow. Adjacent to.

NAAĬ

2819. 奶 38/2 Woman's breast.

2820. 嬭 38/14 Milk. To suckle.
(a) wai-naaĭ 4993. To suckle.
(b) naaĭ-t'aū 4339. Nipple. Teat.
(c) ngeū-naaĭ 3039. Cow's milk.
(d) naaĭ-p'eī 3468. Cream.

2821. 乃 4/2 But. And so.

NAÀM

2822. 揇 64/9 A span. To grasp. (naăm)

NAĀM

2823. 南 24/7 The south.
(a) naām-kīk 1654. The south pole.
(b) naām-yeŭng-kw'ān-t'ó 5194-2137-4384. The East Indies.
(c) naām-hoí 1125. South China Sea.
(d) naām-ping-yeŭng 3301-5194. Antarctic Ocean.
(e) naām-nīng 2901. Nanning.
(f) naām-kīng 1669. Nanking.

2824. 男 102/2 Man. Male. Son. S.

(a) naām-yān 5117.
A man.
(b) naām-nuĭ 2949. Men and women. Both sexes.
(c) naām-shik 3917.
Sodomy.

2825. 喃 $\frac{30}{9}$ To chatter, gabble, repeat after.

2826. 枏 $\frac{75}{4}$ A kind of tree.

2827. 楠 $\frac{75}{9}$

2828. 諵 $\frac{149}{9}$ uf 2825.

NAĂM

2829. 揇 $\frac{64}{9}$ To beat, grasp. (naăm)

2830. 腩 $\frac{130}{9}$
(a) feĭ-t'ò-naăm 759-4402.
Potbelly.

NAÁN.

2831. 赧 $\frac{155}{4}$ To blush.

NAÀN

2832. 攤 $\frac{64}{19}$ To baste, as in sewing.

2833. 蠚 $\frac{142}{19}$ Bite of an insect. Eruptions.

NAĀN

2834. 難 $\frac{172}{11}$ Difficult. Hard. To distress. S. (naân)
(a) naān-waĭ 4999.
To trouble.

NAÂN

2835. 難 $\frac{172}{11}$ Calamity. Distress. (naān)

NAĀP

2836. 納 $\frac{120}{4}$ To present, pay taxes. To receive. S.

2837. 衲 $\frac{145}{4}$ To line, pad, quilt.

NAAT.

2838. 鈉 $\frac{167}{4}$ To burn, sear. Burning hot.
(a) naat.-kai 1517, or naat.-pai 3206.
Soldering iron.

NAĀT

2839. 喃 $\frac{30}{4}$ To stutter. Slow speech.
(a) són-naāt 3691.
Clarionet.

NAAŪ

2840. 錨 $\frac{167}{8}$ An anchor.
(a) naaū-t'úng 4454.
A buoy.

NAAŬ

2841. 撓 $\frac{64}{12}$ To vex, tie up.

NAAÛ

2842. 鬧 $\frac{191}{5}$ Noise. Bustle.

2843. 閙 $\frac{169}{5}$ To scold, revile.
(a) naaû-chung 36..
Alarm clock.

(b) naaû-yeūng-fa 5193-650. Stramonium.

NAÏ

2844. 泥 $\frac{85}{5}$ Soil. Mud.

2845. 坭 $\frac{32}{5}$ Dirt. (neî)

(a) naï-shuí-ló 4004-2404. A mason.

(b) t'aū-naï 4339. Dandruff.

(c) ló-naï 2420. Scurf.

NAÎ To adhere to. Bigoted.

NAK

2846. 囁 $\frac{211}{11}$

(a) nak-ngā 2977. Tongue tied.

NAM

2847. 糈 $\frac{119}{9}$ Delightful.

NĀM

2848. 腍 $\frac{130}{8}$ Tender. Soft. Well cooked.

(a) nām-shîn 3939. Good natured.

2849. 淰 $\frac{85}{8}$ Moist. Soaked. (nâm)

NĂM

2850. 稔 $\frac{115}{8}$ Ripe grain. To hoard.

NĀM

2851. 喭 $\frac{30}{13}$ Muddy. Turbid. Deep sleep.

2852. 腍 $\frac{130}{8}$ Soaked. Satiated.

2853. 淰 $\frac{85}{8}$ To spread. (nam)

NÁN

2854. 撋 $\frac{64}{12}$ To play with, take care of, dally with, defile.

NANG

2855. 能 $\frac{130}{6}$ Unlucky. (nāng)

NÁNG

2856. 褦 $\frac{145}{10}$ To walk on the heels, limp. (nàng)

NÀNG

2857. 褦 $\frac{145}{10}$ To connect, tie. (náng)

NĀNG

2858. 能 $\frac{130}{6}$ Able to. Competent. Ability. Power. (nang)

NAP

2859. 粒 $\frac{119}{5}$ A kernel. C for small things as beads, drops, etc.

2860. 凹 $\frac{17}{3}$ A hollow. Pass. Cavity.

2861. 凹 $\frac{13}{3}$ Concave. Sunken. (aaù)

(a) tsaú-nap 4500. A dimple.

(b) nap-hiu 1089. Collapsed.

NĀP

2862. 洇 $\frac{85}{5}$

(a) nāp-shīk 3925.
  Silly.

2863. 湆 脂 85/9 Sticky.
  Slow.

NAT

2864. 嫩 38/10 Anxious for. To tease, dally with. Lewd.

NAU

2865. 嬲 38/14 | To vex,
2866. 惱 61/9 | irritate, anger. (nŏ)

  (a) nau-nat 2864.
    Irritable.
  (b) nau-shik 3917.
    To scowl.
  (c) nau-nŏ 2929.
    Angry.

NAÚ

2867. 扭 64/4 To turn, twist, wring, sprain.
  (a) naú-t'ung 4458.
    Gripes.
  (b) naú-kéng 1636.
    Testy.
2868. 鈕 167/4 Knob. Button. S.
  (a) nap-naú(nau) 2859.
    Buttons.
  (b) shuí-kwa-naú 4004-2037. Capers.
2869. 紐 120/4 A knot. To tie. S.
  (a) naú-ngaán 2999.
    A loop.
  (b) naú-yeuk。 5178.
    New York.'

NAÛ

2870. 縟 120/10 Smooth. Adorned. Satiated.

NE

2871. 喊 30/16 F—emphatic or demonstrative.

NEĪ

2872. 呢 30/5 See ni.
2873. 尼 44/2
  (a) neī-lōh-hōh 2437-1119.
    Nile River.
2874. 彌 57/14
  (a) neī-ts'oì-à 4801-9
    Messiah.

NEǏ

2875. 你 9/5 Second personal pronoun. You.

NEÎ

2876. 泥 85/5 Bigoted. Mulish. (naī)
2877. 膩 130/12 Greasy. Unctuous.
2878. 餌 184/6 Bait. Cakes. To allure.

NÉNG

2879. 傾 30/11 C for hats.

NEÚNG

2880. 娘 38/7 A young lady.

NI

2881 **呢 30/5** This. F—interrogative.

2882 **誾 158/8** To enter secretly, hide, conceal.

NIK

2883 **匿 23/9** Hidden. Secret. Clandestine.

2884 **搦 64/10** To carry, seize.

2885 **疒 R/104**

2886 **臬 61/11** Evil. Vile.

NĪK

2887 **溺 85/10** To drown. To dote on.

NIM

2888 **拈 64/5** To pick up, carry.
(a) yat-nim-chí 5133-216. A ream of paper.

NĪM

2889 **黏 202/5** Glutinous
2890 **粘 119/5** Sticky. To adhere. (chim)

NÎM

2891 **念 61/4** To ponder, remember. S.
(a) nîm-t'aū 4339. Thought. Motive.

NIN

2892 **犁 5/13**

(a) yám-nin 5095. To suck.

NÍN

2893 **爛 130/19** A slice. Splinter. C for face.

2894 **撚 64/12** To squeeze. (nán)

NĪN

2895 **年 51/3** A year. S.
(a) nīn-k'eī-yát-tsź 1952-5137-4667. Anniversary.

NING

2896 **擰 64/ |** To take, carry,
2897 **擰 64/12** bring. (nîng)

NÍNG

2898 **寧 40/11** Rather.
2899 **寧 40/7** It is better. It is easier.
(a) nîng-hóh 1117. Better that ......
2900 **檸 75/14** Name of a tree.
(a) nîng-mung 2802½. The lemon.
2901 **甯 40/9**

NÎNG

2902 **哝 30/7** To turn, spin,
2903 **擰 64/11** shake. (nîng)
2904 **甯 40/10** S.

-150-

2905. 佞 9/5 Clever. Artful.

2906. 濘 85/14 Mud. Muddy. Marshy.

___

NIP

2907. 吶 30/5 Thin. Flat. Poor.

2908. 吶 30/5 Broken down. (nap)

___

NĬP

2909. 捏 64/7 To fabricate,

2910. 揑 64/9 trump up, knead.

2911. 攝 64/18 To hold up, assist. (ship.)

2912. 鑷 167/18 Forceps. Pincers. To nip, pinch.

(a) siú-nĬp 3674. Tweezers.

2913. 捻 64/8 To pinch, twist with fingers.

2914. 聶 128/12 To whisper. S. (nip.)

2915. 湼 85/9 Black mud. Nirvana.

2916. 臬 132/4 See Ĭt.

2917. 躡 157/18 To step.

___

NĬT

2918. 貎 132/10 To grasp, play with.

___

NIU

2919. 朴 75/3 Slender. Tapering.

___

NĬŬ

2920. 鳥 R 196 A bird.

(a) niŭ-hŏk 1140. Ornithology.

___

NIÛ

2921. 尿 44/4 Urine.

(a) niû paau 3199. The bladder.
(b) oh-niû 3089. To urinate.

___

NŌ

2922. 奴 38/2 A slave. Servant. S.

(a) nō-pŭk 3402. Bond servant.

2923. 孥 39/5 A child.

2924. 儺 9/5

___

NŎ

2925. 惱 61/9 Anger. Vexation. (nau)

2926. 腦 130/9 The brain. Camphor.

(a) nŏ-tseung 4525. The brain.
(b) nŏ-huet.-chung-fung 1212-383-879. Apoplexy.
(c) nŏ-hei-kan 1033-1539. Nerves.

2927. 瑙 96/9 Agate. Jasper. Carnelian.

2928. 弩 57/5 Crossbow.

___

NÔ

2929. 怒 61/5 Anger. Passion.

NOH

2930. 挪 64/7 To fawn over, cajol. (nōh)
*

2931. 挼 64/7 To crumple up, rub.
*

NŌH

2932. 挪 64/7 To handle, move, shift. (noh)
*

2933. 哪 30/7
"

2934. 那 163/4 S. (nǒh, nǎ, nâ)
'"'

NÔH

2935. 糯 119/14 Glutinous or soft rice.
*

2936. 懦 61/14 Weak. Infirm. Imbecile.
*

NOÎ

2937. 内 11/2 Inside. Within. Inner.
(a) noî-yān 5117. My wife.
(b) noî-mô-pô 2729-3342. Department of Home Affairs.
(c) noî-teî-ooî 4125-3143. China Inland Mission
(d) hōh-noî 1119. Hanoi.

2938. 耐 126/3 A period of time. To endure, continue.

2939. 柰 75/5 Resource. Remedy.
*

2940. 奈 37/5 Resource. Remedy.
*

NŌK

2941. 諾 149/9 S.
"'

NONG

2942. 躨 157/20 Calf of the leg. (nōng)
*

NŌNG

2943. 囊 30/19 A large bag. Sack. S.
'

2944. 瓤 97/17 Pulp. Pith. Kernel.
'

NUĔN

2945. 暖 72/9 Warm. Balmy. To warm.

2946. 煖 86/9 Warm. Balmy. To warm.

NUÊN

2947. 嫩 38/11 Young. Tender. Soft. Delicate.

2948. 媆 38/9 Young. Tender. Soft. Delicate.
(a) nuên-tsaí 4482. An infant.
(b) nuên-laām 2167. Light blue.

NUǏ

2949. 女 R/38 Female. A girl. S.
**
(a) nuǐ-yān 5117. A woman.
(b) t'ūng-nuǐ 4463. A virgin.
(c) nuǐ-saì 3590. Son in law.

NŪK

2950. 蹋 157/13 To knead.
*

NUNG

2951. 燶 86 13 To scorch, brown.
   (a) nung-heí-mîn 1031-2687. To scowl.

NŪNG

2952. 農 161 6 To plant, farm, cultivate. S.
   (a) nŭng-hŏk 1140. Science of Agriculture.
2953. 濃 85 13 Strong (liquid). Thick. Dense.
2954. 膿 130 13 Pus. Matter.
   (a) nŭng-ch'ong 578. An abscess.
2955. 襛 115 13 Dense. Thick.

NŪT

2956. 訥 149 4 To stutter. Impediment in the speech.

NG

2957. 吘 30 4 An expletive. Oh! (nḡ)

NǍ

2958. 吘 30 4 } Euphonic particle. Yes.
2959. 悟 61 7 }
2960. 梧 75 7 Kind of tree.
   (a) nḡ-chau 159. Wuchow.
2961. 吾 30 4 I. My.

NǍ

2962. 五 7 ㄨ The numeral 5: common, complicated and running hand forms.
2963. 伍 9 4
2964. 乂 4

   (a) ng-p'oóǐ-tsź 3549-4667. Gall nuts.
   (b) nǧ-fân-mîn 723-2687. Profile.
2965. 午 24 2 ll A.M. to 1 P.M.
   (a) chìng-nǧ 275. Noon.
   (b) sheûng-nǧ 3896. Forenoon.
2966. 迕 162 4 Conflicting. Confused. Disobedient.
2967. 伍 9 4 In fives.
   (a) tuî-nǧ 4253. Ranks.

NĜ

2968. 悟 61 7 To arouse, awake, discern. (nǧ)
2969. 忤 61 4 Obstinate. Perverse. (nǧ)
2970. 悞 61 7 False. To deceive, break a promise.
2971. 誤 149 7 To mistake, mislead, err.
2972. 寤 40 11 } To awake, arouse,
2973. 牢 40 4 }

NGA

2974. 丫 6 2 Distant. (a, ngà)

-153-

NGÁ

2975. 啞 $\frac{30}{8}$ (á)
  (a) ngá-ngá-sheng 3880.
    Squalling.

NGÀ

2976. 丫 $\frac{6}{2}$ (a, nga) To open.
  *
  (a) ngà-keuk。 1638.
    To stride.
  (b) ngà-hoi-keuk。 1124.
    To straddle.

NGĀ

2977. 牙 $\frac{R}{92}$ Teeth. Toothed. Screw thread.S.
  (a) ngā-ch'ōng 586.
    The jaw.
  (b) ch'eūng-ngā 512.
    A tusk.
  (c) tseūng-ngā 4531.
    Ivory.
  (d) seung-ngā 3628.
    Artificial teeth.
  (e) ngā-ts'aat。 4696.
    Tooth brush.
  (f) ngā-shik 3917.
    Buff color.
  (g) ngā-laan-maī 2179-2603. Cochineal.
  (h) kaú-ngā-yeūng 1574-5201. Jagged.
  (i) saam-ngā 3572.
    A tee. (pl)
  (j) t'ung-saam-ngā 4452-3593. A nipple.(pl)
2978. 衙 $\frac{144}{7}$ An office. Government residence. S.
  (a) ngā-moon 2779.
    Yamen.
2979. 芽 $\frac{140}{4}$ A bud. Shoot.
  *   To bud, begin.

  (a) ngā-ts'oì 4800.
    Bean sprouts.
  (b) ngā-sún 3740.
    Sprout. Tenon.
  (c) wōng-ngā-paāk 5070-3178. Colewort.
2980. 禡 $\frac{113}{10}$ The day after new and full moon.

NGĂ

2981. 瓦 $\frac{R}{98}$ Earthenware tiles. Pottery.
  (a) ngă-iū 1390.
    A kiln.
  (b) ngă-t'ūng 4461.
    Earthenware pipe.
  (c) ngă-mín 2687.
    A roof.
  (d) mīng-ngă 2690.
    Oystershell windows.

2982. 雅 $\frac{172}{4}$ Elegant. Refined.
  (a) ngă-tín 4162.
    Athens.

NGÂ

2983. 訝 $\frac{149}{4}$ To obstruct, stop, block.

NGAAĪ

2984. 涯 $\frac{85}{8}$ Shore. Limit.
  *
  (a) mō-ngaaī 2711.
    Boundless.
2985. 捱 $\frac{64}{8}$ To struggle, endure.
2986. 睚 $\frac{109}{8}$
  " "
2987. 崖 $\frac{46}{8}$ Cliff. Precipice.
  " "

-154-

NGAAĪ

2988. 艾 140／2 Artemisia.Moxa.
  * Mugwort. S.
  (a) ngaaī-yūng 5279.
      Moxa punk.
  (b) ngaaī-foō 832.
      Artemisia herb.

NGAĀK

2989. 噛 30／10 Contrary.
              Opposing.
2990. 咈 30／6 Disobedient.
              Against.
2991. 額 181／9 The forehead.
              A fixed number.
2992. 額 181／5 A settled
              portion.

NGAAM

2993. 啱 30／8 Fit.
              Suitable.
  (a) ngaam-ngaam.
      Precisely.Exactly.

NGAĀM

2994. 巖 46／20 Precipice.
              Steep.
2995. 岩 46／5 Rough.
              A cave.

NGAÂM

2996. 讛 149／13 Jargon.
  *   Nonsense.

NGAĀN

2997. 顏 181／9 Countenance.
  *   Color. S.
2998. 擎 64／9 To roll, grind,
  *   play stringed
              instrument.

NGAẮN

2999. 眼 109／6 Eye. Opening.
              Arch. C for
              needle, nail,
              well, etc.
  (a) ngaẩn-chue 314.
      The eyeball.
  (b) ngaẩn-t'ūng-yản 4466-
      5117. The retina.
  (c) ngaẩn-ĭt 1372.
      Opthalmia.
  (d) ngaẩn-foh 765.
      Optical practice.
  (e) ngaẩn-meī 2657.
      The eyebrows.

NGAÂN

3000. 鴈 196／4 Wild goose.
  '   S.

NGAÂNG

3001. 硬 112／7 Hard. Strong.
              Unyielding.
              Obstinate.
  (a) ngaâng-kéng 1636.
      Stubborn.
  (b) ngaâng-haú 1006.
      Foul mouthed.
  (c) ngaâng-hó 1099.
      Really good.

NGAAP

3002. 唊 30／10 To tuck up,
  "   strap.

NGAAT

3003. 齧 211／6 Stench. Niggard-
  "   ly. (ngīt)

NGAĀT

3004. 扤 64／3 To shake, sway,
  "   move. (at,ngat)

NGAAU

3005. 呦 30/5 (aau)
  (a) ngaau-sheng 3880.
    To mew.
3006. 搲 64/11 To scratch.
3007. 胶 109/6 See 306a.

NGAAŪ

3008. 熬 86/11 To continue, endure. (ngō)
3009. 殽 79/8 Mixed. Unsteady.
3010. 餚 184/8 Meats. Delicacies.
3011. 爻 R/89 Lines of diagram.

NGAAŬ

3012. 咬 30/6 To bite, gnaw. (kaau)

NGAI

3013. 嘻 30/14 To urge,
3014. 唲 30/6 importune. Urgently.

NGAĪ

3015. 危 26/4 Dangerous. Peril. Hazard.
  (a) ngaī-hím 1055. Hazardous.

NGAĬ

3016. 蟻 142/13 Ants.
  (a) ngaǐ-t'aū 4339. Anthill.

NGAÎ

3017. 偽 9/12 False. To pretend.
  (a) ngaî-shîn 3939. Hypocritical.
3018. 藝 140/15 Skill. Trade. Handicraft. S.
3019. 毅 79/11 Resolute. Daring.
3020. 巍 46/18 High. Lofty.
3021. 魏 194/8 Exalted. S.

NGAK

3022. 阨 170/4 To cheat, deceive,
3023. 呃 30/4 swindle. (ak)

NGĀM

3024. 唅 30/7 To grunt, mumble, grumble. (hōm)

NGÂM

3025. 啥 30 Feeble.

NGAN

3026. 奀 37/4 Tiny. Puny. On tiptoe. (ngàn)

NGÀN

3027. 奀 37/4 To jerk, dangle, bob. (ngan)

NGĀN

3028. 銀 167/6 Silver. Money. S.
  (a) ngān-chí 216. Paper money. Bank note.

(b) ngān-chik 239, or
ngān-tsak 4487.
Cheek.
(c) ngān-taan 4046.
Bill of exchange.
(d) shuí-ngān 4004.
Mercury.
(e) ngān shuí 4004. Dis-
count. Premium on
exchange.
(f) hon-ngān 1158.
Shroff.
(g) ngān-hōh 1119.
The Milky Way.

NGÂN

3029. 韌 $\frac{178}{3}$ Soft but tough.
3030. 朋 $\frac{130}{3}$ Elastic.
(a) shuí-ngân 4004.
Slops.

NGÃNG

3031. 硬 $\frac{112}{7}$ To groan, growl.
* (ngaāng)

NGAP

3032. 吸 $\frac{30}{4}$ To tattle.
* (k'ap)

NGÃP

3033. 嗒 $\frac{30}{12}$
* To blink, nod,
3034. 扱 $\frac{64}{4}$ beckon.
• (ch'aap。)

NGAT

3035. 扤 $\frac{64}{3}$ To stuff.
* (at, ngaāt)

NGÃT

3036. 兀 $\frac{10}{1}$ To cut off the
' feet, maim. S.

(a) ngāt-ko 1713.
To stand on tiptoe.

NGAU

3037. 鈎 $\frac{167}{5}$
* A hook.
3038. 鈎 $\frac{167}{5}$ (kau)

NGAŪ

3039. 牛 R Cattle.
$\frac{93}{}$ S.
(a) shuí-ngaū 4004.
Water buffalo.
(b) ngaū-naaí-péng 2819-
3276. Cheese.
(c) ngaū-yaū 5149.
Butter.
(d) ngaū-wōng 5070.
Ox bezoar.
(e) mān-ngaū 2612.
A prostitute.
(f) ngaū-shīt-t'iū 3963-
4375. Hydrangea as-
pera.
(g) ngaū-chong 307.
Newchwang.

NGAŬ

3040. 偶 $\frac{9}{9}$ Image. Paired.
* Sudden. To
agree. Joined.S.
(a) ngaŭ-ín 1349.
Accidentally.
(b) ngaŭ-tseūng 4530.
Idols. Images.
3041. 耦 $\frac{127}{9}$ To mate, pair.
S.
3042. 藕 $\frac{140}{15}$ Roots of a cer-
' tain plant.
(a) lín-ngaŭ 2353.
Water lily root.

NGAÛ

3043. 吽 30/4 Dull. Stupid. A dolt.

3044. 䮝 187/10 To gallop wildly. uf 3043.

NGĒ

3045. 喉 30/10 To whine, mutter. (ai, e)

NGI

3046. 噅 30/14 A fib. (ngai)

NGĪT

3047. 齧 211/6 To nibble. Creaking noise. S. (ngaat。)

NGŌ

3048. 擎 64/11 To shake, rattle, move, throw (dice). (ngô)

3049. 搣 64/11

3050. 嗷 30/11 Wailing. Clamor.

3051. 熬 86/11 To simmer, distill, decoct. (ngaaū)

3052. 鰲 195/11 A great fish.

3053. 艠 137/11 Keel.

3054. 螯 142/11 Nippers of a crab.

NGÔ

3055. 傲 9/11 Proud. Haughty.

3056. 搣 64/11 See ngō.

NGŌH

3057. 鵝 196/7 } The goose.

3058. 鵞 196/7 }

(a) ts'ó-ngōh 4777. The common goose.

(b) t'ōng-ngōh 4438. The pelican.

(c) k'eī-ngōh 1962. Penguin.

(d) t'in-ngōh 4355. The crane.

(e) ngōh-mō 2712. A quill.

(f) ngōh-cheūng 191. Webfooted.

(g) ngōh-lún-shĕk-teî 2527-3879-4125. A causeway.

(h) ngōh-haū 1008. Diphtheria.

3059. 訛 149/4 } To deceive,

3060. 譌 149/12 } cheat. Seductive talk.

3061. 蛾 142/7 A moth. S.

(a) tang-ngōh 4094. A moth.

(b) ts'aām-ngōh 4686. Silkworm moth.

3062. 俄 9/7 Sudden.

(a) ngōh-lōh-sz 2437-3763. Russia.

3063. 娥 38/7 Beautiful. A woman's name. S.

3064. 峨 46/7

NGŎH

3065. 我 62/3 Pronoun of the first person. I. We. Me. S.

NGÔH

3066. 餓 184/7 Hungry. Hunger.

3067. 臥 131/2 To lie down. A bedroom.

NGOI

3068. 呆 75/3 Silly. Foolish.

3069. 獃 94/10 Idiotic.

NGOÎ

3070. 外 36/2 Outside. Foreign.
  (a) ngoî-kaau-pô 1494-3342. Department of Foreign Affairs.

3071. 礙 112/14 To hinder, oppose, obstruct, interfere.

3072. 碍 112/8

NGOK

3073. 樂 75/11 Music. Musical instrument. S. (lôk)

3074. 咢 30/6 To turn the head, perk up.

3075. 鱷 195/18 Crocodile. Alligator. Rapacious.

3076. 腭 130/9 The palate.

3077. 鶚 196/9 The osprey.

NGÛN

3078. 岸 46/5 The shore. A bank.

NGÔNG

3079. 昂 72/4 Lofty. Imposing.

NGÔNG

3080. 戇 61/24 Crazy. Stupid.

3081. 憨 61/21 Simple minded.

O

3082. 摸 64/13 To reach.

3083. 爐 86/15 To stew, cook.

Ó

3084. 媼 38/10 An old woman. (wán)

3085. 鷁 195/13 A kind of perch.

Ò

3086. 奧 37/10 Mysterious. Abstruse.
  (a) ò-teî-leî-à 4125-2293-9. Austria.

3087. 澳 85/13 Bay. Cove. Dock.
  (a) ò-moôn 2779. Macao.
  (b) ò-taaî-leî-à 4033-2293-9. Australia.

OH

3088. 阿 170/5 Used as No. 9, which see. S.
  (a) oh-fei-leî-kà 749-2293-1409. Africa.
  (b) oh-ï-laàn 1284-2182. Ireland.

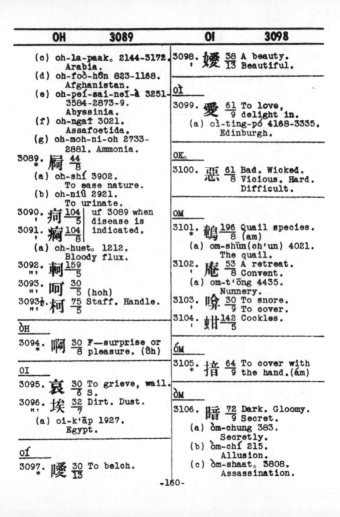

(c) oh-la-paak。 2144-3172.
Arabia.

(d) oh-foò-hŏn 823-1168.
Afghanistan.

(e) oh-pei-sai-neī-à 3251-3584-2873-9.
Abyssinia.

(f) oh-ngaī 3021.
Assafoetida.

(g) oh-moh-ni-oh 2733-2881. Ammonia.

3089. 屙 $\frac{44}{8}$ *
(a) oh-shí 3902.
To ease nature.

(b) oh-niû 2921.
To urinate.

3090. 疴 $\frac{104}{5}$, uf 3089 when disease is
3091. 痾 $\frac{104}{5}$, indicated.

(a) oh-huet。 1212.
Bloody flux.

3092. 軻 $\frac{159}{5}$,,,

3093. 呵 $\frac{30}{5}$,,, (hoh)

3093½. 柯 $\frac{75}{5}$,,, Staff. Handle.

___

ÒH

3094. 啊 $\frac{30}{8}$ * F—surprise or pleasure. (òh)

___

OI

3095. 哀 $\frac{30}{6}$, To grieve, wail. S.

3096. 埃 $\frac{32}{7}$,,, Dirt. Dust.

(a) oi-k'ap 1927.
Egypt.

___

OÍ

3097. 噯 $\frac{30}{13}$ * To belch.

___

3098. 嬡 $\frac{38}{13}$, A beauty.
Beautiful.

___

OÌ

3099. 愛 $\frac{61}{9}$ To love, delight in.

(a) oi-ting-pó 4168-3335.
Edinburgh.

___

OK。

3100. 惡 $\frac{61}{8}$ Bad. Wicked.
Vicious. Hard.
Difficult.

___

OM

3101. 鵪 $\frac{196}{8}$ * Quail species.
(am)

(a) om-shŭn(ch'un) 4021.
The quail.

3102. 庵 $\frac{53}{8}$, A retreat.
Convent.

(a) om-t'ōng 4435.
Nunnery.

3103. 唵 $\frac{30}{9}$, To snore.
To cover.

3104. 蚶 $\frac{142}{5}$, Cockles.

___

ÓM

3105. 揞 $\frac{64}{9}$ * To cover with the hand.(ám)

___

ÒM

3106. 暗 $\frac{72}{9}$, Dark. Gloomy.
Secret.

(a) òm-chung 383.
Secretly.

(b) òm-chî 215.
Allusion.

(c) òm-shaat。 3808.
Assassination.

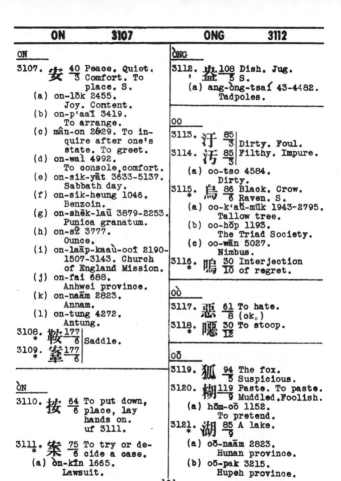

ON

3107. 安 40/3 Peace. Quiet. Comfort. To place. S.
 (a) on-lòk 2455. Joy. Content.
 (b) on-p'aaì 3419. To arrange.
 (c) màn-on 2629. To inquire after one's state. To greet.
 (d) on-waì 4992. To console, comfort.
 (e) on-sik-yàt 3633-5137. Sabbath day.
 (f) on-sik-heung 1046. Benzoin.
 (g) on-shèk-laū 3879-2253. Punica granatum.
 (h) on-sź 3777. Ounce.
 (i) on-laàp-kaaù-ooî 2190-1507-3143. Church of England Mission.
 (j) on-fai 688. Anhwei province.
 (k) on-naām 2823. Annam.
 (l) on-tung 4272. Antung.
3108. 鞍 177/6 Saddle.
3109. 鞌 177/6

ÒN

3110. 按 64/6 To put down, place, lay hands on. uf 3111.

3111. 案 75/6 To try or decide a case.
 (a) òn-kîn 1665. Lawsuit.

ONG

3112. 蚛 108/5 Dish. Jug. 盎 S.
 (a) ang-òng-tsaî 43-4482. Tadpoles.

OO

3113. 汙 85/3 Dirty. Foul.
3114. 污 85/3 Filthy. Impure.
 (a) oo-tso 4584. Dirty.
3115. 烏 86/6 Black. Crow. Raven. S.
 (a) oo-k'aù-mùk 1943-2795. Tallow tree.
 (b) oo-hōp 1193. The Triad Society.
 (c) oo-wàn 5027. Nimbus.
3116. 嗚 30/10 Interjection of regret.

ÒÒ

3117. 惡 61/8 To hate. (ok.)
3118. 噎 30/12 To stoop.

OŌ

3119. 狐 94/5 The fox. Suspicious.
3120. 糊 119/9 Paste. To paste. Muddled, Foolish.
 (a) hōm-oō 1152. To pretend.
3121. 湖 85/9 A lake.
 (a) oō-naām 2823. Hunan province.
 (b) oō-pak 3215. Hupeh province.

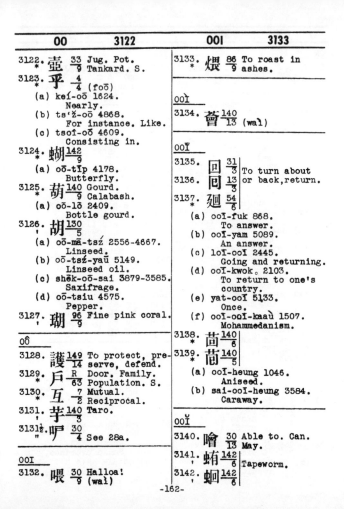

3122. 壺 33/9 Jug. Pot.
* Tankard. S.

3123. 乎 4/4 (foō)
*
  (a) keí-oō 1624.
    Nearly.
  (b) ts'ž-oō 4868.
    For instance. Like.
  (c) tsoí-oō 4609.
    Consisting in.

3124. 蝴 142/9
  (a) oō-tīp 4178.
    Butterfly.

3125. 葫 140/9 Gourd.
* Calabash.
  (a) oō-lō 2409.
    Bottle gourd.

3126. 胡 130/5
'
  (a) oō-mā-tsź 2556-4667.
    Linseed.
  (b) oō-tsź-yaū 5149.
    Linseed oil.
  (c) shēk-oō-sai 3879-3585.
    Saxifrage.
  (d) oō-tsiu 4575.
    Pepper.

3127. 瑚 96/9 Fine pink coral.
'

00̄

3128. 護 149/14 To protect, preserve, defend.

3129. 戶 R/63 Door. Family.
Population. S.

3130. 互 7/2 Mutual.
* Reciprocal.

3131. 芋 140/3 Taro.
'

3131½. 吗 30/4 See 28a.
"

00I

3132. 喂 30/9 Halloa!
(waI)

3133. 煨 86/9 To roast in
* ashes.

001

3134. 薈 140/13 (waI)

00Ī

3135. 回 31/3
3136. 囘 13/3 To turn about
or back, return.

3137. 廻 54/6
*
  (a) ooI-fuk 868.
    To answer.
  (b) ooI-yam 5089.
    An answer.
  (c) loI-ooI 2445.
    Going and returning.
  (d) ooI-kwok。2103.
    To return to one's
    country.
  (e) yat-ooI 5133.
    Once.
  (f) ooI-ooI-kaaù 1507.
    Mohammedanism.

3138. 茴 140/6
*
3139. 蘹 140/5
*
  (a) ooI-heung 1046.
    Aniseed.
  (b) sai-ooI-heung 3584.
    Caraway.

00Ĭ

3140. 噲 30/13 Able to. Can.
May.

3141. 蛕 142/6
3142. 蜖 142/6 Tapeworm.

OOĬ

3143. 會 75/9 To join togeth-er. A meeting.

3144. 会 9/4 Guild. Congrega-tion. Association. Church. S.

(a) ooĭ-t'óng 4435.
　　Meeting place.
(b) nīn-ooĭ 2895.
　　Annual meeting.

3145. 匯 22/11 A draft. Money order. Bill of exchange.

OÓN

3146. 碗 112/8

3147. 椀 75/8 A bowl. Small dish.

3148. 盌 108/5

3149. 腕 130/8 To twist. A joint.
*
(a) shaú-oón 3859.
　　The wrist.
(b) keuk。-oón 1638.
　　Ankle joint.

3150. 剜 18/8 To pare, cut down, dig out.

OŌN

3151. 垣 32/6 A wall. Bulwark. S.
'
3152. 爰 87/5 S.
"'
3153. 援 64/9 To lead.
"'

OŎN

3154. 換 64/9 To change, ex-change, barter.

3155. 玩 96/4 To toy, play with, enjoy. Rare.
*

(a) yaū-oŏn.5151.
　　To ramble about.
(b) koó-oŏn 1796.
　　Curios. Rarities.

3156. 緩 120/9 Slow. Gradually. Indulgent.
'

OŌT

3157. 活 85/6 Alive. Living. Life.

(a) oōt-p'oot。3558.
　　Living. Lively.

PA

3158. 巴 49/1 S.

(a) tá-pa 4027.
　　To slap.
(b) pa-cha 57.
　　Exacting.
(c) pa-kit。1694.
　　To flatter, toady to.
(d) pa-taū-yaū 4116-5149.
　　Croton oil.
(e) pa-shē 3874.
　　The python.
(f) pa-shik-ooĭ 3917-3143.
　　Basel Missionary Society.
(g) pa-līng-ooĭ 2364.
　　Berlin Missionary Society.
(h) pa-sai 3584.
　　Brazil。
(i) pa-nã-mã 2813-2561.
　　Panama.
(j) pa-la-lōng-ka 2145-2460-1409. Paraguay。
(k) pa-t'a-ngōh-nã 4282-3064-2813.Patagonia。
(l) pa-laĬ 2204.
　　Paris.

3159. 爸 88/4 Father.
*

3160. 吧 $\frac{30}{4}$

  (a) pa-paì 3210.
    Clamor.
  (b) pa-mǎ-yaû 2564-5149.
    Coal tar.

PÁ

3161. 把 $\frac{64}{4}$ To grasp. A sheaf. C for fans, knives, etc.

  (a) pá-tìng 4132.
    Tenacious.
  (b) pá-heì 1036.
    Conjuring tricks.
  (c) fóh-pá 767.
    A torch.
  (d) pá-tsúng 4652.
    Sergeant. Captain.

PÀ

3162. 嚛 $\frac{30}{15}$ F—expletive.

3163. 霸 $\frac{173}{13}$ To rule by force, tyran-
3164. 覇 $\frac{146}{13}$ nize, intimi-date. S.

  (a) pà-wǒng 5072.
    The cactus. A tyrant.

3165. 靶 $\frac{177}{4}$ Target. Mark. (pá)

  (a) tá-pà 4027. To hit the target. To execute by shooting.

PÂ

3166. 罷 $\frac{122}{10}$ To finish. Sign of imperative mode. S.

PAAÍ

3167. 擺 $\frac{64}{15}$ To display, ar-range, vibrate.

  (a) tá-paaí-tsź 4027-4667.
    Intermittent fever.

PAAÌ

3168. 拜 $\frac{64}{5}$ To worship, hon-or, make obei-sance.

  (a) paaì-t'ok。 4427. To request as a favor.
  (b) paaì-t'ip。 4365. Visiting card.
  (c) paaì-shaan 3793. To worship at the tombs.

PAAÎ

3169. 敗 $\frac{66}{7}$ Destroyed. De-feated. Ruined.

PAAK。

3170. 百 $\frac{106}{1}$ A hundred. All.
3171.** 佰 $\frac{9}{6}$ Many. Every. S.

  (a) paak。-pá-tsúng 3161-4652. A centurian.
  (b) paak。-tsuk 4636. Centipede.

3172.** 伯 $\frac{9}{5}$ Chief. Father's elder brother. Uncle. S.

  (a) taaî-paak。 4033. Wife's brother in law.
  (b) paak₅kung 1878. Great uncle.

3173. 柏 $\frac{75}{5}$ The cypress.
3174. 栢 $\frac{75}{6}$ Cedar. S.(paāk)

(a) pín-paak$_0$ 3291.
Cypress. Juniper.

(b) paak$_0$-heung-mūk 1046-2795. Cedar.

(c) paak$_0$-tsź-yaū 4667-5149. Juniper seed oil.

(d) paak$_0$-līng 2361. Berlin.

3175. 珀 $\frac{96}{5}$ Amber.

(a) fa-paak$_0$ 650.
Streaked amber.

(b) huet$_0$ -paak$_0$ 1212.
Red amber.

(c) shēk-paak$_0$ 3879.
Heavy yellow amber.

(d) laāp-paak$_0$ 2192. Sparkling yellow amber.

(e) mīng-paak$_0$ 2690. Resinous yellow amber.

(f) shui-paak$_0$ 4004. Pale yellow streaked amber.

3176. 迫 $\frac{162}{5}$ To urge, vex,

3177. 廹 $\frac{54}{5}$ press upon, persecute, (pik)

(a) pik-paak$_0$-sheng 3280-3880. Cracking.

PAĀK

3178. 白 $\frac{R}{106}$ White. Clear. Clean. Plain. S.

(a) paāk-paāk$_0$
Gratuitous.

(b) paāk-t'ip$_0$ 4365.
Anonymous placard or handbill.

(c) paāk-chaū 165.
Daylight.

(d) paāk-wā 4960.
Local dialect.

(e) paāk-t'ōng 4437.
Granulated sugar.

(f) paāk-ts'oî 4800.
Native cabbage. Broccoli.

(g) paāk-lōng 2464.
Surge.

(h) paāk-taaî 4031.
The whites.

(i) paāk-kop$_0$ 1829.
Dove. White pigeon.

(j) paāk-hōk-t'aām 1142-4291. Macao Passage.

3179. 帛 $\frac{50}{5}$ Plain silk. Wealth.

3180. 蔔 $\frac{140}{11}$ | Turnip species.

3181. 菔 $\frac{140}{8}$ |

3181½. 柏 $\frac{75}{5}$ Cedar or cypress. (paak$_0$)

PAAN

3182. 班 $\frac{96}{6}$ Rank. Class. Company. S.

3183. 斑 $\frac{67}{8}$ Striped. Mottled.

(a) paan-kau 1567.
Turtle dove.

3184. 頒 $\frac{181}{4}$ To publish, promulgate, bestow.

3185. 瘢 $\frac{104}{10}$ Eruption. Pustules.

3186. 扳 $\frac{30}{7}$ To turn. (p'aan)

PAÁN

3187. 板 $\frac{75}{4}$ Board. Printing block.

3188. 版 $\frac{91}{4}$ Page of book. Stiff. C.

(a) koó-paán 1796.
Old fashioned. Conservative.

(b) hak-paán 971.
Blackboard.

(c) saam-paán 3574.
Sampan. Small boat.
(d) shĕk-paán 3879.
A slate.
(e) t'in-fa-paán 4355-650.
Ornamental ceiling.
(f) paán-yaū 5149.
Suet.

3189. 哯 $\frac{30}{8}$

PAÀN

3190. 扮 $\frac{64}{4}$ To dress up, disguise.

PAÂN

3191. 辦 $\frac{160}{9}$ To do, manage, perform.

3192. 澷 $\frac{85}{9}$ Mud. Mire. Filth.
(a) paân-ch'ī 535.
A bog.

3193. 瓣 $\frac{160}{14}$ Section. Slice. Flower petals.

PAÀNG

3194. 烽 $\frac{30}{11}$ Bang! (p'aâng)
(a) paâng-peī 3252.
Bandy legged.

PAAT.

3195. 八 $\frac{R}{12}$

3196. 捌 $\frac{64}{7}$

3197. 弎 $\frac{8}{2}$

The numeral 8: common, complicated and running hand forms.

(a) paat.-sin-t'oī 3640-4418.
Octagonal table.
(b) paat.-kok.-yaū 1744-5149. Aniseed oil.

(c) paat.-kok.-ooī 3138.
Star aniseed.
(d) paat.-kok.-yīng 5230.
Octagon.
(e) paat.-tsź 4672. Eight character horoscope.
(f) paat.-tsź-so 3678.
Mustache.
(g) paat.-tsź-keuk. 1638.
Bandy legged.

PAAU

3198. 包 $\frac{20}{3}$ To enclose, wrap up, include. A bundle. S.
(a) paau-fūk 878. A wrapper. Bundle.
(b) paau-laám 2162.
Monopoly.

3199. 胞 $\frac{130}{5}$ Womb. Placenta.
(a) paau-t'oi 4417.
The womb.
(b) paau-i 1248.
The afterbirth.
(c) shui-paau 4004.
A blister.
(d) paau-tsaī 4482.
A vesicle.

3200. 鮑 $\frac{195}{5}$ Kind of dried fish. S.

3201. 勹 $\frac{R}{20}$ To envelope.

PAAÚ

3202. 飽 $\frac{184}{5}$ To eat plenty. Filled. Satisfied. S. (paau)

PAAÙ

3203. 爆 $\frac{86}{15}$ To scorch, crack, burst, bud. (p'aaū)

3204. 豹 $\frac{153}{3}$ Leopard. Spotted felines. (p'aaù)

PAI

3205. 跛 157/5 Lame. Leaning.

3206. 鎞 167/10 See 2838a.

PAI

3207. 閉 169/3 To close, shut up, stop up.

3208. 蔽 * 140/12 To obscure, cover, darken.

3209. 贔 ' 154/14 Strong.

3210. 唄 " 30/11 Noise. Clamor.

PAI

3211. 弊 ' 55/12 Ruined. Spoiled. Worn out. Wicked.
(a) pai-ka-foh 1411-768.
    Bad business!
    A botch!
(b) pai-lok。 2450.
    Bad! Alas!
(c) pai-pëng 3278.
    Abuses. Vices.

3212. 稗 ' 115/8 Weeds. Tares.

3213. 幣 ' 50/12 Wealth. Coin.

3214. 敝 ' 66/8 Unworthy. "My"-self, deprecia-tory.

PAK

3215. 北 21/3 North.
(a) pak-king 1669. Peking.
(b) pak-hoi 1125. Pakhoi. The North Sea.
(c) pak-ping-yeung 3301-5194. Arctic Ocean.

PAN

3216. 奔 * 37/6 To flee, run, elope, hasten.

3217. 檳 * 75/14 Name of tree.

3218. 梹 * 75/7 Betel nut palm.

3219. 檳 * 75/14
(a) pan-lông-suï 2462-3727. Penang.

3220. 濱 85/14 Beach. Shore.

3221. 瀕 85/14 Near to.
(a) pan-kok。 1744. Bangkok.

3222. 啽 " 30/12

3223. 賁 ' 154/5 Valorous. Energetic.

3224. 賓 ' 154/7 A guest.

PAN

3225. 品 * 30/6 Rank. Class. Kind. S.(p'án)
(a) pán-hâng 992. Conduct.

3226. 稟 113/8 To report to a superior.

3227. 稟 115/8 To petition, pay respect to.
(a) pán-taan 4046. A memorial.

PAN

3228. 拚 * 64/8 To braid. (fâng, fing)

3229. 擯 " ' 64/14 To expel.

3230. 嬪 ' 38/14 Imperial con-cubines. Wife.

3231. 殯 ' 78/14 To enshroud, bury.

PÂN

3238. 笨 118/5 Stupid. Doltish. Clumsy. (p'ǎn)

PANG

3233. 崩 46/8 To fall down. Broken.Ruined.
(a) pang-haú 1006. Notch. Harelip.
(b) pang-chìng 278. Menstrual disease.
(c) huet.-pang 1212. Flooding (at child-birth).
(d) pang-sha 3780. Butterfly.

PÂNG

3234. 凭 16/6 To lean on, rely on, trust in.
3235. 嗙 30/12

PAT

3236. 不 1/3 Negative. No. Not. Do not. Is not. S.
(a) pat-siu-fà 3667-650. Indigestion.
3237. 筆 118/6 A pencil. Pen-cil shaped ar-
3238. 笔 118/4 ticles. Style. Penmanship.S.
(a) chué-pat 328. Editor.
(b) ts'an-pat 4712. Own handwriting.
(c) t'it.-pat 4366. Crowbar.
3239. 畢 102 The final. End. Complete. S.
(a) pat-Ip 1368. To graduate.

3240. 篳 118/11 Wicker hedge.
(a) pat-moōn 2779. Wicket gate.

PĀT

3241. 拔 64/5 To pull up, up-root, draw out. (paat.)
(a) tseúng-pāt 4531. Proboscis.
(b) shuēn-t'aū-pāt 3999-4339. A bowsprit.
(c) haaī-pāt 912. Shoe horn.

PAÛ

3241½. 咘 30/4 A swelling. (p'aù)

PE

3242. 啤 30/8 (p'ě)
(a) pe-sūn 3747. Steam whistle.
(b) pe-tsaú 4500. Beer.

PÊ

3243. 嗶 30/14 Particle imply-ing doubt or dissatisfaction. F. (pè)

PEI

3244. 卑 24/6 Humble. Low. Base.
(a) pei-tsîn 4559. Plebian.
3245. 蓖 140/8 Castor oil plant.
(a) pei-mā-yaū 2559-5149. Castor oil.

3246. 悲 $\frac{61}{8}$ To grieve, sympathize with.

3247. 碑 $\frac{112}{8}$ A tablet. Monument.

3248. 陂 $\frac{170}{8}$ A dam. Reservoir.

3249. 萆 $\frac{140}{8}$ A medicinal plant.

PEÍ

3250. 俾 $\frac{9}{8}$ To cause to. To give, allow. By.

3251. 比 $\frac{R}{81}$ To compare with.

  (a) peí-laî-faat. 2207-682.
    Rule of proportion.
  (b) peí-leî-shî 2293-3905.
    Belgium.

3252. 髀 $\frac{188}{8}$ The thigh.

  (a) taaî-peí 4033.
    The hip.
  (b) peí-chip. 282.
    The groin.
  (c) yeùng-peí 5193.
    Leg of mutton.

3253. 彼 $\frac{60}{5}$ Another. Opposite.

  (a) peí-ts'z 4852.
    This and that. One
    to another.

3254. 吡 $\frac{30}{5}$

PEÌ

3255. 秘 $\frac{115}{5}$ Secret. Hidden.

3256. 祕 $\frac{113}{5}$ Private. S.

  (a) peì-lŏ 2424.
    Peru.

3257. 庇 $\frac{53}{4}$ To shelter, protect.

3258. 臂 $\frac{130}{13}$ The upper arm.

  (a) peì-shuí 4004.
    To drain off.
  (b) tiû-peì 4194.
    To swagger.

3259. 痹 $\frac{104}{8}$ Paralysis of limbs.

3260. 痺 $\frac{104}{8}$ Numbness.

3261. 閟 $\frac{169}{5}$ Occult. Secret.

PEÎ

3262. 被 $\frac{145}{5}$ To be the object of. To give to be. To receive. (p'eî)

3263. 備 $\frac{9}{10}$ To prepare for use. To complete, provide against.

3264. 俻 $\frac{9}{8}$

3265. 避 $\frac{162}{13}$ To flee from, avoid, escape.

3266. 啵 $\frac{30}{10}$ Or.

3267. 嚊 $\frac{30}{14}$ F—emphatic.

3268. 嚊 $\frac{30}{12}$

3269. 鼻 $\frac{R}{209}$ The nose.

  (a) peî-koh 1728.
    The nose.
  (b) peî-leùng 2318.
    Bridge of the nose.
  (c) peî-in 1335.
    Snuff.

3270. 笓 $\frac{118}{4}$ Fine comb.

3271. 篦 $\frac{118}{8}$ To comb.

3272. 髲 $\frac{190}{5}$ A wig.

3273. 轡 $\frac{159}{15}$ Reins.

3274. 匕 R 21 Ladle. Spoon.

PEK。

3275. 壁 32/13 A wall. (pik。)

PÉNG--See also ping.

3276. 餅 184/6 Cakes. Pastry.

  (a) pěng-kon 1760.
    Crackers. Biscuits.

PÈNG

3277. 柄 75/5 A handle. Power.

  (a) siù-pèng 3675.
    A laughing stock.

PÊNG

3278. 病 104/5 Sickness. Distress.

PIK

3279. 偪 9/9 To crowd, press upon,
3280. 逼 162/9 urge, oppress.

  (a) pik-shēk-teî 3879-4125. Causeway.

3281. 迫 162/5 To press upon,
3282. 廹 54/5 harass. (paak。)

3283. 碧 112/9 Greenish jade stone.

  (a) pik-yūk 5250.
    Jasper.

3284. 壁 32/13 (pek。)

PĪK

3285. 煏 86/9 To dry by fire. To burn, as pottery.

PIN

3286. 邊 162/15 Side. Bank. Edge.
3287. 边 162/2 Which? What? S.

  (a) fa-pin 650.
    A border.
  (b) pin-kwat 2083.
    A hem.

3288. 鞭 177/9 A whip. To flog, whip.
3289. 辮 120/14 The queue. To plait.
3290. 編 120/9 To twist, plait, braid. (p'in)

PÍN

3291. 扁 63/5 A tablet. Flat. Thin. S.
3292. 匾 23/9 A tablet.

PÌN

3293. 變 149/16 To change, alter,
3294. 变 29/6 transform. S.

PÎN

3295. 便 9/7 Convenient. Handy.
    A side. Place.

  (a) chîng-pîn 274.
    To make ready.
  (b) pîn-shaî 3814.
    Convenient.
  (c) siù-pîn 3674.
    To urinate.

(d) taai-pĭn 4033.
  To ease nature.
(e) pĭn-oŏ 3122.
  Chamber pot.

3296. 辨 160|9 To distinguish between.

3297. 辯 160|14 To discuss, argue.

(a) pĭn-hŏk 1140.
  Logic.
(b) pĭn-pok。 3355.
  To dispute.

3298. 拚 64|5 * To stand in danger of, risk.

3299. 采 R|165 " "

PING—See also peng.

3300. 兵 12|5 Soldier. Military.

(a) ping-tsut 4659.
  Soldiers.
(b) mǎ-ping 2561.
  Cavalry.
(c) pŏ-ping 3341.
  Infantry.
(d) ping-pŏ 3342.
  Board of War.

3301. 冰 15|4 * Frozen. Hard. Ice. Icy.

(a) ping-t'ŏng 4437.
  Candy.
(b) ping-shaan 3793.
  Iceberg.
(c) ping-t'ŏ 4384.
  Iceland.

3302. 咏 30|5 (wĭng)

3303. 冫 R|15 " " " Cold.

PING

3304. 炳 86|5 * Bright. To burn. Luminous.

3305. 丙 1|4 ' Third stem character.

3306. 屏 44|5 To remove, reject.

3307. 秉 115|3 ' To grasp, hold, perform.

3308. 餅 184|6 (péng)

PING

3309. 柄 75|5 Power. A handle.

3310. 开 51|3 * (péng)

3311. 並 1|6 * Two together. United.

3312. 并 51|5 * Moreover. S.

(a) ping-fei 749.
  By no means.
(b) ping-ch'ê 492.
  Moreover.

3313. 併 9|8 ' To compare, compete.

PING

3314. 病 104|5 ' See pêng.

PIT

3315. 必 61|1 ** Certainly. Must.

3316. 臂 148|9 ' Hornlike. Oozing out.

PIT。

3317. 鼈 205|11 ' Kind of turtle. Sea life. S.

PIT

3318. 別 18|5 Different. Other. Separation.

PIU

3319. 標 75 II A notice. Mark.
* To signal, make conspicuous.

3320. 票 113 6 A ticket. Document. Warrant. (p'iù)
*

3321. 鏢 167 II A watch. Timepiece.
*

3322. 彡 R 190 Bushy hair.
" "

PIÚ

3323. 表 145 3 To show forth. A watch. Gauge. Indicator.

(a) piú-chất 152.
   Sister's child.
(b) piú-hing 1070.
   Maternal cousin.
(c) shî-piú 3905, or shî-hak-piú 972.
   Time table.
(d) tîn-piú 4163.
   Voltmeter. Ammeter.
(e) fà-tîn-piú 651.
   Galvanometer.
(f) shuí-piú 4004.
   Water meter.

3324. 裱 145 8 To mount scrolls, repair.
*

(a) piú-ts'eûng-chí 4738-216. Wallpaper.

PIÚ

3325. 𩦡 158 II To push, crowd.
*

PO

3326. 煲 86 15 To boil, cook.

3327. 保 86 9 A pot. Kettle.
*

3328. 鮋 195 7 The ray or skate.
'

(a) wŏng-tím-po 5070-4151.
   Yellow spotted ray.

PÓ

3329. 保 9 7 To preserve, keep, secure against. S.

(a) pó-lǐng 2376.
   To furnish bail.
(b) pó-hím 1055.
   Insurance.
(c) pó-faì 691.
   Premium.
(d) pó-ka 1410.
   Bail.

3330. 補 145 7 To mend, patch, repair, benefit, fill up, amend. A billion.

(a) chik-pó 238.
   To darn.
(b) pó-waì 5003.
   An appendix.
(c) pó-huet。 1212.
   A tonic.

3331. 寶 40 17 A jewel.

3332. 宝 40 5 Precious.

(a) paāk-pó-shēk 3178-3879. Opal.
(b) hūng-pó-shēk 1235 Ruby.
(c) laām-pó-shēk 2167. Sapphire.

3333. 搗 196 4 Bustard. Cockold.
'

3334. 譜 149 13 (p'ó)
' 5

3335. 堡 32 9 Earthworks.
" "

PÒ

3336. 布 $\frac{50}{2}$ Cloth, linen or cotton. Plain silk. S.

(a) paāk-yeūng-pò 3178-5194. Plain calico.

(b) fa-pò 650. Figured chintz.

(c) yàn-fa-pò 5116. Printed calico.

(d) ka-sha-pò 1409-3782. Cambric.

(e) k'eī-pò 1953. Bunting.

(f) ts'o-pò 4775. Sheeting.

(g) yaū-pò 5149. Oil cloth.

(h) pò-cheūng 194. Awning.

(i) pò-fat 727. A swab.

(j) pò-luk-lìn 2503-2350. Brooklyn.

3337. 報 $\frac{32}{9}$ To reply, report, announce, recom-

3338. 报 $\frac{64}{4}$ pense. A letter. Gazette. Newspaper.

3339. 佈 $\frac{9}{5}$ To spread, extend, diffuse.

3340. 埔 $\frac{32}{7}$ Area. Plain. Port. Landing.

PÔ

3341. 步 $\frac{77}{3}$ To walk, step. S.

(a) chí-pô 217. To stop.

(b) shaang-pô 3802. A stranger.

(c) pô-t'aū 4339. A landing place.

3342. 部 $\frac{163}{8}$ A board. Committee. Class. C for books.

(a) pô-tsaí 4482. Pass books.

(b) tsź-pô 4672. The radicals.

3343. 簿 $\frac{118}{13}$ An account book. Register. (pó)

(a) cheūng-pô 192. An account book.

(b) shau-chī-pô 3857-207. Cash book.

3344. 菢 $\frac{140}{8}$ To brood, incubate, hatch.

3345. 暴 $\frac{72}{11}$ Violent. Cruel. Malicious. S.

3346. 捕 $\frac{64}{7}$ To seize, arrest.

POH

3347. 波 $\frac{85}{5}$ A wave. Ripple.

(a) tá-poh 4027. To play tennis or billiards

(b) poh-lōh-kwóh 2437-2097. Pineapple.

(c) poh-lōh-chau 160. Borneo.

(d) poh-sz 3763. Persia.

(e) poh-sź-tûn 3777-4268. Boston.

3348. 坡 $\frac{32}{5}$ Slope of a hill. Embankment.

3349. 玻 $\frac{96}{5}$ Glass. Crystal. Gem.

(a) poh-leī(leī) 2282. Glass.

(b) poh-leī-feī-à 2293-755-9. Bolivia.

3350. 菠 $\frac{140}{8}$ Greens. Spinach.

3351. 啵 $\frac{30}{8}$

PŌH

3352. 播 $\frac{30}{15}$ F—emphatic.

3353. 播 64/12 To sow abroad, publish, promulgate.

POK

3354. 剝 18/8 To skin, peel. (mok。)

POK。

3355. 駮 187/4 To dispute, argue. To join.

3356. 駁 187/6

(a) pok。-maai 2568. To tie or join together.

(b) pok。-shue 3996. To graft.

(c) pok。t'eng 4347. A ferry boat.

3357. 博 24/10 Well versed. Wise. Spacious. Extensive. S.

(a) pok。-sz 3777. Wise men.Philosophers.

(b) pok。-māt-hōk 2636-1140. Physics.

(c) pok。-māt-uén 4910. Museum.

(d) pok。-īn-hōk 1350-1140. Philology.

3358. 膊 130/10 The shoulder.

3359. 癶 30/14

3360. 堡 32/13 A dyke.

PŌK

3361. 薄 140/13 Thin. Poor. Spare. S.

(a) pōk-hōh 1121. Peppermint.

(b) pōk-hōh-ping 3301. Menthol.

3362. 泊 85/5 To moor, be at leisure.

3363. 雹 173/5 Hail.

3364. 鉑 167/5 Leaf metal.

3365. 箔 118/8 A screen of splints.

POM

3366. 椌 75/15 Sound of a cannon.

PONG

3367. 幫 50/14 To help,assist, aid. A class.

3368. 幇 50/9 Fleet. Heap. Pile.

3369. 帮 50/7

3370. 邦 163/4 A state. Kingdom. Country.S.

3371. 鎊 167/7 A broad hoe. Mattock.

3372. 梆 75/7 Watchman's drum or gong. A rail.

PÓNG

3373. 綁 120/7 To bind, tie.

PÒNG

3374. 磅 112/10 A pound. To weigh. (p'ōng)

POOI

3375. 杯 75/4 Drinking vessel. Cup. Tumbler.

3376. 盃 108/4

POOI

3377. 背 130/5 The back. Spine.
To repudiate.
  (a) pooì-tsek。 4511.
    The back.
  (b) pooì-kaaù 1507.
    To apostatize.

3378. 悖 61/7 To rebel
against.
Perverse. S.
  (a) pooì-yīk 5214.
    To revolt.

3379. 輩 159/8 A class. Sort.
*

3380. 輩 159/5 Generation.
*
  (a) paan-pool 3182.
    Colleagues.

3381. 貝 R/154 Precious.
*   Pearl. S.

POOĬ

3382. 焙 86/8 To warm or dry
*   by fire.

3383. 嶅 30/12 Retired. Secret.
*

POON

3384. 搬 64/10 To move, remove.

3385. 攀 64/10 To transport.
  (a) poon-lûng 2544.
    To make mischief.

3386. 般 137/4 A sort. A kind.
*   Manner. Way.
  (a) poon-t'ó 4384.
    Borneo.

3387. 鐇 167/12
" '

POÓN

3388. 本 75/1 The source. Native. Capital.
C for books,

documents, etc.
  (a) shīt-poon 3962.
    To lose in trade.
  (b) poón-hóng 1186.
    This (my) shop.

POÒN

3389. 半 24/5 A half.
  (a) poòn-yê 5176.
    Midnight.
  (b) poòn-pin-ust 3286-
    4937. Half moon.

POÔN

3390. 伴 9/5 A comrade. Associate. To attend
on.

3391. 叛 29/7 To revolt,
*   rebel.

3392. 絆 120/5 To tie, lasso.
'

POOT。

3393. 砵 112/5 A cylinder.
  (a) laû-poot. 2262.
    A funnel.

3394. 鉢 167/5 An almsbowl,
*   Utensil.

POOT

3395. 撥 64/12 To spread,
*   scatter.(p'oot)

3396. 鈸 167/5 Cymbal. Bell.
*

3397. 癶 R/105 To push aside.
" '

POP

3398. 蹼 157/12 (pūk)
*

(a) pŏp-pŏp-t'iù 4371.
To palpitate.

3399. 㗒 㗒 㗒 30/11 Rapping or pop-ping sound.

PUK

3400. 卜 R 25 To foretell. Divination. S.

(a) chim-puk 247.
To cast lots.

3401. 卟 30/2 To snap.

PŪK

3402. 僕 9/12 Servant. Domestic.

3403. 噗 30/14 To fall prostrate.

3404. 踣 157/14 To fall prostrate,

3405. 蹼 157/12 make obeisance. (3405 pŏp)

3406. 瀑 85/15 A waterfall. Cascade. (pô)

PÚNG

3407. 捧 64/8 To hold in both hands. To pre-sent. (fúng)

PÛNG

3408. 膖 182/8 Exhalation. Stench.

P'A

3409. 𧿹 157/4 To squat,crouch, grovel.

P'À

3410. 怕 61/5 To fear, dread. Lest. Probably. S.

(a) p'à-ch'aú 473. Bash-ful. Ashamed.

3411. 帕 50/5 Veil. Handkerchief.

P'Ā

3412. 爬 87/4 To climb, crawl, scrape,scratch, rake. S.

(a) ĭ-p'ā 1280.
Earpick.

(b) hâ-p'ā-so 908-3678.
A beard.

(c) ngaū-yŭk-p'ā 3039-5249. Beefsteak.

3413. 扒 64/2 To climb, catch, hold, paddle.

3414. 耙 127/4 A rake. Harrow.

(a) teng-p'ā 4127.
An iron rake.

3415. 笆 118/7 A bamboo rake.

3416. 琶 96/8 A kind of guitar.

P'AAI

3417. 啡 30/11 To brag.

P'AAÌ

3418. 派 85/6 Branch. Tribe. Sect. To dis-tribute.

P'AAĪ

3419. 排 64/8 To arrange. A rank. Set.

(a) p'aaī-lĭt 2384.
To assort.

(b) p'aaī-kwat 2083.
Ribs. Chops.

(c) yat-p'aaī 5133.
Once.

3420. 牌 91/8 Sign. Notice. Tablet. Card.
- (a) p'aaī-fong 782. A monument.
- (b) ngā-p'aaī 2977. Dominoes.
- (c) chí-p'aaī 216. Pack of cards.
- (d) sóh-p'aaī 3691. Hasp of a lock.

3421. * 桴 75/8 A raft.

3422. 籤 118/11

P'AAK₀

3423. 拍 64/5 To strike, rap, touch.
- (a) p'aak₀-maaī 2568. Together. Side by side.
- (b) p'aak₀-shaú 3859. To clap.
- (c) p'aak₀-paán 3187. Castanets.
- (d) p'aak₀-p'aak₀-hǎ 907. Flapping.

3424. * 魄 194/5 Animal soul.

3425. ' 珀 96/5 Amber. (paak₀)

P'AAN

3426. * 攀 64/15 To pull, drag, climb, implicate.
3427. * 扳 64/14

3428. ' 眅 109/4 Film on the eye.

P'AÀN

3429. ' 襻 145/19 Sash. Band. Loop.

3430. ' 盼 109/4 To regard, long for.

P'AĀNG

3431. 棚 75/8 Scaffolding. Shed. Matshed.

3432. * 蟛 142/12
- (a) p'aāng-k'eī 1959. Small land crab.

3433. ' 膨 130/12 Swollen. Flatulent.

3434. ' 彭 59/9 Strong. S.

P'AǍNG

3435. * 棒 75/8 Staff. Cudgel. To strike.

P'AAU

3436. * 抛 64/4 To throw down, reject.
- (a) p'aau-naaū 2840. To cast anchor.

P'AAÚ

3437. * 跑 157/5 To gallop, run, race.

P'AAÙ

3438. 炮 86/5 To roast or bake.
3439. 砲 112/5 Sound of firing a gun.
3440. 礮 112/16 Cannon. Bomb. Blast.
3441. 爆 86/15 Fireworks. (3441 paaù)
- (a) hoi-p'aaù 1124. To fire a gun.
- (b) hoi-fa-p'aaù 650. A bomb.
- (c) fa-p'aaù 650. Fireworks.
- (d) p'aaù-tseùng 4530. Firecrackers.

(e) p'aaù-t'aū 4339.
  A rocket.
(f) fóh-p'aaù 767.
  Firearms.
(g) p'aaù-I 1280.
  Trunnions.
(h) kei-p'aaù 1601.
  Machine gun.
(i) p'aaù-mǎ 2564.
  Shot.
(j) p'aaù-t'oī 4418.
  A fort.

3442. 泡 85/5 Bubbles. Froth.
  Blister. To
  soak. (p'ò)

3443. 豹 153/3 Leopard.
  (paaù)

P'AAŪ

3444. 刨 18/5 To smooth,
  plane.

3445. 鉋 167/5 A plane.
  (a) p'aaū-fa 650.
  Hair gum.

3445½. 咆 30/5
  To roar,
  howl.
  Furious

P'AI

3446. 批 64/4 To criticize,
  lease, plaster.
  (a) p'ai-p'Ing 3498.
  To review.

P'ÀN

3447. 噴 30/13 To breathe out,
  spout out.
  (a) p'àn-heī 1033.
  To aspirate.

3448. 濆 85/13 To spurt water,
  bubble up.

P'ĀN

3449. 貧 154/4 Poor.
  Impoverished.

(a) p'ăn-k'ŭng 2031.
  Indigent. Poor.

3450. 頻 181/7 To hurry, bustle.
  Incessant.

P'ĂN

3451. 牝 93/2 Female of birds
  and beasts.

3452. 笨 118/5 Thick.
  (pân)

P'ĀNG

3453. 朋 74/4 Friends.
  Companions.
  (a) p'āng-yaū 5160.
  Friends.

3454. 憑 61/12 To lean on,
  trust in.
  (a) p'āng-kuī 1855.
  Proof. Evidence.

3455. 硼 112/8
  (a) p'āng-sha 3779.
  Borax.

3456. 鵬 196/8 Monster bird.
  Roc.

P'AT

3457. 匹 23/2 A pair. A match.
  A mate. C for
  horses, etc.
  uf 3458.
  (a) leŭng-p'at-so 2321-3678.
  A beard.

3458. 疋 R/103 A bolt or piece
  of cloth. C for
  pieces or rolls
  of cloth goods.
  Pair. A mate.
  uf 3457.

3459. 剖 $\frac{18}{8}$ To split asunder. To decide between.
*

P'AÛ

3460. 吥 $\frac{30}{4}$ Spongy. (paû)
*

P'Ě

3461. 啤 $\frac{30}{8}$ To stagger. (pe)
"

P'EI

3462. 披 $\frac{64}{5}$ Spread out. Surface. A cover.
*

3463. 劂 $\frac{18}{5}$ To peel, pare, trim.
'

P'EÍ

3464. 鄙 $\frac{163}{11}$ Low. Mean. Base. Rustic.
'

3465. 痞 $\frac{104}{7}$ Stricture. Costiveness.
'

P'EǏ

3466. 譬 $\frac{149}{13}$ To compare. A simile. Illustration.
*

(a) p'ei-uê 4897.
      A parable.

3467. 屁 $\frac{44}{4}$
'

(a) p'ei-koó 1798.
      The buttocks.
(b) fòng-p'ei 795. To break wind, talk rot.

P'EÌ

3468. 皮 $\frac{R}{107}$ Skin. Leather. Fur. S.

(a) shue-p'eī 3982.
      Book cover.

3469. 疲 $\frac{104}{5}$ Lassitude. Fatigue.
'

3470. 脾 $\frac{130}{8}$ Spleen. Temper.
'

3471. 琵 $\frac{96}{8}$ Kind of guitar.
'

(a) p'eī-p'ā 3416.
      Guitar.
(b) p'eī-p'ā-t'úng 4454.
      A cask.
(c) p'eī-p'ā-sha 3778.
      The ray.

3472. 秕 $\frac{119}{4}$ Blasted grain.
'

(a) p'eī-hong 1175.
      Chaff.

P'EǏ

3473. 被 $\frac{145}{5}$ Bedding. Quilt. Coverlet. (peī)
*

(a) p'ei-taan 4046.
      A sheet.

3474. 婢 $\frac{38}{8}$ Maid servant. Female slave.
*

P'EK.—See also p'ik.

3475. 擗 $\frac{64}{13}$ | To throw, as
*

3476. 撈 $\frac{64}{15}$ | stones, break
* | open.

3477. 劈 $\frac{18}{13}$ To split, rive.
*

P'ENG

3478. 抨 $\frac{64}{5}$ To mend, match, sew. (p'ing)
*

P'ĒNG

3479. 平 $\frac{51}{2}$ Cheap. (p'īng)

P'ENG

3480. 瓶 98|8 Pitcher. Jar.
*
3481. 餅 121|8 Jug, Vase.
* (p'éng)
  (a) fa-p'ēng 650.
       A vase.

P'IK。

3482. 僻 9|13 Quiet. Secluded.
* One sided.
3483. 闢 169|13 To burst forth,
* open up.
  (a) hoi-p'ik 1124.
       The creation.
3484. 劈 18|13 (p'ek。)
*
3485. 擗 64|13 (p'ek。)
*
3486. 辟 160|6 To punish.
' Sovereign.

P'IN

3487. 偏 9|9 Leaning toward.
* Partiality.
  Bias. S.
  (a) p'in-kìn 1663.
       Prejudice.
3488. 篇 118|9 Chapter. Book.
* Leaf of a book.
  C.S.
3489. 編 120|9 (pin, p'ìn)

P'IN

3490. 騙 187|9 To cheat, swin-
* dle, defraud.
3491. 片 R|91 A slice. Strip.
* Piece.
3492. 遍 162|9 Everywhere.
* All.
3493. 徧 60|9 Whole.
* Once.
3494. 抨 64|5 To gauge the
' weights, put
  together.(p'ēng)

P'ING

3495. 聘 128|7 To betroth. Be-
* trothal present.
3496. 娉 38|7 uf 3495.
*

P'ĪNG

3497. 平 51|2 Even. Level.
* Tranquil. S.
  (a) p'ìng-on 3107.
       Peace.
  (b) p'ìng-kwóh 2097.
       The apple.
3498. 評 149|5 To discuss,
' criticize. S.
3499. 抨 64|11 To set at
' rights. Crash-
  ing sound.(ping)
3500. 屏 44|8 A screen.
' Cover. (píng)
3501. 瓶 98|8 See p'ēng.
'

P'IT。

3502. 丿 R|4
"!
3503. 撆 64|12 To wipe off,
' skim.

P'IU

3504. 飄 182|11 To be blown
* about, rocked,
  tossed.
3505. 漂 85|11 To float, drift,
* toss about.
  (p'iù)
3506. 螵 142|11 A chrysalis.
' (piu)

P'IŪ

3507. 漂 85|11 To bleach.
* (p'iu)

3508. 票 113/6 A warrant. Ticket. (piu)

P'IŪ

3509. 瓢 97/11 Calabash. Gourd. Ladle.

3510. 嫖 38/11 Trifling. Wanton. Lewd.

P'O

3511. 鋪 167/7 To spread out, arrange. C.

P'Ó

3512. 普 72/8 Universal. Great.
  (a) p'o-ò-kwok。 3087-2103. Austro-Hungary.
3513. 譜 149/13 A chronicle. Register. List.
  (a) tsūk-p'ó 4638. A clan register.
  (b) mō-p'ó 2711. No truth. At random.

P'Ò

3514. 舖 135/7 } A shop.
3515. 鋪 167/7 } Store. (p'o)

3516. 甫 101/2 A league distance. 10 leÏ. (foó, pó)

P'Ō

3517. 菩 140/8
  (a) p'ō-saat。 3582. An idol. Darling.
  (b) p'ō-t'aI-tsź 4321-4667. Grapes.

3518. 葡 140/9 The vine.
  (a) p'ō-t'ō 4394. Grapes.
  (b) p'ō-t'ō-ngā 2977. Portugal.
3519. 蒲 140/10 Coarse rushes.
  (a) p'ō-k'iū 1990. Duckweed.
3520. 袍 145/5 Long outer robe.

P'Ŏ

3521. 抱 64/5 To embrace, carry in arms, cherish.
3522. 泡 85/5 A bubble.
3523. 疱 85/5 Blister. Froth. (p'aaù)
3523½. 哃 30/8
  (a) shui-p'ŏ-(mIn) 4004-(2678) A sponge.
3524. 鮄 195/5 River porpoise. Torpedo.

P'OH

3525. 盒 75/11 The trunk of a tree. C for trees, shrubs, etc.

P'ÓH

3526. 頗 181/5 Leaning toward. Rather.

P'ÒH

3527. 破 112/5 To break, break through, ruin, destroy.
  (a) p'òh-shuên 3999. Shipwreck.

P'ŌH

3528. 婆 38/8 An old woman. Mother. Dame.

P'OK。

3529. 撲 64/12 To strike down.

  (a) p'ok。-mīt 2701. To extinguish.

3530. 樸 75/12 Rough. Plain. Sincere.

3531. 扑 64/2 To tap, beat, shake.

3532. 朴 75/2

  (a) p'ok。-siu 3669. Epsom salts.

3533. 攴 R/66 To cane.

P'ŌNG

3534. 謗 149/10 To vilify, slander.

P'ŎNG

3535. 旁 70/6 At the side. Near.

  (a) p'ŏng-yān 5117. Bystander.

3536. 傍 9/10 At the side. Near. S.

3537. 磅 157/10 To hurry, rush.

3538. 徬 60/10 Agitated. Fearful.

3539. 膀 130/10 Groin. Loins.

3540. 磅 112/10 Scales. To weigh. (pông)

P'OOI

3541. 坏 32/4 Unburnt brick. (fau)

3542. 胚 130/4 Embryo. Fat.

P'OOÌ

3543. 配 164/3 To pair, mate. A mate.

  (a) p'at-p'ooì 3457. To marry.

3544. 佩 9/6 Pendant. Girdle appendage.

3545. 旆 70/6 Pennon. Pennant.

P'OOĪ

3546. 賠 154/8 To compensate, indemnify.

3547. 培 32/8 To heap up, increase.

3548. 陪 170/8 To bear one company, assist.

  (a) p'ooī-shám-chi-yān 3826-204-5117. Jury.

P'OOǏ

3549. 倍 9/8 To increase. Times.

  (a) paak。-p'ooǐ 3170. A hundred fold.

P'OÒN

3550. 判 18/5 To divide, judge.

3551. 拌 64/5 To reject, separate.

  (a) p'oòn-haì 968. So be it.

  (b) p'oòn-kung 1877. To contract for work.

P'OŌN

3552. 般 108/10 A tray. Vessel. To examine.

(a) p'oŏn-faì 691.
Traveling expenses.
(b) p'oŏn-màn 2629.
To interrogate.
(c) yíng-p'oŏn 5235.
A camp.
(d) haau-kwat-p'oŏn 956-
2083. The pelvis.

3553. 盆 108/4 A bowl. Basin.
* Tub. S.

3554. 磐 112/10 Firm as a rock.
* Stable.
(a) p'oŏn-shĕk 3879.
Solid rock.

3555. 蟠 142/12 To coil up.
'

3556. 槃 75/10 To rejoice.
' uf 3552.

P'OOT。

3557. 撥 64/12 To shake, lift
* up, push aside,
remove. (poŏt)

3558. 潑 85/12 To scatter,
* throw out,
sprinkle.

P'ŌP

3559. 皰 30/8 Roaring sound.
"

P'UK

3560. 仆 9/2 To capsize, fall
* prostrate.

P'UNG

3561. 塳 32/11 Smarting of the
* eyes.

P'ŪNG

3562. 揰 64/9 To collide with,
* meet unexpected-
3563. 碰 112/9 ly. To knock,
* bump, bang.

P'ŪNG

3564. 篷 118/11 Sail. Awning.
* Matshed.

SA

3565. 卅 24/2 Thirty. Abbrevi-
" ation for sam-
shăp.

3566. 繅 120/14 Disorder. Con-
" fused mass.

SAAI

3567. 摋 64/11 To waste.
*
3568. 瀡 85/11
*
3569. 嗺 30/11
*

SAAÍ

3570. 徙 60/8 To change resi-
. dence, remove,
move.

SAAÌ

3571. 嗮 30/11 All. Entire.
" Completely.
(saai)

SAAM

3572. 三 1/2 The numeral 3:
** common, compli-
3573. 叁 28/6 cated and run-
3574. 川 2/2 ning hand forms.
S.
(a) saam-ch'a 401.
A trident.
(b) saam-chek。-shaú 175-
3859. A thief.
(c) saam-sìn-hŏk 3646-
1140. Trigonometry.

(d) saam-shui 4004.
Samshui.

SAÁN

3575. 散 66/8 Broken up. Mis-
* cellaneous. S.
(saàn)

SAÀN

3576. 散 66/8 To scatter, dis-
, perse, dissolve.
(saán)

3577. 傘 9/10 A canopy. Cover.
, Umbrella.

SAAP。

3578. 擸 64/13 Rubbish.
*

3579. 匝 22/3 A revolution.
, Pleasing the
eye.

3580. 颯 182/5 Stormy.
, Sudden.

SAAT。

3581. 撒 64/12 To sow(seed),
, scatter, spill.S.
(a) saat。-hap-la 997-2145.
Sahara.

3582. 薩 140/13 S.
* See 3517a.

3583. 唦 30/15
" 撒
(a) saat。-t'ó-koi-yăn
4383-1738-5117. Sad-
ducees.

SAI

3584. 西 R/146 West. Occiden-
, tal. Foreign. S.
(a) sai-naăm 2823.
Southwest.

(b) sai-pak 3215.
Northwest.

(c) sai-paan-ngā 3182-
2977. Spain.

(d) sai-paak。-leī-à 3172-
2293-9. Siberia.

(e) sai-tsông 4620.
Tibet.

(f) sai-yān-tô 5116-4208.
West Indies.

(g) sai-leī-paak。 2293-
3172. Celebes.

(h) sai-yeūng-yăn 5194-
5117. Portuguese.

3585. 荽 140/7
*
(a) uěn-sai 4925.
Coriander.

(b) tséng-taī-sai 4515-
4071. Ferns.

3586. 犀 93/7
*
(a) sai-ngaū 3039.
Rhinoceros.

(b) sai-kok。 1744.
Rhinoceros horn.

(c) mō-sai 2712.
The yak.

SAÍ

3587. 洗 85/6 } To wash,

3588. 洒 85/6 } cleanse.

(a) saí-laī 2205. Baptism
(not immersion).

(b) saí-p'aaī 3420.
To shuffle cards.

SAÌ

3589. 細 120/5 Small. Fine.
Delicate.

(a) aì-saì 34.
Small of body.

(b) saì-sam 3593.
Heedful. Careful.

3590. 壻 33/9 | Son in law.

3591. 婿 38/9

SAK

3592. 塞 32/10 To block up, stop up, cork.

(a) hoi-maaŭ-sak 1124-2595. To remove the obstructing rushes, i.e. to enlighten the mind.

SAM

3593. 心 R 61 The heart. Center. Mind. Affections.
 **

(a) siú-sam 3674. Careful. Be careful.

(b) sam-kei 1601. Thoughtful.

(c) sam-chŏng 309, or sam-míng 2690. Sane.

(d) t'ung-sam 4452. Tubular.

(e) sam-líng-hŏk 2361-1140. Psychology.

SÁM

3594. 滲 85/11 To scatter, sprinkle.(shàm)
 *

SÂM

3595. 吣 30/7 Disagreeable. Bad.
 "

SAN

3596. 新 69/9 New. Fresh. Recently.

(a) san-sin 3641. New. Fresh.

(b) san-neŭng 2880. A bride.

(c) san-mān-chí 2617-216. Newspaper.

(d) san-ka-poh 1413-3347. Singapore.

(e) san-faŭ 745. Penang.

(f) san-kei-noï-à 1610-2937-9. New Guinea.

3597. 辛 R 160 Bitter. Hard. Toilsome. S.

3598. 薪 140/13 Fuel.
 '

(a) san-shuí 4004. Fuel and water, i.e., salary.

SANG

3599. 僧 9/12 Buddhist priest.

SÀNG

3600. 擤 64/14 To blow the nose, with the fingers.
 *

SAP

3601. 呷 30/5 To suck. Crumbs.
 *

SAT

3602. 膝 130/11 The knee.
 *

SAU

3603. 修 9/8 To repair, improve, adorn. S.
 *

3604. 羞 123/5 To put to shame, feel ashamed.
 *

3605. 脩 130／7 Dried meat.
 *
  (a) sau-kam 1527.
    Salary.
3606. 饈 184／11 Choice food.
 '   Delicacies.

SAÚ

3607. 搜 64／10 To seek, search
 '   out.

SAÙ

3608. 銹 167／7 ｜ Rust. Corrosion.
3609. 鏽 167／12 ｜ To rust.
  (a) t'ŭng-saù 4462.
    Verdigris.
3610. 秀 115／2 Plentiful. Lux-
 *   uriant. Accom-
    plished. S.
3611. 綉 120／7 ｜ Embroidered.
3612. 繡 120／12 ｜ Adorned.
 *   Variegated.
3613. 嗽 30／11 To cough.
 '
3614. 漱 85／11 To rinse the
 '   mouth, gargle.

SE

3615. 些 7／5 A few. Little.
 *   Some.
  (a) se-siú 3674.
    Trifling.

SÉ

3616. 寫 40／12 To write,
 *   sketch.
  (a) sé-tsź 4672.
    To write. A clerk.
  (b) sé-chan 136. To por-
    tray, photograph.

SÈ

3617. 瀉 85／15 To leak, purge.
 *   Dysentery.
  (a) shuí-sè 4004.
    Diarrhoea.
  (b) sè-yaû 5149.
    Castor oil.
3618. 卸 26／6 To lay aside,
 '   unload, deliver,
    retire.
  (a) sè-yâm 5105. To
    retire from office.

SEK₀-See also sik.

3619. 錫 167／8 Tin. Pewter.
 *   solder. S.
  (a) lïn-sek₀ 2350.
    Block tin.
  (b) sek₀-kam 1527.
    Pewter.
  (c) sek₀-pŏk 3364.
    Tin foil.
  (d) sek₀-laān 2182.
    Ceylon.

SENG—See also sing.

3620. 腥 130／9 Rank odor.
 '   Strong smell.

SÉNG

3621. 惺 61／9 ｜ To awake,
3622 醒 164／9 ｜ rouse up.
    (síng)

SEU

3623. 嘯 30／14 Sound of
 "   rustling.

SEUK₀

3624. 削 18／7 To cut, cut off,
 *   scrape.

SEUNG

3625. 相 109/4 Together. Mutual. Reciprocal. (seùng)

3626. 箱 118/9 A box. Chest. Case.

3627.* 霜 173/9 Hoar frost. Frost. Frostlike. Sublime. S.

3628.' 鑲 167/17 To inchase, inlay, glaze window.

3629.' 孀 38/17 A widow. To live alone.

3630.' 礵 112/17 uf 3627.

SEÚNG

3631. 想 61/9 To think, reflect, hope, desire, expect.

SEÙNG

3632. 相 109/4 Likeness. Form.

SIK—See also sek.

3633. 息 61/6 To rest. Quiet. Interest on money. Earnings. S.
(a) siu-sik 3667. News.

3634.' 熄 86/10 To put out, extinguish.

3635. 昔 72/4 Ancient. Formerly. S.

3636.' 惜 61/8 To pity, feel for, regard.
(a) hóh-sik 1117. How sad! Regretable.

3637.* 媳 38/10 Daughter in law.

SIK。

3638. 錫 167/8 See sek。

SIN

3639. 先 10/4 First. Before. Ahead. S.
(a) sin-t'aū 4339. Previously.
(b) sin-chi 205. A prophet.

3640.* 仙 9 Fairies. Geneii. S.

3641.' 鮮 135/6 Fresh. New. Newly slaughtered. S. (sin)

SÍN

3642.' 癬 104/17 Ringworm. Scabby eruption. S.

3643.' 蘚 140/17 Mosses.

3644.' 鮮 195/6 Exhausted. Few. (sin)

SIN

3645.' 先 10/4 To precede. (sin)

3646.' 線 120/9 A thread. Wire.

3647.' 綫 120/8 Clue. Line, (math.)
(a) sin-kung 1878. Informer.

3648.* 鏾 167/12 To castrate a fowl.

3649.' 剸 18/4

3650.' 霰 173/12 Sleet.

SÎN

3651.' 羨 123/7 To desire, long for, admire. S.

SING

3652. 星 72/5 A star. Planet. Point of light. S.
  (a) sing-suk 3736.
      Constellation.
  (b) sing-hei 1033.
      Nebula.
  (c) sò-pá-sing 3684-3161.
      Comet.
  (d) sing-kà-poh 1424-3347.
      Singapore.

3653. 猩 94/9 Large ape. Ourang-outang.
3654. 腥 130/9 See seng.

SÍNG

3655. 省 109/4 To examine, in- vestigate, arouse. (shaáng)
3656. 醒 164/9 See séng.

SÌNG

3657. 姓 38/5 A clan. Surname. S.
3658. 性 61/5 Nature. Disposition. S.
  (a) sìng-hŏk 1140. Mental philosophy.

SIP。

3659. 楔 11/14 To wedge, shim up.

SIT。

3660. 竊 116/17 To steal, pilfer.
3661. 竊 116/4 Privately. Secretly.
3662. 褻 145/11 Irreverent. Impure. Dirty.

(a) sit-tŭk 4261.
    To blaspheme.
3663. 絏 120/6 To fetter. Fetters.
3664. 屑 44/7 Fragment. Trifling.
3665. 洩 85/6 To diminish. To ooze, leak.
3666. 泄 85/5

SIU

3667. 消 85/7 To scatter, disperse.
  (a) siu-yūng 5270.
      To melt.
3668. 銷 167/7 To fuse, dis- solve. Sale. Circulation. S.
  (a) siu-hô 1109.
      To rescind, cancel.
3669. 硝 112/7 Nitre. Saltpetre.
  (a) haām-siu 926.
      Nitre.
  (b) siu-p'eì 3468.
      To tan leather.
3670. 逍 162/7 To ramble, saun- ter, roam.
3671. 簫 118/12 Flute.
3672. 蕭 140/12 Kind of artemisia. S.
3673. 宵 40/7 Dark. Night.

SIÚ

3674. 小 R42 Small. Tiny. Petty.
  (a) siú-taì 4077.
      My humble self.
  (b) siú-shaú 3859.
      A pilferer.
  (c) siú-yăn 5121.
      Preface.

(d) siú-māk 2607.
  Rye.
(e) uĕt-siú 4937.
  29 day month.
(f) siú-luī-sùng 2489-
  3751. Philippines.

___

SIÙ

3675. 笑 118/4 To laugh, smile, laugh at, deride.

(a) siù-wâ 4960.
  Joking.

3676. 嘯 30/12 To whistle.

___

SO

3677. 蘇 140/16 To revive. Cheerful. S.

(a) so-tsaí 4482. Young child. Infant.
(b) so-mūk 2795. Sapan wood.
(c) tsź-so 4670. Sweet basil.
(d) so-kat₀-laān 1833-2182. Scotland.
(e) so-moōn-taap₀-la 2779-4061-2145. Sumatra.
(f) so-chau 159. Soochow.
(g) so-sź 3777. Suez.

3678. 鬚 190/12 Beard. Mustache.

(a) leûng-t'iū-so 2321-4375. Antennae.

3679. 酥 164/5 Crisp. Curd.

3680. 臊 130/13 Rank. Rancid. Stinking.

3681. 穌 115/11 To revive.

3682. 騷 187/10 Trouble. Sad.

___

SÓ

3683. 嫂 38/10 Elder brother's wife. Matron.

___

SÒ

3684. 掃 64/8 To sweep.
3685. 掃 32/8 A broom.

(a) sò-pá 3161 A broom.
(b) kai-mō-sò 1515-2712. Feather duster.

3686. 訴 149/5 To state, inform. A plaint. Plea.

(a) toí-sò 4222. An advocate.

3687. 素 120/4 Commonly. Formerly. Plain. Simple. S.

___

SŌ

3688. 穌 30/16 Ignorant.

___

SOH

3689. 唆 30/7 To incite, stir up.
3690. 梭 75/7 Shuttle. Shuttle like. Swift.

___

SÓH

3691. 鎖 167/10 Lock. Fetters.
3692. 鏁 167/11 To lock.

(a) kwaí-sóh 2061. A latch.
(b) hōh-paau-sóh 1121-3198. A padlock.
(c) t'aap₀-sóh 4307. Foreign padlock.

(d) sóh-shī 3906.
A key.

3693. 瑣 96 Fragments. Min-
' 10 ute. Vexatious.

SOI

3694. 顋 181 9 ⎱ Cheeks.
3695. 腮 130 9 ⎰ Jowl. Jaw.

(a) soi-kaap。 1489.
The cheeks.

3696. 鰓 195 9 Gills of a fish.

SOK。

3697. 索 120 To exact,
* 4 search. A knot.

SONG

3698. 喪 30 Mourning. To la-
' 9 ment. A funeral.
S.

3699. 桑 75 Mulberry tree.
' 6 S.

SÓNG

3700. 嗓 30 The throat.
' 10

(a) sóng-shīk 3925.
The glottis.
(b) hei-sóng 1033.
The larynx.
(c) kwóng-sóng 2107. Can-
tonese dialect.

SÒNG

3701. 喪 30 To lose,
* 9 degrade.

SUEN

3702. 酸 164 Sour. Acid.
' 7

(a) suen-ts'ò 4779.
Vinegar.

3703. 宣 40 To proclaim,
* 6 publish. S.

(a) suen-tò-oot 4207-3143.
Christian and Mis-
sionary Alliance.

3704. 孫 39 Grandson. Des-
* 7 cendants. S.

3705. 痠 104 Aching.
' 7 Painful.

(a) suen-uèn 4930.
Ticklish.

SÚEN

3706. 選 162 To choose, se-
' 12 lect. (suèn)

3707. 損 64 To wound, injure,
' 10 spoil.

SÙEN

3708. 筭 118 8 ⎱ To regard as.
3709. 算 118 8 ⎰ To reckon, calculate.

(a) suèn-faat。 682.
Arithmetic.
(b) suèn-p'oōn 3552.
Abacus.
(c) suèn-mēng 2671.
Fortune telling.

3710. 蒜 140 Garlic.
' 10

SÛEN

3711. 旋 70 To revolve,
' 7 Whirlwind. Dizzy.

SÛEN

3712. 鐫 167 To carve,
' 13 out in stone.

3713. 篆 118 Antique form
' 9 of writing.

SUET₀

3714. 雪 173/3 Snow. Ice.
To avenge. S.
(a) suet₀-ko 1716.
    Ice cream.
(b) suet₀-mō 2726.
    A hood.

SUI

3715. 雖 172/9 Although. Even
if. Supposing.
3716. 需 173/6 Needful. To
need. Supplies.
S.
3717. 須 181/3 Ought.
Necessary.
3718. 胥 130/5 Together. All.
3719. 繻 120/14 Frayed.

SUI

3720. 髓 188/13 Marrow.
(suī)

SUĬ

3721. 碎 112/8 To grind. Fragments. Bits.
Petty.
3722. 歲 77/9 Years.
3723. 崴 46/9 Age. Old.
3724. 粹 119/8 Pure. Unmixed.
3725. 嗉 30/10 Crop or gizzard
of birds.

SUÍ

3726. 緒 120/9 Clue. Thread.

3727. 嶼 46/14 Small island.

3728. 絮 120/6 Cotton. Wool.
Floss.
3729. 髓 188/13 Marrow.
(suī)

SUÍ

3730. 穗 115/12 Ears of grain.
3731. 繸 120/13 A tassel.
3732. 鐩 167/12 A lens.
3733. 遂 162/9 In accord with.
To comply with.
3734. 瑞 96/9 Auspicious.
(a) suī-tín 4162.
    Sweden.
(b) suī-sź 3777.
    Switzerland.
3735. 祟 113/5 Evil spirits.

SUK

3736. 宿 40/8 To lodge. Kept
over night. A
lodge. Stale. S.
(a) suk-sik 3635.
    Formerly.
3737. 粟 119/6 Rice in husks.
S.
(a) suk-maī 2603.
    Corn. Maize.
(b) aang-suk 22.
    Poppy.
(c) aang-suk-tsź 4667.
    White poppy.
3738. 肅 129/8 Respectful
Severe.

SUN

3739. 郇 163/6 S.

-191-

SÚN

3740. 笋 118/4 Bamboo sprouts.

3741. 筍 118/6 Cane sprouts. Tenon.

3742. 榫 75/10 To dovetail, fit into.
 (a) tau-sún 4112.
  To dovetail.
 (b) sún-ngaán 2999.
  To mortise.
 (c) sún-t'aū 4339.
  A tenon.

SÙN

3743. 信 9/7 To believe. Sincerity. Faith. A letter. S.
 (a) sùn-tak 4082.
  Faith. Fidelity.
 (b) sùn-shāt 3854.
  Authentic. True.
 (c) sùn-shēk 3879.
  Arsenic.
 (d) sùn-tsz 4663.
  Postage.

3744. 遜 162/10 Humble. Respectful. Modest.

3745. 囟 31/3 Top of the head.
 (a) sùn-moōn 2779.
  The fontanel.

3746. 汛 85/3 A league. To sprinkle, guard.

3747. 迅 162/3 Quick. Swift.

SUNG

3748. 鬆 190/8 Loose. Slack. To let go.

SÚNG

3749. 慫 128/11 To urge on, incite to.

SÙNG

3750. 送 162/6 To give to, escort, send.

3751. 宋 40/4 S.

SUT

3752. 恤 61/6 Compassionate.

3753. 卹 26/6 To feel for, pity. S.
 (a) sut-koo-uén 1787-4910.
  Orphanage.

3754. 榫 75/11 A bolt. Fastener. Piston.

3755. 率 95/6 To lead, command. In general. All. S.

SZ

3756. 司 30/2 To control, preside over. Overseer. A bureau. S.

3757. 師 50/7 Leader. Model. Teacher. S.

3758. 私 115/2 Private. Partial.
 (a) sz-ka 1410.
  Private.
 (b) sz-tsz 4673.
  Clandestinely.
 (c) sz-ts'uí 4824.
  To embezzle.
 (d) sz-t'ung 4452.
  Illicit intercourse.

3759. 思 61/5 To think, reflect, consider. S. (sz)
 (a) naú-sz-laān 2869-2182.
  New Zealand.

3760. 獅 94/10 The lion.

3761. 絲 120/6 Silk. Fine thread. Wire.

(a) sz-tuên 4245.
    Satin.

3762. 嘶 30 Hiccough. Din.
    12 Chatter.

(a) sz-fung 879.
    Neighing.

3763. 斯 69 This. There.
    8 Any.

(a) sz-pa-taåt 3159-4068.
    Sparta.

(b) aai-sz-laân 13-2182.
    Iceland.

3764. 糸 R Floss silk.
    120

3765. 撕 64 To split, tear,
    12 tease.

3766. 蜊 142 Shells.
    10 Cockles.

SŹ

3767. 死 78 To die, kill.
    2 Death.

(a) haak͘-sź 923.
    Scared to death.

3768. 使 9 To cause. To
    6 use.(shaí,sź)

(a) ch'it͘-sź 563.
    If. Supposing.

3769. 史 30 History.
    2 S.

SẔ

3770. 四 31 The numeral 4:
    2 common, compli-
3771. 肆 129 cated and run-
    8 ning hand forms.
3772. 乂 4
    1

(a) sẔ-fong 779.
    Square. Everywhere.

3773. 思 61 Thoughts. Mean-
    5 ing. Ideas.(sz)

3774. 使 9 A messenger.
    6 (sẔ,shaí)

(a) t'in-sź 4355.
    Angel.

3775. 肆 129 To exhibit. Pro-
    8 fligate. Dissi-
    pation. S.

SẔ

3776. 事 6 A matter.Affair.
    7 Work. Duties.
    Business.

(a) yaû-sẔ 5159.
    Busy.

(b) sẔ-t'aû 4339.
    Master.

(c) sẔ-tsaí 4482.
    Servant.

3777. 士 R Scholar.Officer
    33 Gentleman. S.

SHA

3778. 沙 85 Sand. Sandy.
    4
3779. 砂 112 Granulated. S.
    4

(a) faû-sha 743.
    Quicksands.

(b) sha-t'aan 4293.
    Shallows.

(c) sha-laû 2262.
    Filter of sand.

(d) sha-chí 216.
    Sandpaper.

(e) sha-t'êng 4347.
    Small flat boat.

(f) p'oôn-sha 3553.
    Borax.

(g) pó-sha 3331.
    Emery.

(h) sha-shat 3851.
    Sand flea.

(i) heî-sha 1033.
    Ammonia.

(j) sha-shî 3905. Sarsa-
    parilla (drink).

(k) sha-ohui 357.
Sandpiper. Snipe.
(l) sha-kai 1515.
Sand grouse.
(m) tsuí-sha 4627.
Sardine.
(n) sha-maáng 2586.
File fish.
(o) sha-kaù 1582.
Grapnel.
(p) sha-ch'ān 469.
Saucy.
(q) sha-mîn 2687. The
Shameen, Canton.

3780. 紗 120/4 Gauze. Crepe.
' Sarcenet.

3781. 痧 104/7 Cholera.
'

3782. 裟 145/7 Buddhist
' surplice.

SHÁ

3783. 耍 126/3 To sport, play.
*
(a) shá-t'ò 4393.
A puzzle (toy).

3784. 灑 85/19 To sprinkle,
scatter, spill.

3785. 嗄 30/9 To waive. Cer-
" tainly. Verily.

SHAAÌ

3786. 曬 72/19 To dry in the
*
3787. 晒 72/6 sun. To get sun-
* stroke.

SHAAÏ

3788. 舐 135/6 To lick, lap.
'
3789. 餂 135/8

SHAAK

3790. 搡 64/10 To seek out, se-
* lect, feel with
the hand.
(a) t'aàm-shaak 4287.
To explore.

SHAAM

3791. 衫 145/3 Coat. Skirt.
Garment.
(a) shaam-k'am 1905.
Lapel.

3792. 彡 R/59 Feathers.
" '

SHAAN

3793. 山 R/46 Mountain. Hill.
Gravegrounds.
Wild. S.
(a) shaan-tûng 4280.
A tunnel.
(b) shaan-chuk-kwóh 364-
2097. Mangosteen.
(c) paaì-shaan 3168.
Worship at the
tombs.
(d) shaan-sai 3384.
Shansi province.
(e) shaan-tung 4272.
Shantung province.

3794. 閂 169/1 To bar, close.
A bar, Bolt.

3795. 刪 18/5 To expunge, can-
* cel, erase, re-
ject.
(a) shaan-ch'uē 593.
To repeal.

3796. 珊 96/5 Coral.
*
(a) shaan-oō 3127.
Coral.

SHAÀN

3797. 訕 149 —3 To slander, revile.

3798. 疝 104 —3 Hernia.

3799. 沺 85 —3

　(a) shaàn-t'aū 4339.
　　Swatow.

SHAĀN

3800. 潺 85 —12 Expectoration.

3801. 孱 39 —9 Feeble.

SHAANG

3802. 生 R —100 Living. Raw. Unripe. Life. To give birth, beget, produce. S. (shang)

　(a) shaang-kwóh 2097. Unripe or uncooked fruit.
　(b) shaang-tsź 4672. The verb.
　(c) shaang-ì 1258. Business. Occupation.
　(d) shaang-kam 1527. Chancre.
　(e) moōn-shaang 2779. Disciple.
　(f) sin-shaang 3639. Sir. Teacher. Mr.
　(g) shaang-māt-hŏk 2636-1140. Biology.
　(h) shaang-mêng-hŏk 2671. Ontology.

3803. 牲 93 —5 Animals. Sacrificial victims. (shang)

SHAÁNG

3804. 省 109 —4 Frugal. Saving. A province. S. (sing)

　(a) shaáng-shëng 3883. Provincial city.

3805. 揹 64 —9 To scour.

SHAAP。

3806. 焾 86 —6 To rail at, irritate.

SHAĀP

3807. 煠 86 —9 To boil or fry in oil.

SHAAT。

3808. 殺 79 —6 To kill, slay, To finish.

3809. 刷 18 —6 To brush, sweep away, clean. A brush.

　(a) ngā-shaat。 2977. Tooth brush.

SHAAU

3810. 梢 75 —7 Rudder. End of branch.

SHAAÚ

3811. 稍 115 —7 A little. To sprout slowly.

SHAAÙ

3812. 哨 30 —7 An outpost. A guard. To patrol, project.

SHAI

3813. 篩 118/10 Bamboo sieve. To sift, strain.

SHAÍ

3814. 使 9/6 To use, send, employ, cause.
3815. 哘 30/8 (sź, sź)
3816. * 駛 187/5 To sail a boat, navigate.
3817. * 駛 187/6 To hasten, turn quickly.

SHAÌ

3818. 世 1/4 A generation. Age. World.
(a) shaì-toǐ 4222. Generation.
(b) kam-shaì 1526. The present world. This age.
3819. * 勢 19/11 Power. Powers.
3820. * 勢 19/11 Authority. Force.
(a) kot͜-shaì 1832. To castrate.

SHAÎ

3821. * 誓 149/7 To swear, take an oath.
3822. * 噬 30/13 To eat, gnaw, snarl.

SHAM

3823. 深 85/8 Deep. Intense. Abstruse. Very.
3824. * 參 28/9 Ginseng. S.

3825. * 森 75/8 Kind of tree or wood. Pride of India.

SHÁM

3826. 審 40/12 To investigate, try, judge. S.
(a) shám-p'oòn 3550. To judge.
3827. * 嬸 38/15 Wife of father's younger brother.
(a) à-shám 9. A nurse.

SHÀM

3828. ' 滲 85/11 To leak, soak through. (sám)

SHÂM

3829. 甚 99/4 Deeply. Very.

SHAN

3830. 身 R/158 The body.
(a) oǒn-shan 3154. To change clothes.
(b) on-shan 3107. Employed.
(c) faat͜-shan 681. To reach puberty.
3831. * 伸 9/5 To stretch out or forth, extend. S.
(a) shan-uen 4908. To redress a grievance.
3832. ' 申 102/1 To report, explain. Time period 3 to 5 P.M. S.
3833. ' 紳 120/5 Sash. Girdle.

(a) shan-k'am 1905.
Gentry.

___

SHÀN

3834. 呻 30/5 To whine.
"

___

SHĀN

3835. 神 113/5 Diety. Divine. Spirit. GOD. S.
(a) ka-shān 1410.
Household gods.
(b) tsing-shān 4560.
Energy. Vitality.
(c) shān-tŏ-hŏk 4207-1140.
Theology.
(d) shān-oô 3129.
Kobe.
3836. 臣 R/131 Minister.States- man. Servant. Vassal. S.
*
3837. 晨 72/7 Morning. Dawn.
*
3838. 辰 R/161 A time period of two hours. Time. 7 to 9 A.M.
'

___

SHĀN

3839. 慎 61/10 To take care. Cautious. At- tentive. S.
*
3840. 腎 130/8 (shĕn)
'
(a) noî-shān 2937.
Kidneys.
(b) ngoî-shān 3070.
Testicles.
(c) shān-nōng 2943.
The scrotum.
(d) aapₛ-shān 24.
Duck's gizzard.

___

SHANG—See also shaang.

3841. 坳 100/7 Relatives by affinity.
'
3842. 笙 118/5 Pan pipes.
'

___

SHAP

3843. 濕 85/14 Moist. Wet.
3844. 淫 85/10 Damp. Shady.
*

___

SHĀP

3845. 十 R/24 The numeral 10:
**
3846. 拾 64/6 common and com- plicated forms.
(a) shāp-fan 696.
Complete. Perfect.
3847. 什 9/2 Sundry. Miscel- laneous. Ten.
3848. 拾 64/6 To gather up, collect.
*

___

SHAT

3849. 失 37/2 To lose, err. A fault.
(a) shat-keuk。 1638.
To trip.
3850. 室 40/6 Dwelling. Inner room. Apartment. wife.Concubine.
*
3851. 虱 142/2 Louse.
*
3852. 蝨 142/2 Bug. Flea.
*
3853. 瑟 96/9 Lute.
"'

SHĀT

3854. 實 $\frac{40}{11}$ True. Sure.

3855. 寔 $\frac{40}{9}$ Certainly. Solid.

3856. 实 $\frac{40}{5}$ S.

(a) shāt-tsoī 4609.
Verily. Really.

SHAU

3857. 收 $\frac{66}{2}$ To receive, gather, bring

3858. 収 $\frac{29}{2}$ to a close. To harvest, store away.

(a) shau-meī 2663.
The last. Finally.
(b) shau-maaī 2568.
To store up.
(c) shau-kot。 1832.
Harvest.
(d) shau-līm 2346.
Shrouding.

SHAÚ

3859. 手 R $\frac{R}{64}$ Hand. Arm. A hand(workman).

(a) shaú-chaang 94.
The elbow.
(b) shaú-ngaǎn-kwat 2999-2083. The wrist.
(c) shaú-tsok。 4610.
Handicraft.
(d) haān-shaú 934.
Unemployed.
(e) shaú-faat。 682.
Sleight of hand.
(f) shaú-ts'eung 4736.
A pistol.

3860. 首 R $\frac{R}{185}$ The head. Chief. Beginning. S.C.

3861. 守 $\frac{40}{3}$ To keep, guard. Observe. S.

SHAŪ

3862. 瘦 $\frac{104}{10}$ Lean. Thin. Poor.

3863. 獸 $\frac{94}{15}$ Animals. Beasts. Brute. (shaû)

SHAŪ

3864. 愁 $\frac{61}{9}$ Anxiety. Grief.

SHAÛ

3865. 受 $\frac{29}{6}$ To receive, endure, abide.

3866. 授 $\frac{64}{8}$ To give, confer, impart. S.

3867. 壽 $\frac{33}{11}$ Longevity. Old age. S.

3868. 售 $\frac{30}{8}$ To sell, dispose of.

SHE

3869. 賒 $\frac{154}{7}$ To buy or sell on credit.

SHE

3870. 捨 $\frac{64}{8}$ To let go, give, reject. uf 3871.

(a) she-hó 1099.
Excellent.

3871. 舍 $\frac{135}{2}$ To abandon, give as alms. (she)

SHE

3872. 舍 $\frac{135}{2}$ Place of abode. Lodge. To lodge. (she)

3873. 赦 $\frac{155}{4}$ To pardon, forgive. S.

SHĒ

3874. 蛇 $\frac{142}{5}$ A serpent. Snake. S.

-198-

(a) shē-mooī 2769.
   Strawberry.
(b) shē-p'ŏ-lāk 3521-2218.
   Raspberry.

___

SHĚ

3875. 社 113/3 Tutelary diety.
   Village.Society.

3876. 唶 30/8 See 3870a.

___

SHĒ

3877.* 射 41/7 To shoot out,
   discharge,
   radiate.

3878. 麝 198/10 Musk deer.'

___

SHĒK

3879.** 石 R 112 Stone. Rock.
   Firm. S.
(a) ts'ing-shēk 4764.
   Granite.
(b) wān-shēk 5027.
   Veined marble.
(c) fa-fán-shēk 650-713.
   Variegated marble.
(d) keung-shēk 1643½.
   Petrified rock.
(e) laī-shēk 2213.
   Coarse sandstone.
(f) shēk-shī 3902. Broken
   stone. Concrete.
(g) shēk-ko 1715.
   Gypsum.
(h) shēk-ko 1714.
   Plaster of Paris.
(i) faū-shēk 743.
   Pumice.
(j) shēk-i 1248.
   Lichens.
(k) shēk-paan 3182.
   Garoupa.

(1) shēk-kaū-kung 1574-
   1878. Rock fish.
(m) shēk-nuī 2949.
   Barren woman.
(n) shēk-lūng. 2532. Stone
   dragon. Sheklung.
(o) shēk-p'aaī-waan 3419-
   4971. Aberdeen.

___

SHENG—See also shing.

3880. 聲 128/11 Sound. Tone.
   Noise.
3881. 声 33/4 Reputation.
   Rumor.S.(shing)
(a) sheng-p'òh 3527.
   Hoarse.
(b) sheng-hōk 1140.
   Acoustics.
(c) sheng-sik-fa 3633-650.
   Acacia.

___

SHÉNG

3882.* 覡 147/7 Sorcery.
(a) shéng-kung 1878.
   A wizard.
(b) shéng-p'òh 3528.
   A witch.

___

SHĒNG

3883. 城 32/7 A city. Inside
   the walls. S.
   (shīng)

___

SHEUK。

3884.' 沕 85/3 Careless.
   Soft(cooked).

___

SHEUNG

3885. 傷 9/11 To injure,wound.
   Distressed. S.

(a) sheung-fung 879.
Cold. A cold.

3886. 雙 172 A pair. Couple.
10 Two. S.

3887. 商 30 To deliberate,
8 consult. A mer-
chant. S.

(a) sheung-mô 2729.
Commerce.

3888. 觴 148 Wine cups.
11

SHEÚNG

3889. 賞 154 To reward, be-
8 stow, confer
upon.

SHEŪNG

3890. 常 50 Constant. Per-
8 manent.Always.S.

(a) p'ing-sheung 3497.
As usual. Ordinary.

3891. 裳 145 Lower garments.
8 Clothing.

3892. 嘗 30
11 To taste, prove.

3893. 嚐 99 S.
8

3894. 償 9 To indemnify.
15

SHEŪNG

3895. 上 1 To rise up, as-
2 cend, go up.
(sheung,sheung)

SHEÚNG

3896. 上 1 Above. Top. Pre-
2 ceding.Previous.

(a) sheung-hoi 1125.
Shanghai.

3897. 尚 42 Still. And be-
5 sides.Superior.

SHI

3898. 施 70 To grant, be-
5 stow aid, con-
fer on. S.

(a) shi-ka-koh 1409-1728.
Chicago.

3899. 詩 149 Song. Poem.
6 Ode. S.

3900. 屍 44 A corpse.
6

3901. 尸 R Corpse. Effigy.
44 Useless. S.

SHÍ

3902. 屎 44 Excreta. Dung.
6

(a) shí-haang 940.
Latrine. Privy.

SHÌ

3903. 試 149 To try, test,
6 verify.

3904. 弒 56 To assassinate,
9 murder a super-
ior.

SHĪ

3905. 時 72 Time. Season.
6 S.

(a) tsik-shī 4533.
Immediately.

(b) tong-shī 4230.
Then. At that time.

(c) shī-hing 1072.
Fashionable.

(d) shī-haû 1015.
Time.

(e) shī-piú 3323. Time
table. Time slip.

(f) shī-ling-fung 2378-
879. Monsoon.

3906. 匙 21 Key. Spoon.
9 (ch'ī)

3907. 鰣 195/10 Herring.

3907½. 鰣 195/6 (ch'ī)

SHǏ

3908. 市 50/2 A market. Fair.
  (a) shǐ-tsǔk 4637. Vulgar.
  (b) shǐ-tséng-wâ 4515-4960. Slang.
  (c) shǐ-ts'ó 4789. Execution ground.

SHÎ

3909. 是 72/5 Such. This. Then. Certain. Positive. S.
  (a) shî-mân 2629. Responsibility.

3910. 示 R/113 To make known. An edict. S. (k'eī)

3911. 視 147/5 To look at, see, regard. S.
  (a) miǔ-shî 2706. To despise.

3912. 豉 151/4 Salted beans. Relishes.
  (a) shî-yaū 5149. Soy sauce.

3913. 嗜 30/10 To relish, lust for.

3914. 侍 9/6 To serve, wait on.

3915. 蒔 140/10 To transplant.

3916. 氏 R/83 Clan. A woman. S.

SHIK

3917. 色 R/139 Color. Beauty. Lustful pleasures.

  (a) shik-shuí 4004. Color. Tint.

3918. 識 149/12 To know, understand, be acquainted with. S.

3919. 飾 184/5 To paint, adorn, gloss over.

3920. 餙 184/7 Beauty.

3921. 式 56/3 Form. Pattern. Type. S.

3922. 釋 165/13 To loosen, set at liberty. S.
  (a) shik-kaaù 1507. Buddhist sect.

3923. 適 162/11 To reach to. Just then. Now.
  (a) shik-chīk 243. Just then.

3924. 骰 188/4 Dice. (t'aū)

SHĪK

3925. 食 R/184 To eat, consume.
  (a) shīk-tsẑ-kei 4673-1623. To board oneself.
  (b) shīk-chaai 69. To abstain from animal food.

3926. 蝕 142/9 Eclipse. To eat away.

SHÍM

3927. 閃 169/2 To flash, dodge. S.

3928. 陝 170/7 (haāp)
  (a) shím-sai 3584. Shensi province.

SHIN

3929. 搧 64/10 To strike, flog.

SHIN

3930. 扇 63/6 A fan. Leaf of a door. To fan.

3931. 諞 149/10 To persuade, beguile, wheedle.

3932. 碢 112/10 To polish, glaze, calender, slip.

3933. 騸 187/10 To geld, castrate. (shîn)

3934. 搧 64/10 To fan, strike.

3935. 蹁 157/10 To slip, slide.

SHÍN

3936. 蟬 142/12 Cicada. Broad locust.

SHǏN

3937. 鱔 195/12 ⎫ The eel.
3938. 鱔 195/12 ⎭

(a) fóh-shǐn 767. Electric eel.
(b) wōng-shǐn 5070. Mud eel.

SHÌN

3939. 善 30/9 Good. Righteous. Clever. Expert. S.

3940. 擅 64/13 To act on one's own authority, assume, usurp.

3941. 繕 120/12 To write, copy.

SHING—See also sheng.

3942. 升 24/2 To rise, ascend. A pole. A pint.

3943. 昇 72/4 To rise, ascend.

3944. 陞 170/7 To ascend, rise in office.

SHÍNG

3945. 聖 128/7 ⎫ Holy. Sacred. Perfect. Divine.
3946. 圣 29/3 ⎭ Sage. Prince of. S.

(a) shíng-lìng 2361, or shíng-shàn 3835. The Holy Spirit.
(b) shíng-pei-tak-póh 3253-4081-3335. St. Petersburg.

3947. 勝 19/10 To conquer, overcome, excel. (shing)

SHĪNG

3948. 成 62/2 To finish, perfect, complete. S. (shěng, ch'íng)

(a) shīng-yāt 5137. The entire day.

3949. 繩 120/13 ⎫ A string.
3950. 繩 120/8 ⎭ A line. Cord.

3951. 誠 149/7 Sincere. Faithful.

(a) shīng-sam-shóh-uên 3593-3977-4932. Amen.

3952. 承 64/4 To receive, bear, hold.
(a) shīng-kai 1522. To continue.
(b) shīng-chuê 339. To sustain.

3953. 乘 4/9 To mount on, ride, ascend. (chīng)
(a) shīng-faat 682. Rules of multiplication.

(b) shǐng-shǐ 3905. **To im-**
prove the moment.

3954. 盛 108 Abundant. Com-
7 plete.S.(shìng)

(a) shǐng-king 1669.
Shengking. Moukden.

3955. 丞 1 To aid.
5 Assistant.

(a) shǐng-seùng 3632.
Cabinet minister.

SHǏNG

3956. 剩 18 To remain over.
9 Left overs.
Surplus.

3957. 盛 108 Plenty. Great.
7 S. (shǐng)

(a) shǐng-shuè 3987.
Your home.
(b) shǐng-waì 5018.
Your favor.

3958. 乘 4 A chariot.
9 C. (shǐng)

SHIP。

3959. 涉 85 To concern,pore
* 7 over, wade. S.
3960. 攝 64 To hold, assist,
* 18 attract. (nǐp)

(a) ship。-shēk 3879.
Magnet.
(b) ship。-lìk 2330.Attrac-
tion. Magnetism.

3961. 燁 86 Luxuriant.
12

SHǏT

3962. 賒 154 Loss.
* 6 To lose.
3963. 舌 R Tongue. Clapper.
* 135 S.
3964. 折 64 See ch'it。
* 4 uf 3962.

SHIU

3965. 燒 86 To burn, roast.
12 Feverish.

SHIÚ

3966. 少 42 Few. Seldom. De-
1 ficient in.
(shiù)

SHIÙ

3967. 少 42 Young.
1 Immature.

SHIŪ

3968. 韶 180 Harmony. S.
"ˈ 5

SHIÛ

3969. 紹 120 To introduce,
'ˈ 5 connect. S,
3970. 肇 129 To begin.
"ˈ 8

SHÓ

3971. 數 66 To count, cal-
11 culate. (shò)

SHÒ

3972. 數 66 An account. Num-
11 ber. Amount.
(shó)

(a) shò-hòk 1140.
Arithmetic.

SHOH

3973. 疏 103 Separated.
' 7 Distant. Lax.
3974. 疎 103 Opening between.
* 7 Coarse. S.

3975. 蔬 140/11 Edible plants.
* Vegetables.

3976. 梳 75/7 A comb. To comb
* or dress hair.

SHÓH

3977. 所 63/4 A place. Build-
** ing. That. That
which. Where?
What? S.

(a) shóh-shĬk 3925.
That which is eaten.
Eatables.

(b) shóh-yaŭ 5159. That
which is, or which
one has.

SHOK。

3978. 索 120/4 To exact. (sok。)
*

3979. 欶 76/7 To suck, rinse,
* absorb.

3980. 朔 74/6 First day of
' the moon. (sok。)

SHÓNG

3981. 爽 89/7 Cheerful.Lively.
* Crisp. To air,
dry.

SHUE

3982. 書 73/6 Book. Letter.
Writing. Docu-
ment.

(a) shue-tsuì 4633.
Preface.

(b) shue-laŭ 2248.
Bookstore. Library.

(c) shue-koón 1820.
Schoolhouse.

(d) shue-sùn-koón 3743.
Postoffice.

(e) shue-keì 1627.
Secretary.

(f) kóng-shue 1779.
To lecture, preach.

(g) tŭk-shue 4258.
To study, study
aloud. Education.

3983. 舒 135/6 Ease. To open
out, expound.S.

(a) shue-fŭk 874.
Good spirits.

(b) shue-shŭk-lĬk 4009-
2330. Resiliency.

3984. 輸 159/9 To lose, be
* beaten.

(a) shue-tó 4199.
To bet.

(b) m̄-shue-fŭk 2551-874.
To dislike. Disaf-
fection.

SHUÉ

3985. 鼠 R/208 Rat. Mouse.
Rodent species.

(a) lŏ-shué 2420.
The rat.

(b) shēk-shué 3879.
Field mouse.

(c) k'uĬ-shué 2021.
Water rat. Vole.

(d) so-shué 3680.
Musk rat.

(e) t'Ĭn-shué 4356.
Mole.

(f) foo̱i-shué 845, or
kwóh-shué 2096, or
sung-shué 3748.
The squirrel.

(g) wŏng-shué-lŏng 5070-
2459. Weasel.

(h) ngān-shué 3028.
Ermine.

(i) shué-foo̱ 835.
Wood louse.

(j) lŏ-shué-Ĭ 2420-1280.
A noose.

3986. 暑 72/9 Summer heat. Hot.

SHUÈ

3987. 處 141/5 A place.

3988. 噓 30/11 (ch'uè, ch'ué)

3989. 恕 61/6 To forgive, show mercy. Indulgent.

3990. 庶 53/8 All. Common. People. S.

SHUĒ

3991. 藷 140/16 Bulbs.

3992. 薯 140/14 Tubers.

(a) shuē-tsaí 4482. Potatoes.

(b) faan-shuē 655. Sweet potatoes.

3993. 殳 R/79 Weapons.

SHUĚ

3994. 墅 32/11 Lodge in a field.

3995. 署 122/9 See ch'uě.

SHUÊ

3996. 樹 75/12 A tree. Trees in general. S.

3997. 竪 117/8 Upright. To set up, establish. S. uf 3998.

3998. 豎 151/8 Slave. Low. Stupid. Vulgar. S.

SHUĒN

3999. 船 137/5 A boat. Ship.

4000. 舡 137/3 Junk. S.

(a) fóh-shuēn 767. A steamer.

(b) lūn-shuēn 2518. Propellor driven ship.

(c) mǐng-lūn-shuēn 2690. Paddle wheel steamer.

SHUET。

4001. 說 149/7 To speak, talk, discourse.

(a) shuet。-wâ 4960. Talk.

(b) ín-shuet。 1341. To speak, give address.

SHUI

4002. 衰 145/4 To decay, decline, fail.

4003. 夊 R/35 To saunter.

SHUÍ

4004. 水 R/85 Water. S.

(a) shuí-taaí 4033. High tide.

(b) shûn-shuí 4022. Favorable tide.

(c) shuí-fa 650. Spray.

(d) haú-shuí 1006. Spittle. Saliva.

(e) shuí-shaú 3859. Sailor.

(f) shuí-hôh-sìn 1119-3646. Log line.

(g) shuí-chaì 117. A cock. Valve in pipe.

(h) tá-p'íng-shui 4027-3497. To work with a level. (surv.)

(i) ngān-shui 3028. Discount. Exchange.

(j) shui-tin-kaán 4159-1475. Hydrophobia.

(k) shui-sin-fa 3640-650. Narcissus.

(l) shui-sìng 3652. Planet Mercury.

(m) shui-s² 3777. Suez.

SHUÌ

4005. 税 $\frac{115}{7}$ Taxes. Duties. Revenue. S.
*

SHUÍ

4006. 誰 $\frac{149}{8}$ Who. Whom. What. Anyone. A one. S.

4007. 垂 $\frac{32}{5}$ To hand down, droop, suspend.

SHUÎ

4008. 睡 $\frac{109}{8}$ To sleep, lounge.

SHUK

4009. 縮 $\frac{120}{11}$ To confuse, contract, shrink. S.

(a) shuk-maaì 2568. To concentrate.

(b) shau-shuk 3857. To condense.

(c) shuk-heì 1033. To sob.

4010. 叔 $\frac{29}{6}$ Father's younger brother. Uncle. S.
*

SHŪK

4011. 熟 $\frac{86}{11}$ Ripe. Cooked. Mature. Intimate with. Skilled.

(a) shūk-t'aàn 4300. Coke.

4012. 屬 $\frac{44}{18}$ Belonging to. Connected with.

4013. 属 $\frac{44}{9}$ Allied. Related.

4014. 贖 $\frac{154}{16}$ To redeem, ransom. S.
*

4015. 蜀 $\frac{142}{7}$
" "

SHŪN

4016. 純 $\frac{120}{4}$ Pure. Sincere. Unmixed. Uniform.

(a) shūn-chîk 242. Artless.

4017. 脣 $\frac{130}{7}$ The lips.
*

4018. 唇 $\frac{30}{7}$
*

4019. 醇 $\frac{164}{8}$ Rich. Pure. Liberal.

4020. 酓 $\frac{164}{5}$
'

4021. 鶉 $\frac{196}{8}$ Quail. (ch'un)
'

SHÙN

4022. 順 $\frac{181}{3}$ To follow. Convenient. Obedient. In sympathy with.

SHŪNG

4023. 崇 $\frac{46}{8}$ To honor, reverence. S.
*

(a) shūng-taaì 4033. Sublime.

SHŪT

4024. 術 144/5 A trick. Device.
*

4025. 述 162/5 To publish, nar-
* rate, declare,
state.

4026. 朮 75/1 Kind of plant.
'

TÁ

4027. 打 64/2 To strike, beat,
** whip, do, make,
play, cause.
(a) tá-chaai 69.
To say mass.
(b) yat-tá 5133.
A dozen.

4028. 哆 30/5 A dozen.
"

TAAI

4029. 獃 94/10 Idiotic.
* (ngoì)

TAAÍ

4030. 歹 R/78 Bad. Perverse.
"'

TAAÌ

4031. 帶 50/8 To lead, bring.
" A girdle. Zone.
S
(a) hōn-taal 1164.
Frigid zone.
(b) wan-taal 5020.
Temperate zone.
(c) maāt-taal 2591.
Carter.
(d) taal-shui 4004.
To pilot. A pilot.
(e) hoí-taal 1125.
Edible seaweed.

4032. 戴 62/14 To wear on the
* head, sustain.

TAAÎ

4033. 大 R/37 Great. Noble.
** Eminent.Big. S.
(a) taaî-ying-kaaù-ooî
5222-1507-3143.
Church Missionary
Society.
(b) taaî-sai-yeūng 3584-
5194.Atlantic Ocean.
(c) taaî-lìn-waan 2350-
4971. Dalny.

4034. 呔 30/3
"

TAAM

4035. 擔 64/13 To carry on a
4036. 担 64/5 pole. To bear,
4037. 咁 30/8 sustain.
(taàm)
(a) taam-pó 3329.
To go security.
(b) taam-pó-sùn 3743.
Registered letter.

TAÁM

4038. 膽 130/13 Gall bladder.
4039. 胆 130/5 Courage.Bravery.
S.
(a) taám-chap 148.
Bile.
(b) taám-faān 671.
Blue vitriol.
(c) lūng-taám-tsʻó 2532-
4777. Gentian.

TAÀM

4040. 擔 64/13 A burden.
4041. 咁 30/8
"

4042. 淡 85/8 Insipid. Flat. Dull. (t'aǎm)

4043. 啖 30/8 To bite. A bite.

4044. 陷 30/8 Morsel. Bait. S.

4045. 澹 85/13 Insipid. Luke-warm. Dull. (taǎm)

TAAN

4046. 單 30/9 Single. Odd. Alone. Only.

4047. 单 24/6 Bill. Receipt. Commercial doc-ument. S.

  (a) pó-taan 3329. Insurance policy.

4048. 丹 3/3 Carnation. Pill. Drug. Remedy.S.

4049. 玗 32/4

4050. 癉 104/12 Distressed. Diseased.(t'aán)

TAÁN

4051. 蛋 142/5 Eggs. Testes. Aborigines.

4052. 疍 103/5 Boat people. (taân)

  (a) taán-wŏng 5070. Yolk.

TAÀN

4053. 誕 149/7 A birthday.

4054. 誔 149/7 To boast, brag.

4055. 旦 72/1 Morning. Dawn.

TAÂN

4056. 但 9/5 But. Only. How-ever. Still. S.

  (a) taân-faān 667. All. Whoever.

4057. 蛋 142/5 Aborigines.Boat people. Eggs. (taân)

  (a) taân-ka 1410. The river boat people. A low fellow.

4058. 彈 57/12 Bullet. Pill. Ball. (t'aân)

  (a) taân-kung 1883. A spring.

  (b) taân-kung-sóh 3691. A spring latch or lock.

TAAP。

4059. 搭 64/12 To add on, pile up, erect (a building),board train or boat.

4060. 搭 64/10

  (a) taap。-haak。 921. Passengers.

  (b) taap。-chuê 339. To lodge.

  (c) taap。-shĭk 3925. To board with.

4061. 答 118/6 To answer, respond to.

4062. 荅 140/6

  (a) pò-taap。 3337. To repay, requite.

TAĀP

4063. 踏 157/8 To tread on, stamp down.

4064. 蹋 157/10

4065. 沓 85/4 To place on top, pile up. A pile. S.

TAAT。

4066. 笪 118/5 C for land, spots, marks, etc. Bamboo mat. To flog.

4067. 撻 64/11 To throw.

TAAT

4068. 達 162/9 To open. To see through, inform.
(a) taāt-ī-mān 1284-2616. Darwin.

4069. 噠 30/13

TAI

4070. 低 9/5 To bend down, stoop, lower.

TAÍ

4071. 底 53/5 The underside. End. Finally.
(a) tò-taí 4203. Finally.
(b) taí-kó 1722. Printer's copy.

4072. 抵 64/5 To push against, To oppose.
(a) taí-chuê 339. To endure.
(b) taí-chaí 117. To boycott.

4073. 詆 149/5 To slander, defame.

4073g. 提 64/9 See t'aí.

TAÌ

4074. 帝 50/6 The Supreme Ruler. Gods.
(a) sheúng-taì 3896. GOD. Gods.

4075. 渧 85/9 To drip, ooze.

TAÎ

4076. 第 118/5 Gradation. Class. Order. Number.
(a) taî-(î)-yeúng (1287)-5201. Another kind.

4077. 弟 57/4 Younger brother.

4078. 遞 162/10 To bear to hand to, transmit, exchange.

4079. 隸 171/9 See laî.

4080. 隷 171/7

TAK

4081. 得 60/8 To obtain, get. Can.

4082. 德 60/12 Virtue. Goodness.
(a) 16-tak-ooî 2426-3143. Lutheran Church.

TĀK

4083. 特 93/6 Only. Alone. Specially. Purposely.
(a) tāk-tang 4096. Purposely. Intentionally. Solely.

4084. 杙 75/3 Peg. Stake.

TAM

4085. 泵 85/5 To exceed. (tam)

TÁM

4086. 揞 64/10 To beat, throw down. To drive (as a stake).

TĂM

4087. 泵 85/5 To drop down, sag.

4088. 㰱 30/15

   (a) tăm-tui 4248.
      Slouching.

TÂM

4089. 畜 40/8 To trample.
   *   (t'ăm)

   (a) tâm-tâm-chuền 347.
      To revolve.

TAN

4090. 墩 32/12 A heap.
   *   Tumulus.

4091. 墪 32/12 Beacon mound.
         uf 4092.

   (a) t'uēn-tan 4444.
      Buttocks.

   (b) yat-tan 5133.
      One ton.

TÁN

4092. 朶 R/75 Stump of a tree.
   '   See 4090.

   (a) ch'eung-moōn-tán 499-
      2779. Window sill.

   (b) fung-kaû-tán 879-1598.
      Beginning of a
      typhoon.

   (c) sz-tán 3761.
      Silk winders.

   (d) chaaī-tán 71. Unlucky
      day. Debtor. Bank-
      rupt.

4093. 蟺 157/13 Depot. Store.
      House.

   (a) tán-ka 1410.
      Monopolist.

   (b) tán-p'ò 3514.
      House of assigna-
      tion.

   (c) tán-wán 5024.
      Place securely.

TANG

4094. 燈 86/12 Lamp. Lantern.

4095. 灯 86/..2 Light.

   (a) tang-taám 4038.
      Lamp chimney.
      Electric bulb.

   (b) tang-sam 3593.
      Lamp wick.

4096. 登 105/7 To ascend, mount,
   *   advance. S.

   (a) tang-kung 1878.
      Rangoon.

TÁNG

4097. 等 118/6 A class.
      To wait.

TÀNG

4098. 凳 16/12 A stool.

4099. 櫈 75/14 Bench.

TÂNG

4100. 戥 62/9 Small steelyard
   *   for weighing
      silver.

4101. 蹬 157/14 To be sorry for.
   "   To tread on.

TAP

4102. 嗒 30/10 To hang down.
   "   Absent minded.
      (t'aap₀)

TĀP

4103. 搭 64/12 To strike.
  " (taap。)

TAT

4104. 吔 30/5 To dab.
  "

TĀT

4105. 突 116/4 To rush out,
  * appear suddenly.
  (a) tāt-tāt. Trembling.
4106. 凸 17/4 Projecting. In
  * relief. (taāt)

TAU

4107. 兜 10/9 A sack. Bag.
  *
  (a) tau-heí 1031.
      To tilt.
  (b) tau-mau 2640.
      Repulsive.
  (c) tau-t'ò 4402.
      A stomacher.
4108. 揪 64/11 To seize, grasp,
  ' raise up, gath-
      er in.

TAÚ

4109. 斗 R/68 A peck. Measure.
  * Dipper. Vessel.

TAÙ

4110. 鬥 R/191 To wrangle, con-
4111. 鬧 191/4 test, fight,
      wrestle.
4112. 鬮 191/14 To play at.

4113. 竇 116/15 A hollow.Sluice.
  ' Duct. Hole.
4114. 魓 30/11 Cave. Den.
  * Nest. (taù)

4115. 抖 64/4 To touch, work
  " in wood.

TAÙ

4116. 荳 140/7 Beans. Peas.
  (a) ts'ing-taû 4764.
      Green peas. String
      beans.
  (b) taû-kok。 1744.String
      beans. Peas in pod.
  (c) ts'aān-taû 4695.
      Kidney beans.
  (d) pin-taû 3286.
      (French) beans.
  (e) pín-taû 3291.
      Lentils.
  (f) siú-taû 3674.
      Fitch.
  (g) taû-k'aù 1933.
      Nutmeg.
  (h) taû-k'aù-fa 650.
      Mace.
4117. 豆 R/151 A trencher.
  * Tray.S.uf 4116.
4118. 痘 104/7 Small pox.
  *
  (a) shuí-taû 4004.
      Chickenpox.
  (b) taû-tseung 4523.
      Lymph.
  (c) taû-p'eī 3468.
      Pockmarked.
4119. 逗 162/7 To loiter,
  ' dawdle. S.
4120. 竇 116/15 See taù.
4121. 嘖 30/10
  "
  (a). lò-taû 2420.
      Father.

TE

4122. 爹 88/6 Father.
  " "Daddy".

TĔ

4123. 嗲 30/10 Lazy.

TEÎ

4124. 哋 30/6 Sign of plural.

4125. 地 32/3 Earth. Ground. Place. uf 4124.
  (a) teî-hŏk 1140. Geology.
  (b) teî-king-tò 1668-4208. Longitude.
  (c) teî-fŭk 876. Lintel.
  (d) teî-chî 216. Title deed.
  (e) teî-chung-hoî 383-1125. Mediterrean Sea.

TĒK

4126. 糴 119/16 To buy rice or grain.

TENG—See also ting.

4127. 釘 167/2 A nail. Bolt. To nail. (tèng)

4128. 疔 104/2 Boil. Pimple. Syphilitic sore.

TÉNG

4129. 頂 181/2 The top. Peak. To exceed. Very. C.

TĒNG

4130. 矴 112/2 To stone, strike. To nail. (tìng)

4131. 揈 64/8 To throw, pelt, smash.

TĔNG

4132. 定 40/5 To fix. Decided. (tìng)
  (a) tĕng-ngãn 3028. Bargain money.
  (b) tĕng-ts'an 4712. To betroth (of man).

TEU

4133. 嗾 30/13 Sound of a trumpet.

TEÚ

4134. 朵 75/2 C for flowers, flame, etc. (tŏh)

TEUK

4135. 啄 30/8 Birds eating. To peck, preen.

4136. 斲 69/13 To cut up, mince.

TEUNG

4137. 啄 30/14 To peck, blink the eyes.

TI

4138. 啲 30/8 Some. A little.

4139. 的 106/3 A few. (4139 tik)
  (a) kòh-ti 1734. Those.
  (b) ni-ti 2881. These.
  (c) faai-ti 651½. Quicker. Quickly.

TIK

4140. 的 106/3 Clear. Time. A little. (ti)

(a) tik-kòm-toh 1758-4215.
   A very little.Least.
(b) tik-yaŭ-a-toh 5148-4-
   4215. Equador.

4141. 滴 85 II Drop. Mite.
* To drip.

4142. 嫡 38 II Wife. Consort.
*

TĬK

4143. 敵 66 II In opposition. An enemy. To oppose.

4144. 荻 140/7 Rushes. Sorghum.
*

4145. 滌 85/10 To wash,cleanse, reform.
'

4146. 覿 147/15 Face to face.

4147. 笛 118/5 Fife. Flute. (tēk)
'

4148. 迪 162/5 To lead forward, follow.
'

4149. 狄 94/4 S.
"ı'

4150. 糴 119/16 See tēk.

TÍM

4151. 點 203/5 A dot. Point.

4152. 點 203/5 Speck. Mark.
'

4153. 点 86/5 Comma. Hour. To light, as a lamp. How?

(a) tím-shŏ 3972.
   To reckon.
(b) tím-ni 2881.
   How? What?
(c) tím-kaaí 1436. How do you explain it? What is the meaning?
(d) tím-sam 3593. Pastry. Refreshments.

TĬM

4154. 店 53/5 An inn. Tavern Shop.

(a) tsaú-tìm 4500.
   A restaurant.

4155. 玷 96/5 A flaw. To disgrace, bump, touch.
*

(a) tìm-oo 3114.
   To sully.

4156. 佔 9/5 To secure, appropriate.(chìm)
'

TÎM

4157. 掂 64/8 Straight. Along a path.
*

TIN

4158. 瘨 104/10 Crazy. Raving.

4159. 癲 104/19 Mad. Vicious.

4160. 顛 181/10 Confused. Upset. Calamity. Top. uf 4159.
*

4161. 巔 46/19 Peak. Apex.
'

TÍN

4162. 典 12/6 Canon. Rule. Records. Constant. To mortgage.

(a) yan-tín 5108.
   Grace.
(b) tsź-tín 4672.
   Dictionary.

TĬN

4163. 電 173/5 Lightning. Electricity.

(a) tìn-lô 2426.
   Electric circuit.

(b) tîn-hŏk 1140.
Electrical science.

(c) tîn-sìn 3646.
Electric wire.

(d) tîn-k'aū 1938.
Dynamo.

(e) tîn-ch'e 491.
Motor. Electric car.

(f) tîn-ch'ī 535.
Battery.

(g) tîn-pò 3337.
Telegram.

(h) tîn-wà 4960.
Telephone.

(i) tîn-shuĕn 3999.
Motor boat.

4164. 殿 79/9 A large hall.
* Palace. Temple.

4165. 奠 37/9 To pour out, of-
* fer libations.
Settled.

4165½. 墊 32/11 To advance mon-
* ey, repay, fill
up.

(a) î-tîn 1256.
A cushion.

4166. 靛 174/8 Indigo.
* Blue dye.

4167. 甸 102/2 To rule, culti-
"¹ vate.

TING—See also teng.

4168. 丁 1/1 Individual. Per-
' son. To sustain.
S.

(a) ping-ting 3300.
A soldier.

(b) ting-heung 1046.
Cloves.

(c) ting-heung-fa 650.
The lilac.

(d) ting-fong-ch'ek。 779-
496. Cubic foot.

4169. 玎 96/2 Jingling noise.
'

TÍNG

4170. 鼎 R 206 A tripod.
'

TÌNG

4171. 矴 112/2 To drop anchor.
* An anchor stone.
(tèng)

4172. 訂 149/2 To settle, ad-
* just, collate,
edit.

4173. 梃 115/7
*

(a) tiu-tîng 4186.
Perverse.

(b) ts'z̄-tîng 4860.
Persimmon stem.

TĪNG

4174. 錠 167/8 Ingot.
' Trencher.

TĪP

4175. 碟 112/9 Plate. Saucer.
*

4176. 疊 102/19 To reiterate,
* fold over,

4177. 叠 29/11 pile up,
* accumulate.

4178. 蝶 142/9 Butterfly.
*

TIT。

4179. 跌 157/5 To fall,
' tumble.

TĪT

4180. 秩 115/5 Decorum, Method.
* Order. S.

4181. 帙 50/5 Book cover.
' Wrapper.

-214-

TIU

4182. 丟 $\frac{1}{5}$ To throw away, cast down, lose.
  (a) tiu-kā 1424. To blast reputation, lose face.
  (b) tiu-tsź-ngaǎn 4672-2999. To talk learned.

4183. 彫 $\frac{59}{8}$ *
4184. 雕 $\frac{172}{8}$ * To engrave, carve, polish. (t'iù)

4185. 凋 $\frac{15}{8}$ Fading. Falling. Withered.

4186. 刁 $\frac{18}{1}$, Perverse. Truculent. Aggressive. Depraved. S.
  (a) tiu-foó 835. A shrew. Virago.

4187. 貂 $\frac{153}{5}$ The sable. S.
  (a) tiu-shué 3985. Marten.

TIÚ

4188. 屌 $\frac{44}{6}$ * Term of abuse. Penis.

TIÙ

4189. 吊 $\frac{30}{3}$
4190. 弔 $\frac{57}{1}$, To suspend, hang, mourn, console.
  (a) tó-tiù 4123. To procrastinate.
  (b) mân-tiù 2629. Execution by hanging.
  (c) faat-yeūng-tiù 681-5193. Epilepsy.
  (d) tiù-chung-fa 385-650. Bellflower.

4191. 釣 $\frac{167}{3}$ * Hook. To angle, fish with rod. S.

TIÙ

4192. 調 $\frac{149}{8}$ To change about. A tune.

4193. 銚 $\frac{121}{6}$ * Black glazed earthen jar.

4194. 掉 $\frac{64}{8}$, To shake, toss, move.

TO

4195. 刀 $\frac{R}{18}$ Knife. Sword.
  (a) to-yūk 5249. The blade.
  (b) yat-to-chí 5133-216. A quire of paper.

4196. 都 $\frac{163}{9}$ Even. Also. Capital. S.
  (a) to-tuk 4255. Military Governor General.

TÓ

4197. 倒 $\frac{9}{8}$ ** To fall over, invert, upset. Action accomplished.
  (a) tó-hāng 986. To walk backwards.
  (b) tó-t'àn 4330. To recoil.
  (c) tó-tsò 4592. Bankrupt.

4198. 島 $\frac{46}{7}$ * An island. (t'ó)

4199. 賭 $\frac{154}{9}$ * To wager, gamble.

4200. 擣 $\frac{64}{14}$, To pound in a mortar.

4201. 到 $\frac{18}{14}$ uf 4197.

4202. 禱 $\frac{113}{14}$ See t'ó.

TÒ

4203. 到 $\frac{18}{6}$ 162 To reach to, get, come to. Until. S. (tó)
**

4204. 妒 $\frac{38}{5}$ Jealous.
*

4205. 妬 $\frac{38}{4}$ Envious.
*

4206. 蠹 142 Bookworm. $\frac{16}{16}$ Rice weevil.
(a) tò-uē 4872.
A "bookworm".

TÔ

4207. 道 162 A path. Way. $\frac{9}{9}$ Road. Doctrine. C.
(a) tô-leỸ 2285. Doctrine.
(b) tô-ì-hŏk 1292-1140. Ethics.
(c) tô-kaaù 1507. Taoism.
(d) tô-t'oỸ 4423. Intendant of Circuit.

4208. 度 53 A measure. Standard. C for doors, etc. S. (tŏk)

4209. 盜 168 Robbery. A robber. Pirate.
*

4210. 導 41 To lead, guide. $\frac{13}{13}$
*

4211. 渡 85 To ford. A ferry $\frac{9}{9}$ or passage boat.
'

4212. 杜 75 A kind of wood. $\frac{3}{3}$ To stop, cut off. S.
'

4213. 蹈 157 To tread on, $\frac{10}{10}$ disregard.
'

4214. 鍍 167 To gild, plate. $\frac{9}{9}$

TOH

4215. 多 36 Many. Much. $\frac{3}{3}$ S.
**

(a) toh-tsʻ2 4854. Often.

TÓH

4216. 躲 158 To get out of $\frac{6}{6}$ the way, evade, escape.

4217. 朵 75 A bunch. Cluster. $\frac{2}{2}$ C for flowers
*

4218. 朵 75 and things hanging. (teú) $\frac{2}{2}$
'

4219. 垛 32 Portico. Buttress. Battlements. $\frac{6}{6}$
'

TÔH

4220. 惰 61 Lazy. Indolent. $\frac{9}{9}$ Careless.
*

4221. 墮 32 To fall down, $\frac{12}{12}$ decay. Ruin.
*

TOỸ

4222. 代 9 A generation. $\frac{3}{3}$ To act instead of one. In behalf of. S.
**
(a) toỸ-paān 3191. Attorney.
(b) toỸ-shŭk 4014. To atone.

4223. 待 60 To behave toward, treat. $\frac{6}{6}$
'
(a) táng-toỸ 4097. To await.

4224. 袋 145 A bag. Sack. $\frac{5}{5}$ Pouch. Purse. Pocket.
'
(a) kaú-lūng-toỸ 1571-2532. Cartridge box.

4225. 玳 96 Tortoise shell. $\frac{5}{5}$
'

4226. 瑇 96 $\frac{9}{9}$
'

(a) toî-mooî 2778.
Tortoise shell.

4227. 隶 R To reach to.
ᵐ, 171 Surplus.

TŌK

4228. 度 53 To measure, cal-
6 culate, guess.
(tô)

4229. 鐸 167 A kind of bell.
, 13

TONG

4230. 當 102 Suitable. Just
8 then. To act as,
be. S. (tòng)
(a) tong-shî 3905.
At that time.
(b) taam-tong 4035.
To undertake.

4231. 璫 96 Pendant. Jing-
, 13 ling bell. Rat-
tle.

TÓNG

4232. 黨 203 An association.
* 8 Clan. Faction.
Party.
(a) tóng-uê 4893. Adher-
ent. Partizan.

4233. 擋 64
* 13 ┐To obstruct,
│withstand,
4234. 攩 64 │oppose.
* 20 ┘

TÒNG

4235. 當 102 To regard as,
* 8 value, pawn.
(tong)
(a) tòng-aat。 26.
A pawnshop.

4236. 湯 162 To pass by,
, 9 fall, miss.

(a) tòng-tsź-mǎ 4667-2561.
A race horse.

4237. 擋 64 To oppose.
, 13 (tóng)

TÔNG

4238. 蕩 140 Vast. Vagrant.
* 12 To wander, stray,
waste. S.

4239. 溫 108 To move, plas-
* 12 ter, smear, put
on. S.

TUEN

4240. 端 117 Principles. Doc-
* 9 trines. Affairs.
Origin. Head. S.

TUẾN

4241. 短 111 Short. Brief.
* 7

TUẼN

4242. 斷 69 To determine.
14 Decidedly.
Assuredly.
(tuẽn, t'uẽn)

TUẾN

4243. 段 79 Part. Piece.
* 5 Section. C. S.

4244. 斷 69 To cut off,
* 14 break off, stop.
(tuẽn, t'uẽn)

4245. 緞 120 Satin. Thick
* 9 silk.
(a) taaî-fa-tuẽn 4033-
650. Damask.
(b) kǔk-tuẽn 1875.
Brocade.

TUET。

4246. 凹 18 Conical.
ᵐ 5 Tapering.

TUĔT

4247. 奪 37/11 To take by force.

TUI

4248. * 堆 32/8 A heap. A mass. Pile. To heap.

TUÍ

4249. 對 41/11 A scroll. To push together, combine. (tuí)

TUÌ

4250. 對 41/11 Opposite to. Facing.

4251. 对 41/11 To respond. A pair.
(a) tuì-tuì. To tally, compare.

4252. , 碓 112/8 Foot pestle. To pound (rice).

TUÎ

4253. 隊 170/9 Group. Squad. Company. Drove. Herd. C.

4254. , 兌 10/5 To exchange, barter.

TUK

4255. 督 109/8 To oversee, rule, lead, warn. S.
(a) tsúng-tuk 4652. Provincial Governor General.

4256. , 篤 118/10 Sincere. Firm. Stable. Pure.
(a) tuk-sùn 3743. Faith. Assurance.

4257. , 尻 44/3 Bottom. Rump. Buttocks.

(a) kwāt-tuk-lô 2086-2426. Cul-de-sac.

TUK

4258. 讀 149/15 To read aloud, study. S.

4259. 獨 94/13 Only. Solely. Alone. Solitary.
(a) tŭk-t'aŭ-kung 4339-1878. Widower.

4260. , 毒 80/4 Poison. Virus. To hate.
(a) tŭk-haŭ 1006. Spiteful.
(b) pìn-tŭk 3295. Venereal ulcer.

4261. * 瀆 85/15 To trouble, defile, insult, profane.

4262. * 讟 149/22 To slander, abuse, hate.

4263. , 犢 93/15 Calf. Heifer. Sacrificial victim.

TUN

4264. , 敦 66/8 Honest. Generous.

4265. * 墩 32/12 See tan.

TÚN—See tán.

TÙN

4266. , 撣 64/12 To throw off, shake off.

4267. 燉 86/12 To steam, cook by steaming.

TÛN

4268. * 頓 181/4 To bow, prostrate, stop, knock. S.

4269. 鈍 167 Dull. Blunt.
* — 4 Stupid.
  (a) tûn-t'oi 4417.
    A dunce.

4270. 頓 30
" — 13

4271. 沌 85 Confused.
" ' — 4 Chaotic.

TUNG

4272. 東 75 The east. Host.
* — 4 Chief. Master. S.
  (a) tung-ka 1410. Head of
    house or firm.
  (b) tung-naām 2823.
    Southeast.
  (c) tung-pak 3215.
    Northeast.
  (d) tung-hoí 1125.
    East China Sea.
  (e) tung-king. 1669.
    Tokyo. Tongking.
    Mukden.

4273. 冬 15 Winter.
* — 3 S.
  (a) yǎn-tung 5122½
    Honeysuckle.

TÚNG

4274. 懂 61 To understand.
' — 13

TÙNG

4275. 凍 15 Cold. Icy.
' — 8 To freeze.

4276. 棟 75 Ridgepole.
' — 8 Beam. Stake.
  (a) tùng-k'eī 1962.
    Perpendicular.

TǓNG

4277. 動 19 To move, affect,
' — 9 influence.

  (a) tǔng-ts'iū 4773
    Crow bar.
  (b) tǔng-lĭk-hōk 2330.
    Dynamics.

4278. 洞 85 To see through,
* — 6 perceive.

4279. 峒 30 A cave.
* — 9 Cavity.

4280. 峝 46 Cavern.
' — 6 Tunnel.

4281. 戙 62 uf 4277.
" ' — 6

T'A

4282. 他 9 Other. Another.
* — 3 He. They.

T'AAÌ

4283. 太 37 Too. Very. Term
* — 1 of respect. S.
      (t'aaî)
  (a) t'aaî-p'īng-hoí 3497-
    1125.
    Pacific Ocean.

4284. 泰 85 Prosperous.
' — 5 Exalted.

T'AAǏ

4285. 艃 137 Rudder.
" — 11

T'AAM

4286. 貪 154 Covetous.
" — 4 Greedy.

T'AÀM

4287. 探 64 To visit, feel
* — 8 with the hand,
    search out, try,
    spy, sound.

T'AĀM

4288. 談 149/8 To talk. Talk. Language. S.

4289. 痰 104/8 Phlegm. Mucus.

4290. ' 燂 86/12 To heat, singe, dry.

4291. " 潭 85/12 Deep. Deep pool.

T'AĂM

4292. 淡 85/8 Watery. Weak. (taăm)

(a) t'aăm-shuí 4004. Fresh water.

T'AAN

4293. * 灘 85/19 Rapids. Sand bank. Shoal.

4294. * 攤 64/19 To open, divide, spread out. gamble. (naàn)

(a) kwóh-t'aan 2097. Fruit stall.

(b) shik-t'aan 3924. Dice.

T'AÁN

4295. 癱 104/19 Palsy. Paralysis. Numbness.

4296. 坦 32/5 Level place. Quiet. S.

4297. * 袒 145/5 To bare, strip, disclose.

4298. ' 燀 104/12

4299. ' 疸 104/5

(a) wŏng-t'aán 5070. Jaundice.

(b) t'aán-tsui 4625. Erysipelas.

T'AÀN

4300. 炭 86/5 Coal. Charcoal. S.

(a) teî-mĭn-t'aàn 4125-2687. Peat.

(b) shuí-fóh-t'aàn 4004-767. Charcoal.

(c) t'aàn-taăm 4038. Lignite. Jet.

4301. * 嘆 30/11

4302. 歎 76/11 To sigh, moan.

(a) hó-t'aàn 1099. Luxurious.

T'AĀN

4303. 壇 32/13 An altar. Sacrificial area.

4304. * 彈 57/12 To strike, play instrument, accuse. (taăn)

4305. 檀 75/13 S.

(a) t'aān-heung-mŭk 1046-2795. Sandal wood.

(b) t'aān-heung-shaan 3793. Hawaiian Is.

T'AĂN

4306. * 灘 85/19 Marsh. Flat. Tidelands. (t'aan)

T'AAP。

4307. 塔 32/10

4308. 墖 32/12 A tower. Spire. Pagoda. S.

4309. 磴 112/8 A jar. Mortar.

4310. ' 鰨 195/10 See t'aat。.

T'AAT。

4311. 撻 * 64/13 To strike, flog, lose money.

4312. 鰨 ' 195/10 (t'aap。)
 (a) t'aat。-sha- uē 3778-4872. Sole.

T'AI

4313. 梯 * 75/7 Ladder. Steps. Stairs.
 (a) t'ai-t'oi 4423. Landing.

T'AÍ

4314. 睇 109/7 To gaze, look at, observe.

4315. 體 188/13 Body. Trunk. Substance. Appearance.
 (a) t'ai-t'ip。 4364. To sympathize with.
 (b) t'ai-hōk 1140. Anatomy.
 (c) t'ai-kung-hōk 1879. Physiology.
 (d) t'ai-pìn-hōk 3293. Morphology.
 (e) t'ai-mìn 2687. Reputation.

T'AÌ

4316. 替 73/8 To substitute for. In place of. For.

4317. 剃 * 18/7 } To shave.

4318. 髯 * 190/7 }

4319. 涕 85/7 To weep, drivel.

4320. 嚏 ' 30/15 To sneeze, snivel, hiccough.

T'AÏ

4321. 提 64/9 To raise, lift, bring forward. (tai)
 (a) t'aī-fòng 799. To beware. Watch against.
 (b) t'aī-pāt 3241. To advance.
 (c) t'aī-tuk 4255. Commander in Chief.
 (d) t'aī-kaal 1442. Extradition.

4322. 啼 30/9 To cry, wail. Cry of fowl or bird.
 (a) t'aī-huk 1223. To weep and wail.

4323. 題 * 181/9 Title. Theme. To discuss.
 (a) t'aī-heí 1031. To mention.
 (b) t'aī-mēng 2669. To nominate.
 (c) ts'im-t'aī 4745. To subscribe.

4324. 蹄 ' 157/9 A hoof.
 (a) taaī-sha-t'aī 4033-3778. Elephantiasis.

T'AǏ

4325. 娣 ' 38/7 Younger sister. A boy.

T'ÀM

4326. 噤 * 30/13 To deceive. (kàm)

4327. 咄 " 30/5 uf 4326.

T'ǍM

4328. 氹 85/I A pool.

T'AN

4329. 吞 $\frac{30}{4}$ To swallow, gulp down, appropriate.

T'ÀN

4330. 褪 $\frac{145}{10}$ To disrobe, slip off, move back, draw in.
  (a) t'àn-huî 1221. To shove along.
  (b) t'àn-haû 1013. To move back, reverse.
  (c) t'àn-lat 2238. To slip off.
  (d) t'àn-kong 1776. Piles.

4331. 撴 $\frac{64}{13}$ To put down.

T'ĀNG

4332. 籐 $\frac{118}{15}$ Vines. Creepers.

4333. 藤 $\frac{140}{15}$ Rattan.
  (a) tsź-t'āng 4670. Wistaria chinensis.
  (b) mō-īp-t'āng 2711-1367. Dodder.
  (c) t'āng-p'aaī 3420. Cane shield.
  (d) tá-t'āng 4027. To bind with rattan.

T'AP

4334. 諮 $\frac{149}{10}$ To mutter.

T'AU

4335. 偷 $\frac{9}{9}$ To steal, pilfer. By stealth.

T'AÚ

4336. 唞 $\frac{30}{7}$ To gasp, breathe, rest.

4337. 抖 $\frac{64}{4}$ (4337 taù)

T'AÙ

4338. 透 $\frac{162}{7}$ To see through, pass through. (t'aŭ)
  (a) t'aù-fóh 767. To kindle a fire.

T'AŪ

4339. 頭 $\frac{181}{7}$ Head. Top. Chief. First.
  (a) t'aū-lô 2426. Vocation. Calling.
  (b) t'aū-p'eī 3468. Scurf.

4340. 投 $\frac{64}{4}$ To throw, fling, give over. S.
  (a) ch'ut-t'aū 648. To put up at auction.
  (b) t'aū-hōng(kòng) 1188. To surrender.

4341. 骰 $\frac{188}{4}$ Dice. (shīk)

4342. 丶 $\frac{R}{8}$ Above.

T'EK₂—See also t'ik.

4343. 踢 $\frac{157}{8}$ To kick, stumble against.

T'ENG—See also t'ing.

4344. 聽 $\frac{128}{16}$ To hear, listen, obey. (t'ing)

4345. 听 $\frac{30}{4}$

4346. 廳 $\frac{53}{22}$ Court. Hall. Parlor. Station. Lodge.

T'ĔNG

4347. 艇 137/7 Small boat. Boat.
  (a) p'oŏn-t'ĕng 3552. Cargo boat.

T'EÙ

4348. * 唾 30/8 To spit. (t'òh)

T'IK—See also t'ek.

4349. ' 剔 18/8 To scrape off, pick out.
4350. ' 惕 61/8 To respect, revere. To place, put.

T'IM

4351. 添 85/8 Also. More. To add to.

T'ĪM

4352. 甜 99/6 Sweet. Agreeable.
4353. ' 恬 61/6 Peaceful. Still.

T'ĬM

4354. ' 餂 184/6 To taste.

T'IN

4355. ** 天 37/1 Heaven. Sky. Day. Celestial.
  (a) hó-t'in 1099. Fine weather.
  (b) t'in-hâ 908. The earth. The world.
  (c) t'in-heï 1033. Atmosphere.
  (d) yat-t'in 5133. A day.

  (e) t'in-t'ŏng 4435. Heaven.
  (f) t'in-sz̀ 3774. Angel.
  (g) t'in-mân 2616. Astronomy.
  (h) t'in-wŏng-sing 5072-3652. Planet Uranus.
  (i) t'in-taï 4071. Nadir.
  (j) t'in-moŏn-tung 2779-4273. Asparagus.
  (k) t'in-fa 650. Smallpox.
  (l) t'in-tsun 4643. Tientsin.

T'ĪN

4356. 田 102/R Fields. Lands. S.
4357. * 塡 32/10 To fill in, fill up, level off.

T'ING

4358. 聽 128/16 To hear, obey. (t'eng)
  (a) t'ing-yāt 5137. Tomorrow.

T'ÌNG

4359. * 聽 128/16 To allow, wait, await, follow. (t'èng, t'eng, t'ing)

T'ĪNG

4360. 停 9/9 To stop, rest, cease, delay.
4361. * 亭 8/7 A resting place. Portico. Arbor. Pavilion.
4362. * 庭 53/7 Inner court. Hall. Family rooms. (t'ĕng)

4363. 蜓 142/7 Kind of lizard.

T'IP。

4364. 貼 154/5 To paste up, affix, attach to.

4365. 帖 50/5 Card. Bill. Document.

T'IT。

4366. 鐵 167/13 Iron.

4367. 鉄 167/5 Firmness. S.

(a) shaang-t'it。 3802. Cast iron.

(b) shŭk-t'it。 4011. Malleable iron.

(c) t'it。-kaap。 1488. Ironclad.

(d) t'it。-lõ 2426. Railroad.

(e) t'it。-kwai 2063. A rail.

(f) paāk-t'it。 2063. Tin.

(g) k'ap-t'it。 1926. Iron magnet.

(h) t'it。-faàn 671. Sulphuret of iron.

(i) t'it。-wā-fán 4958-713. Acetate of iron.

(j) t'it。-lõk 2454. Black oxide of iron.

4368. 饕 184/9 Gluttonous.

T'IU

4369. 挑 64/6 To bear a load, irritate, mix up, provoke.

4370. 佻 9/6 Weak. Unsteady.

T'IŪ

4371. 跳 157/6 To leap, jump, bound, bounce, dance.

4372. 越 156/6 To hop, jump. uf 4371.

4373. 糶 119/19 To sell grain.

4374. 彫 59/8 To engrave, carve. (tiu)

T'IŪ

4375. 條 75/6 C of things long and slender.

4376. 条 75/3

(a) t'iū-chaàl 117. Trigger.

4377. 調 149/8 To harmonize, adjust, blend. (tiû)

(a) t'iū-chî 235. Medical treatment.

T'O

4378. 饕 184/13 Gluttonous.

4379. 叨 30/2 Covetous. Anxious for.

T'Ó

4380. 土 R 32 Earth. Soil. Place. Local. Native. S.

(a) t'ó-iu 1379. Isthmus.

(b) t'ó-kok。 1744. A cape of land.

(c) t'ó-sing 3652. Planet Saturn.

(d) t'ó-Ĭ-k'eĬ 1280-1955. Turkey.

4381. 禱 113/14 To pray, entreat. (tó)

4382. 討 149/3 To search, ask for, beg.

4383. 吐 30/3 Phonetic. See t'ò, t'òh.

4384. 島 46/7 An island. (tó)

___

T'ò

4385. 吐 30/3 To pour out, throw up. S. (t'òh)

4386. 套 37/7 A covering. Case. Noose. Trap. To trap. C.

4387. 菟 10/10 } Hare.
4388. 兔 10/5 } Rabbit.

4389. 菟 140/8 Dodder species.

___

T'ō

4390. 徒 60/7 Disciple. Associate. Vainly.
(a) moōn-t'ō 2779. Disciple.
(b) t'ō-taī 4077. Apprentice.
(c) t'ō-īn 1349. Vainly. Without cause.

4391. 逃 162/6 To flee, escape, abscond.

4392. 桃 75/6 Peach species. S.
(a) yìng-tsuí-t'ō 5223-4627. Beaked peach.
(b) ha-māt-t'ō 899-2638. Khamil peach.
(c) yeūng-t'ō 5195. Carambola.
(d) t'ō-kaau 1495. Peach gum.
(e) shēk-sīn-t'ō 3879-3640. Orchis.

(f) t'ō-hūng 1235. Carnation.
(g) kaap̥-chuk-t'ō 1485-364. Oleander.
(h) t'ō-uě 4891. Olibanum.

4393. 圖 31/11 Plan. Chart. Map. Scheme. Plot.

4394. 萄 140/8 Grape vine.

4395. 塗 32/10 Mud. Mire. Dirt. To daub, blot out. S.

4396. 途 162/7 Road. Path. Pursuit. Journey.

4397. 淘 85/8 To scour, wash out.

4398. 荼 140/8 A bitter herb.

4399. 陶 170/8 Pottery furnace. Kiln.

4400. 屠 44/9 A butcher. To slaughter. S.

4401. 翿 124/14 A banner.

___

T'ŏ

4402. 肚 130/3 Stomach. Abdomen.
(a) t'ŏ-fuk 870. Belly. Bowels.
(b) siú-t'ŏ 3674. Bladder of animals.
(c) ngaū-t'ŏ 3039. Tripe.
(d) yaū-t'ŏ 5159. Pregnant.

___

T'OH

4403. 拖 64/5 } To drag, lead,
4404. 扡 64/5 } involve, raise up.
(a) t'oh-shuěn 3999. Tugboat.

T'ÓH

4405. 安 38/4 Settled. Secure.
* Quiet. Ready.
(t'ŏh)

(a) t'ŏh-tòng 4235.
Correct. In order.

T'ÒH

4406. 唾 30/8 Spit. Saliva.
*

4407. 吐 30/3 To spit.
" (t'eŭ)

T'ŎH

4408. 駝 187/5 Camel.
* Hump-backed.

(a) t'ōh-pooì 3377. Hump-
backed. Bent over.

4409. 馱 187/4 To bear on the
* back. To impreg-
nate.

(a) t'ōh-t'ŏ 4402.
Pregnant.

4410. 鉈 167/5 A weight.
'

(a) tiù-t'ōh 4189.
Plumbline.

4411. 砣 112/5 A stone roller.
' Weight.

4412. 鴕 196/5
'

(a) t'ōh-niŭ 2920.
The ostrich.

4413. 陀 170/5
" '

4414. 佗 9/5 uf 4408
' and 4409.

T'ŎH

4415. 柁 75/5 Helm. Tiller.
'

4416. 舵 137/5 Rudder. (t'aaŸ)
*

T'OI

4417. 胎 130/5 The womb. Preg-
* nant. Congenital.

(a) t'oi-tûng 4277.
Quickening.

(b) t'oi-i 1248.
Placenta.

(c) shēk-t'oi 3879.
Barren.

(d) chue-t'oi 314.
Pearl mussel.

(e) mīn-t'oi 2676.
Cotton quilt.

T'OĪ

4418. 檯 75/14 A table.
*

4419. 枱 75/5
'

(a) ì-t'oĪ 1287.
Second hand.

(b) yat-t'oĪ 5133.
A table full.

(c) paat-sin-t'oĪ 3195-
3640. Octagon table.

4420. 撞 64/14 To carry on a
' pole between
two or more
4421. 抬 64/5 persons. To
raise up, move.

4422. 臺 133/8 Terrace. Turret.
* Platform. Stage.
Title of re-
spect. S.

(a) kóng-shue-t'oĪ 1779-
3982. Pulpit.

(b) p'aaù-t'oĪ 3438.
A fort.

(c) t'oĪ-waan 4971.
Formosa.

4423. 台 30/2 Eminent.
* Honored. S.

(a) hing-t'oĪ 1070.
Brother. Comrade.

4424. 苔 140/5 Moss. Lichen.
'

T'OĬ

4425. 殆 78/5 Dangerous. Nearly. Negligent. Idle.

4426. 怠 61/5 (4426 toĭ)

T'OK。

4427. 托 64/3 } To support, grasp, carry.

4428. 拓 64/5 }

   (a) fa-t'ok。 650. Calyx.

   (b) t'ok。-laāt-sz 2194-3756. A "Trust".

4429. 託 149/3 To commit to, entrust with, charge with.

T'ONG

4430. 劏 18/13 To kill, slaughter.

   (a) t'ong-hoi 1124. To rip open.

   (b) shaang-t'ong 3802. To cut up alive.

   (c) t'ong-sź-ngaū 3767-3039. A footpad.

4431. 湯 85/9 Soup. Broth. Gravy. Hot water. S.

T'ÓNG

4432. 倘 9/8 If. Supposing.

   (a) t'óng-yeūk 5181. If it be. If so.

T'ÒNG

4433. 燙 86/12 To iron, scald, blister.

4434. 撗 64/15 To open (sliding windows).

T'ŌNG

4435. 堂 32/8 Hall. Court. Chapel. Meeting place.

4436. 唐 30/7 Exaggerated. Boastful. S.

   (a) t'ōng-shaan 3793. China.

   (b) t'ōng-yān 5117. Chinese.

4437. 糖 119/10 Sugar. Sweets.

   (a) paāk-t'ōng 3178. Refined sugar.

   (b) t'ōng-shui 4004. Molasses. Syrup.

4438. 塘 32/10 A pool. Tank. Embankment.

   (a) yat-t'ōng-lō 5133-2426. A league.

4439. 棠 75/8 Crabapple tree.

   (a) ch'un-hoí-t'ōng 629-1125. Begonia.

4440. 螗 142/10 Kind of cicada.

   (a) t'ōng-mei 2655. Dragon fly.

4441. 螳 142/11

   (a) t'ōng-lōng 2466. The mantis.

4442. 膛 130/11 The thorax. Breast. Hollow.

T'UĔN

4443. 團 31/11 A lump. Cake. Cluster. C.

4444. 臀 130/13 The seat. Rump. Buttocks.

T'UĚN

4445. 斷 69/14 To cut off, break off. (tuĕn)

T'UET。

4446. 脱 130/7 To strip, remove, escape, avoid.

___

T'UI

4447. 推 64/8 To push, decline, shirk, avoid. (ch'ui)

___

T'UÍ

4448. 腿 130/10 Thigh. Leg. Ham.

___

T'UÌ

4449. 退 162/6 To put away, remove, retreat, decline.

___

T'UĪ

4450. 頹 181/7 Used up. Feeble. infirm.

___

T'UK

4451. 禿 115/2 Bald. Bare. Blunt. S.

___

T'UNG

4452. 通 162/7 To go through, perceive. All. The whole.

  (a) t'ung-chi 205.
    To inform.
  (b) t'ung-pò 3337.
    To advertise.
  (c) t'ung-sz̤ 3776.
    An interpreter.
  (d) t'ung-ch'é-kaì 493-
    1521. Average.
  (e) tá-t'ung 4027.
    To bribe.

___

  (f) t'ung-shue 3982.
    Almanac.
  (g) t'ung-lung 2529. A
    hole through. A vent.
  (h) in-t'ung 1334.
    Chimney pipe.

4453. 通 140/11 Kind of plant used to make paper.

  (a) t'ung-chí 216.
    Rice paper.
  (b) t'ung-mô 2726.
    Pith hat.

___

T'ÚNG

4454. 桶 75/7 Cask. Tub. Pail. Chest. Box. *

4455. 統 120/6 To command, rule. The whole. All. S. *

  (a) t'úng-kaì 1521.
    To sum up.
  (b) t'úng-taal 4031. To
    be in command of.

4456. 埔 32/7 Pit. Grave. *

4457. 捅 64/7 To stick into, punch into.

___

T'ÙNG

4458. 痛 104/7 Pain. Ache. Illness. Distress. Intense. S.

___

T'ŪNG

4459. 同 30/3 Altogether.

4460. 仝 9/3 With. United. S.

  (a) t'ūng-yān-ooî 5119-
    3143. United Brethren Church.

4461. 筒 118/6 Pipe. Tube. Duct.

  (a) fóh-yeùk-t'ūng 767-
    5183. Cartridge.

(b) maǎn-fa-t'ūng 2576-
650. Kaleidoscope.
(c) mǎn-pêng-t'ūng 2629-
3278. Stethoscope.
(d) ǐ-t'ūng 1280.
Telephone receiver.

4462. 銅 167/6 Copper. Brass.

(a) wŏng-t'ūng 5070.
Brass.
(b) hūng-t'ūng 1235.
Copper. Arsenide
of nickel.
(c) t'ūng-lāk 2217. Sul-
phate of copper.
(d) t'ūng-lŏk 2454.
Oxide of copper.

4463. * 童 117/7 Lad. Student.
Virgin. S.

(a) t'ūng-shaang 3802.
Student.

4464. 僮 9/12 Slave boy or
girl. A youth.

4465. 桐 75/6 Varnish tree.

(a) t'ūng-yaū-fooi 5149-
847. Putty.

4466. ' 瞳 109/12 Pupil of the
eye.

4467. ' 篸 118/11 Hairclasp. Pin.

4468. 篸 118/12 To pin, peck.
(ch'aǎm)

4469. * 暫 72/11 Temporarily.

(a) tsaǎm-shǐ 3905.
For a while.
(b) tsaǎm-ch'è 492.
Meanwhile.

4470. * 鏨 167/11 A small chisel.
To cut, enchase.
(tsaǎm)

4471. ' 趲 156/19 To urge, hasten,
put to flight.

4472. 讚 149/19 To praise, eulogize, commend.

(a) tsaàn-meǐ 2661.
To praise, extol.

4473. * 濺 85/19 To spatter,
splash, recoil.
(tsaàn)

4474. ' 贊 154/12 To assist, aid,
second. S.

4475. ' 雜 172/10 Mixed. Confused.
Miscellaneous.

(a) tá-tsaáp 4027. Man of
all work. A coolie.
(b) tsaáp-keuk。 1638.
Buffoonery.

4476. ' 習 124/5 To practice. A
custom. Habit.S.

4477. ' 集 172/4 To collect, gather. An assembly.
S.

4478. ' 楫 75/11

(a) tsaáp-mūk 2795.
Kind of hard wood.

4479. " 甲 13/3 See 1493a.

4480. ' 擠 64/14 To press upon,
push. (chai)

(a) tsai-yúng 5263. A
throng. To throng.

4481. ' 劑 18/14 To adjust, trim,
compound.

TSAÍ

4482. 仔 9/3 A son. Boy.
** Little. A diminutive particle.
(a) tsaí-nuí 2949.
    Children.
(b) nuí-tsaí.
    A girl. Daughter.
(c) kaú-tsaí 1574.
    A puppy.
(d) chue-tsaí 312. Small
    pig. Emigrant sold
    like a pig.
(e) fóh-shuên-tsaí 767-
    3999. Steam launch.
(f) heung-kóng-tsaí 1046-
    1780. Aberdeen.

TSAÌ

4483. 祭 113/6 Sacrifice.
* Worship. S.
(a) tsaI-sz 3756.
    A priest.
4484. 濟 85/14 To aid, help,
* relieve.
4485. 際 170/11 Intercommunication. A place.
' Limit.
(a) kaau-tsaI 1494. Intercourse of friends.
4486. 嚌 30/14 Too. Superlative degree.
*

TSAK

4487. 則 18/7 Rule. Law. Conjunction. Then.
", (tsik)
(a) shî-tsak 3909.
    So then.
(b) I-tsak.1287.
    Secondly.
(c) tsak-kʻēk 1970.
    To amuse.
1487½. 鰂 195/9 A species of
', fish.

(a) hoí-tsak 1125.
    Variety of perch.
(b) kam-tsak 1527.
    Red tailed bream.

TSĂM

4488. 浸 85/7 To immerse,
* soak. Deep.
(a) tsăm-laí 2205.
    Baptism. Immersion.
(b) tsăm-sùn-ooí 3743-
    3143.Baptist Church.

TSANG

4489. 憎 61/12 To hate, detest.
(a) tsang-oò 3117.
    To abhor. To hate.
4490. 增 32/12 To add to, increase.
4491. 曾 73/8 Great(grandson
' etc.) To increase. S.
    (tsʻāng)
(a) tsang-tsó 4587.
    Great grandfather.
4492. 罾 122/12 Square lifting
' net.

TSÀNG

4492½. 甑 98/12 Boiler. Caldron.
'

TSÂNG

4493. 贈 154/12 To give, present,confer on.
*.

TSAP

4494. 執 140/11 A little. Tuft.
', A pinch. Things
    close together.
    (chap)

TSĀT

4495. 疾 104/5 Illness.Disease.
Urgent. S.
(a) tsāt-yăn 5117.
A leper.
(b) tsāt-haú 1006.
To haggle.

4496. 蒺 140/10 Gorze. Furze.
Caltthrops.

4497. 嫉 38/10 Envy. Jealousy.

TSAU

4498. 撤 64/8 To grasp, beat
the watch,fight.

TSAÚ

4499. 走 R/156 To run, go hurriedly, travel,
depart.

4500. 酒 164/3 Spirits. Liquor.
Wine.
(a) hak-tsaú 971.
Port wine.
(b) hŭng-tsaú 1235.
Claret.
(c) paāk-tsaú 3178.
Sherry or hock.
(d) pá-laān-teî-tsaú 3166-
2181-4125. Brandy.
(e) fóh-tsaú 767.
Alcohol.
(f) tsaú-tsuèn 4623.
Corkscrew.
(g) tsaú-tsĭk 4546.
Banquet.

TSAÙ

4501. 奏 37/6 To report to
superiors. To
perform (in
music).

4502. 縐 120/10 Wrinkled.
(ơh'aaū)

(a) tsaù-sha 3780.
Crape.

4503. 皺 107/10 Wrinkles.
Furrows.

TSAÛ

4504. 就 43/8 Now. Then.
Forthwith. S.

4505. 袖 145/5 A sleeve.
To sleeve.

4506. 驟 187/14 Quick. Suddenly.
To race.

TSE

4507. 嗟 30/10 To sigh.

TSÉ

4508. 姐 38/5 Elder sister.

TSÈ

4509. 借 9/8 To lend, borrow,
suppose.
(a) tsè-taan 4046. Promissory note. Bond.
(b) tse-ì 1258.
Metaphor.

TSÊ

4510. 謝 149/10 To give thanks,
take leave, decline. S.

TSEK₂—See also tsik.

4511. 脊 130/6 The spine.
A ridge.

4512. 績 120/11 To spin, twist.
Merit. (tsik)

4513. 瘠 104/10 Lean. Emaciated.
Meager. S.(tsik)

TSĒK

4514. 蓆 140/10 A mat. Matting.
*

TSÉNG--See also tsing.

4515. 井 7/2 Well. Deep pit.
* S.
(a) yat-tséng 5133.
100 square or cubic feet.

TSĔNG

4516. 淨 85/8 | Pure. Spotless.
4517. 淨 15/8 | Clean. (tsĭng)

TSEUK。

4518. 雀 172/3 Birds.
(a) shī-shān-tseuk。 3905-3838. Canary.
(b) ngǎ-tseuk。 2981. House sparrow.
4519. 鵲 196/8 Jackdaw. Jay.
* Magpie.(ts'euk。)
4520. 爵 87/14 Rank of nobil-
' ity.
(a) kung-tseuk。 1878. Duke.
(b) haū-tseuk。 1009. Marquise.
(c) paak。-tseuk。 3172. Earl.
(d) tsź-tseuk。 4667. Viscount.
(e) naām-tseuk。 2824. Baron.

TSEŪK

4521. 嚼 30/18 To chew,
' ruminate.

TSEUNG

4522. 將 41/8 Sign of future tense. Will. Shall be. S.
(a) tseung-loī 2445.
In the future. Presently.
(b) tseung-kān 1549.
Nearly. About to.
4523. 漿 119/11 Flour paste.
* Starch.
4524. 漿 85/11 Syrup. Broth.
' Starch. Pasty.

TSEÚNG

4525. 槳 75/11 An oar.
Keelboard.
4526. 奬 37/11 To aid, exhort.
'

TSEÙNG

4527. 醬 164/11 Condiment.
* Sauce.
4528. 將 41/8 Military com-
' mander.(tseung)

TSEŪNG

4529. 匠 22/4 Mechanic. Workman. Artisan. S.
(tseúng)
4530. 像 9/12 Likeness.Image.
* Idol.
4531. 象 152/5 Elephant. Image.
Star.
(a) tseūng-p'eī 3468.
India rubber.
4532. 橡 75/12 Oak. Chestnut
' oak.

TSIK--See also tsek.

4533. 卽 26/7 That is. Which is. Now. Then. Near. S.

(a) tsik-haak。922.
　　Immediately.
(b) tsik-haî 968.
　　That is. Just so.

4534. 跡 157/6

4535. 速 162/7 | Trace. Footprint.

4536. 迹 162/6 | Mark. Appearance.

4537. 蹟 157/6 | Stain.

(a) î-tsik 1293.
　　Miracle.

4538. 積 115/11 | To pile up, hoard, store, gather together.

4539. 漬 85/11 | Soaked. Steeped in. Dyed.

4540. 績 120/11 | See tsek.

TSIK。

4541. 鶺 196/10 | The wagtail.

4542. 脊 130/ | See tsek。

4543. 瘠 104/10 | See tsek。

TSĪK

4544. 藉 140/14 | Confused. To lean on, depend on, avail oneself of. S.

4545. 寂 40/8 | Silent. Still. Quiet.

4546. 席 50/7 | A mat. Feast. Banquet.(tsēk)

4547. 夕 R/36 | Evening. Dusk. Late. S.

4548. 籍 118/14 | List. Register. Record. S.

4549. 蓆 140/10 | See tsēk.

TSIM

4550. 尖 42/3 | Pointed. Sharp. Acute. Clever. Point. Tip.

TSÎM

4551. 漸 85/11 | By degrees. To imbue. (tsîm, tsìm)

(a) tsîm-tsîm.
　　Gradually.

TSIN

4552. 煎 86/9 | To fry, grill, decoct. (tsìn)

4553. 箋 118/8 | Note paper. Tablet.

TSÎN

4554. 翦 124/9 | To cut off, shear, cut, remove.

4555. 剪 18/9 |

(a) tsîn-yūng 5272.
　　Velvet.

TSÌN

4556. 箭 118/9 | An arrow. Dart.

4557. 薦 140/13 | To introduce, recommend, raise.

4558. 荐 140/6 | To repeat, recur, introduce, recommend.

4558½. 煎 86/9 | To decoct.

TSÎN

4559. 賤 154/8 | Ignoble. Low. Mean. Cheap. S.

(a) tsîn-yān 5117.
　　Low fellow.

TSING

4560. 精 119/8 Essence of vitality. Excellent. Fine. Semen.

(a) tsing-shǎn 3835. Vigor. Energy.

(b) tsing-kung 1877. Skilled workman.

(c) tsing-tsai 4482. A shrewd fellow.

4561. 晶 * 72/8 Crystal. Pure and bright.

(a) wǒng-tsing 5070. Indian topaz.

(b) māk-tsing 2606. Smoky quartz.

(c) laām-tsing 2167. Beryl.

(d) tsź-shuí-tsing 4670-4004. Quartz amethyst.

(e) t'ō-shik-shuí-tsing 4392-3917-4004. Bohemian ruby.

4562. 睛 109/8 Pupil or ball of the eye.

(a) ngaǎn-tsing 2999. The iris.

(b) paāk-tsing 3178. White of the eye.

(c) tsing-chue 314. Crystalline lens.

(d) p'aan-tsing 3428. Cataract.

TSÍNG

4563. 井 7/2 See tséng.

TSÌNG

4564. 淨 85/8 Pure. Spotless. Clean. (tsěng)

4565. 凈 15/8 Clean. (tsěng)

(a) tsîng-haí 968. Only.

4566. 靜 174/8 Quiet. Still. Peaceful.

(a) tsîng-hǒk 1140. Statics.

4567. 靖 117/8 To plan, regulate. Quiet. S.

4568. 窜 116/4 To entrap.

TSIP₀

4569. 接 64/8 To receive, succeed, splice. S.

(a) tsip₀-shaang-p'ǒh 3802-3528. Midwife.

TSIT₀

4570. 節 118/9 Joint. Verse. Festival. S.

(a) shī-tsit₀ 3905. Periods of time.

(b) tsit₀-chaí 117. Temperate.

(c) ts'ing-tsit₀ 4763. Chaste.

4571. 卩 R/26 A joint.

TSĪT

4572. 截 62/10 To cut off, stop, divide.

4573. 捷 64/8 Quick. Prompt. Active. S.

TSIU

4574. 蕉 140/12 Banana. Plantain.

4575. 椒 75/8 Pepper. Peppery. S.

4576. 礁 112/12 Rocks in water.

4577. 焦 86/8 Scorched. Dried up. S.

-234-

(a) tsiu-t'aàn 4300.
  Coke.

TSIÚ

4578. 勦 18/11 To destroy, ex-
  * terminate.
4579. 勦 19/11 To harass,
  ' trouble.

TSIÙ

4580. 燋 86/12 To wound by
  ' fire. To char,
  scorch.

TSIÛ

4581. 嘐 30/12 | To chew,
  *
4582. 嚼 30/15 | masticate.
  *

TSO

4583. 租 115/5 To rent, lease.
  Rent. Tax.
  (a) shap-tso 3843.
    Rent paid in kind.
4584. 糟 119/11 Sediment. Dregs.
  * Remains of malt.
  S.
4585. 遭 162/11 To encounter,
  * meet, endure.
  A turn.

TSÓ

4586. 早 72/2 Morning. Early.
  Previous. Before.
  (a) tsó-shān 3838.
    Good morning!
  (b) tsó-nīn 2895.
    Formerly.
  (c) tsó-tsó.
    Very early.
4587. 祖 113/5 Ancestor.
  * Founder. S.

4588. 棗 75/8 Jujube.
  * Date. S.
4589. 組 120/5 To knit, fasten
  ' together, or-
  ganize.
4590. 藻 140/16 Duckweed.
  ' Pond weed.

TSÒ

4591. 竈 116/16 | Furnace.
  '
4592. 灶 86/3 | Range. Hearth.
  *

TSÔ

4593. 做 9/9 To do, act,
  ** make. To be.
  (a) tsô-heî 1031.
    Finished.
4594. 造 162/7 To create, orig-
  ' inate, build, do.
  (a) tsô-chuế 328.
    Author. Originator.
4595. 皂 106/2 | Black. Menials.
  '
4596. 皂 106/2 | Servants.
  ' | Runners.

TSÓH

4597. 左 48/2 The left. Dep-
  ' uty. Error. S.

TSÒH

4598. 佐 9/5 To aid, assist.
  '

TSÔH

4599. 座 53/7 Couch. Seat.
  ' Throne. C.
  (a) yat-tsôh-t'aap. 5133-
    4307. A pagoda.

4600. 坐 $\frac{32}{4}$ See ts'ŏh.

(d) hó-tsoî 1099. Happily.
Fortunately.

TSOI

4601. 災 $\frac{86}{3}$ Calamity.
* Affliction.

4602. 灾 $\frac{86}{3}$ Divine
* judgment.

4603. 栽 $\frac{75}{6}$ To plant,
* set out.

4604. 哉 $\frac{30}{6}$ Expletive of
, praise or sur-
prise.

(a) shîng-tsoi 3945.
Holy!

(b) wôh-tsoi 5062.
Woe!

TSOÍ

4605. 宰 $\frac{40}{7}$ To rule, con-
, trol, slaughter
animals. S.

(a) chué-tsoí 328.
Ruler. Lord.

4606. 載 $\frac{159}{6}$ A year.
, (tsoî)

TSOÌ

4607. 再 $\frac{13}{4}$ Again.
Repeated.

4608. 載 $\frac{159}{6}$ Contained in.
* Recorded in. S.
(tsoí)

TSOÎ

4609. 在 $\frac{32}{3}$ To be, be pres-
** ent. Living at.
On. In.

(a) tsoî-tsoî.
Everywhere.

(b) m̄-tsoî 2551.
Not here. No need.

(c) tsoî-noî 2937.
Included. Within.

TSOK.

4610. 作 $\frac{9}{5}$ To make, do, act,
be, become. S.

TSŎK

4611. 昨 $\frac{72}{5}$ Recently. Late-
ly. Yesterday.
S. (tsok。)

4612. 鑿 $\frac{167}{19}$ A chisel.

4613. 錯 $\frac{167}{8}$ To chisel,
" gouge out.

TSONG

4614. 贓 $\frac{154}{18}$ Spoils.
*

4615. 賍 $\frac{154}{6}$ Booty.
* Plunder.

4616. 賕 $\frac{154}{14}$ To take bribes.

TSÒNG

4617. 葬 $\frac{140}{9}$ To bury.

4618. 塟 $\frac{140}{9}$

TSÔNG

4619. 臟 $\frac{130}{18}$ Chief viscera.
Entrails.

4620. 藏 $\frac{140}{14}$ Storehouse.
" '

TSUEN

4621. 尊 $\frac{41}{9}$ Honorable.
* Noble. S.

TSUÉN

4622. 纂 $\frac{120}{14}$ To seize, edit.
,

TSUEN

4623. 鑽 167 $\frac{167}{19}$ To bore, pierce.
* A bit.
(a) tsuen-shĕk 3879.
Diamond.

TSUĔT

4624. 絕 $\frac{120}{6}$ To cut off, sev-
er, destroy,
stop.

TSUI

4625. 疽 $\frac{104}{5}$ Deep seated
, ulcer. Abscess.
(a) ngaām-tsui 2994.
Cancer.

4626. 蛆 $\frac{142}{5}$ Maggots.
,

TSUÍ

4627. 嘴 $\frac{30}{12}$ Bill of bird.
* Mouth. Spout.
Pointed.

4628. 咀 $\frac{30}{5}$ To suck.
" uf 4627.

TSUÌ

4629. 最 $\frac{73}{8}$ Best. Very.Most.
* Excellent. Com-
plete.

4630. 醉 $\frac{164}{8}$ Drunk.
* Intoxicated.

TSUÍ

4631. 罪 $\frac{122}{8}$ Fault. Sin.
* Punishment.

4632. 聚 $\frac{128}{8}$ To gather,
* assemble.
(a) tsui-tsaāp 4477.
Assembly. Meeting.

4633. 序 $\frac{53}{4}$ Series.
* In order. S.

4634. 叙 $\frac{29}{7}$ To converse,
"' discuss.
4635. 敍 $\frac{66}{7}$
"'
(a) tsui-leî-à 2293-9.
Syria.

TSUK

4636. 足 $\frac{R}{157}$ Foot. Enough.
* Complete. S.

TSŬK

4637. 俗 $\frac{9}{7}$ Common. Plebian.
* Colloquial.
Vulgar.

4638. 族 $\frac{70}{7}$ Class. Tribe.
* Clan.

4639. 續 $\frac{120}{15}$ To join on, con-
, nect,succeed to.

TSUN

4640. 遵 $\frac{162}{12}$ To obey, con-
* form to.

4641. 樽 $\frac{75}{12}$ Bottle. Vase.
*

4642. 罇 $\frac{121}{12}$ Goblet.
*

4643. 津 $\frac{85}{6}$ To pass over,
, ford. Overflow.
Saliva.
(a) tsun-yĭk 5216.
Secretion.

TSÙN

4644. 進 $\frac{162}{8}$ To advance, en-
* ter.

TSÛN

4645. 盡 $\frac{108}{9}$ To exhaust. All.
* Entire. S.
(a) tsûn-t'aū 4339.
The very last.

(b) tsûn-tei 4124.
   Wholly.

TSUNG

4646. 宗 40/5 Ancestor. Origin. Sort. S.

4647. 蹤 157/11 Footprint. Trace.

4548. 踪 157/8 Vestige. To follow, imitate.

4649. 棕 75/8 Kind of palm.

4650. 椶 75/9 Coir. Brown color.

4651. 鬃 190/8 High head dress. Wig. Mane.

(a) chue-tsung-mō 312-2712
   2712. Bristles.

TSÚNG

4652. 總 120/11 To unite in one. All. Generic.

4653. 摠 64/11 Generally. Still. Certainly.

(a) tsúng-shò 3972.
   Total.

(b) tsúng-lei 2282.
   To superintend.

(c) tsúng-t'aū 4339.
   Foreman.

(d) tsúng-tuk 4255.
   Governor General.

(e) tsúng-t'úng 4455.
   President of a republic.

TSÙNG

4654. 縱 120/11 Lenient. Indulgent. To loose, tolerate.

(a) tsùng-ln 1349.
   Supposing.

(b) tsùng-sź 3768. Seeing that. Although.

TSÚNG

4655. 訟 149/4 Litigation. Action at law.

4656. 從 60/8 To follow. Attendants. (ts'úng)

4657. 頌 181/4 To praise, laud, eulogize. S.

4658. 誦 149/7 To chant, read, recite.

TSUT

4659. 卒 24/6 A soldier. Deputy. The end.

(a) tsut-chi 204.
   Finally.

TSZ

4660. 滋 85/10 Sap. To enrich, moisten, sprout.

(a) tsz-yún 5258. To mollify, fertilize.

(b) tsz-yik 5204.
   To benefit.

4661. 蚳 142/6 Hairy insects.

4662. 螆 142/10

4663. 資 154/6 Property. Capital.

4664. 孜 39/4 Ever active.

(a) tsz-sheng 3880.
   Buzzing.

4665. 貲 154/5 Property. Valuables. To redeem.

4666. 茲 140/6 This. Here. It. Now.

TSŹ

4667. 子 R/39 Boy. Son. Posterity. Seeds. Sir. Time period 11 P.M. to 1 A.M. S.

(a) tsź-saì 3589.
   Careful. Minute.

4668. 姊 $\frac{38}{5}$ Elder sister.
**

4669. 姉 $\frac{38}{5}$
.

4670. 紫 $\frac{120}{5}$ Purple. S.
.

4671. 滓 $\frac{85}{10}$ Sediment. Dregs.
'

TSŹ

4672. 字 $\frac{39}{3}$ Letter. Symbol.
**   Character. S.
   (a) tsź-hô 1109.
      Chop. Label.
   (b) tsź-mín 2687.
      Literally.

4673. 自 $\frac{R}{132}$ From. Self.
**   Personally.
   (a) tsź-kei 1623.
      (My)self.
   (b) tsź-hân 981.
      Remorse.
   (c) tsź-tsûn 4645.
      To suicide.
   (d) tsź-tsź.
      Gradually.
   (e) tsź-laàp. 2190.
      Independent.

4674. 嗣 $\frac{30}{10}$ Heirs. Poster-
*   ity. To connect.
       S.
   (a) tsź-tsź 4667.
      An adopted son.

4675. 祀 $\frac{113}{3}$ To sacrifice.
.

4676. 伺 $\frac{9}{5}$ To attend, wait
*   on, examine.

4677. 寺 $\frac{41}{3}$ Hall. Monastery
.   Temple.

4678. 巳 $\frac{R}{49}$ Time period 9
.   to 11 A.M.

4679. 牸 $\frac{93}{6}$ Females of cer-
'   tain animals.

4680. 飢 $\frac{184}{2}$ Food.
'   }

4681. 飼 $\frac{184}{5}$ To eat.
.

TS'AĀK

4682. 賊 $\frac{154}{6}$ A thief.
        Robber.

TS'AAM

4683. 參 $\frac{28}{9}$ To blend, mix
*   consult.(sham)

TS'AÁM

4684. 慘 $\frac{61}{11}$ Cruel. Inhuman.
        Distressing.
        Grief.
   (a) ts'aám-sam 3593.
      Shocking.

4685. 篸 $\frac{118}{11}$ Basket. Hod.
        Skuttle.(tsaam,
        ch'aám,ts'aàm)

TS'AĀM

4686. 蠶 $\frac{142}{18}$
'   } The silkworm.

4687. 蚕 $\frac{142}{4}$
.

4688. 巉 $\frac{46}{18}$ Rugged. Craggy.

4689. 慚 $\frac{61}{11}$
'   } Ashamed.

4690. 慙 $\frac{61}{11}$
.

4691. 讒 $\frac{149}{18}$ Calumny.
'   To slander.

TS'AAN

4692. 餐 $\frac{184}{7}$
.   } A meal. To eat.

4693. 飡 $\frac{184}{2}$
'

TS'AÀN

4694. 粲 119/7 Fine rice. Pure.

   (a) ts'aàn-t'aū 4339.
      Worthless fellow.

TS'AĀN

4695. 殘 78/8 To injure, ruin. Cruel.

   (a) ts'aān-yán 5114.
      Remorseless. Cruel.

TS'AAT。

4696. * 擦 64/15 To brush, polish. A brush.

TS'AI

4697. 妻 38/5 A wife.

4698. * 凄 15/8 Intense cold. Distressing.

4699. 淒 85/8 Afflicted. Miserable.

   (a) ts'ai-leūng 2315.
      Distressing.

4700. * 悽 61/8 Grief. Sorrow. Suffering.

4701. ' 棲 75/8 To roost, rest,

4702. ' 栖 75/6 sojourn. A roost.

TS'AÌ

4703. 切 18/2 The whole of. (ts'it。)

4704. * 砌 112/4 To lay, as bricks. To place, arrange.

TS'AĪ

4705. 齊 R 210 Equal. Even. All. A class. S. (chaai)

   (a) ts'aī-peī 3263.
      Prepared, Ready.

4706. 蠐 142/14 Grub. Maggot.

   (a) ts'aī-ts'ō 4788.
      Grub. Larva.

TS'AĬ

4707. ' 鯗 195/5 Fish variety.

   (a) wŏng-meī-ts'aĬ 5070-
      2663. Yellow tail
      mullet.
   (b) paāk-ts'aĬ 3178.
      Greenish mullet.

TS'AM

4708. * 侵 9/7 To invade, usurp, put in, stick in. S.

TS'ÁM

4709. ' 寢 40/11 To lie down to sleep, cease.

TS'ĀM

4710. * 尋 41/9 To seek for, ask for. (k'ām)

4711. 鱘 195/12 Sturgeon.

TS'AN

4712. 親 147/9 Personal. Close to. Relatives.

   (a) ts'an-shaú 3859.
      With (my) own hands.
   (b) ts'an-tsuí 4627.
      To kiss.
   (c) tĕng-ts'an 4131. To
      hit, as with a stone.

TS'ĀNG

4713. 曾 73/8 Past. Finished. Done. (tsang)

(a) m̄-ts'āng 2551.
Not yet.

(b) yă-ts'āng 5083.
Already.

4714. 層 44 A layer. Story
12 of a house.
Degree.

(a) kaak。-ts'āng 1448.
Strata.

___

TS'AP

4715. 葺 140 To repair,
9 thatch, cover.

4716. 戕 62 To lay aside
9 weapons. To cut
off, tread down.
S.

4717. 緝 120 To pursue,
9 catch.

___

TS'AT

4718. 七 1
** 一
The numeral 7:
4719. 柒 75 common, compli-
5 cated and run-
4720. 杀 8 ning hand forms.
一

(a) yat-yat-ts'at-ts'at
5133. Worthless.

4721. 漆 85 Lacquer tree.
* 11 Varnish. Paint.

(a) yaū-ts'at 5149. Paint.
To paint, varnish.

4722. 膝 130 See sat.
* 11

(a) ngaū-ts'at-ts'ó 3039-
4777. Hyssop.

4723. 屾 46 The penis.
" 屮 2

___

TS'AU

4724. 秋 115 Autumn.
4 Harvest. S.

4725. 鞦 177 To swing.
9 A swing.

___

4726. 鰍 195 ⎫
鰍 9 ⎬ Eel. Lizard.
4627. 鰌 195 ⎭
鰌 9

(a) hoí-ts'au 1125.
Sea serpent. Dragon.

(b) hoí-ts'au-uē 4872.
Whale.

(c) ts'au-uē-kwat 2083.
Whalebone.

___

TS'AÙ

4728. 湊 85 To collect, at-
9 tend to, attend
on.

(a) ts'aù-ngaam 2993.
Just the thing.

(b) wâ-maaī-ts'aù 4960-
2568. Sweeping as-
sertion.

___

TS'AŪ

4729. 囚 31 A prisoner. To
* 2 imprison.(ch'aū)

___

TS'È

4730. 斜 68 Uneven.
* 7 Slanting. (ts'ē)

___

TS'Ē

4731. 斜 68 Oblique. Aslant.
* 7 Uneven. (ts'è)

(a) ts'ē-mān 2619.
Twilled.

4732. 邪 163 Wicked. Demon-
* 4 iacal. Depraved.
Erroneous.

(a) ts'ē-kaaū 1507.
Heresy.

___

TS'EK。-See also ts'ik.

4733. 瘌 104 Pricking pain.
* 9 Ache.

-241-

TS'ĒNG--See also ts'ing.

4734. 請 149/8 To request, invite, engage.
(a) ts'éng-à 8.
Good bye.

TS'EUNG

4735. 槍 75/10 Spear. Lance. Weapon. *

4736. 鎗 167/10 Spear. Gun. Pistol. Opium pipe. *

TS'EŪNG

4737. 搶 64/10 To take by force, rob, ravish.

TS'EŪNG

4738. 牆 90/13 A wall.

4739. 墻 32/13

4740. 詳 149/6 To discuss, judge. Minutely detailed. *

4741. 祥 113/6 Felicity. Good luck.

4742. 爿 R/90 To split wood. "'"

TS'IK

4743. 戚 62/7 Relatives by affinity. Grieved. S. *

4744. 刺 18/6 To pierce, stab, wound. To tattoo. To pole a boat. (ts'z) '

TS'IK。

4744½. 癡 104/8 See ts'ek。

TS'IM

4745. 簽 118/13 To subscribe, sign, endorse, label.

4746. 籤 118/17 Divining slip. Lot. Warrant. Ticket.

4747. 剆 18/14 To cut, stick in. '

4748. 劖 18/17 '

4749. 憸 61/13 Insinuating. Flattering. "'"

4750. 纖 120/17 Small. Fine. Delicate. "'"

TS'ĬM

4751. 僭 9/12 To arrogate to oneself, usurp. '

TS'ĪM

4752. 摺 64/12 To grasp, pick out, draw out. '

4753. 潛 85/12 To dive, hide. To do secretly. '

TS'IN

4754. 千 24/1 A thousand. **

4755. 仟 9/3 Many. All.

4756. 遷 162/12 To remove, move, transfer, change. S. (4757 hui)

4757. 迁 162/3 *

4758. 韆 177/15 A swing. To swing.

TS'ÍN

4759. 淺 85/8 Shallow. Easy. Simple.
(a) ts'ín-paāk 3178. Very simple.

TS'ĬN

4760. 前 18/7 In front. Before (of time or place). First.

4761. 錢 167/8 A coin. Cash.

4762. 木 4/2 Money. S.

TS'ĬNG

4763. 清 85/8 Pure. Clear. Honest. Correct. S.

(a) ts'ing-ch'ŏh 574. Settled. Right.Good.

(b) ning-ts'ing 2896. Take entirely.

4764. 青 R/174 Color of nature. Green. Blue. Black.

(a) ts'ing-oŏt 3157. Verdant.

(b) ts'ing-yŭk 5250. Sapphire.

(c) uĕn-ts'ing 4918. Black.

(d) ts'ing-nĭn 2895. Springtime of life. Youth.

(e) ts'ing-nĭn-ooî 3143. Young Men's Association.

(f) kai-taân-ts'ing 1515-4057. White of egg.

(g) ts'ing-t'ó 4384. Tsingtao.

TS'ÍNG

4765. 請 149/8 See ts'éng.

TS'ĪNG

4766. 情 61/8 Feelings. Affections. Emotions. Lust.

(a) ts'ing-uĕn 4632. Voluntary. Willingly.

(b) ts'ing-leî 2285. Common sense.

(c) ts'ing-yÍng 5230. Aspect.

(d) ts'ing-yaū 5148. Motive.

(e) toh-ts'ing 4215. Amorous.

(f) ts'ing-yân 5117. Adulterer.

(g) yān-ts'ing 5117. A permit. Favor.

(h) sz-ts'ing 3758. Fornication.

4767. 晴 72/8 Clear. Cloudless.
*

TS'IP。

4768. 妾 38/5 Concubine. Handmaid. S.
'

TS'IT。

4769. 切 18/2 To cut, carve. Earnest. Urgent. (ts'aî)

TS'IŨ

4770. 誚 149/7 To blame, scold, ridicule.
*

4771. 肖 130/3 Like. Similar. To imitate.

4772. 俏 9/7 Similar.Pretty. Scraping.

TS'IŪ

4773. 鍪 167/9 A spade. To
*
4774. 鍬 167/9 shovel, spade, dig out.

TS'O

4775. 粗 119/5 Coarse. Rough. Rude.

-243-

4776. 操 64/13 To manage, hold
* to. To drill. S.

TS'ó

4777. 草 140/6 Grass. Plants.
Vegetation. S.

  (a) ts'ó-ch'eüng 510.
    A meadow.

  (b) ts'ó-tsź 4672. Grass
    characters. The run-
    ning hand Chinese
    writing.

  (c) ts'ó-kó 1722.
    Rough sketch.

4778. 艸 R/140 Plants.
"'

TS'ò

4779. 醋 164/8 Vinegar.

4780. 躁 157/13 Hasty. Violent.
*

4781. 趮 156/13 Irascible.
*

4782. 燥 86/13 Dry. Parched.
*

TS'ō

4783. 嘈 30/11 Noise. Clamor.

4784. 譄 149/11 Uproar. Din.

4785. 槽 75/11 Manger. Trough.
* Groove.

  (a) tsaú-ts'ō 4500.
    A distillery.

  (b) ts'ō-chue. 312.
    To rear pigs.

4786. 漕 85/11 Watercourse.
* Whirlpool.
To transport.
by water.S.

4787. 艚 137/11 A junk.
"'

4788. 螬 142/11 Grubs in fruit.
'"

4789. 曹 73/7 S.
"'

TS'OH

4790. 搓 64/10 To rub, roll be-
* tween the hands.
(ch'aai)

TS'ÒH

4791. 錯 167/8 Mistake. Error.
Wrong.

4792. 銼 167/7 File. Rasp. To
* file. (ch'òh)

TS'ǑH

4793. 坐 32/4 See tsôh.

TS'OI

4794. 啋 30/8 Interjection.
"

4795. 啋 30/11 Fie!
" To billingsgate.

TS'OI

4796. 彩 59/8 Variegated.
* Brilliant.Lucky.

  (a) ts'oí-tseuk。-fa 4518-
    650. Larkspur.

  (b) hó-ts'oí 1099.
    Happily.

4797. 採 64/8 To pluck,
* select.

  (a) ts'oí-shĕk 3879.
    To quarry.

4798. 睬 109/8 To take notice
* of.

4799. 朵 165/1 To pluck, take.
"' S.

TS'OI

4800. 菜 140/8 Vegetables. Herbs. Food in general.

(a) shaang-ts'oi 3802. Lettuce.

(b) paāk-ts'oi 3178. Native cabbage.

(c) yĕ-ts'oi 5173. Greens.

(d) yĕ-ts'oi 5169. Foreign cabbage.

(e) yĕ-ts'oi-fa 650. Cauliflower.

(f) haām-ts'oi 926. Sauerkraut.

4801.* 賽 154/10 To contest, exhibit, rival.

4802." 嘖 30/17

TS'OĪ

4803. 財 154/3 Property. Wealth. Valuables. Presents.

(a) ka-leī-ts'oī 1414-2276. Curry stuff.

4804.* 才 R 64 Ability. Talent. Power. Genius. S.

4805.• 材 75/3 Material. Stuff. Ability.

4806.* 裁 145/6 To make clothes, cut out, calculate.

(a) ts'oī-fūng 894. To tailor.

TS'ONG

4807. 倉 9/8 Granary. Storehouse.

(a) fòh-ts'ong 771. A godown. Warehouse.

4808.* 艙 137/10 Compartments of vessel. Hod.

4809.* 蒼 140/10 Azure. Color of sky. Sky. S.

(a) k'ūng-ts'ong 2035. Firmament.

4810. 鯧 195/8 ⎫ The pomfret.

4811. 鎗 195/10 ⎭

TS'ŌNG

4812.* 藏 140/14 To conceal, store up, hoard. (tsŏng)

TS'UEN

4813. 村 75/3 A village. Hamlet.

TS'UÈN

4814. 寸 R 41 An inch. S.

(a) ch'ek₀-ts'uèn 496. Dimensions. Measurments.

TS'UÈN

4815. 全 11/4 All. Complete. Entire. Perfect. S.

4816.* 存 39/3 To preserve, remain, continue.

(a) ts'uèn-kan 1539. Counterfoil. Stub.

4817.• 泉 85/5 A spring. Fountain.

4818.• 痊 104/5 Cured. Recovered.

4819."• 銓 167/6 To estimate, select.

TS'UET₀

4820.' 捽 64/8 To grasp, clutch, butt.

4821. 撮 $\frac{64}{12}$ To gather up.

   (a) ts'uet₅-tük 4261.
     Avaricious.

TS'UI

4822. 推 $\frac{9}{11}$ To urge, hasten, press upon.

4823. 趨 $\frac{156}{10}$ To run after, follow, hasten.

TS'UÍ

4824. 取 $\frac{29}{6}$ To take, appropriate, receive.

TS'UÌ

4825. 娶 $\frac{38}{8}$ To take a wife, marry.

4826. 趣 $\frac{156}{8}$ Agreeable. Amusing. To hasten.

4827. 翠 $\frac{124}{8}$ Kingfisher. Bluish.

4828. 脆 $\frac{130}{6}$ Delicate.

4829. 脆 $\frac{130}{6}$ Brittle. Crisp.

TS'UÏ

4830. 隨 $\frac{170}{13}$ To follow, comply with. S.

4831. 徐 $\frac{60}{7}$ Dignified. Sedate.

TS'UK

4832. 速 $\frac{162}{7}$ Haste. Quick. (tsik)

4833. 促 $\frac{9}{7}$ Urgent. Contracted.

   (a) ts'uk-chik 238.
     The house cricket.

4834. 簌 $\frac{118}{11}$ Dense growth.

4835. 籔 $\frac{118}{11}$ A sieve.

TS'ŪN

4836. 循 $\frac{60}{9}$ To revolve, according with, sooth.

   (a) ts'un-tô-ooi 4207-
     3143. Wesleyan Mission.

4837. 巡 $\frac{47}{4}$ To patrol, go on circuit or beat.

4838. 巡 $\frac{47}{3}$

   (a) ts'un-ting 4168.
     Patrol. Police.

   (b) ts'un-shuen 3999.
     Guard boat.

   (c) ts'un hang 986.
     To encompass.

4839. 旬 $\frac{72}{2}$ Decade. Period of ten days.

   (a) ng-ts'un-tsit₀ 2962-
     4570. Pentecost.

4840. 紃 $\frac{120}{3}$ Silk bands. A spindle.

4841. 馴 $\frac{187}{3}$ Tame. Docile.

4842. 秦 $\frac{115}{5}$ S.

4842½. 鱒 $\frac{195}{12}$ Kind of fish. Roach.

TS'UNG

4843. 聰 $\frac{128}{11}$ To understand. Acute.

4844. 聰 $\frac{128}{9}$ Quick. Smart.

4845. 葱 $\frac{140}{9}$ Onion species.

   (a) ts'ung-t'au 4339.
     Onions.

   (b) sai-heung-ts'ung 3589-
     1046. Chives.

4846. 璁 $\frac{96}{11}$ Turquois.

4847. 瑽 $\frac{96}{11}$

   (a) ts'ung-hang 989.
     Emerald.

TS'ŪNG

4848. 從 $\frac{60}{8}$ To follow, obey, agree with. From. S. (tsŭng)

  (a) ts'ŭng-ts'In 4760. Formerly.

4849. 松 $\frac{75}{4}$ Pine tree. S.

  (a) ts'ūng-heung 1046. Resin.

  (b) kom-ts'ūng-heung 1750. Spikenard.

  (c) ts'ūng-tsit-yaū 4570-5149. Turpentine.

  (d) ts'ūng-shuê-ko 3996-1714. Pitch.

  (e) ts'ūng-t'aap 4307. Pine cones.

4850. 叢 $\frac{29}{16}$ Crowded. Bush. Thicket. S.

TS'Z

4851. 疵 $\frac{104}{5}$ Flaw. Fault. Defect. Malady. Scab.

  (a) hak-ts'z 971. A mole.

4851½. 磁 $\frac{112}{10}$ Magnetic ore. (ts'z̄)

TS'Ź

4852. 此 $\frac{77}{2}$ This. Now. Here.

TS'Z̀

4853. 賜 $\frac{154}{8}$ To bestow, confer upon, give.

4854. 次 $\frac{76}{2}$ A time. Second in order. A turn. Next. S.

4855. 刺 $\frac{18}{6}$ To prick, stab, dig into.

4856. 莿 $\frac{140}{8}$ A thorn. S.

  (a) fán-ts'z̀ 713. Pimple.

  (b) keI-ts'z̀ 1605. Sarcasm.

  (c) òm-ts'z̀ 3106. Innuendo.

4857. 廁 $\frac{53}{9}$ A privy.

4858. 厠 $\frac{27}{9}$ Night stool.

4859. 束 $\frac{75}{2}$ A thorn. Spike.

TS'Z̄

4860. 柿 $\frac{75}{4}$ Persimmon.

  (a) kai-sam-ts'z̄ 1515-3593. Small red persimmon.

  (b) ngaū-sam-ts'z̄ 3039. Large red persimmon.

  (c) nām-ts'z̄ 2848. Soft flat persimmon.

4861. 辭 $\frac{160}{12}$ To decline, refuse, take leave.

4862. 詞 $\frac{149}{5}$ Word. Phrase. Style. Term.

4863. 磁 $\frac{112}{10}$ Magnetic iron ore. (ts'z)

  (a) ts'z̄-shêk 3879. Loadstone.

4864. 瓷 $\frac{98}{6}$ Earthenware. Porcelain.

4865. 慈 $\frac{61}{10}$ Gentle. Tender. Parental love.

  (a) ts'z̄-pei 3246. Compassionate.

  (b) ts'z̄-oI 3099. Affectionate love.

  (c) ts'z̄-sam 3593. Compassionate.

4866. 臍 $\frac{130}{14}$ The navel.

  (a) ts'z̄-taaI 4031. Umbilical cord.

4867. 茨 $\frac{140}{6}$ Thatch. To thatch. S.

TS'Z	4868		UE	4873

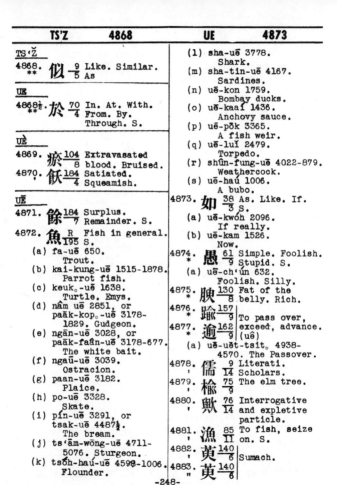

TS'Ž

4868. 似 9/5 Like. Similar.
** As

UE

4868½. 於 70/4 In. At. With.
** From. By.
Through. S.

UÈ

4869. 瘀 104/8 Extravasated blood. Bruised.
4870. 飫 184/4 Satiated. Squeamish.

UĒ

4871. 餘 184/7 Surplus. Remainder. S.
4872. 魚 R 195/8 Fish in general. S.

(a) fa-uē 650.
   Trout.
(b) kai-kung-uē 1515-1878.
   Parrot fish.
(c) keuk₀-uē 1638.
   Turtle. Emys.
(d) nâm uē 2851, or paăk-kop₀-uē 3178-1829. Gudgeon.
(e) ngān-uē 3028, or paăk-faân-uē 3178-677. The white bait.
(f) ngaū-uē 3039.
   Ostracion.
(g) paan-uē 3182.
   Plaice.
(h) po-uē 3328.
   Skate.
(i) pín-uē 3291, or tsak-uē 4487½.
   The bream.
(j) ts'âm-wōng-uē 4711-5076. Sturgeon.
(k) tsŏh-haú-uē 4598-1006.
   Flounder.

(l) sha-uē 3778.
   Shark.
(m) sha-tin-uē 4167.
   Sardines.
(n) uē-kon 1759.
   Bombay ducks.
(o) uē-kaai 1436.
   Anchovy sauce.
(p) uē-pŏk 3365.
   A fish weir.
(q) uē-luī 2479.
   Torpedo.
(r) shûn-fung-uē 4022-879.
   Weathercock.
(s) uē-haú 1006.
   A bubo.

4873. 如 38/3 As. Like. If. S.

(a) uē-kwóh 2096.
   If really.
(b) uē-kam 1526.
   Now.

4874. 愚 61/9 Simple. Foolish. Stupid. S.
*
(a) uē-ch'ún 632.
   Foolish. Silly.

4875. 腴 130/8 Fat of the belly. Rich.
*

4876. 踰 157/9 To pass over,
*
4877. 逾 162/9 exceed, advance.
* (uē)
(a) uē-uĕt-tsit₀ 4938-4570. The Passover.

4878. 儒 9/14 Literati. Scholars.
'
4879. 楡 75/9 The elm tree.
'
4880. 歟 76/14 Interrogative and expletive particle.
'
4881. 漁 85/11 To fish, seize on. S.
'
4882. 黄 140/6 Sumach.
'
4883. 黄 140/6 Sumach.
"

(a) shĭk-chue-uē 3925-322.
Sumach.

4884. 輿 159 / 10 To maintain, contain. The earth. People.

4885. 甎 116 / 9 Thickness of brick.

(a) taan-uē 4046.
Single brick wall.

4886. 余 9 / 5 S.
" '

4887. 禺 114 / 4 Beginning.
" '
S.

4888. 雨 R / 173 Rain. Showers.

4889. 與 134 / 8 With. Together with.

(a) uě-k'ăp 1927.
Also.

4890. 語 149 / 9 Words. Sayings.
* To converse.

4891. 乳 5 / 7 Milk. Breasts.
* To suckle.

(a) ngaū-uě-tŭng 3039-4275. Blancmange.

4892. 宇 40 / 3 The four quarters. World. Sides of house.
*

4893. 羽 R / 124 Long feathers. Plumes. Whip. S.

(a) uě-sha 3780.
Camlet.

4894. 禹 114 / 4 S.
" '

4895. 預 181 / 4 To prepare, provide against.

(a) uê-liû 2400.
To anticipate.

(b) uê-peî 3263.
To prepare.

4896. 遇 162 / 9 To meet, happen, occur. S.

(a) uê-cheŭk 184.
To meet with.

4897. 喻 30 / 9 To teach, understand, communicate, illustrate. S.

4898. 諭 149 / 9

(a) p'eî-uê 3466. Illustration. Parable.

4899. 愈 61 / 9 To surpass, exceed, cure,
*

4900. 愉 61 / 9 become convalescent.
*

4901. 寓 40 / 9 To reside, sojourn. An allegory.

4902. 御 60 / 8 To drive horses, manage, control. Attendants, S.

(a) uê-laū 2261.
Tamarix chinensis.

4903. 譽 149 / 14 To praise, extol. S.

4904. 茹 140 / 6 Roots. To eat herbs. Greedy.

4905. 踰 157 / 9 To pass over, overstep,

4906. 逾 162 / 9 exceed, advance. (uē)
*

4907. 冤 14 / 9 To oppress,
*

4908. 寃 40 / 9 wrong. Act of injustice.
*

4909. 淵 85 / 8 Gulf. Ravine. Abyss. Deep. S.

4910. 院 170 / 7 A hall. Building. Establishment. (uên, uén)

(a) tin-kw'ŏng-uén 4159-2143. Insane asylum.

4911. 婉 38 / 8 Docile. Tender. Yielding.
'

4912. 苑 140/5 Elegant. Tare.

UÈN

4913. 怨 61/5 Indignant with. To regret, grumble, complain.

UĚN

4914. 緣 120/9 Hem. Selvage. Cause. Connection.

(a) uēn-koó 1809.
A reason.

4915. 完 40/4 Finished. To finish, complete.

4916. 園 31/10 Garden. Orchard. Park.

4917. 圓 31/10 Round. Circular. A dollar.

(a) uēn-t'uēn 4443.
Globular.

(b) taaî-uēn 4033.
A dollar.

(c) poòn-uēn 3389.
A half dollar.

4918. 元 10/2 First. Origin. Principle. A dollar. S.

4919. 原 27/8 Origin. Source. Cause. S.

4920. 源 85/10 Source of a stream. Spring.

4921. 鉛 167/5 Lead.

(a) hak-uēn 971.
Lead.

(b) paâk-uēn 3178.
Spelter. Pewter.

(c) uēn-seung 3627.
Acetate of lead.

(d) uēn-taan 4048.
Red oxide of lead.

(e) uēn-pat 3237.
Lead pencil.

(f) uēn-p'ìn 3491.
Leads. (pr).

4922. 員 30/7 An official. C for things round.

4923. 丸 3/2 Pill. Pellet. Ball. S.

4924. 沿 85/5 Follow along. Continue. Along the way.

4925. 芫 140/4

(a) uēn-sai 3585.
Caraway.

4926. 玄 95 R Dark. Deep. Profound. S.

4927. 懸 61/16 To tie up, suspend. Anxiety.

4928. 苑 140/3 A sedgy plant.

4928½. 鳶 196/3 A kite.

UĚN

4929. 遠 162/10 Far. Distant. Remote.

4930. 頓 159/9 Weak. Soft.

4931. 軟 159/4 Yielding. Pliable.

UÈN

4932. 願 181/10 To desire, wish for, long for.

4933. 縣 120/10 Governmental district. S.

4934. 愿 61/10 Loyal. Good. Careful. Sincere. uf 4932.

4935. 院 170/7 A hall, building. Establishment. (uěn, uén)

UET。

4936. 乙 R/5 To mark. Stem. Carved. S.

UĒT

4937. 月 R 74 The moon. A month. S.
(a) uēt-fân-p'aaī 724-3420. Calendar. Almanac.

4938. 越 156 5 To pass over, exceed. S.
(a) uēt-hó 1099. Still better.
(b) uēt-naām 2823. Annam.

4939. 悅 61 7 To take pleasure in, please, submit.
(a) uēt-mān-sam 2618-3593. Popular.

4940. 穴 R 116 Cave. Cavern. Recess. Den.

4941. 曰 R 73 To speak. It is said. The meaning of.

4942. 閱 169 7 To look over, review, as troops.

4943. 粵 119 6
(a) leŭng-uēt 2321. The two Kwong provinces.

UK

4944. 屋 44 6 House. Dwelling. Abode.
(a) uk-k'eī(k'eī) 1949. Home. House.
(b) uk-poòl 3377. Top of a house.

UNG

4945. 壅 32 13 To dung, cover up. (úng, yúng)

ÚNG

4946. 擁 64 13 To push, shove, crowd. (ung, yúng)

ŪNG

4947. 甕 98 13 Earthenware pitcher. Jar.

4948. 瓮 98 4 Circular opening. (aàng)

WA

4950. 呱 30 Wail. Cry. F— implying doubt.

4951. 譁 149 Clamor.

4952 嘩 30 12 Hubbub. (wâ)

4953. 娃 38 6 Beautiful woman. Baby.

4954. 哇 30 6 Wanton. To coax. To vomit.

WÁ

4955. 嗠 30 13 Patios. It is said. 4960 also used.

4956. 刷 18 9 To hack to death. Slicing to death.

4957. 摬 64 10 To grasp, scratch.

WĀ

4958. 華 140 8 Beauty. Splendor. Elegance. S.
(a) wā-meī 2661. Beautiful. Splendid.
(b) wīng-wā 5049. Glory.
(c) chung-wā 383. China.

4959. 樺 75 12 The birch.

WÂ

4960. 話 149 6 Language. Words. Speech. To speak. (wá)

-251-

4961. 畫 102/7 A picture. Drawing.
*

4962. 囬 102/3 Painting.
* (waāk)

WAAĪ

4963. 懷 61/16 Bosom. Affections. To cherish. S.
*

4964. 槐 75/10 Locust tree. S.
,

WAAÎ

4965. 壞 32/16 To spoil, ruin, destroy.
.

WAAK

4966. 或 62/4 Perhaps. Or. Uncertain.
.

 (a) waāk-ché 169. Perhaps.

4967. 畫 102/7 To draw, paint, plan. A stroke in writing. Mark. (wâ)
*

4968. 惑 61/8 Doubt. To delude, tempt, deceive.
.

4969. 劃 18/12 Graving tool. To carve, cut out, mark.
*

WAAN

4970. 彎 57/19 To draw, as a bow. Curved. Bent.
*

 (a) waan-kúng 1886. An arch.

4971. 灣 85/22 Bay. Cove. Anchorage.
*

 (a) waan-pōk 3362. To anchor.

 (b) waan-chaap。 97. To moor.

WAĀN

4972. 還 162/13 To return, repay. Still.
*

 (a) waān-shaú 3859. To retaliate.

4973. 頑 181/4 Stupid. Mulish. Fun.
*

 (a) waān-shá 3783. Play. Amusement.

4974. 環 96/13 Ring. Ornament. To encircle.
*

4975. 鐶 167/13 Ring. Bracelet.
*

WAĂN

4976. 挽 64/7 To lead, regain, revert, pull, recover. (waán)
.

4977. 鯇 195 The tench.
,

 (a) hak-waán 971. Black tench.

 (b) hak-shēk-waán 3879. Red fin tench.

WAÂN

4978. 患 61/7 Misfortune. Distress. Calamity.
.

4979. 宦 40/6 Official. Government servant.
,

4980. 幻 52/1 Phantom. Artifice.
,

WAĀNG

4981. 橫 75/12 Crosswise. Perverse. At the side. S.

 (a) waāng-pan 3220. Yokohama.

WAÂNG

4982. 橫 75/12 Perverse. Obstreperous. Evil. S.
*

-252-

(a) waâng-yīk 5214.
Perverseness.

(c) waî-noî-sui-laât
2937-3734-2194.
Venezuela.

WAAT₂

4983. 挖 $\frac{64}{6}$ To scoop out,
 * gouge, dig, pick.

WAÌ

4992. 慰 $\frac{61}{11}$ To soothe, com-
 * fort.

4993. 喂 $\frac{30}{9}$
 " To feed, suckle,

WAĀT

4984. 滑 $\frac{85}{10}$ Smooth. Slippery. Artful. S.
(a) waāt-shēk 3879.
 Soapstone.

4994. 餧 $\frac{184}{9}$ rear or breed
 * animals.

4995. 餒 $\frac{184}{8}$
 *

WAI

4985. 威 $\frac{38}{6}$ Majesty. Pomp.
 * Awful. Beauti-
 ful.
(a) wai-lāk-sź 2217-3777.
 Wales.

4996. 穢 $\frac{115}{13}$ Dirt. Filth.
 * To defile.

4997. 畏 $\frac{102}{4}$ To fear, dread,
 ' respect. Awe.

4998. 薈 $\frac{140}{13}$ To flourish.
 ' Luxuriant. (ool)

4986. 喊 $\frac{30}{9}$ Exclamation,
 " calling to a
 person. Hello!

WAÍ

4987. 諉 $\frac{149}{13}$
4988. 詒 $\frac{149}{9}$ To defame,
 * vilify.
(a) waí-p'òng 3534.
 To backbite, slander.

WAÎ

4999. 爲 $\frac{87}{8}$ To be, do, make.
 * S. (waî)

5000. 惟 $\frac{61}{8}$ But. Only.
 * To be.

5001. 圍 $\frac{31}{9}$ To surround,
 * enclose.

5002. 違 $\frac{162}{9}$ To oppose, dis-
 * obey.

5003. 遺 $\frac{162}{12}$ To bequeath,
 * leave behind,
 loose. S.

4989. 諉 $\frac{149}{8}$ To evade, shirk,
 excuse, retract.
(a) t'ui-waí 4447.
 To evade, excuse.

4990. 毀 $\frac{79}{9}$ To ruin,
 * destroy.

4991. 委 $\frac{38}{5}$ To sustain, give
 " over to. S.
(a) waí-shāt 3854.
 Certain. Really.
(b) waí-k'uk 2029.
 Grievous. Unjust.

5004. 帷 $\frac{50}{8}$ Curtain. Screen.
 * Vail. Tent.
(a) waî-mōk 2746. Cloth
 partition. Tent.

5005. 幃 $\frac{50}{9}$ Curtain. Women's
 * apartments.

5006. 維 $\frac{120}{8}$ To connect, fas-
 * ten, observe.

5007. 桅 $\frac{75}{6}$ A mast. Tree.
 *

5008. 囗 $\frac{R}{31}$ An enclosure.
 '

5009. 韋 $\frac{R}{178}$ Thongs. S.
 "'

-253-

WAĬ

5010. 諱 149/9 To conceal, avoid using (name). (faì)
*

5011. 葦 140/9 Kind of rush. Reed.
'

5012. 緯 120/9 Parallels of latitude. The woof.
'

  (a) waĭ-tô 4208. Latitude.

WAÎ

5013. 為 87/8 Because. The reason of. By means of. (waĭ)
**

5014. 位 9/5 Seat. Throne. site. C for persons.

5015. 衛 144/9 To defend, preserve, guard. S.

  (a) waî-shaang-hŏk 3802-1140. Hygiene.

5016. 慧 61/11 Wisdom. Intelligence. Sagacity.

5017. 謂 149/9 To inform, explain. Meant. S.
*

5018. 惠 61/8 Kindness. Grace. Favor. S.
*

5019. 胃 130/5 Stomach. Digestion.
*

  (a) waî-haú 1006. Appetite.

WAN

5020. 溫 85/9 Warm. Gentle. Benign. S.
*

  (a) wan-yaū 5152. Meek.

5021. 瘟 104/10 Epidemic. Plague.
*

  (a) wan-yĭk 5215. Pestilence. Plague, particularly bubonic.

  (b) wōng-wan-pĕng 5070-3278. The plague.

  (c) wan-ngaū 3039. Rinderpest.

  (d) wan-tuĭ-t'aū 4249-4339. Plague take him!

5022. 縕 120/10 uf 5026.
'

WÁN

5023. 搵 64/10 To seek, search. To dip.

5024. 穩 115/14 Firm. Stable. Secure.

  (a) wán-chân 141. Secure. Good.

  (b) wán-p'ōh 3528. A midwife.

5025. 媼 38/10 An old woman. (ó)

WÀN

5026. 韞 178/10 To hold, keep, Store up.(wán)
'

WĀN

5027. 雲 173/4 Clouds. S.

  (a) wān-shĕk 3879. Marble.

  (b) wān-mŏ-hok₂ 2720-1138. Mother of pearl.

  (c) wān-naām 2823. Yunnan province.

5028. 魂 194/4 Spirit. Soul. Ghost. Mind. Wits.

5029. 匀 20/2 Equal. Alike. Once.

5030. 芸 140/4 A fragrant plant.

5031. 云 7/2 To speak.
" '

WĂN

5032. 允 10/2 To believe, put confidence in, sanction. *
(a) wăn-chŭn 376. To authorize, assent to.

5033. 尹 44/1 To rule, oversee. True. S. "'

5034. 殞 78/10 To die, perish. "'

WÂN

5035. 運 162/9 To turn. Turn of destiny. Transport. Commerce. *
(a) wân-hōh 1119. A canal for commerce.

5036. 暈 72/9 To be dizzy, giddy. A halo. *
9 (wan, wăn)
(a) wân-lông 2468. Sea sickness.

5037. 混 85/8 Confused. Turbid. Disorderly. To confound. '

5038. 諢 149/9 To joke, jest. *

5039. 韻 180/10 Rhyme. Symmetrical. "'

WAT

5040. 屈 44/5 To bend, stoop. Oppression. Grievance. S. *

5041. 鬱 192/19 Dense growth. Depressed. *

5042. 欝 75/22 Anxious. Despondent. Grieved. S. *

5043. 爩 86/29 To smoke out, bleach with sulphur smoke. '

WĀT

5044. 核 75/6 Fruit stone. Pits. Kernel. (hăt) *

5045. 搰 64/10 To dig, stir up. '

WE

5046. 喂 30/9 An exclamation, calling attention. "

WĪK

5047. 域 32/8 A state. Country. "'
(a) wīk-toh-leî 4215-2293. Victoria, B.C.

WING

5048. 掹 64/5 To throw aside, or away. *

WĪNG

5049. 滎 75/10 Glory. Splendor. S. *

5050. 栄 75/6 Glory. Splendor. S. *

WĬNG

5051. 永 85/1 Eternal. Forever. S.

WÎNG

5052. 咏 30/5 To sing, hum. Chant. (5052 ping)

5053. 詠 149/5 To sing, hum. Chant.

WIT

5053½. 搣 64/10 Creaking. "

WOH

5054. 鍋 167/9 Pot. Boiler. Pan. *

(a) woh-teng 4127.
Rivets.

5055. 籭 118/9 Shallow splint tray.

5056. 窩 116/9 Nest. Nook. Den.

(a) woh-chaāk 80.
Zinc.

5057. 蝸 142/9 Snail. Poor hovel.

(a) woh-ngaū 3039.
Common snail.

5057½. 膈 130/9 Addled.

WÓH

5058. 搲 64/9 To throw away. (wǒh)

WŌH

5059. 和 30/5 Together. In harmony. Peace. S. (wôh)

(a) wōh-mūk 2797.
Concord.

(b) wōh-sheûng 3897.
Buddhist priest.

5060. 禾 R 115 Grain or rice growing.

WǑH

5061. 搲 64/9 To spoil. Spoiled. (wóh)

WÔH

5062. 禍 113/9 Calamity. Woe. Misfortune.

5063. 啝 30/8 F—denoting a quoted statement.(wòh,wóh)

5064. 和 30/5 To respond, rhyme. To compound, mix properly. In accord with.

5065. 盃 108/5 To compound.

WŌK

5066. 鑊 167/14 Caldron. Boiler. Pan.

5067. 獲 94/14 To catch,obtain, seize, arrest.S.

WONG

5068. 尢 R 43 Crooked. Deformed.

WÓNG

5069. 枉 75/4 Wrong. Crooked. To suffer wrong.

(a) wóng-faî 691.
In vain. Useless.

WŌNG

5070. 黃 R 201 Yellow. Imperial. S.

(a) wōng-kwa 2037.
Cucumber.

(b) taaî-wōng 4033.
Rhubarb.

(c) wōng-p'eî 3468. A native fruit,wongpei.

(d) mō-teî-wōng 2712-4125.
Digitalis.

(e) wōng-niū 2920.
Oriole.

(f) wōng-ngaū 3039.
Ordinary cattle.

(g) wōng-uē 4872.
Kind of herring.

(h) t'āng-wōng 4333.
Gamboge.

(i) kaú-wōng 1574.
Dog bezoar.

(j) wōng-hoî 1125.
The Yellow Sea.

(k) wōng-pò 3340.
Whampoa.

5071. 皇 106/4 Emperor. Great. August. Divine. S.

5072. 王 R/96 King. Ruler. Prince. S.

5073. 磺 112/12 Sulphur.
*

5074. 蝗 142/9 Locust species.
*
(a) wōng-ch'ūng 646. The common locust.

5075. 癀 104/12 Jaundice.
'

5076. 鰉 195/9 Sturgeon.
'

5077. 凰 16/9 Fabulous bird.
"'

5078. 徨 60/9 Doubtful. Irresolute.
"'

WŎNG

5079. 往 60/5 To go, proceed.
5080. 徃 60/5 Formerly. To travel.

WÔNG

5081. 旺 72/4 Brilliant. Vigorous. Prosperous.
*

5081½. 王 R/96 To govern. (wōng)
'

YA

5082. 吔 30/3 An exclamation. F.
"

YĂ

5083. 也 5/2 Also. F.
*
(a) yă-ts'āng 4713. Already.

YÂ

5084. 廿 24/1 Abbreviation for ī-shāp, 20.(yê)

YAAK。

5085. 喫 30/9 To eat, swallow.
"

YAAP。

5086. 揜 64/7 To raise.
"

YAĪ

5087. 吟 30/4 Bad. Inferior.
"

5088. 曳 73/2 Flexible.
"'

YAM

5089. 音 R/180 Sound. Tone. Communication. News.

5090. 陰 170/8 Shade. Dark. Female.
*

5091. 隂 170/9 Negative principle.
*
(a) yam-kung 1879. Hard lines!
(b) yam-oô 3129. Vagina.

5092. 髟 190/4 Curls. Tresses. (yām)
*

5093. 欽 76/8 Imperial. To respect.
'

5094. 歆 76/9 To enjoy. Savor of offerings.
"'

YÁM

5095. 飲 184/4 To drink, swallow. (yăm)
(a) yám-shīk-hōk 3925-1140. Dietetics.

YÀM

5096. 蔭 140/11 Shade. To shelter, protect.

YÂM

5097. 淫 85/8 Lewd. Obscene. Dissolute.

5098. 婬 38/8 Vicious. To go to excess, debauch.

5099. 髥 190/4 A fringe. Ledge. To haul up.(yam)

5100. 吟 30/4 To hum, intone.

5101. 壬 33/1 Smart. Artful.

5101½. 袵 145/6 Lapel of garment. A hanging. uf 5104. (yăm)

YĂM

5102. 泲 85/6 To dip, souse.

5103. 飲 184/4 To dip. (yám)

5104. 衽 145/4 Lapel of garment.

YĂM

5105. 任 9/4 To bear,sustain. An office. A trust. A fathom. S.

5106. 賃 154/6 To lease, rent, hire.

YAN

5107. 因 31/3 Cause. Reason. Because. For. S.

5108. 恩 61/6 Grace. Favor. Kindness. Tenderness. S.

(a) yan-tín 4162. Grace. Favor.

5109. 殷 79/6 Full. Rich.Abundant. Earnest.S.

5110. 慇 61/10 Pained. Grieved. Anxious.

5111. 姻 38/6 Relatives by marriage.

5112. 茵 140/6 Padded mat. Cushion. Kind of tree.

5113. 昕 109/4 To see indistinctly, look fixedly.

YÁN

5114. 忍 61/3 Patience. Endurance. S. (yăn)

(a) yán-noî 2938. To endure, be patient.

5115. 隱 170/14 Hidden. Retired. Private. S.

5115½. 人 R/9 See yăn.

YÀN

5116. 印 26/4 To print, seal, mark. A mark. S.

(a) yàn-tô 4208. India.

(b) yàn-tô-yeūng 5194. Indian Ocean.

YĀN

5117. 人 R/9 Man. Human. Person. S.

(a) hak-yān 971. Negro.

(b) yān-chúng-hŏk 391-1140. Ethnology.

(c) yān-luî-hŏk 2494. Anthropology.

5118. 仁 9/2 Gentleness. Mercy. A kernel. Seed. S.

(a) yān-oì 3099. Charity.

5119. 寅 40/8 To treat well. Time period 3 to 5 A.M.

5120. 几 R/10 Humane.

(b) hó-yắp-t'aŭ 1099-4339. Affable.

(c) yắp-tsĭk 4548. To be naturalized.

YAT

YĂN

5121. 引 57/1 To lead, guide, quote. A preface.

(a) p'aaŭ-yán 3438. A fuse.

5122. 廴 R/54 To go far.

5122½. 忍 61/3 See yán.

5133. 一 R/1 The numeral 1: common, compli-

5134. 壹 33/9 cated, an older form, and run-

5135. 弌 56/1 ning hand form. A unit. Unity.

5136. 弌 R/2 Whole. First. S.

YÂN

5123. 孕 39/2 Pregnant. With child.

5124. 刃 18/1 A weapon. Blade. Sword. To kill.

5125. 仞 9/3 A measure. Fathom.

5126. 韌 178/3 Tough. Strong. Pliable. (ngấn)

5127. 釁 164/18 Grievance.

YĀT

5137. 日 R/72 The sun. A day. Daily.

(a) yāt-poón 3388. Japan.

5138. 逸 162/8 To indulge, let loose. Ease. Leisure.

5139. 溢 85/10 Overflowing. Surplus. To flow out.

5140. 液 85/8 Fluid. Secre- tions. (yĭk)

YAP

5128. 揖 64/9 To bow politely, salute.

5129. 泣 85/5 To weep, lament. Tearful.

5130. 邑 R/163 District. City. Hamlet. Camp.

5131. 翁 124/6 Harmonious. To write.

(a) ngaăn-yap-mō 2999- 2712. Eyelash.

YAU

5141. 憂 61/11 Grieved. Anxious. Depressed. Sad. S.

5142. 幽 52/6 Quiet. Retired. Obscure. S.

5143. 優 9/15 To excel, play with. Fully. S.

YĂP

5132. 入 R/11 To enter, put into.

(a) yắp-moŏn 2779. To en- ter, make beginning.

5144. 休 9/4 To rest, desist. To put away. Move. S.

5144½. 麀 198/2 A doe. Roe.

YAÚ

5145. 朽 75/2 Decayed. Worn out. Used up.

5146. 内 R 114 Step. Track.

YAÙ

5147. 幼 52/2 Young. Tender. Delicate.

YAŪ

5148. 由 102/1 From. By. To permit.
(a) yau-la-wai 2145-4985. Uruguay.

5149. 油 85/5 Oil. Grease. Paint. To oil, paint.
(a) chue-yau 312. Lard.
(b) shĕk-nŏ-yau 3879-2926. Bitumen.
(c) fóh-yau 767. Naptha.
(d) t'ōng-fóh-yau 4431. Carron oil.
(e) yau-mŭk 2795. Teak.

5150. 泅 85/5 To swim.

5151. 遊 162/9 To saunter, roam, travel.
(a) yau-mŭk 2796. Nomads.

5152. 柔 75/5 Pliant. Yielding. Tender. Mild.

5153. 猶 94/9 Yet. Still. As if. S.
(a) yau-t'aai 4283. Judea, Jewry.

5154. 郵 163/8 Postoffice. Lodge.
(a) yau-ching 277. Postal service.

5155. 游 85/9 To travel, wander, float, swim.

5156. 疣 104/4 A swelling. Wen.

5157. 蚰 142/5
(a) yau-ín 1358. The earwig.

5158. 尤 43/1 Criminality.

5158½. 柚 75/5 See 2503b. (yaû)

YAǓ

5159. 有 74/2 To have, possess. There is. Affirmation. S.

5160. 友 29/2 Friend. Companion. Friendly.

5161. 誘 149/7 To allure, lead, tempt.

5162. 酉 164/7 Time period 5 to 7 P.M. Ripe. Mellow. S.

YAÛ

5163. 叉 R 29 Also. Again. Yet again.

5164. 右 30/2 The right hand. Right side. The place of honor. S.

5165. 祐 113/5 Divine care.

5165½. 佑 9/5 To protect, care for. uf 5165.

5166. 柚 75/5 Variety of fruit tree.
(a) yaû-tsź 4667. The pummelo.

5167. 宥 40/6 To forbear, forgive. S.

5168. 釉 165/5 Glaze. Enamel.

YĒ

5169. 椰 75/7 ⎫
*   ⎬ The cocoanut
5170. 椰 75/9 ⎭ tree.
*

(a) yē-tsź 4667.
Cocoanut.

(b) yē-tsź-tsaú 4500.
Arrack.

(c) yē-shuí 4004.
Cocoanut milk.

(d) yē-ts‘oì 4800.
Foreign cabbage.

5171. 爺 88/9 Sir. Gentleman.
*   Term of respect.

5172. 耶 128/3
"'

(a) Yē-So 3681.
JESUS.

(b) yē-lō-saat₀-laǎng.
2426-3581-2187.
Jerusalem.

YĚ

5173. 野 166/4 Waste country.
Desert. Savage.
Rude. Wild. Some-
thing. A thing.

(a) mat-yě 2635.
What?

(b) haǎn-yě 934. An ordinary thing. Inconse-
quential.

(c) yě-ts‘ó 4777.
Weeds.

(d) yě-yàn 5117.
A savage.

(e) yě-tsaí 4482.
A bastard.

(f) yaú-yě 5159.
There is something.

5174. 惹 61/9 To provoke. To
'   irritate, delude,
attract.

5175. 嘢 30/11 Something.
"   A thing.

YÈ

5176. 夜 36/5 Night. Late.

5177. 贏 154/13 To win, gain,
*   excel. (yéng,
yíng)

YEUK₀

5178. 約 120/3 A covenant. Bond.
Agreement. S.

(a) yeuk₀-taan 4046.
A bond.

(b) yeuk₀-mok₀ 2744. About.
Approximately.

(c) yeuk₀-lō-ooí 2420-3143.
Reformed Presbyter-
ian Church.

5179. 躍 157/14 To jump, leap,
*   hasten. (yeūk)

5180. 葯 140/9 Orris root.
*   uf 5183.

YEŪK

5181. 若 140/5 If. Supposing.
Like. As to.

5182. 弱 57/7 Weak. Feeble.
Infirm.

5183. 藥 140/15 Drugs, Medicine.
*   S.

(a) yeūk-tsaú 4500. Tinc-
ture. Liquid medi-
cines.

5184. 虐 141/3 To be harsh. To
*'   maltreat, op-
press.

5185. 籲 214/9 To call, cry,
*   groan.

5186. 龥 118/20 To entreat,
*   harmonize.

5187. 龠 R 214 A flute.
"'

5188. 瘧 104/10 Hot or cold
"'   fits. Intermittent fever.

5188½. 鑰 167/17 Lock. Key.
"'   Bolt.

YEUNG

5189. 秧 115/5 Shoots. Young plants.

5190. 殃 78/5 Calamity. Crime. Mishap.

YEÚNG

5191. 抰 64/5 To shake,

5192. 映 72/5 Bright. Reflection.

YEŬNG

5193. 羊 R123 Sheep. Goat.
  (a) mīn-yeŭng 2676. Sheep.
  (b) shaan-yeŭng 3793. Goat.
  (c) ko-yeŭng 1715. A lamb.
  (d) yeŭng-kok.-fung 1744-879. Whirlwind.
  (e) yeŭng-tiù 4190. Epilepsy.
  (f) yeŭng-shēng 3883. Canton.

5194. 洋 85/6 The ocean. Vast. Foreign.

5195. 楊 75/9 Poplar. Aspen. S.
  (a) ch'ik.-yeŭng. 547. The alder.
  (b) yeŭng-t'ō 4392. Carambola.
  (c) yeŭng-mooi 2767. Arbutus.

5196. 陽 170/9 Positive principle. Male. Sun. S.
  (a) yeŭng-māt 2636. The penis.

5197. 揚 64/9 To display, publish, raise. S.

  (a) yeŭng-tsź-kong 4667-1771. Yangtsekiang.

YEÚNG

5198. 養 184/6 To bear, as children. To nourish, rear, raise. S. (yeŭng)

5199. 仰 9/4 To look up, respect.

5200. 癢 104/15 To itch, scratch. S.

YEŬNG

5201. 樣 75/11 Model. Sort. Kind. Pattern. Manner.

5202. 讓 149/17 To give way, yield, resign.

5203. 釀 164/17 To brew, mince,

YIK

5204. 益 108/5 Advantage. Benefit.

5205. 益 108/5 Profit. To increase. S.
  (a) ts'éng-yik 4734. To ask further.

5206. 抑 64/4 To put down. Else. Or.
  (a) yik-waāk 4966. Or else. Or.

5207. 憶 61/13 To recollect, remember, reflect.

5208. 臆 130/13 The breast. Heart. Feelings.

5209. 噎 30/17 Rancid.
  (a) tá-sz-yik 4027-3759. To belch.

YĪK

5210. 亦 8/4 Also. Moreover. S.

5211. 役 60/4 To serve. Petty official. Employee.

(a) chik-yĭk 239. Occupation. Duties.

5212. 翼 124/11 Wings. To shelter, assist. S.

5213. 譯 149/13 To interpret, translate.

5214. 逆 162/13 To rebel, resist, oppose.

5215. 疫 104/4 Pestilence. Epidemic.

5216. 液 85/8 Secretion. Exudation. (yāt)

5217. 繹 120/13 To unravel, unfold, explain.

5218. 驛 187/13 A courier. Post. Mail.

5219. 弋 56/R An arrow. To aim, shoot.

5220. 易 72/4 To modify, change. (ĭ)

YING

5221. 應 61/13 Right, Proper. Ought.S.(yĭng)

(a) ying-koi 1737.
Ought. Should.

(b) ying-shĭng 3952.
To promise.

5222. 英 140/5 Excellent. Valiant. Brave. S.

(a) p'ō-kung-ying 3519-1878. Dandelion.

(b) ying-kwok 2103.
British Empire.

(c) ying-kaak-laān 1450-2182. England.

(d) ying-mân 2616.
English language.

(e) ying-naĭ 2844.
Portland cement.

5223. 鷹 196/13 Falcon. Eagle. Hawk.

5224. 嬰 38/14 An infant. To entangle. S.

5225. 鸚 196/17 Parrot.

5226. 櫻 75/17 Cockatoo.

5227. 瑛 96/9 The cherry.

5227. 瑛 96/9 Quartz. Crystal.

YING

5228. 影 59/12 Image. Shadow.

(a) ying-seûng 3632.
To photograph.

YING

5229. 應 61/13 To respond, echo. fulfil.

(a) yìng-îm 1329.
To fulfil.

YING

5230. 形 59/4 Appearance.Form. To give form.

(a) ying-chat 150.
Matter. Elements.

(b) yĭng-hŏk 1140.
Geometry.

5231. 刑 18/4 To punish. Punishment.

5232. 仍 9/2 Still. Yet.

(a) yĭng-în 1349.
Still is. After all.

5233. 迎 162/4 To meet, receive a guest.

(a) yĭng-tsĭp 4569. To receive, entertain.

5234. 贏 154/13 To profit, gain, win.(yēng, yê)

5235. 營 86/13 Military post. Camp. To scheme. S.

-263-

5236. 蠅 142/13 Fly species.

5237. 蝇 142/8 (ying)

(a) oō-ying(yīng) 3115.
House fly.

5238. 凝 15/14 To congeal.Hard.
Fixed. (k'īng)

5239. 盈 108/4 Full. To fill overpass. S.

YĪNG

5240. 認 149/7 To recognize, confess.

YUI

5241. 桜 75/7 A tree. Hazelnuts.

YUÌ

5242. 蜹 142/8 Gnats.Wriggling. Swarming.

YUǏ

5243. 蕊 140/12 Stamens.Pistil.

(a) fa-yuǐ 650.
Pistil.

(b) fa-fán-yuǐ 713.
Stamens.

(c) fa-yuǐ-shék 3879.
Dolomite.

5244. 蕊 85/16 Sap.

YUÎ

5245. 裔 145/7 Posterity. Descendants. Frontier. Skirt. S.

5246. 鋭 167/7 Sharp pointed. Acute. Glib.

YUK

5247. 喐 30/8 To move,shake.

5248. 郁 163/6 S.

YŪK

5249. 肉 R/130 Flesh. Meat. Pulp of fruit.

5250. 玉 R/96 Jade stone. Gem. S.

(a) hak-yūk 971.
Fossil jet.

(b) ts'ing-yūk 4764.
Sapphire.

(c) ch'ik-yūk 547.
Jacinth.

(d) yūk-tsaam-fa 4468-650.
Tuberose.

5251. 褥 145/10 Mattress. Cushion. (yuk)

5252. 慾 61/11 To lust,

5253. 欲 76/7 passionately desire.

5254. 獄 94/10 Prison. Jail. To sentence, imprison.

(a) teî-yūk 4125.
Hell.

5255. 辱 161/3 To disgrace, shame, insult, defile. S.

5256. 育 130/4 To bear,nurture, rear, foster. S.

5257. 浴 85/7 To wash, purify.

YŪN

5258. 潤 85/12 To moisten, ben- efit, fertilize.

5259. 閏 169/4 Intercalary period.

5260. 膶 130/12 The liver.

YUNG

5261. 翁 124/4 Venerable. Old man. S.

5262. 癰 104/18 Malignant boil. Abscess.
  (a) yung-tsui 4625.
    Cancer.

YÚNG

5263. 擁 64/13 To crowd, crush, embrace. (úng)

5264. 湧 85/9 To flow rapidly, rise, bubble up.

5265. 壅 32/13 To bank up, obstruct. Heap. Manure. (úng)

5266. 蛹 142/7 Chrysalis of silkworm.

5267. 踊 157/7 To leap, skip, exult.

5268. 朧 130/13 To bulge out. A swelling

YŪNG

5269. 容 40/7 To contain, endure. Appearance. Contents.
  (a) yūng-î 1291.
    Easy. Easier.
  (b) yūng-maaû 2599.
    Appearance.

5270. 鎔 167/10 Mold. Die. To smelt, fuse, melt, cast.

5271. 濃 85/13 Strong (of liquids. Thick. (nūng)

5272. 絨 120/6 Floss. Down. Woollen.

  (a) taaî-yūng 4033.
    Broadcloth.
  (b) fóh-yūng 767.
    Tinder.

5273. 庸 53/8 To use. Service. Constant. Common.

5274. 榕 75/10 The banyan tree.

5275. 融 142/10 | To blend,

5276. 螎 142/10 | combine.

5277. 戎 62/2 Military. Weapons. Troops.

5278. 蓉 140/10 Hibiscus.
  (a) oh-foô-yūng 3088-833.
    Poppy.

5279. 茸 140/6 Luxuriant. Deer's horns.

5280. 稬 115/10 Over ripe.

YŬNG

5281. 勇 19/7 Bravery. Daring. Courage.
  (a) yŭng-sẑ 3777.
    A warrior.

YÛNG

5282. 用 R/101 To use, employ. Expenses.

NOTES

NOTES

RADICAL INDEX

Explanation and Notes

In this index all the characters which are treated in this dictionary are listed according to the Radical system. Under each Radical the heavy face figures set to the right of the column indicate the number of strokes, in addition to the Radical, for the characters listed below. The numbers appearing below each character are the numerical reference to the serial numbers of the characters in the dictionary.

In some cases the character appears more than once in the dictionary, the reference being given in the index for each occurrence. The first reference in such cases, usually indicates the most common use of that character.

In some very few cases a character is listed in this index under two different Radicals; one being the "authorized", as indicated in the body of the dictionary, and the other being an "unauthorized", but nevertheless commonly found placement in typographical lists.

For the benefit of beginners in study of the Chinese characters a few remarks may be helpful.

Counting the "strokes" in most of the characters is just plain and easy, but inasmuch as there are many characters in which the stroke count as made by Chinese authorities is not what it apparently should be, if the character one is looking for is not found under the counted number of strokes, it is well to scan the listings under one less or one more stroke than such count.

It should be borne in mind that in a great many cases what the Westerner would take to be two strokes is counted as but one. For instance: The character 口 hau, Radical 30, is reckoned as three strokes, not four. First is the left down stroke |; Second is the upper cross and right down stroke ㄱ; and, Third is the lower horizontal stroke — to complete the character. There are numerous other similar

111.

cases of what we might term two strokes merged into one. Note that the 〕 as in 司(3756) is one stroke, while 〕 as in 可(1117) is two strokes.

Certain variations in arrangement of strokes which are simply variations in writing the same character should be made note of. For instance: ᅳand ‑‑are usually one and the same thing; as in 言 or 言. Likewise 八 may appear as ㇆ ; 亡 as 匕 ; 夕 as 爫 ; 丆 as 刀 ; etc. Illustrations might be multiplied, but just this much here to indicate that characters sought for may be found with a variation in arrangement of some of the strokes.

One other remark may be pertinent. In a character in which two or three Radical forms appear as component parts, the most prominent appearing one may or may not be the Radical under which it is listed, hence it may be sought under the other Radicals, if not located at once.

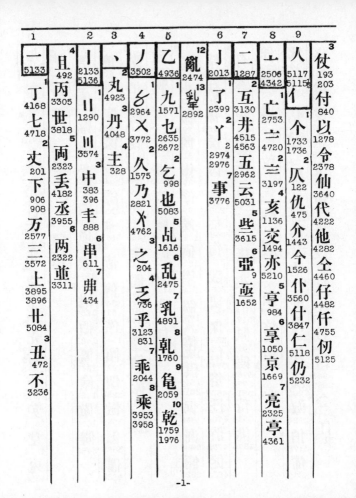

1	2	3	4	5	6	7	8	9	

1 — 一 [4] 5133
[1] 丁 4168
[2] 七 4718
丈 201
下 906 908
万 2577
三 3572
上 3895 3896
[3] 廿 5084
丑 472
不 3236

2 — 且 [4] 492
[1] 丙 3305
世 3818
[5] 両 2323
丢 4182
[6] 丞 3955
两 2322
並 3311

— 丨 2133 5136
[1] 刂 1290
川 3574
[3] 中 383 396
[6] 丰 888
[7] 串 611
弗 434

3 — 、 5136
[1] 丸 4923
丹 4048
[3] 主 328

4 — ノ 3502
[1] 彡 2964
乂 3772
[2] 久 1575
乃 2821
[4] 乆 4762
之 204
[4] 乏 736
[7] 乎 3123 831
[8] 乖 2044
[8] 乘 3953 3958

5 — 乙 4936
[1] 九 1571
[2] 乜 2635 2672
乞 998
也 5083
乱 1616
[7] 乱 2475
[8] 乳 4891
[9] 乾 1760
亀 2059
[10] 乾 1759 1976

— 亂 [12] 2474
乿 [13] 2892

6 — 亅 2013
[1] 了 2399
[2] 丫 2974 2976
[7] 事 3776

7 — 二 1287
[2] 互 3130
井 4515 4563
五 2962
云 5031
些 3615
[9] 亞
亜 1652

8 — 亠 2506 4342
[1] 亡 2753
[2] 亢 4720
亥 3197
[4] 交 1136
亦 1494
[5] 亨 5210
享 984
[6] 享 1050
京 1669
[7] 亮 2325
亭 4361

9 — 人 5117 5115
[1] 亻
个 1733 1736
[2] 仄 122
仇 475
介 1443
今 1526
[5] 仆 3560
什 3847
仁 5118
仍 5232

— 仗 [3] 193 203
[1] 付 840
以 1278
[2] 令 2378
仙 3640
代 4222
他 4282
仝 4460
仔 4482
仟 4755
仞 5125

儿 5120
- **1** 兀 3036
- **2** 元 4918 / 允 5032
- **3** 充 634 / 兄 1070
- **4** 兆 294 / 兌 1227 / 光 2105 / 先 3639 3645
- **5** 克 973 / 免 2681 / 兌 4254 / 兎 4388

14
儕 421 / 儔 484 / 儒 4878
15 償 3894 / 優 5143
16 儲 594 / 儳 4571

12
儍 456 / 儸 4751 / 傿 1701 / 儷 1812 / 僞 3017 / 僕 3402 / 僧 3599 / 儘 4464 / 像 4530
13 儀 1267 / 價 1421 / 僵 1643 / 儉 1659 / 儆 1674 / 僻 3482

10
僭 456 / 傅 837 / 傢 1411 / 傑 1696 / 備 3263 / 傍 3536 / 傘 3577
11 債 71 / 傳 348 / 儡 613 / 僅 1543 / 傾 1977 / 僂 2254 / 傲 3055 / 傷 3885

9
側 121 / 偵 272 / 偉 1343 / 假 1419 / 偈 1422 / 偕 1434 / 健 1666 / 偶 3040 / 借 4509 / 停 4360 / 偷 4335 / 做 4593

倫 2515 / 們 2784 / 俾 3250 / 倏 3264 / 倂 3313 / 倍 3549 / 修 3603 / 倉 4807

8
值 243 / 倡 503 / 倣 792 / 俯 818 / 俸 891 / 倖 995 / 候 1015 / 倚 1255 / 偺 1596 / 個 1731 1734 / 倦 1843 / 俱 1847 / 俗 2015 / 倨 1862 / 偪 2088 / 倆 2324

7
俘 809 / 俠 950 / 係 968 / 侯 1009 / 徑 1683 / 俐 2296 / 侶 2490 / 侮 2722 / 俄 3062 / 便 3295 / 保 3329 / 信 3743 / 俗 4637 / 侵 4708 / 俏 4772 / 促 4833

6
侏 321 / 侈 522 / 侃 1161 / 依 1247 / 佳 1433 / 供 1882 / 俐 1890 / 例 2207 / 佬 2404 / 來 2445 / 佰 3171 / 佩 3544 / 使 3768 3774 / 侍 3914 / 佻 4370

3
伴 3390 / 伸 3831 / 但 4056 / 低 4070 / 佗 4414 / 佐 4598 / 作 4610 / 似 4676 / 余 4886 / 位 5014 / 佑 5165½

休 5144 / 仰 5199
5 佔 252 4156 / 住 339 / 佛 735 / 何 1120 / 伽 1418 1947 / 佶 1797 / 佢 2026 / 伶 2363 / 你 2875 / 佞 2905 / 做 2924 / 伯 3172 / 佈 3339

4
仲 399 / 份 724 / 伐 737 / 伏 768 / 伕 876 / 伊 1253 / 价 1445 / 伎 1634 / 件 1665 / 企 1962 / 伎 2614 / 伍 2963 2967 / 会 3144 / 任 5105

#	部首	字
11	兒 1266 [6]	兔 4387 [9], 兜 4107 [12], 競 1673 [14]
12	入 5132 [2]	内 2937 [4], 全 4815 [6], 兩 2321 [14], 㒼 3659
13	八 3195 [2]	兮 966 [4], 公 1878 [6], 六 2504, 共 1892, 兵 3300 [6], 其 1955, 具 1856, 典 4162 [8], 兼 1655
14	冂 2090 [2]	冇 2719 [3], 册 423, 回 2861, 回 3136, 甲 4479 [4], 再 4607 [7], 冑 166, 冒 2731 [9], 冕 2683
15	冖 2674 [3]	冠 1155 [7], 冢 642 [8], 袜 2223, 冥 2694, 冤 4907
	冫 3303 [3]	冬 4273, 冲 635 · 1816 · 1827 [8], 决 2011, 冰 3301 [5], 况 797, 冷 2187 [8], 净 144, 准 376, 凉 2315, 凌 2362, 凋 4185, 凍 4275, 净 4517 · 4565
	凄 4698 [9]	減 1458, 凝 1979 · 5238 [14]
16	几 1609 · 1611	凡 667 [1], 几 668 [3], 凭 3234 [7], 凰 5077 [9], 凱 1127 [10], 凳 4098 [12]
17	凵	凶 1230 [1], 凹 2860 [3], 出 648 [9], 凸 4106 [4], 函 929 [6]
18	刀 4195	刁 4186 [1], 刃 5124 [3], 分 696 · 723, 切 4769 [4], 刊 1160 [6], 列 2384 [4], 刎 2625, 刑 5231
5	初 572	刲 1688, 刼 1689, 利 2293, 別 3318, 刨 3444 [6], 剌 3463, 判 3550, 刜 3795 [4], 刳 4246
6	制 117	剎 446, 刐 585, 刻 922, 券 1211, 刮 1559, 刮 2056, 剌 3649, 刷 3809, 到 4201 · 4203, 刺 4744 · 4855

19 (刀/力)

[7]
剋 974
剌 2196
削 3624
剎 4317
則 4487
前 4760
[8]
剹 351
剗 432
剳 1298
剛 1772
剙 2743 3354
剜 3150
剖 3459
剔 4349

[9]
剩 3956
剪 4555
副 4956
[10]
創 584
剴 1129
割 1832
[11]
剺 433
剸 540
剿 4578

[12]
劃 4969
[13]
劍 1658
劇 1970
劈 2259
劊 3477 3484
劋 4430
[14]
劑 4481
[17]
劖 4747
劗 4748

力 2330
[2]
功 1209
[3]
加 1409
劾 1879
[4]
劣 2478
[5]
助 299
劫 1690
劬 2022
[6]
効 963
劭 1002

[7]
勅 546
勁 1687
勉 2682
勇 5281
務 2729
[9]
勘 1149
勒 2217
動 4277
[10]
勗 706
勞 2408
勝 3947

[11]
勤 1917
募 2732
勢 3819
勢 3820
勦 4579
[14]
勳 705
[15]
勵 2158
勴 2210
[17]
勸 1207

20 (勹)

勹 3201
[1]
勺 181
[2]
勾 1568
勿 2639
匀 5029
[3]
包 3198
[4]
匈 1229
[6]
匊 1869

21 (匕)

匕 3274
化 651
北 3215
匙 537 3906

22 (匚)

匚 3579 [3]
匡 1179
匠 4529
匣 948
匭 753
[11]
匯 3145
[12]
匱 2071

23 (匸)

匸 3457 [2]
區 2018
匿 2883
匾 3292

24 (十)

十 3845
[1]
千 4754
廿 5084
午 2965
卅 3565
升 3942
[3]
半 3389
[4]
卍 2582

[6]
卓 498
協 1083
卑 3244
單 4047
卒 4659
南 2823
[10]
博 3357
[7]
卍

25　卜 3400
- ³ 占 247 / 251
- 卡 1893
- ⁶ 卦 2043

26　卩 4571
- ³ 卯 2598
- ⁸ 危 3015
- 印 5116
- ⁵ 卵 2527
- ⁶ 卷 1838 / 1842
- 卸 3618
- 卹 3753
- ⁷ 即 4533
- ⁹ 卿 1074

27　厂 ⁷
- 厚 1014
- ⁸ 厘 2276
- ⁹ 原 4919
- 厠 4858
- ¹⁰ 厨 591
- ¹² 厨 591 / 厭 1310 / 1311
- ¹³ 属 2216

28　厶 2644 ³
- 去 1221 / 1217
- ⁸ 叁 3573
- ⁹ 参 3824 / 4683

29　又 5163 ¹
- ² 叉 401
- 反 661 / 及 1927
- 收 3858 / 友 5160
- ⁶ 圣 3946
- ⁸ 变 3294 / 受 3865
- 叔 4010 / 取 4824
- ⁹ 叛 3391 / 叙 4634
- ¹¹ 叠 4177
- ¹⁶ 叢 4850

30　口 1006 ³
- 只 176 / 右 220 / 叶 241
- 召 293 / 叶 1084 / 号 1110
- 可 1117 / 古 1796 / 句 1853 / 叩 1931
- 叻 2334 / 另 2379 / 叼 2818 / 卟 3401 / 司 3756 / 史 3769

叩 4379
- 台 4423
- 右 5164
- ³ 吁 4189
- 吓 907
- 后 1016
- 向 1053
- 合 1193 / 1831
- 吱 1381
- 吉 1560
- 吃 1563 / 999
- 叫 1709
- 各 1743
- 吏 2295

名 2669 / 2695
- 吠 4034
- 吊 4189
- 吐 4385 / 4383 / 4407
- 同 4459
- 吧 5082

⁴ 呀
- ⁸ 呃 3023
- 吱 209
- 吨 374
- 吵 449
- 吹 614
- 吽 695
- 听 3131
- 吧 3160
- 呸 3460 / 3241½
- 吞 4329
- 听 4345
- 吩 5087
- 吟 5100

君 2074
- 吕 2489
- 吻 2622
- 味 2794
- 咼 2839
- 呾 2957 / 2958
- 吾 2961
- 呻 3043

⁵ 咋
- 周 156
- 呪 164
- 咒 164½
- 呎 168 / 176½
- 哢 762
- 呼 802
- 咐 822
- 呷 942
- 呵 1114 / 3093
- 呌 1286
- 呑 1415
- 咎 1587
- 咁 1758
- 咕 1794 / 1805

垃 2236
- 呡 2615
- 味 2666 / 2673
- 命 2671 / 2698
- 味 2789
- 呢 2872 / 2881
- 咖 2907
- 呵 2908
- 呦 3005
- 吐 3254
- 咆 3445½
- 咝 3601
- 呻 3834
- 咧 4028
- 呫 4104

嗎 2562
嚜 2989
唊 3002
鳴 3116
噉 3266
嗓 3700
嚛 3725
嗜 3913
嗒 4102
噎 4121
嗲 4123
嗟 4507
嗣 4674

喂 4993
　 5046
　 5132
　 5085

10
啞 10
嗌 14
嗾 33
　 649
　 3045
嗙 78
嗼 407½
嚐 519
嗑 943
鞡 1043
嗰 1732
喰 1908
喰 2456
嗋 2522

喏 1904
喬 1991
喇 2144
喱 2273
嘵 2328
肇 2814
喃 2825
嘩 3103
喪 3698
　 3701
嚶 3785
善 3939
單 4046
喇 4279
啼 4354
嗆 4897
喊 4986

9
喈 173
　 1681
喳 3876
喘 606
嗉 684
喚 864
喂 902
喊 925
　 975
喉 965
喉 1008
喜 1030
喝 1199
喧 1202
嗳 1378
喋 1427
喀 1903

售 3868
啣
商 3887
㕭 4037
啐 4041
啖 4043
啗 4044
啄 4135
啲 4138
唾 4348
　 4406
啋 4794
唰 5063
啒 5247

唐 4436
員 4922

8
啞 6
　 10
　 40
　 2975
啐 93
啁 105
啜 349
啍 373
唱 507
啡 752
啾 1184
啟 1900
啓 1901
皎 2034
唪 3815

啁 2093
啦 2146
商 3876
啉 2222
咽 2514
問 2629
嗑 2630
啊 2783
㕭 2993
啊 3094
啩 3189
啤 3242
　 3461
唪 3351
咆 3523½
唳 3559

7
唉 32
吮 134
哲 285
咀 297
哮 954
哼 982
唏 1018
哈 3024
　 3025
哪 2933
唙 1185
哭 1223
唻 1486
呦 1691
哥 1728
咯 1871
咽 2136

哈 2188
　 2232
　 2234
哩 2270

6
咸 928
哈 997
哐 1021
响 1048
哀 1243
品 3225
咃 4124
哉 4604
哇 4954

嗦 2990
咬 3012
㖞 1500
哯 3014
咢 3074
哀 3095

咥 4327
咀 4626
呱 4950
㖊 5052
响 3302
和 5059
哝 5064
啄 1928
　 1131
唎 2387
咯 2450
　 1748
啤 2545
唰 2600
　 2602
咪 2604
哶 2648
唎 2654
咯 2670

11	拾	12	嘶	13	顳	15	14	16	18	口 5008	9 圜 5000	土 4380

11
嘔 54
噈 149
嗒 515
嘛 1215
嘉 1413
嘅 1600
墂 1615
嘍 2244
嘐 2416
嘛 2554
嗌 2632
嘆 2745
嗊 2879
嗷 3050
嗺 3194
嗰 3210

拾
啥 3399
啡 3417
噓 3571
嗺 3569
嗽 3613
嘗 3892
嘛 3988
兜 4114
嘆 4301
嘈 4783
彩 4795
嘢 5175

12
揸 58
嘲 106
鈰 382
喥 417
嘻 1022
嘵 1089
噎 1370
嗷 1753
嘮 2403
揖 3033
噁 3118
啦 3222
棒 3235
嗺 3268
唸 3383
嘯 3676

嘶 3762
噍 4581
嘴 4627
嘩 4952
嘘 1215

13
器 1035
噫 1250
噤 1531
嘩 1907
嚛 4326
嘵 1738
賑 4955
嗅 2094
嗝 2102
呤 2360
咯 2370
呧 2431
嗲 2851
曖 3097
噲 3140
噴 3447
噬 3822
嚏 4069
嚓 4133

顳 4270

14
喂 195
嚇 923
鳴 3013
噚 3046
嗅 2737
罷 3243
臓 3267
噠 3359
嘆 3403
嚅 3583
啜 3623
啄 4088
嘖 4137
嚌 4486

15
嘷 381
嘈 1426
嚟 2050
嚓 2200
嚟 2737
嚲 3243
嘫 3267
嚛 3688

17
齋 1246
謦 1316
齇 1597
嚩 2150
闌 2179
嚷 4802
嚛 5209

16
嚨 45
雖 914
嗎 1051
嘾 1529
嘫 2155
嚨 2535
喊 2871
斂 3688

21
嘱 367

22
嚖 1462

18
嘴 15
遮 168
嘮 1090
嚏 2199
嚼 4521

19
嚇 2149
囉 2432

口 5008
四 479
四 4729
四 3770
回 3135
囚 3745
因 5107
国 2104
困 2134
固 1810
圈 1201
國 2103

9 圜 5000
圓 4916
圓 4917
圖 4393
圕 4443

土 4380
地 4125
在 4609
址 218
坏 740
坏 3541
坊 782
坑 940
坎 1146
均 2077
坍 4049
坐 4600
坐 4793

						33	34	35	36	37	

土（續）

Column 1 （[5]–[7]）:
- [5] 坏 425 / 坷 1118 / 坤 2129 / 坭 2845 / 坡 3348 / 垂 4007 / 坦 4296
- [6] 垢 1580 / 垣 3151 / 梁 4219
- [7] 埕 560 / 埋 2568 / 埃 3096 / 埔 3340 / 城 3883

Column 2 （[8]）:
- 涌 4456
- [8] 執 147 / 埠 745 / 埯 1303 / 基 1606 / 堅 1660 / 堝 1778 / 培 3547 / 埽 3685 / 堆 4248 / 堂 4435 / 域 5047

Column 3 （[9]–[10]）:
- [9] 場 510 / 堪 1143 / 堰 1344 / 堯 1397 / 塄 1435 / 堡 3335 / 報 3337
- [10] 塚 641 / 塊 652 / 堍 1891 / 塞 3592 / 塔 4307 / 塡 4357 / 塋 4395 / 塘 4438

Column 4 （[11]）:
- [11] 塵 469 / 塢 511 / 墝 1150 / 境 1676 / 墺 1981 / 墓 2727 / 墅 3561 / 墊 3994 / 墫 4165½

Column 5 （[12]）:
- [12] 壋 360 / 壚 718 / 墳 1214 / 墩 2606 / 墊 4090 / 塾 4265 / 塹 4091 / 墮 4221 / 塔 4308 / 增 4490

Column 6 （[13]–[16]）:
- [13] 墾 979 / 壁 3275 / 墼 3284 / 壇 3360 / 墻 4303 / 壈 4739 / 甕 4945 / 壅 5265
- [14] 壓 25 / 壕 1108
- [15] 壘 2492
- [16] 壞 2140 / 壟 2541 / 壤 4965

士（33）
- 士 3777
- [1] 壬 5101
- [4] 壯 309 / 壳 1137 / 声 3881
- [9] 壺 3122 / 壻 3590 / 壹 5134
- [11] 壽 3867

夂（34）
- 夂 1573

夊（35）
- 夊 4003
- [7] 夏 909
- [11] 夐 2033

夕（36）
- 夕 4547
- [2] 外 3070
- [3] 多 4215
- [5] 夜 5176
- [8] 夠 1583 / 梦 2809
- [11] 夥 769 / 夢 2808

大（37）
- 大 4033
- [1] 夫 801 / 天 1386 / 太 4283 / 夭 4355
- [2] 失 3849
- [3] 夷 1268 / 夸 2112
- [4] 夾 1485 / 奀 3026 3027
- [5] 奉 897 / 奇 1950 1612 / 奈 2940

大（37，續）
- [6] 契 1902
- [7] 奔 3216 / 奏 4501
- [8] 套 4386 / 奢 491 / 奠 4165
- [10] 奧 3086
- [11] 奩 2343 / 奪 4247 / 奬 4526
- [13] 奮 722

女

女 2949

[2]
奶 2816
奴 2819

[3]
妃 2922
好 751
她 1099
妁 1100
奸 1467
妄 2760
如 4873

[4]
妆 302
妨 784
妖 1380
妓 1632
妗 1916
妙 2708

妒 4205
妥 4405

[5]
始 523
姑 1786
姆 2725
妹 2765
妺 2776
姓 3657
妬 4204
姐 4508
姊 4668
姉 4669
妻 4697
姜 4768
委 4991

[6]
姪 152
姣 961
姨 1270
姦 1466
姝 1505
姤 1588
姬 1617
娀 1644
娃 3474
威 4953
姻 4985
娗 5111

[7]
媤 1635
娟 1836
娩 2685
娘 2880

[6]
娥 3063
娉 3496
娣 4325
娼 502
婚 3591
嫌 698

[10]
嫁 835
嫌 1317
嫁 1423
媾 1589
媿 2125
婢 2166
婆 2260
娑 3528
婉 4825
婷 4911
媛 5098
嬲 2864
媼 3084
嬀 5025
媳 3637
嫂 3683
嫉 4497

[9]
媚 2667
媛 2948
媒 2772
婿 3591

[11]
嬙 188
嫵 2583
嫺 2947
嬈 3510
嫽 4142

[12]
嫻 935
嬉 1025
嬌 1701

[13]
嬡 3098

[14]
嬭 2820
嬲 2865
孀 3230
嬰 5224
嬌 3827
嬔 3629

[19]
孌 2473

子

子 4667

[1]
孔 1232

[2]
孕 5123
孖 2552
字 4672
存 4816
孛 808
孝 960
孜 4664

[5]
孤 1787
季 2066
孟 2589
孥 2923
孩 1133

[7]
孫 3704
孰 2650
挐 2684

[9]
孱 3801

[13]
學 1140

[14]
孾 1735

[16]
孿 1376
孽 1377

宀

宀 2679

[3]
宅 83
安 3107
守 3861
宇 4892

[4]
宋 3751
完 4915

[7]
宜 1265
官 1815
宝 3332
实 3856
定 4132
宗 4646

客 921
宣 3703
室 3850
宦 4979
宥 5167
害 1135
宴 1346
家 1410
宫 1884
宁 2899
宵 3673
宰 4605
容 5269

寄 1629
寇 1935
密 2638
宿 3736
宙 4089
寂 4545
寅 5119
富 823
寒 1164
寐 2668
甯 2901
寋 3855
寓 4901
寃 4908

宀 (continued)

[10] 寥 2904
[11] 寨 72
察 444
寡 2038
寞 2748
寧 2898
寤 2972
實 3854
寢 4709

[12] 寬 857
寮 2392
寫 3616
審 3826
[16] 寵 640
[17] 寶 3331

41 寸 4814

[2] 对 4251
寺 4677
封 880
[7] 射 3877
專 344
將 4522 / 4528
[9] 尋 1913 / 4710
尊 4621
[11] 對 4249 / 4250
[13] 導 4210

42 小 3674

[1] 少 3966 / 3967
[3] 尖 4550
[5] 尚 3897

43 尢 5068

[1] 尤 5158
[8] 就 4504

44 尸 3901

尺 496
尹 5033
[2] 尻 956
尼 2873
[3] 居 4257
[4] 局 1875 / 2030
尾 2653 / 2663
尿 2921
屁 3467
[5] 届 1446
居 1846
屈 5040

尸 (continued)

[6] 屍 3900
屎 3902
屛 4188
屋 4944
展 260
屐 1969
屑 3664
[8] 屝 3089
屏 3306 / 3500
[9] 屬 4013
屠 4400
[11] 屢 2487

[12] 履 2291
層 4714
[18] 屬 4012
[21] 屭 37

45 中 3793

46 山

[2] 屼 4723
[5] 岡 1775
岩 2995
岸 3078
峒 4280
[7] 峰 889
峽 945
峨 3064
島 4198 / 4384
[8] 崎 1948
崙 2523
嵒 2524
崖 2987

山 (continued)

崩 3233
崇 4023
[9] 嵌 1157
嵐 2168
歲 3723
嶇 2020
[14] 嶄 1271
嶺 2377
嶁 3727
[17] 巍 3020
巉 4688
[19] 巔 4161
[20] 巖 2994

47 川 604

[3] 州 159
巡 4838
[4] 巡 4837
巢 451

工 1877
- 巧 958
- 巨 1863
- 左 4597
- 巫 2714
- 差 400 / 411

己 1623
- 己 1279
- 巳 4678
- 巴 3158
- 厄 214
- 巷 1182 / 1190

巾 1537
- 布 3336
- 市 3908
- 帆 672
- 希 1020
- 帛 3179
- 帕 3411
- 帙 4181
- 帖 4365
- 帝 4074
- 緷 2287
- 帮 3369
- 師 3757
- 席 4546

帳 194
- 常 3890
- 帶 4031
- 帷 5004
- 幅 869
- 帽 2726
- 幀 3368
- 幛 5005
- 幌 794
- 幔 2579
- 幙 2746
- 幕 2747

幢 588
- 幡 659
- 幣 3213
- 幟 533
- 幪 2339
- 幫 3367

干 1761
- 平 3497 / 3479
- 年 2895
- 幵 3310
- 幸 993
- 并 3312
- 幹 1768

幺 1382
- 幻 4980
- 幼 5147
- 幽 5142
- 幾 1624 / 1610

广 1306
- 庄 308
- 座 4599
- 床 587
- 庇 3257
- 序 4633
- 府 814
- 庚 1554
- 庙 2710
- 底 4071
- 店 4154
- 度 4208 / 4228

庫 827
- 庭 4362
- 康 1177
- 庵 3102
- 庶 3990
- 庸 5273
- 廁 4857
- 廈 910
- 廉 2342
- 廊 2461
- 廓 776

廛 552
- 廠 579
- 廚 592
- 廢 690
- 廣 2107
- 廟 2709
- 廩 2228
- 廳 4346

廴 5122
- 延 1352
- 廻 3177
- 迴 3282
- 建 1664
- 廻 3137

廾 1888
- 弄 5084
- 弇 2544
- 弇 1304
- 弊 3211

弋 [5219]	弓 [1883]	彊 [13] [1648] [1965] / 彌 [14] [2874] / 彎 [19] [4970]	彐 [1524] / 彡 [3792]	彳	徒 [8] [3570]	徵 [12] [270]	心 [3593]	怎 [5] [130]	恥 [6] [525]	悔 [7] [853]
式 [5135]	弔 [4190]	彝 [15] [1273]	形 [5230]	役 [5211]	得 [4081]	徹 [567]	必 [3315]	怯 [1080]	恃 [542]	悍 [1171]
式 [1289]	引 [5121]		彥 [1364]	征 [269]	從 [4848]	德 [4082]	志 [230]	怡 [1269]	恍 [793]	悟 [2959] [2968]
弑 [3921]	弗 [731]		彫 [4374] [4183]	彼 [3253]	御 [4656] [4902]	徽 [688]	忌 [1631]	急 [1558]	恨 [981]	悄 [2970]
弒 [3904]	弛 [527]		彩 [4796]	往 [5079]	復 [747] [875]		忘 [2754]	怪 [2048]	恆 [987]	悖 [3378]
	弟 [4077]		彭 [3434]	徃 [5080]	徧 [3493]		忙 [2755]	怒 [2929]	恒 [988]	悅 [4939]
	弦 [1354]		彤 [189]	很 [977]	循 [4836]		忍 [5114]	怕 [3410]	恰 [996]	患 [4978]
	弩 [2928]		影 [5228]	後 [1013]	徨 [5078]		忠 [384]	性 [3658]	恐 [1231]	
	弱 [5182]			律 [2546]	徭 [1396]		快 [651]	思 [3759] [3773]	恭 [1881]	
	張 [185]			待 [4223]	微 [2656]		念 [720]	怠 [4426]	息 [3633]	
	強 [1964] [1966] [1647]			徑 [1682]	徬 [3538]		忽 [726]	怨 [4913]	恤 [3752]	
	彌 [4058] [4304]			徒 [4390]			念 [2891]		恕 [3989]	
				徐 [4831]			忤 [2969]		恬 [4353]	
									恩 [5108]	

						戈 2095		戶 3129	手 3859	找 108

Radical 心 (continued)

8
悵 200 · 愓 352 · 惜 707 · 悔 1300 · 惧 1858 · 悶 2786 · 惘 2787 · 惡 3100 / 3117 · 悲 3246 · 惜 3636 · 惕 4350 · 悽 4700 · 情 4766 · 惑 4968 · 惟 5000

惠 5018
9
恕 1058 · 恢 1085 · 意 1258 · 感 1755 · 惱 2866 / 2925 · 愛 3099 · 惶 3621 · 想 3631 · 愁 3864 · 惰 4220 · 愚 4874 · 愈 4899 · 愉 4900 · 惹 5174

10
愴 581 · 慌 780 · 愷 1126 · 慅 1395 · 愧 2124 · 慄 2547 · 慎 3839 · 慈 4865 · 愿 4934 · 愬 5110 · 逮 5053

11
慳 933 · 慰 1040 · 慶 1076 · 慮 2495 · 慢 2578 · 慕 2728 · 應 2886 · 慘 4684 · 慚 4689 · 慇 4690 · 慰 4992 · 慧 5016 · 憂 5141 · 慾 5252

12
憒 582 · 憤 721 · 憒 851 · 憲 1068 · 慣 2054 · 憐 2351 · 憫 2621 · 憑 3454 · 憎 4489

13
懈 919 · 懇 976 · 憾 1156 · 憨 1918 · 懂 4274 · 憶 4749 · 憶 5207 · 應 5221 / 5229

15
懲 562
16
懿 1260 · 懶 2185 · 懵 2801 · 懸 4927 · 懷 4963
18
懼 1857
19
戀 2476
21
戁 3081
24
戀 3080

Radical 戈 (62)

戈 2095
2
成 3948 · 戎 5277 · 戒 1437 · 我 3065 · 或 4966
6
戝 4281
7
戚 4743
8
戟 1653
9
戡 1151 · 戥 4100 · 戢 4716

10
截 4572
2
戲 1037 · 戮 2512
12
戰 263
13
戲 1036
14
戳 497 · 戴 4032

Radical 戶 (63)

戶 3129
4
房 798 · 戽 829 · 戾 2500 · 所 3977 · 扁 3291
6
扇 3930
11
扈 2486

Radical 手 (64)

手 3859
4
才 4804
1
扎 102
2
扒 3413 · 扑 3531 · 打 4027
6
扔 48 / 3004 · 戾 3035
11
扠 403 · 扞 1172 · 扣 1930 · 扛 2002 · 托 4427

找 108 · 抓 109
1
折 283 · 抄 447 · 扯 493 · 抔 741 · 扶 830 · 扻 1147 · 技 1633 · 抗 1785 / 2003 · 扳 2623 · 扭 2867 · 扱 3034 / 443 · 把 3161

支
207

19
攤 2433
攣 2470
攤 4294
攙 2832

20
攪 1502
攤 4234

21
攬 2171

24
攫 2573

16
攏 778
攔 2147
攏 2538

17
撓 428
攔 2180

18
攪 607
攔 2127
攝 3960
2911

15
擲 82
擴 777
擾 1403
擠 2193
擢 2381
擤 2734
2738
擺 3167
攀 3426
撈 3476
攪 4434
擦 4696

14
擠 116
4480
擬 1281
攔 1749
攝 2169
擎 2170
擯 3229
攀 3427
擭 3600
擣 4200
擡 4420

13
擣 3578
擅 3940
擔 4035
4040
撻 4311
擷 4331
擋 4233
4237
操 4776
擁 4946
5263

13
擇 80
擿 1481
擈 1533
擊 1651
撤 1651½
撿 1656
據 1855
擒 1912
擎 1982
撇 2307
擄 2422
擘 2572
盥 2631
換 3082
瓣 3476
3485

12
攝 2897
播 3353
撲 3529
145
撥 3395
3557
擎 3503
撒 3581
撕 3765
搭 4059
4103
擎 4266
撏 4752
撮 4821

12
撞 310
撐 436
439
撑 437
揸 494
撤 564
撫 817
橋 1704
1711
撬 1710
撈 2198
2402
播 2264
撩 2389
2394
撓 2841
撚 2854
2894

撥 3006
擎 3048
撒 3049
3056
摒 3499
撓 3567
擔 4067
攬 4108
摠 4653

11
摘 79
摺 282
摳 1929
捥 1974
摑 2049
摟 2258
摺 2265
捷 2355
摘 2401
捫 2502
摩 2733
摸 2739
2744
捽 2896
2903
挈 2998

擎 3385
搜 3607
損 3707
撡 3790
撞 3929
搧 3934
搭 4060
揲 4086
搶 4737
搕 4957
搵 5023
揖 5045
捛 5053½

75（木）

梢 3810　梳 3976　梯 4313　桝 4454　梛 5169　桜 5241

[7]
桅 213　梵 680　菜 709　械 917　梟 1092　梗 1555　椈 1746　梁 2318　桹 2463　梅 2767　梨 2779　梧 2960　梻 3218　梆 3372　梭 3690

[6]
桃 2106　框 2114　栗 2548　案 3111　栢 3174　桑 3699　條 4375　桃 4392　桐 4465　栽 4603　栖 4702　桅 5007　核 5044　栞 1001 1195　栄 5050

[6]
桂 153　株 318　桁 941　栲 959　校 964　栩 1219　栘 1274　栭 1275　格 1450　栟 1518　根 1538　桔 1561　桀 1698　柏 1943　桂 2067

枴 2045　柳 2261　某 2642　奈 2939　柯 3093　柏 3173 3181　柄 3277 3309　柁 4415　桔 4419　柴 4719　柔 5152　柚 5166 5158½　枹 810

柿 4860　柾 5069
[5]
枳 151 222　査 405 419　柱 596　枯 803　柙 949　枵 1091　染 1325　枷 1412 1428　架 1424　柬 1474　柩 1599　柑 1751

極 100　枕 128 131　枝 206　杵 597　杼 602　枌 708　枋 783　杭 1189　果 2096　林 2226　枚 2773　枏 2826　板 3187　杯 3375　東 4272　松 4849

[3]
杖 202　杈 402　杉 427　東 624　杏 994　杞 1626　杆 1762　杠 1783　李 2288　朴 2919　呆 3069　代 4084　杜 4212　条 4859　朽 5145　村 4813

木 2795　朩 4092
[1]
札 103　未 2665　末 2792　本 3388　朮 4026
[2]
朱 316　机 1602　朴 3532　朶 4134　朵 4217　束 4218

74（月）

月 4937　有 5159
[2]
服 874 1224　朋 3453
[6]
朕 133　朔 3980　朗 2467
[7]
朓 2764　朏 129　朝 287 569　期 1952 1614
[14]
朦 2805
[16]
朧 2539

73（日）

日 4941
[1]
凸 1493　曲 2029 1224　曳 5088
[3]
更 1550 1557 1479 46
[6]
書 3982
[7]
曼 2581　曹 4789
[8]
替 4316　曾 4713 4491　最 4629
[9]
會 3143

[14]
曛 704　曜 1407　曚 2804
[15]
曠 2141
[19]
曬 3786

8	榲	9	10	11	櫽	12	13	14	16	欠	14
	2087				4478					1056	

椏 5
棧 90
棹 114
棹 182
植 244
根 429 435 441
椎 621
棻 757
棗 1034
椅 1256
棘 1650
極 1654
棺 1817
棋 1956
棊 1957
棍 2079

楄 2087
棉 2676
椚 2751
棃 2778
椀 3147
棑 3421
棚 3431
棒 3435
森 3825
棟 4276
棠 4439
椒 4575
棗 4588
棕 4649
棲 4701

9
楨 271
楚 574
楮 598
椿 630
楓 886
椵 1209
楦 1210
業 1368
楷 1894
棟 2359
楣 2659
楠 2827
樓 4650
楡 4879
椰 5170
楊 5195

10
榨 62
槌 622
槌 754
構 1591
槁 1724
槀 1725
榦 1769
椰 2462
槙 2542
槃 3556
樺 3742
槍 4735
槐 4964
榮 5049
榕 5274

11
樟 187
椿 304
樞 595
槿 1545
槩 1997
槼 1998
樓 2248
櫃 2252
榴 2253
樑 2317
樂 2455
樅 3073
橫 2713
標 3319
弇 3525
榟 3754

櫽 4478
槳 4525
槽 4785
樣 5201

12
橙 440
橈 1392
機 1601
橄 1756
橱 1844
橜 1845
橋 1989
橫 2073
橘 2085
橘 2252
樸 3530
樹 3996
橡 4532
樽 4641
樺 4959
橫 4981 4982

13
樫 557
橄 1003
橝 1318
橝 1420
橝 1657
橝 4305

14
櫂 113
櫫 1305
櫃 2072
櫝 2175
檬 28021
檸 2807
檳 2900
檳 3217
檳 3219
檖 4099
檀 4418

15
櫓 2421
櫓 3366

16
櫬 468
櫫 2412
櫂 2536
櫝 2537

17
欅 1852
欄 2177 2181
櫻 5226

18
權 2007

21
欖 2162

22
欝 5042

欠 1056
2
次 4854
7
欷 859
欸 3979
17
欄 5253
8
款 860
欺 1019
欽 5093
18
歐 1086
歃 5094
10
歌 1729
11
歐 51
歃 4302

14
欮 4880
15
歇 354
18
歡 856

止 217	歹 4030	殳 3993	毋 2716	比 3251	毛 2712	氏 3916	气 1039	水 4004	池 535 [3]	沈 457 [4]	治 235 [5]
正 [1] 275 266	死 [2] 3767	段 [5] 4243	母 [1] 2720		毡 [5] 254	民 [1] 2618	氛 [1] 710	氹 [1] 4328	汎 666	沉 458 135	沾 246
此 [2] 4852	殀 [4] 1387	彀 [6] 1139	每 [3] 2774		毫 [7] 1104		氣 [6] 1033	永 5051	汗 1168	沖 636	沼 290
步 [4] 3341	殆 [5] 4425	殺 3808	毓 [4] 2811		毬 1937			汁 [2] 148	汞 1244	汲 1925	注 338
武 [4] 2723	殊 5190	殷 5109	毒 4260		氈 [13] 253			氾 665	江 1771	決 2012	泛 663
歪 [5] 2652	殖 [8] 245	殼 [8] 1139						求 1936	汙 3113	沒 27921	法 682
歲 [9] 3722	殘 4695	殽 3009							污 3114	沐 2799	況 796
歷 [10] 2333	殞 [10] 5034	殿 4164							汛 3746	沙 3778	沸 732 654 694
歷 [12] 2332	殭 [13] 1644	毀 [13] 4990							汕 3799	沓 4065	汽 1041
歸 [14] 2057	殮 2346	毆 [11] 55							汋 3884	沌 4271	河 1119
	殯 [14] 3231	毅 [14] 3019									沽 1791
											泪 2498
											泯 2627
											沫 2791

水(氵)（續）

【14】灌 300 ／ 灂 866 ／ 濠 1106 ／ 濫 2176 ／ 濘 2906 ／ 濱 3220 ／ 濵 3221 ／ 濕 3843 ／ 濟 4484
【15】瀑 3406 ／ 瀉 3617 ／ 瀆 4261
【16】瀦 326 ／ 瀚 1170 ／ 瀨 2159 ／ 瀝 2329 ／ 瀛 2301 ／ 瀜 2336 ／ 濾 5244
【17】瀾 2183
【18】灌 1826
【19】灘 3784 ／ 灘 4293 ／ 灑 4306 ／ 瀆 4473
【22】灣 4971

火 767

火 767
【2】灰 845 ／ 灯 4095
【3】灼 183 ／ 灸 1586 ／ 灶 4592 ／ 災 4601 ／ 灾 4602
【4】炙 240 ／ 炒 448 ／ 炊 616 ／ 炕 1183 ／ 炕 2004 ／ 炉 2407 ／ 炎 1323
炸 67
【5】炷 337 ／ 热 1374 ／ 炬 1860 ／ 炯 2091 ／ 炳 3304 ／ 炮 3438 ／ 点 4153 ／ 炭 4300
【6】烝 268 ／ 烜 1205 ／ 烘 1242 ／ 烟 1335 ／ 烈 2386 ／ 烙 2452 ／ 烕 2702
烏 3115 ／ 焰 3806
【7】烽 890 ／ 焉 1337 ／ 熙 1359 ／ 焗 1876 ／ 焗 2092
【8】焚 719 ／ 焰 1324 ／ 然 1349 ／ 無 2711 ／ 焙 3382 ／ 焦 4577
【9】照 291 ／ 煮 329 ／ 煩 669 ／ 煇 687 ／ 熙 1026 ／ 煙 1334 ／ 煉 2356 ／ 煤 2766 ／ 煖 2946 ／ 煨 3133 ／ 煏 3285 ／ 煲 3327 ／ 煠 3807 ／ 煎 4552 ／ 煎 4558
【10】熏 702 ／ 熊 1239 ／ 熄 3634
【11】熒 1077 ／ 熱 1372 ／ 熱 1373 ／ 熾 2511 ／ 熬 3008 ／ 熟 3051 ／ 熟 4011
【12】燀 110 ／ 燔 670 ／ 燄 1326 ／ 燕 1347
【13】燭 366 ／ 燼 2951 ／ 燥 4782 ／ 營 5235
【14】燻 703 ／ 燿 1408
【15】爐 3083 ／ 爆 3203 ／ 爍 3441 ／ 爗 3326
【16】爛 1328 ／ 爐 2406
【17】爛 2186
【19】爥 2436
【29】爥 5043

爪 107

爪 107
【4】爭 92
【5】爬 3412 ／ 爰 3152
【8】爲 4999
【9】爲 5013
【14】爵 4520

父 836

父 836
【4】爸 3159
【6】爹 4122
【9】爺 5171

爻 3011

爻 3011
【7】爽 3981
【10】爾 1284

	97	98	99	100	101	102		103	104		
	瓜 2037	**瓦** 2981	**甘** 1750	**生** 3802	**用** 5282	**田** 4356	**番** 656	**疋** 3458	**广** 2885	**疒** 66	**痔** 236

Column **97** 瓜 2037 (11):
瑾 1546
瑠 2256
璃 2282
璁 4846
(12) 璊 2256
(13) 璐 4231
環 4974
(15) 瓊 1983

Column **98** 瓦 2981 (11):
瓠 3509
(17) 瓢 2944

(4) 瓮 4948
(6) 瓷 4864
(8) 瓶 3480 3501
(11) 瓴 343
(12) 甌 53 甂 4492
(13) 甕 4947
(14) 甖 21

Column **99** 甘 1750 (4):
甚 3829
(6) 甜 4352
(8) 甞 3893

Column **100** 生 3802 (6):
產 430
(7) 甥 3841

Column **101** 用 5282 (1):
甪 2197 2238
(2) 甫 821 3516

Column **102** 田 4356 (1):
甲 1488
申 3832
由 5148
(2) 男 2824
甸 4167
(3) 回 4962
(4) 界 1438
畏 4997
(5) 畜 625
留 2247
畝 2643

Column 番 656 (6):
異 1293
(5) 略 2308
畧 2309
畾 2246
2253
(7) 番 655
畫 4961 4967
(8) 當 4230 4235
(14) 疆 1641
(19) 畾 4176

Column **103** 疋 3458 (6):
疌 4052
(5) 疏 3973 疎 3974
(9) 疑 1263

Column **104** 广 2885 (2):
疒 4128
疢 1584
疝 3798
(4) 疥 1447
疣 5156
疫 5215

Column 疒 66 (5):
症 278
疹 463
痷 693
痈 1752 疛 3090
病 3278 3314
疲 3469
疽 4299
疾 4495
疽 4625
疕 4851

Column 痔 236 (6):
痕 980
痊 4818
痣 233
痢 2299
瘈 3705
痧 3781
痦 3465
痘 4118
痛 4458

				105	106	107	108	109		
				戊 3397	自 3178	皮 3468	皿 2696	目 2798		

8
癌 7
痴 517
麻 2227
瘋 2558
痾 3091
痹 3260
痰 4289
痢 4733 4744
瘀 4869
9
瘇 393
瘋 882
瘕 901
痕 1010
瘩 2810
痹 3259

10
瘡 578
痳 3185
瘦 3862
瘨 4158
瘠 4513 4543
瘟 5021
瘟 5188
11
瘴 198
瘵 418
瘤 2257
瘻 2267
瘰 2434

12
癇 936
癎 1475
瘺 2268
療 2395
癆 2414
癉 4050 4298
廣 5075
13
癟 2110
14
癡 516

15
癢 5200
16
癲 2154
癰 2302
17
癬 3642
18
癱 5262
19
癩 4159
癵 4295

105 戊 3397
4
癸 2069
7
發 681
登 4096

106 自 3178
1
百 3170
7
皁 4595
皂 4596
3
的 4139 4140
4
皆 1431
皇 5071
5
皋 1720
6
皎 1506
7
皓 1112

107 皮 3468
10
皴 4503
13
皺 261

108 皿 2696
盅 387
盃 3376
盆 3553
盈 5239
盎 3112
盌 3148
益 5204 5205
盂 5065
盒 1194
盖 1741 1995
盆 2123
盜 4209

109 目 2798
3
直 242
盲 2585
看 1158 1162
眉 2657
盼 3430
相 3625 3632
盹 3428
省 2797 3655
盺 5113
眨 98
眞 136

6
眯 305
眾 395
眷 1840
眠 2680
眼 2999
眵 3007
7
睇 4314
8
睦 2797
睡 4008
督 4255
睛 4562
睬 4798

10
睸 715
瞎 1004
11
瞭 438
瞞 2782
瞳 4466
13
瞽 1806
矇 2209
瞿 2025
矓 2806
19
矖 2208

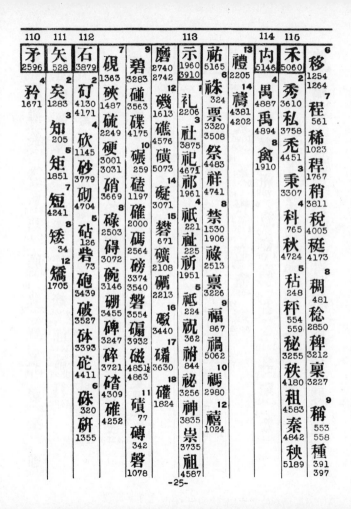

110 · **111** · **112** · **113** · **114** · **115**

110 矛 2596
- [4] 矜 1671

111 矢 528
- [2] 矣 1283
- 知 205
- [5] 矩 1851
- [7] 短 4241
- [8] 矮 34
- [12] 矯 1705

112 石 3879
- [2] 矴 4130
- 矷 4171
- [4] 砆 1145
- 砂 3779
- 砌 4704
- [5] 砧 126
- 砦 73
- 砲 3439
- 破 3527
- 砵 3393
- 砒 4411
- [6] 硃 320
- 研 1355

石（续）
- [7] 硯 1363
- 硤 1487
- 硫 2249
- 硬 3001　3031
- 硝 3669
- [8] 硪 2503
- 碍 3072
- 碗 3146
- 硼 3455
- 碑 3247
- 碎 3721
- 碴 4309
- 碓 4252

石（续）
- [9] 碧 3283
- 碰 3563
- 碟 4175
- [10] 碾 259
- 磋 1197
- 確 2000
- 碼 2564
- 磅 3374　3540
- 磐 3554
- 碥 3932
- 磁 4851½　4863
- [11] 磧 77
- 磚 342
- 磬 1078

磨 2740　2742
- [12] 礎 1613
- 礁 4576
- 磺 5073
- [14] 礙 3071
- 礬 671
- 礦 2108
- 礫 2213
- [16] 礮 3440
- [17] 礴 3630
- [18] 礱 1824

113 示 1960　3910
- [1] 礼 2206
- [3] 社 3875
- 祀 4671
- 祁 1961
- [4] 祉 225
- 祈 1951
- [5] 祗 224
- 祝 362
- 祔 844
- 祕 3256
- 神 3835
- 祟 3735
- 祖 4587

祐 5165
- [6] 祩 324
- 票 3320　3508
- 祭 4483
- 祥 4741
- [8] 禁 1530　1906
- 祿 2513
- [9] 禀 3226
- 福 867
- 禍 5062
- [10] 禔 2980
- [12] 禧 1024

[13] 禮 2205
- [14] 禱 4381　4202

114 内 5146
- [4] 禹 4887
- 禺 4894
- [8] 禽 1910

115 禾 5060
- [2] 秀 3610
- 私 3758
- 禿 4451
- 秉 3307
- [4] 科 765
- 秋 4724
- [5] 秔 248
- 秤 554　559
- 秘 3255
- 秫 4180
- 租 4583
- 秦 4842
- 秧 5189

禾（续）
- [6] 移 1254　1264
- [7] 程 561
- 稀 1023
- 稈 1767
- 稍 3811
- 稅 4005
- 稃 4173
- 稠 481
- 稔 2850
- 稗 3212
- 稟 3227
- [9] 稱 553　558
- 種 391　397

禾
稼 1429
稿 1722（10）
稟 1723
穀 1865
稻 5280
穟 1176（11）
稽 1899
穌 3681
積 4538
穗 3730（12）
穡 2955（13）
穢 4996
穩 5024（14）

穴 4960
究 1585（2）
空 1226 / 1234
穹 2035
穿 603（4）
穵 2530
窀 2531
窃 3661
突 4105
窋 4568
窄 76（5）
窒 154（6）

（7）
窗 499
窓 501
窖 1512（13）
窘 2135
窟 729（8）
窳 500（9）
窣 4885
窩 5056（10）
窬 862
窨 1390
窯 1391
窮 2031
窺 2122（11）

（12）
窿 863
竄 608（13）
簽 1096 / 1988
竅 2032
竇 4113 / 4120（15）
竈 2529（16）
竊 5056
竉 4591
竊 3660（17）

立 2190
站 86（5）
竜 2532
章 186
竟 1677（7）
童 4463
竪 3997（8）
靖 4567
竭 1986（9）
端 4240
竸 2237（12）
競 1686（15）

竹 364
竻 2218（2）
竿 1764
笊 112（4）
笏 733
笐 3238
笘 3270（8）
笑 3675
笋 3740

（5）
筦 518
符 832
笭 1577
笠 2235
笨 3232
笶 3452
笙 3842
笪 4066
第 4076
笛 4147

（6）
策 424
筭 1517
筋 1539
筐 1181
筆 3237
筍 3741
答 4061
等 4097
筒 4461
筴 340（7）
筵 1351
笵 1490
笵 3415

（8）
筍 97
箏 143
箒 163
箍 805
箇 2115
箕 1607
箝 1972
箘 1735
管 1819
箊 2165
箚 3271
箔 3365
算 3708
箙 3813

（9）
篊 124
築 368
箸 341
範 679
篇 3488
箱 3626
篆 3713
箭 4556
節 4570
篙 5055
篤 1717（10）
篔 2543
簀 4256

（11）
勒 2219
篦 2283
篾 2700
撢 3422
篳 3240
篷 3564
篸 426
簆 4467
簐 4685
籔 4834
簇 4835
簡 1473（12）
簫 3671
簪 4468

（13）
簾 1319
簿 2338
簙 3343
簽 4745
籌 480（14）
籃 2164
籍 4548
籐 4332
籙 2513（15）
籠 2533
籤 4746（16）
籮 2438（17）
籬 2277（19）
籲 5186（20）

米 2603	粮 [7] 2312	糟 4584	糸 3764	紙 [4] 216	絮 104	絞 [5] 1503	絺 [6] 1028	綻 [7] 89	緯 [8] 1452	縊 [9] 38	繁 [10] 673
来 2446	粱 2319	糧 [12] 2311	系 [1] 970	紛 701	終 388	結 1694	經 1482	綢 478	緘 1456	縕 452	縲 894
粉 713	粲 4694	糯 [14] 2935	糾 [2] 1581	紡 787	紬 399½	絜 1695	絹 1668	練 2358	縐 4502	緻 231½	纍 2481
粃 3472	粹 3724	糲 [16] 4126	紅 [3] 1235	級 1924	紿 485	給 1923	絹 1841	緊 1541	縣 2677	緵 361	縡 2549
粘 249 2890	精 4560	糴 4150	紀 1625	紋 2619	紱 1353	絳 1782	綠 1941	綦 1618	緬 2686	縝 464	縪 2584
粒 2859	糈 2847	糶 [19] 4373	紃 4840	納 2836	累 2493	絡 2496	綱 2130	綱 1774	緩 3156	縛 775	縮 4009
粗 4775	糊 3120		約 5178	紐 2869	絆 3392	線 2453	綁 3373	綾 2371	編 3290	縟 2870	績 4512
粧 303	糕 [10] 1716			素 3687	細 3589	線 3663	綉 3611	綸 2525	線 3646	縣 4933	縫 4540
粥 365	穀 1864			索 3697	絮 3728	絲 3761		綠 2507	緒 3726	縝 5022	總 4652
粟 3737	糖 4437			紗 3780	紳 3978	統 4455		綿 2678	緞 4245		縱 4654
粵 4943	糞 [11] 717			純 4016	紹 3969	絕 4624		網 2759	緝 4717		
	糠 1175				組 4589	絨 5272		綾 3647	緣 4914		
	糜 2658				紫 4670			綑 3950	緯 5012		
	糢 2717							維 5006			
	漿 4523										

| | | 121 | 122 | 123 | 124 | 125 | 126 | 127 |

[12]
織 238
繙 658
續 848
繞 1405
繑 1993
繚 2396
繡 3612
繢 3941
[13]
繪 849
繫 969
繭 1470
繳 1706
繱 3731
繩 3949
繹 5217

[14]
繾 1066
繼 1522
辮 3289
緤 3566
繻 3719
纂 4622
[15]
纏 264
纓 550
纘 2118
纗 2142
纝 2383
纍 2483
續 4639
[16]
纜 2174
纖 4750
[21]
纘 2173

缶 738 (121)
[3] 缸 1770
缺 2010
[6] 缾 3481
缿 4193
[8] 罃 1777
罌 44
[11] 罍 1079
罏 2148
[12] 罇 4642
[14] 罌 22
[18] 罐 1823

网 2762 (122)
[3] 罕 1159
罔 2763
[6] 罘 739
罛 1790
[8] 罟 1807
罩 111
置 231
罧 2231
罪 4631
[9] 署 601
3995
罰 734

[10] 罵 2567
[2] 罷 3166
詈 4492
[14] 羅 2437
[17] 羈 1621
[19] 羇 1620

羊 5193 (123)
[2] 羌 1645
美 2662
[14] 羔 1715
[17] 羗 2661
[11] 羚 2368
[13] 羞 3604
着 184

[7] 羲 1292
羣 2137
羨 3651
羹 1552
[11] 義 1029
[13] 羶 256
羸 1551

羽 4893 (124)
[4] 翟 531
翅 532
[5] 翁 5261
翎 2372
[11] 習 4476
翕 5131
翡 761
[9] 翠 4827
翦 4554
[10] 翰 1169

[11] 翏 1251
翼 5212
[12] 翻 657
翹 1992
[14] 耀 1406
翾 4401

老 2420 (125)
[36] 考 957
者 169

而 1262 (126)
[3] 耎 3783

耒 2447 (127)
[4] 耗 1101
耕 1480
[3] 耙 3414
[9] 耦 3041

耳 1280	11 聯 2471	聿 2550	肉 5249	4 肢 208	5 胐 1799	6 脂 211	7 脚 1639	8 脹 94	9 腫 392	10 膏 1454	13 膿 1803
3 耶 5172	3 聳 3749	8 肅 3738	2 肌 1608	肺 692	脉 2609	脒 319	脛 1684	腓 196	腸 513	膊 1714	膁 2344
耻 526	聲 3880	肆 3771 3775	肋 2161 2221 1539½	肥 759	胡 3126	脅 1082	胴 2294	腓 760	腹 870	膀 3358	臉 2347 2348
耿 1556	聰 4843	肇 3970	3 肘 162	肪 785	胞 3199	胸 1228	腩 2771	腐 842	膆 1296 1308	膝 3539	膾 2954
5 聊 2391	12 職 239		肝 1763	肯 985	背 3377	胭 1336	膈 3605	腔 1178	腰 1379	腿 4448	臂 3258
7 聘 3495	聶 2914		肛 1776	肩 1661	胥 3718	胳 1451	脣 4017	腕 1295	腳 1638	11 鬎 631	臊 3680
聖 3945	16 聾 2534		肕 3030	股 1798	胆 4039	脈 2608	脫 4446	脺 1307	腩 2830	膠 1495	膽 4038
8 聞 2617	聽 4344 4358 4359		肚 4402	肧 3542	胎 4417	能 2858 2855		脍 1366	腦 2926	膜 2740	臀 4444
聚 4632			肖 4771	育 5256	胃 5019	脊 4511 4542		腃 2848 2852	腥 3620 3654	膝 3602 4722	臆 5208
聰 4844						胞 4828		腕 2926	膈 3076	膣 4442	臃 5268
						脆 4829		脾 3149	膃 3695	膚 811	14 臍 4866
								膊 3470	膕 5057½	12 膩 2877	15 臘 2191
								腎 3840		膨 3433	16 臚 2418
								腴 4875		膕 5260	18 臟 4619
											19 臠 2893

131	132	133	134	135	136	137	138	139	140		
臣 3836	自 4673	至 227	臼 1944	舌 3963	舛 609	舟 161	艮 1547	色 3917	艸 4778	芝 212[4]	芋 599[5]
臥 3067[2]	臭 474[4]	致 228[3]	舀 1404[4]	舍 3871 3872[2]	舞 2721[8]	舡 4000	良 2314		艾 2988[2]	芻 573	范 680½[2]
臨 2224[11]	臬 1375 2916[4]	臺 4422[8]	春 386	舐 3788		舫 790[4]	艱 1465[11]		芍 179[3]	花 650	苦 813
	皐 1719[5]		舅 1942[7]	舒 3983[6]		航 1187			芎 2752 2757	芳 786	苛 1116
	皋 1721		與 4889[8]	舖 3514[7]		般 3386			芊 3131	芬 711	苡 1285
	臲 2918[10]		興 1072 1075[8]	舔 2337[8]		舱 2233[5]			芄 4928	芙 833	苜 1576
			擧 1849[11]	餳 3789[9]		船 3999				芥 1439	茄 1946 1414 1954
			舊 1594[12]	舘 1820[10]		舵 4416				芹 1919	苴 1789½
				礫 2306[11]		艇 4347[7]				芽 2979	苓 2366
				讕 2153[16]		艋 2588[8]				芫 4925	茅 2595
						艙 4808[10]				芸 5030	茂 2645
						艛 3053[11]					苗 2704
						艕 4285					茉 2793
						艚 4787					苘 3139
											苔 4424

13	12	11	10	9	8		7		6	
薷 920	蕃 673	蔗 171	蒸 267 280	蓍 336 177	菠 3350	菖 504	莊 307	茨 4867	茱 322	苑 4912
薏 1097	蕘 1398	蔦 1339	蓄 626	葷 700	菩 3517	菲 755	莖 990	黄 4882	茶 409	若 5181
薏 1259	蕆 1967	蔻 1933	蒿 1098	葍 872	菀 4389	菸 1338	荷 2116	茹 4883	荒 781	英 5222
薑 1640	蕎 1990	蔪 2220	蓋 1740 1994	葑 887	萄 4394	菫 1544	莧 1121 1123	茵 4904	茯 877	
蕿 2082	蕘 2023	蔓 2240	蒯 2047	葒 1241	茶 4800	菰 1789	莫 1362	茸 5112	薁 1272	
蕾 2499	蔽 3208	蓮 2353	蒙 2803	葉 1367	菥 4856	菊 1867	莢 1492	葺 5279	茭 1497	
蔴 2560	蕭 3672	蔆 2373	蒲 3519	蔞 1384	華 4958	菌 2132	莞 1822		荆 1672	
薄 3361	蕩 4238	蔴 2557	蒜 3710	葭 1416		菱 2373	莉 2297		荔 2211	
薩 3582	蕉 4574	蔄 2559	蒔 3915	韮 1579		菓 2097	莨 2320		荖 2242	
薪 3598	蕊 5243	蒟 3180	蒺 4496	葛 1833		萌 2634	莫 2741 2749		茗 2697	
薦 4557		蔬 3975	蓆 4514 4549	葵 2128		萊 2448	莓 2769		茴 3138	
薈 4998		蓮 4453	蒼 4809	落 2454		菔 3181	荾 3585		荅 4062	
3134		蓻 4494	蓉 5278	萬 2576		菘 3245	荳 4116		荐 4558	
				葫 3125		菫 3249	荻 4144		茲 4666	
				葡 3518		菏 3344	茶 4398		草 4777	

| 14 | 16 | 虍 虫647 | 蛆4626 | 蜇286 | 蜘210 | 蝌766 | 螞2565 | 蟲646 | 蠔1105 | 血1212 |

右→左 各欄

第一欄（14）
藍 2167
蘝 2706
薯 3991
藉 4544
藏 4620
4812
15
藩 672
藜 2203
藝 3018
藕 3042
藤 4333
藥 5183

第二欄（16）
蘤 773
蘆 2409
蘇 3677
藷 3991
藻 4590
17
蘭 2182
蘚 3643
19
蘿 2440

第三欄（虍）
虍
2 虎 815
虐 5184
4 虔 1975
處 3987
589
590
虛 1213
7 號 1109
虜 2423
11 虧 686
2121

第四欄（虫 647）
虫 647
2 虱 3851
虹 1237
4 蚓 1320
蚣 1444
蚊 2613
蚤 4687
5 蚱 68
蛀 334
蚶 1321
蛉 2369
蚶 3104
蛇 3874
蛋 4051
4057

第五欄（蛆 4626）
蛆 4626
蚰 5157
6 蛛 317
蜂 1784
蛤 1830
蛩 2036
蛔 3142
蛕 3141
蛓 4661

第六欄（蜇 286）
蜇 286
蜉 744
6 蜂 883
蜆 1064
蜓 1358
蜋 2466
蛾 3061
蜎 4015
蜓 4363
蛹 5266

第七欄（蜘 210）
蜘 210
蛻 1643
蜚 1958
蜞 1959
蜫 2076
蜢 2587
蜜 2637
蜀 5237
蛸 5242

第八欄（蝌 766）
蝌 766
蝙 873
蝦 899
蝐 1088
蝘 1342
蝠 2655
蝁 2756
蝴 3124
蝨 3852
蝕 3926
蝶 4178
蝸 5057
蝗 5074

第九欄（螞 2565）
螞 2565
螟 2693
螄 3766
螈 4440
螎 4662
融 5275
螏 5276
11
蟄 155
螽 390
螫 544
螺 2443
螓 2761
蝸 5057
螯 3054
螵 3506
螳 4441
蟖 4788

第十欄（蟲 646）
蟲 646
蟯 1915
蟀 2024
蟛 2419
蟛 3432
蟠 3555
蟬 3936
13
蟹 916
蠍 1087
蟶 1646
蟪 1914
蠃 2444
蟻 3016
蠅 5236

第十一欄（蠔 1105）
蠔 1105
蠐 4706
15
蠢 632
蠨 674
蠟 2192
16
蠹 4206
17
蠹 884
蠱 1800
蠲 1837
18
蠶 4686
蠻 2833

第十二欄（血 1212）
血 1212
5 衃 2610
6 衆 395

誌 234	諄 375	諸 315	謙 1054	證 276	譖 455	讒 4691		**3**	**5**	**3**	**2**
誨 854	詔 548	諕 789	諢 1399	識 1605	讙 1065	**19**		豈 1032	象 4531	豺 420	貞 265
誠 1441	誹 758	諷 893	詞 1730	謠 2084	護 3128	讚 4472		**4**	**7**	豹 3204 3443	負 839
誥 1727	課 772	諧 915	講 1779	誷 3060	譽 4903	**20**		豉 3912	豪 1107	**9**	貢 1889
誶 2715	諒 2327	諲 1203	謎 2605	識 3918	賣 4258	讖 1069		**8**	**9**	貂 4187	財 2649
誤 2971	論 2528	諺 1365	謗 3534	譁 4951	**16**	**22**		豎 3998	豬 313	**7**	財 4803
誓 3821	誰 4006	調 1371	諷 3931	**13**	儲 476	讘 4262		**11**		貍 2281	**4**
誠 3951	諲 4054	諫 1476	諾 4334	議 1282	讐 477			豐 881		貌 2299	責 75
說 4001	談 4288	謀 2641	謝 4510	警 1675	讕 549			**17**		**9**	販 664
誕 4053	調 4192	諾 2941	**11**	譫 2996	讌 1348			艷 1332		貓 2593	貨 771
誚 4770	諾 4377	諞 2828	謳 49	譬 3466	變 3293			**20**		**18**	貧 3449
誦 4658	請 4734	諭 4898	謫 84	謫 3334	**17**			豔 1331		貛 858	貪 4286
語 4890	諉 4765	諲 4988	譽 1079½	譅 3513	讖 454			**22**			
誘 5161	誘 4989	諢 5010	謹 1542	讌 454	讓 5202			豔 1333			
認 5240		謂 5017	謬 2646	譯 5213							
		諱 5038	譜 4784								

5	6	8	10	赤 547	走 4499	趣 4826	足 4636	6	9	11	14
賑 462	賄 850	質 150	購 1593	4	2	10	2	跟 1536	踵 394	蹙 2388	躊 487
貯 600	賈 1804	232	賽 4801	赧 2831	赴 841	趖 488	趴 2817	跎 1949	踹 415	蹕 2640	躀 3404
費 691	賂 2428	賙 157	11	赦 3873	3	趨 4823	3	跪 2070	蹅 633	蹟 4537	蹬 4101
賀 1122	賍 3962	賬 192	賺 88	7	起 1031	13	趵 1565	跨 2113	蹄 4324	蹤 4647	躍 5179
貳 1288	賍 4615	賦 828	贅 359	赫 924	赶 1765	趱 4781	4	路 2426	踰 4876	12	15
貽 1277	資 4663	賢 1356	12	赭 170	13	19	趾 226	跳 4371	踱 4905	蹯 675	躔 551
貫 1825	賊 4682	賣 2570	贊 4474		趁 466	趲 4471	跰 1566	跡 4534	10	蹺 1093	17
貴 2065	賃 5106	賠 3546	贈 4493		超 568		跁 3409	7	蹊 489	蹻 1707	躙 2178
買 2569	7	賞 3889	13		6		5	踊 5267	蹉 967	蹭 2117	18
貿 2647	賓 3224	5177	贏 5234		越 4372		距 2028	8	蹇 1662	蹴 2163	躑 2917
費 3223	賒 3869	賤 4559	14		越 4938		跛 3205	踭 95	蹐 3537	蹶 3398	20
貼 4364		賜 4853	贔 3209		7		跑 3437	踞 1861	蹋 3935	3405	躦 2942
貲 4665		9	贓 4616		趙 295		跌 4179	踏 4063	蹈 4064	13	
		賴 2156	15		趨 1766			踢 4343	蹈 4213	躇 595½	
		賭 4199	贖 4014					踪 4648		躅 2950	
			18							蹇 4093	
			贓 4614							躁 4780	

身 3830
- 3 躬 1885
- 6 躲 4216
- 8 軃 35
- 聞 2882
- 11 軀 2019
- 軆 3325

車 490
- 3 軌 2063
- 軍 2075
- 軒 1059
- 4 軛 17
- 軟 4931
- 軸 371
- 軫 465
- 軺 2005
- 軻 3092
- 輋 3380

- 6 較 1508
- 載 4606
- 軾 4608
- 7 輔 843
- 輕 1042
- 1071
- 8 輟 355
- 輝 685
- 輦 2349
- 輪 2518
- 輩 3379

- 9 輻 871
- 輸 3984
- 輗 4930
- 10 轄 1000
- 輿 4884
- 11 轉 346
- 347
- 轆 2501
- 12 轍 565
- 轎 1703
- 1712
- 14 蟲 2081
- 15 轡 3273
- 16 轤 2415

辛 3597
- 5 辜 1788
- 7 辣 2195
- 辤 2194
- 辦 3191
- 辨 3296
- 12 辭 4861
- 14 辯 3297

辰 3838
- 3 辱 5255
- 6 農 2952

辵 (走)
- 2 边 3287
- 迁 1216
- 过 2101
- 3 迅 3747
- 巡 4837
- 4 返 662
- 近 1549
- 迎 5233

- 5 迦 1417
- 迫 3176
- 3281
- 逞 556
- 迪 4148
- 6 追 356
- 迭 1276
- 迷 2601
- 送 3750
- 逃 4391
- 退 4449
- 迹 4536
- 逆 5214

- 7 這 174
- 逐 370
- 逸 556
- 逢 895
- 逗 1484
- 1685
- 述 1939
- 逛 2055
- 2119
- 連 2350
- 逭 3670
- 逗 4119
- 透 4338
- 途 4396
- 通 4452
- 速 4535
- 4832
- 造 4594

- 8 週 158
- 進 4644
- 遊 5138
- 9 遺 27
- 遄 610
- 遏 905
- 過 2100
- 逼 3280
- 遍 3492
- 遂 3733
- 達 4068
- 道 4207
- 遏 4236
- 逾 4877
- 4906
- 遇 4896

違 5002
- 遊 5035
- 遊 5151
- 10 遣 1063
- 遙 1400
- 遛 2263
- 遜 3744
- 遞 4078
- 遠 4929

- 11 遮 167
- 適 536
- 3923
- 遭 4585
- 12 遵 2398
- 選 3706
- 遶 4640
- 遷 4756
- 遺 5003
- 13 邀 1383
- 邁 2571
- 避 3265
- 還 4972
- 15 邊 3286

邑 5130
- 那 2815 (4)
- 邦 2934
- 邪 3370
- 邪 4732
- 郊 1496 (6)
- 郁 3739
- 郁 5248
- 郤 1963 (7)
- 郡 2080
- 郎 2460

部 3342
- 郭 2104 (3)
- 郵 5154
- 都 4196
- 鄉 1045 (10)
- 鄙 3464
- 鄭 2516 (12)
- 鄰 2516

酉 5162
- 酌 178 (3)
- 配 3543
- 酒 4500
- 酋 676
- 酣 1795
- 酥 3679
- 酖 281
- 酗 4020 (12)
- 酬 482 (11)
- 醇 483
- 醱 1511 (7)
- 酷 1225
- 酵 2160
- 酸 3702

醯 1294
- 醇 4019 (1)
- 醉 4630
- 醋 4779
- 醒 3622 (9)
- 　　 3656
- 醯 63 (10)
- 醲 473
- 醫 1249 (11)
- 醬 4527
- 釀 5203 (17)
- 釁 5127 (18)

釆 3299
- 采 4799 (1)
- 釉 5168
- 釋 3922 (13)

里 2285
- 重 398 (2)
- 重 645
- 野 5173 (4)
- 量 2313 (5)
- 量 2326
- 釐 2275 (11)

金 1527
- 針 123 (2)
- 釘 568
- 釜 820
- 釘 4127
- 釧 612 (3)
- 釵 414
- 釦 1934
- 釣 4191
- 釬 1168
- 鈈 18 (4)
- 釸 101
- 鈔 450
- 鈉 2838
- 鈕 2868
- 鈍 4269

5
- 鉏 575
- 鈎 1569
- 銜 1932
- 鉸 3037
- 鈷 1971
- 鈴 2367
- 鈞 3038
- 鉑 3364
- 鉢 3394
- 鈸 3396
- 鉋 3445
- 鐵 4367
- 鉈 4410
- 鉛 4921

6
- 銃 644
- 鉥 327
- 銜 930
- 銓 1510
- 銚 1897
- 銘 2691
- 銀 3028
- 銅 4462
- 銓 4819

7
- 鋤 576
- 鋒 885
- 鋏 1491
- 鎧 2758
- 鋪 3511
- 鋃 3515
- 銹 3608
- 銷 3668
- 銼 4792
- 銳 5246

8
- 錐 357
- 錘 619
- 錦 1528
- 鋼 1773
- 鍋 1814
- 鋸 1854
- 錄 2509
- 錨 2840
- 錫 3619
- 　　 3638
- 錠 4174
- 錯 4613
- 錢 4761
- 錯 4791

9
- 鍼 125
- 鍾 389
- 鎛 1440
- 鍵 1667
- 鍊 2357
- 鐶 4214
- 鏊 4773
- 鍬 4774
- 鍋 5054

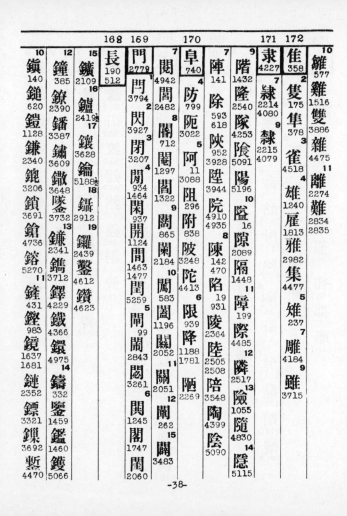

182

風 879

5 颯 3580

8 颶 1598
颸 1859
飈 3408

11 飄 3504

183

飛 750

5 飜 764

184

食 3925

2 飢 1604
飮 4680
飧 4693

4 飯 677
飽 3202
飫 4870
飲 5095　5103

5 飾 3919
飼 4681

6 餉 1049
餃 1499
餌 2878
餅 3276　3308

4 餁 4354
養 5198

7 餓 3066
餘 3920

5 餐 4692
餘 4871

8 餚 932
館 1821
餜 2099
餑 3010

餕 4995

9 餞 1012
餈 4368
餵 4994

10 餚 1038
餚 1718

11 饉 3606

12 餽 91
饒 1401
饑 1603

13 饗 1052
饕 4378

14 饜 1313

185

首 3860

186

香 1046

11 馨 1073

187

馬 2561

3 馮 896
馳 538
馱 4409

4 馴 4841
駁 3355

5 駐 335
駕 1425
駛 3816
駝 4408

6 駭 1132
駱 2451
駿 3356
騁 3817

8 駪 1330
騎 1945　1954

9 騙 3490

10 騫 1060
騮 2243
騰 3044
騷 3682
騙 3933

11 驅 2017
驟 2441

12 驍 1094　1702
驕 1699

13 驗 1329
驚 1670
驘 2442
驛 5218

14 驟 4506

16 驢 2480

188

骨 2083

2 骫 1622

4 骰 3924　4341

5 骷 804
骸 1130

7 骾 1921

8 髀 3252

13 髓 3720　3729
體 4315

189

高 1713

髟 3322	鬥 4110	鬯 509	鬲 2335	鬼 2061	魚 4872	鯉 2289	鮞 1402	鱗 2520	鳥 2920	鴻 1238	鶴 1142

[190] 髟 3322
- [4] 髡 5092, 5099
- [5] 髮 683
- 髭 3272
- [6] 髻 1519, 1523
- [7] 髟弟 4318
- [8] 鬆 3748
- 鬃 4651
- [12] 鬚 3678

[191] 鬥 4110
- [4] 鬪 4111
- [5] 鬧 2842
- [14] 鬭 4112

[192] 鬯 509
- [19] 鬱 5041

[193] 鬲 2335

[194] 鬼 2061
- [4] 魁 847
- 魂 5028
- 魄 3424
- [8] 魏 3021
- [11] 魔 2735
- [14] 魘 1309

[195] 魚 4872
- [4] 魷 460
- 魴 800
- 魯 2424
- [5] 鮓 60
- 鮃 539
- 鮒 844½
- 鮑 3200
- 鮨 3524
- [6] 鮪 852
- 鮫 1498
- 鮮 3641, 3644
- 鯗 3907½
- 紫 4707

[196] [7] 鯉 2289
- 鯆 3328
- 鯢 4977
- [8] 鯨 1980
- 鯪 2375
- 鯛 4811
- [9] 鰕 900
- 鰔 1757
- 鰓 3696
- 鯽 4487½
- 鰍 4726
- 鮨 4727
- 鰉 5076

[10] 鮞 1402
- 鰊 2053
- 鰣 3907
- [8] 鰨 4310, 4312
- 鯧 4811
- [11] 鰰 345
- 鰱 2354
- 鰻 2580
- 鰲 2628
- 鰵 3052

[12] 鱗 2520
- 鱧 3937
- 鱔 3938
- 鱘 4711
- 鱒 4842½
- [13] 鱣 258
- 鱟 1017
- 鱷 3085
- [15] 鱸 2382
- [16] 鱸 2413
- [18] 鱷 3075

鳥 2920
- [2] 鳧 834
- 鳩 1567
- 鳳 898
- 鳴 2692
- 鳶 4928½
- 鴉 3000
- 鴇 3333
- [5] 鴨 24
- 鴈 408
- 鴎 521
- 鴣 1792
- 鴒 2365
- 鴕 4412

[6] 鴻 1238
- 鴿 1829
- 鵑 1835
- 鴯 1870
- 鵝 2724
- 鵝 3057
- 鵞 3058
- [8] 雛 379
- 鶴 3101
- 鵬 3456
- 鶉 4021
- 鵲 4519
- [9] 鶚 3077
- 鶯 43

鶴 1142
- 鵒 1393
- 鶺 1515
- 鷂 4541
- [11] 鷗 52
- 鶙 172
- 淮鳥 380
- 鷥 1252
- 鷸 2397
- [12] 鵰 938
- [13] 鸇 258
- 鷺 2429
- 鷹 5223
- [17] 鸚 5225
- [19] 鸞 2472

197	198	199	200	201	202	203	204	205	206	207	208
鹵 2425	鹿 2510	麥 2607	麻 2556	黃 5070	黍	黑 971	黹	黽 2624	鼎 4170	鼓 1802	鼠 3985

197	198	199	200	201	202	203	204	205
7 覰 1469	2 麀 5144	4 麩 807	4 麼 689		3 黎 2204	4 默 2611		11 鼈 3317
9 鹹 926	5 塵 330	5 麵 812	3 麾 2736		5 黏 250 2889	5 黜 399		
10 鹺 1471	6 麤 2660	麪 2689			11 黐 514	點 4151		
13 鹽 1314	8 麗 2212	8 麴 1874				點 4152		
鹼 1472	10 麝 3878	9 麵 2688				8 黨 4232		
	12 麟 2526							

209	210	211	212	213	214
鼻 3269	齊 4705	齒 524	龍 2532	龜 2058	龠 5187

209	210	211	212	213	214
3 鼾 1165	3 齋 69	6 齦 1540	6 龕 1144		8 籲 5185
		齧 3003 3047			
		11 齫 2846			

NOTES

ENGLISH INDEX

This section of this book brings an English-Cantonese Dictionary within the covers of one volume. In compiling this Index the aim has been to take the material in the main section of the book and make it of the largest availability from the English side. In making use of this Index, it should be borne in mind that it is an Index, making that which has been compiled for one purpose available in an additional way. It has not started as a compilation of an English Chinese dictionary, and seeming incongruities can be laid to that fact.

Explanatory Notes

The numbers in this Index refer to the numerical designation of entries in the main Chinese-English section of the work.

For instance, 3123 indicates a reference to the single character designated by that serial number.

3123b indicates a reference to phrase (b) listed under this character number 3123.

The following arrangements and abbreviations are used:

1923, 387b. Two or more references separated by a comma indicates that each is a distinct reference and that either one is a translation for the English word. The first number given indicates the most common colloquial translation, if there be any choice.

3293-3917. Two or more references connected by hyphen indicate the combination of these different characters (or phrase characters), into one phrase as the complete translation sought.

(1409,4490). This arrangement indicates that two separate references may be used alone or combined into one phrase in the order given.

1674-(3621). An indicated phrase with one of the references
(4609)-908. in parenthesis means that the reference in the parenthesis may or may not be used.

[715,3067]-798. This arrangement indicates that either of the references inside the brackets may be used in combination with the reference outside the brackets.

128,a. Separating the numerals and phrase letter by a comma indicates, as in this case, that 128 alone, or phrase 128a, may be used as equally appropriate.

C-. With reference given use 整 chíng, 做 tsò, or other word of like import.

-D. With reference given use diminutive 仔 tsaí or 子 tsź.

D-. Prefix reference given with diminutive such as 小 siú or 細 saì.

-G. Add word indicating gender, as 公 kung or 牯 koó, for male, and 母 mǒ or 姆 ná for female.

-K. Add possessive particle 嘅 kè, or other.

-L. Add 佬 ló, or other word of similar import.

N-. Make a negative of the reference given according to the sense by the use of 唔 m̄, 不 pat, 無 mó, or 冇 mǒ, etc.

S-. }
-s. } Use words indicating the superlative degree, as 至 chì, 極 kǐk, etc.

-Y. According to the required sense add words indicating individual, as 人 yān, 者 ché, 頭 t'aū, etc.

-pt. Add word indicating past tense, as 咀 chǒn, 曉 hiu, etc.

/ indicates that the reference given is not the translation of the English word, but that the term sought for may be made by using this reference and phrasing it with other characters.

(gr) denotes that the reference is to a grammatical particle, the use of which gives the sense of the English word against which it appears.

(tr) denotes that the reference given is a transliteration, not a translation of the English.

<u>Geographical Names</u> are not in the main Index, but will be found grouped by themselves at the end.

In the first edition of this work, the parts of speech were uniformly indicated against the different entries. However, with the freedom with which words in Cantonese are used as nouns or verbs, or otherwise in so much of the language, it has seemed that the "parts of speech" indications in the Index rather led to confusion than to clarity. Hence in this edition, this feature has been eliminated. However, in such cases as occur, in which some distinction must be indicated the following signs are used:

        * to indicate a verb.
        ' to indicate an adjective.
        " to indicate an adverb.

NOTE: A few phrases are designated (l) in the book. As small (l) and figure (1) appear the same, such phrases are indicated by use of a capital (L), as 409L.

A	ABO	ACA

A

a, 5133.
abacus, 3709b.
abandon* 3871-1034.
abashed* 2124.
abate* 1458a.
abbey, Buddhist,
  735-4677.
--,Tauist 4207-1818.
--,Roman,
--, Tauist,
  4207-1818.
--, Roman, 3603-
  4207-4910.
abbot, Buddhist,
  201b.
--, Tauist, 190a.
abbreviate,*
  1458-4241.
abbreviated writ-
  ing, 1458b.
abdomen, 4402.
abet* 3367-299.
abhor* 4489-1311.
abide*(stay), 339.
-- (endure) 3865.
ability, 1768a,
  4804-2357, 2330b.
abjure* 3821-4932-
  (4624).
able to, 3140,2858.
aboard, 4609, 965.
abode, 4944a.
abolish, 690-593.
abominate,*227-4489.
aborigines,
  4380-5117.
-- boat people,
  4057.
-- of China,
  2704-4667.
abortion, 430d,
  4221-4417.
abound* 5158-4215,
  881-3954.

about (nearly)
  1998a, 5178b,
  3896-908.
--(concerning),
  2528a, 1927.
--(around), 156a.
-- to, 4522b.
--, to gad, 2119a.
above, 3896.
abreast, 3423e.
abridge* 1473a.
abroad, " 3070.
abrogate* 690.
abrupt, ' 4105-1948.
abruptly, "
  4105-1349.
abscess 2954a.
abscond* 4391,4216.
-- with money,
  1031d.
absence, leave of,
  1726h.
absent, N-4609.
--minded, 4102.
absolutely, 3315-
  4132, 4652.
absolve,* 3873.
absorb,* 3979.
abstain,*1437.
--from animal food,
  3925.
abstracted, ' 2754c.
abstruse,
  3823-(3086).
absurd, N-2285b.'
abundance,
  2032a, 823.
abundant, 881a.
abuse (scold)*
  2298a.
--(mistreat),
  4695-1135.
--(misuse),
  2474-5282.
abuses, 3211,c.
abyss,3823-4909.

acacia, 1527c,
  3881c.
academy, 1141a.
accede, *5032,
  4960-985.
accelerate,* 1766a.
accept,* 3857-2836.
access,
  1117a-[2200,5132]
accessory, 4656-678
accidental,
  1258c, 3040a.
acclimated, 874b.
acclivity,
  4731-3348.
accompany, 4459-
  2568-1221, 3548.
accomplice,
  4656-678.
accomplish,*
  3948-(4504).
accomplished, '3610.
accomplishment,(gr).
  184, 4197.
accord (peace),
  3625-5059.
--with, in, 1247.
accordance with,in,
  291b.
according to,
  1247b, 291b.
accordingly,
  1753-4504.
accordion, 879g-D.
accost, *553-802.
account, 3972-2798.
  192a.
--,(bill) 4046.
--book, 3343a.
--of, on,
  5107-5013.
accounts, to reckon
  up, 152la.
accountable,'3909a.
accountant, 191a.
accumulate,* 4538-
  2568, 4477-2568.

accurate, N-4791.
accusation,
 1726-311.
accuse,* 1726.
-- a superior, to,
 1880a.
— falsely, 2715.
accustomed to,
 2054-4011.
acetate of copper,
 671e.
-- — iron, 4367i.
-- — lead, 4921c.
ache, 4458,4733.
achieve,*
 3948-(4504).
achievement,
 3948-1879.
acid, 1964a.
—,' 3702.
—, carbolic,
 474b, 1409d.
—, nitric, 1964b.
acidify, * C-3702.
acknowledge,*5240.
acme, 227, 1654.
aconite, 3131-4339.
acorn, 2548c.
acoustics, 3881b.
acquaint,* 4452a.
acquaintance,
 4011-3918.
acquainted (accus-
 tomed), 4011.
—, mutually,
 3625-3918.
— with, 3918.
acquiesce*4960-985.
acquire* 4081-4197.
acquit,3826-N-4631,
 3922-795.
acre, Chinese,2643.
acrid, 2165.
across (crosswise),
 4981.
—, to go, 2100.
act,*4593,986.

— (make, become),
 4610.
—, an, 3776.
— as, 4230.
— in behalf of,
 4222.
acting appointment,
 601a.
action (conduct)
 986a.
—(movement),
 1849-4277.
— accomplished,
 (gr) 4197.
— at law,
 4655-4862.
actionable, 1117a-
 1726.
active, 651½, 2363,
 3859-651½.
—, ever, 4664.
actor, 1037d.
acumen, 2690b.
acute(clever)2363a.
—(pointed)
 (4550,5246).
—(understanding)
 4843.
—angle, 1744a.
adage, 4637-5002.
adamant,1773,4623a.
Adam's apple,1008c.
adapt, C-1193.
add on (pile) 4059.
— to, (1409,4490).
added on, 4351.
adder, 677b, 4260-
 3874.
addict to,
 344-2729.
addition, 1409-682.
additional, 4351,
 2379a, 1287.
addled, 5061.
address,* 553-802.
—(house number),
 2780b.

— a letter, 3616-
 3743-3468.
—, to give an,
 4001b.
adept, 4011-3859.
adequate,1583-3814.
adhere,* 514,
 2889-1541.
adherent, 4232a.
adhesive,' 514.
adhesive, 1495.
adieu, 986b.
adipose, 759.
adjacent,838-1549.
adjoining, 1920.
adjourn, 4172-1952.
adjure, 681-3821.
adjust, C-4481,
 C-2993.
adjutant, 826-4528.
administer, 1819.
administration,277.
admiral,
 11251-4033-4528.
admiralty, 11251.
admire, 3842-3651.
admit, 3250-5132.
—(acknowledge),
 5240.
admonish,1675-1437.
ado, 4215-3776,
 4783-4475.
adopt, 2190-1292-
 4667, 2190-2693a.
adopted father,
 1902a.
— mother, 1902b.
— son, 4674a.
adore, 4023-3168.
adorn, 3603-3919.
adrift, 3505-2245.
adroit, 3939-4560.
adulation,548-2667.
adult, 4033-5117.
adulterate, 1929.
adulterer, 4766f.

ADU	AFF	AFT
adulterous, 1466-3100.	affair, 3776-1768.	—, to look, 4314-1811.
adultery, 1466a.	affairs, 1368a.	afterbirth, 1013e, 3199b, 4417b.
advance,*4760-1221, 4644.	affect,*(1755,4277).	afterglow, 4355-1235.
—goods on credit, 3869.	—(concern) 2051,f.	aftermath, 1013b-3776.
— money, 4509.	affection, 4766.	afternoon, 908a, 20b, 165b.
advantage (place), 1099-3987.	affectionate, 1373e,3823-4766.	afterwards, 1013b,1349b.
—(profit), 5204, 2293c.	affectionate love, 4865b.	again, (4607,875),5163.
advent, 2200-4203.	affections, 513a, 3593.	—(back), 831.
—(of Christ), 1781c.	affiance, 4132b.	—, to do 4593-2100.
adventure, 986c.	affiliate, 1694-4712.	against(by), 3423a.
—,* 986c, 3551.	affinity,5111-4712.	—(leaning), 15.
adversary,475-4143.	affirm, 4960-968.	—(opposing), 2989.
adverse, 2989,1230.	affirmation, (gr.) 968, 5159.	—, over 2687b.
adversity, 813,a.	affix, 4364.	—, to run 2118-4712.
advert to, 4321-1031.	—(as a seal) 1923.	agate, 2563a.
advertise, 4452b, 3337-1726.	afflict, 2740a.	age, 1625b, 3722, 1554.
—(post bills) 4364-288c.	affliction, 813a, 4601-2835.	—, the 3818, 1438a.
advertisement, 1726a.	affluent, 881,a.	—, present 3818b.
advice(counsel), 1207-2616.	afford, 2569-4081.	aged, 2420-4033.
—(information), 4452a,1663-3918.	affray, 1494g, 2842-1494.	agent, 4222a-Y.
advisable, 1099-4593.	affright,* 923-(780).	aggravate, C-645.
advise, 1207.	affront,* 2362a.	aggressive, 4186,1227-3100.
advocate, 3686a.	afire, 767-3965.	aggressor, 3639-4027-Y.
adz, 816a.	aflame, 1235-767.	agile, 1042-651½.
aeolian harp,1048c.	afloat, 743.	agitate, 5247-4277,1389.
Aeolus, 879c.	afoot, 3341.	agitated,3538-5078.
aerated water, 1121f.	aforesaid, 4760-1779.	aglow, 1235-1372.
aerial, 1226-383-K.	aforetime, 3639-3905.	ago, 4760, 3639.
aerolite, 2245c.	afraid, 3409, 1231a,780.	agony, S-813.
aeroplane, 1602b.	African, 3088a-Y, 5117a.	agree(harmony), 5059-1193.
afar, 4929.	aft, 1013-(3286).	—(promise), 5221b.
affable, 1099-3625-4889, 5132b.	after, 1013.	— with,1193.
	— all, 5232a, 4071a.	
	— inquiry, 1585a.	

-3-

AGR	ALE	ALL

AGR

agreeable, 1193b.
—(liking),
  1193-3593.
—(taste),4352.
—(willing), 856a.
agreement
  5178, 1193a.
agriculture,
  1480-397.
—, science of
  2952a.
aground, to run
  1184, 1749-4759.
ague, 681-2187.
ah! 1, 3094.
aha! 902b.
ahead, 3639, 4760.
ahoy! 4986.
aid,* 3367-299.
ail, 5159-3278,
  4458.
Ailanthus glandu-
  losa, 630b.
aim,*1053-376.
aim, 2798-4140.
air, 1033.
—,* 2469a.
air plant, 2182c.
airs, to put on,
  1181.
airy, 2316b.
ajar, 1124-4140.
akin, 4459-5201.
alabaster, 2620.
alacrity, 3157a.
alarm, 1670a.
—(arouse)
  1674-3621.
— olock, 2843a.
alas! 32a, 3211b.
albatross,
  1125-3057.
albumen, 4764f.
alcohol, 4500e.
alder, 5195a.
ale, 4500.
ale house, 4154a.
alert, 1542a.

ALE

aleurites, 2548c.
algae, edible 683c.
algebra,4222-3972a.
alias, 3318-2669.
alien, 2104c-Y.
alight,* 2454.
alike, 5133-5201,
  4868-5029.
alive, 3802-3157.
alkali, 1314.
all, 975a, 3571,
  1743, 1431.
—(complete) 3846a,
  4815, 4705.
—(crowd), 395.
—(every), 1736a,
  4056a.
—(many),3170,2576.
—(throughout),
  4452.
—(utmost), 4645.
—along, 2426a.
— around, 156a.
— of (us, them),
  1410c.
—(polite address),
  2384a.
— states, 2104b.
— that there is,
  2015.
allay, 217.
allegiance,
  384-3593.
allegory,
  4901-1350, 4898a.
alleviate, C-1042.
alley, 1152.
alliance, 2471a.
Alliance Mission,
  3703a.
allied, 4012.
— troops, 2471b.
alligator,
  3075-4872.
allocate, 3108-696.
allot. 696-3418.
allow, 376,
  5148-4081.

ALL

alloy, 1527-4070.
alloy,* 1929.
allude, 1779-1927.
allure, 5121-5161.
allusion, 3106b.
ally,* 1694-4712.
ally, 3453a.
almanac, 4452f,
  4937a.
almighty, 2711d.
Almighty, The
  4815-2858-169.
almond, 994a.
almost,400b, 92d.
alms, to give
  156b, 3898-3870.
— bowl, 2409a.
aloes, 2409b,1046f.
aloft, 3896-1713.
alone, 4259,
  1787-4259.
—(single) 4046.
—(widowed), 3629.
along a path,
  4157, 242.
—(with),4459-2568.
alongside, 3536.
—, to go 2568.
aloof, 2274.
aloud, 4033-3880.
alpaca, 3256a-5193.
alphabet,4672-4339.
already, 1279a,
  5083a.
alright, 4593-4081.
also, 4196, 5163,
  4351, 5210,1262a.
altar, 4483-4303.
alter, (1739,3293).
altercate, 3297b,
  15a.
alternately(every
  other one), 2163b.
—(succession)
  2518a.
Althoea rosa,2128b.
although,3715-1349,
  4654a.

ALT	AMU	ANI
altitude, /1713.	amusing, 4826, 1117-3675.	animation, 4560a.
altogether, 1892-2568, 975a.	analyze, 957a, 444-3854.	animosity, 981, 4489.
alum, 671a.	anarchy, 4033-2474.	aniseed, 3139a.
—, burnt, 671b.	anatomy, 4315b.	— oil, 3197b.
— shale, 671f.	ancestor,4587-4646.	—, star, 3197c.
always, 3905-3905, 3890-3905.	anchor, 4366-2840, 4171.	ankle, 1638b.
am, 968.	—, to 4971a, 4171.	— joint, 3149b.
amah, 9b, 3827a.	—, to cast 3436a.	anklet, 1638-18.
amass, 4538-2568.	—, to weigh 2174d.	annals, /613,/230.
amateur, N-4011-3859.	anchorage, 4971, 1780.	annex, *1409.
amaze, 1670-184.	anchovy sauce, 48720.	annihilation,2057d.
ambassador, 3774-3836, 411.	ancient, 1796, 1595,3635.	anniversary, 2895a.
amber, 819a, 3175.	and, 1927, 1892, 5163, 4889a.	annotate,333,/3616.
ambergris, 2532f.	and(nought,0)2304.	announce, 1726, 3337, 613.
ambition, 230a.	anecdote, /1796-3776.	annoy, 669a.
ambush, 876-3300.	anemone, sea 2059d.	annual, 2774-2895.
amen, 6-2783, 9m, 3951a.	anesthetic, 2558c.	— meeting, 3144b.
amend, 1739-275.	anew, 4607.	annul, 527,690-593.
amends, to make 3546-3330.	angel, 3774a.	annular,4917.
amethyst,4670-5250.	anger, (2865,2929), 2925.	anoint, 406.
amiable, 1117-3099.	—,to 2865.	anonymous placard, 3178b.
amid, 1955b,4609c.	angle, 1744a.	another, 3318, 1289a, 4282.
amiss, N-153.	—, acute 1744b.	— kind, 4076a.
ammonia, 3088g, 3779i.	—, obtuse 1744d.	answer, 3137a.
ammunition, 767L, 644a.	—, right 1744c.	—(speak), 4061.
among them, 1955b, 4609c.	—, * 4191-4872.	—(suit), 184.
amorous, 4766e.	angry, 2866c.	—, an 3137b.
amorphozoa, 1602d.	—, to get 1033d, 681-2029.	ant, 3016.
amount, 3972, 1892-1521.	anguish, S-4458.	antagonism, /4143.
amour, 4766-4339.	animal soul,3424.	antarctic, 2823.
ample(means), 823a.	animalculae,2656b.	ante-, 3639.
—(room), 2107a, 2107-4033.	animals, 1910a.	anteater, scaly 603b.
amputate,1832-1221.	—(domestic),625a.	antecedents, 2445-2331.
amulet, 832b.	—(catlike), 2280.	antechamber, 1160-4361.
amuse, 1124b,1970a.	—(wild)5173-3863.	antelope, 2368a.
amusement, 4973a.	animate, 3749-1031.	antennae, 3678a.
		anthill, 3016a.
		anthracite, /2766.
		anthropology, 5117c.
		anti-, 4250,4143.

ANT	APP	APT
anticipate, 4895a.	apparel, 1248a.	apt to, 3140.
antidote, 1436b.	apparent, 1117a.	aquatic, /4004.
antique form of	apparition, 1062d.	aqueduct, /2021.
writing, 3713.	appeal, 1936.	aquiline nose, 43c.
antiquities,	— higher,	arbitrate,
1796-2636.	1233-1751.	1878-4242.
antiquity,	appear, 1061-648.	arbitrator, 5059-Y.
1796-3905.	— suddenly, 4105.	arbor, 2316a.
antler, 1744j.	appearance, 5269b.	Arbutus, 5195c.
anus, 1776a,	(5230,311).	arch, 4970a, 2999.
3902-729.	appease, 3633-1033.	archaeology, 1796c.
anvil, 4366-126.	appeased, 3497.	archangel,
anxiety, 2040a,	append, 1674.	4355f-190.
5141-2495.	appendage, girdle	archer, 4556-3859.
anxious, 5141-	3544.	architect,
2495, 2040-3593.	appendix, 3330b.	4967-4487-Y.
— for, 2864.	appetite, 5019a.	archway, 1886a.
anxiously look for,	applaud, 1199-4796.	arctic, 1654a.
2764.	apple, 3497b.	ardent, 1373,e.
any, 2635.	—, Adam's 1008c.	— love, 4458-3099.
— (some), 4139.	—, custard 2211b.	arduous, 2834.
anyone, 2635-4006.	apply(ask), 1936.	are, 968.
anything,2635-5173.	—(put on), 4364.	—(in), 965.
anyplace,3286-3987.	—(use),5282.	area, 3340, 4066.
anytime, 1624a.	— medicine, 806a.	arena, 510.
anywhere,3286-3987.	appoint, 563c.	argue, 3297b,2528c.
apart, 2274, 3973.	appointed time,	argus pheasant,
apartment, 798.	1952.	2472a.
apartments, women's	appointment,acting	arid, S-1759.
5005.	601.	arise, 1031b.
apathy,N-1755-4277.	apportion,696-1124.	aristocracy, 1410d.
ape, 2243a.	appraise,1797-1421.	arithmetic,
aperient, 1042f.	apprehend(arrest)	3709a, 3972a.
aperture,1006,2529.	2151, 363.	ark(boat), 161a.
apex, 4161-4129,	—(understand)	—(of Israel) 2072.
4550.	1095-2690a.	arm, 3859.
aphrodisiacs, 798a.	apprentice,	—, fore 3859-162.
apiece, 2774.	1013-3802,4390b.	—, upper 3859-3258.
apocalypse, 2611a.	apprise, 4452a.	armchair,
Apollyon, 2061a.	approach, 4522b.	1494k, 1256a.
apologize, 1436c.	appropriate, 4824.	armful, 2169.
apoplexy, 2926b.	—(fit),1193-3814.	armor, 1488a,2123a.
apostatize, 3377b.	approve, 383b.	armored cable,
apostle,3774-4390.	approximately,	2174b.
apothecary,	5178b.	armory, 2075b.
5063-1046-Y.	apricot, 994.	armpit, 1451a.
apparatus, 1411a,	April, 3770-4937.	arms, below the
1035b.	apron, 2139a.	1082.

ARM	ART	ASS
—(weapons), 3300-1035.	artless, 4016a.	assay, 957-1329, 1329-2100.
—, fire 767k.	arts, magic 2714a.	assemble, 4632,a.
army, 2075.	as, 1099b,4868, 291b.	assembly, 4632a, 3143.
—, Chinese 2508a.	as usual, 3890a.	assent, 4960-985, 5032,a.
—, Salvation 1582d.	asafoetida, 3088f.	assert, 4960-968.
aroma, 1311.	asbestos, 845d.	assess, 1797a.
around, 156a.	ascend, 3895,3942, 4096.	assets, 1368c.
arouse,(3621,2968).	ascent, 3895-2426.	assign, 939b.
arrack, 5170b.	ascertain,405-2690.	assignation, house of 4093b.
arraign, 1726.	ascetic, 2357a.	assist, 3367-299.
arrange, 3107b, 3167, 3511.	ascribe to, 2057.	assistant, 768c.
array, battle 141.	ashamed,1663-525b, 3410a.	—(general work), 4475a.
arrears, 2121a.	ashes, 845.	—(vice officer), 1038.
arrest(stop), 217.	ashore, to go 2568a,3895-3078.	assize, 1815-1281-1421.
—(custody) 2151, 363, 23.	aside, 3535.	associate,* 3625-5122, 2447b.
arrive, 4203.	—, lay 3858b.	—, 4459-3390.
arrogant,1699-3055.	ask, 2629,	association, 3143, 4232.
arrogate, 4751-723.	—(beg),1936.	assort, 3419a.
arrow, 4556.	—(invite), 4734.	assuage, 1437.
arsenal, 2075b.	— after, 2629-[3107,1015].	assume(suppose), 1278a.
arsenic. 3743c, 1350c.	— for favor, 3168a.	— falsely, 1419b.
—, sulphuret of 1240a.	— further, 5205a.	assuming, 3940-4673.
arsenide of nickle, 4462b.	— riddles, 1796b.	assurance(faith), 4256a.
arson, 795c.	askew, 2652.4731.	—(presumption), 4038.
art(skill) 3018, 958.	aslant, 4731.	assure, 4036a.
artemisia, 2988.	asleep, 715b.	assuredly, 4242, 2096a.
artery, 1819h.	asp, 4259-3874.	asthma, 606b.
artful, 2044-958, 4984.	asparagus, 4355j, 2532e.	astonish,1670-1950.
article,1665,2636a.	aspect, 4766, 1678-3917.	astonishing, 1950b.
artifice, 2062b.	aspen, 5195.	astound, 923-780.
artificial, 3859-4610.	asperse, 4988a.	astraddle, 2976b.
— flowers, 216j.	asphalt,4125-2329a.	astray, 4238-3849.
— teeth, 2977d.	aspirate, 3447a.	astringent, 3857-3843-5183-2400.
artillery, /3438.	ass, 2480.	
—man, 3438-3859.	assail, 1880.	
artisan, 4529.	assassin, 4855-921.	
artist, 2708a, 958-4529.	assassinate, 3106c.	
	assault, 1880-4027.	
	—(bodily harm) 4027-1638-2083.	

AST	ATT	AUX
astrology, 247a.	attorney-general, (H.K.) 2546b.	auxiliary, 3367.
astronomy, 4355g.	attract, 5121.	avail(profit) 5159-5204.
astute, 2690b.	— (as magnet),3960.	— one's self of, 466.
asunder, /2274, /3973.	attraction, 3960b.	avarice, 4286-2166.
—, to split 3459.	attractive force, 1926a.	avaricious, 981a, 933.
asylum, 4910.	auburn, 1200a.	avenge, 477a.
at, 965, 4609.	auction sale, 925b.	avenue, /1430.
— last, 1585a, 4659a.	—, to put up at 4340a.	aver, 4960-968.
— once, 4533a, 3905a.	audacious, 1754, 4033-4038.	average, 4452d, 494b.
— present, 1262b.	audible, 4344-4081.	averse, N-383b.
— times,5159-3905.	audience, 395-(5117).	avert, 296, 2681.
— that time,4230a.	audit, 957c.	aviation, 750-986-1140.
— the side, 3535.	auditor, 957c-Y.	avocation, 1368a.
ate, 3925-pt.	— general, 957c-3756.	avoid, (4446,2681).
athirst, 1636-1198.	auger, 3161-4623.	—(flee) 3265.
atlas, 4125-4393-3982.	aught, 4140.	— using, 5010.
atmosphere, 4355c.	augment,1409,4351.	avouch, 5240-136.
atom, 2656c.	augur, 247.	avow, 242-4960.
atone, 4222b.	august, 5071.	await, 4097,4223a, 4359.
atrocity, /4695a.	August, 3195-4937.	awake(naturally), (715)-3621.
attach, 4364-1549.	aunt, maternal 1270-2720, 9e.	—(spiritually), 3621-2968.
attachment, 4364-3593.	—, paternal 1786-2720.	—(watchful) 1674-(3621).
attack, 1880-1549.	auspicious, 1560.	awaken, 1709-3621.
attain, 4081-4197.	austere, 1875-3738.	aware, 205-4203.
attempt, /3903-119.	authentic, 3743b.	away, 2274, 1221.
attend(give attention) 2247b.	author, 4594a.	—, brush 2056.
— on, 874a.	authority, 2007a, 3819.	—, run 4499.
— to, 2285a.	authorize, 5032a.	awe, 4997-1857.
attendance, /4609.	autobiography, 1625d.	awful(majesty), 4985.
attendants, 1536a.	autoboat, 4163i.	—(terrible), 1494h.
attention, to give 2247b.	autocar, 490e,m.	awhile, 5133-[141-907].
attentive, 3589b, 1918a.	autocrat, /3164a.	awkward(rude),4775.
attest, 4610-276.	autocycle, 4163-490h.	—(unskilled), N-3859-3018.
attic, 4129-2248.	autograph, 3238b.	awl, 357.
attire, 301a.	automobile, 490e,m.	awning, 194b.
attitude, 5269.	autumn, 4724-(4355).	
attorney, 311c.		
—, to act as 4222a.		

AWR	BAI	BAN
awry, 2652.	bail,*3329a,4036a.	—(bump), 3562.
axe, 816a.	bait, 2878.	bangle, 18.
—, pick 816b.	—(allure), 5121-5161.	banian, 5279.
axis, 371.		banish, 2629-2075.
axle, 371a.	—(harass), 2834a.	bank(for money),
ay, 968-(2450).	baize, 4775-4033-2881.	3028-[1186,3514].
azelea, 1835b.		—(shore), 3078,
azure, 4809-3917.	bake, 1876.	3286.
	balance, 4355-3497.	— note, 3028a.
	—(left over),3956.	— up, to 5265.
B	—(steelyard), 558.	bankrupt, 4197c.
	— for silver, 2276c.	banner, 1953,4401.
babble, 2416a, 4783-449.	bald, 2105, 4451.	—(large), 4401.
	baldhead, 2105g.	—(sign), 3319.
baby, 3677a.	bale, 3198, 2130.	bannerman, 1953b.
bachelor, 2665b.	—,* [2130,3198]-339.	banquet, 4500g,
back, the 3377.		1351-4546.
—(behind), 1013.	— out(water), 829.	banter, 846a,1649b.
—(reverse), 4330b.	ball, 1937.	banyan, 5274.
— on, turn the 3377.	—(tr) 3347.	baptism(immersion),
	—, cannon 3441i.	4488a.
—, turn 655, 662.	—, eye 4562.	—(not immersion),
backbite, 4988a.	—, play 3347a.	3587a.
backbone, 1379b.	ballad, 2029.	Baptist Church,
back-door, 1013-2779.	ballast, 75-4608.	4488b.
	balloon, 1042e.	baptize, 3898-(3587,4488).
backslide, 3377b.	balmy, 2945.	
backstitch, 1932.	balsam, 215e,898a.	baptized, to be
backward,1053-1013.	bamboo, 364.	3865-(4488,3587).
—, to walk 4197a.	— basket, 2438.	bar(of a door),
bacon, 1335e.	— pipe for smoking	3794, 27.
bacteria, 2656b.	1515m.	—(barrier), 2051.
bad, N-1099.	— pole, 364-1717.	—,* 3794.
—(poor), 5087.	— sieve, 3813.	—(impede), 296a.
—(spoiled), 474, 2186.	— sprouts, 364c.	barb, 3037.
	banana, 4574.	barbarian, 2574-1268.
—(wicked), 3100.	band(tie), 4031.	
—(exclamation), 3211b.	—(company), 3182, 4253.	barbarous, 2574.
		barbel, 1413a.
— business! 3211a.	— box, 216-1194.	barber, 4317-4339-Y.
badge, 1627e.	bandage, 264-4031.	
badger, 858a,313c.	—,* 264, 3198.	bare, 547, 2105, 2435.
baffle, 296a.	banditti, 753-4232.	
bag, 4224, 2943.	bandylegged, 3197g, 3194a, 1684a.	—, to lay 2743.
—,*4027-4197,363.		barefaced, 2347a.
baggage, 986d.	bane, 4260.	barely, 1543.
bail, 3329d.	bang! 3194.	bargain, 3479.
		—,* 1779-1421.

BAR	BAT	BEA
— money, 4132a.	battle, 193a.	beauty, female
bark,* 695.	— array, 141.	3917.
—(of tree), 3468.	battlefield, 263c.	beaver, 2442b.
barley, 2607d.	bawdy-house, 502b.	becalmed, N-879-
—, pearl 1259a.	bawl, 802-925.	3816,4359-879.
barn, 4356-308.	bay, 4971, 3087.	because, 5107-
barometer, 125g.	bayonet, /1658.	(5013).
baron, 4520e.	be, 968,4999,4230.	beche-de-mer,1125g.
barracks, 73a,	—(become) 4610.	beckon, 3033.
3300-798.	—(do), 4593.	becloud, C-2805.
barrel, 4454.	— in, 965, 4609.	become, 681, 3948,
barren land, 4513-	beach, 1125-3286.	4999.
4380.	beacon, 1335f.	—(grow), 3802.
— woman, 3879m.	bead, 314.	becoming(fit),
— womb, 4417c.	beak, 4627.	1193b.
barricade, 2181.	beam, 2317-2795,	bed, 586-(3187).
barrier, 2051,99.	427.	— to make a 587b.
—(hindrance),296b.	—,* 681-1719.	bedbug, 474a.
barrister,	bean curd,4116-842.	bedding, 587a,3473.
4033-311c.	— sprouts, 2979a.	bedfellow, 128d.
barrow, wheel 4901.	beans, 4116.	bedroom,(715,3067)-
barter, 4254-3154.	—, french 4116d.	798.
base(bottom), 4071.	—, kidney 4116c.	bee, 883a.
—(foundation),	—, salted 3912.	—, queen, 2637d.
1606, 1638, 4090.	—, string 4116a.	beehive, 2637e.
—(humble), 1054a,	bear, 1239a.	beef, 3039-5249.
3464.	—(carry), 4035.	— steak, 3412c.
—(worthless),	—(two men), 4420.	beer, 3242b.
5087, 4300.	—(endure), 3865,	beeswax, 2192a,
Basel Missionary	5114a.	2637c.
Society, 3158f.	— on back, 2649.	beet(greens),
basement, 2411a.	— a child, 3802.	1235-1362a.
bashful, 3410a.	— one company,	beetroot, 1235e.
basil, sweet 3677c.	3548.	beetle, 1488b.
basin, 3553.	beard, 3412b.	—, dung 1643.
—, small 3146.	beasts, 3863.	befall, 184a.
basket, 2164, 2438,	—(domestic),625a.	befit, C-1193b.
2235.	— and birds,	before, 3639,4760.
bastard, 5173e.	1910a.	—(early), 4586.
—(abusive), 2058f.	beat, 4027, 4086.	—(formerly), 3639-
baste, 2832.	—(defeat), 4027-	3905.
bastinado, 4027-	3169.	—(in front),2687a.
3187-4667.	—(patrol), 4837.	— dawn, 2804.
bat, 750a.	—(chunam), 386b.	— hand, 4895-3639.
bathe, 3587-3830.	beau, 1818e.	befoul, C-3114a.
battery(electric),	beautiful, 1099-	befriend, 291-1811.
4163f.	4314,4958a,2661,	beg(alms), 998.
—(guns), 3441j.	4985.	—(request), 1936.

-10-

BEG	BEL	BES
— pardon, 1737a.	belong, 4012, 2051.	besotted, 699-2601.
beget, 3802.	beloved, (3977)-3099.	bespeak, 4132.
beggar, 298a.	below, 4071-906, 908.	best, 696a, S-1099,
begin, 1031a, 1124.	belt, 1379a.	4076-5133.
— to write, 2454a.	bemoan, 3246-3095.	bestow, 3898, 4853,
— work, 1877g.	bemuddle, 3120-4395.	157.
beginning, 523a,	bench, 4098.	bet, 3984a.
3860.	—(magistrate's),	betelnut, 2462a.
— with, 1031.	1878-3111.	—pepper, 2247.
begone! 493, 1566f.	bend, a 2029b.	betony, 773a.
begonia, 4439a.	—,* 2029a, 5040.	betroth(of men),
begrime, C-3114a.	— down, 4070.	4132b.
beguile, 1019-	— to breaking, 283.	—(of women), 1218a.
(4968).	beneath, (4609)-908.	betrothal presents,
behalf, in 4316-	benefactor, 5107-	3495.
(4222).	328.	better, 1099a, 1557-
behave, 986.	beneficent, 985-	1099.
— toward, 4223,	3752.	—, still 4938a.
1158a.	benefit, 5204.	— than, 2101e.
behavior, 986a,	—(grace), 5108-81.	— that, 2899a.
3225a.	—,* 4660b.	between, 383a.
behead, 85-4339,	benevolence, 5118a.	bevel, 4731.
3808-4339.	benighted, /971a.	bewail, 3095-1223.
behind, 1013.	benign, 5020.	beware, 4321a.
— time, 536.	bent, 2029, 29.	bewildered, 2601c,
—, to leave 2247a.	— back, 4408a.	3593-2474.
behold, 4314.	—(inclination),	bewitch, 2601.
behoof, 2293c.	/985, 230a.	beyond, 2100.
behoove, 521la.	benumb, C-2558.	bezoar, dog 50701.
being(existence),	benzoin, 3107f.	—, cow 3039d.
5159.	bequeath, 5003,	bias(partiality),
—(life), 2671a.	2247a.	3487.
belabor, 4027-4756.	berate, 2567, 2842.	—(slanting),
belch, 3097.5209a.	bereaved, 3701-3849.	4731, 2652.
beleaguer, 5001-	beriberi, 1639j.	bib, 2241c.
2134.	berries, 2769, 2148.	Bible, 1668c.
belfry, 2248a.	berth, (798, 586)-	bicycle, 490h.
beleive, 3742.	5014.	bid(order), 697a,
beleiver, 3742-	beryl, 2507-5250,	367.
4207-Y.	2256a.	—(invite), 4734.
bell, 385, 236Q.	beseech, 976-1936.	—(offer), 648.
—, small tinkling	beset, 5001-339.	bide, 4097.
2367.	beside, 2568, 121-	bier, 1599-1424.
belladonna, 1946c.	3286.	big, 4033.
bellflower, 4190d.	besides, 1262a, 593,	bigonia, 2362b.
bellow, 802-925.	2379a, 398, 4351.	bigoted, 2876.
bellows, 879h.	besiege, 5001-2134.	bile, 4039a.
belly, 4402, a.	besmear, 406.	bill(beak), 4627.

BIL	BIT	BLE
—(invoice, etc.) 4046.	bite, 4043.	bleed, 2245-1212.
— of exchange, 3028c,3145-4046.	—,* 3012.	blemish, 903a.
— of lading,2171b.	— of insect, 2833.	blend, 1929a.
billiards, 3347a.	biting, 2194.	bless, 362a.
billingsgate,4794.	bits, 3721.	blessed, 4081-362a.
billion, 3330.	bitter, 813.	blessing, 867.
billows, 2468.	—(toilsome), 3597.	blight, 4695,3211.
bin, 2071.	bittern, 2429b.	blind, 2585-(2999).
bind, 104,3373, 2130.	bitumen, 2329a, 5149b.	blinds(bamboo) 2338.
— books, 4127.	bituminous sulphur, 2249d.	—(venetian),1369a.
— with rattan, 4333d.	bivalve, 1064a.	blink(eyes), 3033.
binding(of books), 3468a.	black, 971.	—(light), 3927.
—(of clothes), 2139-3286.	— oxide of iron, 4367j.	bliss, 867.
biography, 311a, 1350b.	— thrush, 408a.	blister, 3442, 3199c.
biology, 3802g.	blackboard, 3188b.	—,* 4433, 681-3199c.
birch, 4959.	blackguard, 2186b.	bloated, 392.
bird,(4518,2920).	blacking, shoe 913g.	block, 1596,4339.
— cage, 2533b.	blackleg, 2401e.	—(pulley), 2437c.
—, cluck of 1871.	blackmail, 2217a.	—(stop), 3592.
—, crest of 1523.	blacksmith, 4027-4366-L.	—, printing 3187.
—, cry of 2692.	bladder, 2921a.	— up, 2457.
— eating, 4135.	—(of animals), 4402b.	blockade, 296-3592.
birdlime, 515a.	—, disease of 2227.	blockhead, 2795-3040-Y,5087-2404.
birds and beasts, 1910a.	—, gall 4038.	blood, 1212.
bird's nest, edible 1340c.	blade, 4195a.	—(kindred) 2608.
birth, 3802.	blame, 4631.	— vessels, 1539a.
birthday,3802-5137. 4053.	—,* 2048, 75.	bloody flux, 3091a, 2299b.
biscuit, 1760d.	blameless, N-4631.	bloom, 1124c.
bishop, 1455a.	blanc-mange, 4891a.	blot out, (4395)-2790.
—(Rom.C.), 15071.	blank, 1226-3178.	blotter, 216g.
bishopwort, 773a.	blanket, 254b.	blow, 4027.
bit(little), 4140.	blaspheme, 3662a.	—,* 614.
—(piece), 652.	blast, 3879-3438.	— pipe, 614b.
—(time), 907.	— reputation, 4182a.	— the nose, 3600.
—(tool), 4623.	blaze(flame), 767b.	— out, 614-2701.
— of bridle, 1971a.	—(conflagration), 767a.	blown about, 3504.
bitch, 1574-G.	blazing, 2386,2586.	blue, 2167.
	bleach, 3507-3178.	—, light 2948b.
	bleat, 2651.	— vitrol, 4039b.
		blunder, 4791.
		blunt,N-2293,4269.
		blur, 2717a,2806.

BOW	BRE	BRI
bowl, 3146, 387.	break,* C-2186,	—, bit of 1971a.
—, alms 3394.	283, 3527.	brief, 4241.
bowsprit, 3241b.	—(as bread), 2572.	brigand, 4682.
box, 3626, 2542.	— off, 4445.	bright,2105-(2690).
—, covered 1194.	— — with fingers,	brightness, 2105-
—,* 2008c.	2699.	1406.
— wood, 1852a.	— open, 3475.	brilliant, 2105d.
Boxers, the 2008d.	— out, 681, 648.	brim, 1981.
boy, (2824)-4482,	— the law, 678.	brimstone, 2249b.
4667.	— wind, 3467b.	brine, 926-4004.
—(servant),3776c.	breakfast,4586-677.	bring, 2896, 2433,
boycott, 4072b.	bream, 4872i, 800-	2888, 2812.
bracelet, 3859-18.	4872.	—(lead), 4031.
braces, 824-4031.	breast, 1228-4760.	— forward, 4321.
brackish, 926.	—(of woman),2819.	brinjal, 1946b.
brad, 3589-4127.	breastplate, 1637c.	—, hairy 2037k.
brag, 1671a,2111.	breath, 1006e.	brink, 3286, 2615.
braggart,2111-1006.	breathe, 4336-1033.	brisket, 2771,5249.
braid,* 3290,3228.	— out, 3447a.	bristles, 4651a.
brain, 2926a.	breech, 1013-3286.	brittle, 4828.
brake, 2518-117.	—(of body), 4444.	broad, 865, 2107a.
bramble,1672a,2218.	breeches, 824.	— locust, 3936.
bran, 1175a.	breed, 430c.	broadcloth, 5272a.
branch, 206.	— horses, 625c.	brocade, 4245b.
— office, 696c.	breeze, 879-D.	brocolli, 3178f.
brand,* 2452-5116.	brethren, 1070a.	brogue, 4380-4287.
—, fire- 3161c.	brevier(type),	broil, 92.
—(mark), 5116.	3195-1109.	—,* 3965.
—(trade mark),	brew, 5203.	broken, 2186,3233.
2606-4339.	bribe, 850a.	—(maimed), 2010.
brandish, 2721.	—,* 4452a	—(scattered),3575.
brandy, 4500d.	brick, 342.	broker,1668a,383-Y.
brass, 4462a.	— kiln, 1390.	bronchocele, 3058h.
brassica, 4800b.	— layer, 2844a.	bronchitis, 1033e.
brave, 5281.	— tea, 409L.	bronze, 4462a.
bravery, 4038,5281.	—, thickness of	—(color), 1796-
bravo! 1099.	4885.	4462-3917.
brawl, 92a.	bricks, to point	brooch, 1905a.
brawn, 2330.	2623b.	brood,*3344-(4051).
bray, 2480b.	brick wall, single	brook, 1898.
braze, 4462-1168½.	4885a.	broom, 3685a.
brazen faced,2347a.	bride, 3596b.	broth, 4431.
brazier, 4027-	bridegroom, 2460a.	brothel, 502b, 73.
4462-Y.	bridge, 1989.	brother, 1070a.
—(pan), 4300-4109.	— of nose, 3269b.	—, elder 1070
breach, 2529.	—, suspension	2404a, 1728.
bread, 2688b.	4189-1989.	—, younger 2404b,
breadth, /865.	bridle, 1642.	4077.

-14-

BRO	BUI	BUS
—, father's younger 4010.	build, 1031, 1664-4594.	—, thorny 1650.
— in law, husband's 4697-1942.	building, 1463, 4910-3977.	bushel, 4109.
— — —, wife's 3172a.	bulb, 4339.	business,3776-1768.
brow, 2991.	—(tubers), 3991.	—(calling), 1368a.
browbeat, 922a.	bulging, 1803.	—(concern), 2051.
brown, 4649-3917.	bulky, 4033.	—(trade), 3802c.
—,* 2951.	bull, 3039-G.	bustle, 3450-2522.
brownie, 2281b.	bullet, 4058.	busy, 3776a,N-934a.
bruise, 415.	bullock, 3039-D.	—(diligent),1917a.
bruised, 4869.	bully, 902.	but, 4056-(968).
brush, 4696, 3809.	bulrush, 2409.	butcher, 4400-Y.
—,* 4696, 653.	bulwarks, 2181a.	—,* 4430.
—, tooth 2977e.	bump, 3562.	— bird, 2397a.
brute, 1910a.	bumptious, 2004-3419.	butler, 1819b.
brutish, 3863-3593.	bunch(bundle),3161.	butt,* 627a.
bryony, 2037j.	—(of flowers), 4217, 2033.	butter, 3039c.
bubble, 3522.	—(of keys), 2232.	— dish, 3039c-387.
— up, 3448.	bundle, 3198, 102, 624.	butterfly, 3124a, 3233d.
bubbling, 2078.	bung, 151, 3592.	buttocks, 3467a, 4257.
bubo, 4872s,2767h.	bungler, 2478-1877-Y.	button, 2868.
buck, 2510-G.	bunk, 586-5014.	— hole, 2780c.
bucket, 4454.	buoy, 2840a,304a.	buttress, 4219.
buckle, 1930-4031-4974.	bunting, 3336e.	buy, 2569.
—,* 1930.	burden, 4040.	— on credit,3869.
buckwheat, 2607a, 1744h.	burglary, 2690d.	buzz, 4664a.
bud, 2794, 2979, 2222.	bureau(office), 3756.	buzzing ears,1280d.
—,* 3203, 2794.	—(toilet), 303a.	by(along,through), 4027.
Buddha, 735.	burial spot, 2727.	—(near), 1549,121.
Buddhism, 735a.	burn, 3965.	—(the passive), 3258.
Buddhist abbot, 201b.	—(brand), 2452.	—(use), 5282.
— nun, 1786d.	—(sear), 2838.	— and bye, 2578-2578.
— priest, 5059b, 3599.	burning, 1372,2838.	— measure, 4242.
— sect, 3922a.	burnish, 2740-2105.	— no means, 3312.
— stanzas, 1525.	burnt alum, 671b.	bylaws, 186a.
buff color, 2977f.	burrow, 4113.	bypath, 1683a.
buffalo, water 3039a.	burst, 3203.	bystander, 3535a.
buffoon, 472.	— forth, 3483.	byword, 4637-4890.
buffoonery, 4475b.	bury, (4617,2568).	
bug, 2795f, 3851.	—(conceal), 2568.	
	— alive, 1462a.	
	bush, 3996-D,4850.	

CAB	CAL	CAN

CAT	CEL	CHA
cathartic, 3617-5183.	celery, 1919a.	chalk, 713f.
catholic, 3512-4355b.	celestial, /4355.	challenge, 5174-4143.
-- Church, 1507g.	cell, 798-D.	chamber, 798.
catkins, willow 2261c.	cellar, 241la.	--, council 1747.
catlike animals, 2280.	cement, 845-1495.	-- pot, 3295e.
	--(concrete),3879f.	chameleon, 1342a.
cattle(cow), 3039.	--(Portland),5222e, 1235g.	chamois, 2368a.
--(in general), 625a.	--, * 1694.	chamomile, 1867c.
--(ordinary),5070f.	cemetery, (5090)-3793.	champion,1107-1696.
--, to tend 1158-3039.	censer, 1046-2406.	chance, 3040a.
catty, 1534.	censor, 1468-1815.	chancre, 3802d.
caul, 2750c.	censure, 75d.	change(alter) 1738-(3293).
cauliflower, 4800e.	census, 423a.	--(chemical), 3293-(651).
caulk, 96a.	-- ticket, 2780.	--(exchange), 3154.
cause, 1809b.	cent, 3640.	--(money), 108.
--, * 3814, 2378, 3250.	center, 3593, /383.	--(position), 4192-(346).
causeway, 3280a, 3058g.	centipede, 3171b.	-- clothes, 5830a.
cauterize, 1584, 2056c.	centurion, 3171a.	channel, 2426c.
caution, 1674-1437.	century, 1625c, 3170-2895.	chant, 5100, 1729.
cautious, 1542a, 3593a.	cereals,2607c,1864.	-- prayers, 2891-1668.
caught, 363-4197.	ceremony, 2206a.	chaotic, 5037-4271.
-- in a fork, 401.	certain, 4132,3854, 2096c.	chapel, 2206L, 867c-4435.
cavalry, 3300b.	-- one, a 2642.	chapped, 425.
cave, 2529, (2994, 4940), 4278.	certainly, 3909-3315, 4242.	chapter, 186.
cavil, 363a.	certificate(character), 4557-3982.	char, 3965-971, 4580.
cayenne, 2195b.	--(examination), 1329b.	character, 986a, 3225a.
cease, 4359-(3633), 217.	certify, 276.	--(letter), 4672.
ceasing, without 1086a.	cesspool, (4004)-4328.	charcoal, 1669a.
cedar, 3173b.	chafe, 4696.	charge(blame), 75.
cedrela odorata, 630a.	chafer, 3778-3936.	--(trust with), 840a.
ceiling, 3188e.	chaff,1175,3472a.	--, electric 634a.
celandine,205-2720.	--, wheat 2607g.	--, official 75a.
celebration,/1075a.	chagrin, 5041-1033.	-- on account, 3895-3972.
celebrity, 2669-3880.	chain, 2352, 2357.	chariot, 2561-490, 1848.
	chair, 1256.	charity, 5118a.
	--, arm 1256a.	charm, 832b.
	--, coolie, 801b, 4421-1703-Y.	charming,4939-1258.
	-- cushion, 4165½a.	
	--, sedan 1703.	

COA	COI	COL
coachman, 490-801.	coil up, 3555-2568.	color, 3917,a.
coagulate, 1694c.	coiled wax taper,	colorwash, 845a.
coal, 2766a.	2192g.	— * 3684-845a.
— mine, 940a.	coin, 4761.	colt, 2561-D.
— oil, 767j.	—, cash 2612,4761.	coltsfoot, 860b.
— tar, 3160b.	—, cent 3640.	column(of letters),
coalesce,3802-2568.	—, dollar 2612,	1186.
coarse, 4775.	4917b.	—(pillar), 596.
coast, 1125-3286.	—, five cent 723b.	coma,699-4008-3278.
coat, 3791	—, ten cent 1104b.	comatose, 2754d.
—(heavy), 2240.	—, twenty cent	comb, 3976.
—(of paint), 4488.	1104d.	—, fine 3270.
coax, 5121-4960.	coincide, 1193.	combat, 1494g.
cobbler,3330-922-Y.	coinciding, 2993.	combative, 4110-
cobra, 945a, 884e.	coir, 4649.	1033.
cobweb, 210a-2759.	coition,798b,1494e.	combine, 5059-1193.
cochineal, 2977g.	coke, 4577a,4011a.	come, 2200, 2445.
cockroach, 1493a.	cold, 2187, 4275.	— back, 875.
cock, 1515-G.	—(indifferent),	— down(as from
—(tap), 4004g.	2187a.	heaven), 1781-
— a gun, 2573-	—, a 3885a.	2224.
1515k.	coleopterous,1488b,	— to, 4203.
— of a gun, 1515k.	2494.	comedy, 3675-1036.
cockatoo,3178-5225-	colewort, 2979c.	comely, 1099-4314.
2724.	colio, 4402-4458.	comet, 3652c.
cockcrow, 1515g.	collapsed, 2861b,	comfits, 4437-4058.
cockles, 3766-3104.	3233.	comfort, 3107d.
cockroach, 1493a.	collar, 1636b.	comfortable, 3107a.
cockscomb, 1516a.	—(yoke), 17.	comic, 1099-3675.
cock's spur, 2028a.	— bone, 3692d-	comma, 4151.
cocoa(tr),1713-1713.	2083.	command, 697a.
cocoanut, 5170a.	collate, 4250-2100.	—, in 4455b.
— milk, 5170c.	colleagues, 3380a.	commander, 4339-Y.
cocoon, 1470.	collect(gather),	— in chief, 4321c.
codfish, 2628-4872.	4632-2568.	—, military 4528,
cod liver oil,4872-	—(money) 3857.	3300-4339.
1763-5149.	— by force, 269a.	commandments, 1441-
code(secret),1525.	college,1140a,1140-	2671.
coerce, 1966-3279.	4435.	commelina, 364e.
coffee(tr), 1415a.	collide, 3625-3562.	commemorate, 3323-
coffer dam, 99a.	colloquial, 4637.	1627.
coffin, 1817a.	—, 4637-4960.	commence, 1031a,
cog, 524.	collusion, 4459-	1124.
cognomen, 1109b.	2641.	commencement, 523a.
cogwheel, 524-2518.	colon, 4033-513.	commend, 4472.
cohabit, 4459-	colonel, 4683-4528.	—(recommend),
(798,1846).	colonize, 335.	1850a.
cohere, 514-2568.	colony, 4012-2103.	comment, 333-1436.
coiffure, 1523.		

condole, 4189-4992.
conduct, 986a, 3225a.
—,* 4031, 5121.
conduit, 4461, 2021.
cone, [4246, 3740]-
  5230.
—, pine 4849e.
confederate, 4459-
  2633.
confer (give), 4853.
— (consult), 127a.
confess, 5240.
— (Rom. Cath.),
  1726j.
confide, 3743-4427.
confident, 3743b,
  1772a.
confine, 23-339,
  2134a.
confirm, C-4132.
confiscate, 1815d.
conflagration, 767a.
conflict, 193a,
  1494g.
—,* 310a.
conform, /291b.
confound, 4027-5037.
confounded, 2474-
  (3571).
confront, /2687b.
Confucian sacred
  books, 1668c.
Confucianism, 1232b.
Confucius, 1232a.
confuse, (1403)-
  2474.
confused, 2190b,
  2528e.
confute, 3355-4197.
congeal, 1979.
congee, 365.
congenial, 1193-
  3593.
congenital, 4417-
  3802.
congou tea, 409r.
congratulate, 1881-
  1030.

congregate, 4632a.
congregation,
  3143, 4632a.
congress, 4632a,
  3143.
— (national), 2103-
  3143.
— (sexual), 1494e.
congruous, 2993.
conical, 4246.
conjecture, 1797.
conjunction, 3143-
  1193.
— (gr), 1927.
conjuring tricks,
  3161b.
connect, 3356a,
  4569-4639.
connected with,
  4012, 2052f.
conquer, 4027-5234.
consanguinity,
  2083-5249-4712.
conscience, 2314-
  3693.
conscious, 4167-
  1745.
consent, 376, /988.
consequence, 2052-
  970.
consequently, 4673-
  1349.
— (therefore),
  1278b.
conservative,
  3188a.
consider (think),
  3759-3631.
— (regard), 3708,
  4235.
considerably, 2308-
  2308.
considerate, 5159-
  3593, 4315a.
consideration, 4314-
  2687.
consignee, 3876-
  771-Y.

consignor, 2454-
  771-Y.
consist of, 2937-
  5159.
consistent with,
  1193.
console, 3107d.
conspicuous, 4314-
  4081-1663.
conspire, 1694-2633.
constable, 411a.
constant, 1086a.
constantly, 3905-
  3905.
— current, 2245g.
constellation,
  3652a.
constipation, 3295d-
  1694.
constitute, 2190.
constitution, 1068a.
constrain, 2682a.
construct, 1031,
  4594.
consul, 2376a.
— general, 4652-
  2376a.
—, vice 826a.
consult, 3887-2313,
  127a.
consume, 3814-3571.
— (spend), 691.
consummate, 3948.
— marriage, 2138b.
consummately, 3846a.
consumption, 692a,
  2414a.
contact, /2568.
contagious, 613-
  1325.
contain, 2006a.
contained in 4608.
contemn, 1019.
contemplate, (3759)-
  3631-907.
contemptible, 1117-
  [3117, 3464].
contend, 92.

CON	CON	COR
content, 3107a.	convulsions, 471-	— (in general),
contents, 3977-4608.	628-3278.	5060.
contest, 92.	coo, 1794-1794.	— (on foot), 1515L.
continent, 4033-159.	cook, 768b, 592b.	cornelian, 2563a.
continually, 2247c,	— * 329.	corner, 1744,a.
3905-3905.	— (boil), 3326.	— of the mouth,
continue, /2938.	cooked, 4011.	2622.
continuous, 3625-	cookhouse, 592a.	cornice, /3646.
2350.	cookie, 3276-D.	coroner, 1330a-1815.
continuous current,	cool, 2187.	corpse, (3767)-3900.
2245f.	— (indifferent),	corpulent, 759b.
contraband, 3758-	2187b.	corral, 2181.
771.	— (pleasant),	correct, N-4791,
contract, 1193a.	2315.	4405a.
— * 2190-5178.	coolie, 1794a.	— (right), 275.
— (lessen), 4009.	—, chair 801b.	—, * 1739-275.
— for work, 3551.	—, house 1819d.	correspond, 3625-
contracted, 76.	—, shop 4475a.	4459.
contradict, 3297b.	coolies, to sell	—, * 4452-3743.
contrary, 669a, 2989.	2570c.	correspondent,
contrast, 3625-4250.	cooper, 805-4454-L.	4452-3743-Y.
contribute, 3250.	cooperate, 1083a.	corridor, 2461.
— (money), 1834-	copious, 4215, 881.	corroborate, /276.
(3028).	copper, 4462,b.	corrode, 3608-4965.
contrition, 4673-	—, acetate of	corrosion, 3608.
4913.	671e.	corrupt, 842a.
contrive, 648-682a.	—, sulphate of	cosey, tea 409-
control, 1819,117.	671d.	1908.
contumely, 2362a.	copperas, 4764-671.	cosmetics, 713e.
convenient, 3295b.	coppersmith, 4462-L.	cosmogony, 1124e.
convent, 3102a.	copulate, 798b,	cost, 1421a.
convention, /3143.	1494e.	costs, 3814-5282.
converse, 2528b,	—, of animals 391b	costiveness, 3295d-
1779-4001a.	copy, 1722.	1694.
conversation, 4001a,	— * 447-3616.	costly, 2065.
1350a.	— (imitate), 1140.	costume, 301a.
convert, 3293-651,	—, original 1722a,	cot, 586-D.
651b.	4071b.	cottage, D-4944.
—, a 1507e-Y.	—, printer's 1722.	cotton, 2676a.
convex, 4106.	coral, 3796.	— cloth, 3336.
— lens, 1637f.	cord, 3948.	— quilt, 4417e.
convey, 3384.	cordial, /856a, /384.	— yarn, 2676-3780.
convict, 678-Y.	core, 3593.	couch, 586.
—, * 4132-4631.	coriander, 3585.	cough, 1928.
convince, 3493-4197.	cork, 151.	—, wheezing 606a.
convolvulus, 550b.	—, * 3592.	council, 3143, 1747a.
convoy, 3750-986.	— screw, 4500f.	— chamber, 1747.
	corn, 3737a	counsel, 1207.
	-24-	

COU	COX	CRE
counsellor, 311c.	coxwain, 3810-	creep, 2178.
count,* 1521a,3971.	[1878, 1877].	creeper, 2178-4332.
countenance, 2687-	coyote, 1574a.	creeping sensation,
2599.	cozy, 3107-2945.	2558b.
—,* 291-1811.	crab, 916.	cremation,719-3965.
counter, 2073d.	—, small 3432a.	crescent,3596-4937-
counterfeit, 1419-	— apple tree,4439.	5230.
4593.	crack, 2148.	cress, 1919b.
counterfoil, 4816a.	—,* C-2385, 425.	crest, 1816, 1523.
counterpane, 3473-	crackers, 3276.	crevice, 2148.
2687.	—, fire 3441d.	crib, 2177.
country, 1045b.	cracking, 2334a.	—(bed), 586-D.
—(nation), 2103.	craft(skill), 3018.	cricket, 4833a.
county, 814,5130.	crafty, 1504,1467a.	—(game), /3347a.
couple(pair),4250.	cram, 2785-(3854).	crime, 4631.
—(double), 3886.	cramps, 471a.	criminal, 678-Y.
courage, 4038,	cramped, 2134-3279.	crimp, 2046a.
1763a, 5281.	crane, 1142,3058d.	—,* 4502-2568.
courageous, 4033-	crank, 1503c.	crimson, 1235a.
4038.	crape, 4502-3780.	cripple, 3205-1638.
courier, 411, 5218.	crash, 2081,3194.	crisp, 4827.
course,(4207)-2071.	crate, 2235.	criticise, 3446,a.
court, 569.	crater, 767g-1006.	crockery,1770-2981.
—(hall),4435,4346.	crave, 1936.	crocodile, 3075-
—, inner 4362.	crawfish, 900d.	(4872).
—(law), 2978a.	crawl, 2178, 3412.	crooked(bent),2029.
— yard, 2461.	crawling things,	—(position),N-275,
courtesies, to ex-	2076b.	2652.
change 2206d.	crayon, 713f-3237.	crop, 3858c, 3857-
courtesy, 2616c.	crazy, 4158, 3080.	5060.
cousin, /1070a.	creaking, 2334a,	— of bird, 3725.
cove, 4971, 3087.	3047.	cross,' 2865,c.
covenant, 5178.	cream, 2820d.	—, 1424a.
—,* 2190-5178.	crease, 452.	—(go), 2100.
cover, 1994.	create. 584a.	—(irritate) 1649a.
—, book 3468a.	creation, 3483a.'	— river, 1125a.
—,* 1908, 167.	creator, 584a-328.	— the legs, 1494i.
—(close), 3208.	credit(believe),	— wise, 4981.
— with the hand,	3743.	croton oil, 3158d.
3105.	—, buy or sell on	crouch, 3409, 876.
covered dish,1155b.	3869.	croup, 954a.
covering,3468,4386.	—, get goods on	crow, 4a.
coverlet, 3473.	2151d.	—,* 4322.
covet, 4286-(2166).	creditor, 71a.	crowbar, 3238c,
covetous,4286-3593.	credulous, 1291-	4277a.
cow, 3039-G.	3743.	crowd, 2137.
coward, N-4038.	creed, 3743-1668.	—,* 5263, 3279.
coxcomb, 1516a.	creek, 638, 1478.	crown, 1816a.

CRU	CUN	CUS

CRU

— (top), 4129.
crucify, 4127-/1424a.
cruel, 4695a,2586.
cruet, 2666b.
cruise, 4837.
cruiser, 4837b.
crumble, /3721.
crumbs, 3601-3721.
crumple, 452.
crush(press), 64, 5263.
— (to breaking), 415.
crust, 3001-3468.
crusty, 3100.
crutch, 2045a.
cry(call), 1709, 1378.
— (weep), 925,1223.
— of animal,2692.
— of bird, 4322. 2692.
crystal, (4004)-4561.
crystalline lens, 4562c.
cub, /4482.
cube, 2190-779.
cubic foot, 4168d.
cubicle, 798-D.
cubit, 162.
cuckold, 2059g.
cockoo, 1835a.
cucumber, 2037a, 5070a.
cud(to chew), 657-4777.
cudgel, (2795)-3435, 2079.
cue, 3289.
cuff, 4505-100b.
—,* 2008c.
culdesac, 2088a.
culpable, 1117-75.
culprit, 578-Y.
cultivate,1480-397.
cumber, /296.

CUN

cunning(crafty), 2062a.
— (skilful), 958.
cup, 3375.
cupboard,3146-2071.
cur, /1574.
curb, 2217.
—,* 1819e.
curd, 2819-1694.
—, bean 4116-842.
curdle, 1694c.
cure, 1249-(1099).
curios, 3155b.
curious, 1020b.
curl, 2470a.
— up, 1566a.
curly hair, 1839a.
currants,314-3517b.
current, (4004)-2245.
—, electric 2245d.
—, constant 2245g.
—, continuous 2245f.
—, intermittent 2245h.
— price,3905-1421.
—,primary 2245e.
—, strong 1541b.
— use, 4452-5282.
curry powder,1640c.
— stuff, 1414a.
curse, 164a,2298a.
curtain, /2338.
—, mosquito 194a.
curved, 2029b.
cushion, 5251-D, 4165-a.
cuspidor, 1824a.
custard apple, 2211b.
custom, 2120a.
—(tribute), 4005.
customer, (2569)-921.
customs dues,4005.
— house, 2052c.
—, maritime 2052a.

CUS

— service, 2052b.
—, to pass 2052d.
cut, 1832, 4769.
—(shear), 4554.
— off, (85,4445), 3624.
— out, 4806.
— the throat, 2790a.
— up, 1436, 4136.
— up alive,4430b.
—, short 1683a.
cuttlefish, 186b, 2606.
cyathiform, 2182d.
cyclone, 3711-879, 879a.
cyclopedia, 2494a.
cylinder, 3393.
— of engine,3552.
cymbal, 3396.
cypress, 3174a.

D

dab, 4104.
—(fish),3778-2589-4872.
dabble in, 2544.
dace, 5070-2663-2520.
daddy, 4122-4122.
dagger, 4241-1658.
dahlia, 179a.
daily, 4435-4435.
dainties, 2666.
dainty dish, 2319b.
dais, 3111-4418.
dally with, 2854-2864.
dam, 3248.
—(mother), 2312.
—,* 3592-3248.
damage, 4965.
damask, 4245a.

DAM	DEA	DEC
dame, 3528.	deacon, 147-3776.	decision, 328b.
damn, 164a.	dead, 3767-pt,	deck, 3999-2687.
damp, 3843.	2101b.	declare, 4960-3854.
damson, 2767c.	deaf, 1280e.	—(make known),
dance, 2721a.	deal, 1099-4215.	613.
dandelion, 5222a.	—(wood), 427-2795.	—(show),3323-2690.
dandle, 1389a,	—,* 1494c.	declaration of war,
2265a.	dealer, wholesale,	263a.
dandruff, 2845b.	1804a.	decline, 4447-4861.
danger, 3015a.	dear(loved), 3977-	declivity, 4731-
danger! 1055a.	3099.	3348.
dangerous, 1055.	—(in price),2065.	decoct, 4552.
dangle, 3027.	— me! 32a.	decorate, 301-274.
dare, 1754.	dearth, 1603,a.	decorum, 1267-338.
daring, 4033-4038.	death, 3767.	decoy, 5121-5161.
dark, (?1.	—(ruin) 3767-2753.	— birds, 301c
—, about 2804.	— rattle, 494a.	decrease, 1457a.
darkened, 2805.	— warrant, 2671b.	decree, 2671-2378.
darkness, 971a.	debate, 92-2528.	decrepit, /2420-
darling, 4458-	debauch, 4151-3113.	/5182.
3099-Y.	debility,4930-5182.	dedicate, 1882-897.
darn, 3330a.	debit note, 1980-	deduct, 1457, 593.
dart, 4556.	4046.	— tare, 2712d.
—,* 3927.	debt, 71.	deed, 986a.
Darwin, 4068a.	—, sue for 1726c.	—(document), 1902,
dash, 635-(310).	debtor, 71b.	4125d.
date(time), /1109.	debts, 1056b.	deep, 3823.
—(fruit), 4588.	decade, 4839.	— sleep, 2851.
—, fixed 1952a.	decalogue, 3845-	deer, 2510.
daub, 4395-3113,	1441.	deer's horn, 5279.
406.	decamp, 4449-3265.	defame, 4988a.
daughter, 2949,	decant, 3258.	defeated,3169,5234.
4482b.	decapitate, [85,	defect, 686a,1056a.
—(your),4754-1527.	3808]-4339.	defend, 3329-3128.
— in law,3637-835.	decapitation, 275a.	defendant, 1726f.
dawn, 2105a.	decayed, 2768-2186.	deficiency, 1056a,
day, 5137, 4355d.	deceased, 3767-Y.	686a.
— after tomorrow,	deceit, 2062a.	defile, 3113-2775.
1013a.	deceitful, 2062a.	—, a 3793-945.
— of month, 1109.	deceive, 3022,4326,	definite, 4132.
—, entire 3948a.	1019.	deflect, 346-4731.
—, every other	—(delude), 2601,a.	deformed, 473-2048.
2163a.	December, 3845-	defraud, 3022-3490.
daylight, 2105b,	1287-4937.	deft, 958a.
3178c.	decency, 1193-2205.	defy, 1649-4110.
day's work, 1877b.	decide, 4132.	degenerate, 908-
dazzle, 438.	decidedly, 4242,	2245.
dazzling, 2105d.	4132.	

DEG	DEN	DES
degrade(rank), 1781b.	dentist, 2977-765-1249c.	— (intention),328b.
— one's self, 4182-2687.	denude, C-547.	— (plot), (1521)-2641.
degree(class), 4097.	deny, N-5240.	designate, 553.
— (level), 4714.	— one's self,973a.	designation, 1109, 4672a.
— (measure), 4208.	depart, 1221,4499.	desirable, /1099.
— (rank), 1924.	department, 3342, 3756.	desire, 3631,4932.
—, superlative, (gr),1654,227, 3849a.	— (political or geographical), 159.	— (covet), 4286.
degrees, by 4551a.	depend on, 1255a.	desist, 4360, 1086, 217.
delay, 536.	deplorable, 3636a.	desk, [3616a,3982]-4418.
delegate,* 1494f.	deport, 3384-1221.	desolate,1787-1164.
deliberate,' 4045-4132.	deportment, 986a.	despair, 4624-2764.
—, *3887-2313,127a.	depose, 1449-238.	despatch, 2616-3982.
delicate, (1701)-2947.	deposit, 4235-4339.	— (telegram),4163g.
delicacies, 137-3606.	— (place), 795.	— * 4027-681.
delicious, 1750b.	depot, 4093.	— (goods, letter), 1629.
delighted, 856a.	— (station), 86b, 490-86.	desperate, 2711c.
delineate,4967-648.	depraved,4732,3100.	despicable, 1117-3117.
delirium, 2143-2735c.	depreciate, 4314-1042.	despise, 726b, 3911a.
— tremens, 2735b.	depress, 25.	despond, 3849-2764.
deliver, 1494.	depressed, 5141-2786.	dessicate, 1779b.
— (save),1582.	deprive, 4247.	destination, 1221-1053.
delude, 2601a, 1800a.	depute, 1063.	destiny, 2671.
deluge, 1236a.	deputy, 825.	destitute, 2031, 3449a.
demand, 2629-4824.	deranged, 2474.	destroy, C-4965, 4990-2186.
—, in 3905c.	— (mentally), 4158.	— (break), (3527, 2186).
demeanor,2687-1006.	deride, 1037a.	— (utterly), 4578-2701.
demented, 4158.	derive, 4081-4197.	destruction, 2701-2753.
demolish, 422-3571.	descend, (1781, 2454.)	detach, (696)-1124.
demon, 2735, 2061.	descendants, 1013d, 4667-3704.	detached, 2274.
demonical, 4732.	describe, [215, 3616]-648.	detail, in 370-5133.
demur, N-985.	desecrate, 3662a.	detain, 2246.
demurrage, 2101c.	desert, 2141a,5173.	detect, 405-648.
den,2529,4113,4940.	— (merit), 1879a.	detective,3106-411.
denomination,4672a.	—, * /4499.	
denote, 215-3854.	deserve, 5223-3865.	
denounce,1233-1726.	design, 1258-4530, 4961.	
dense, 2638.		
dent, 2860.		

DET	DIC	DIN
deter, 2180-296.	— playing, 82a.	dine, /3925.
deteriorate, 4002-4965.	dictate, 367-522.	dinner, 4033-4692.
determination, 2012a.	— to a writer, 1006-3866.	dip in, 4488.
determine, 4132.	dictionary, 4162b.	— the finger in, 4151.
determined, 2190a.	dictum, 3001-4960.	— up, 728-1031.
detest, 4489-3117.	die, 3767, 2101b.	diphtheria, 3058h.
detract, 1779-3707.	diet,* 1437-1006.	dipper, 4109,1138.
devastation, 781-690.	dietetics, 5095a.	direct, 242.
develope, 681-648.	diety, 3835.	—,* 215g.
—(photo), 1062f.	differ,92,696-3318.	—(command), 697a.
developer(ph), 1062g.	difference, 696-3318.	direction, 1053, 4339.
deviate, 986-400.	—, a little 92d.	directly, 4533.
device, 682a,1521.	different, N-4459.	director, 243a.
devil, 2061,a.	—, very 400c.	directory, 3657-2669-2509.
devise, 648-682a.	differential calculus, 696c.	dirt(earth), 2844.
devoid of, 2711.	difficult, 2854, 3100.	—(dung), 3902.
devolve, 1494-2454.	—(abstruse), 3823.	dirty,3113a,2148d.
devoted, 384-3593.	difficulty, 1465a.	disabled, N-2858.
devour, 4329.	diffident, 3743-2551-2100.	disaffected, 3984b.
devout, 1680-1975, 3951-3593.	diffuse, (3339)-3576.	disagree, 3625-92.
dew, 2427b.	dig, 2086, 4983.	—(not alike), N-4250.
dexterous, 958a.	digest, 3667-651.	disagreeable, 473, 3595.
diabetes, 2225b.	digitalis, 5070d.	disappear, 1663d.
diabolical, 1380b.	dignified, 4985-1316.	disappoint, 310b.
diadem, 2683,1816a.	dignity, 4985-1267.	disapprove, N-383b.
diagnose, 461.	dike, 1606.	disaster,4601-2835.
diagonal,4731-3646.	dilate, 436-1124.	disavow, N-5240.
diagrams, the eight 3195-2043.	dilatory, 2578.	disband, 3576.
dial, 2064a,2122b.	dilemma, 2321-2834.	disburse, 648, 207.
dialect, 3178d, 4380-4960.	diligent, 1917,a.	discard, 4182-1034.
dialogue,3625-2528.	dilute, 1502b.	discern, 1663.
diameter, 1683b.	dim, 2806.	discernment, 2690b.
diamond, 4623a, 1527h.	dime, 1104b,c.	discharge, 648,795.
dianthus, 364g.	dimensions, 512-865, 4814a.	— cargo, 771a.
diaphanous, 4338-2105.	diminish, 1457,a.	disciple, 2780e, 4390a.
diarrhoea, 3617a.	diminutive, 3674-3589.	discipline, 1507-682.
diary, 1627c.	dimple, 2861a.	disclose, 2427a. 1062c.
dice, 3924-(4667), 4294b.	din, 4784-449, 3160a.	discomfit, 4027-3169.
		discomfort,N-3107a.

discontinue,4445,
N-4593.
discordant, N-5059,
N-2993.
discount, 4004i.
—,* 1930.
discouraged,
N-3107a.
discourse, 1779,
4001b.
discourteous,2205e.
discover, 405-648.
discredit, N-3743.
discreet,4667-3589.
discrepant, N-4250.
discretion, 1542a.
discriminate, 696-
3318.
discuss, 2528c.
disdain,3911a,1311a.
disease, (4495)-
3278.
—, bladder 2227.
—, bowel 2299.
—, scrofulous
2434.
—, skin 2154.
—, wasting 2414.
disembodied spirit,
2061.
disengage, 1436-
1124.
disentangle, 1436-
2238.
disengaged, 934a.
disgrace,3604-5255,
4155a.
—,* 2362a.
disguise,1419-3190.
disgust, 4489-1311.
disgusting, 1117-
3117.
dish, 3146, 4175.
dishes, 3146-4175
disheartened, 3593-
2110.
dishonest, N-136-
3593.

dishonor, 2362a.
— a bill, N-5240-
4046.
disinclined,N-3631.
disinfect, 1436-
1325.
disinfectant, 474b,
/5183.
disinherit, 648.
disk, 2518.
— of moon, 2387.
dislike, N-383b.
— a person, 3984b.
dismay, 4033-1670a.
dismiss, 795,1217.
disobedient, 3378a.
disobey, N-4344-
4960.
disordered, 2190b,
2528e.
disown, N-5240.
disparage, 1779-
4070.
disparity, 400.
dispatch,2616-3982.
—(telegram),4163g.
—* 4027-681.
—(goods, letter),
1629.
dispensary, 5183-
798.
dispense, 3898.
— with, 2681.
disperse, 3576-
(1124).
display, 1061-648.
displeased, N-383b.
dispose(arrange),
3107b.
disposition, 3658-
4766.
dispute, 3297b, 92.
disquietude,
N-3497a.
disregard, 1042d,
N-1811.
disreputable,
3849-4315.

disrepute, N-2669-
3880.
dissemble, 61-4594.
disseminate, 613.
dissimilar, N-4868.
dissipate, 3576,
650j.
dissipated, 795d.
dissolute, 795d.
dissolve, 651-1124,
(3668,3576).
dissuade,1208-1437.
distant, 4929.
distaste,1663-4292.
distend, 185a.
distil, 268.
distillery, 4785a.
distinct, 2690.
distinguish, 696-
3318.
distinguished,
1099-2669-3880.
distorted, 2652.
distress, 1465a,
4978-2835.
distressed, 36a.
distressing, 813a,
3597-813.
distribute, 3418.
district, 4933.
distrust,3759-1263.
disturb, 1502-4277,
1502a.
disturbance, make
3802-3776.
ditch, (940,2021).
ditty, 1729.
diuretic,2293-4004-
5183.
dive,* 2668a.
diverge, /401.
diverse, 1624-5201.
—(not alike),
N-4459.
divert, 5121-1124.
— the mind, 1124-
3593.
divide, 696-(1124).

DIV	DON	DRA
divination, 3400a.	don't, 2604,N-1099.	dragon's blood, 2552f.
divine, 3835-K.	dooms-day, 3826a-5137.	
—,* 247, 3400a.	door, 2779-(1006).	drain, 940b, 2021.
— blessing, 867.	— frame, 2114.	— off, 3258a.
divining blocks, 1513-3375.	— latch, 2061f.	drake, 24-G.
division, 696.	—, side 2780a.	draught, see draft.
—(political), 159.	— keeper, 1158-2780-Y.	draughts, 1956.
divorce, 648i.	— sill, 429.	draw, 2151, 2584.
divulge, 4960-/-205.	— way, 2779-1006.	—(influence),5121.
dizzy, 5036.	dose, 874g, 4481.	—(picture, etc.) 4967, 3616.
do, 4593, 986.	dot, 4151.	—(up, out), 471.
— not,2604,N-1099.	dote on, 2887-3099.	— bow, 4970.
docile, 4841.	dotted, 4151-4151.	— in, 4330.
dock, 3999-3087.	double,' 3886,2552.	— lots, 147a.
—,* 1184-3999.	—, 2321-3549.	— sword, 3241.
doctor, 1249c.	—*1409-5133-3549.	— towards, 2573.
doctrine, 4207a, 1507.	—(fold), 282.	— water, 4027-4004, 1925.
document, /3982.	doubt, 3759-1263.	drawer, 2073b.
—, commercial 4046.	doubtful, N-4132.	drawers, 2937-824.
dodder, 4333b.	doubtless, N-4791.	drawing, 4961.
dodge, 3927.	dough, 681-2688.	— room, 921-4346.
doe, 2510-D.	dove, 3178l.	drawl, 2151-512/.
dog, 1844.	—, turtle 3183a.	dread, 780, 3410.
— bezoar, 5070l.	dovetail, 3742a, 1494j.	dreadful,2293-1135.
— fish, 4179-4197-3778.	down, /2712.	dreadfully, 2051g.
— rose, 4439-22-650.	—,*" 2454,908.	dream, 2808.
dogged, 3001a.	— stairs,2248-908.	—,* 681-2808.
dogmatic, N-1263.	dowry, 303a.	dreamer,681-2808-Y.
doleful, 36a.	doze, 996a.	dreary, 3208-36.
dolichos, 1833.	dozen, 4027b.	dredge,* 2198.
doll, 1878d.	drab, 2548-3917.	dregs, 59a.
dollar, 3028-4761.	draft(drawing), 1722.	drench, 3843-3571.
—, one 2612a, 4917b.	—(drink), 5133-4043.	dress, 301a.
dolt, 3043-D.	—(order), 3145-4046.	—,* 177-1248a.
domestic, 1410.	—(ship's) 3925-/-4004.	— the hair, 3976.
— animals, 625b.	—(wind), 4452-879.	dressing case, 1637b.
dominate, 57-2007a.	drag, 2151,4403.	dribble, 2306.
dominoes, 2083f, 3420b.	—(in water), 2198.	dried, 1759.
done, 4593-[4915, 1031]	dragon, 2532.	— duck, 2191a.
	— fly, 4440a.	— fruit, 1760b.
donkey, 2480.	— well tea, 409cc.	— meats, 2191.
		— orange skins, 2085a.
		— prunes, 2767b.

DRI	DRY	DUP
— sausage, 2191b.	dry, 1759,1167.	duplicity, 1287-3593.
— up, 1759-3571.	—,* C-1759.	durable, 1904.
drift, 3505-2245.	—(by heat), 1167.	during,/2937,/1463.
drill, 4623-4627.	— by fire, 3382.	dusk, 699a, 13a.
—* 603, 4623.	— in air, 2469a.	dust, 469,a, 2792.
—(practice), 4776.	— in sun, 3786.	—,* 653.
drink, 5095.	— rot, 803a.	— pan, 2193a-431.
drinking vessel, 3375.	duality in nature, 5090-5196.	duster, 3685,b. dusty from travel, 469b.
drip, 2262a.	duck, 24.	duties(customs), 4005, 1049-3028.
drive(force), 1765.	—, Bombay 4872n.	—(occupation), 5211.
—(horse), 3816.	—, dried 2191a.	
—(nail), 4027.	—, Muscovy 24b.	duty, 3388-723.
—(push), 4447.	—, Teal 24a.	—, official 75a.
—(stake), 4086.	—, wild 24a.	dwarf, 34-D.
— out, 370a.	duckling, 24c,D-24.	dwell, (1846,339).
drivel, 4319.	duckweed, 3519.	dwelling, 339a.
drizzle, 2656-4888.	duct, 4461.	dwindle,4551a-4009.
droll, 4826.	due, 4203-1952.	dye, 1325-3917.
drollery,4826-4960.	—(owing), 1056.	dynamics, 4277b.
dromedary, /2451a, 4259-889-4408.	—(proper), 5221-4230.	dynamite, 67-5183. dynamo, 4163d.
droop, 4007.	—, over- 2101c.	dynasty, 569a.
—(decay), 4002.	dues, customs 4005.	dysentery, 2299a, 3617.
drop, 4141.	—, tonnage 450b.	dyspepsia, 3236a.
—,* 2262a.	—, transit 450a.	dysury, 3295c-3236-4452.
—(fall), 4179.	duke, 1878-(5171), 4520a.	
—(hang down) 4087.	dull, N-2293.	
—(let go), 795.	—(blunt), 3803.	
— anchor, 3436.	—(business), 4042.	E
dropsy, 392a,1800b, 196a.	—(gloomy), 2806, 459a.	
dross, 3902, 59a.	—(indifferent), 2187a.	
drought, 1167.	—(stupid), 3043.	each, 2774.
drove, 4253.	duly, 1247-1952.	—(all), 1743.
drown, 457-3767.	dumb, 6-(1006).	— time, 895a.
drowsy, 715a.	dumfound, 924-4712.	eagerly, 976a.
drub, 3435-4027.	dummy, 6-D.	eagle, 3835-5223.
drudgery,3597-813/.	dumplings, 1716.	ear, 1280-(D).
drugs,5183-(4805).	dun, 3279-2433.	— lobe, 1280b.
drugstore,5183-798.	dunce, 4269a.	— of corn, 3730.
drum, 1802.	dung, 717, 3902.	— pick, 3412.
drummer, 4027-1802-L.	—,* 4945-717.	— ring, 1280-4974.
drumstick, 622c.	— beetle, 1643.	— wax, 1280c.
drunk, 4630-4500.	dungeon, 2411a.	
drunkard, 2186-4500-Y.	dung-hill,717-4248.	

EAR	ECO	EIG

EAR

— wig, 5157a.
earl, 4520c.
early, 4586.
earn, 88.
earnest,1918,1373e.
earnestly, 976a.
earnings, 3633,
2293a.
earth(dirt), 2844.
—(globe), 4125-
1938.
—(ground), 4125.
—(world), 4355b.
earthen jar, 560.
earthenware, 2981-
(1035).
— tiles, 2981.
— pipe, 2981b.
earthquake, 138b.
earthworm, 4125-
2532.
ease, 3107,a.
—,* 795-3748.
— nature, 3295d,
648e, 3089b.
easier, 5269a.
east, 4272.
easy, 1291.
eat, 3925, 5085.
— lunch, 20a.
— plenty, 3202.
eating house,1713d.
eatables, 2636c.
eau de cologne,
2427c.
eaves, [1318,5099]
1006.
ebb tide, 1760f,
570b.
ebony, 2767e,206c.
ebullition, 2078-
1031.
echo, 1048a.
eclipse, 3926.
ecliptic,5070-4207.
economical, 1659,
933a.

ECO

economize, 1659-
5282.
edge, 3286.
—(brink), 3286.
— of knife, 1006,
885.
edged tools, 2293e.
edible, 1117,a,-
3925.
— berries, 2769.
— fungus, 2795e.
— mallows, 2128a.
— plants, 4800.
— toadstools,
1996d.
— seaweed, 4031e.
edict, 1726b.
edify, 5198-3593.
edit, 1514-4172.
editor, 3238.
educate, 1507-5198.
educated, 2616a,
3982g.
education, 2729a.
eel, 3937-(4872).
—, conger 1125-
2580.
—, electric 3938a.
—, mud 3938b.
effect, 2096.
effectual, 1879c.
effeminate, 2811a.
effervesce, 681-
2078.
efficacious, 1879c.
efficacy, proven
963b.
effluvia, 474-1033.
effigy, 3040b.
—, paper 216h.
effort. 648-2330.
egg, 4051,2527,631.
—, fowl's 1515-
4051.
— plant, 2037b.
— shell,4051-1137.
egret, 2429a.
eight, 3195.

EIG

eighteen,3845-3195.
eighteenth, 4076-
3845-3195.
eighth, 4076-3195.
eightieth, 4076-
3195-3845.
eighty, 3195-3845.
either, 4966.
eject, (1765)-648.
elapsed, 2100-1089.
elastic, 3029.
elbow, 3859a.
— chair, 1256a.
—, pipe 496d.
elder, 4033.
—, an 190-2420.
—(older), 2420-
2100.
— brother, 2404a.
— brother's wife,
3683.
— sister, 9h.
elect, (1468,3706).
electric, 4163.
— battery, 4163f.
— bulbs, 4095a.
— car, 490e.
— charge, 634a.
— circuit, 4163a.
— current, 2245d.
— dynamo, 4163d.
— eel, 3938a.
— force, 2330a.
— light,4163-4094.
— motor, 4163e.
— telegraph,4163g.
— telephone, 4163h.
— torch, 4163-366.
— tram, 490e.
— wire, 4163c.
electrical science,
4163b.
electricity, 4163-
(1033).
elegant, 2616-2982,
2303.
elegance, /4958.
elements, 4918-150.

ELE	EME	ENC
— of learning, 572-1140.	emery, 3779g.	encourage, 1802a, 1207-(2682).
elephant, 4531.	— cloth,3779-3336.	encroach,4708-252.
elephantiasis, 4324a.	emetic, 681-54-5183.	encumber, 2496-359.
elevate, 1849.	emigrate, 648-3070.	encyclopedia,2494a.
elevated,1713.	emigrant coolies, 4482d.	end, (3857)-2663.
eleven, 3845-5133.	eminent, 1713,4621.	—, an 4339.
eleventh, 4076-3845-5133.	emolument, 887.	—,* 3857, 217.
elf, 1380a,2243b.	emotions, 4766.	— of the world, 2792a.
eligible,1193-5282.	emperor, 5071-4074.	endeavor, 648-2330.
ellipse, 512-4917.	emphatic, 976-3880.	—(try), 3903.
elliptical language, 3804-2616.	empire, 4355b.	endless, N-4645.
	employ(use), 3814, 5282.	endowments, 4804.
elk, 4033-2510.	—(engage), 4734.	endurance, 5114.
elm, 4202.	employed, 3830b.	endure,5114a,4072a.
elongate, C-512.	employee, 768c.	enduring, 1904.
elope, 4499-2426.	employer, 3776b.	enemy, 475-4143.
eloquence, 1006f.	employment, 1438a, 4339a.	energetic, 2454b.
eloquent, 1744m.	—(labor), 1877a.	energy, 2330.
else(besides), 2379a.	—, permanent, 1877f.	enfold, 2239-339.
elsewhere, 3318-3987.	—, to look for 108a.	enforce, 1966,3814.
emaciated, 3862.	empower, 3250-2007.	engage(employ), 4734.
emancipate, 795.	empress, 5071-1016.	—, see betroth.
embankment, 1606-(5001).	— dowager, 5071-4283-1016.	engaged, N-934a, 3776a.
embargo, 1530-217.	empty, 1226-(1213).	engagement, 5178.
embark, [3895,2454, 4059]-3999.	—,* C-1226.	engine, 1602a.
embarrass, 2496.	emulate, 4110-1140.	—, fire 490c.
embellish, 3603-3919.	emys, 4872c.	— house 490-798.
embers, 767-3958.	enact, 563, 4610.	—, steam 490d.
embezzle, 3758c.	enamel, 2456a.	engineer, chief 490k.
emblem, 1109,1627e.	enamelled ware, 2456a-1035.	—, 2nd 1287-490.
embossed, /4106.	encamp, 97-5235.	English, 5222.
embrace, 3521.	encampment, 3552c.	— language, 5222d.
— an opportunity, 466.	encircle, [5001, 2050]-339.	engraft, 206b.
embroider,3611-650.	enclose, 5001-339.	engrave,4183-(972).
embroil, 1502a.	enclosure, /4916.	engross, 2171-2568.
embryo, 572-4417, 3542.	encoffin,3857-2346.	enigma, 3106-4890.
	encompass,5001-339.	enjoin, 367-822.
emerald, 2506-5250.	encore, 4607/.	enjoy, 1050.
emerge, 648-2200.	encounter, 184a.	enlarge, C-4033.
		enlarged, 2107-865.
		enlighten, 291-(2105).
		enlist, 288.

ENL	EPS	ETH
—(military),4593-3300.	epsom salts, 3532a.	—(medical), 2558c.
enmity, 475-4913.	equal, 2077-3497, 4459/.	ethics, 4207b.
enormous,3829-4033.	equanimity, 3593-4132.	ethnology, 391a.
enough, 1583,4636.	equator, 547a.	etiquette, 2205b.
enquire, 2629.	equinox, autumnal 4724-696.	eulogize, 4472-(4657).
enrage, 1649a.	—, vernal 629b.	eunuch, 1297-5117.
enraptured, 2399a-856a.	equitable, 1878a.	— of palace,1461a.
enshroud,3857-2346.	erase, 2056a.	euphorbium, 2220a.
ensign, 1953.	erect, 1962.	evacuate,3384-1226.
ensnare, 2453a.	—,* 1031.	— the bowels,648e, 3089a.
ensure, 3329a.	ermine, 3985h.	evade, 4989a.
entangle, 1922b, 2118a.	err, /4791.	evaporate, (3942)-3576.
enter, 5132.	error, 4791.	even, 3497, 4705.
— on account, 3895-3972.	erupt, 648.	—(likewise),4196.
entertain, 288d, 1494b.	eruption,3185,2833.	— if, 3715-1349.
entice,5121-(5161).	—, scabby 3642.	evening, 13a, 2575.
entirely,3571,4645-4125.	erysipelas, 4299b.	event, 3776-(4766).
entitled to, 5221-4081.	escape, [4391,4216]-3265.	eventually, 3857-2663.
entrails, 513-(4619).	—(as water), 2262.	ever(any time), 1624a.
entrance, (2779, 1006).	eschatology, 2447e, 2528g.	—(continually), 1086a.
entrap, 2759.	escort, /3750.	—(eternally), 5051-4929.
entrapped, 5132-[1201a, 2533].	escutcheon, 3691-3419.	everlasting, 5051-(4929).
entreat, 976-1936.	essay, 2616-186.	— life, 5051-3802.
entrust, 1494f.	essence, 4560.	every, 2774.
— with, 840a.	essential, 1541a.	—(all), 1743-3170.
enumerate, /1124.	establish, 563c, 2190.	— one, 1736a.
enunciate,1779-648.	establishment, 1875, 4910.	— other day,2163a.
envelope, 880b.	estate, 430a,1368b.	everywhere, 3772a, 3987-3987.
—,* 3198-339.	esteem(consider), 1278a.	evidence,1006-1882.
envy, 4204-1631.	—(respect), 4621-(1680).	—(proof), 3454a.
ephidra, 2557c.	— lightly, 1042,d.	evident, 2690a, 1062a.
epidemic, 3905-278.	estimate, 2313a, 1797.	evil, 3100.
epidendrum, 2182c.	estuary, 1006c.	evolve, 1341b.
epilepsy, 4190c.	et cetera, 5163-5159-4351.	ewe, 5193-G.
epistle,3743-(102).	eternal, 5051-4929.	ewer, 4004-3480.
epitaph, 234a.	ether,(tr)1278-4283.	exact, 2993a.
epithet, 3318-1109.		—,* 471-2743.
epitome, 4033-2308.		

EXA	EXE	EXP
—(extort), 2217a.	execute, 4593-3948.	experienced, 4011-
exacting, 3158b.	execution, 275a.	3859, 2420c.
exactly, 2993a.	—(beheading), 85-	experiment, 3903-
exaggerate, 1779-	3767.	1061.
650f.	—(hanging), 4190b.	expert, 958a.
exaggeration, 650f.	— ground, 511a.	—(well versed),
exalt, 1849-1713.	executioner, 3808-	3939-4560.
exalted, 1713.	3859.	expiate, 4014.
examination, 957b.	executor, 3952-	expire, 3447a.
examine, 957a.	3191-Y.	—(die), 4624-1033.
—(investigate),	exempt, 2681.	—(time), 2785.
405a.	exercise(move), 986.	explain, 1436.
—(judicially),	—(practice), 4476-	explanation, 1436-
3826-(2629).	2358.	682.
—(look at), 4314.	exert, 681-722.	explode, 65, 4027-
—(officially),	— strength, 648-	3438.
1330.	2330.	explore, 3790a.
example, 5201-4667.	exhalation, 3408-	explosion, 3194.
exasperate, 1649a.	(1033).	export, 648c.
excavate, 2086.	exhaust, 4645.	expose, 1061-648.
exceed, /2100.	— of engine, 3767-	expostulate,1207a.
exceedingly, 2399a.	1033.	expound, 1779-1436.
excel, 3947-2100.	exhausted, (1584)-	express, 1779-648.
5234.	2110.	expression, 5230.
excellency(title),	exhibit, 1061-648.	expressly, 4083a.
4033-5117.	exhort, 1207.	expunge, 406-1221.
excellent, 696a.	exigency,1541-1558.	exquisite, 2708.
except, 593.	exist, 4609,5159.	extant, 3977-4609.
excepting,593-1089.	exit, 1221-2426,	extend, 3831-1124.
excess, 2100/.	2779.	—(lengthen),3831-
—(bad), 795d.	eject, 1765-(648).	512.
excessive, 2100-	exorbitant, 2100f.	—(widen), 3831-
4339.	exorcise, 370b.	865.
exchange, 4004i.	— by incantations,	extensive, 2107a.
—, * (4254)-3154.	1670c.	extenuate, 1457-
—(money), 108.	expand, 185a.	1042.
—, bill of 3028c,	expect, 2764,215h,	exterior,3070-2687.
3143-4046.	2400a.	exterminate, 4578-
excite, 1649,1502a,	expectoration,	2701.
1802a.	4004d.	external, 3070.
exclaim, 802-925.	expedient, 3295,b.	extinguish, 3634,
exclude, 593-648.	expel, 1765-648,	3529a.
exclusive atten-	370a.	extol, 4472a.
tion, 344	expend, 3814-691.	extort,2217a,1922.
excrement, 3902.	expenses,3814-5282.	extra, 2379a.
excruciating, 4684.	—, traveling	extract, /648, 63.
excuse, 1663-2327,	2426b,3552a.	extradition, 4321d.
4989a, 4989-4861.	expensive, 2065.	extradite, 4321d.

EXT	FAI	FAS
extraordinary, 1450-3070.	—(just) 1878a.	fashion, 860a.
—(strange), 1950b.	— tide, 4004b.	fashionable, 3905c.
extravagant, 491.	— wind, 4022-879.	fast, 651½.
extravasted blood, 4869.	fairies, 3640.	—(firm), 3854.
extreme, 1654.	faith,3743a,4256a.	—,* 1530-3925, 3925b.
extremely, 2399a, 227-1654.	faithful, 384-3593.	fasten, 3373.
extricate, 4446-2238.	falcon, 1931-5223.	—(a door), 3794.
exudation, 5215.	fall, 4179,4103.	fastener(bolt), 3754.
eye, 2999.	—(drop), 2454.	fat, 5149.
— ball, 2999a.	—(stumble),2054,c.	—,' 759.
— brows, 2999e.	—, cause to 931.	fate, 4355-2671.
— lashes, 5131a.	— down, 3233.	father, 836a.
— lids, 1996b.	— in torrents, 2225.	—, adopted 1902a.
— socket, 1180a.	— into, 931.	—, step 1902a.
	— over, 4197.	— in law,3070-836.
	— prostrate, 876.	fatherless, 1787.
F	— short, 92.	father's elder brother, 3172.
	false, 1419, 3017.	— younger brother, 4010.
	falsehood, 4033-4960.	fathom, 5105,5125.
fable, 4901-1350.	falsely, 1419a.	—,* 453-4228.
fabric, 3336.	—, assume 2731.	fatigue, 1584-2110.
fabricate, 1419-4610.	falsify, 61a.	fatten, 5198-759.
face, 2687.	fame, 2669-(3880).	faucet, 4004g.
facile, 5269a.	family, 1410a.	fault(blemish), 903a.
facility, /1291.	famine, 1604a.	—(mistake), 4791.
facing, 2687b.	famishing, S-3066.	—(sin), 4631.
— toward, 1053.	fan, (879)-3930.	favor, 5108,4766a.
fact, 3854-3776.	—,* 4027-3930, 3557.	favorable, 4022.
faction, 4232.	—(electric), 4163-(879)-3930.	— tide, 4004b.
factory, 1186.	— palm, 2128e.	favorite, 640-3099.
faculty, 1768a.	fanatic, /2143, /4158.	fawn over, 2930-2854.
fade, 346-3917.	fancy, 383b.	fear, 3410, 1231a.
faded, 4695-1089.	fantan, 657-4294.	fearful, 780.
fagged, 2110.	far, 4929.	feasible, 1117a.
faggot, 3161-419.	fare, 16391, 490-691.	feast, [1351,4500]-4546.
fail, N-4197,690.	farewell, 986b.	feather, 4518-2712.
—(bankrupt), 4197c.	farm, 4356-308.	— duster, 3685b.
faint, 3849-5028.	—,*1480-4356.	February,1287-4937.
—,' 4930-5182.	farmer,1480-4356-L, 2952-801.	feces, 3902.
fair, 3908,1214.	farmhouse, 308.	fee, 2120-3028.
—(clear), 4763.	fascinating, 5159-5121.	feeble, 4930-5182.

FEE

feed, 826.
—(care for),5198.
—(give food), 4993.
feel, 1745, 1663.
— with the hands, 2738.
feelings,4766,513a.
feet, 1638.
—, bound 102a.
feign, 61.
felicity, 867.
feline, 2592.
—, spotted 3204.
fell(cut down) 85.
felled timber,1762.
felled tree, 2087.
fellow, 2404.
—(comrade), 4459-3390.
— students, 501f.
— townsman, 1045c, 4459-1045.
fellowship, 1494b, 3625-1494.
felon, 678-Y.
felony, 4033-4631.
felt, 2712f.
female, 2720,2811, 2949.
—(girl), 2949.
—(woman), 2949-5117.
— sex, 5090-2494.
— relatives,2776.
— slave, 3474.
— world, 1438b.
fence, 2181,2277, 5001.
—(sword play), 1658c.
— off, 2180.
fencing,(art), 1658b.
fender, 2360.
ferment, 681-1511.
fern, 3585b.
ferocious, 1227, 2586.

FER

ferry, 4211-4339.
ferryboat, 3356c.
fertile, 759,d.
fertilize, 4660a.
fervent, 1372.
fester, 3802-578.
festival,4570-1952.
fetch, 2896.
fetid, 474.
fetter, 3691.
fetters 2390.
fetus, 3542-(4417).

feud, 92a.
feudal territory, 880.
fever, 1373d.
—, intermittent 3167a.
—, to have 681-1373.
feverish,1372,1077.
few, 3966, 3615a, 1624, 4138.
fib, 4033-4960.
fiber, 3761, 2619.
—, muscle 1608a.
fickle N-4132-3593.
fiction, 3674-4001.
fictitious, 1419.
fiddle, 1372.
—, play the 2998-1353a.
fidelity, 384-3593.
fidgety, 3693-3721.
fie! 4794.
field, 4356.
—(area), 511.
— mouse, 3985b.
— glass, 16371.
fiend, 3100-2061.
fierce, 2586-2386.
fife, 4981-4147.
fifteen, 3845-2962.
fifteenth, 4076-3845-2962.
fifth, 4076-2962.
— moon, 2253b.

FIF

fiftieth,4076-2962-3845.
fifty, 2962-3845.
fig, 2711g.
fight(war), 263, 193a.
—, * 1494g, 1424b.
— fire, 1582b.
figurative, 3466a.
figure,5230-(4530).
— of speech,3466a.
figures(pattern), 2619.
filament, 3761.
file, (3161)-4792.
—,* 4792.
file fish, 3779a.
filial, 960-(4022).
fill, 634-2785.
— in, 4357.
filled, 3202.
fillet of beef, 3039-2261.
film, 2750.
—(ph.tr.) 752-2229.
— on the eye, 3428.
filter, 3779c.
—,* 1448-4763.
filth, 2148d.
filthy, 3113a.
fin, 531.
final, 3858a.
— particle, 2294a.
finally, 4071a, 1595a.
find, 5023-4197.
— out, 405-648.
fine, 5147-3589.
—(pretty), 2303.
—,* 734-(3028).
— comb, 3270.
— weather, 4355a.
finger, 3859-215.
— bowl, 3859-387.
— nail, 215d.
— ring, 1437a.

FIN	FIR	FLA
finish(complete), 4593-3948.	— rate, 4129-1099.	flail, 4027-5060-3435.
finished, 4593a, 4593-4915.	fish, 4872.	flake, 3491.
finite, 939c.	—,* 2433-4872.	flame, 767b.
fir(tree), 4849.	—(angle), 4191-4872.	flannel, 682c,3674-5272.
—(wood), 427.	— for(grapple), 2198.	flap, 1994.
fire, 767.	— glue, 1495a.	flapping, 3423d.
—(conflagration), 767a.	— roe, 2527.	flash, 3927.
—,* 3965.	— scales, 2520.	flask, 4641.
— a gun, 3441a.	— weir, 4872p.	flat, 3497.
— arms, 767k, 3441f.	— with rod, 4191-4872.	—(thin), 3291.
— bed, brick 1183.	fisherman, 2433-4872-Y.	—(taste), 4042.
— crackers, 3441d.	fishing rod, 1764a.	— lands, 4306.
— engine, 490c.	fishy smell, 4872-3620.	flatter, 548-2667.
—, fight 1582b.	fissure, 2148a.	flatulent, 3433.
— fly, 767-5236.	fist, 2008a.	flavor, 2666.
— hose, 1008e.	fistula, 3802-603.	flaw, 903a.
—, kindle 4338a.	fit, 3849-5028, 4190c.	flax, (3589)-2556.
— man, 1582b-Y.	—,'2993,1193,184.	flay, 2743-(3468).
— man(stoker), 3965-767-Y.	fitch, 4116f.	flea, 1574b.
— place, 767f.	fitful, 762.	flee, 4499.
—, to set 795c.	fitting, 1193/.	fleece, 5193-2712.
— tea, 448d.	fittings,1411-3802.	fleet, 3367.
— wood, 419.	five, 2962.	—,* 651½.
— works, 3438c, 1335a.	— cent coin, 723b.	flesh, 5249.
firm(fast), 3854.	— to seven a.m., 2598.	— color, 547.
—(stable), 5024a.	fives, in 2962,a.	fleshy tumor,2257a.
—(strong), 1660-1810.	fix, 4872a.	fleur-de-lis,3124a-650.
—(business),1186, 1878f.	—(settle), 4132-(3854).	flexible, 4930, 5040-4081.
firmament, 4809a.	fixed axis, 371c.	flick, 4349-1221.
firmly, 3854.	— date, 1952a.	flighty, 4369-4311.
first, 4076-5133.	— number, 2991-3972.	fling, 763, 5048, 4182.
—(beginning) 572.	flabby, 3748-3460.	flint, 767p.
—(position), 4339.	flag, 1953.	float, 743.
—(time), 3639.	—, signal 1953a.	flock, 2137.
— born, 190-4482.	—, sweet 504.	flog, 3288-4027.
— day of the moon, 3980.	flageolet, 3671.	flood, 4004a.
— month, 266a.	flagstaff, 1953-1762.	—, the 1236a.
— quarter, 1354a.	flagstone, 3188d.	—,* 197.
		flooding at child-birth, 3233c.
		floor(story), 2248.
		boards, 2248e.

FLO	FON	FOR
—, ground 4125-2248.	— —(love), 4458-3099.	foreman, 4339-Y, 2171a.
— joists,2248-141.	fontanel, 3745a.	forenoon, 2965b, 165a.
—, threshing 511.	food, 2636c, 768a.	forerunner, 2017a.
floss silk, 3761-(5272).	fool, 3068-Y.	foreshore, 1125-4293.
flounder, 4872k.	foolish, 4874a.	foreskin,5196-3468.
flour, 713,2688a.	foot, 1638.	forest, 2226a.
— paste,4523-3120.	—(measure), 496.	foretell,3639-1779.
flourishing, 2645-3957.	— pad, 1484a.	forever, 5051-4929.
flow, 2245.	— prints, 1639f, 1639-511c.	forfeit, /734.
flower, 650.	—, sole of 1639d.	forge, 4027-4366-2406.
— buds, 2979,2222.	— stool,1639-4063-4098.	—,* 4027-4366.
— garden,650-4916.	for(because), 5107-(5013).	—(counterfeit), 1419/.
flowers, artificial 216j.	—(in behalf of), 4316, 4222.	forget, 2754a, N-1627a.
— of sulphur, 2249c.	forage, 2312a.	forgive, 3873-2681, 857a.
flowering, 650.	forbearance, 5114a, 857a.	fork, 206d.
fluctuating,N-4132, 2464.	forbid, 1530-(217).	forked, (2)-401.
flue, 4452h.	force, 2330.	forlorn, 1787-4259.
fluent, 2245a.	—,* 2682a,1966.	form, (5250,2599).
fluid, /4004.	—, attractive 1926a.	formality, mere 2206c.
flurried, 780-2755.	—, electric 2330a.	former, 1594,3639.
flush, 681-1235.	—(rape), 1466b.	formerly, 4848a, 5079, 3635.
flute, 3671, 4981-4147.	—, rob by 1688.	fornication, 4766h, 1576a.
flutter, 3529-5212.	—, take by 4247.	forsake, 4182-1034.
—, in a 3593-2474.	— water, 1826.	fort, 3441j.
flux, bloody 2299b.	forceps, 1971.	fortified camp, 73.
fly,* 5236,a.	ford, 3341-3959.	forth, 648.
—,* 750.	fore, 3639, 4760.	forthwith, 4504.
flying machine, 1602b.	forearm, 3859-162.	fortieth, 4076-3770-3845.
foam, 743-50.	forefinger, 215b.	fortress, 72.
foe, 475-4143.	forego, 3871/.	fortunate, 1560.
fog, 3106-2730.	forehead,2991-4339.	fortunately, 4609d, 4796b.
foil, 3364.	foreign, 5194,656, 2447o.	fortune, 2671.
fold, /2181.	—(occidental), 3584.	— telling, 3709c.
—(increase), 3549.	— Affairs, Department of, 3070a.	— teller, 3709c-Y.
—,* 282.	— nations, 2104c.	forty, 3770-3845.
foliage, 1367-2645.	foreigners, 3584-Y, 2104c-Y.	forward, 4760.
follow,1536-(4830).		
—(imitate), 1140.		
folly, 3069-3776.		
fond of, 1100.		

FOR	FRA	FRU
—(bold),4033-4038.	fray, 1494g.	—, citrus 2085.
foster, 5198.	freak, 1950b/.	—, dried 1760b.
foul, 3113a.	freckled,3183-4151.	—, preserved
— mouthed, 3001b.	free, 4673-328.	2097b.
— wind, 2989-879.	—,* 795.	— stall, 4294a.
found(establish)	-- school, 1292-	— stone, 5044.
2190.	1140.	—, to produce
—(metals), 332.	freely, 3178a.	2096d.
foundation, 1606-	freeze, 2187e,4274.	—, unripe 2097a.
(218), 1638-	freight(goods),771.	fry, 4552-(448).
founder, 4594a.	—(payment), 1638i.	— in oil, 110.
fountain, 4817.	French, 682b/.	frying pan, 5066.
four, 3770.	— beans, 4116d.	fuel(coal), 4300.
— points, the	frequently, 2487a,	—(wood), 419.
3772a.	1575a.	Fukienese, 1141d.
— square, 3178a/.	fresh, 3596a.	fulfil, 5229a.
fourteen,3845-3770.	— fruit, 2097a.	full, 2785.
fourteenth, 4076-	— water, 4292a.	—(of food), 3202.
3845-3770.	freximus chinensis,	fully, 3571,4645b.
fourth, 4076-3770.	2192c.	fume, 2842, 1033d.
—, one 723a.	friction,3625-2740.	fumigate, 702.
fowl(birds), 4518-	Friday, 2206g-2962.	fun, 4973a.
2920.	friends, 3453a.	fundamental, 1538-
—(chicken), 1515.	to make 1494a.	3388.
—, cry of 4322.	friendly, 3593-1099.	funeral, 3698-3776,
—, pip of 1921a.	friendship,1494,d.	3750-4617.
fox, 1848a.	frighten, 923.	fungus, 2132,2795e.
--, striped 2594b.	frightened, 1670a,	funnel, 3393a.
foxglove, 2712e.	780.	—(chimney), 4452h.
foxlike animals,	frightful, 1117-	fur, 3468.
2280.	3410.	— garments, 1940.
fraction, 696.	frigid zone, 4031a.	furious, 2143.
fracture, 3233.	fringe, 5099.	furl, 1839-2568.
fragile, 1291-2186.	fritters, to make	furlough, 1422.
fragment, 3721.	2456-713.	—, ask 1726h.
fragrance, 1048.	frivolous, 743a.	—, give 795a.
fragrant,1073-1048.	frog, 1515i,1830a.	furnace,(767)-2406.
frail, 4930-5182.	frolic, 4973a.	—(portable), 879j.
frame, 1424.	from(out of), 5148,	furnish, 4705a-
—(surrounding),	4848-4673.	1411a.
2114.	—(where),1053,965.	furniture, 1411a.
—, door 2779-2114.	front, 2687a.	furred tongue,
frankincense, 4891-	frontier, 1676a.	2294b.
1046.	frost, 3627.	furrow, 2202d.
frantic, 4158-2143.	froth, 3522, 50.	further, 5163,169b.
fraternity, 3143.	frozen, 3301,4275.	—(distance), 4989-
fraud, 1019a.	frugal, 3804-1659.	4138.
fraudulent, 1467a.	fruit, 2097,2096.	

FUR	GAM	GAT

FUR

furthermore, 1262a.
fury, 2929-2143.
furze, 4496.
fuse, 5121a.
—,* 3963-5270.
fussy, 743a.
futile, 4390c.
future, 4522a.
— tense(gr), 4522.

G

gabble, 2416a.
gable, /1523.
gad about, 2119a.
gad fly, 2756.
gag, 2795-2162.
—,* [1972,3592]-1006.
gage, 377-4487.
gaiety, 673-4958.
gain, 2293,c.
—* 88.
gait, 3341-986.
galangal ginger, 2314.
gale, 879a.
gall, 4038,a.
— bladder, 4038.
— nuts, 2792-b, 2964a.
gallant(heroic), 5222-1240.
gallery, /2248.
gallipot, 1155a.
gallon(tr), 1409a.
gallop, 3437.
gallows, 4189-5117-1424, 38-1424.
galvanized iron, 5056a-4366.
galvanometer,3323e.
gambier, 2320a.

GAM

gamble, 4199-4761, 82b.
gambler, 4199-(4761)-Y.
gambling game,656d.
— house,656d-1820.
gamboge, 5070h.
game(meat), 2666c.
—(play), 1875.
—, to play 4973a.
—, make 1037b.
— of rolling coppers, 2502b.
gander, 3058-G.
gang, 4253.
gangrene,3767-5249-3278.
gaol, see jail.
gap, 1006.
gape, 1114a.
garble, 1779-2652.
garden,(650)-4916.
gardener, 650b.
gardenia, 1420.
gargle, 2456-1006.
garland, 650-2726.
garlic, 3710-4339.
garment, 3791.
garments, 1248a.
—, fur 1940.
garoupa, 3879k.
garret, 2248-D, 4129-2248.
garrison, 3300.
garrulax thrush, 2657a.
garter, 4031c.
gas, coal 2766b.
— meter, /3323.
— works,767-4515-1878f.
gases, 1033a.
gash, 3885-1006.
—,* 1832,3885.
gasoline, 2766c.
gasp,471b,608-1033.
gate, 99-(1006), 2780.

GAT

—, sluice 99a.
—, wicket 3240a.
gatekeeper, 1158-2779-Y.
gather(meet), 4632.
— together, 3857, 4538, 147.
gauge, 3323.
gauze, 3780.
gaze, 4314-(4132), 1818a.
gazelle, 2368a.
gazette, 3337.
gear, 768.
—(mech.) 2518-524.
gecko, 2479c,1830.
gelatine, 1495.
geld, 1298,3820a.
gem,5250,3331-3879.
gender, [2824,2949]-2494.
—,* 3802.
genealogy, 970a.
general, 4928-2075.
generally, 3890a.
—(together), 4652-1892.
generate(as animals), 391b.
—(produce), 3802.
generation, 3818a.
generous,4033-2313.
genial, 5020-5059.
genii, 3640.
genius, 4804.
genteel, 1099-2205.
genial, 4039c.
—, yellow 2353c.
gentile, 1293-3370-Y.
gentle, 5020a.
gentleman(teacher), 3802f.
—(old),2420-5171.
—(young), 3632-1878.
gentlemen! 2384a, 2384-1878.

GEN	GIV	GNA
gently, 1042b.	— (present), 3750.	gnaw, 3012-3047,
gentry, 3833a.	— address, 4001b.	2514.
genuine, 136.	— attention, 2247b.	go, 1221, 986.
geography, 2285e.	— birth, 3802.	— and return,
geology, 4125a.	— thanks, 1755a.	2447b.
geomancy, 879d.	— trouble, 1403.	— away, 493.
geometry, 5230b,	gizzard, 3840.	— out, 648b.
1624e.	glad, 856a.	— between, 383-Y.
geranium, 1046d.	glance, 4314-907.	goal, 2798-4140.
—, flowering	glare, 2105-2586.	goat, 5193b.
5194-2128.	glass, 3349a.	gobble, 2477c.
germ(seed), 2979,	— (lens), 1637.	goblet, 4641.
391, 5118.	— (tumbler), 3349a-	GOD, 3835, 4074a.
germs, 2656b,2132a.	3375.	gods, 4074,a,
german silver,	—, looking 1637a.	2061-3835.
3178-4462.	glaze, 3932 C-4984.	godown, 4807a.
germinate, 681-	— (set glass),3628.	going and return-
2979.	glazed tile, 2256b.	ing, 3137c.
get, 4081-(4797),	gleam, 3927.	goitre, 4033-1636-
2433.	glib, 2293-1006.	3436.
ghost, 2061.	— (slippery) 4984.	gold, (5070)-1527.
giant, 1712-2404.	glimmer, /3927.	— fish,1527-4872.
gibberish, /2514.	glitter, 681-2105.	— leaf, 1527a.
giddy, 4339-5036.	globe, 1937.	golden pheasant,
gift, 3750-2205.	—, lamp 111a.	1515b.
gigantic, 4033.	—, the 4125-1937.	gone, 1217a.
giggling, 1025b.	globular, 4917a.	gong, 2439.
gild,4214-1527.	gloomy, 3106.	gonorrhea, 372a.
gilt, 1527-3917.	glorify, 2057-5049.	good, 1099.
gills, 3696.	glorious,5049-1406.	— (as a child),
gimlet, 3859-4623.	glory, 5049-(2105),	2044.
ginger, 1640.	4958b.	— (righteous),3939.
—, preserved	glossy, 2303a.	— (stable), 5024a.
1640b.	gloss over, 3919.	—, really 3001c.
—, stem 1640a.	glottis, 3700a.	— bye, 4734.
ginglymus joint,	glove, 2235a.	— —(by host),
1521b.	—, * 2235a.	986b.
ginseng, 5117-3824.	glow,681-1235-1372.	— —(by visitor),
giraffe, 4408-3204.	glow worm,295-2105-	4793-1.
gird, 624-339.	646.	— for nothing,
girder, 141.	glue, 1494.	2401d.
girdle, 4031,1379a.	glutinous, 514.	— morning, 4586a.
girl, 2949-D.	glutton, 4033-3925-	— natured, 2848a.
—, slave 2765-D.	5072.	—, spirits, in
—, singing 502.	gluttonous, 4286-	3983a.
—, street 2222b.	3925.	— tempered, 1636d.
give, 3250.	gnash, 3012-2977.	goods, 771, 2636d.
— (confer), 4853.	gnats, 2613-(D).	

GOO	GRA	GRA
— on credit,to get 2151d.	granary, /4807.	gray, 1200a, 845-3917.
goose, 3057,a.	grand 1713-4033.	grease,(1714)-5149.
—, wild 3000-l (3057).	— child, 3704.	greasy, (759)-2877.
gore, 627b.	— daughter, 3704-2949.	— quartz, 2192f.
gorgeous, 4958b.	— father, 9f.	great, 4033.
gormandize, 3925-2101f.	— mother, 9g.	— uncle, 3172b.
gorze, 4496.	— son,3704-(4667)	greedy, 4286-3593.
gospel, 867c.	granite, 650f, 3879a.	Greek,1020c-2104-Y, 1020-2293-2873-Y.
gossip, 934d.	grant, 4853.	green, 2507-3917, 4764.
—,* 1779-934d.	granulated, 3778.	— peas, 4116a.
gouge, 4612.	grapes, 3517b.	— vitrol, 2507b.
—,*4983, 4612.	grapnel, 3779o.	greens, 1362a,3350-4800.
gourd, 2037, 3125.	grapple, 2198.	greet, 2629-1015.
—, bottle 3125a.	grasp, 57,147,2812.	grey, 1200a, 845-3917.
—, orange 2037h.	—(embrace),2169.	grief, 5141-2786.
gout, 1638-879.	grass, 4777.	grievance, 4991b.
govern, 1819a.	— cloth, 909a, 2557b.	grieved, 5141-3864.
government, 2104a.	—, dried 1497.	grievous(heavy), 645.
— office, 2978,a.	—, green, 2507a.	—(lamentable), 3636a.
—, powers of 147e.	— hopper, 2587a.	grievously, 1494h.
governmental science, 1669b.	— sandals, 913b.	grill, 448.
governor, 4653d.	— spear 781a.	grimace, 2652-2687.
— general, 4653d, 117c.	grate, 4366-2406.	grind, 2740.
—, military 4196a.	—,* 2056b.	grindstone, 2740-4195-3879.
gown, 512-3791.	grateful, 1755a.	gripes, 2867a.
grace(mercy),4162a.	gratified, 6513-2455.	gristle, 2083d.
graceful, 2982.	gratis, 3178a.	grits, 2607e.
grackle, 1728b.	gratitude, 1755-3593.	gritty, 4031-3778.
gradation, 4097, 4076, 1924.	gratuitous, 3178a.	groan, 4507-3465. 3031.
grade, 1432a.	grave, 718-2727, 3793.	grocery, 4475-771-3514.
gradually, 4551a.	—,' 1316-3738.	groin, 3252b.
graduate, 3239a.	— clothes, 3867-1248.	groom, 2561a.
graft,* 3355b.	—(weighty), 645.	groove, 940,2261.
grain, 1864.	gravegrounds, 3793.	—,* 2261f.
—, a 2859.	gravestone, 2727-3247.	grope, 2738.
—, bearded 2607.	gravel, 3778.	gross, 4775-(4033).
—, ears of 3730.	—(disease), 2227a.	grotesque, 1950-2048.
—, growing 5060.	gravity, 1926a.	
— of wood, 2619.	gravy, 148.	
grammar, 2616e.		
gramophone, 2247d.		
grampus, 1980-4872.		

GRO	GUM	HAI
ground, 4125,4380.	gumboil, 1752a.	—, dress the 3976.
— nut, 650d.	gums, 2977-1540-	— gum, 3445.
group, 4253.	5249.	— pin, 4467,/123.
—,* 2137.	gun, 4736, 3674-	— press, 1523-25.
grouse, sand 3779L.	3438.	— tuft of 1523.
grove, 2226,a.	—(cannon), (4033)-	hairy brinjal,
grovelling, 908d.	3438.	2037k.
grow, 3802, 190-	— boat, [3438,	Hakkas, 921b.
4033.	3300]-3999.	hale, 309a.
— from a slip,	— cap, 2726a.	half, 3389.
442a.	— cock, 1515k.	— dollar, 4917c.
grub, 647a.	gunpowder, 767L.	— moon, 3389b.
grudge, 4913-981.	— tea, 409z.	— witted, 2220b.
gruel, 365.	gush, 3441-648.	halibut,4033-48721.
grumble,2222a,3024.	gust, 141-879.	hall, 4346, 4435,
grunt, 3024, 3047.	gut, 513.	4910.
guano, 4518-3902.	gutta percha,3002-	—, public 1821b.
guarantee, 4036a,	3996-1495.	halliards, 2287a.
2691.	gutter,/(940)-2021.	halloa! 3132,4986.
guard, (1158)-3861.	gypsum, 3879g.	halo, 5036.
— against, 4321a.	gyves, 1638-2390.	halt, 4360-1638.
— boat, 4838b.		—(limping), 3205-
guardian, 1819a-Y.		1638.
guava, 656b.	**H**	halter,2533c,2383b.
gudgeon, 4872d.		ham, 767n.
guess, 1797, 413.		hamlet, 4813.
guest, (5117)-921.	ha! 902.	hammer, 619.
guide, 5121-2426,	habit, 2054-(4476).	—,* 4027, 4086.
4031.	habitable,339-4081.	hammock, 4189-586.
guild, 1186, 3143.	habitual, 2054.	hamper, 2235.
guile, 2062a.	hack, 4136,3624.	—,* 296a.
guilt, 4631.	haddock, 5070-4967.	hand, 3859.
guilty, 5159-4631.	hades, 5090-1463.	—,* 1494.
guise, 301a, 2599.	haematite iron ore,	— bill, 288c.
guitar, 3471a.	170a.	— cuffs,3859-2390.
gulf, 4033-4971.	haft, 3277.	—, left 4597.
—(abyss), 3823-	haggle, 4495.	—, right 5164.
4909.	haikwan taels,	—, running 4777b.
gull, 52.	2052e.	handful, 57.
—,* 1019a.	hail, 3363.	handicraft, 3859c,
gullet, 1008a.	—,* 2454-3363.	3018.
gully, 940, 2021.	—(call), 288.	handkerchief,1537a.
gulp, 4329.	hair, 2712.	handle, 3277.
gum, (3996)-1495.	— of the head,	—,* 2738, 4115.
— benjamin, 3107f.	4339-683.	handmaid, 3474.
— camphor, 187a.	— cloth,2712-3336.	handrail, 830-3859.
—, hair 3445a.	—, curly 1839a.	handsome,1424-3819,
—, peach 4392d.		2661.

HAN	HAR	HEA
handwriting, 3238-4534.	harsh, 977, 914.	healthy, 309a.
—, own 3238b.	hart, 2510-G.	heap, 4090, 4248.
handy, 3295b.	hartshorn, 2510-5279.	—* 4248-2568, 2231.
hang, 4189.	harvest, 3858c.	hear, (4344,2617).
— down, 4102.	—, wheat 2607h.	hearing, hard of 2534.
— up, 2039.	hash, 448b.	hearsay, 2617a.
— up to dry, 2469.	hasp, 3037.	hearse, 3698-1848.
hanging, 4189-1636.	— of look, 3420d.	heart, 3593.
hanker after, 4286.	haste, 1558-4769.	hearth, 767f-3879.
happen, 4896,a.	hasten, 4826,1766a.	heartily, 1750-3593.
happily, 4609d, 4796b.	hasty, 1008d,1558.	heat, 1372-(1036).
happiness, 867.	hat, 2726.	—,* C-1372.
happy, 856a, 5159-867.	—, pith 4453b.	—, prickly 693a.
harass,2833a,2137a.	hatch, 3999-2779, 1994.	heathen, 3168-3040b-Y.
harbor, 1779-1006.	—* 3344.	heaven, 4355,e.
—,* 5056-4812.	— artificially, 3382.	— kingdom of 4355-2103.
hard, 3001.	hatchet, 816a.	heavily, 4033.
—(difficult), 2834,3100.	hatchway, 3999-1006.	heavy, 645.
— lines! 5091a.	hate, 4489, 981.	hedge, 2277.
— of hearing, 2534.	— bitterly, 720a.	hedgehog, 313b.
harden, C-3001.	hateful, 1117-3117.	heed, 2246b.
hardly, 1543,92d.	haughty, 1699-3055.	heedful, 3589b.
hardship, 1465a.	haul, 494.	heedless, N-2246b, N-3589b.
hardy, 1964-1664.	have, 5159.	heel, 1638-94.
hare, (5173)-4387.	havoc, 4695-1135.	heifer, 3039-G-D.
harebell, 2367a.	hawfinch, 21921.	height, /1713.
harelip, 3233-1006.	hawk, 2557h.	heighten, C-1713.
harlot, 502a.	hawker, 3674-664.	heir, 4674,a.
harm, 1135,3885.	—, to turn 2177b.	hell, 5254a.
harmless, 784a.	hawser, (4033)-2173.	hellebore, 2409b, 2203a.
harmonize, C-5059, 2057a.	hawthorn, 222.	hello, 4986,3132.
harmony, 5059-(2797).	hay, 1760c.	helm, 4285,4415.
harness, 1035b.	hazard, 3015,a.	—, to port the 2573.
—,* 2953-231.	—,* 1754.	helmet, 4339-2123.
harp, 143.	hazardous, 3015a.	helmsman,57-4285-Y.
—, aeolian 1048c.	haze, 5027-2730, 904.	help, 3367-299.
harpischord, 143.	hazel nut, 5241.	— no 2711c.
harpoon, 3321,4872-401.	he, 2026.	help! 1582a.
harrier, 1393.	head, 4339,3860.	helping hand, 3367-3859.
harrow, 2202b,3414.	—, top of 3745.	hem, 3287b.
	headache, 4339-[4458,4733].	
	headstrong, 3001a.	
	heal, 1249-(1099).	

HEM	HIL	HOL
—, 4369a.	hill, 3793,2364.	—, ask 1726h.
hemp, 2556.	hilt, 3277.	—, give 795a.
hen, 1515-G.	nim, 2026.	hollow, 2529,4113,
—, cackle of	himself,2026-4673a.	2860.
1566e.	hinder, 296,a.	hollyhock, 2128b.
hence, 1809a.	hindermost, 3858a.	holy, 3945.
her, 2026.	hinge, 1510.	holy! 4604a.
herbs, 4777-4800.	hint, 1110d.	HOLY SPIRIT, 3946a.
—(medical), 5183-	— at, 3106b.	homage, to offer
4777.	hip, 3252a.	897.
herd, 2137.	hippocampus, 1125f.	home, 2157.
herdsman, 2796-Y.	hippopotamus,2561k.	—(family dwelling)
here, 2881-3987.	hire(wages), 5117-	339a.
hereafter, 4852-	1877.	—(house), 4944a.
1013.	—(rent),4583,5106.	— Affairs, Dept.
heresy, 4732a.	— men, 4734.	of 2937a.
heretofore, 1053-	his, 2026-1600.	homeless, N-339a,
2445.	history, 1627d,	2057c.
hernia, 513d.	2333b.	homemade, 2177a.
hero, 1107-1696.	hit, 4027-(184).	hone, [2740,570]-
heron, 2429.	— with stone,	3879.
herring,5070g,3907-	4131-4488.	—,* 2740-2293.
4872.	hitherto,1053-2445.	honest, 2420-3854.
hesitate,3759-1263.	hive, 2637e.	honey, 2637.
—(in speaking),	hoar frost, 3627.	honeycomb,2637-798.
2514a.	hoard, 4538-2568.	honeysuckle, 4273a.
heterodoxy, 1293-	hoarse, 3881a.	1526-3028-650.
1507.	hoax, 1037b.	hong, 1186.
hew, 4136, 3624.	hobgoblin, 2243b,	honor, 4621-2065.
hibernate, 4753-	1380a.	—,* 4621-(2065),
4812.	hock, 4500.	1680.
hibiscus(rosa),	hod, 4685.	— parents, 960-
1235c.	hoe, 576a.	1680.
—(mutabilis),833a.	—,* 575.	hood, 3714b.
—(manihot),2128c.	hog, 312.	hoof, 4324.
—(syriaca), 735c.	hoist, 493.	hook, 1569, 3037.
hiccough, 1370a.	— sail, 2287b.	hoop, 2700, 805.
hidden, 4812-2568.	Hoklos, 1141d.	—,* 805.
hide, 3468.	hold, 4608.	hoot, 1199-(3880).
—,* 4812-2568.	—,* 57.	hooting owl,2222c.
— one's self,2887-	—(contain), 301.	hop, 4371.
2568.	— fast, 339b,1486.	hope, 2764,215h.
hideous, 473-2599.	— in the mouth,	—,* 2764, 3631.
high, 1713.	1152.	horizon, 1639h.
— peak, 1669.	hole, 2529, 1006.	horn, 1744.
— price, 2065.	holiday, 795a-5137.	—, deer's 2510-
— road, 2561g.	—(gala day),1713e-	5279.
— tide, 4004a.	5137.	hornet, 884c.

HOR	HOW	HUS
hornlike, 3316, 1744-5230.	more, 1120a.	husks,1175.
horoscope characters, 3197e.	— sad! 3636a.	husky voice, 3880a.
horrible,4698-4684.	however, 3715-1349.	hut, 2595-4944.
horse, 2561.	howl, 1709-925.	Huxley, 924a.
— power, 2561i.	hubbub, 3160a,1203.	hyacinth, 2563b.
— racing, 3437-2561.	hug, 2169.	hydrangea aspera, 3039f.
— radish, 2330c.	hull grain, to 386.	hydraulics, 4004-682.
— shoe, 2561-1485.	— of a ship, 3999-3830.	hydrophobia, 4004j.
—, to ride 1954.	human, 5117.	hygiene, 5015a.
— whip, 2561b.	— kind, 2494b.	hymn, 3945-3899.
horses, to breed 625c.	humane, 4865-3593.	—, to sing 507-3899.
hose, 2591.	humble, 1054a.	hypocrite, 3017a-Y.
—(tubing), 1008.	— self, my 3674a.	hypocritical,3017a.
hospital, 1249b.	humbug, 908e.	hyson skin tea, 409x.
host, 4272a.	—,* 4326.	— tea, 409u.
—(many), 2075.	humility, 1054a.	— tea, old 409v.
hostage, (5117)-232.	humming sound, 2082.	— tea, young 409w.
hostess,2949-4272a.	humorous,1117-3675.	hyssop, 4722a.
hostler, 2561a.	hump(on animal), 1661.	
hot, 1372.	humpback, 4408a.	
—(acrid) 2194.	humpbacked, 4408a.	I
—(feverish), 1372, 1077.	hundred, 3170.	
— weather, 1373a.	hundredth, 4076-5133-3170.	
hotel, 921b.	hunger, (1603)-3066.	I, 3065,
hound, 2380-1574.	hungry, 4402-3066.	ice, 3714, 3301.
hour, 4151-385.	hunt, 2380a.	— berg, 3301b.
—, quarter 2056.	hurrah! 1099.	— cream, 3714a.
—, to strike 480a.	hurricane, 879a,b.	— house, 3714-579.
house, 4944-a.	hurried, 4832,2755.	— water,3714-4004.
— coolie, 1819d.	hurry, 1766/651½/.	icy, S-4275.
—, customs 2052c.	hurt, 3855-1135.	idea, 1258a.
—, eating 1713d.	—(pain), 4458.	—(plan), 682a.
—, mercantile 1186.	husband,201a,1878c.	identical, 3625-4459.
— of assignation 4093b.	— strength, 626a.	idiom, 1779-548.
— tax, 2276b.	—, to marry a 1423, 2780f.	idiot, 3068-Y.
household, 1410.	husband's sister, 1786.	idiotic, 4874a.
— gods, 3835a.	— mother, 1786.	idle, 934.
hovel, 2392.	husbandman, 2952-801.	—(lazy), 2185a.
how? 4153,b.	hush! 2604-3880.	— fellow, 1250a.
— many? 1624c.	— up, to 167c.	idol, 3517a,3040a.
— much less, or	husk, 1137.	—, clay 1878e.

IF	IMM	IMP
if, (4432)-5181.	immortality, 5051-3802.	imposter, 1419b, 2079a.
— rsally, 4873a.	immutable, 3236-1739.	imposts, 450a.
ignis fatuus,2061b.	imp, 2061-D.	impotence, N-2330.
ignite, 184b.	impair, 3707.	impoverished,3449a.
ignoble, 4559.	impart, 613-(3250).	impracticable, N-4081.
ignorance, 2803b.	impartial, N-3487-3593.	imprecation, 164,a.
ignorant, N-1663-3918.	impatient, N-5114a.	impregnate, 4409.
iguana, 1830b.	impeach, 1726,2199.	impress, 4027-5116.
ill, 5159-3278.	impede, 296a.	—(the mind), 1649.
—(bad), N-1099.	impediment to speech, 2956.	imprison, 2134-5132-1455.
illegal, N-1193-2546a.	impel, 4822, 4946.	imprisoned, 4793-1455.
illegitimate,3758a.	imperative,S-1541a.	improbable, 2834-3743.
— child, 5173e.	imperfect, 1056a.	improper, N-[184, 2993].
illicit, 3758.	imperial,5093,5071.	improve, C-1099a.
— intercourse, 1466, 3758d.	— proclamation, 292.	impudent, 3779p.
ill-natured, 2866a.	— gunpowder tea, 409aa.	impure,N-1693-4564.
illness, 3278-(4458).	imperious, 3163-1033.	in, 965, 4609.
illtreat, 1135.	impersonate, 1419/.	— debt, 2121a.
illumine, 291-(2105).	impertinent, 3779p.	— order to, 2200.
illustrate, 3323-2690.	impetuous, 3658-1558.	inaccurate, (5159)-4791.
illustration,4898a.	implement, 1035b.	inadequate, N-1583.
ill-will, 981.	implicate, 2495a, 318a.	inadvertently, N-1745.
image, 3040b.	implore, 976-1936.	inattentive, N-2247b.
—(shape), 5230.	—(as beggar), 998.	inauspicious, N-1560.
—(picture), 5228.	imply, 3106b.	incalculable,2032a.
imagine, 3631.	impolite, 2206e.	incantation, to exorcise by 1670c.
imbecile,2936-5182.	import, 5132-1006.	incapable, N-3140.
imbue with, 246-1325.	importance, no 2016b.	incarnate, 1781c.
imitate,1140-(657).	important, 1541a.	incarnation, 1781c.
imitation, 1419.	imported, 2447c.	incendiarism, 795c.
immaculate, N-903a.	imports, 5132-1006-771.	incense, 1046.
immature, 3967.	importune, 3013, 1086a-1936.	—,* 1649a.
immediately, 3905a, 4533a.	impose, 1409.	— sticks, 1046a.
immense, S-4033.	— upon, 1019a.	incessantly,1086a.
immerse, 4488,134.	impossible, 3236-2858.	incest, /1466.
immersion(baptism), 4488a.		inch, 4814.
immodest,3849-2205.		
immoral, N-275.		

INC	INC	IND
inchase, 1157,3628.	incurable, 682e.	indulgent, **4654**,
incident,3776-4766.	—(disease) N-	857.
incidental, 3040a.	1249-4081.	industrious, 1917a.
incision, 2426e.	indebted, 1056.	inert, N-3140-5247.
incisor, 2779-2977.	indecent, 749-2205.	inexhaustible,
incite,3749-(3689).	indeed, 3855a.	2032a.
incivility, 2206e.	indefinite, N-939b.	inexpensive, 3479.
inclined,4731,2652.	indelible, N-2238-	inexperienced,
121.	4081.	3802-3859.
— to be sick,	indemnify,3546-657.	inexplicable, N-
3631-54.	indemnity, 3546-	1436-4081.
— to do, 985,3631.	3028.	inexpressible,
inclose, 3198-2568.	independent, 4673-	1779-N-4203.
—(surround), 5001-	[328,2190].	inextricable, 1436-
339.	index,2509a,2798a.	N-2238.
include, 3198-2006.	India, Pride of	infamous, 474, 473.
included, 4609c.	813b.	infant, 3677a,
including, 2350-	— ink, 2606.	2948a.
2568.	— rubber, 4531a.	infanticide, 3808-
incoherent talk,	indian corn,3737a.	1266.
2996-4960.	— topaz, 4561a.	infantry, (3341)-
incombustible, N-	indicate, 215f.	3300.
3965-4081.	indicator, 3323.	infatuated, 2601b.
income, 5132-3633.	indict, 1726-586.	infect, 1325-3278.
incompatible,	indifferent, 2187a.	infectious, 3140-
N-5059.	indigent, 3449a.	1325.
incompetent,N-3140.	indigestion, 3236a.	inferior, 908-4097.
incomplete, N-4705.	indignant, 1156a,	—(goods), 5087.
incomprehensible,	4913.	infernal, 5254a-K.
N-1095-4081.	indignation, 2865-	infinite, N-939,
inconceivable,	981.	2032a.
3631-N-4203.	indigo, 2167a.	infirm, 2936-5182.
inconclusive, 2665-	indisposed,N-3107a.	inflamation,(1693)-
4132.	—(disinclined),	1372.
incongruous, N-	N-3631.	inflate, 1802b.
[2993,1193,4250].	indissoluble, N-	inflexible, 3001.
inconsistent, N-	651-4081.	inflict, 1832,1409.
[1193,2285].	indistinct,N-2690a.	influence, 1755-
inconstant, N-4132.	individual, 5117,	4277, 651b.
inconvenient, N-	5014, 1734.	influenza, 3885a/.
779d.	—(by itself),	inform,4452a,3686.
incorrect, 4791.	2379-4673.	informer, 3647a.
increase, 1409-	indivisible, N-	infuse, 635.
(4215).	723-4081.	— tea, 635a.
incredible, 404a,	indolent, 2185a.	ingenious,4560-958.
2834-3743.	indorse, 4745.	ingot, 4174.
incubate, 3344.	induce, 2378,5121.	ingratitude, 2754b.
		ingulf, 4329.

INH	INQ	INS
inhabit,1846-(339).	inquire,(788)-2629.	instigate, 3689-
inhabitant, 1846c.	— after one,3107c.	3749.
— of country,	inquiry, after	instinct,3388-3658.
3388-4125-Y.	1585a.	institute, 4910.
— of world,3818-Y.	inquisitive, 1099-	—,* 563,c.
inhale, 1926.	788-2629.	instruct, 1507.
inharmonious, N-	insane, 681-4158.	—(command), 697a.
5059.	insanity, 4158.	instruction, 1507a.
inherent, 3802-	insane asylum,	instructor, 3802f,
4609c.	4910a.	1507b.
inherit, 3952,4674.	insect, 646,2076b.	instrument, 1035b.
inheritance, 1368b.	— wax, 2192b.	—, string 1353a.
inhuman,4695a-3593.	insecure, N-5024a.	—, wind 879g.
iniquitous, N-	insensible, 3849-	— to play 4304,
4207,a.	5028.	1911b.
iniquity,4631-3100.	inseparable, 696-	insufferable, N-
initiate, 2207a.	4081.	5114-4081.
—(introduce),5121-	insert, (442)-5132.	insufficient, N-
5132.	inside,2484-(4339),	1583.
injure,(3707)-1135.	2937.	insult, 2362a,1019.
injurious, 2293-	insight, 1663-3918.	insurance, 3329b,
1135.	insignificant,	1340e.
injury, 3885, 1135.	3615a, 2656c.	— policy, 4047a.
ink, 2606.	insincere, N-136-	insure, 2569-3329a.
—, foreign 2606a.	3854.	—(guarantee),
—, liquid 2606a.	insipid, 4042,4292.	4037a.
— stand, 2606b.	insist, 3315-1388.	insurrection, 4610-
— stone, 1363a.	inshare, 2453a.	2474.
— well, 2606c.	insoluble, N-651-	intact, 4815.
inland, 2937-4125.	4081.	integrity, 3951-
inlay, 3628.	—(problem), N-	3854.
inlet, 1125L.	1436-4081.	intellect, 2361-
inmost, S-[3823,	insolvent, 71d.	4804.
2937].	inspect, 405a.	intelligence, 1663-
— heart,3823-3593.	—(view), 4314.	3918.
inn, 1086b, 921b.	inspector, 1455a.	—(news), 3633a.
innate, 3802-4609c.	inspiration, 2611a.	intelligent, 2690b.
inner, 2937, 2638.	inspire, 1926-1033.	intelligible, 2690a.
innocent, N-4631.	—(urge), 1649.	intemperance, 1100-
innocuous, N-4260.	instalment(payment)	4500.
innovate,3596-5132.	696-4972.	intemperate, 795e.
innovation, 3596-	instant, 4533a.	intend, 3631.
4593/.	—(month), 3388-	Intendant of Cir-
innuendo, 4856c.	4937.	cuit, 4207d.
innumerable, N-	instantly, 4533a.	intense, 3823,4458.
3972-4081.	instead of, (4316,	intensely, 1099.
inoculate, 397a.	4222).	intention, 1258,a,
inquest, 1330a.	instep, 1639c.	328b.

intentionally, 4083a.
intentness, 344-3593.
inter, 4617-(2568).
intercalary, 5259.
intercede, 4222-1936.
intercept, 2180-339.
interchange, 3625-3154.
intercourse, 1494b, 2447b.
—, commercial 1494c, 2447b.
—, friendly, 2447b.
—, illicit 1466, 3758d.
—, sexual 1494e, 798b.
—, social 2447b.
interdict,1530-217.
interest(attention) 2247b.
—(concern),2052,f.
—(profit), 5204.
— on money,2293,a.
—, compound 2293b.
interesting, 1099-4344.
interfere, 296b.
interference,4215-3776.
interim, 3905-1463.
interior,2937,2484, 383,a.
interlace, 1494-1409.
interleave, 1448a.
intermediate, 383a.
intermittent, 141-141.
— current, 2245h.
— fever, 3167a.
internal, 2937.
international, 2104b.

— law, 1718b-1618-682.
interpose, 5132-383a.
interpret(explain), 1436, 613-4960.
—(translate), 658-5213.
interpreter, 4452c, 658-5213-Y.
interrogate, 3552b.
interrogative(gr), 2648,2881.
interrupt, 296.
intersect, 3625-1494.
interstice, (3973, 2148).
interval, 1463.
intervene, 5132-383a.
interview, 2687-1663.
intestine, 513.
—, large 1776.
intestines, urinary, 513c.
intimacy, 1494d.
intimate,3625-4011, 4711.
—,* 1726-205.
— with. 4011.
intimidate, 902a, 902-3164.
intimidation,1231-923.
into, 5132.
intoxicated, 4630-(4500).
intoxicating, 3140-4630.
intractable,N-3865-1507.
intrepid,4038-3593, 5281.
intricate, 2834-(1436).

intrigue, 2062-61.
—,* 4369-3689.
introduce, 1663a.
—(a customer), 1849a.
—(a subject), 4323a.
—(recommend), 1850a.
— into, 5121-5132.
introduction(to a book), 3674c.
—(recommendation), 4556-216.
intrude, [310,442]-5132.
inundate,4004-4488, 197.
inundation, 4004a, 1236a.
invade, 4708-5132.
invaluable, S-2065.
invariable, 3236-1739.
inveigh, 2842.
inveigle,1569-5121.
invent, [119,584]-4594.
inventory, 2636f.
invert, 4197-346.
investigate, 405,a.
—(judicially), 3826-2629.
invigorate, 3330-2330.
invitation card, 4734-4365.
invite, 4734.
invoice, 771-4046.
invoke, 362.
involve, 4403-2496.
inward, 2937.
— thoughts, 513a.
irascible, 1636e.
iris, 4562a.
—(flower), 2754e.
— pumila, 2182a.

IRO	IT	JAW
iron, 4366.	— is easier, 2898.	—(cheek), 3695.
—,* 4433.	itch, 2154.	jawbone, 2052i.
—, acetate of 43671.	—,* 980.	jay, 4519.
—, cast 4367a.	itching, 980a.	jealous, 4204-1631.
—, clad, 4367c.	item, 4375.	jealousy,4497-4204.
—(for clothes), 4433-4109.	items, 2798.	jeer, 1037h.
— magnet, 4367g.	itinerary,2426-561.	JEHOVAH, 5172-5064-
—,malleable 4367b.	ivory, 2977c.	4958.
— ore, haematite 170a.	ivy, 4332.	jelly, 4275.
		—(animal), 1716.
— —, magnetic 4863.		—(fruit),2097-148.
—, oxide of 4367j.	**J**	jenny, 2480-G.
—, soldering 2838a.		jeopardy, 3015a.
—, sulphate of 671c.		jerk, 763, 3027, 2867.
—, sulphuret of 4367h.	jacana, 1515d.	jessamine, 2793a.
—, to puddle 448a.	jacinth, 5250c.	jest, 3675a.
— worker, 4027-4367-L.	jackal, 1574a.	—,* 1779-3675a.
irrational,N-4766b.	jackass, 2480-G.	JESUS, 5172a.
irregular, 2474.	jackdaw, 3115-4519.	jet, 4300c.
irrelevant,N-2051f.	jacket,(4241)-3791.	— fossil 5250a.
irremediable,2711c, 2711-682.	jade, 5250.	— of water, 3877-4004.
irresolute, N-328b.	—, greenish 3283-(5250).	jetty, 2564b,2561j.
irrespective,2528d.	jagged, 2977h.	Jew, 5153a.
irreverent, 3662.	jail, 1455-(798).	jewel, 3331-3879.
irrigate, 2225a.	jailbird, 1455b.	jewelry, 3860-3919.
irritable, 2866a.	jailer, 1819,1158-1455.	jigger, 3779h.
irritate, 1649a.	jam, 2097b.	jingle, 2090a,2081b.
irritated, 1869a.	—,* 3279-(3854).	jinricksha, 490b.
is, 968.	January, 266a.	— coolie, 490b-Y.
—(have), 5159.	jar, 560, 21.	job, 1665.
— not, 3236,N-968.	—,* 138a.	— work, 1877e.
isinglass, 1495a.	—(large), 1770, 4947.	jog, 3562.
island, 1125b.	—(vase), 3480.	— along, 488-488.
ism, 2528.	—(covered), 1155a.	joggle, 3048,5247.
isolated,2379-4673.	jargon, 2996-4960.	join, 3356,a.
issue, (681,648).	jasmine, 2793a.	— the church, 1507e.
isthmus, 4380a.	jasper, 3283a.	joint, 4570.
it, 2026.	jatropha, 4465.	—, ginglymus 1521b.
— being so, 1628b.	jaundice, 4299a.	— stock,1193-3388.
— is better, 2898.	jaunt, 648-5151.	joist, (2248)-141.
	java sparrow,1871a.	joke, 3675a.
	javelin, 3859-4556.	—,* 1779-3675a.
	jaw, 2977a.	jolly, 867b.

JOL	JUT	KIL
— time, 1075a.	jut, 4106-(648).	kilogramme, 1606b.
jolt, 1264a.	juvenile, 2947.	kilometer, 1606c.
jonquil, 4004k.		kind, 5201,2494.
josspaper, 4918-		—,' 1099-3593.
3331.		kindle fire, 4338a.
jostle, 3562-5247.	**K**	kindling, 419.
jot, 4151.		kindness,5018-3099.
journal, 1627c.		—(benevolence),
journey, 2426-561.		5118a.
jowl, 3694a.		—, profound 1238b.
joy, 651½-2455,	kaleidoscope,2577b.	kindred, 4712-4743.
4134a.	keel, 3999-(4071)-	—(blood), 2608.
joyful, 651½-2455.	2083.	king, 5072.
jubilee, 1030-2895.	keelboard, 4525.	king crab, 1017.
judge, 3826-3776-	keen, 2293.	kingdom, 2103.
1815.	keep(detain), 2246-	kingfisher, 2460b.
— * 3826a.	(339).	— feathers, 4827-
—(criticize),	—(feast), 4593.	2712.
1282a.	—(observe), 3861.	kinsman, 2824-4712.
— in the matter,	—(preserve) 3329.	kinswoman, 2949-
589a.	—(put by), 3858b.	4712.
judgment,4132-3111.	—(rear) 5198.	kiss, 4712b.
— day, 3826a-5137.	—(watch), 1158.	kitchen, 591a.
jug, 3480,3122.	— watch, 1550c.	— garden, 4800-
jugglery, 543a.	keg, 4454.	4916.
juice, 148.	kerchief, 1537.	kite, 2161.
jujube, 4588.	kernel, 5044,2859,	—, to fly 795-
July, 4718-4937.	5118.	2161.
jumble, 2474.	kerosene, 767j.	—, singing 143b.
jump, 4371.	ketchup, 3912a.	knapsack,3377-4224.
junction,3625-1494-	—(foreign), 1946a-	knave, 2105-2079.
3987.	148.	knead, 2950, 412.
June, 2504-4937.	kettle, 3326.	knee, 3602-4339.
jungle, 4850-2226.	—, tea 409f.	— cap, 3602-4339-
junior, 3967-2895,	key, 3692d.	2083.
1013-3802.	— hole,3692d-2999.	kneel, 2070-(908).
juniper, 3174a.	khamil peach,4392b.	knife, 4195.
— seed oil, 3174c.	kick, 4343.	—, clasp 282a.
junk, 3999.	kid, 5193b-D.	—, pocket 4195-D.
Jupiter, 2795g.	kidnap, 2046-4031.	knit, (4369)-238.
jury, 3548a.	kidnapper, 2046a.	knob, 2868,314a.
just,' 1878a.	kidney beans,4116c.	knock, 4027,3423.
—," 2993a, 4504.	kidneys, 3840.	— against, 3562.
— right, 275d.	—(animal), 1379c.	knot, 1694a,2383.
— so, 4533b.	kill, 4027-3767,	—, loose 2383b.
— then, 3923a.	3808.	— in wood, 45.
justice, 1878a,b.	—(slaughter) 4430.	—, to tie 4027-
justify,1279a-1292.	kiln, 1390, 2981a.	1694.

KNO	LAM	LAN
knotty log, 45a.	lama(Tibet), 2144a.	—, magic 3877-5228-4094.
know, 205, 3918.	lamb, 5193a-D, 5193c.	— slide, 4094-3491.
—(understand), 1095.	lame, 3205-1638.	lap, 3602-4339-3987.
knowledge, 1663-3918.	lament, 4322a.	—, * 2153, 3788.
known, to make 3910.	lamentable, 3636a.	lapel, 3791a.
knuckle, 2008b, 2383a.	lamp, 4094.	lapse, 2100.
kodak, 5228-3626.	—(electric bulb), 4094a.	larboard, 3999-4597.
kotow, 1930a.	— black, 1335d.	lard, 5149a.
	— chimney, 4094-4461.	larder, 2636c-798.
	— globe, 111a.	large, 4033.
	— saucer, 87a.	lark, 2557g, 2365b.
L	— shade, 111a.	larkspur, 4796a.
	— wick, 4094b.	larva, 4706a.
	—, to light, 4151-4094.	larynx, 3700.
	lampoon, 3178-447.	lascivious, 1100-3917.
label, 4672a, 1109-3319.	lance, 4735.	lash, 3288.
labor, 1877a.	lancet, 1124-578-4195.	lass, 2949b.
—(travail), 430.	land, 4125.	last, 913d.
—, in 2224-430.	—(cultivated), 4356.	—, * 3814-4081.
—, * 4559-1877.	—, by 4027-2426.	—, ' 3858a.
laborer, 1887-Y.	— army, 2508a.	—(day of time), 2792.
laborious, 3597-813.	—, * 3895-3078.	—(week), 3639.
labrax, 2413a.	landing, 2564b, 3341c.	—(year), 1594.
labyrinth, 2029c.	—(on stairs), 4313a.	—(yester-) 4611.
lac, 59b.	—, to make 2568a.	lasting, 1904, 1660a.
lace, 3287a.	landlord, 4125-328.	latch, 3692a, 2061f.
—, shoe 913f.	—(field), 4356-328.	— lock, 4058b.
lacerate, 109-2186.	—(house), 4944-328.	—, * 3692-(339).
lack, 1056.	—(inn), 4154- 328.	late, 536, 2578.
lacking, N-1583.	lands, 4356.	—(past date), 2101c.
lacquer, 4721.	land-tax, 4125-4005.	— at night, 5176.
— ware, 4721-1035.	lane, 1190.	— in the day, 20.
lad, 2404c, 2614a.	language, 4960.	lath, 2795-3491.
ladder, 4313.	—(speech), 1006-5089.	— and plaster wall, 1419-4738.
lade, 2454-771.	—, bad 2186b.	lathe, 490g.
lading, bill of 2171b.	languid, 2110.	—, to turn in a 490.
ladle, 1138, 112a.	lantern, 2533d.	latitude, 5012a.
lady(married), 2816a.		lattice, 1450a, 2277b.
—(unmarried), 1786b.		latrine, 3902a, 4857-3977.
lady's toilet, 303a.		laud, 4472-4657.
lake, 3121.		

LAU	LEA	LEA
laudanum, 4c-4500.	leads(pr), 4921f.	—, to obtain 2433-
laugh, 3675.	leaf, 1367.	4766g.
laughable, 1099-	—, gold 1527a.	leaven, 1511.
3675.	— metal, 3364.	leavings, 59.
laughing stock,	— of book, 3488,	lecherous, 1100-
3277a,2767f.	1367.	3510.
launch, 3999a-D.	— of door, 3930.	lecture, 3982f.
—,* [648, 4447]-	— fan, 2128-3930.	ledge, 3879-4418.
4004.	league, 4438a,3516-	ledger, 4096-1627-
laurel, 2067b.	3746.	3343.
lavatory,3587-2687-	—(combine), 2471-	lee,908-879-3295.
3554.	1193.	leech, 1958a.
—(room), 3587-3830-	leak, 2148.	— line of sail,
798.	—,* 2262.	2396.
lavish, 3527-691.	lean, 3362.	leeks, 1578-(4800).
law, 682, 2546a.	—* 13-(2568).	leer, 1744n.
—, martial 2075a.	—, upon, 1247a,	lees, 59, 3029.
—, to go to 1815c.	1255a.	left, 4597.
lawsuit, 3111a.	leaning toward,	— overs, 3956.
lawyer, 311c.	3487.	leg, 1638.
lawsonia, 215e.	leap, 4371.	—(ham), 4448.
lax, 3748.	— year, 5259-2895.	—, calf of 2037m,
—(morally),3593-	learn, 1140.	1638a.
3748.	learned, 3356-1140.	— of mutton,3252c.
laxative, 2656a.	—(clever), 2690b.	legs, to cross the
lay(as brick),4704.	learning, 2616a.	1494i.
— bare, 2743.	lease, 3446.	legacy, 5003/.
— by, 4812-(2568).	—,* 4583-(5106).	legal, 2207c.
— down office,	least, S-3674.	legation, 5093-411-
3618a.	—, 4140a.	2978a.
— hands on, 3110.	leather, (4011)-	legend, 1796-4890.
—(place), 795,116.	3468.	leggings, 825a.
—(recline), 715.	leave, 2274, 1221.	legion, 2075.
—(spread out),	— ask for 4734-	legislate,563-2207.
3167.	1422.	legitimate(proper),
— table,3167-4418.	— a space, 1234.	184, 275.
— tiles, 1996c.	— behind, 2246,a.	legumes, 4116.
layer, 4714.	— —(bequeath),	leisure, 934.
lazy, 2185a.	5003.	—, at 934a.
lead, 4921,a.	—(let alone),	leisurely, 2578-
—,* 4031,5121.	5148-4081.	2578.
— by the hand,	— of absence,	lemon, 2900a.
4403.	1726h.	lemonade, 2900a-
— ore, 2352.	—(of steamer),	4004.
— pencils, 4921e.	1124a.	lend, 4509.
leader, 4339-2798.	—(permit), 4766g.	length, 512/.
—(newspaper),2528-	— port, 648c. •	—, a 4375.
4001.		lenient, 857-3989.

LEN	LIB	LIG
lens, 1637,d,3732.	library,3982b,3982-798.	lignite, 4300c.
—, concave 1637e.	—(books), 3982-4538.	like, 1099b,4868.
—, convex 1637f.	lice, 3851.	—,* 383b.
— of eye, 4562c.	—, to crack 2781a.	liking, 856a.
lentils, 4116e.	license, 3420, 147-291.	likely,1998a,1573a.
leopard, 3204.	—,* 648-3420.	likeness, 5230-311.
leper, 2558a-Y, 4495a.	licensed opium, 1335L.	—(image), 4530.
leprosy, 2558a.	licentiousness, 4286-3917.	—(photo), 3632.
leprous, 681-882.	lichee, 2211a.	likewise,5210,5163.
less, 3966.	lichen, 3879j,4423.	likin tax, 2276a.
lessen, 1457,a.	lick, 3788, 2337.	lilac, 4168c.
lesson, 772.	licorice, 381a.	— convolvulus, 2532b.
lest, 1231a.	lid, 1994.	lily,3170-1193-650.
let(allow), 5148-4081.	lie, 4033-4960.	—, water 2353a.
— go, 795.	—,* 1779-4033-4960.	limb, 208-(4315).
— house, 648f.	— down, 715.	lime, 845.
— loose, 3748.	lieutenant, 826, 3861-3263.	—(fruit), 2900a.
lethargy, 699-4008.	life, 2671a.	—, bird 515a.
letter, 3743, 880a.	— belt, 743b.	— kiln, 845-1390.
—(a character), 4672.	lift, 4189-4422.	— stone, 845-3879.
—, registered 4036b.	—,* 471.	— water, 3879-845-4004.
lettuce, 4800a.	— off, 1984.	limit, 939.
level, 3497.	—(the head), 4035.	"Limited", 939c.
— off, 4357, 432.	— water, 829.	limp, 1566d.
—, to find 4004.	light(bright),2105.	limpet, 2444c.
lever, 4754-1534-4084.	—(color), 4759.	line, 3646.
— watch,1954-2561-3321.	—(weight), 1042.	—(cord), 3949.
levity, 1042c.	—, 2105.	—(stroke), 4967.
levy, 471.	—,a 4094, 767.	—,*(pad), 2857.
lewdness, 3510.	— fire, 4336,4338.	lineage, 1522.
lexicon, 4162b.	— lamp, 4151.	linen, 2556,b.
liable for, 3909a.	— of, to make 726b.	— thread, 2557a.
liabilities, 1056b.	lighthouse 4094-[4307,2248].	liner, 767-4000b.
liar, /4033-4960.	lightly, 1042b.	linger, 2263a.
libations, to offer 4165.	—, to esteem 1042,d.	liniment,5183-1714.
libel, 4987-2669.	lightning, 2303b, 3927-4163.	lining, 2484.
liberal, 3411.		link, 2350-4974.
liberate (3922)-795.		—,* 1930-2350.
liberty, 4673-328.		linotype, 147-4672-1602a.
		linseed, 3126a.
		— oil,3126b,2557e.
		lintel,4125c.
		—, window 499-2657.

LIO	LOA	LON
lion, 3760.	loafer, 2401d.	longitude, 4125b.
lioness, 2720-3760.	loan, 4509-1191.	longsuffering,
lips, 1006-4017.	—,* 4509.	5114a.
liquid,4004-(2494).	loathe, 4490-1311.	look, 4314.
—,' 4004.	loathsome, 1117-	— after, 1158.
liquidate, 4564-	3117.	— for, 5023.
3972.	lobby, 2779-1006-	—(hope), 2764.
liquidation, 4294-	4346.	looking glass,
3972.	lobe of ear, 1280b.	1637a.
liquor, 4500.	lobster, 900d.	loom, 238b.
liquorice, 1750a.	local, 4380, 3388-	loop, 2869s.
list, 2798.	4125.	loophole, 2148b.
—(register), 423.	— dialect, 3178d.	loose, 3748.
listen, 4344.	— products, 430b.	—,* 1436-2238,
literally, 4672b.	location, 590.	795.
literary, 2616a.	look, 3691.	loosely, 2190b.
literati, 3982g-Y.	—, bolt 2063-3691.	lop off, 1832-1221.
literature, 2616,b.	—(canal), 99a.	loquacious, 1006h,
litharge, 2637f.	—,* 3691-2568.	4215-1006.
litigation, 92c.	locker, 2071.	loquat, 2412a.
little, 4138,3966.	locomotive, 490d.	lord, 328.
—(small), 3589.	locust, 5074a.	Lord's Supper,
—, very 4140a.	— tree, 4964.	2575b,3945-4692.
live, 3802.	lodge, 1086b.	lordship,4033-5117.
—(dwell), 1846a,	—(society), 3143-	lore, 2616a.
339.	1820.	lose, 1663d, 3849.
— alone, 3629.	—,* 1086-3736,339,	—(in game) 3984.
— stock, 625a,	4060b.	—(in trade),3388a.
3803-1006.	lodger, 921-D.	— color,3293-3917.
livelihood, 2100-	lodging house,	— face, 4182a.
5137.	1086b.	loss, 686a.
—, to seek 5023-	loft, 2248.	—(in trade),3388a.
4339a.	lofty, 1713.	lost, 1663d.
lively, 3157a,3981.	log, 427,2795-4339.	—(ruined), 2753,
liver, 1763, 5260.	— book,3999-1627c.	457.
livid, 4764-971.	—, knotty 419a.	lot(drawing), 480.
living, 3802,3157a.	— line, 4004f.	—(ground), 4066-
— things, 2636b,	logic, 3297a,2669a.	4125.
1006a.	LOGOS, 4207.	—(life), 2671.
lizard,1321a,1830b.	loins, 1379, 1296a.	—(many), 4215.
Lloyd's, 3999-2729-	loiter, 2265a.	lots, to draw 147a.
3143.	lonely, 2187, 1797-	lotion, 3587-5183.
loach, 3115-4872.	4259.	lottery ticket,
load, 4040,4420.	long(space), 512.	1829a.
—,* 301.	—(time),2938,1575.	lotus, 2353a.
loadstone, 3960a,	— for, 4932,2476a.	— nuts, 2603e.
4863a.	longevity,512-3867.	loud, 4033-3880.
loaf, 2689b.		

MAI	MAL	MAN

MAI

maim, 2010a.
maimed, 2010.
main, 4033, 275.
— road, 2561g.
— spring, 681-
4375.
maintain,3329-4616.
—(support), 5198.
maize, 3737a.
majestic,4985-1316.
majesty, 4985-1316.
majority,4033-3389.
—(age), 3948-4168.
make, 4593, 274,
4027.
— angry, 1649a.
— bed, 587b.
—(cause), 2378.
—(compel), 2682a,
1966.
— conspicuous,
3319.
—(create), 4594.
—known, 3337,3910.
— light of, 726b.
—(mental work),
4610.
— money, 681-4803.
— obeisance, 3168.
—(proclamation),
648.
— profit, 88.
—(provoke), 1649.
— ready, 3295a.
— sport of, 2544a.
— trouble, 3802-
3776.
— up accounts,
1521a.
— waste, 690.
maker, 4594a.
malady, 3278-278.
malaria, 198-1033.
male and female,
5090-5196.
male(beasts),1878,
1801.
—(birds), 1878.

MAL

—(human), 2824.
—(boy), 2824-D.
—(man), 2824a.
— relatives,1070a.
— sex, 5196-2494.
malefactor, 678-Y.
malevonent, [1227,
971]-3593.
malicious, 1227-
3100.
malignant, 3100-
4260.
— boil, 5262.
mall, 621a.
malleable iron,
4367b.
mallet, 621a.
mallows, 2128a.
malt, 2607-2979.
mama, 2553-2553.
mammon, 4761-4803.
man(human), 5117.
—(male) 2824a.
— of all work,
4475a.
— of war, 263b,
3300-3999.
manacles, 3859-
2390.
manage, 2285a,3191-
2285.
manager, 57a.
Manchu, 2785a-Y.
mandarin, 1815b.
— orange, 320b.
mane, 4651.
mange, 3802-4661.
manger, 2561-4785.
mangle, 3932-3336-
1601.
—(spoil), 4695.
mango, 2751a.
mangosteen, 3793b.
manhood, 3948-5117.
maniac, 4158,2143.
manifest, 771-4046.
—,* 1061,b.
manifold, 673.

MAN

manihot, 2128c.
manipulate, 4027.
manis, 603b.
mankind, 2494b.
manly, 2074-4667.
manner, 5201.
manners,2204,2120a.
manslaughter, 2971-
3808.
mantel-piece 767f-
2991.
mantis, 4441a.
mantle, 4033-2240.
manual, 3859.
— labor,3859-4610.
manufactory, 119a-
579.
manufacture, 119a.
manure, 717.
—,* 2454-717.
manuscript, 3616-K,
3859-447.
many, 4215, 3170.
—?, how 1615c.
— thanks, 4215-
4510.
map, (4125)-4393.
maple, 886-3996.
mar, 3707-4965.
marble, variegated
3879c.
—, veined 3879b.
March, 3572-4937.
—,* 3341-986.
mare, 2561-G.
margarite, 137a.
margin, 3286.
marigold, 1867a.
marine,1125/,4004/.
— risk, 4004-1055.
mariners, 4004c.
marines,4004-3300c.
maritime customs,
2052a.
mark, 1627e, 4967.
—,* 4027-1109,
4967.

MAR	MAS	MEA
—(scar), 980.	—, school 3802f.	meager, 4513.
—(observe), 4314-	—, ship 4000-328.	meal, 4692, 677.
136.	— workman, 837a.	—(flour), 713.
—, trade 1627e.	masticate, 4581,	mealy-mouthed 526a.
market,(1430)-3908,	4521.	mean(base), 4559.
2177.	mat, 4514.	meaning, 1258a.
— price,3908-1421.	—(cushion), 4165½.	means, 682a,779b.
— town, 1214.	— sail, 2287.	—, by no 4242-N-
marking line, 2606-	— shed, 579b.	968.
4109.	—, to build	meanwhile, /4459-
marquis, 4520b.	4059-3431.	3905, 4469b.
marriage, 698-5111.	match, 419b.	measles, 648-2558.
— engagement,	—, * 1193.	measure, 4109.
4132b.	mate, 769a.	—,* 4228,2313.
married woman, 835.	—, first 768d.	meat, 5249.
marrow, 3720,2083e.	—, second 768e.	—, dried 2191.
marry, 3543a.	—,* 3543.	—, salt 2191.
—(of couple),3948-	material,4805-2400.	mechanic, 4529.
4712.	maternal aunt, 9e.	mechanics, 1602a-
—(of man), 4825.	— cousin,3323b	1140.
—(of woman), 1423,	— uncle, 1942.	mechanism, 1602a.
2780f.	mathematics, 3972a,	medal, 3889-3420.
Mars(planet), 7671.	1120b.	meddle, 2285a.
marsh, 3779b,81.	matrix, 2713.	mediator, 383-
mart, 745-4339,	matron, 3683,2725.	[5117,3329]
(1430)-3908.	matter(affair),	medical books,5183-
marten, 4187a.	3776-1761.	3982.
martial, 2723.	—(elements),5230a.	— practice, 765a.
— law, 2075a.	—(pus), 2954.	— prescription,
marvel, 1950-3776.	—(substance), 150.	5183-4046.
—,* 1663-1950b.	—,* 681.	— treatment,4377a.
marvellous, 1950b,	—, no 2016b,2528d.	medicines, 5183-
404a.	—, serious 2052g.	(4805).
masculine gender,	matting, 4514.	—(liquid), 5183-
5196-2494.	mattook, 575.	4004.
mash, 412-2186.	mattress, 586-5251.	—(pill),5183-4923.
mask, 1139c.	mature, 4011.	—(plaster), 5183-
mason, 2845a.	—,* 3948-4011.	1714.
—, 4027-3879-L.	maul, 55.	—(powder), 5183-
mass, 4443, 1596.	maxim, 125h.	713.
—, to say 4027a.	May, 2962-4937.	—(tincture),5183a.
masses, the 908-	— 1117a, 4081.	— science of
2618.	—(able), 3140.	1249a.
massacre,3808-2512.	—(as a wish),4932.	—, to apply 806a.
massive, 1014a.	— I trouble you,	—, to take 874f.
mast, 5007.	669b.	medieval, 383-3818.
master, 328-(5117).	me, 3065,	meditate,3759-3631.
—(employer),3776b.	meadow, 4777a.	

MIL	MIS	MOL
—, sugar 171d.	misinterpret, 1436-4791.	mold, 2713.
millet, 2603c.	mislead, 5121-4791.	moldy, 2712b.
million, 3170-2576.	misprint,5116-4791.	mole, 3985e.
millstone, 2742-3879.	mispronounce, 1779-4791.	—(on skin), 971-233.
mimic, 1140.	misreport, 3337-4791.	— cricket, 4380-1574.
mince, 4136.	misrepresent, 1779-2652.	molest, 2333a.
mind, 3593,5028.	miss, 1786b.	mollify, 4660a.
—, * 4314-339.	—* 3849, N-4198.	molt, 4446-2710.
—, to speak one's 1779a.	— the road, 787-4791.	moly, 2793a.
mindful, 5159-3593.	missionary, 613a-Y.	moment, 907, 141.
mine, 2108.	mist, (5027)-2730.	monarch, 5072.
—, * 2086.	mistake, 4791,400a.	monastery, Buddh-ist, 4677.
—(poss.) 3065-K.	—* 4593-4791.	—, Roman 3603-4207-4910.
—(explosive),2479.	mistaken,1ʹ97-4791.	—, Tauist 1818.
—, coal 940a.	mister(Mr.) 3802f.	Monday, 2206 j.
mineral, 1527-3879.	mistress(Mrs.) 2816a.	money, (3028,4761), 1527.
minister, 3836.	—, kept 1902e.	— order, 3028c.
—, * 147-3776.	mistrust, 1263a,	—, paper 3028a.
—(ambassador), 5093-411.	misunderstand,4344-4791.	moneyless, N-4761.
—, cabinet 3955a.	mite, 4140a,1104.	Mongol, 2803c-Y.
—, gospel 2796a.	mix, 1929a, 1502a.	mongrel, 391c.
mint, 1875a.	—(adulterate) 1929-3778.	monk, 3599,5059b.
—(plant), 1046e.	mixed, 2474,2193a.	monkey, 2243a.
—, * 332.	moan, 4507-4301.	monopolist, 4093a.
minus, 92.	mob,3170-3657-2474.	monopolize, 4093-771.
minute, 696,2673a.	mock, 1037b.	monopoly, 3198b.
—, 2656-3589.	model, (2713)-5201.	monsoon, 3905f.
minutely, 4667a.	moderate, N-4215-N-3966.	month, 4937.
miracle, 4537a, 1950a.	modern, 1526, 3596.	—, 29 day 3674e.
mirage, 1125c.	— times,1549-3818.	—, 30 day 4937-4033.
mire, 2844-(3192).	modest, 5159-2342-525.	—, first 266a.
mirror, 1637,a.	Mohammedanism, 3137f.	monument, 3420a.
mirth, 651--2455.	moist, 3843.	—(image), 4530.
miscarriage, 3674-430.	moisten, C-3843, 5258,2225a.	mood, 3593-4766.
miscellaneous,4475, 3847.	molasses, 4437b.	moody, 1802-1033.
mischief, to make 3385a.		moon, 4937-(2105).
miser, 933c.		— at quarter, 1354.
miserable, 4699a.		—, first day of 3980.
misery, 813a.		
misfortune, 1465a, 5062.		

MOO	MOT	MUL

MOO

—, half 3389b.
—, wane of 2010g.
moor, 3362.
mop, 727a.
mope, 681-2786.
moral, 3939.
morals, 986a.
more, 1557, 398, 4351.
moreover, 797a, 4351, 5163.
morning, 287.
—, early 4586.
—, good 4586a.
morose, 5090-457.
morphine, 4c-4560.
morphology, 4315d.
morrow, 2690c, 4358a.
morsel, 4043.
mortal, 3140-3767.
mortar, 386a.
—(plaster), 845.
mortgage, 4235.
— deed, 4162-1902.
mortgagee, 4162-328.
mortification, 803b.
—(gangrene), 5249-3767.
mortise, 3742b.
mosque, 3137f-2206L.
mosquito, 2613.
— net, 194a.
moss, 2769a, 683b.
most, 4215, 4629, 227.
mostly, 4215.
moth, 3061a.
mother, 2720a, 2720-4712.
—, adopted of 1902b.
— in law, 3070-2720.
—, step 1013c.
— of pearl, 5027b.
motion, 4277, 986.
—(parliamentary), 1282-4240.

MOT

motive, 2891a.
motor, 490, 1602a.
—(electric), 4163e.
— car, 490e.
mottled, 3183.
motto, 4323-1853.
mould, 2713.
mouldy, 2712b, 2768.
moulding, /3646.
moult, 4446-2712.
mound, 4248.
—, beacon 4090.
mount, *, 3895.
—(photo), 3324.
mountain, 3793.
mourn, 3095-1223, 4189-3698.
mourning apparel, 3698-874.
—, to go into 874d.
—, to lay off 874e.
mouse, 3985a-D.
—, field 3985b.
mouth, 1006.
— of river 1771a.
—, to stop 1972.
mouthful, 1006j, 4043.
move, 5247-(4277) 2502.
—(remove), 3384.
— back, 4330.
moving power, 1601.
mow, 432.
moxa, 2988.
Mr. 3802f.
Mrs. 2816a.
much, 4215.
—, too 2101f.
mucus, 4289.
mud, 2844.
muddled, 3120.
muddy, 372.
muff, 1886-3859-4386.
mugwort, 2988.

MUL

mulberry, 3699.
mule, 2441a, 2480.
mulish, 2876.
mullet, 4707.
multiplication, 3953a.
multiply, 3953.
multitude, (2137, 395).
mumble, 3024.
mumps, 66a.
munificient, 1014-398.
murder, 1227-3808.
murderer, 1227a.
murmur, 2528e, 2222a.
muscle, 1608-(5249), 1539.
— fibre, 1608a.
—, voluntary 1608b.
muscovy duck, 24b.
museum, 3357b.
mushroom, 2132.
music, 3073-5089.
musical instrument, 3073.
musicians, 614c.
musk, 3878-1046.
— deer, 3878.
— melon, 2037f.
— rat, 3985d.
musket, 4736.
muslin, 2676-3780.
mussel, 1064a.
—, pearl 4417d.
Mussulman, 2734d.
must, 3315-4132.
mustache, 3197f.
mustard, 2195a, 1439a.
— plant, 1439-4800.
musty, 1176c, 47-4965.
mute, 6-(1006).
mutilate, 4695-1135.
mutiny, 3391-5214.
mutter, 4334-3045.

mutton, 5193-5249.
— chops, 5193-
3419b.
—, leg of 3252c.
mutual, (3130)-3625.
muzzle, 1006,4627.
—,* 2235c.
my, 3065-K.
— country, 3388-
2103.
— humble self,
3674a.
— lad! 2404c.
— self, 4673a.
— shop, 3388b.
myriad, 2576.
myrrh, 2792-a.
mysterious, 1950.
mystery, 3086-2708.
myth, 1213a.
mythology, 2061e.

N

nadir, 4355i.
nail, 4127.
—, finger 215d.
—, toe 215d.
—,* 4127, 4130.
naked, 547,b.
—(bare), 2105.
name, 2669.
—(business),4672a.
—(surname),3657.
—,* 1709,a.
namely, 4533.
nandina domestica,
364f.
nankeen cloth,547d.
nap, 2712.
—(sleep), 996a.
nape of neck, 1191.
napkin,table
1537,c.
naptha,2766c,5149c.

narcissus, 4004k.
narcotics, 2601d.
narrate, 613,4025-
648.
narrow, 76.
nasturtium, 1121b.
nasty, 474.
nation, 2103,3370.
national affairs,
2729b.
nations, foreign
2104c.
native, 3388-4125.
4380.
—, 3388-4125-Y.
— place, 1045b.
natural, 4355-3802.
— philosophy,
1450d.
naturalized, to be
5132c.
naturally, 4673-
1349.
nature, 3658.
—, good 2848a.
naught(0), 2304.
naughty, N-1099.
nausea,[3140,3631]-
54.
nautilus, 2444a.
naval, 4004-3757.
nave(of wheel),
3593.
navel, (4402)-4866.
— cord, 4866a.
navigate, 3816.
navy, 1125i.
nay, N-968.
near, 1549,1920.
nearly, 400b, 92d.
—(time), 4522b.
neat, 4705-274.
—(clean), 1759a.
nebula, 3652b.
necessary, 1388,
1541a.
neck, 1636.
— bone, 1451.

— lace, 1636-2357.
— tie, 1636a.
necrosis,3767-2083.
need, 1388.
—, no N-3814.
needle,(2999)-123.
—, magnetic 123e.
needless, N-3814.
needy, 2031-736.
nefarious,474-3100.
negative(gr), 2719,
2551, 2711,3236.
— charge, 634b.
— principle, 5090.
neglect, N-2285.
neglected(orphaned)
1787.
negligent, N-3593a.
negotiate, 3191-
2285.
negro, 5117a.
neigh, 3762a.
neighbor,782a,
neighbor, 782a,
1045a,2286a,2517a.
neighboring, 1448c.
nephew, 152.
Neptune, planet
1125.
nerves, 2926c.
nervous(timid),780.
—(irritable),
1636c.
nest, 451, 4113.
—, edible bird's
1340c.
net, 2759, 2437a.
— weight,4564-645.
—, mosquito 194a.
nettle rash, 879-
2833.
neutralize poison,
1436b.
nevertheless, 3715-
1349.
new, 3596.
—(fresh), 3596a.

NEW	NIT	NOS
news, 2617b,3633a.	nit, 631d.	nostril, 3269-2529.
newspaper, 3596c, 5137-3337.	nitre, 3669,a.	not, 2551,2719, 3236.
next, 1289a.	nitric acid, 1964b.	— yet, 2665,a.
— month, 908-4937.	nitrogen,4042-1033.	— here, N-965- 3987, 4609b.
—(near), 1920.	no, 2711, 2551-968.	notable, 749a.
— time, 908b.	—(none), 2719.	notch, 3233.
— week,4076-1780g.	— help for it, 2711c.	—,* 1832-1006.
— world, 2447d.	— importance, 2016b.	note(borrower's), 4509a.
— year, 648-2895.	— matter, 2016b.	—(letter), 3743.
nibble, 3047.	— need, N-3814, 4609b.	—(sound), 5089.
nice, 1006.	— objection, 784a.	—, bank 3028a.
— looking, 4958a, 4958-2212.	— truth, 3513b.	— paper, 4553.
nickle,arsenide of 4462b.	nobility, 4520.	—* 1627.
nickname, 650e.	noble, 4621, 4033.	nothing, 2719-5173.
nicotine, 1335g- 4260.	nod, [4151,3033]- 4339.	—, a good for 2401c.
niece, 152b.	noise, (4033)-3880, 1047.	notice, 3319,1726a, 3420.
niggardly, 933.	noisome, 4260, 474.	—,* 1745.
night,(5176)-2575.	noisy, 4783,1047.	notification, 3337- 4046.
— dress, 569,b- 3791.	nomads, 5151a.	notify, 3337-205, 4452a.
—, last 4611-2575.	nom-de-plume, 3318-2669.	notion, 3631-4339.
— mare, 2735a.	nominate, 4323b.	notoriety, 1031- 2669.
— soil, 3902.	none, 2719, 2711.	notwithstanding, 3715-1349.
— stool, 3902a, 4857.	— greater, 2749a.	nought, 2719-5173.
—, towards 13a.	nonpareil(type), 1109a.	—(0), 2304.
— watches, 1550.	nonsense,2996-4960.	noun, 3854-4672.
— watchman, 1158b.	nook, 1744,a.	nourish, 5198.
— work, 1877c.	noon, 2965a, 20b.	novel, 3674-4001.
nimble, 651-.	noose, 3985j,1694b, 1968a.	—,' 3596, 1950.
nimbus, 3115c.	—,* 1968-339,2050.	novelty, 3596-5201.
nine, 1571.	north, 3215.	November,3845-5133- 4937.
nineteen,3845-1571.	— pole, 1654a.	novice, 9L, 3596- 3859.
nineteenth, 4076- 3845-1571.	—east, 4272c.	now, 1262b, 1526, 4873b.
ninetieth, 4076- 1571-3845.	—west, 3564b.	now! 2814.
ninety, 1571-3845.	nose, 3269,a.	noxious, 3100,4260.
ninth, 4076-1571.	—, bridge of 3269b.	nozzle, 4627.
nip, 2912, 1973.	—, roman 43c.	nude, 547,b.
nippers, 1971.	—, stop up 1302a.	
nipple, 2820b.	nosegay, 3641-650- 1938.	
—(pl) 2977j.		
nirvana, 2915-3552.		

NUG	OAR	OBS
nugatory, 4390c, 690.	oar, 4525, 2421.	—(as a pipe), 3592.
nugget, 1527-4339.	— lock, 4525-1280.	obtain, 4081-(4197),
nuisance, 474-2636.	oath, 3821-4932.	2433.
null, 686,4390c.	—, take an 681-	obtuse, 4269.
nullah, 3793-940.	3821.	— angle, 1744d.
numbed, 2558.	oatmeal, 2607c.	obviate, 2681.
number, 3972.	oats, 2607b.	obviously, 4235-
—(no.) 4076,1109.	obedient, 4344-4960.	2687.
—, * 3971.	—(compliant),4022.	occasion, 1601c.
—, fixed 2991	—(child), 2044.	—(time), 3419.
numbers, 2798a.	obeisance, 3168,	—, * 3814.
numeral,2798a-4672.	2206g.	occasionally, 5159-
numerically, 291-		3905.
2798.	obey, 4344-4960.	occidental, 3584.
numbness, 2558.	object, 2636a.	occiput, 128c.
nun, 1786c.	— * 4129-3355.	occult, 3255-2638.
—, Buddhist 1786d.	— of, to be the	occupants, 1846b.
—, Roman, 3603-	3262.	occupation, 1368a,
4207-2949.	objection, no 784a.	1877a.
—, Tauist 1786e.	obligation, 3388-	occupy, 1846,a.
nunnery, 3102a.	723.	occur,4896,a.
nurse, 9b, 3827a.	—(debt), 192a.	occurrence, 3776.
—, * 2819a.	oblige, 2682a.	ocean, (5194,1125).
—(carry), 3521.	obliged, much 4215-	ochre, 170,a.
—, wet 2553a.	4510.	
—, dry 1760e.	obliging, 4022.	o'clock, 4151-385.
nurture, 5198.	oblique, 4731,2652.	octagon, 3197d.
nut, 1001a.	obliterate, 2701-	octagonal table,
—, betel 2462a.	3571.	3197a.
— cracker, 1001a-	oblong, 512-779.	October, 3845-4937.
1971.	obloquy, 2362a.	ocular, 2999-1663.
—, lotus 2603e.	obscene language,	oculist, 2999d-
— machine 2444f-	2186b.	1249c.
2713.	obscure, 2777.	odd(over), 2304,
— shell, 1137.	obscured,2805-2777.	1624.
nutmeg, 4116g.	obsequies, 3698-	—(single), 4046.
— orange, 1561b.	2205.	—(strange), 1950.
nux vomica, 2561L.	observatory, 2616d-	odds and ends,3601-
	4422.	3721.
	observe, (4314,	ode, 3899.
	1663).	odious, 1117-3117.
O	—(keep), 3861.	odor(bad), 474.
	obsolete, 1594,	—(pleasant), 1046.
	690.	of, 1600.
oak, 4532.	obstacle, 296b/.	off(distant), 2274.
oakum, 2557d.	obstinate, 3001,a.	—, to go 1221.
—(native), 364-	obstruct, 296a,	offence, 4631.
3761.	2180-339.	

OFF	OLD	OPE
—, to take 1663-2048.	—(of things), 1594.	— school, 1821a.
offend, 4081-4631, 678.	— fashioned,3188a.	— sliding window, 501d.
offer, 3250, 648.	—, to grow 190.	opening, 2999,1006, 2529.
—(as a present), 3750-(3250).	olea fragrans, 2067c.	— between, 3973.
—(as an offering), 1067.	oleander, 4392g.	opera glass, 16371.
— libations, 4165.	olibanum, 4399h.	operation, 1877a.
offering,4483-2636. 482.	olive, 1756a.	—(surgical), 1832-278.
office(building), 1820.	— seed, 2162c.	ophthalmia, 2999c.
—(official building), 2978a.	ology, 2528.	opthalmoscope, 405-1637g.
—(position), 5105.	omelet, 1515-4051-3276.	opiate, 228-4008-5183.
—(room), 3616a-2248.	omen, 294-4339.	opinion, 1663c.
—(situation), 239.	omit, 2155, 2245.	—, your 1713a.
—, branch 696c.	omnipotent, 2711d.	opium, 4c, 2603f.
—, post 3982d.	omnipresent,2711f.	— dross, 4c-3902.
—, to lay down 3618a.	omniscient, 2711e.	— licensed 1335L.
officer, 1815.	on, 965,4609,3896.	— pipe, 1335m.
—, acting 601a.	once, 192b, 3137e, 3419c, 907.	— raw 4d.
official,1815-3776.	one, 5133.	opponent,4250-4339.
—, an 1815.	—(single), 4046.	opportunely, 2993a.
— charge, 75a.	—, a 169.	opportunity, 1602c.
— duty, 75a.	—, 'quarter, 1744i.	—, to embrace an 466.
— post 2010.	—, that 1732a.	oppose, 4250, 4072, 296.
officiating, 601-2285.	— to another, 3253a.	opposing(wind). 2989.
officious, 4215-3776.	— to 3 P.M. 2665.	opposite, 2687b.
offing, 1125-2687.	one's self, 4673a.	—(contrary), 3625-661.
often, 4215a,2486.	onion, 4845a.	oppress,902,25-339.
ogle, 1744n.	only, 4046-(968), 4259, 176.	oppresion, 922a.
oh! 33,a.	ontology, 3802h, 2528f.	oppressive, 1922a.
— dear! 33a.	oolung tea, 409p.	optical practice, 2999d.
oil, 5149.	onward, 1053-4760.	optician, 4594-1637g-Y.
— cloth, 3336g.	ooze, (3316)-2262.	optics, 2105e.
— well, 767h.	opal, 3332a.	optimist, 2455b.
ointment, 1714,a.	opaque, N-4338-2105.	optional,4630-3295.
old(age), 3722.	open, 1124.	or, 5206a, 3266.
—(ancient), 1796.	—(as a book),1984, 2572.	oral, 1006-1779.
—(of persons), (2420,4033).	—(break), 422.	orange, common 440.
	— door, 1302c.	
	— out, 185.	
	—, pry 1710.	

oxide of copper, 4462d.
— of lead, red 4921d.
oyster, 1105a.
— bed, 1105b.
— shell windows, 2981d.

P

pace, 3341.
pacify, 2378-5059.
pack, 301.
—(bundle up), 3198.
— of cards, 3420c.
— wrapper, 2650a.
package, 3198.
packet, D-3198.
packthread, 2556-3949.
pact, 1193a,5178.
pad, 2837.
paddle, 1392.
—,* 3413.
— wheel steamer, 4000c.
paddock, 2561f.
paddy, 5060.
padlock, 3692b.
—, foreign 3692c.
page of book,3187.
pagoda, 4307.
pail, (4004)-4454.
pain, 4458.
painful, 813a,4458.
paint, 5149,4721a.
—* 4721a.
—(picture), 4967.
painter, 4721a-L.
pair, 4250.
—,* 3543-1193.
—, in 3886.
palace, 1884-4164.

palanquin, 1703.
palate, 3076.
palaver, 1213-4960.
pale, 3178.
paling, 2181-1762.
palisade, 2181a.
pall, 1817-111.
—,* 3849-2666.
pallid, 4764-3178.
palm, 4649, 2106-2463.
—, fan 2128.
— of hand, 191.
palmleaf thatching, 2128f.
palpitate, 3398a.
palsy, 882-4295.
paltry, 3615a.
pamphlet, 3982-D.
pan, 5054,5066.
pancake, 5149-4552-3276.
pancreas,4352-5249.
pane, 652, 3491.
panelled, 1799a.
— door, 2037L.
pangolin, 603b.
panic, 923-(3808).
pansy, 1544a.
pant, 606.
panther, 3204.
pantomime, 1037-2721.
pantry, 2636c-798.
pants, 824.
paochung tea, 409q.
papa, 9a.
papaya, 2037i.
paper, 216.
— effigies, 216h.
— mulberry, 598.
—, news 3596c.
—, note 4553.
—, rice 4453a.
—, sized 216a.
parable, 3466a.
parade ground, 1508c.

paradise, 2455a.
—, bird of 4518-5071.
paragraph, 4243, 4570.
parallel, 3286-986.
— of latitude, 5012.
paralysis, (882)-4295.
paramour, 4766f.
parapet, 5001-4738.
parasite,1629-3802.
parasol, 167-D.
parboil, 329-3389-4011.
parcel, 3198.
—,* 696-1124.
parch, 1183.
parched, 1759-(4782).
parchment, 5193-3468-216.
pardon,3873-(2681), 857a.
—, beg 1737a.
pare, 3446, 3463.
paregoric, 217-4458-5183.
parents, 836-2720.
park, 4916.
parliament, 2103-3132, 1282b.
parlor, 921-4346.
paroquet, 43b.
paroxysm, 471-628.
parrot, 5225-2724, 43b.
— fish, 4872b.
Parsee, 3178-4339-Y.
parsley, 1919c.
parsnip, 2440e.
parson, 2796a.
part, 723.
—* (696,1124).
—(go away), 2274-1124.

PAR	PAS	PAT
partake, 5159-723.	— money, 16391.	patron, 5108-328.
partial, 5159-3487.	passenger, 4060a.	patronize, 3367-
partiality, 3487-	passed time, 1668d.	467.
3593.	passion(anger),	pattens, 1969.
partially, 1624-	2929.	pattern, 5201-
723.	—(desire), 4766-	(4667).
participate, 5159-	5252.	patties, 1744o.
723.	— flower, 879n.	pauper, N-1255a.
particularize,370c.	passionate, 767-	pause, 1086-(907).
particle, 4140,	3658.	pave, 3511-3879-
2656,c.	passive, N-5247.	3187.
—(gr), 1213-4672.	passover, the	pavement,3879-2426.
parti-colored,4475-	4877a.	paving stone,3188d.
3917.	passport,2426-3508,	pavilion, 4361.
particular, 4667a.	291a.	paw, 3863-191,107.
—(important),	password, 1110d.	pawn, 4235, 26.
1541a.	past, 2101-1089,	— broker,4235-328.
particularly,4083a.	1279a.	— shop, 26, 4235-
parties to case,	— tense(gr), 297,	3514.
1726g.	1089,2399.	— ticket, 26a.
parting, 2274-3318.	paste, 4523-3120.	pay, 648-3028, 207,
— of the way,3572-	—,* 2889, 4364,	1494.
401-2426.	3324.	— taxes,2836-4005.
partition, 1448-	pasteboard, 216-	— respects, 2629-
3187.	3530.	1015.
—,* 1477.	paster, 3324-4529.	— wages, 2312a.
—, cloth 5004a.	pastor, 2796a.	— day, 2312a-5137.
partisan, 4232a.	pastry,4153d,2689c,	peace, 3497a, 5059-
partner, 769a,4459-	3276.	(2797).
3390.	—(covered dish),	peaceful(quiet),
partridge, 172a.	2059e.	4566.
party, 4232.	pasture, 2796-4776.	peacefully, 3107.
—, republican	pat, 3423.	peach, 4392.
2618c.	patch, 3330.	— gum, 4392d.
— spirit, 4232-	— work, 3478.	peacock, 1232c,
1033.	path, D-2426.	1515c.
pass, /216.	pathology, 3278-	— feather, 1232c-
—(gate), 99.	2528.	2712.
—,* 2100-(1221).	patience, 5114a.	peak, 3793-4129.
— book, 3342a.	patient, to be	peaked, 4550.
— by, 2100.	5114a.	peanuts, 650d.
— customs, 2052d.	patois, 4380-4960.	pear, russet 2279a.
— the night,2101a.	patrimony, 1368b.	—, native 2279b.
passage, 2426,2779,	patriot, 3099-2103-	pearl, 137a.
1190.	Y.	— barley, 1285a,
—(on ship), 3999-	patrol, 4837a.	1259a.
5014.	—,* 405-1430, 648-	—, mother of
— boat,4211-(3999).	4837.	5027b.

PEA	PEN	PER
— mussel, 4417d.	penholder, 3237-1762.	percolate, 3828-2262.
peas, 1121d,4116a.	peninsula, 3389-4384.	percussion cap, 2726a,
—, trestle for 2277a.	penis(common term), 4723.	perdition, 458a-3987.
peasant, 1045a-Y.	—(polite term), 5196a.	peremptory, 1541.
peat, 4300a.	penitence,853-3593.	perennial,158-2895.
pebble, 631c,3879-D.	penknife, 4195-D.	perfect, 3948-4815.
peck, 4109.	penmanship, 3237.	—,* 3948.
—,* 4135, 4137.	pennant, 1953-4031.	perfectly, 3846a.
pecul, 5133-3170-1534.	pennib, 3237-4627.	perfidious, 1467a.
pedestal, 596.	penniless, N-2635-4761.	perforate, 603.
pedler, 664-D.	penny, 4033-4462-4761.	perform, 986,4593.
peddler's boat, 2392a.	pennyroyal, 3879-3361a.	— in music 4501.
peel, 3468.	pension, 512-2311.	perfume,1046-[5149, 2400].
—,* 2743-3468.	pentagon,2962-1744-5230.	perhaps, 4966a.
peep, 2122-4287.	pentecost, 4839a.	peril, 3015a.
peerless, N-4250.	penurious, 933.	period, 4151.
peevish, 2866a.	peony, 4048a-650.	— of time, 3905d.
peg, 4127-4084,2796-4127.	people, 5117-4124.	periodic,2518-3905.
Pekeo tea, 409t.	—(population), 1006b.	periodical(monthly) 4937-3337.
pelf, 4761-4803.	—, the 2618,2104d, 3170-3657.	—(quarterly),2066-3337.
pelican, 3058b.	—, to sell 2570b.	periosteum, 2083-2750.
pellet, 4058-4667.	pepper, 3126d.	perish, 2701-2753.
pelt, 3802-3468.	—, powdered 2792b.	perishable, 1291-4965.
—,* 4131.	peppermint, 3361a.	peritoneum, 513-2750.
pelvis, 3552d.	peppers, 2195b.	periwig, 1419-4339-683.
pen, 3237.	peppery, 4575.	perjure, 681-5069-3821.
—(enclosure), 2181.	per, 2774.	perjury, 5069-3821.
—, foreign 2606a-3237.	peradventure,4966a.	permanent employment, 1877f.
penal law,5231-682.	perambulate, 5151-986.	permeate,4452-4338.
penalty, 734a.	perceive,1745-4081.	permit,4766g-(216).
penates, 3835a.	—(see), 1663.	—* 377.
pencil, 3237.	perceptible, 4314-4081-K.	—(let alone), 5148-4328.
—, lead 4921d.	perch, 4701.	pernicious, 2293-1135.
— shaped articles, 3237.	—(fish),2413-4872.	
—, slate 3879-3237.	perchance, 4966a, 3040a.	
pending, 2665-4132.		
pendulum, 3167.		
penetrate, 4452.		
penguin, 3058c.		

PER	PHA	PIC
perpendicular, 4276a.	phantom, 1380,a.	—(type), 3845-1287-4672.
perpetrate, 986, 4593, 4610.	pharmacology, 5183-1140.	pick(choose), 1468.
perpetual, 5051.	pharmacy, 5183-798.	—(as fruit), 79.
perpetuity, 5051-4929.	pharisee, 684a.	— up, 147,2888.
perplexed, 669a.	pheasant, 1515a.	pickax, 816b.
perquisites, 2120-3028.	—, argus, 2472a.	picket, 304.
perroquet,3674-43b.	—, golden, 1515b.	pickle, 1366-926.
persecute,2135-370, 3280-1135.	—, peacock, 1515c.	pickled, 926.
persimmon, 4860.	phenomenon, 4531.	pickles, 2097c.
persist,1086a-1388.	philology, 3357c.	pickpocket, 442d, 402a.
person, 5117,5014.	philosopher, 3357a.	picture, 4961.
—(body), 3830.	philosophy, 285a.	pictures for children, 1878d.
—, in 4712-3830.	—, mental 3658a.	picul, 4040, 5133-3170-1534.
personal,4712,3388.	—, natural 1450c.	pidgin English, 926a.
perspicacious, 2690b.	phlegm, 4289.	pie, 2059e.
perspicuous, 2690a.	phoenix, 898.	—(bird), 1030a.
perspiration,1168.	phonetic,5089-4672.	piece, 652.
perspire, 648-1168.	— system,5089-682.	—(bit), 3721.
persuade,1207-874.	phonetics, 3880-5089-1140.	—(of cloth), 3458.
perturb, 1403-2474.	phonograph, 2247d.	—(work), 1877e.
peruse, 4258,1158.	phonography, 1458b-3616.	pier, 2564b.
pervade, 4452-508.	photmia serrulata, 2192d.	pierce, (1559,603), 4623.
perverse,2946,4981, 2029.	photograph, 3632.	piety, filial 960.
pervious,4338-4081.	—. * 5228a,3616b.	—, religious 1975-1680.
pestilence, 5021.	photographic plate, 5228a-3491.	pig, 312.
pestle, 386-(596).	phrase, 1853.	— basket, 2533a.
—, foot 4252.	phraseology, 1853-682.	—, small 4482d.
petal, 650-3491.	phrenology, 3632-2926.	— stye, 312-4113.
petition, 3226.	phthisis, 692b, 2414a.	pigeon, 3178i.
petrified rock, 3879.	physic, 5182.	—, wild 3183a.
petrify, 3293-5013-3879.	physical,5159-5350.	pigment, 2997-2400.
petroleum, 3879-5149.	physician, 1249c.	pigmy, 34-D.
petruding, 4106.	physics, 2636l, 3357b.	pigs, to rear 4785b.
petticoat, 2937-2139.	physiognomy, 3632.	pigtail, 3288.
petty, 3674,3615a.	—(science), 3632-1140.	pike, 4735.
pew, 4793-5014.	physiology, 4315c.	—(fish), 4872g.
pewter,3619b,4921b.	piano, 1911a.	pile, 2230, 4248, 4059.
	pica(bird), 1030a.	—(accumulate), 4538.

PIL	PIS	PLA
— driver, 622a.	pistil, 650c.	—(country), 3497-
piles(wooden), 304.	pistol, 3859f.	4919.
—(disease), 236a,	piston, 167, 3754.	—(even), 3497.
4830d.	pit, 4328, 4291.	—, to make 1062b.
pilfer, 3674b.	—, deep 4515.	plaintiff, 1726e.
pilferer, 3674b,	pitch, 3160b,4849d.	plait, 3290.
3574b.	— dark, 971b.	—, * 4027-3290.
pilgrim, 5151-921.	— out, 403.	plan, 682a.
pill, (5183)-4923,	pitcher, 4004-560.	—(map), 4393.
4058.	—, earthenware	— * 2641.
—, was coated	4947.	—(counsel), 127a.
2192h.	— plant, 313e.	plane(surface),
pillage, 4737-1688.	pitchfork,5060-401.	3497-2687.
pillar, 596.	pith, 3996-3593.	—(tool), 3445.
pillory, 1412.	— hat, 4453b.	—, * 3444.
pillow, 128a.	— paper, 4453a.	— mensuration,
—, * 131.	pithy, 5159-2330.	779a.
— case, 128b.	pitiless,3001-3593.	planet, 986e.
pilot, 4031d.	pitiful, 1117b.	— Jupiter, 2795g.
pimp, 2059g.	pits, 5044.	— Mars, 7671.
pimple, 4856a.	pitted(pocked),	— Mercury, 4004L.
pin, (4033)-4339-	4118a.	— Neptune, 1125h.
126.	pity, 2351-3752.	— Saturn, 4130c.
pin together,1445.	—, 1117b,2351a.	— Uranus, 4355h.
pinafore, 2139a.	pivot, 371.	— Venus, 1527f.
pincers, 1971.	placard, 4365.	plank, 3187.
pinch, 4494.	—, anonymous	plant, 4777.
—, * 2912, 2699.	3178b.	—, * 397.
pine(tree), 4849.	—, street 288c.	plantago, 490L.
—(wood), 427.	place, 3987, 4125-	plantain, 4574.
— cones, 4849e.	779.	plaster, 845.
pineapple, 3347.	—(building, etc),	—(medical), 1714a.
pink(flower),2440f.	3977.	— of paris, 3879h.
pinnacle, 4129.	—(as in the first	—, * 4239, 2623a.
pint, 3942.	place), 4487.	plat, 3228.
pioneer,1124-2426/.	—(position), 5014.	plate, 4175.
pious, 1975-(3593).	— of records,2071.	—, iron 4366-3187.
pip(seed), 5044.	—, * 116,3110,795.	— photographic
— of fowl, 1921a.	— on top, 4065.	/3491.
pipe, 4461, 1008.	placenta, 4417b,	—, * 4214.
—, earthenware	3199b, 1013f.	platform,4422,3431.
2981b.	placid, 5059-1033.	platinum,3178-1526.
— elbow, 496d.	plagiarism, 447-	play, 4973a.
—, opium 1335m.	3660.	—(theatrical),
—, suction 1926b.	plague, 5021a.	1037.
—, water 1008f.	—, * 2834a.	— * 4973a,661.
— clay,4452h-2844.	plaice, 4872g.	—(at cards), 4027.
pirate, 1125-4682.	plain, 2690a.	

PLA	PLU	POL
—(at dice), 82a.	plummet, /4411.	—(ceremonial),
—(instrument),	plump, 759c.	2206a.
4304.	plunder, 4614.	political science,
— organ, piano,	—,* 4027-1688,	2104e.
1911b.	2310.	politics,2103-3776.
—(stage), 4593-	plunge, 4340.	pollen, 713a.
1037.	plural(gr), 4124.	pollute, 3113-2775.
— tennis, 3347a.	Pluto, 1322a.	polygamy,4215-4825.
—(wind instrument)	pneumatics, 1033b.	polygon, 4215-1744-
614.	pocket, 4224.	5230.
player, 1037d.	— glass, 1637a.	polypus, 3269-2132.
playful, 2054b.	pockmarked, 4118c.	pomatum, 4339-683-
plea, 311b, 3686.	pod, 4116-1492.	5149.
pleasant, 4081b,	poem, 3899.	pomegranate, 2252a.
1099.	poet, 3899-5117.	—, flowering 767q.
please(request),	poetess, 3899-2949.	pomfret, 4810-4872.
669b.	poignant,2194,813.	pommel, 4027.
pleased, 856a.	point, 4550.	pomp, 673-4958.
pleasure,651½-2455.	—(dot), 4151.	pond, 535, 4438.
plebian,4637,3244a.	— of fact, 1955c.	ponder, 3631,2891.
pledge, 4235-4339.	— of light, 3652.	ponderous,645-4033.
—,* (3110)-4235.	—,* 215.	pongee, 478.
plenary, 2785.	— bricks, 2623b.	—, raw 478a.
plentiful, 881a.	pointed, 4550,4627.	—, soft 478b.
plenty, 3957,4215.	poison,4260-(2636).	—, undyed 1470b.
plethora, 309c.	poisonous, 4260.	pony, D-2561.
pliable, 5152-4930.	poke, 4855,2394.	pool, 535, 4438,
pliers, 1971-D.	poker, 767-3435.	4328.
—, cutting 4554-	pokeweek, 872.	poor, 2031, 3449a.
1971.	pole, 1764,3942.	—(emaciated),3862.
plight, 4125-5014.	—, north 1654a.	—(in quality),
—,* 4235,5221b.	—, south 2823a.	5087.
plot, 1521.	— cat, 2594a.	—(thin), 3361.
—(lot), 4066.	—,* 436.	pope, 1507h.
—(plan), 4393.	polianthes, 5250d.	poplar, 5195.
—,* 2641.	police, 411a.	popping sound,3399.
plough, 2201.	—(H.K.,Shameen)	poppy, 3737b,5278a.
—,* 2202c, 1480.	2507c.	populace,3170-3657.
—share, 2202a.	— whistle, 1515j.	popular, 4939a.
pluck,* 2631.	policy, insurance	population, 1006b,
—(fruit), 79.	4047a.	1335c.
plug, 151,3592.	polish, 5149.	porcelain, 4864-
—,* 3592-339.	—,*2740-2105,4696.	(1035).
plum, 2767, 2288.	polite, 5159-2205-	porch, 2248b.
plumage, 4518-2712.	2599.	porcupine, 313a,b.
plumbing, 1008f-	politeness, 2205-	pores, 2712a, 1988.
3776.	2599.	pork, 312-5249.
plumbline, 4410a.		

POR	POS	PRE
porpoise, 313d.	posterity, 4667-3704, 1013d.	preacher, 613a-Y.
porridge, 2607c.	postman, 3743-411.	precarious, 3015a.
port, 1780-(1006)-745-(4339).	postpone, 4447-536.	precaution, /4321a.
—, leave 648c.	postscript, 4607-3237.	precede, 3645.
— the helm, 2421c.	pot, 3122.	precedent, 2207b.
— wine, 4500a.	—(boiling), 3326.	preceding, 2897, 3639.
porter(at door), 1158-2779.	—(large cooking), 5054, 5066.	precept, 1507a.
—(carrier), 4035-4040-L.	—, chamber 3295e.	precincts, 1676a.
portfolio, 1485b.	—, tea 409g.	precious, 3331-(3381).
portico, 2461,4361.	potash, 1471.	precipice, (2987)-2994.
portion,(723,4667).	potatoes, 3991a, 1121e.	precise, 275.
Portland cement, 5222e, 1235g.	—, sweet 656a.	precisely, 2993a.
portly, 759b.	potbelly, 2830a.	preclude, 2681-228.
portmanteau, 1485c.	potency, 2330.	precocious, 2195c.
portrait,3632,4530.	potent, 5159-2330.	predecessor, 3639/.
portray, 3616b.	pottage, 4431,1551.	predict, 3639-1779.
Portuguese 3584h.	pottery, 2981-(1035),1770-2981.	predisposed, 3639-1053.
position, (4125)-5014.	pouch, 1121a, 4224.	pre-eminent, 648-395.
positive, 3854.	poultice,5183-1714.	preen, 4135.
— charge, 634c.	poultry, 1515-24.	pre-engaged, 3639-5221.
— principle,5196.	pound, 3374.	preface, 3674c, 3982a.
positively, 5133-4132.	— * 4086,4027.	prefect, 205a.
posse, 309b.	—(as rice), 386.	prefecture, 814.
possess, 5159.	pour, 4197, 127.	prefer, 2898-4932.
possessed, 2601.	pout, 4106-4627.	pregnant,4963-5123, 4409a.
possessions, 3977-5159.	poverty, 3449a.	prejudice, 3487a.
possessive(gr), 1600, 204.	powder, 713, 2792.	premature, 4586.
possible, 1117,a, 4081a.	power, 2007a, 4804-2858.	premises, 339-3977, 1186.
post, 304.	—(strength), 2330.	premium, 3889.
—(mail), 5218.	—, moving 1601.	—, insurance 3329a.
—(military), 5235.	powerless, N-2330.	— on exchange, 3028e.
— office, 5154a-1875, 3982d.	practically, 1117-5282.	prepare, 4895b.
—(pillar), 596.	practice,4476-2358.	— food, 329.
—(position), 2010.	—, medical 765a.	prepared, 4705.
postage, 3743d.	—, sharp 1875c.	prepay, 3639-1494.
poster, 288b,c.	praise, 4472,a.	Presbyterian church, 190b.
posterior, 1013.	prance, 4371.	
	prawns, 900c.	
	pray, 1951a.	
	preach, 613a,3982f.	

PRE	PRI	PRO
prescription, 5183-779.	—, Jewish 4483a.	probe, 123.
presence, 2687a.	—, Roman Catholic 836b.	proboscis, 3241a.
present(place), 965, 4609.	—, Tauist 4207-3777.	procedure, 682a, /986.
—(time), 1526.	primary current, 2245e.	proceed, 4760-1221.
—(gift),2205-2636.	— school, 1141c.	process, 682a.
—,* 3750.	prime, 4076-5133.	procession, /648-5151.
— offering, 1067.	— minister, 4605-3632.	proclaim, 3703-613.
— age, 3818b.	primitive, 4919-3388.	proclamation,1726b.
— world, 3818b.	primrose, 2353b.	procrastinate,4447-536, 4190a.
presently, 4504, 4522a.	prince,(2074)-5072.	procure, 2433.
preserve,3329,3861.	princess, 2074-328.	procurer, 2059g.
preserves, 2097b.	principal, 4339.	procuress, 2553b.
preside over, 1819a.	—(money), 3388-(4761).	prodigal, 491-4958.
preside over, 1819a.	principally, 4215.	—, a 2468-4607.
president, 3143-4339.	principle, 4207a.	prodigious, S-4033.
— of republic, 4653d.	print, 980b.	prodigy, 4560-2048.
press, 2071.	—,* 5116-4672.	produce, 430b.
—, oil 62.	printed calico, 3336b.	—,* (3802,648), 430.
—, printing 5116-4672-1602a.	printer's chase, 2114a.	—(as fruit), 1694, 3802.
—,* 25-604, 3279, 77, 62.	— copy, 1722.	produce fruit, 2096d.
— together, 1485a.	printing blocks, 3187.	product, /2636.
pressing,1558-4769.	— office, 5116-3982-1875.	—, local 430b.
prestige,2671-3880.	prior, 3639.	products of the soil, 430b.
presume, 1754.	prison, 1455-(798).	productions, 430.
pretend,1419/3017.	prisoner, 1455-678, 479.	profane, 3662a.
pretty, 1056-4314, 2303.	private, 3758a.	profess, 4671-553.
prevail, 5234.	privately, 3758b.	profession, 1368,a.
prevent, 296.	privileges, 2293c.	professor, 1507b, 3802f.
previous,3896,3639.	privy, 3902a,4857.	profile, 2964b.
previously, 3639a. 4895-3639.	— council, 1747a.	profit, 5204,2293c.
price, 1421a.	prize, 3889-(4853).	—,* 88.
—(value), 243.	—(pry), 1711-1031.	profitable, 5159-5204.
prick, 1559,4855.	probably, 1998a, 4966a,2041,3409.	profligate, 795d.
prickles,2218,4855.	probation, 3903-1330.	profound, 3823.
prickly heat, 693a.		— kindness, 1238b.
pride, 3055-1033.		profusion, 4215.
— of India, 813b.		progeny, 4667-3704, 1013d.
priest, Buddhist 5059b.		

prognosticate, (247)-3400.
progress,4760-4644.
prohibit, 1530-217.
project, 4106-648.
prolapse, 360a.
prolific, 881,4215-3802.
prologue, 3674c.
prolong, C-512.
prominence, 4106.
promise, 5221b.
promissory note, 1984-4046.
promontory, 3793-4627, 4380b.
promote, 1409, 299.
—(in rank), 4321.
prompt, 651½-4573.
promulgate, 613-1779.
pronoun of first person, 3065.
—, second person, 2875.
—, third person, 2026.
pronounce, 1779-648.
pronunciation, 1001-5089,1971b.
proof, 3454a.
—, printer's 1722.
prop, 436, 4129.
propagate,3802-648.
—(as doctrine), 613.
propel, 4447-4760, /986.
— with oars, 113.
propeller, 3106-2518,2663-490.
— driven boat, 4000b.
proper, 184, 1193.
property, 430a, 4803,2636d.

prophecy,4895-1350.
prophet, 3639b.
prophetess, 2949-3639b.
propitiate, 5059-657.
propitious, 1560.
proportion, rule of 3251a.
propose, 648-328b.
proprietor, 328, 4272a.
propriety, 2205.
prosecute, 1726d.
prosecutor, 1726e.
proselyte, 1739-1507-Y.
prospect, 1678a.
—(as miner), 4287.
prospectus, 4570-2308.
prosper, 1072a,681-4803.
prosperous, 1072a.
prostitute, 502a, 3039e.
—, to become 2570d.
prostrate, 3404-4197.
protect, 3329-(5165).
protest, 1726-3686.
Protestant churches 1507d.
protuberant, 4106.
proud, 1699-3055.
prove, 1330-648.
proverb, 4637-4890.
Proverbs, book of 125h.
provide, 1923.
—(prepare), 4895b.
province, 3804.
provincial city, 3804a.

provisions, 2636c, 768a, 10061.
provoke, 1649.
prow, 3999-4339.
proxy, 4222-2285.
prudence, 229a.
prune,*/1832,3804.
prunes 2767a,2288.
—, dried 2767b.
prunus japonica, 2288a.
pry(spy), 2122a.
— up, 1710.
psalms, 3945-3899, 3899-3488.
psychology, 3593e.
puberty, 3830c.
—, female 4355-2069.
—, male 3948-4463.
public, 1878.
—, the 2618,3170-3657.
— road, 1815a.
publish(as books), 648/.
—(propagate),3703-613.
pucker(lips),2600.
—(wrinkle), 4502.
pudding, 2689c.
puddle, 4328.
— iron, 448a.
puff, 133, 141.
puffed up, 1699-3055.
pull, 2151, 2631, 2584.
—(pick), 79.
— to pieces, 422.
— up, 3241.
pullet, 1513e, 1515-Y.
pulley, 2437d,2501.
pulp, 5249,2944.
pulpit,4422a,1341a.
pulse, 4116.

PUL	PUS	QUA
—(blood), 2608.	pus, 2954.	quality, 3658-150,
pulverize, /3721.	push, 4946, 4447.	/4097.
pumice, 38791.	— off, 436.	quantity,3972,4394-
pummelo, 2503a,	pustules, 3674-578.	3966.
5166a.	put, 116,795,3110.	—(math). 1624e.
pump, 493-4004-	—(affix), 4364.	quarrel, 92, 15a.
1601a.	— down, 2454.	quarrelsome, 977.
pumpkin, 2037d.	— forth,648.	quarry, 3879-2108.
punch, /310,/4612.	— into, 5132.	—,* 4797a.
punctual,1247-1952.	— on(as plaster),	quarter hour,2056d.
punctuate, 4151-	4239.	—, one 723a,1744i.
1853.	— on(as seal),	— year, 2066.
puncture, 1559,123.	1923.	—,* 1086-3736.
pungent, 2194.	— on trestles,	quartz, 4004-4561.
punica granatum,	2457.	— amethyst, 4561d.
3107g.	— out, 3634.	—, greasy 2192f.
punish, 734, 75b.	— to shame, 3604.	—, smoky 4561b.
punishment, 734a.	— together, 1485a.	quash, 3529a.
—, capital 275a.	— up at auction,	quassia, 2795a.
punk, moxa 2988a.	4340a.	quay, 2561j.
punkah, 879-3930.	putchuk, 2795d.	queen, 5071-1016.
puny, 3589a.	putrid, 474,842a.	— bee, 2637d.
pup, 4482c.	putty, 4465a.	queer, 1950,2220b.
pupil, 1141b.	puzzle(toy), 3783a.	quell, 2701.
— of eye, 2999a.	pygmy, 34-4482.	quench, 2701.
puppet show, 2061d.	pyramid, 4550-779-	— thirst, 1436a.
puppy, 4482c.	5230.	query, 2629-4960.
purchase, 2569.	python, 3158e.	quest, 4710.
pure, 4763-1693,		question,2629-4960.
4016.		—* 2629.
—(chaste), 265.		—(doubt), 3759-
—(clean), 1760a.	**Q**	1263.
purgative, 3617-		queue, 3289.
5183.		quick, 651⅓.
purgatory, 2357b.	quack, 310c.	—(clever), 2363a.
purge, 3617.	—,* 23-23.	—(hasty) 1558.
purify, C-1693.	quadrangular,3772a.	—(living), 3802.
purple, 4670-3919.	quadrant, 496d.	quickening, 4417a.
purpose, 328b,230a.	quadruped, /3863.	quicker, 4139c.
purposely, 4083a.	quaff, 5095.	quicklime, 845b.
purse, 1121a, 3028-	quail, 3101a.	quickly, 4139c.
4224.	—,* 3849-230.	quickness of under-
— the lips, 2703.	quaint, 1796-2048.	standing, 2361b.
purslane, 1362b.	quake, 138a.	quicksands, 3779a.
pursue, (356,1765).	—, earth 138b.	quicksilver, 3028d.
— animals, 2380.	qualified, 2858,	quiet, (3107)-4566.
pursuit, 1368a.	1117a.	—(peaceful), 3497.

QUI	RAD	RAN
—(rest), 3633.	radishes, 2440d.	ranks, 2967a, 141.
quietly, 4566-4566.	radium, 5246-150.	rankle, /3593-2078.
quietness, 3497a.	radius, 3389-1883b.	ransom, 4014.
quill, 3058e.	raffle, 3048-3924.	rant, 2143-1779.
quilt, 3473.	raft, 3421.	rap, 3423, 953.
—, cotton 4417e.	rafter, (941)-1746.	rapacious, 3075.
—,* 2837.	rag, 2186-3336.	rape, 1466b.
quilted,2837.	rage, 720-2929.	rapid, 1558-4832.
quince, 2037i.	raging, 2143.	rapids, 4293.
quinine, 1527e.	rail, 4367e.	rapping sound,3399.
quinsy, 3058h.	—(bird), 364-1515.	rapture,2599a-856a.
quire of paper,	—,* 2298a.	rare, 1020a.
4195b.	railing, 2180-1762.	rarities,1950-2636,
quirk, 2867-1521.	railway, 4367d.	3155b.
quit,217,1086,3857.	— station, 86b.	rascal, 1467c.
— work, 795b.	rain, 4888.	rash, 2143, 743a.
quite, 3846a.	—,* 2454-4888.	rasp, 4792.
—, not 92d.	rainbow, 1237.	raspberry, 3874.
quiver, /4224.	rainy looking,459a.	rat, 3984a.
—,* 138.	raise, 1031,1849.	— trap,3984a-2533.
quorum, 4033-3389.	—(as pay) 3942.	rate, 1421.
quote, 5121-(4025).	—(rear), 5198.	—, tax 1049.
	— wall, 2230.	rather, 2899a,3526.
R	raised(in relief),	ratify, 4132/.
	4106.	rations, 2311,1049.
rabbet, 2261.	raisins,1760-3517b.	rattan, 4332.
—,* 5132-2261.	rake, 3414.	—, bind with
rabbit, 3178-4387.	—(man), 6501.	4333d.
rabble, 908-2618.	—(bamboo), 3415.	rattle, 2223.
rabid, 2143,4159.	—(iron), 3414a.	—,* 2502, 3048.
race, 2494, 391.	—,* 3412.	—, death 494a.
—,* 3437.	ram, 5193-G.	— snake,1048-2663-
—, horse 4236a.	—,* 386, 310.	3874.
races, 3437-2561.	ramble, 5151-986,	rave, 2143/.
rack, 1424.	2055.	ravelled, 2474.
racket, 4783.	rampart, /1606.	raven, 3115-4, 4a.
racking, 813a.	rancid, 3620-474,	ravenous, 3066-S.
racquet, tennis	5209.	ravine, 1866a,940.
3347a-3187.	random, 3513b,2474.	raving, 4158.
radiate, 3877.	range(stove), 767f,	ravish, 4737.
radiation, 3576-	4591.	—(force), 1466b.
1372.	—(mountain), 2377.	raw, 3802.
radicals, the	rank,3680,3620,474.	— metals, 2108.
3342b.	—(grade), (4097,	ray(light), 3877-
radio, 3857-5089-	1924).	2105.
1601.	—(position), 3225.	—(fish), 3471c,
	—(row), 1186.	3328.

RAZ	REC	REF
razor, 4317-4195.	recently, 3596, 1546-2445.	reference to, with 2528a.
reach, 4203.	recipe, 779b.	refine, 2356.
—(comparison), 1927.	reciprocal, 3130-3625.	refined, 2982.
— with hand, 3082.	recite, 2891.	refit, 3603-274.
read(aloud), 4258.	reckon, 4153a,3708.	reflect(as light), 661-291.
—(silently), 4314.	— accounts, 1521a.	—(think), 3631.
readily, 1291.	reclaim, 2433-657.	reform, 1739-275, 2057b.
ready, 4705a,3295.	recline, 715.	Reformed Presbyterian Mission, 5178c.
— made, 1361b.	recognize, 5240.	refrain,* /1437, /5114.
— money, 1361c.	recoil, 4197b,4473.	refresh, 3330,3981.
—, to make 3295a.	recollect, 1627a,b.	refreshments,4153d.
real, 136.	recommend, 1850a.	refuge, 4216-3265-3987.
reality, 136-3854.	—(advise), 1207.	refund, 4972.
really,3855a,2096a.	recommendation, 4557-3982.	refuse, 59a.
— good, 3001c.	recompence, 3337.	—,* 4447-4861, N-4569.
realm, 2103,a.	reconcile, 5059/.	refute, 3355-5234.
ream, 2130,2888a.	recondite, 3086-2708.	regain, 4081-657.
reap, 3858c,1832.	reconnoitre, 4027-4287.	regard,* 1811,3752.
reaping instrument, 2339.	record, 2509.	— as, 1278a,3708, 4235.
rear, 2663, 1013-3295.	—,* 1627.	regardless, 2528d.
—(as building), 1031.	recorded in, 4608.	regards, 2629-1015.
—(raise), 5198.	recoup, 4707-657.	regatta, 4110-3999.
reason(cause), 1809b.	recover, 4081-657.	regeneration, [4607, 645]-3802.
—(principle), 4207a.	—(from illness), 1099-657.	regiment, 5235.
—,* 2528.	recruit, 3596-3300.	region, 4125-779.
reasonable, 5159-4207a, 2285b.	—,* 288-3300.	register, 423.
rebel,* 661.	rectify, 274-275.	—,* 423b, 333a.
— against, 3378.	rectum, 513b.	registered letter, 4036b.
rebellion, 2474.	recumbent, /13.	regret, 853a, 3636.
rebels, 5214-4682.	recur, /5163,/4607.	regretable, 3636a.
rebound, 4473-1031.	red, 1235.	regular, 1247-682, 275.
rebuild, 4607-1031.	reddish, 547.	regulate, 589-235.
rebuke, 75d.	redeem, 4014.	regulations, 2120-2207, 186a.
recant, 661-1006.	redress a grievance 3831a.	reign, 4593-5072.
recede, 4449,4330b.	reduce, 1457.	reimburse,4972-657.
receipt, 3858-4046.	reed, 2409-4149.	
receive, 4569-3857.	reel, 2501.	
—(as teaching), 3865.	—,* 787.	
receiver, telephone 4461d.	refer, 215.	

REI	REM	REP
rein, 3273-4339.	remiss, /2185a.	—(speak), 4061.
reindeer, 2510a.	remit(as sentence),	report(rumor),879f.
reinforce, /299.	795.	—(sound), 1047,
reinstate, /657.	—(forgive), 3873-	3366.
reiterate, 2222a.	2681.	—(written), /2509.
reject, 4182-1034.	—(relax), 3748.	—,* 3337, 3226.
rejoice, 856a,651½-	—(send), 1629.	repose, 3107-4566.
2455.	remnants,3956,3721.	represent(in place
rejoiner, 3137b.	remonstrate, 1208a.	of), 4222.
relapse,/4607,/875.	remorse, 4673b.	—(stand for),
relate, 1779.	remorseless, 4695a.	4610-968.
related, 4712.	remote, 4929.	—(symbolize),
—(belonging to),	remove(by shears),	3319-2690.
4012.	4555.	repress, 25, 117,
relatives, 4712-	—(from office),	1530, 974.
4743.	1449.	reprimand,75d,4960.
—, male 1070.	—(move), 3384.	reprisal, 3337-875.
relax, 3748.	—(put away), 593,	reproach,5255-2567.
release, 795.	4446.	reproduction, or-
relent, /853.	remunerate, 3546-	gans of 3802-245-
relevant, 2052f.	657.	1035.
relic, 5003-2636.	rend, 2385.	reprove, 75d,4960.
relict, 2038-835.	renew, C-3596.	reptile, 2178d,646.
relief, in 4106.	rent, 4583.	republic, 2618b.
relieve, 1582-4484.	—(torn), 2186.	republican party,
religion, 1507.	— paid in kind,	2618b.
religious, 1680-	4583a.	repudiate, 3377.
1975.	repair, 274a, 3603-	repulse, 4027-4449.
relinquish, 3870.	274, 3330.	repulsion, 2027-
relish, 2666d.	repay, 4972-657,	2330.
—,* 3913,205-2666.	4062a.	repulsive, 4107b.
reluctant, 2185.	repeal, 3795a.	reputation, 2669-
rely on, 1247a.	repeat, 4607/.	2880, 4315e.
remain, 2247-339.	—(as lesson),2891.	—, to blast 4182a.
— over, 3956.	repeatedly, 4607-	request, 3977-1936-
remainder, (4871)-	3572, 2486.	K.
3956.	repel, 1604a.	—,* 1936-4734.
remark(observe),	repent, 853-1739.	—,as favor, 3168a.
4314-1663.	repetition, 359a.	require, 3717-1388.
—(speak), 4960.	repine, 4913.	requite, 4062a.
remarkable, 749a,	replace, 3107-657.	rescind, 3668a.
1950.	—(make good),3330-	rescue, 1582,555a.
remedy, 682a.	657.	research, 957a.
—(medicine), 5183.	replant, 4607-397.	resemble, 4868-.
remember, 1627a,	replenish,2779-657.	resentment, 4913-
1625a.	reply, 3137b.	981.
remind, 4321-3621.	—,* 3137a,3337.	— to cherish
		1156a.

reserve, 2247-655.	restaurant, 4154a, 1713d.	retrograde, 4197-986.
reserved, 3823-457.	—(light lunch), 409d.	return, 655, 662, 3135.
reservoir, 4435, 535, 626b.	resting place, 4361.	—(restore), 4972.
reside, 1846a.	restitution, 3546-3331.	— to one's country, 3137d.
residence, 339a.	restive, 29-1636.	reunite, 1193-657-2568.
resign, 1726i.	restless, 2710-2898-2938.	reveal, 1061-648.
—(be submissive), 874, 3983a.	restoration, 875-3135.	revel, 2842-4500.
resiliency, 3983b.	restore, 4976-3135.	revelation, 2611a, 1901a.
resin, 4849a.	—(save), 1582-657.	revenge, 477a.
resist, (2004)-2027, 4233.	restrain, 2016a, 2134a,1819e,1530.	revenue, 827a,4005.
resistance, 296.	restrict, 939a.	reverberation,5229-1047.
resolute,1660-3593.	restriction, 743.	revere, 1881-1680.
resolve, 328b.	results, 2096,d.	reverence, (1881)-1680.
—,* 4132-328b, 2190.	resume, /657.	reverse, 2687b.
resonance, 1047-3658.	resurrection, 875a.	—,* 4330b, 661.
resonant, 1047.	resusitate, 875a.	revert, 2057-661.
resound, 1047.	retail trade, 3674-3802c.	review, 4607-4942.
—(echo), 3135.	retain, 2246.	— troops, 4942-4776.
resource,1221-2426.	retake, 2433-657.	— book, 3446a.
—, no 2711c.	retaliate, 4972a, 4062a.	revile, 2842,4988a.
respect, 1680.	retard, 296b.	revise, 3603-1739.
respectable, 5159-4315d.	retch, 4610-54.	revive, 875-3677.
respectful, 1881-1680.	retina, 2999b.	revoke, 690-593.
respecting, 2528a.	retinue, 1536a.	revolt, 3378a,3391.
respects, to pay 3168-1015.	retire, 4449,3618.	revolting, 4698-4684.
respiration, 802-1926.	retired, 4440-4566, 2611.	revolution, 2474.
respite, 1086-3905.	retirement, 4566-383.	—(circuit), 156, 3135.
resplendent, 2105-2105.	retort, 4972-1006.	revolve, 4089a,346.
respond, 4061.	retrace, 3135-3341.	revolver, 2506a, 2350a.
—(answer), 3137a.	retract, 657-1006.	reward, 3889-4853.
responsibility, 4035-4031,3909a.	retreat, 5115-3987.	—(bonus), 650g.
responsible, 3909a.	—,* 4449.	—, * 3287-(4853).
rest, (3107,3633).	retrench,1457-3804.	rewrite, 4607-3616.
—(remainder),3956.	retribution, 3337-5229.	reynard, 2281a.
—* 3633, 4336, 1086, 4360.	retrieve, 4081-657.	rhetoric, 1006f.
		rheum, 4289.

RHE	RIG	ROA
rheumatism, 879L.	— hand, 5164.	roam, 5151.
rhinocerous, 3586a.	righteous, 1292,	roar, 954.
rhubarb, 5070b,	3939.	roaring, 2081.
2314b.	righteousness,	roast, 3965, 3133.
rhyme, 1084.	1878b.	rob, 4737.
rib, 2221,b,2221a.	rigid, 3001.	— by force, 1688.
ribs, 3383b.	rigorous,1316-1541.	robber, (4209)-4682.
ribbon, 4031.	rill, D-1119.	robe, 3791,3520.
rice, broken 2603d.	rim, 3286.	robust, 758a,309a.
—, cooked 677.	rinderpest, 5021c.	rock, 3879, 3554a.
—, glutinous 2935-	ring, 1201.	—,* /3167.
2603.	—, finger 1437a.	— fish, 3879L.
—, growing 5060.	— leader, 4339-	— honey, 2637b.
— hulled 2603.	2798.	rocked, 3504.
— paddy, 1864.	—,* 4027-385.	rocket,1031c,3441e.
— paper, 4452a.	ringlet, D-4974.	rocking chair,
—, to buy 2603h.	ringworm, 2154a.	2502-1256.
—, to sell 2603i.	rinse, 2456.	rocky, 4688-2994.
— weevil, 4206.	riot, (2472)-2842-	rod, 2079, 1764.
rich, 823-1014.	3776.	—, fishing 1764a.
— man, 4803-328.	—,* 2472-2842.	roe(deer), 2510-D.
riches, 4803-3179.	rip, 2385.	—(fish), 631b.
rickety, 1264a.	— open, 4430a.	rogue, 4682-D,
ricksha, 490b.	ripe, 4011.	753-D, 2186-D.
rid, 2238.	ripen, 190-4011.	roll, 1838.
riddle, 2605.	— by keeping, 56a.	—,* 346, 2502.
—, to ask 1796b.	ripple, 2619b.	— up, 1839.
ride, in vehicle	rise, 3895, 1031,	roller, 2501.
4793.	3943.	— stone 2131a.
— on animal, 1954.	rising, 4610-2474.	rollers, 4033-2468.
ridge, 4511.	— tide, 570a.	rolling pin, 2998-
—(in field), 2301.	risk, 3551.	2688-2079.
— pole, 2317.	risky, 1055.	Roman Catholic,
ridicule, 525-3675.	rite, 2205a.	1507g.
ridiculous, 1117-	Rites, Board of	— — priest,
3675.	2206f.	836b.
riding whip, 2561b.	rival, 475, 4250-	— nose, 43c.
rifle, (3711)-4736.	4339.	roof, 2981c, 4944-
rifled(grooved),	rivalry, 3652-92.	3377.
5132-2261.	rive, 3477.	room,798,4346,1463.
rift, 2148.	river, 1119, 1771,	—(space), 4125-779.
rigging, 2287a.	1125.	roost, 4701.
right, 184.	rivet, 5054a.	—,* 2640.
—(correct), 275,	—,* 2564c.	root, 1538,a.
1099, 2993.	rivulet, 1898.	—, China 876a.
—(just), 275d.	road, 2426.	—, Szechuen 877c.
—(righteous),1292.	—, public 1815a.	
— angle, 1744c.		

ROO	RUD	RUS

ROO

rootlet, 1967.
rope, 3949.
—(cable), 2173.
rose, 2770a.
— apple, 3518a-2097.
rosewood, 2279c.
rosin, 4849a.
rot(dry), 803a.
—(damp), 2768.
rotate, 2518-347.
rotation, 2518a.
rotten, 2768-2186.
rouble, 2417a.
rouge, 1336-211.
—,* 406-1336-211.
rough, 914.
—(coarse), 4775.
— draft, 1722.
round, 4917.
rouse(from sleep), 3621.
—(provoke), 1649.
rout, 2474-4499.
route, 4207-2426.
rove, 5151.
rover, 5151-Y.
row, 1186, 2196.
—(disturbance), 2843-3776.
—,* 113.
rowdies, 753a.
rowlock, 4525-1638.
royal, 5072-2074.
rub, 406.
—(grind), 2740, 4696.
— between hands, 412.
— out, 2590,2790.
rubber, India 4531a.
rubbish, 2193a.
rubble, 2574a.
ruby, 3332b.
—, Bohemian 4561e.
rudder, 4285,4415.
ruddy, 1235.

RUD

rude(rough), 4775, 1473.
—(impolite),2206e.
rudiment, /572.
— of learning, 3674-1140.
rue, 474b.
—, 853.
rueful, 36a.
ruffian, 1227-4390.
ruffle, 4502-2568.
rug, 253.
rugged, 4688, 1948.
—(as speech), 2221c.
ruin, 3527-3169.
—* 3169-(4965), 2010a.
ruined, 3169,457.
rule, 2120a, 186a.
—(measure), 496.
—(law), 682.
—* 1819a.
—(as paper) 1477b.
— of proportion, 3251a.
ruler, 5072,4605, 328.
rumble, 2081.
rumor, 879f,1280f.
rump, 2663-2532-2083.
rumple, 452.
run, 4499.
—(as water), 2245.
—(race), 3437.
— against, 2118.
— aground, 2004.
runner, 411.
running, 4499,2245.
— hand, 4777b.
— knot, 3985j.
rupture, 2385.
—(hernia), 513.
rural, 1045b.
ruse, 2062b.
rush, 4095b-4777.

RUS

—.* 635-4105.
rushes, 4777.
rust, 3608.
—,* 3802-3608.
rustic, 1045b.
rustling,3778-3778, 3623.
rut, 2063,a, 565.
rye, 3674d.

S

sabbath, 3107e.
sable, 971-4187.
sack, 4224, 2943.
— cloth, 4775-2557b.
sacking, 3336-3198.
sacred, 3945.
sacrifice, 4483-2636.
—* 1067-4483.
—(part with),2764.
sad, 36a,5141-3864.
—. how 3636a.
saddle, 2561d.
sadness, 36a,5141-3864.
safe, 1485d,4367-3626.
—, 5024a.
safflower, 1235c.
saffron, 1235d.
sagacious, 2363.
sage, 3945-Y.
sago, 2603a,b.
said, the 1737.
—, it is 4955.
sail, 2287.
—,* 3816.
—, hoist 2287b.
—, to set 1124a.
— cloth, 672a.

-85-

SAI	SAN	SAV
sailing ship, 5007-3431-3999.	sandal wood, 4305a.	—(wild), 2574, 5173.
sailor, 4004c.	sandals, grass 913b.	save, 1582, 555a.
salad, 4800a.	sandpiper, 3779k, 1846e.	— life, 1582a.
salary, 3605a.	sane, 3593d.	saving, 933, 3804.
sale, 648-2570.	sanguine, 4215-2764-K.	Saviour, 1582c.
salesman, 2570a.	sanitary, 5015-3802.	savor, 2666d.
salient, 4106-648-2200.	sanity, 4673-4609.	saw, 1854.
saline, 5159-1314-2666.	sap, 148, 5244.	—,* 1440, 2151a.
saliva, 4004d.	sapan wood, 3677b.	sawdust, 1176b.
sally, 4499-648.	sapphire, 5250b, 3332c.	saxifrage, 2420d, 3126c.
salmon, 2561-5160-4872.	sarcasm, 4856b.	say, 1779, 4960.
saloon, 921-4435.	sarcenet, 1841, 3780.	— mass, 4027a.
salt, 1314.	sardine, 3779m, 4872m.	sayings, 4890.
—,' 926.	sardius, 2563a.	scab, 2810.
—,* 1366.	sarsaparilla, 877a.	scabbard, 1139b, 1658a.
saltmarsh, 1315b.	—(water), 3779j.	scaffold, 3431, 1424.
saltpetre, 3669.	sash, 4031.	scald, 2511.
salts, epsom 3532a.	Satan, 2061a.	scale(balance), 4355-3497.
salty, 926.	satchel, 1692-4224.	—(musical), 5089-1450.
salubrious, 1099-4004-4380.	satiated, 3202.	—(of map), 3543-682.
salutation, 2206d.	satin, 4245, 3761a.	scales(fish), 2520.
salute, 2206d, 4734-3107.	satire, 4856b.	scaly(flaky), /3491.
—(by guns), 2206-3438.	satisfied, 4081b, 3593-4636.	— anteater, 603b.
salvation, 1582.	saturate, 4488-4338.	scamp, 2079a.
Salvation Army, 1582d.	Saturday, 2206g-2504.	scamper, 4499, 3216.
salve, 1714a.	Saturn, 4380c.	scan, 4314-444.
same, 4459, 5133-5201.	sauce, 4527, 3912a.	scandal, 473-3776.
sampan, 3188c.	—, anchovy 4872o.	scandalous, 473.
sample, 5201-(4667).	saucer(foreign), 409-4175.	scanty, /76, /3966.
sanctify, 4610-3945.	—(native), 409-3999.	scar, 980.
sanction, 376.	—, lamp 87a.	scars about eyes, 2630a.
sanctuary, 3945-3977.	saucy, 3779p.	scarce, 3966.
sand, 3778.	sauerkraut, 4800f.	scarcely, 1543.
— bank, 4293.	saunter, 934-5151.	scare, 923.
— flea, 3779h.	sausage(pork), 513e.	— to death, 3767a.
— grouse, 3779L.	—, dried 2191b.	scarf, /1537.
— paper, 3779d.	savage, 5173d.	scarlet, 1235.
— stone, 3879e.	—(ferocious), 1227.	scatter, 3576.
		—(as seed), 3581.
		—(as water), 3784.
		scene, 1678-4531.

SCE	SCR	SEA
scent, 1046.	scrape, 2056, 3624.	seaman, 4004c.
—,* 3269-2617.	— together, 2477a.	seamstress, 57-123-K.
scented capers, 409y.	scratch, 109, 3006.	sear, 2838.
sceptical, 4215-1263.	scream, 925, 1709.	search, 5023.
schedule, 423.	screen, 2338.	— out, 4287, 405.
scheme, 2641.	—,* 167.	season, (4355)-3905.
—, wily 2062b.	screw, 2444f.	—,*(cure), 1759-3981.
schism, 696-2779.	—(propellor), 490-(1367).	—,* [2454,4192]-2666d.
scholar, 3982g-Y.	—, cork 4500f.	seasonable, 3905.
—(pupil), 1141b.	— driver, 2444f-3446.	seasoning, 2666d.
school, 3982c,1141-4435. 1141a.	— thread, 2977.	seasons, the 2066.
—, primary 1141c.	scribble,2474-3616.	seat, (4599)-5014.
—, middle 383c.	scribe, 3982g-Y.	—(chair), 1256.
—, to open 182la.	scrimp, 4241-3966.	secede, 4624, 2274, 648.
— fellow, 3982-5160.	scrip, D-4224.	secluded, 3383.
— master, 3802f.	scrofula, 2302,a.	second, 1287a.
— mistress, 2949-3757.	scroll, 1838, 4249.	—* 4474-3948,3367-299.
— of fish, 4253.	scrolls, to mount 3324.	— hand, 4419a.
science,(765)-1140.	scrotum, 3840c.	— rate, 1287-4097.
scissors, 1510a.	scrub, 4696, 3587-2590.	— son, 1289c.
scoff, 1605a.	scruple(doubt), 3759-1263.	— son's wife, 1289d.
scold, 2842,2567.	scrutinize, 405a.	secondly, 4487b.
—(grumble), 2222a.	scuffle, 92a.	secret, 2638, 3106, 3758.
scoop, /1137.	scull,* 2421a.	secretary, 1304e, 3982e.
—,* 4983.	scum, 743-2792.	secrete, /2882.
scope, 4033-1258.	scurf, 2845c,4339b.	secretion, 4643a.
scorch, 3965-2951.	scythe, 2340c.	secretly, 3758-3106a.
scorn, 1311a.	sea, (5194)-1125.	sect, 1507-2779.
scorpion,884d,544a.	— anemone, 2059d.	section, 4243.
scoundrel, 2105-2079.	— serpent, 4726a.	secular, /1438a.
scour, 3805, 4397.	— sickness, 5036a.	secure, 5024a.
scourge, 3288.	— slugs, 1125g.	securely, 1541.
scout(disdain), 1311a.	— weed, 1125d.	security, 4035a.
—(spy), 306-907.	— —, edible 403le.	sedan chair, 1703.
scowl, 2866b.	seal, 445b, 1125e.	— — poles, 1703-3942.
—,* 2866b,2951a.	—(stamp), 5116.	sedate, 307-1680.
scraggy, 3862-648-2083.	—, to affix 1923-5116.	sediment, 59a.
scramble, 1912a.	— up, 880.	
scrap, 3721.	sealing wax, 767m.	
	seam, 2471d.	

SED	SEN	SEV
sedition, 4610-2474.	—(judicial), 3191.	—(grevious), 398, 645.
seditious, 1403-2474.	sentiment, 1258, 1663e.	sew, 2471.
seduce, 5121-5161.	sentinel, 3812-Y.	sewer, 940b.
sedulous, 1917a.	separate, 2379a.	sewing machine, 490f.
see, (4314,1663).	—,* 696-(1124).	sex, 5090-5196.
seed, 391.	separated, 2274.	sexes, both 2824b.
—(kernel),5044, 5118,4667.	September, 1571-4937.	sextant, 496c.
—, canary 2603c.	sepulchre, 718-2727.	sexual, 2824b/.
seeing that, 1628a.	sequel, 1013-3776.	— intercourse, 798b,1494e.
seek, 5023, 108-4710.	sequester, 447,880.	shabby, 3244a.
—(beg), 1936.	serene, 3107-4566.	shackles, 2352a, 2390.
seem, 4868.	serf, 2922a.	shad, 2204a.
seen, 2101d.	serge, 1200.	shaddock, 2503b.
seer, 3639b.	sergeant, 3161d.	shade, 5090-(36).
see-saw, 4355-3497-1424.	serious, 1494h, 2052g.	—(lamp), 111.
seethe, 4552, 2131.	serpent, 3871.	shadow, 5228.
—(boil), 2078.	—, sea 4727a.	shaft, 1762, 3277.
seize, 363, 2151.	servant, 864b.	shaggy, 3748-2712.
seldom, /3966.	—(boy), 3776c.	shake(as dice), 3048.
select, 1474-3706, 80, 1468a.	—, bond 2922a.	—(move), 5247.
selenite, 4926b.	serve, 874a.	—(swing), 1389.
self, 4673a.	sesamum, 212a.	—(the head), 2902.
selfishness, 3758-3593.	—, ground 2559a.	—(tremble), 138.
sell, 2570.	set, 826, 3182.	shaky, 743, 1264a.
— on credit, 3869.	—,* 116, 795.	shale, alum 671f.
— people, 2570b.	— sail, 1124a.	shall(future), 4522.
selvage, 3286,4914.	— type, 147b.	—(must), 3315.
semen, 4560, 391.	— up, 2190.	shallow, 4759.
semi-, 3389.	settle, 4132.	shallows, 3779b, 2301a.
send, 1629.	settlement, 745-4339.	sham, 61b.
—(a person), 4027-681.	seven, 4718.	—,* 61.
— forth, 681.	seventeen, 3845-4718.	shame, 526b.
— off, 493.	seventeenth, 4076-3845-4718.	—, put to 3604.
senile, 2420-2895.	seventh, 4076-4718.	shanty, 2392.
senior, 190.	seventieth, 4076-4718-3845.	shape, 5230.
sensation, 1745.	seventy, 4718-3845.	share, 724, 696.
senna, 4964-1367.	sever, 1832-4241.	—,* 696.
sense, 1663-3918.	several, 1624,b.	shark, 4872L.
sensible,1745-4081.	severe, 1316-3738.	sharp, 2296,651½c.
sensual, 3758-5252.		—(pointed), 4550.
sentence, 1853.		—(quick), 2363a.

SHA	SHI	SHO
— practice, 1875c.	shire, 3804.	showy, 1421b,3419-
sharpen, 2293f.	shirk, 4989a,4216-	511, 1713e.
sharper, 4984-2079.	3270.	shred, 2186-4375.
shatter, 4027-3721.	shirt, 3791.	shrew, 3100-3528,
shave, 4317.	—, under [1168,	4235a.
—(plane), 3444.	2937]-3791.	shrewd, 25571.
— whole head,683a.	shirting,5194-3336.	— fellow, 4560c.
shavings, 3444-419.	shiver, 2187d.	shriek, 1709-3880.
—, gum 3445a.	shoal, 3779b.	shrike, 2397a.
shawl, 2241a.	shook, 138-4277.	shrill, 978a.
she, 2026.	shocking, 4684-	—(creak), 2094.
sheaf, 3161.	(3593).	— call, 1378.
shear, 4554.	shoe, 912.	shrimp, 899.
shears, 1510a.	— blacking, 913g.	— trap, 1577.
sheath, /1137.	— horn,913c,3241c.	shrimps, dried
shed, 579a, 3431.	— lace, 913f.	900b.
sheen, 2105-1406.	— last, 913d.	shrine, 1144,2709.
sheep, 5193.	— sole, 913e.	shrink, 4009a.
— fold, 5193-2181.	—, wooden 1969.	shrive, /1457.
sheer, 4565a.	shoot, 2979.	shrivel, 452.
sheet, 3473a.	—,* 3877, 4027.	shroff, 3028f.
—(paper), 185.	— cane 1497a.	shroud, 3858-1248.
shelf, 1450b.	shop, 3514, 4154,	shrouding, 3858d.
shell, 1138.	1875.	shrub, 34-3996.
—, bivalve 1064a.	— coolie, 1819d.	shrubs, collection
—, tortoise 4226a.	— sign, 288a.	of, 2226.
—, univalve 2443.	—, tea 409e.	shrug, 4009/.
shellac, 59b.	shore, 3078.	shudder, 4027-138.
shelter, 167, a.	— up, 2457, 436.	shuffle(as cards),
shepherd, 2796-	short(length),4241.	3587b.
5193-Y.	—(stature), 34.	shun, 3265.
sheriff, 613-3508-	— cut, 1683a.	shut, 3794,3207.
1815.	—, to fall 92.	— the door, 1302b.
sherry, 4500c.	shorthand /1457b.	shutters, 499-3188,
shield, 167,3420.	shot, 3441l,4058-	501c.
—, cane 4333.	4667.	shuttle, 3690.
shift, 3384, 3154,	should, 5221a.	shuttlecook, to
5247.	shoulder,3358-4339.	play 1340d.
shin, 4760-2344.	— blade, 2083b.	sick, 5159-3278.
shine, 681-2105,	shout, 1199, 1709.	—(nauseated),
291.	shove, 4946,4330a.	3631-54.
ship, 3999.	—(pole), 436.	sickle, 2340a.
— master, 3999-	shovel, 431.	sickness, 3278.
328.	show, 1713e.	side, 3286, 3536.
—, to board	—,* 215f,1061-648.	—, at the 4981.
2454c.	—, puppet 2061d.	— door, 2780a.
shipwreck, 3527a.	shower, 1274a.	
shipwright, 3999-		
4529.		

SIE	SIN	SKE
siege, lay 5001-339.	sincerity, /3743.	skeleton, 2083-4315.
sierra, 2377.	sinew, 1539.	sketch, 4961.
siesta, 715-20.	sing, 507.	—,* 3616, 4967.
sieve, 3813-(4109).	singe, 3965-2951.	—, rough 4777c.
sift, 3813.	singing girls, 502.	skewer, 434.
sigh, (4507)-4301.	— kite, 143b.	skilful, 958.
sighing, 4507-4301.	single, 4046.	skill, (4804)-3018.
sight, 2999-1663.	—(minded), 344.	skilled, 4011,
sightless, 2585.	— brick wall,	2708a.
sightly, 1099-4314.	4885a.	— workman, 4560a.
sign, 1627b.	singular, 1950b.	skimmer, 112a.
—(board), 3420.	sinister, /2062b.	skin, 3468.
—(omen), 294.	sink, 457.	—, thin 2750.
—, shop 288a.	sinner, 4631-Y.	—,* 3354.
—,* 4745.	sip, 2654, 349.	skip, 4371.
signal, 1109,3319.	siphon, 1744k.	skirmish, D-263.
— flag, 1953a.	sir, 3802f.	skirt, 2139.
signet, 819.	sirs, 2384a.	— of coat, 3791-2663.
silence, 2719-3880.	sister, elder 9h.	skull, 1139a.
—, to keep 1153a.	—, younger 91.	—(bare), 804a.
silent, 4564-4566.	—, husband's 1786.	skuttle, 4685.
silica, bamboo	— in law, 1270.	sky, 4355.
364b.	sister's child,	skylark, 2365e.
silk, 3761.	3323a.	skylight, 501b.
—, cloth 478.	sit, 4793.	skyward, 1053-4355.
—, thick 4245.	— up in bed,1566c.	slab, 652.
— winders, 4092c.	site, 4125-5014.	— of stone, 3188d.
— worm, 4686.	sitting room,	slack, 3748.
— — moth, 3061b.	4346.	— water, 2578.
sill, 429.	situated, 4609.	slacken, 3748.
silly, 632a,3068.	situation(place),	slag, 4366-3721.
silver, 3028.	4125-5014.	slake, 1436.
similar, 4868.	—(office), 239-5105.	—(lime), 681.
simile, 3251-4890.	six, 2504.	slam, 635-310.
simper, 2187c.	sixteen, 3845-2504.	slander, 4988a.
simple(easy),1291,	sixteenth, 4076-3845-2504.	slang, 3908b.
5269a, 4759.	sixth, 4076-2504.	slanting,4731,2652.
—(foolish),4874a.	sixtieth, 4076-2504-3845.	slap, 3158a, 2049.
— minded, 632b.	sixty, 2504-3845.	slash, 85.
simply, 3236-2100,	size, 4033-3589.	slat, 805.
4259, 2711b.	—(glue), 1495.	slate, 3188d.
sin, 4631-(3100).	skate, 4872h.	slatternly, 2768a.
since(seeing it is)	—,* 3932.	slaughter, 4430.
1628a.	skein, 103.	slave, 2922-3550.
sincere,3951-[3854-3593].		—, female (2922)-3474.

SLA	SLO	SMO
— girl, 2765-4482.	slovenly,2155-2272.	smooth, 4984.
slay, 3808, 4027-3767.	—(in dress),2151e.	—,* C-4984.
sled, 4403-1703.	slow, 2576.	—(plane), 3444.
sleek, 4984-81.	—(late), 536.	smother, 1875,d.
sleep, 715,b,4008.	slowly, 2578-2578.	smudge, /3113.
sleepy, 715a.	slug, 3269-4319-647.	smuggle, 4499-3758.
sleeve, 4505.	—, sea 1125g.	smuggled goods, 3758-771.
sleight of hand, 3859e.	sluggard, 2185a-Y.	smut, 3113-2775.
slender, 5147-3589.	sluggish, 2185a-K,120.	snaffle, 2561-1642.
slice, 3491, 652, 2893.	sluice, 4113.	snail, 2444b.
slide, 3935.	— gate, 99a.	snake, 3874.
slight,' 3674-3674.	slumber, 4008.	snap, 3400.
—,* 726b.	slur, 4155,a.	—(break),* 4445, 283.
slightly,2308-2308.	slush, 2844-3192.	snapper, 2190c.
slily, /2062.	slut(dog), 1574-G.	snappish,1558-3658.
slim, /3862.	sly, 2401c.	snare, 1201a.
slime, 2844/.	—, on the 907a.	snarl, 3822.
sling(weapon), 750-4411.	small(quantity), 3966.	snarling of dogs, 978.
—(for carrying), 2453,2650a.	—(size),3589,3674.	snatch, 4737.
slip, 2979.	small pox,648-4118.	sneak off, 4391-3265.
—,* 3935.	smart, 2363a.	sneer, 2187c.
— off, 4330.	—(as of a child), 2093.	sneeze, 998b,1928a.
—, grow from 442a.	— as a monkey, 2243b.	sniff, 1926-1033.
— knot, 1694b.	—,* 1663-4458.	snip, 4554-(4445).
slippers, 4403-912, 913a.	smarting eyes,3561.	snipe, 3779k.
slipper boat,2233a.	smash, 4027-3721.	snivel, 4320, 3979-3269.
slippery, 4984-(2266).	smear, 406, 4239.	snore, 494c.
slipstitch, 4457-3646.	smell(bad), 474.	snort, 3447-3269.
slit, 2385, 2148.	—(fragrant), 1046.	snot, 3269-4319.
—,* 2385-1124.	—, strong 3620.	snout, 4627, 3269.
sliver, 3491.	—,* 2617.	snow, 3714.
slobber,2245-4004d.	smelt,* 3667a,2356.	snub, 4241.
slope, 4731.	smilax pseudo China 877b.	snuff, 3269c.
slops, 3030a.	smile, 1152-3675.	snug, 3107-5024.
sloppy,3843-(4984).	smite, 4027.	so(with adj. or adv.), 1758.
sloth, 2795-1574.	smith, 4529.	—(with verb),1753.
slothful, 2185a.	smoke, 1335.	soak, 4488, 3843.
slouching, 4088a.	—(meats), 702.	soaked, 2851.
slough, 3843-2844.	—(tobacco), 1335k.	soap, 656c.
	smoky, 5159-1335, 971.	soapstone, 4984a.
		soar, 1713-750.

SOB	SOL	SOU
sob, 4009c.	solicitor, 311d.	soul, 2361a.
sober, 3621-4132.	solicitude, 2040a.	sound, 3880-(5069).
sociable, 1099-	solid, 3854, 3001.	— * 1047.
3625-4889.	solitary, 4259,	—(asleep), 2851.
social intercourse,	1787, 2038.	soundly, 645.
2447b.	solstice, 227b.	soup, 4431.
society, 3143.	soluble, 1117-3667-	—, thick 1551.
sock, (4241)-2591.	651.	sour, 3702.
socket, 4113.	solve, 1436-(2690).	source, 4920-4339.
—, eye 1181a.	some, 4139, 1624.	souse, 5102.
sod, 4777-3468.	— one, 3420-Y.	south, 2823.
soda, 1315a.	somersault, 1535a.	— pole, 2823a.
—, sulphate of	something, 5173,	southeast, 4272b.
4926a.	934b,2635.	southwest, 3584a.
— water, 1121f.	sometimes, 5159-	souvenir,1627-2636.
sodomite, 1902f	3905.	sovereign,328,5072.
sodomy,1466c,2824c.	son, (2824)-4482,	sow, 313-G.
sofa,587,4008-1256.	4667.	sow,* 3581.
soft, 2848.	—, adopted 4674a.	soy, 3912a.
— and pliable,	— in law, 2949c.	space, 1463, 4125-
4930.	—, second 1289c.	779.
softly, 1042b.	song, 1729-D,2029e.	spacious, /885.
soil, 2844, 4380.	sonorous, 1048b.	spade, 431.
—,* C-3113.	soon, N-1624-2938,	—(small), 4773.
sojourn, 1629a.	4504.	span, 2822.
sojourner, 921.	sooner, 4586-4138.	—(pair), 4250.
solace, 3107d.	soot, 1334-2766,	spank, 3423,2049.
solanum, 1946.	767e, 2401b.	spare, 3361.
solder, (1168½)-	soothe, 3107d.	sparing, 3804.
3619.	soothsayer,3400a-Y.	spark, 7671,c.
—,* 1168½.	sophistry, 958b.	sparkle, 767d.
soldering iron,	sorcerer,2824-2714-	sparrow, 2557f.
2838a.	3802f.	—, house 4518b.
soldier, 3300,a,	sorcery, 2714a.	—, Java 1870a.
4168a.	sore, 578.	sparse, 3966.
— uniform, 2042a.	—, 4458.	spasm, 471a.
soldierly, 5281.	sorely, 398.	spatter, 1700,4473.
sole(fish), 4312a.	sorghum, 4144.	spawn, 631b.
—,' 4046, 4259.	—, sweet 2409a.	speak, 1779.
— of foot, 1539d.	— vulgare, 2319a.	—(address), 4001b.
— of shoe, 913c.	sorrow, 37a, 5141-	spear, 4735.
solely, 4259-968,	2786.	speargrass, 781a.
3236-2101.	sorrowful, 37a.	special, 4083a.
solemn, 1316-3738,	sorry, 36a.	specie, 3028-4761.
1881-1680.	sort, 5201,2494.	species, 2494,391.
solemnize, 2206d.	sot, 2186-4500-Y.	specify, 4960-3854.
solicit, 1936.	souchong tea, 409s.	specimen,5201-4667.

SPE	SPI	SPR
specious talk, 958-1350.	spire, 4307, 2248a.	spray, 4004c.
speck, 4151.	spirit, 2362, 5028, 3835.	—(sprig), 206.
speckled, 4151-4151.	—(disembodied), 2061.	spread about, 2245.
spectacle, 1678.	spirits(alcoholic), 4500.	— open, 4294.
spectacles, 1637g.	—(animal), 4560a.	— out, 3167, 3511.
spectre, 2061.	spiritless, 3849-5028.	spring, 4058a.
spectrum, 2105f.	spit, 4406.	—(moving power), 1601.
speculate, 448,c.	spite, 4913-981.	—(of watch), 682-4375.
speculum, /1637.	spiteful, 4260a.	—(of water), 4920-(4817).
speech, 4960,4001a.	spittle, 4004d.	—(season), 629.
speechless, 6.	spittoon, 1824a.	—, * 4371.
speed, /651½.	splash, 1700,4473.	springtime of life, 4764d.
speedily, 4533a.	spleen, 2344a,3470.	— water, 3793-4004.
speedy, 651½a.	splendid, 4958a.	sprinkle, 3794,1700.
spell, 4769-5089.	splendor, 5049-2105.	sprite, 1380.
spelter, 4921b.	splice, 3356,a.	sprout, 2979, 2794.
spend, (3814,691).	splinter,3491,2893.	—,* 2634, 648/
—(of time), 2101.	split, 2385.	sprouts(edible), 3740.
spendthrift, 2468-4667.	—* 3527, 2385, 1145, 3477.	spry, 1042-651-.
sperm, 4560.	spoil, 274b.	spume, 743-3439.
spermatozoa, 4560-646.	—(break), C-2186.	spunk, 767-1033.
spew, 4406, 54.	spoils, 4614-2636.	spur, 2028.
sphere, 1938.	spokes, 871.	—,* 4343.
spice, 1046-2400.	sponge, 3522a.	spurious,1419,3017.
spices, the five 2666a.	— cake, 1515h.	spurt, 3448.
spider, 1915b,210a.	spongy, 3460.	—, to make a 1868.
— web, 317a, 210a-2759.	sponsor, 4035-1410.	sputum, 4004d.
spike, 4859, 4127.	spool, 2501.	spy, 3646-Y, 4287-4667.
spikenard, 4849b.	— of thread,2501a.	—,* 2122a, 306.
spill, 2245, 2262, 4197.	spoon, 537a, 1551.	— glass, D-1637i.
spin, (787)-4512.	—, tea 409h.	squabble, 15a,92,a.
— around, 4089a.	sport, 4973a.	squad, 4253.
spinach,1362a,3350.	—, make 2544a.	squalling, 2975a.
spindle, 4840.	sportsman, 2380-Y.	squander, 651-3576, 3576-4761.
spine, 1379b.	spot, 4151, 4851.	squanderer, 2468-4667.
spinet, D-1911.	—(place), 4066.	square, 3772a,779.
spinning machine, 787-1601.	spotless, 4564.	—, carpenter's 496d.
— wheel, 787-490.	spout, 4627.	squash, 2037.
spinster,2420-2949.	—(downpipe), 4004-4785.	
spiral, 2444e.	—,* 3447, 284.	
	sprain, 2867-3885.	

SQU	STA	STE
squat, 2640.	stanchion, 436.	steal, 4335, 3660.
squeaking, 2094.	stand, 1962,a.	stealth, 4335.
squeamish, 4870.	— on tiptoe,1566b.	steam, 4004-1033.
squeeze,25,62,1485.	standard, 4208.	—,* 268.
—(extort), 2217a.	—(flag), 1953.	— boiler, 268a.
squint, 4509-2999.	standstill, 4360-	— launch, 4000a-D.
squire, 3802f.	3633.	— whistle, 3242a.
squirrel, 2490a,	stanza, 4570,3899.	steamer, 4000a.
3985f.	staple, 2552-4127.	— paddle wheel
squirt, 284.	4366-1280.	4000c.
stab, 1559.	star, 3652.	steamship, 2518b.
stability,413-1810.	— aniseed, 3197c.	steed, 2561.
stable, 2561e.	starboard, 3999-	steel, 1773.
—(secure), 5024a.	5164.	steelyard,558,4100.
stack, 4248.	— the helm, 2421b.	steep, 4731.
staff, 1764,2045a.	starch, 4523.	—,* 4488.
stag, 2510-G.	stare, 305.	steeple,4307,2248a.
stage, 4422, 2554.	start, 1031, 1124,	steer, 3933-3039.
— of a journey,86.	681.	—,* 57-4285.
stagger, 3461.	startle, /923.	steersman, 57-4285-
staging, 1424,3431.	starvation, 3066-	Y, 3811-1878.
stagnant, 536a.	3767.	stem, 1762,206,
stain, (980,4534).	state, 2103.	2116.
—,* 1325-3113.	—(condition),4766-	—,* 296a.
staircase, 2248e.	3819.	stench, 474.
stairs, 2248e.	—,* 4960.	stenography, 1458b-
stake, 4084, 304,	statesman, /3836.	3616.
4276.	statics, 398-1140,	step, 3341.
stalactite, 385-	4566a.	—(stair), 1924.
4891-3879.	station, 3830-723.	—,* 986.
stalagmite, 3879-	—, railroad 86b.	— father, 1522a.
586.	—, military 73a.	— mother, 1013c.
stale, 3736,1594.	stationary, N-5247.	— ladder, 4313.
stalk, 1762,206.	stationery, 216-	— over, 2163.
stall, /2181.	2400.	stern, 1316-3738.
—, fruit 4294a.	statue, 3040b.	—, 3999-2663.
stallion, 1801a.	statuettes, 1878d.	stethoscope, 4461c.
stamens, 650c.	stature, 5230-4530.	stew, 3143, 3083.
stamina, 3593-2330.	statute, 2546a.	steward, 1819c.
stammer, 2221.	statutes(code),	stick(branch), 206.
stammering, 2514a.	1068.	—(walking, etc.),
stamp, 5116.	stave, 4454-3187.	2079,2045a.
—(postage), (tr)	stay, 4097, 2246.	—(pierce), 1559.
3777-4036.	stead, 4222, 4316.	—(adhere), 514,
— on, 4063.	steadfast, 1660a.	2889.
— duty, 5117-1834.	steadily, 4551a.	sticky, 2810,2863.
stanch, 328-1810.	steady, 5024a.	stiff, 3001,1555.
—,* 217.	steak, beef 3412e.	

STI	STO	STR
stiffen, 2378-3001.	stone, 3879.	straightway, 3905a.
stiff neck, 2199a.	— (seed), 5044.	strain, 1448b.
stiffnecked, 29-1636.	—, ink 1363a.	strainer, 2437b, 2262b.
stifle, 1875, d.	— roller, 2131a, 4411.	strait, 945.
still,'(3107)-4566.	—,* 4130.	—,' 76.
—," 398,4938, 5232a, 1557.	stonecutter, 4027-3879-2404.	straitened, 2135.
stillborn, 3767-4417.	stool, 4098.	stramonium, 2843b.
stilson wrench, 1971c.	—, to go to 648e.	strange, 1950b.
stilts, 3355-1638-2079.	stoop, 3118-4070.	—(to a place), 3802-3070.
stimulants, 1649c.	stop, 3592,151,117.	stranger, 3341b, 921.
stimulate, 3749-1031. 1649.	—* 217,1086,4360, 117,3341a.	strangle, 2217b,38.
sting, 4127, 123.	— up, 3592, 3207.	strap, 3468-4031.
—,* 4855.	— work, 1877h.	—,* 3002.
stingy, 933.	stopper, 151.	strata, 4714a.
stink, 474-1033.	store(shop), 3514.	stratagem, 779c.
stinking, 474.	—* 4538-2568, 3858b.	straw, 5060-1759.
stink-pot,845-3326.	storehouse, 771b, 579.	— hat, 4775-2726.
stint, 939a.	storekeeper, 1819-4807.	strawberry, 3874, 2769a.
stipend, 3605a.	stores(provisions), 768a.	stray, 4238-3849.
stipple, 4151-4967.	stork, 3178-1142.	streaks, 815-3183-2619.
stipulate, /4132.	storm, 4027-879.	stream, 1898,a.
stipulations, 5178-4375.	story, /1796.	—(current), 4004-2245.
stir, 1502, 5247.	—(floor), (4714)-2248.	streamer,1953-4031.
—(as in cooking), 2401a.	— to tell a 1796a.	street, 1430.
— up, 3689.	stout, 4560-309.	—, small 1190.
stirrup, 2561c.	—(fat), 759a.	— girl, 2222b.
stitch, 123-3341.	—(strong), 1660a.	— placard, 2880.
—,* 4127, 2471.	stove, 767f,1876a.	strength, 2330.
—, back 1932.	—(portable), 879j.	strengthen, 3330-2330.
stock, 771.	stow, 501-2568.	strenuous, 1918a.
—(butt), /4339.	straddle, 2976b.	stress, 398.
—(share), (1798)-723.	straggle, 986-3576.	stretch, 2631.
stockings, 2591.	straight, 242,275, 4157.	— forth, 3831.
stocks, 1639h,1412.	—, not 2652.	strew, 3581, 3576.
stolid, 4269.	straighten, C-275.	strict, 1316-1541.
stomach, 4402.	straightforward, 242.	stride, 4033-3341.
— ache, 4402-4458.		—,* 2976a.
stomacher, 4107c.		strife, 3625-92.
		strike, 4027.
		—(clap), 3423.

STR	STU	SUB
— (kick), 4343.	student, 1141b.	subscribe, 4323c.
— (stone), 4130.	studious, 1917a-1140.	subsequent, /1013.
— against, 310.		subside, /3633.
— an average, 494b.	study, 1140,3982g.	subsidiary, 299.
— out, 2790.	— aloud, 3982g.	subsist, 5198-3802.
— the hours, 480a.	stuff, 4805-2400.	substance, 150,2636.
string, 3949.	— (useless), 690-2636.	substitute, 4222/.
— (of beads, etc.), 611.	stumble against, 4343.	— for, 4316.
—, * 1825a.	stump, 2087a.	subtle, 958, 2708.
— beans, 4116a.	stun, 1670b.	subtract, 1457.
— of a lute, 1353.	stunt, 296-3802.	subtraction, 1457-682.
stringy, 4215-1538.	stunted, 34.	suburbs, 3883-3070.
strip, 4375,3491.	stupified, 3849-5028, 2601/.	—, western 2052j.
—, * 4446.	stupendous, S-4033.	subvert, 1977-4197.
striped, 2261e, 3183-2619.	stupid, 632a.	succeed(accomplish) 4081-3948.
— fox, 2594b.	stupidity, 2595-3592.	— (follow), 4569-4593, 1522.
stripling, 3967-2895.	sturdy, 4033/.	successive, 2508-4639.
strive, 3625-92.	sturgeon, 4872j.	successor, 1522-Y.
stroke, 4967.	stutter, 2263c, 2839.	succinct, 1473a.
— (blow), 4027.	sty, 312-2181.	succumb, 874.
— the beard, 2477a.	style(fashion), 3905c.	such, 1753.
stroll, 2055, 5151.	—, literary 2616e.	— and such a one, 2642.
strong(firm), 1660a.	—, the written 2285c.	suck, 349,3979.
— (hard), 3001.	—, * 553, 1709.	suckle, 4993,2892a.
— (of fire), 2586.	suavity, 5020a.	suction pipe, 1926b.
— (of liquid), 5271.	sub, 908, 826.	sudden, 726a.
— (of wind), 4033.	subdue, 3947-874.	suddenly, 4506, 726a-(1463).
— (physically), 309, a, 5159-2330.	subject, 4323-2798.	sudorific, 681-1168-5183.
— (pungent), 2194.	—, * 4027-874.	suds, 1469-4004.
— current, 1541b.	subjection, 874.	sue, 311c.
strop, 1199-4195-3468.	sublimate, 3627.	— (ask), 1936.
—, * 1199.	sublime, 4023a.	— for debt, 1726c.
structure, 1463, 4910,3977.	submarine cable, 2174a.	suet, 3188f,1379d.
struggle, 92,a.	submerge, 4488.	suffer, 3865.
strychnine, 2561L.	submission, 4022-874.	— (permit), 376.
stubble, 5060-1759-4339.	subordinate, /4012.	suffering, 3597-813.
stubborn, 3001a.	suborn, 2569-567.	suffice, 1583.
stucco, 3879h.	subpoena, 276-5117-3320.	sufficient, 1583-(3814).
stud, 2868a.		
— horse, 625c.		

SUF	SUM	SUP
suffocate, 1875d.	—,* 1726.	supreme, 227-3896.
sugar, 4437a.	sun, 5137, 1093a.	— ruler, 4074.
— candy, 3301a.	—,* 3786.	supremely, 1654,
— cane, 171.	sunbeam, 2105-3877.	3846a.
— mill, 171d.	sunburn, 3786-971.	sure, (2000)-3854.
suggest, 4323a.	Sunday, 2206i.	surely, 5133-4132.
suggestion, 1207.	Sunday School, 328-	surety, 4036a.
suicide, 4673c.	5137-1141a.	—(the person),
suit, 3226.	sunder, 696-1124.	3329d.
—(of clothes),	sundial, 2064a,	surface, 2687.
4446.	2122b.	surge, 3178g.
—,* 1193.	sundries, 3601-3721,	surgeon, 765b-1849c.
suitable, 2993,	3847-2637.	surgery, 765b.
1193,b.	sundry, 4475,3847.	surly, 2574, 2459-
suite, 1536a.	sunflower, 2128d.	3658.
suitor, 1936-Y,	sunken, 2860.	surmise, 1797.
1726e.	sunrise, 5137-648.	surname, 3657.
sulky, 1802c.	sunset, 5137-2454.	—, your 1713b,
sullen, 1796d.	sunshine, 2105b.	2065a.
sully, 4155a.	sunstroke, 1373b.	surpass, 3947-2100.
sulphate of copper,	sup, 5085, 942.	surplus, 3956,4871.
671f 4462c.	super-, 2100,3896.	surprise, /1670,
— — iron, 671c.	superb, S-1099.	/923.
— — soda, 4926a.	superficial, 4759.	surprising, 1950b.
sulphur, 2249a.	superfluous, 2101f.	surrender, 4340b.
—, bituminous	superintend, 4255-	surreptitious,
2249d.	2285.	3758, /3106.
—, flowers of	superintendent,	surround, 5001-339.
2249c.	1455a.	survey, 405a.
—, red gangue	superior, 3896-	— land, 2313-4125.
2249e.	(4097).	surveyor general,
sulphuret of arse-	superlative, 1654,	1877i.
nic, 1240a.	227.	survive, 398-3802.
— — iron, 4367h.	supernatural, /2048.	suspect, [413,3759]-
sulphuric acid,	supper, 2575b.	1263, 3410.
2249a-1964a.	supplicate, 976-	suspend, 2039,4189.
sultry, 3986-[36,	1936.	—(stop), 4360,217.
1372].	supplication,1951a.	suspenders, 824-
sum, 1892-1521.	supplies, 3716.	4031.
— up, 4455a.	supply, 1882-1923.	suspense,2039-3593.
summary, 4652-2507.	support(uphold),	suspicion, 3759-
sumach, 4882.	830a.	1263.
summer, 909-4355.	—(nourish), 5198.	sustain,830a,3952b,
— house, 2316a.	suppose, 1797-	4035.
summit, 4129.	(2326).	sustenance, 5095-
summon, 293, 613-	supposing, 3768a.	3925.
1709.	suppress, 25-117.	swab, 727a.
summons, 3508.		

SWA	SYC	TAK
swaddle, 550.	sycee, 2619d.	—(lead a person), 4031.
swagger, 3258b.	syllable, 696-5089.	— a wife, 4825.
—, noisy 1567b.	syllabus, 1473a.	— away, 4824.
swallow, 1340a.	symbol, 1627e.	— by force, 4247, 4737.
—, * 4329.	symbolize, 3323-2690.	— care of, 1811.
swamp, 3192a.	sympathize, /1117b.	— entirely, 4763b.
swan, 1238-1870.	— with, 4315a.	— leave, 4861.
swarm, 2137.	sympathy with, in 4022.	— medicine, 874f.
swart, 971.	synagogue, 3144a.	— off, 2238.
sway, 2007a.	syphilis, /4128.	tale, /1796.
—, *3004, 5247.	syphilitic sores, 2767g.	— bearer, 1006-3973.
swear, 681-3821.	syphon, 564a,1744k.	talent, 1768a,4804.
—(curse), 164a.	syringe, 284a.	talisman, 832.
sweat, 1168.	syrup, 4437b,4524.	talk, 4001a,4287.
—, * 648-1168.	system, 682.	—, * 1779.
sweep, 2421.	Szechuen root,877c.	—, learned, 4182b.
—, *3684.		talkative, 1100-1779.
sweeping assertion, 4728b.		tall, 1713.
sweet, 4352.	**T**	tallow, 5193-5149.
— basil, 3677c.		— tree, 3115a.
— bread,3039-5044.	T-shape, 4168-4672.	tally, 480.
— flag, 504.	table, 4418.	—, * 832a, 4251a.
— heart, 1528d.	—, octagonal 3197a.	talons, 107.
— potato, 3991b.	— cloth,4419-3336.	tamarisk, 2261a, 1818b.
— sorghum, 2409a.	— napkin, 1537c.	tamarix chinensis, 4902a.
sweets, 4437.	tablet, 3420.	tame, 4011,4851.
swell, 4033-2468.	tack, 4127-D.	tamp, 386.
—, * 392-1031.	—, * 4127.	tampering, 3859-4215.
swelling, 392,2257, 3241½.	—(nautical),1929b.	tan, 3669b, 1294.
swift, 651½.	tackle, 1035-5282.	tangle, 2474.
swim, 5150-4004.	tact, 2690-2285.	tank, 4438, 535.
swimming(dizziness) 4339-5036.	tadpole, 2479b, 3112a.	tankard, 3122.
swindle, 3123.	tael, 2321.	tanner, 3468-4529.
swine, 312.	—, Haikwan 2052e.	Taoism, 4207c.
swineherd,2796-312.	taffeta, 1841.	taotai, 239a.
swing, 4725-4758.	tail, 2663.	tap(water), 4404-1006, 2529-4339.
—, * 1389-(3167).	tailor, 4806a.	—, * 3423.
—(throw off), 763.	taint, 1325.	—(let out), 795.
switch, 3288.	take, 2433.	tape, 4031.
—(electric, etc.), 117.	—(in hand), 2896, 2888.	
swivel, 346-3755.		
swoon, 3849-5028.		
sword, 1658, 4195.		

TAP	TEA	TEA
taper, D-366.	—, Campoi 1468b.	tease, 2834a,2864.
—, coiled wax 2192g.	— canister, 409-1824.	—(comb), 3809.
tapering,4246,4550.	—, Congou 409r.	—(as cotton),4304.
tapestry, 650-253.	— cup, 409-3375.	teasing, 2432.
tapeworm, 3141-646.	—, Dragon Well 409cc.	teat, 2820b.
tapioca, 2603a.	—, green 409o.	tedious, 512a.
tapir, 3178-3204.	—, gunpowder 409z.	tee, 29771.
tar, 3160a.	— house, 409d.	teem, /2785.
tardy, 536, 2578.	—, Hyson 409u.	teens, 3246-1624.
tare, to deduct 2712d.	—, — skin 409x.	teeth, 2977-(524).
tares, 3212.	—, imperial gun-powder, 409aa.	—, artificial 2977d.
target, 3165-4667.	— kettle, 409f.	teething, 648-2977.
tariff, 4005-4707.	— leaves, 409a.	telegram, 4163g.
tarnish, 2105c.	— merchant, 409j.	telegraph(electric) 4163g.
taro, 3131-4342.	—, old Hyson 409v.	telegraphy, 4163g-1140.
tarpaulin, 3160b-3336.	—, Oolung 409p.	telephone, 4163h, 879.
tart, 3702.	—, Paochung 409q.	teleology, 1694d.
tartan, 1957c.	—, Pekeo 409t.	telescope, field 16071.
Tartar, 2785a.	— picker,79-409-Y.	—(astronomical), 4355g-1637.
task, 1877-772.	— plant, 409b.	tell, 4960, 1779, 1709.
tassel, 3731.	— pot, 409g.	temper, 3658-4766.
taste, 2666,d.	— poy, 4091.	—, good 1636d.
—,3892.	—, red 409n.	temperament, 513a.
tasteless, 4292.	—, scented capers 409y.	temperate, 4570b.
taster, tea 409k.	— shop 409e.	— zone, 4031b.
tattered, /2186.	—, Souchong 409a.	temperature, 2187-1372-723.
tattle, 3032.	— spoon, 409h.	tempest, /879.
tattooed, 2619c.	—, taster, 409k.	temple, 2709, 4164.
taunt, 1605a,1605-4770.	—, to fire 448d.	— keeper, 362b.
tavern, 4154a.	—, to infuse 636a.	temporal, 3818b.
tawdry, 2105-2687.	—, water fairy 409bb.	temporarily, 4469-3905.
tawny, 2420e.	—, young Hyson 409w.	tempt, 3903-4968, 5121-5161.
tax, 4005, 1049.	teach, 1507.	temptation, 5161-4968.
—,* [3857,2836]-1049.	teacher, 3802f, 1507b, 3757.	ten, 3845.
—, house 2276b.	teaching, 1507a.	— cents, 1104a.
— in kind, 2311.	teak, 5149e.	— cent coin, 1104b,c.
—, likin 2276a.	teal, 24a.	
taxes, to pay 2836.	team, 3040.	
tea, 409.	tear, 2572-2186.	
—, Bohea, 1273a.	tears, (2999)-2497.	
—, black 409m.		
—, brick 409L.		

TEN	TER	THE
— days, 4839.	terror, 1670a.	therapeutics, 2395a, 1249-682.
— feet, 201.	test, 3903-(1329).	there, 1734-3987.
—, over 2304a.	testament, /5178, 5003-3982.	there! 2814.
— thousand, 2576.	testicles, 3840b, 2527b.	there is, 5159.
— years, 4839.	testify, 270.	thereabout, 3896-
tenable, 1117-3861.	testimony, 270-1855.	908, 4597-5164.
tenacious, 3161a.	testy, 2867b.	thereafter, 4852-
tenant, (3514)-921.	text, 2798b.	1013.
tench, 4977-4872.	textile, /239.	therein, 1955b.
tend, 1158.	texture, /2619.	thereon, 4609-3896.
—(wait on), 874a.	than, 2100.	thereupon, 4868½-
— cattle, 2796.	thank, 4510.	3909.
tendency, 1053.	— you, 1737a, 669b, 4215-4510.	thermometer, 125f.
tender, 2848, 2947.	thankful, 1755-5108.	these, 4139b.
—(young), 5147.	thankless, 2754-	thesis, 2798b.
—(bid), 3320.	5108.	they, 2026-4124.
—(boat), 3356c.	thanks, to give 1755a.	thick, 1014.
—, * 4340.	that, 1731.	—(of liquid), 2953, 1694.
tenderly, 4458-3099.	— is, 4533a.	—(close), 2638.
tendon, 1539.	— one, 1732a.	thicket, 34-2226.
— of elbow, 94.	— which), 3977.	thickness, 1014.
— of heel, 94.	—(in order that), 2200.	thief, 4682-3574b.
tendrils, 2178c.	thatch, 1994-2595, 2128f.	thieve, 4335.
tenet, 4207a.	thaw, 3667.	thigh, 4033-3252.
tenfold, 3845-3549.	the, 1731.	thill, 1783.
tennis, 3347a.	theater, 1037c.	thimble, 125b.
tenon, 3740-4339, 2979b.	theatrical, 4593- 1036.	thin, 3361.
tenor, 4033-1258.	thee, 2875, 1284.	—(lean), 3862.
tense, 1541.	theft, 4335-5173.	—(watery), 1023.
tension, 3697-2330.	theine, 409-150.	thing, 2636a, 5173.
tent, 194c.	their, 2026-4124-K.	think(suppose), 1797.
tentative, /3903.	them, 2026-4124.	—(reflect), 3759- 3631.
tenth, 4076-3845.	—, among 1955b	third, 4076-3572.
—, one 3846a-5133.	theme, 2798b.	—, one 3572-723- 5133.
tepid, 2945.	then, 1734-141-3905, 4504, 3905b.	thirst, 1198.
term(time), 939- 1952.	thenceforth, 4673- 1013.	thirsty, 1636-1198.
—(word), 4960-4339.	theology, 3835c.	thirteen, 3845-3572.
—, * 553, 1708a.	theory, 682.	thirteenth, 4076- 3845-3572.
termination, 3858a.		
terminology, 2669a.		
terrace, (4355)- 4422.		
terrible, (S)-1494h.		
terrific, 1117-3410.		
terrify, 923.		

THI	THR	TIE
thirtieth, 4076-3572-3845.	—, to cut the 2790a.	— up, 103.
thirty, 3572-3845, 3565.	throb, 4371.	tier, 4714.
this, 2881.	throe, S-4458.	tiffin, 20a.
— and that, 3253a.	throne, (5072)-5014.	tiger, 815a.
thistle, 2203b.	throng, 2137.	— lily, 1839b.
thong, 3468-4031.	—, * 4480.	tight, 1541.
thorax, 1228/.	throttle, /117.	—, very 992a.
thorn, 4855, 2218.	—, * 2217b.	tiles, 2981.
thorns, 1672a.	through, 4452, 5148.	—, glazed 2256b.
thorough, 4452.	throw, 4182, 5048.	—, to lay 1996c.
thoroughfare, 4452-2426, 1430.	— dice, 82.	till, 4761-2071.
thoroughly, 4645b, 3571.	— down, 4086.	—, 4203.
	thrum, 4304.	—, * 1480.
those, 4139a.	— the guitar, 143a.	tiller, 4285-3277.
thou, 2872, 1284.	thrush, black 408a.	tilt, 4107a.
though, 3715-1349.	—, white eyed 2657b.	timber, 427.
thought, 2891a, 1258a.	—(disease), 2186a.	—(in general), 2795-2400.
thoughtful, 3593b.	thrust, 48, 442.	timbrel, D-1802.
thoughts, inward 513a.	thumb, 215a.	time, 3905-(1015).
	thump, 4086, 983.	—, appointed 1952.
thoughtless, N-3593b.	thunder, 2479.	—, at that 4230a.
thousand, 4754.	— without rain, 1169a.	—, passed by, 1668e.
—, ten 2576.	Thursday, 2206g-3770.	—, period of 141.
thousandth, 2275.	thus, 1753.	—, periods of 4570a.
thrash, 4027.	tibia, 1684-2083.	—, present 1526.
thread, 3646.	tick, 585-5251-4224.	—, slip, 3905e.
—, * 603.	ticket, 3320, 3508.	—, table, 3905e. 3323c.
—, linen 2557i.	—, census 2780b.	
—, screw 2977.	—, lottery 1829a.	timely, 4586.
—, spool of 2501a.	ticklish, 3705a.	times, 192, 4854, 3135.
threaten, 923.	tide, 570-4004.	timid, 2936-5182.
three, 3572.	—, ebb 1760f.	tin, 3619, 4367f.
thresh, 4027-5060.	—, favorable 4004b.	—, block 3619a.
threshing floor, (5060)-511.	—, high 4004a.	— ore, 2352.
	— lands, 4306.	tincture, 5183a.
threshold, 429.	tidings, 3633a, 2617b.	tinder, 5272b.
thriftless, 743-4339.	tidy, 4705-274.	tine, 401-524.
thrifty, 933b.	tie, 4031.	tinfoil, 3619c.
thrill, /138.	—, * 3373.	tinge, 1325.
thrive, 681-4068.	—(join), 3355a.	tinkling, 2360.
throat, 1008,a.	—(knot), 1694.	tinsel, 1527b.
		tint, 3917a.
		tiny, 3026, 3589-3674.

TIP	TOM	TOT
tip, /4550.	tomtit, 2397.	total, 4652a.
— toe, 1566d.	ton, 4091b.	totally, 4645b.
— —, stand on 1566b, 3036a.	tone, 3880-5089.	touch, 2733,4155.
tired, 2110.	tongs, 767-1971.	touching,3423-2568.
tiresome, 512a, 2496b.	tongue, 2294.	tough, 3029.
titillate, 109.	—, furred 2294b.	tour, 648-3070.
title, /2669,4621-1109.	— tied, 2846a.	tow, 2151b, 4403.
— deed, 4125d.	tonic, 3330c.	towards, 1053.
— page, 2687c.	tonight, 1526-2575.	towel, (2687)-1537.
titter, 1025a.	tonnage dues, 450b.	tower, 1713c,4307.
tittle tattle, 359c.	tonsil, 1008-1001.	towing path, 2174c.
to, 2100.	tonsure, 2454d.	town, 5130, 4813, 3883.
—(unto), 4203.	too, 2101f, 4283, 4486.	toy, 1878d.
—(in order to), 2200.	— much, 2101f.	— with, 2544a.
—(against), 4250.	tools, 1035b.	trace, (4647)-4534.
toad, 1915a.	—, edged 2293e.	track(mark), 4534.
toadstools, 1996d.	tooth, 2977.	—(railway), /3646.
toady, 3158c.	— ache, 2977-4458.	tract(small book), D-3982.
toast, 1183.	— brush, 2977e.	—(religious), 2616f.
tobacco, 1334,g.	— paste,2977-1714.	—(of land), 4066.
— shop, 1335l.	— pick, 2977-4745.	tractable, 4344-4960.
—, scented 1335j.	— powder, 845c.	trade(business), 3802c.
today, 2636g,1526-5137.	toothed, 2977.	—(handicraft), 3018.
toe, 1638-215.	top,4129-4339,3896.	—, * 2569a.
— nail, 215d.	topaz, Indian 4561a.	—, Board of 1875b.
together, 1892-2568, 2350a.	topic, 2798b.	—, in the 1186b.
—(mutual), 3625.	torch, 3161c.	— mark, 1627e.
toil, 1877a,2408.	torment, 813-2834.	—, wholesale 1186a.
toilsome, 3597-813.	torn, 2186.	tradesman, 3514-1410.
token, 1627e.	tornado, 2532-879.	trading company, 1878f.
tolerate,5105-4848, 5114.	torpedo(fish),3524-4872.	tradition,1006-613.
toll, 2100-2426-4761.	—(naval), 2479a, 4872.	traffic, 3802c.
tomato,1946a,1561e.	torrent, 1558b.	train(railway), 490d.
tomb, 718-2727, 3793.	torrents, to fall in 2225.	—, 1507-5198.
—, to worship at 3168c.	torrid, 1372.	—, to board 4059.
tomorrow, 4358a, 2690e.	— zone, 1372-4031.	trait, / 3987.
	tortoise, 2058.	
	— shell, 4226a.	
	tortuous, 1834a.	
	torture, 986-5231.	
	toss, 3436.	
	— about, 3505.	

TRA	TRE	TRI
traitor,/1466-2570-328.	treachery, /1467.	trifling, 934c, 1266a,3615a.
tram, electric 490e.	treacle, 4437b.	trigger, 4376a.
trample, 415a.	tread, 986.	trigonometry,1744g, 3574c.
trance, 5132-2601.	— underfoot, 415a.	trim, C-4705.
tranquil, 3497.	treason, 2641a.	—(cut), 1832,4554.
tranquility, 3107-3497,4283-3497.	treasure, 3028, 4803-3179.	trip, 3849a.
transact, 3191.	—, a 3331-3538.	tripang, 1125g.
transaction,(3191)-3776.	treasury, 3028-827.	tripe, 4402c,1367a.
transcendentalism, 568a.	treat, 4223.	triple, 3572-3549.
transcribe, 447.	treatise, D-3982, 186.	tripod, 4170.
transfer,1494-2100.	treatment, medical 4377a.	trippingly, 1042-3341.
transfigure, 3293-651.	treaty, 5059-5178.	triumph, 1126-1729.
transform,4594-651.	tree, 3996-(2795).	trivial, 3615a.
transgress, 678.	trellis, 2277a.	trocar, 125d.
transient, 4469a.	trellised, 2162c.	troops, 2075.
transit, 1668-2100.	tremble, 138.	tropics, 1372-4031.
— dues, 450a.	trembling, 4105a.	trot, 2263b.
translate,658-5213.	tremens, delirium 2735b.	trouble,1465a,3776-(1768).
transmigration, 2518c.	trench, 940.	—,* 2834a, 1403.
transmit, 1629, 1494, 613.	trencher, 4117.	troublesome, 691b.
transparent, 4338-2105.	trend, 1053.	troublous, 2474.
transplant, 442.	trespass, 678.	trough, 4785.
transport, 3384.	trestles, to put on 2457.	trousers, 824.
transpose, 4192-346.	trial, 3903.	trout, 4872a.
transverse, 4981.	—(of a case), 1878-3111,/3826.	trowel, 845-537.
trap, 2533.	triangle, 1744f.	truant, 4391-1140.
trash, 2193b.	triangular, 1744e.	truculent, 4186-2574.
travail, 430-4458.	tribe, 207a, 4638.	true, (136,3854), 3743b.
travel, [5151,648]-986.	tribulation, 4978-2835.	truly, 136-968.
traveler, 986-2488.	tribunal,1878-3111.	trump up, 2909.
traveling expenses, 3552a, 2426b.	tribute, 1889.	trumpet, 1110c, 1043a.
traverse, 2100.	trick, 2062b,1875c, 2029d.	—, conch shell 2444d.
tray, 4427-3552.	—,* 5037.	trundle, 2501d.
—, covered 1194.	tricks, conjuring 316lb.	trunk, 2542,3826.
treacherous, 2062a.	tricky, 2266a, 2029c, 1683d.	—(body), 3826.
	trident, 3574a.	—(elephant's), 3241.
	trifle, 934-3776.	trunnions, 3441g.
	—,* 2393.	trust(charge),5105.

TRU	TUR	TYR
—(corporation), 4428b.	— in lathe, to 490.	tyranny, 3164-4207.
—,* 1255a, (3743, 2156).	—(veer), 346b.	tyrant, 3164a.
trustworthy, 2420-3854, 1508b.	turncoat, 347a.	tyre, 2518-805.
truth, 136-2285.	turner, 490j.	tyro, 572-1140.
—, in 1955c.	turning lathe,490g.	
try, 3903.	turnip, 2440a.	
—(a case), 3826.	turpentine, 4849c.	# U
tub, 3552, 4454.	turquoise, 4846.	
tube, 1819, 4461.	turret, 4422.	udder, 4891-4224.
tubers, 3991.	turtle, 4872c,3317.	ugly, 473, N-1099-4314.
tuberose, 5250d.	turtledove, 3183a.	ulcer, 578a.
tubular, 3593e.	tusk, 2977b.	—, venereal 1752b.
tuck up, 3002.	tutor, 190-1507.	ulcerate, 3802-578.
Tuesday,2206g-1287.	twang, 2119b.	ulterior,3070,1013.
tuft, 4494.	tweak,2913.	ultimately, 4071a.
— of hair, 1523.	tweezers, 1490a, 2912a.	ultramarine, 735d.
tug, 4403, 2151.	twelfth, 4076-3845-1287.	umbilicus, 4866.
tuition, 3982-1527.	twelve, 3845-1287.	umbrage, 3119-1263.
tumble, 4180.	twentieth, 4076-1287-3845.	umbrella, 167.
— down, 2182c.	twenty, 1287-3845.	un, Many words with this prefix being simple negatives of words found elsewhere are not given under this initial.
— over, 2117.	— cent coin,1104d.	
tumbler, /3375.	twice, 2321-3135, 1289b.	
tumor, fleshy 2257a.	twiddle, 2854.	
—, vascular 2257c.	twigs, 2116a.	unable, N-[2858, 3140].
tumult, 4783-2842.	twilight, 5070-704.	unaccountable,1436-N-4081.
tumulus, 4090.	twilled, 473la.	
tune, 4192.	twine, 3949-D.	unaccustomed, N-2054.
—,* 1508d.	twinkle, 3927.	unacquainted, N-3918.
tunnel, 3793a.	twins, 2552-4482, 2470.	unanimous, 5133-3593.
turban, 1503.	twist, 2867, 1503.	unaware, N-1797.
turbid, 372.	two, 1287.	unbelief,3236-3743.
turbot, 4872k.	—,*2321.	unbiased, N-3487.
turbulence, 2474.	—(double), 3886, 2552.	unbind, 1436-2238.
tureen, 4431-4107.	type, 4572-2859.	unblemished,N-903a.
turf, 4777-3468.	—(symbol), 3323.	unblushing, 2347a.
turkey, 767o.	—, to set 147b.	unbounded, N-939.
tumeric, 5070-1640.	typefounder, 332-4672-Y.	unbutton,1436-2868.
turn, 346.	typhoon, 879b.	unceasing, 1086a.
—(as a screw), 1503, 2867.	tyrannize, 3163.	
— back, 3135,661.		
— corner, 346a.		
—, in 2518a.		

UNC	UNI	UPR
uncertain, N-4132.	unimportant, 934c, N-1541a.	uproar, 2145a,449, 4783.
uncivilized, 5173.	union, /1193.	uproot, 3241.
uncle, 9c,d.	unit, 5133, 4046.	upset, 4197.
unclean, N-1760a.	unite, 1193-2568.	upstairs, 2248c.
unclothe,1436-1248.	united, 4459.	urethra, 2921-1819.
uncomfortable, N-3107a.	—(allied), 2471.	urge, 3013, 3279, 4822.
uncommon, 749a.	United Brethren, 4460a.	urgent, 1558, 1541.
unconscious, 3849-5028.	unity, 5133.	urgently,976a,3013.
uncooked, 3802.	univalve shellfish, 2443.	urinate(polite), 3295c.
uncovered, 2105.	universal, 3512.	—(common), 2921b.
undecided, N-4132.	university, 4033-1141a.	— unconsciously, 2159a.
under, 906,a,965.	unjust, N-1878a.	urinal, 2921-3122, 4857-3977.
undergo,3865.	unlimited, N-939.	urinary intestines, 513c.
underhand, 907a.	unload, 771a.	urine, 2921.
understand, 1095, 2690a.	unloose, 1436.	—, stringy 2227c.
—(having learned), 5918.	unlucky, N-4796b.	urn, 4309.
—(perceive), 1745.	unmannerly, 2206e, 2245b.	us, 3065-4124.
understanding, quickness of 2361b.	unmixed, 4016-3724.	usage, 2120a.
undertake, 4230b.	unnecessary,N-3814.	use,* 3814, 5282, 1895.
undo, 1436.	unoccupied, 1226.	useful, 3295-5282.
undoubted, 2711a.	unorthodox, 4732.	useless, N-5282.
undress, 1436-1248.	unreasonable,2574b.	usual, 3890a.
unemployed, 3859d.	unripe, 2665-4011, 3802.	usually, 3890a.
uneven, 4732, N-3497.	unroll, 260.	usurp, 3164-251, 4751.
unexpected, 1258c.	unskilled, 2054a.	usury, 2293-645.
unfair, N-1878a.	unthankful, 2754b.	utensil, 1035a.
unfaithful, 1700a, N-384-3593.	untidy, 215le.	uterine, 4459-3199.
unfinished, N-3948.	untie, 1436.	uterus, 4417, 3199.
unfit, N-1193.	until, 227a.	utility, 5159-5282.
unfold, 1436-1124.	unusual, 749a.	utmost, S-1654.
ungovernable, 117d.	unyielding, 3001.	utter, 1779-648.
ungrateful, 2754b.	up, 3895.	utterly, 4645b.
unhappy, N-867.	upbraid, 2842.	
unhealthy, N-3981.	uphill, 3895,2834.	
unicorn, 74.	uphold, 830a.	
uniform, 4016,4459-5201.	uplift, 1849.	**V**
—, soldier's 2041a.	upon, 3896, 4609.	
	upper, 3896.	
	upright(position), 1962-2190.	vacancy(official), 2010.
	—(right), 275.	

VAC	VAS	VER
—, to fill 2010c.	vassal, 4656-Y.	verdant, 4764.
—, to make 2010b.	vast, 3829-4033.	verdict, 3550.
vacant, 1226.	vat, /4454.	verdigris, 3609a.
vacate, 3384-1226.	vault(cellar),	verge, 2615.
—(an office),	2411a.	verify, 3903-1330.
3618,a.	vaunt, 2111-4033.	verily, 2000-3854.
vacation,1422,795a.	veal, 3039-D-5249.	vermicelli, 2688
vaccinate, 397a.	veer, 346,b.	713b.
vaccine, (3039)-	vegetable, 4800.	vermillion, 316.
4118b.	vegetation, /4777.	—, light 1235b.
vacuous, 1226.	vehement, 2586.	— powder, 320c.
vacuum, 4645-1226.	vehicle, 490.	vermin, 647.
vagabond,753,2057c.	veil, 1994-2687-	vernacular, 4380-
—, a 2186-D.	3780.	4960.
vagina, 430d.	—,* 167.	vernal, 629.
vagrant, 4238.	vein, 1819i.	— equinox, 629b.
vague, 663,a,2707.	velvet, 4555a.	verse(poetry),3899.
vain, 1226, 301b,	vend, 2569.	—(stanza), 4570.
1213-743.	venerable, 2420.	versed in, 4011,
vainly, 4390c.	venerate,4621-1680.	3357.
valance, 869a.	venereal, 629d.	vertebrae, 4511-
vale, 1866,a.	— ulcer, 4260b,	2083.
valerian, 1133a.	1752b.	vertex, 4129.
valiant,5281-1754.	venery, 2949-3917.	vertigo, 4339-5036.
valid, 4405a.	venetians, 501c.	very, 1099, 3823.
valise, 3468-3626,	vengeance, 477a.	— early, 4586c.
3468-4224.	venison, 2510-5249.	— little, 4140a.
valley, 1866.	venom, 4260.	vesicle, 3199d.
valor, 5281-1033.	venomous, 4260.	vessel(utensil),
valuable, 2065-398.	vent, 4452g, 1221-	1035a,4109,3552.
valuation, 1797-	2426.	—(ship), 3999.
1421.	ventilate, 4452-	—, blood 1539a.
value, 1421.	879.	vest, 3377-3593.
—, of 243.	ventilator, 1033-	vestige, 980.
—,* 1797-1421.	4452.	veteran, 2420-3859.
valve, 117, 1301.	venture, 1754,3551.	vex, 669a,2841.
van, 3639-885.	venus, 1527f.	vexation, 2925.
vanquish, 3947.	veracity,2420-3854.	via, 1668-2100.
vantage, 2293c.	verandah, 2248b,	viands, 2636c.
vapor, 1039.	4355-4422.	vibrate, 3167,138.
variance, 92.	verb, 3802b.	vice, 3100,3211c.
varicose, 196-4033.	verbal, /1006.	—(tool), 1491a.
various, 1743-5201.	verbatim, 370d.	—(instead of),826.
varnish, 4721a.	verbiage, 359b.	— consul, 826a.
vary, 3293.	verbose, 359a.	viceroy, 4653d.
vase, 650-4641,	verbosity, 4215-	vicinity, /1920.
3480.	4960.	vicious, 3100.

WAR	WAT	WED

WAR

warn, 1674-1441.
warp, 1668-3646.
—, to form the, 1481.
warped, 2470, 29.
warrant, 3508.
—, * 3198.
warrior, 5281-3777.
wart, 1010,677c.
wary, 1542.
wash, 3587.
— basin,2687-3553.
— board, /3187.
— stand,2687-3553-1424.
—, white 845a.
washer, 1438a.
washerman, 3587-1248a-L.
wasp, 884b.
waste, 781-5173, 2141-5173.
—, * 691, 3567.
watch(timepiece), 3323.
—(time), 1550.
—, * 4314, 1158.
— against, 4321a.
—, to keep 1550c.
watchful, 1542a.
watchman, 1158b, 1550a, 207b.
watchman's drum, 3372.
watchtower, 1550b.
watchword, 1110d.
water, 4004.
—, * 2225.
—, aerated 1121f.
— buffalo, 3039a.
— chestnut, 2548a.
— closet, 4857-3977.
— cress, 1919b.
— fairy tea,409bb.
— fall, 3406.
—, fresh 4292a.
— lily, 2353a.

WAT

— melon, 2037c.
— — seeds, 2037g.
— meter, 3323f.
— pipe, 1008f.
— —(for smoking), 1515m.
— rat, 3985c.
— spout, 2532a.
waters, 1125.
watery, 4292,1023.
wattles, 1816b.
wave, 2468,3347.
—, * 1389-3167.
wax, 2192.
— candle, 366a.
— coated pills, 2192h.
—, insect 2192b.
—, sealing 767m.
— tree, 271a.
way, 2426, 4207.
— method, 682a.
we, 3065-4124.
weak, 4930-5182.
—(timid), 2936-5182.
—(watery), 4292.
wealth, 4761-4803, 823a.
wean, 4445-2819.
weapon, 4735,2293e.
wear clothes, 603a.
— on the head, 4032.
weary, 2110, 1584a.
weasel, 3985g.
weather, 4355-3905.
—, fine 4355a.
—, hot 1373c.
— cock, 4872r.
— glass, 125g.
weave, 238.
web, 2755.
—, spider 317a, 2755.
— footed, 3058f.
wed, 3543a.

WED

—(of couple),3948-4712.
—(of man), 4825.
—(of woman), 1423, 2780f.
wedding,698-(1351).
wedge, 4550-96.
—, * 3659.
Wednesday, 2206g-3572.
wee, 3589-3674.
weed, 5173-4777.
—, * 1097, 2631.
week, 2206g.
weep, 925, 2245-(2999)-2497.
— and wail, 4322a.
weeping willow, 2261b.
weevil, 2603g.
weigh, 558, 2313, 3374.
— anchor, 2174d.
weight, 2564,4411.
weighty, 645.
weir, fish 4872p.
—, waste 99a.
weird, 2048.
welcome, 856-5233.
weld, 5270-2568.
welfare, 3497a.
—, to ask after 3107c.
well, 4515.
—," 1099.
— cooked, 2848, 4011.
— oil 767h.
— then, 1349a.
— versed, 3357, 4011.
wen, 5156.
Wesleyan Mission, 4836a.
west, 3584-(3286).
western suburbs, 2052j.

WET	WHI	WIL
wet, 3843.	—, steam 3242a.	willing, 985.
— nurse, 2553a.	whit, 5133-4138.	willingly, 4766a,
whale, 4727b,1980-	white, 3178-(3917).	1750-3593.
4872.	— of egg, 4764.	willow, 2261.
whalebone, 4727c.	— of eye, 4562b.	— catkins, 2261c.
wharf, 2561j.	whitebait, 4872e.	—, weeping 2261b.
what? 2635a,3286.	whites, 3178h.	wily scheme, 2062b.
—(that which),	whitewash, 845a.	win, 5234.
3977.	who? 2635b,3286/.	wind, 879.
whatever, 4056a.	whoever, 4056a.	—, * 1993-2568.
wheat, 2607.	whole, 3948, 4815.	— about, 550.
— chaff, 2607g.	wholesale, 1186a,	winding, 2029b.
— harvest, 2607h.	1804a.	windlass, 2501c.
wheel, 490a,2501b.	wholesome, 3981.	windmill, 879-2740.
— barrow, 490i.	wholly, 4645b,3571.	window, 499.
wheezing, 901a.	whore, 1850b,502a,	—, oyster shell
— cough, 606.	3039e.	2981d.
whelp, 1574-D.	whosoever, 4056a.	— sill, 4092a.
when? 1624a.	why? 4151c,2635c.	windpipe, 2029b.
where? 3286-3987.	wick,4095b.	wine, 4500.
—(demonstrative),	wicked, 3100.	wing, 5212.
3977.	wicker hedge, 3240.	wink, 98.
wherefore, 1278b.	wicket gate, 3240a.	winnow, 614a.
whereupon, 4504.	wide, 865.	winnowing machine,
whet, 2293f.	widen, C-865-4138.	2073c, 8791.
whether, 3236-2528.	widgeon, 1252.	winter, 4273-4355.
whetstone, 2213,	widow, 2038-835.	wipe, 2590.
2740-4195-3879.	widower, 4259a.	— out, 2790.
which? 3286/.	width, 865.	wire, 3646.
— is, 4533.	wield, 57.	—, electric 4163c.
while, 907, 141.	wife, 4697, 2420b.	— gauze,4366-3780.
—, for a 4469a.	wig, 3272.	wisdom, 229a.
whine, 3045.	wild(untamed),5173.	wise, 229a, 3357,
whinny, 3762.	—(mad), 2143.	2690a.
whip, 3288.	— cat, Siberian	wish, 3631.
—, * 3288-4027.	2281c.	—(must have),
—, riding 2561b.	wildly, 2474.	1388.
whirl, 4089a.	wilderness, 1496a,	—(hope), 2764.
whirlpool, 4197-	2141a.	—(expressing a
4786-4004.	wile, 2062b.	wish), 4932.
whirlwind, 2061c.	wilful, 1810a.	wistaria chinensis,
whisk, 653.	will(determination)	4333a.
whiskers, 3678,	328b.	witch, 3882b.
3412b.	—(testament), 367-	witchcraft, 2714a.
whiskey, 1864-4500.	3982.	with, 4459, 1892,
whistle, 1515j.	—(future tense),	2568.
—, * 614a.	4522.	withered, 1759-803.

WIT	WOR	WRI
within, 1463, 2484, 2937.	—, job 1877e.	wriggle, 1834a.
without, 3070-4339.	workman, 1877-Y.	wring, 2867-1759.
— cause, 4390e.	—(hand), 3859.	wrinkle, 2619a.
withstand, 4233-339.	—, master 837a.	—* 4502-(2568).
witness, 276.	—(skilled), 4529, 4560b.	wrist, 3149a, 3859a.
wits, 5028.	Works, Board of Public, 1877i.	write, 3616.
wizard, 3882a.	world, 1438a.	—, begin to 2454a.
woe, 5062.	—(earth), 4355b.	— between the lines, 2148c.
woe! 4604b.	—(globe), 4125-1938.	writer(author), 4610-3982-K.
woebegone, 36a.	—, end of 2792a.	writhe, 628.
woeful, 4699a.	—, female 1438b.	written style, 2285c.
wolf, 420a.	—, next 2447d.	writing, 4672.
wolf's bane, 3115-4339.	worldly customs, 3818-4637.	—, a 3982.
woman, 2949a.	worm, 646.	wrong, 4791.
—, married 835.	wormeaten, 334-2186.	—, to commit 678.
—, old 3528.	worse, 3211.	wry, 2652.
womb, 4417, 3199, a.	worship, 3417, 2206g.	
wonder, 2048, 1663-1950.	—(with incense), 1046b.	**Y**
wonderful, 1950a, b.	— at the tombs, 3793c.	
wont(accustomed), 2054.	—, Christian place of 2206k.	yak, 2284a.
wood, 2795.	worst, S-3100.	yamen, 2978a.
—, fire 419.	worth, 243.	yard(measure), 2564a.
—, cut, 2795-3187.	worthless, 2186, N-5282.	—, ship's 1783.
— louse, 647b.	worthy, 1555.	yarn, 3780, 3646.
—, to work in 4115.	— of, 1143.	yawn, 925a, 1114a.
wooden, 2795-K.	would, 3631, 4932.	year, 2895.
— shoes, 1969.	wound, (3885, 1135).	years(age), 3722.
woof, 5012-3646.	wrangle, 92, 15a.	yearn, 4458-3631.
wool, 5193-2712.	wrap, 3198.	yeast, 1511a.
woollens, 5272.	wrapper, 3198a.	yell, 4033-925.
word(spoken), 4960.	wrasse, spotted 2413b.	yellow, 5070.
—(written), 4667.	wren, 2397.	— chrysanthemum, 2367b.
work, 1877a.	wrench, 2444f-619, 1971.	— gentian 2353c.
—, * 4593-1877.	—, stilson 1971c.	— spotted ray, 3328a.
—, begin 1877g.	wrestle, 4110.	yelp, 695.
— in wood, 4115.		yes, 968.
— levels, 4004h.		yesterday, 4611-5137, 1913a, 2636h.
—, night 1877d.		
—, one day's 1877b.		
—, stop 1877h.		
worker, 1877-Y.		

YET	YOU	ZEB
yet, 398.	— sister, 91.	zebra, 815b.
—, not 4713a.	your, 2875-K.	zenith, 4355-4129.
yew tree, 754.	— favor, 3957b.	zigzag, 204-4672.
yoke, 17.	— home, 3957a.	zinc, 5056a.
yolk, 4052a.	yourself, 4673a.	
you, 2875.		zodiac, 551a,5070-4207.
young, 3967-2895, 2947, 5147.		zone, 4031.
— child, 3677a.	Z	—, frigid 4031a.
— lady, 1786b.		
— men's associa-tion, 4764e.		—, temperate 4031b.
younger brother, 2404b.	zeal, 721-2330.	—, torrid 1372-4031.
	zealous, 1918.	

GEOGRAPHICAL NAMES

Geographical Names

Aberdeen, 3879o, 4482e.
Abyssinia, 3088e.
Aden, 9s.
Afghanistan, 3088d.
Africa, 3088a.
Amazon, 9q.
America, 9o.
—, United States of 650k, 2662a.
Amoy, 910a.
Anhwei, 3107j.
Annam, 3107k, 4938b.
Antarctic Ocean, 2822d.
Antung, 3107L.
Arabia, 3088c.
Aral Sea, 926b.
Arctic Ocean, 3215c.
Argentine, 9r.
Armenia, 9p.
Asia, 9n.
Athens, 2982a.
Atlantic Ocean, 4033b.
Australia, 3087b, 1527j.
Austria, 3086a.
Austro-Hungary, 3512a.
Bangkok, 3221a, 2581a.
Belgium, 3251b.
Berlin, 3174d.
Bocca Tigris, 815c.
Bolivia, 3349b, 2734a.
Bombay, 2589b.
Borneo, 3347c, 3386a.
Boston, 3347e.
Brazil, 3158.

Bremen, 2734c.
British Empire, 5222b.
Brooklyn, 3336j.
Burmah, 2686a.
Calcutta, 2690e.
California, 1527i.
Cambodia, 1527L.
Canada, 1409b.
Canton City, 2107e, 5193f.
— Province, 2107c.
Celebes, 3584g.
Ceylon, 3619d.
Chefoo, 1335n.
Chekiang, 284b.
Chicago, 3898a.
Chihli, 242a.
Chili, 229b.
China, 383d, 4968c.
Chosen(Korea), 287a.
Chusan, 161b.
Cochin China, 1494L.
Colombo, 1117c.
Constantinople, 2074a.
Cuba, 1796e.
Dalny, 4032c.
Denmark, 4048-2607.
Dumbell Island, H.K. 160b.
Dutch Folly, 1125k.
East China Sea, 4272d.
East Indies, 2823b.
Ecuador, 4140b.
Edinburgh, 3099a.
Egypt, 3096a.
England, 5222c.
Europe, 51a.
Foochow, 867d.
Formosa, 4422c.
France, 682b.
Fukien, 867e.
Fusan, 820a.
Galveston, 1407c.

Germany, 4081c.
Glasgow, 1448a.
Gobi, 2095a.
Greece, 1020c.
Greenland, 1450e.
Greenwich, 1450f.
Hague, The 1125p.
Hainan, 1125m.
Haiphong, 1125n.
Hangchow, 1189a.
Hankow, 1163a.
Hanoi, 2937d.
Hanyang, 1163b.
Harbin, 997a.
Hawaiian Islands, 4305b.
Hoihow, 1125L.
Holland, 1121c.
Honam, Canton 1119a.
Honam Province, 1119a.
Hong Kong, 1046h.
Hunan, 3121a.
Hungary, 1229a.
Hupeh, 3121b.
Iceland, 3763b, 3301c.
India, 5116a.
Indian Ocean, 5116b.
Indies, East 2822b.
—, West 3584f.
Ireland, 3088b.
Italy, 1258d.
Japan, 5137a.
Java, 107a.
Jerusalem, 5172b.
Judea, 5153a.
Kansu, 1750c.
Kiangsi, 1771b.
Kiangsu, 1771c.
Kirin, 1560a.
Kiu Kiang, 1573b.
Kobe, 3835d.
Kongmoon, 1771d.
Korea, 287a.
Kowloon, 1573c.

GEOGRAPHICAL NAMES

Kwangsai, 2107d.
Kwangtung, 2107c.
Kweichow, 2065b.
Kweilin, 2067c.
Kwong Provinces,
  the Two 4943a.
Lhasa, 2145b.
Loh Fau, 2437d.
London, 2515a.
Luzon, 2489a.
Macao, 3087a.
Macao Passage,
  3178j.
Madagascar, 2561r.
Malacca, 2561q.
Malay, 2561o.
Malaysia, 2561p.
Manchuria, 2785a.
Manila, 2561n,
  2489a.
Marseilles, 2552c.
Mediterranean Sea,
  4125c.
Mesopotamia, 2662b.
Mexico, 2606e,
  2607i.
Moluccas, 2734b.
Mongolia, 2803c.
Moscow, 2606f.
Moukden, 3954a,
  4272e.
Nagasaki, 190c.
Nanking, 1669c.
Nanning, 2823e.
Newchang, 3039g.
New Guinea, 3596f.
New York, 2869b.
New Zealand, 3759a.
Nile River, 2873a.
North Sea, 3215b.
Norway, 2930a.

Pacific Ocean,
  4283a.
Pakhoi, 3215b.
Panama, 3158i.
Paraguay, 3158j.
Paris, 3158L.
Patagonia, 3158k.
Peking, 3215a.
Penang, 3596e,
  3219a.
Persia, 3347d.
Peru, 3256a.
Philippines, 3674f,
  756a.
Port Arthur, 2488a.
Portugal, 3518b.
Rangoon, 4096a.
Red Sea, 1235h.
Rome, 2437e.
Roumania, 2437f.
Russia, 3062a.
Sahara, 3581a.
Saigon, 1889a.
St. Petersburg,
  3946b.
Samshui, 3574d.
San Francisco,
  1527k.
Scotland, 3677d.
Shameen, Canton,
  3779q.
Shanghai, 3896a.
Shansi, 3793d.
Shantung, 3793c.
Sheklung, 3879n.
Shengking, 3954a.
Shensi, 3928a.
Siberia, 3584d.
Singapore, 3596d,
  3652d.

Soochow, 3677f.
South China Sea,
  2823c.
Spain, 3584c.
Sparta, 3763a.
Straits Settlements
  1125p.
Suez, 3677g,4004m.
Sumatra, 3677e.
Swatow, 3799a.
Sweden, 3734a.
Switzerland, 3734b.
Syria, 4635a.
Szechuen, 604a.
Taku, 1791a.
Tibet, 3584e.
Tientsin, 4355L.
Tongking, 4272e.
Tokyo, 4272e.
Tsingtao, 4764g.
Turkey, 4380d.
United States of
  America, 650k,
  2662a.
Uruguay, 5148a.
Venezuela, 4991a.
Victoria, B.C.,
  5047a.
Vladivostock,
  1125o.
Wales, 4985a.
West Indies, 3584f.
Whampoa Island,
  160a.
Whampoa, 5070k.
Wuchow, 2960a.
Yangtsekiang,5197a.
Yellow Sea, 5070j.
Yokohama, 4981a.
Yunnan, 5027c.